American Casebook Series
Hornbook Series and Basic Legal Texts
Nutshell Series

of

WEST PUBLISHING COMPANY
P.O. Box 3526
St. Paul, Minnesota 55165
October, 1983

ACCOUNTING

Faris' Law and Accounting in a Nutshell, approximately 392 pages, 1984 (Text)

Fiflis and Kripke's Teaching Materials on Accounting for Business Lawyers, 2nd Ed., 684 pages, 1977 (Casebook)

Siegel and Siegel's Accounting and Financial Disclosure: A Guide to Basic Concepts, 259 pages, 1983 (Text)

ADMINISTRATIVE LAW

Davis' Cases, Text and Problems on Administrative Law, 6th Ed., 683 pages, 1977 (Casebook)

Davis' Basic Text on Administrative Law, 3rd Ed., 617 pages, 1972 (Text)

Davis' Police Discretion, 176 pages, 1975 (Text)

Gellhorn and Boyer's Administrative Law and Process in a Nutshell, 2nd Ed., 445 pages, 1981 (Text)

Mashaw and Merrill's Introduction to the American Public Law System, 1095 pages, 1975, with 1980 Supplement (Casebook)

Robinson, Gellhorn and Bruff's The Administrative Process, 2nd Ed., 959 pages, 1980, with 1983 Supplement (Casebook)

ADMIRALTY

Healy and Sharpe's Cases and Materials on Admiralty, 875 pages, 1974 (Casebook)

Maraist's Admiralty in a Nutshell, 400 pages, 1983 (Text)

AGENCY—PARTNERSHIP

Fessler's Alternatives to Incorporation for Persons in Quest of Profit, 258 pages, 1980 (Casebook)

AGENCY—PARTNERSHIP—Continued

Henn's Cases and Materials on Agency, Partnership and Other Unincorporated Business Enterprises, 396 pages, 1972 (Casebook)

Reuschlein and Gregory's Hornbook on the Law of Agency and Partnership, 625 pages, 1979, with 1981 pocket part (Text)

Seavey's Hornbook on Agency, 329 pages, 1964 (Text)

Seavey and Hall's Cases on Agency, 431 pages, 1956 (Casebook)

Seavey, Reuschlein and Hall's Cases on Agency and Partnership, 599 pages, 1962 (Casebook)

Selected Corporation and Partnership Statutes and Forms, 556 pages, 1982

Steffen and Kerr's Cases and Materials on Agency-Partnership, 4th Ed., 859 pages, 1980 (Casebook)

Steffen's Agency-Partnership in a Nutshell, 364 pages, 1977 (Text)

AMERICAN INDIAN LAW

Canby's American Indian Law in a Nutshell, 288 pages, 1981 (Text)

Getches, Rosenfelt and Wilkinson's Cases on Federal Indian Law, 660 pages, 1979, with 1983 Supplement (Casebook)

ANTITRUST LAW

Gellhorn's Antitrust Law and Economics in a Nutshell, 2nd Ed., 425 pages, 1981 (Text)

Gifford and Raskind's Cases and Materials on Antitrust, 694 pages, 1983 (Casebook)

LAW SCHOOL PUBLICATIONS—Continued

ANTITRUST LAW—Continued

Oppenheim, Weston and McCarthy's Cases and Comments on Federal Antitrust Laws, 4th Ed., 1168 pages, 1981 (Casebook)

Posner and Easterbrook's Cases and Economic Notes on Antitrust, 2nd Ed., 1077 pages, 1981, with 1982–83 Supplement (Casebook)

Sullivan's Hornbook of the Law of Antitrust, 886 pages, 1977 (Text)

See also Regulated Industries, Trade Regulation

BANKING LAW

Lovett's Banking and Financial Institutions in a Nutshell, approximately 406 pages, 1984 (Text)

White's Teaching Materials on Banking Law, 1058 pages, 1976, with Case and Statutory Supplement (Casebook)

BUSINESS PLANNING

Epstein and Scheinfeld's Teaching Materials on Business Reorganization Under the Bankruptcy Code, 216 pages, 1980 (Casebook)

Painter's Problems and Materials in Business Planning, 2nd Ed., approximately 1035 pages, 1984 (Casebook)

Selected Securities and Business Planning Statutes, Rules and Forms, 485 pages, 1982

CIVIL PROCEDURE

Casad's Res Judicata in a Nutshell, 310 pages, 1976 (text)

Cound, Friedenthal and Miller's Cases and Materials on Civil Procedure, 3rd Ed., 1147 pages, 1980 with 1982 Supplement (Casebook)

Ehrenzweig, Louisell and Hazard's Jurisdiction in a Nutshell, 4th Ed., 232 pages, 1980 (Text)

Federal Rules of Civil-Appellate-Criminal Procedure—West Law School Edition, 343 pages, 1983

Hodges, Jones and Elliott's Cases and Materials on Texas Trial and Appellate Procedure, 2nd Ed., 745 pages, 1974 (Casebook)

Hodges, Jones and Elliott's Cases and Materials on the Judicial Process Prior to Trial in Texas, 2nd Ed., 871 pages, 1977 (Casebook)

Kane's Civil Procedure in a Nutshell, 271 pages, 1979 (Text)

Karlen's Procedure Before Trial in a Nutshell, 258 pages, 1972 (Text)

Karlen, Meisenholder, Stevens and Vestal's Cases on Civil Procedure, 923 pages, 1975 (Casebook)

CIVIL PROCEDURE—Continued

Koffler and Reppy's Hornbook on Common Law Pleading, 663 pages, 1969 (Text)

McBaine's Cases on Introduction to Civil Procedure, 399 pages, 1950 (Casebook)

Park's Computer-Aided Exercises on Civil Procedure, 2nd Ed., 167 pages, 1983 (Coursebook)

Shipman's Hornbook on Common-Law Pleading, 3rd Ed., 644 pages, 1923 (Text)

Siegel's Hornbook on New York Practice, 1011 pages, 1978 with 1981–82 Pocket Part (Text)

See also Federal Jurisdiction and Procedure

CIVIL RIGHTS

Abernathy's Cases and Materials on Civil Rights, 660 pages, 1980 (Casebook)

Cohen's Cases on the Law of Deprivation of Liberty: A Study in Social Control, 755 pages, 1980 (Casebook)

Lockhart, Kamisar and Choper's Cases on Constitutional Rights and Liberties, 5th Ed., 1298 pages plus Appendix, 1981, with 1983 Supplement (Casebook)—reprint from Lockhart, et al. Cases on Constitutional Law, 5th Ed., 1980

Vieira's Civil Rights in a Nutshell, 279 pages, 1978 (Text)

COMMERCIAL LAW

Bailey's Secured Transactions in a Nutshell, 2nd Ed., 391 pages, 1981 (Text)

Epstein and Martin's Basic Uniform Commercial Code Teaching Materials, 2nd Ed., 667 pages, 1983 (Casebook)

Henson's Hornbook on Secured Transactions Under the U.C.C., 2nd Ed., 504 pages, 1979 with 1979 P.P. (Text)

Murray's Commercial Law, Problems and Materials, 366 pages, 1975 (Coursebook)

Nordstrom and Clovis' Problems and Materials on Commercial Paper, 458 pages, 1972 (Casebook)

Nordstrom and Lattin's Problems and Materials on Sales and Secured Transactions, 809 pages, 1968 (Casebook)

Nordstrom, Murray and Clovis' Problems and Materials on Sales, 515 pages, 1982 (Casebook)

Nordstrom's Hornbook on Sales, 600 pages, 1970 (Text)

Selected Commercial Statutes, 1379 pages, 1983

Speidel, Summers and White's Teaching Materials on Commercial and Consumer Law, 3rd Ed., 1490 pages, 1981 (Casebook)

LAW SCHOOL PUBLICATIONS—Continued

COMMERCIAL LAW—Continued

Stockton's Sales in a Nutshell, 2nd Ed., 370 pages, 1981 (Text)

Stone's Uniform Commercial Code in a Nutshell, 507 pages, 1975 (Text)

Uniform Commercial Code, Official Text with Comments, 994 pages, 1978

UCC Article 8, 1977 Amendments, 249 pages, 1978

UCC Article 9, Reprint from 1962 Code, 128 pages, 1976

UCC Article 9, 1972 Amendments, 304 pages, 1978

Weber and Speidel's Commercial Paper in a Nutshell, 3rd Ed., 404 pages, 1982 (Text)

White and Summers' Hornbook on the Uniform Commercial Code, 2nd Ed., 1250 pages, 1980 (Text)

COMMUNITY PROPERTY

Mennell's Community Property in a Nutshell, 447 pages, 1982 (Text)

Verrall and Bird's Cases and Materials on California Community Property, 4th Ed., 549 pages, 1983 (Casebook)

COMPARATIVE LAW

Barton, Gibbs, Li and Merryman's Law in Radically Different Cultures, 960 pages, 1983 (Casebook)

Glendon, Gordon, and Osakwe's Comparative Legal Traditions in a Nutshell, 402 pages, 1982 (Text)

Langbein's Comparative Criminal Procedure: Germany, 172 pages, 1977 (Casebook)

COMPUTERS AND LAW

Mason's An Introduction to the Use of Computers in Law, approximately 200 pages, 1984 (Text)

CONFLICT OF LAWS

Cramton, Currie and Kay's Cases-Comments-Questions on Conflict of Laws, 3rd Ed., 1026 pages, 1981 (Casebook)

Scoles and Hay's Hornbook on Conflict of Laws, Student Ed., 1085 pages, 1982 (Text)

Scoles and Weintraub's Cases and Materials on Conflict of Laws, 2nd Ed., 966 pages, 1972, with 1978 Supplement (Casebook)

Siegel's Conflicts in a Nutshell, 469 pages, 1982 (Text)

CONSTITUTIONAL LAW

Engdahl's Constitutional Power in a Nutshell: Federal and State, 411 pages, 1974 (Text)

CONSTITUTIONAL LAW—Continued

Lockhart, Kamisar and Choper's Cases-Comments-Questions on Constitutional Law, 5th Ed., 1705 pages plus Appendix, 1980, with 1983 Supplement (Casebook)

Lockhart, Kamisar and Choper's Cases-Comments-Questions on the American Constitution, 5th Ed., 1185 pages plus Appendix, 1981, with 1983 Supplement (Casebook)—reprint from Lockhart, et al. Cases on Constitutional Law, 5th Ed., 1980

Manning's The Law of Church-State Relations in a Nutshell, 305 pages, 1981 (Text)

Miller's Presidential Power in a Nutshell, 328 pages, 1977 (Text)

Nowak, Rotunda and Young's Hornbook on Constitutional Law, 2nd Ed., Student Ed., 1172 pages, 1983 (Text)

Rotunda's Modern Constitutional Law: Cases and Notes, 1034 pages, 1981, with 1983 Supplement (Casebook)

Williams' Constitutional Analysis in a Nutshell, 388 pages, 1979 (Text)

See also Civil Rights

CONSUMER LAW

Epstein and Nickles' Consumer Law in a Nutshell, 2nd Ed., 418 pages, 1981 (Text)

McCall's Consumer Protection, Cases, Notes and Materials, 594 pages, 1977, with 1977 Statutory Supplement (Casebook)

Selected Commercial Statutes, approximately 1360 pages, 1983

Spanogle and Rohner's Cases and Materials on Consumer Law, 693 pages, 1979, with 1982 Supplement (Casebook)

See also Commercial Law

CONTRACTS

Calamari & Perillo's Cases and Problems on Contracts, 1061 pages, 1978 (Casebook)

Calamari and Perillo's Hornbook on Contracts, 2nd Ed., 878 pages, 1977 (Text)

Corbin's Text on Contracts, One Volume Student Edition, 1224 pages, 1952 (Text)

Fessler and Loiseaux's Cases and Materials on Contracts, 837 pages, 1982 (Casebook)

Freedman's Cases and Materials on Contracts, 658 pages, 1973 (Casebook)

Friedman's Contract Remedies in a Nutshell, 323 pages, 1981 (Text)

Fuller and Eisenberg's Cases on Basic Contract Law, 4th Ed., 1203 pages, 1981 (Casebook)

LAW SCHOOL PUBLICATIONS—Continued

CONTRACTS—Continued

Jackson and Bollinger's Cases on Contract Law in Modern Society, 2nd Ed., 1329 pages, 1980 (Casebook)

Keyes' Government Contracts in a Nutshell, 423 pages, 1979 (Text)

Reitz's Cases on Contracts as Basic Commercial Law, 763 pages, 1975 (Casebook)

Schaber and Rohwer's Contracts in a Nutshell, 2nd Ed., approximately 409 pages, 1984 (Text)

Simpson's Hornbook on Contracts, 2nd Ed., 510 pages, 1965 (Text)

COPYRIGHT

See Patent and Copyright Law

CORPORATIONS

Hamilton's Cases on Corporations—Including Partnerships and Limited Partnerships, 2nd Ed., 1108 pages, 1981, with 1981 Statutory Supplement and 1984 Supplement (Casebook)

Hamilton's Law of Corporations in a Nutshell, 379 pages, 1980 (Text)

Henn's Cases on Corporations, 1279 pages, 1974, with 1980 Supplement (Casebook)

Henn and Alexander's Hornbook on Corporations, 3rd Ed., Student Ed., 1371 pages, 1983 (Text)

Jennings and Buxbaum's Cases and Materials on Corporations, 5th Ed., 1180 pages, 1979 (Casebook)

Selected Corporation and Partnership Statutes, Regulations and Forms, 556 pages, 1982

Solomon, Stevenson and Schwartz' Materials and Problems on the Law and Policies on Corporations, 1172 pages, 1982 with 1983 Supplement (Casebook)

CORPORATE FINANCE

Hamilton's Cases and Materials on Corporate Finance, approximately 721 pages, 1984 (Casebook)

CORRECTIONS

Krantz's Cases and Materials on the Law of Corrections and Prisoners' Rights, 2nd Ed., 735 pages, 1981, with 1982 Supplement (Casebook)

Krantz's Law of Corrections and Prisoners' Rights in a Nutshell, 2nd Ed., 384 pages, 1983 (Text)

Popper's Post-Conviction Remedies in a Nutshell, 360 pages, 1978 (Text)

Robbins' Cases and Materials on Post Conviction Remedies, 506 pages, 1982 (Casebook)

Rubin's Law of Criminal Corrections, 2nd Ed., 873 pages, 1973, with 1978 Supplement (Text)

CREDITOR'S RIGHTS

Epstein's Debtor-Creditor Law in a Nutshell, 2nd Ed., 324 pages, 1980 (Text)

Epstein and Landers' Debtors and Creditors: Cases and Materials, 2nd Ed., 689 pages, 1982 (Casebook)

Epstein and Sheinfeld's Teaching Materials on Business Reorganization Under the Bankruptcy Code, 216 pages, 1980 (Casebook)

Riesenfeld's Cases and Materials on Creditors' Remedies and Debtors' Protection, 3rd Ed., 810 pages, 1979 with 1979 Statutory Supplement and 1981 Case Supplement (Casebook)

Selected Bankruptcy Statutes and Rules, approximately 400 pages, 1984

CRIMINAL LAW AND CRIMINAL PROCEDURE

Cohen and Gobert's Problems in Criminal Law, 297 pages, 1976 (Problem book)

Davis' Police Discretion, 176 pages, 1975 (Text)

Dix and Sharlot's Cases and Materials on Criminal Law, 2nd Ed., 771 pages, 1979 (Casebook)

Federal Rules of Civil-Appellate-Criminal Procedure—West Law School Edition, 343 pages, 1983

Grano's Problems in Criminal Procedure, 2nd Ed., 176 pages, 1981 (Problem book)

Israel and LaFave's Criminal Procedure in a Nutshell, 3rd Ed., 438 pages, 1980 (Text)

Johnson's Cases, Materials and Text on Substantive Criminal Law in its Procedural Context, 2nd Ed., 956 pages, 1980 (Casebook)

Kamisar, LaFave and Israel's Cases, Comments and Questions on Modern Criminal Procedure, 5th ed., 1635 pages plus Appendix, 1980 with 1983 Supplement (Casebook)

Kamisar, LaFave and Israel's Cases, Comments and Questions on Basic Criminal Procedure, 5th Ed., 869 pages, 1980 with 1983 Supplement (Casebook)—reprint from Kamisar, et al. Modern Criminal Procedure, 5th ed., 1980

LaFave's Modern Criminal Law: Cases, Comments and Questions, 789 pages, 1978 (Casebook)

LaFave and Scott's Hornbook on Criminal Law, 763 pages, 1972 (Text)

Langbein's Comparative Criminal Procedure: Germany, 172 pages, 1977 (Casebook)

Loewy's Criminal Law in a Nutshell, 302 pages, 1975 (Text)

LAW SCHOOL PUBLICATIONS—Continued

CRIMINAL LAW AND CRIMINAL PROCEDURE—Continued

Saltzburg's American Criminal Procedure, Cases and Commentary, 2nd Ed., approximately 1169 pages, 1984 (Casebook)

Saltzburg's Introduction to American Criminal Procedure, 702 pages, 1980 with 1983 Supplement (Casebook)—reprint from Saltzburg's American Criminal Procedure, 1980

Uviller's The Processes of Criminal Justice: Investigation and Adjudication, 2nd Ed., 1384 pages, 1979 with 1979 Statutory Supplement and 1983 Update (Casebook)

Uviller's The Processes of Criminal Justice: Adjudication, 2nd Ed., 730 pages, 1979. Soft-cover reprint from Uviller's The Processes of Criminal Justice: Investigation and Adjudication, 2nd Ed. (Casebook)

Uviller's The Processes of Criminal Justice: Investigation, 2nd Ed., 655 pages, 1979. Soft-cover reprint from Uviller's The Processes of Criminal Justice: Investigation and Adjudication, 2nd Ed. (Casebook)

Vorenberg's Cases on Criminal Law and Procedure, 2nd Ed., 1088 pages, 1981 (Casebook)

See also Corrections, Juvenile Justice

DECEDENTS ESTATES

See Trusts and Estates

DOMESTIC RELATIONS

Clark's Cases and Problems on Domestic Relations, 3rd Ed., 1153 pages, 1980 (Casebook)

Clark's Hornbook on Domestic Relations, 754 pages, 1968 (Text)

Krause's Cases and Materials on Family Law, 2nd Ed., 1221 pages, 1983 (Casebook)

Krause's Family Law in a Nutshell, 400 pages, 1977 (Text)

Krauskopf's Cases on Property Division at Marriage Dissolution, approximately 220 pages, 1984 (Casebook)

EDUCATION LAW

Morris' The Constitution and American Education, 2nd Ed., 992 pages, 1980 (Casebook)

EMPLOYMENT DISCRIMINATION

Player's Cases and Materials on Employment Discrimination Law, 878 pages, 1980 with 1982 Supplement (Casebook)

Player's Federal Law of Employment Discrimination in a Nutshell, 2nd Ed., 402 pages, 1981 (Text)

EMPLOYMENT DISCRIMINATION—Continued

See also Women and the Law

ENERGY AND NATURAL RESOURCES LAW

Rodgers' Cases and Materials on Energy and Natural Resources Law, 2nd Ed., 877 pages, 1983 (Casebook)

Selected Environmental Law Statutes, 768 pages, 1983

Tomain's Energy Law in a Nutshell, 338 pages, 1981 (Text)

See also Environmental Law, Oil and Gas, Water Law

ENVIRONMENTAL LAW

Bonine and McGarity's Cases and Materials on the Law of Environment and Pollution, approximately 892 pages, 1984 (Casebook)

Findley and Farber's Cases and Materials on Environmental Law, 738 pages, 1981, with 1983 Supplement (Casebook)

Findley and Farber's Environmental Law in a Nutshell, 343 pages, 1983 (Text)

Hanks, Tarlock and Hanks' Cases on Environmental Law and Policy, 1242 pages, 1974, with 1976 Supplement (Casebook)

Rodgers' Hornbook on Environmental Law, 956 pages, 1977 (Text)

Selected Environmental Law Statutes, 768 pages, 1983

See also Energy and Natural Resources Law, Water Law

EQUITY

See Remedies

ESTATES

See Trusts and Estates

ESTATE PLANNING

Kurtz' Cases, Materials and Problems on Family Estate Planning, 853 pages, 1983 (Casebook)

Lynn's Introduction to Estate Planning, in a Nutshell, 3rd Ed., 370 pages, 1983 (Text)

See also Taxation

EVIDENCE

Broun and Meisenholder's Problems in Evidence, 2nd Ed., 304 pages, 1981 (Problem book)

Cleary and Strong's Cases, Materials and Problems on Evidence, 3rd Ed., 1143 pages, 1981 (Casebook)

Federal Rules of Evidence for United States Courts and Magistrates, 327 pages, 1983

LAW SCHOOL PUBLICATIONS—Continued

EVIDENCE—Continued

Graham's Federal Rules of Evidence in a Nutshell, 429 pages, 1981 (Text)

Kimball's Programmed Materials on Problems in Evidence, 380 pages, 1978 (Problem book)

Lempert and Saltzburg's A Modern Approach to Evidence: Text, Problems, Transcripts and Cases, 2nd Ed., 1296 pages, 1983 (Casebook)

Lilly's Introduction to the Law of Evidence, 486 pages, 1978 (Text)

McCormick, Elliott and Sutton's Cases and Materials on Evidence, 5th Ed., 1212 pages, 1981 (Casebook)

McCormick's Hornbook on Evidence, 3rd Ed., approximately 1128 pages, 1984 (Text)

Rothstein's Evidence, State and Federal Rules in a Nutshell, 2nd Ed., 514 pages, 1981 (Text)

Saltzburg's Evidence Supplement: Rules, Statutes, Commentary, 245 pages, 1980 (Casebook Supplement)

FEDERAL JURISDICTION AND PROCEDURE

Currie's Cases and Materials on Federal Courts, 3rd Ed., 1042 pages, 1982 (Casebook)

Currie's Federal Jurisdiction in a Nutshell, 2nd Ed., 258 pages, 1981 (Text)

Federal Rules of Civil-Appellate-Criminal Procedure—West Law School Edition, 343 pages, 1983

Forrester and Moye's Cases and Materials on Federal Jurisdiction and Procedure, 3rd Ed., 917 pages, 1977 with 1981 Supplement (Casebook)

Merrill and Vetri's Problems on Federal Courts and Civil Procedure, 460 pages, 1974 (Problem book)

Redish's Cases, Comments and Questions on Federal Courts, 878 pages, 1983 (Casebook)

Wright's Hornbook on Federal Courts, 4th Ed., Student Ed., 870 pages, 1983 (Text)

FUTURE INTERESTS

See Trusts and Estates

HOUSING AND URBAN DEVELOPMENT

Berger's Cases and Materials on Housing, 2nd Ed., 254 pages, 1973 (Casebook)—reprint from Cooper et al. Cases on Law and Poverty, 2nd Ed., 1973

See also Land Use

IMMIGRATION LAW

Weissbrodt's Immigration Law and Procedure in a Nutshell, approximately 240 pages, 1984 (Text)

INDIAN LAW

See American Indian Law

INSURANCE

Dobbyn's Insurance Law in a Nutshell, 281 pages, 1981 (Text)

Keeton's Cases on Basic Insurance Law, 2nd Ed., 1086 pages, 1977

Keeton's Basic Text on Insurance Law, 712 pages, 1971 (Text)

Keeton's Case Supplement to Keeton's Basic Text on Insurance Law, 334 pages, 1978 (Casebook)

Keeton's Programmed Problems in Insurance Law, 243 pages, 1972 (Text Supplement)

York and Whelan's Cases, Materials and Problems on Insurance Law, 715 pages, 1982 (Casebook)

INTERNATIONAL LAW

Henkin, Pugh, Schachter and Smit's Cases and Materials on International Law, 2nd Ed., 1152 pages, 1980, with Documents Supplement (Casebook)

Jackson's Legal Problems of International Economic Relations, 1097 pages, 1977, with Documents Supplement (Casebook)

Kirgis' International Organizations in Their Legal Setting, 1016 pages, 1977, with 1981 Supplement (Casebook)

Weston, Falk and D'Amato's International Law and World Order—A Problem Oriented Coursebook, 1195 pages, 1980, with Documents Supplement (Casebook)

Wilson's International Business Transactions in a Nutshell, 2nd Ed., approximately 490 pages, 1984 (Text)

INTERVIEWING AND COUNSELING

Binder and Price's Interviewing and Counseling, 232 pages, 1977 (Text)

Shaffer's Interviewing and Counseling in a Nutshell, 353 pages, 1976 (Text)

INTRODUCTION TO LAW

Dobbyn's So You Want to go to Law School, Revised First Edition, 206 pages, 1976 (Text)

Hegland's Introduction to the Study and Practice of Law in a Nutshell, 418 pages, 1983 (Text)

Kinyon's Introduction to Law Study and Law Examinations in a Nutshell, 389 pages, 1971 (Text)

See also Legal Method and Legal System

JUDICIAL ADMINISTRATION

Carrington, Meador and Rosenberg's Justice on Appeal, 263 pages, 1976 (Casebook)

LAW SCHOOL PUBLICATIONS—Continued

JUDICIAL ADMINISTRATION—Continued

Nelson's Cases and Materials on Judicial Administration and the Administration of Justice, 1032 pages, 1974 (Casebook)

JURISPRUDENCE

Christie's Text and Readings on Jurisprudence—The Philosophy of Law, 1056 pages, 1973 (Casebook)

JUVENILE JUSTICE

Fox's Cases and Materials on Modern Juvenile Justice, 2nd Ed., 960 pages, 1981 (Casebook)

Fox's Juvenile Courts in a Nutshell, 3rd Ed., approximately 260 pages, 1984 (Text)

LABOR LAW

Gorman's Basic Text on Labor Law—Unionization and Collective Bargaining, 914 pages, 1976 (Text)

Leslie's Labor Law in a Nutshell, 403 pages, 1979 (Text)

Nolan's Labor Arbitration Law and Practice in a Nutshell, 358 pages, 1979 (Text)

Oberer, Hanslowe and Andersen's Cases and Materials on Labor Law—Collective Bargaining in a Free Society, 2nd Ed., 1168 pages, 1979, with 1979 Statutory Supplement and 1982 Case Supplement (Casebook)

See also Employment Discrimination, Social Legislation

LAND FINANCE

See Real Estate Transactions

LAND USE

Hagman's Cases on Public Planning and Control of Urban and Land Development, 2nd Ed., 1301 pages, 1980 (Casebook)

Hagman's Hornbook on Urban Planning and Land Development Control Law, 706 pages, 1971 (Text)

Wright and Gitelman's Cases and Materials on Land Use, 3rd Ed., 1300 pages, 1982 (Casebook)

Wright and Webber's Land Use in a Nutshell, 316 pages, 1978 (Text)

See also Housing and Urban Development

LAW AND ECONOMICS

Goetz' Cases and Materials on Law and Economics, approximately 460 pages, 1984 (Casebook)

Manne's The Economics of Legal Relationships—Readings in the Theory of Property Rights, 660 pages, 1975 (Text)

LAW AND ECONOMICS—Continued

See also Antitrust, Regulated Industries

LAW AND MEDICINE—PSYCHIATRY

Cohen's Cases and Materials on the Law of Deprivation of Liberty: A Study in Social Control, 755 pages, 1980 (Casebook)

King's The Law of Medical Malpractice in a Nutshell, 340 pages, 1977 (Text)

Shapiro and Spece's Problems, Cases and Materials on Bioethics and Law, 892 pages, 1981 (Casebook)

Sharpe, Fiscina and Head's Cases on Law and Medicine, 882 pages, 1978 (Casebook)

LEGAL HISTORY

Presser and Zainaldin's Cases on Law and American History, 855 pages, 1980 (Casebook)

See also Legal Method and Legal System

LEGAL METHOD AND LEGAL SYSTEM

Aldisert's Readings, Materials and Cases in the Judicial Process, 948 pages, 1976 (Casebook)

Bodenheimer, Oakley and Love's Readings and Cases on an Introduction to the Anglo-American Legal System, 161 pages, 1980 (Casebook)

Davies and Lawry's Institutions and Methods of the Law—Introductory Teaching Materials, 547 pages, 1982 (Casebook)

Dvorkin, Himmelstein and Lesnick's Becoming a Lawyer: A Humanistic Perspective on Legal Education and Professionalism, 211 pages, 1981 (Text)

Fryer and Orentlicher's Cases and Materials on Legal Method and Legal System, 1043 pages, 1967 (Casebook)

Greenberg's Judicial Process and Social Change, 666 pages, 1977 (Coursebook)

Kempin's Historical Introduction to Anglo-American Law in a Nutshell, 2nd Ed., 280 pages, 1973 (Text)

Kimball's Historical Introduction to the Legal System, 610 pages, 1966 (Casebook)

Mashaw and Merrill's Introduction to the American Public Law System, 1095 pages, 1975, with 1980 Supplement (Casebook)

Murphy's Cases and Materials on Introduction to Law—Legal Process and Procedure, 772 pages, 1977 (Casebook)

Reynolds' Judicial Process in a Nutshell, 292 pages, 1980 (Text)

See also Legal Research and Writing

LAW SCHOOL PUBLICATIONS—Continued

LEGAL NEGOTIATION

Edwards and White's Problems, Readings and Materials on the Lawyer as a Negotiator, 484 pages, 1977 (Casebook)

Williams' Legal Negotiation and Settlement, 207 pages, 1983 (Coursebook)

LEGAL PROFESSION

Aronson's Problems in Professional Responsibility, 280 pages, 1978 (Problem book)

Aronson and Weckstein's Professional Responsibility in a Nutshell, 399 pages, 1980 (Text)

Mellinkoff's The Conscience of a Lawyer, 304 pages, 1973 (Text)

Mellinkoff's Lawyers and the System of Justice, 983 pages, 1976 (Casebook)

Pirsig and Kirwin's Cases and Materials on Professional Responsibility, 3rd Ed., 667 pages, 1976, with 1981 Supplement (Casebook)

Schwartz and Wydick's Problems in Legal Ethics, 285 pages, 1983 (Casebook)

Selected Statutes, Rules and Standards on the Legal Profession, approximately 220 pages, 1984

Smith's Preventing Legal Malpractice, 142 pages, 1981 (Text)

LEGAL RESEARCH AND WRITING

Cohen's Legal Research in a Nutshell, 3rd Ed., 415 pages, 1978 (Text)

Cohen and Berring's How to Find the Law, 8th Ed., 790 pages, 1983. Problem book by Foster and Kelly available (Casebook)

Dickerson's Materials on Legal Drafting, 425 pages, 1981 (Casebook)

Felsenfeld and Siegel's Writing Contracts in Plain English, 290 pages, 1981 (Text)

Gopen's Writing From a Legal Perspective, 225 pages, 1981 (Text)

Mellinkoff's Legal Writing—Sense and Nonsense, 242 pages, 1982 (Text)

Rombauer's Legal Problem Solving—Analysis, Research and Writing, 4th Ed., 424 pages, 1983 (Coursebook)

Squires and Rombauer's Legal Writing in a Nutshell, 294 pages, 1982 (Text)

Statsky's Legal Research, Writing and Analysis, 2nd Ed., 167 pages, 1982 (Coursebook)

Statsky's Legislative Analysis: How to Use Statutes and Regulations, 216 pages, 1975 (Text)

Statsky and Wernet's Case Analysis and Fundamentals of Legal Writing, 2nd Ed., 441 pages, 1984 (Text)

Teply's Programmed Materials on Legal Research and Citation, 334 pages, 1982. Student Library Exercises available (Coursebook)

LEGAL RESEARCH AND WRITING—Continued

Weihofen's Legal Writing Style, 2nd Ed., 332 pages, 1980 (Text)

LEGISLATION

Davies' Legislative Law and Process in a Nutshell, 279 pages, 1975 (Text)

Nutting and Dickerson's Cases and Materials on Legislation, 5th Ed., 744 pages, 1978 (Casebook)

Statsky's Legislative Analysis: How to Use Statutes and Regulations, 216 pages, 1975 (Text)

LOCAL GOVERNMENT

McCarthy's Local Government Law in a Nutshell, 2nd Ed., 404 pages, 1983 (Text)

Michelman and Sandalow's Cases-Comments-Questions on Government in Urban Areas, 1216 pages, 1970, with 1972 Supplement (Casebook)

Reynolds' Hornbook on Local Government Law, 860 pages, 1982 (Text)

Stason and Kauper's Cases and Materials on Municipal Corporations, 3rd Ed., 692 pages, 1959 (Casebook)

Valente's Cases and Materials on Local Government Law, 2nd Ed., 980 pages, 1980 with 1982 Supplement (Casebook)

MASS COMMUNICATION LAW

Gillmor and Barron's Cases and Comment on Mass Communication Law, 3rd Ed., 1008 pages, 1979 (Casebook)

Ginsburg's Regulation of Broadcasting: Law and Policy Towards Radio, Television and Cable Communications, 741 pages, 1979, with 1983 Supplement (Casebook)

Zuckman and Gayne's Mass Communications Law in a Nutshell, 2nd Ed., 473 pages, 1983 (Text)

MILITARY LAW

Shanor and Terrell's Military Law in a Nutshell, 378 pages, 1980 (Text)

MORTGAGES

See Real Estate Transactions

NATURAL RESOURCES LAW

See Energy and Natural Resources Law, Environmental Law, Oil and Gas, Water Law

OFFICE PRACTICE

Hegland's Trial and Practice Skills in a Nutshell, 346 pages, 1978 (Text)

Strong and Clark's Law Office Management, 424 pages, 1974 (Casebook)

LAW SCHOOL PUBLICATIONS—Continued

OFFICE PRACTICE—Continued

See also Legal Interviewing and Counseling, Legal Negotiation

OIL AND GAS

Hemingway's Hornbook on Oil and Gas, 2nd Ed., Student Ed., 543 pages, 1983 (Text)

Huie, Woodward and Smith's Cases and Materials on Oil and Gas, 2nd Ed., 955 pages, 1972 (Casebook)

Lowe's Oil and Gas Law in a Nutshell, 443 pages, 1983 (Text)

See also Energy and Natural Resources Law

PARTNERSHIP

See Agency—Partnership

PATENT AND COPYRIGHT LAW

Choate and Francis' Cases and Materials on Patent Law, 2nd Ed., 1110 pages, 1981 (Casebook)

Miller and Davis' Intellectual Property—Patents, Trademarks and Copyright in a Nutshell, approximately 400 pages, 1983 (Text)

Nimmer's Cases on Copyright and Other Aspects of Law Pertaining to Literary, Musical and Artistic Works, 2nd Ed., 1023 pages, 1979 (Casebook)

POVERTY LAW

Brudno's Poverty, Inequality, and the Law: Cases-Commentary-Analysis, 934 pages, 1976 (Casebook)

LaFrance, Schroeder, Bennett and Boyd's Hornbook on Law of the Poor, 558 pages, 1973 (Text)

See also Social Legislation

PRODUCTS LIABILITY

Noel and Phillips' Cases on Products Liability, 2nd Ed., 821 pages, 1982 (Casebook)

Noel and Phillips' Products Liability in a Nutshell, 2nd Ed., 341 pages, 1981 (Text)

PROPERTY

Aigler, Smith and Tefft's Cases on Property, 2 volumes, 1339 pages, 1960 (Casebook)

Bernhardt's Real Property in a Nutshell, 2nd Ed., 448 pages, 1981 (Text)

Boyer's Survey of the Law of Property, 766 pages, 1981 (Text)

Browder, Cunningham, Julin and Smith's Cases on Basic Property Law, 3rd Ed., 1447 pages, 1979 (Casebook)

Burby's Hornbook on Real Property, 3rd Ed., 490 pages, 1965 (Text)

PROPERTY—Continued

Burke's Personal Property in a Nutshell, 322 pages, 1983 (Text)

Chused's A Modern Approach to Property: Cases-Notes-Materials, 1069 pages, 1978 with 1980 Supplement (Casebook)

Cohen's Materials for a Basic Course in Property, 526 pages, 1978 (Casebook)

Cunningham, Whitman and Stoebuck's Hornbook on the Law of Property, Student Ed., approximately 808 pages, 1984 (Text)

Donahue, Kauper and Martin's Cases on Property, 2nd Ed., 1362 pages, 1983 (Casebook)

Hill's Landlord and Tenant Law in a Nutshell, 319 pages, 1979 (Text)

Moynihan's Introduction to Real Property, 254 pages, 1962 (Text)

Phipps' Titles in a Nutshell, 277 pages, 1968 (Text)

Uniform Land Transactions Act, Uniform Simplification of Land Transfers Act, Uniform Condominium Act, 1977 Official Text with Comments, 462 pages, 1978

See also Housing and Urban Development, Real Estate Transactions, Land Use

REAL ESTATE TRANSACTIONS

Bruce's Real Estate Finance in a Nutshell, 292 pages, 1979 (Text)

Maxwell, Riesenfeld, Hetland and Warren's Cases on California Security Transactions in Land, 3rd Ed., approximately 646 pages, 1984 (Casebook)

Nelson and Whitman's Cases on Real Estate Transfer, Finance and Development, 2nd Ed., 1114 pages, 1981, with 1983 Supplement (Casebook)

Osborne's Cases and Materials on Secured Transactions, 559 pages, 1967 (Casebook)

Osborne, Nelson and Whitman's Hornbook on Real Estate Finance Law, 3rd Ed., 885 pages, 1979 (Text)

REGULATED INDUSTRIES

Gellhorn and Pierce's Regulated Industries in a Nutshell, 394 pages, 1982 (Text)

Morgan's Cases and Materials on Economic Regulation of Business, 830 pages, 1976, with 1978 Supplement (Casebook)

Pozen's Financial Institutions: Cases, Materials and Problems on Investment Management, 844 pages, 1978 (Casebook)

See also Mass Communication Law, Banking Law

LAW SCHOOL PUBLICATIONS—Continued

REMEDIES

Dobbs' Hornbook on Remedies, 1067 pages, 1973 (Text)

Dobbs' Problems in Remedies, 137 pages, 1974 (Problem book)

Dobbyn's Injunctions in a Nutshell, 264 pages, 1974 (Text)

Friedman's Contract Remedies in a Nutshell, 323 pages, 1981 (Text)

Leavell, Love and Nelson's Cases and Materials on Equitable Remedies and Restitution, 3rd Ed., 704 pages, 1980 (Casebook)

McCormick's Hornbook on Damages, 811 pages, 1935 (Text)

O'Connell's Remedies in a Nutshell, 364 pages, 1977 (Text)

York and Bauman's Cases and Materials on Remedies, 3rd Ed., 1250 pages, 1979 (Casebook)

REVIEW MATERIALS

Ballantine's Problems

Black Letter Series

Smith's Review Series

West's Review Covering Multistate Subjects

SECURITIES REGULATION

Ratner's Securities Regulation: Materials for a Basic Course, 2nd Ed., 1050 pages, 1980 with 1982 Supplement (Casebook)

Ratner's Securities Regulation in a Nutshell, 2nd Ed., 322 pages, 1982 (Text)

Selected Securities and Business Planning Statutes, Rules and Forms, 485 pages, 1982

SOCIAL LEGISLATION

Brudno's Income Redistribution Theories and Programs: Cases-Commentary-Analyses, 480 pages, 1977 (Casebook)—reprint from Brudno's Poverty, Inequality and the Law, 1976

Hood and Hardy's Workers' Compensation and Employee Protection in a Nutshell, approximately 243 pages, 1984 (Text)

LaFrance's Welfare Law: Structure and Entitlement in a Nutshell, 455 pages, 1979 (Text)

Malone, Plant and Little's Cases on Workers' Compensation and Employment Rights, 2nd Ed., 951 pages, 1980 (Casebook)

See also Poverty Law

TAXATION

Dodge's Federal Taxation of Estates, Trusts and Gifts: Principles and Planning, 771 pages, 1981 with 1982 Supplement (Casebook)

TAXATION—Continued

Garbis and Struntz' Cases and Materials on Tax Procedure and Tax Fraud, 829 pages, 1982 with 1984 Supplement (Casebook)

Gunn's Cases and Materials on Federal Income Taxation of Individuals, 785 pages, 1981 with 1983 Supplement (Casebook)

Hellerstein and Hellerstein's Cases on State and Local Taxation, 4th Ed., 1041 pages, 1978 with 1982 Supplement (Casebook)

Kahn's Handbook on Basic Corporate Taxation, 3rd Ed., Student Ed., 614 pages, 1981 with 1983 Supplement (Text)

Kahn and Gann's Corporate Taxation and Taxation of Partnerships and Partners, 1107 pages, 1979, with 1981 Supplement (Casebook)

Kragen and McNulty's Cases and Materials on Federal Income Taxation, Vol. I: Taxation of Individuals, 3rd Ed., 1283 pages, 1979 with 1983 Supplement (Casebook)

Kragen and McNulty's Cases and Materials on Federal Income Taxation, Vol. II: Taxation of Corporations, Shareholders, Partnerships and Partners, 3rd Ed., 989 pages, 1981 with 1983 Supplement (Casebook)

Lowndes, Kramer and McCord's Hornbook on Federal Estate and Gift Taxes, 3rd Ed., 1099 pages, 1974 (Text)

McNulty's Federal Estate and Gift Taxation in a Nutshell, 3rd Ed., 509 pages, 1983 (Text)

McNulty's Federal Income Taxation of Individuals in a Nutshell, 3rd Ed., 487 pages, 1983 (Text)

Posin's Hornbook on Federal Income Taxation of Individuals, Student Ed., 491 pages, 1983 (Text)

Rice's Problems and Materials in Federal Estate and Gift Taxation, 3rd Ed., 474 pages, 1978 (Casebook)

Rice and Solomon's Problems and Materials in Federal Income Taxation, 3rd Ed., 670 pages, 1979 (Casebook)

Rose and Raskind's Advanced Federal Income Taxation: Corporate Transactions—Cases, Materials and Problems, 955 pages, 1978 (Casebook)

Selected Federal Taxation Statutes and Regulations, 1255 pages, 1983

Soboloff and Weidenbruch's Federal Income Taxation of Corporations and Stockholders in a Nutshell, 362 pages, 1981 (Text)

LAW SCHOOL PUBLICATIONS—Continued

TORTS

Christie's Cases and Materials on the Law of Torts, 1264 pages, 1983 (Casebook)

Green, Pedrick, Rahl, Thode, Hawkins, Smith and Treece's Cases and Materials on Torts, 2nd Ed., 1360 pages, 1977 (Casebook)

Green, Pedrick, Rahl, Thode, Hawkins, Smith, and Treece's Advanced Torts: Injuries to Business, Political and Family Interests, 2nd Ed., 544 pages, 1977 (Casebook)—reprint from Green, et al. Cases and Materials on Torts, 2nd Ed., 1977

Keeton's Computer-Aided and Workbook Exercises on Tort Law, 164 pages, 1976 (Coursebook)

Keeton, Keeton, Sargentich and Steiner's Cases and Materials on Torts, and Accident Law, 1360 pages, 1983 (Casebook)

Kionka's Torts in a Nutshell: Injuries to Persons and Property, 434 pages, 1977 (Text)

Malone's Torts in a Nutshell: Injuries to Family, Social and Trade Relations, 358 pages, 1979 (Text)

Prosser and Keeton's Hornbook on Torts, 5th Ed., Student Ed., approximately 1052 pages, 1984 (Text)

Shapo's Cases on Tort and Compensation Law, 1244 pages, 1976 (Casebook)

See also Products Liability

TRADE REGULATION

McManis' Unfair Trade Practices in a Nutshell, 444 pages, 1982 (Text)

Oppenheim, Weston, Maggs and Schechter's Cases and Materials on Unfair Trade Practices and Consumer Protection, 4th Ed., 1038 pages, 1983 (Casebook)

See also Antitrust, Regulated Industries

TRIAL AND APPELLATE ADVOCACY

Appellate Advocacy, Handbook of, 249 pages, 1980 (Text)

Bergman's Trial Advocacy in a Nutshell, 402 pages, 1979 (Text)

Goldberg's The First Trial (Where Do I Sit?) (What Do I Say?) in a Nutshell, 396 pages, 1982 (Text)

Hegland's Trial and Practice Skills in a Nutshell, 346 pages, 1978 (Text)

Jeans' Handbook on Trial Advocacy, Student Ed., 473 pages, 1975 (Text)

McElhaney's Effective Litigation, 457 pages, 1974 (Casebook)

Nolan's Cases and Materials on Trial Practice, 518 pages, 1981 (Casebook)

Parnell and Shellhaas' Cases, Exercises and Problems for Trial Advocacy, 171 pages, 1982 (Coursebook)

TRUSTS AND ESTATES

Atkinson's Hornbook on Wills, 2nd Ed., 975 pages, 1953 (Text)

Averill's Uniform Probate Code in a Nutshell, 425 pages, 1978 (Text)

Bogert's Hornbook on Trusts, 5th Ed., 726 pages, 1973 (Text)

Clark, Lusky and Murphy's Cases and Materials on Gratuitous Transfers, 2nd Ed., 1102 pages, 1977 (Casebook)

Gulliver's Cases and Materials on Future Interests, 624 pages, 1959 (Casebook)

Gulliver's Introduction to the Law of Future Interests, 87 pages, 1959 (Casebook)—reprint from Gulliver's Cases and Materials on Future Interests, 1959

McGovern's Cases and Materials on Wills, Trusts and Future Interests: An Introduction to Estate Planning, 750 pages, 1983 (Casebook)

Mennell's Cases and Materials on California Decedent's Estates, 566 pages, 1973 (Casebook)

Mennell's Wills and Trusts in a Nutshell, 392 pages, 1979 (Text)

Powell's The Law of Future Interests in California, 91 pages, 1980 (Text)

Simes' Hornbook on Future Interests, 2nd Ed., 355 pages, 1966 (Text)

Turrentine's Cases and Text on Wills and Administration, 2nd Ed., 483 pages, 1962 (Casebook)

Uniform Probate Code, 5th Ed., Official Text With Comments, 384 pages, 1977

Waggoner's Future Interests in a Nutshell, 361 pages, 1981 (Text)

WATER LAW

Trelease's Cases and Materials on Water Law, 3rd Ed., 833 pages, 1979 (Casebook)

See also Energy and Natural Resources Law, Environmental Law

WILLS

See Trusts and Estates

WOMEN AND THE LAW

Kay's Text, Cases and Materials on Sex-Based Discrimination, 2nd Ed., 1045 pages, 1981, with 1983 Supplement (Casebook)

Thomas' Sex Discrimination in a Nutshell, 399 pages, 1982 (Text)

See also Employment Discrimination

WORKERS' COMPENSATION

See Social Legislation

CASES AND MATERIALS
ON
LAW AND ECONOMICS

By
Charles J. Goetz
Joseph M. Hartfield Professor of Law
University of Virginia School of Law

AMERICAN CASEBOOK SERIES

WEST PUBLISHING CO.
ST. PAUL, MINN.
1984

Library of Congress Cataloging in Publication Data

Goetz, Charles J.
  Cases and materials on law and economics.

  (American casebook series)
  Includes index.
  1. Law—United States—Cases.   2. Economics.
I. Title.   II. Series.
KF385.A4G59   1983   349.73   83–21787
                            347.3
ISBN 0-314-76541-7

Preface

The relatively brief history of the Law-Economics nexus has already produced a number of excellent books, running the gamut of treatises, collected articles, and expository works. Many of these have been pressed into service—with varying degrees of success—as teaching materials. These pages nonetheless represent the first attempt to present economic analysis in a way that mirrors the traditional law school casebook format.

The materials in this book do not presume any prerequisite level of economic knowledge; the important conceptual tools are introduced gradually and applied to a series of increasingly sophisticated problems. For some students, certain unfamiliar concepts and perspectives will at first seem to present formidable technical hurdles. In fact, however, the technical economics involved never rises above a very modest level that is soon amply accessible to anyone who merely perseveres.

The cases, problems, and textual matter have been selected to teach those important economic concepts that have wide applicability in Law. The substantive areas of application are primarily illustrative and do not pretend to survey the depth and breadth of contemporary Law and Economics scholarship. A supplementary reading list, organized by applied areas of Law, is supplied as a Bibliographical Appendix, although this list is itself intended to be suggestive rather than comprehensive. Areas with strong economic overtones—such as antitrust and tax policy—have deliberately been somewhat under-represented in both the text and the bibliography precisely because their economic content is so apparent.

The content of the book has been developed in classes at the University of Virginia since 1975. The first three chapters contain essential concepts that probably should be treated in the order presented. The remainder of the material is somewhat more conducive to selective "skipping around." Although the number of pages may seem slimmer than a standard casebook, experience has indicated that they represent an over-full semester's agenda.

The author would find it impossible to enumerate all of his colleagues, past and present, who have patiently initiated a curious—in many senses of the word—economist into the mysteries of the Law. Thomas Bergin, Stephen Saltzburg and Warren Schwartz should nonetheless be singled out for their generosity with both time and insights. Finally, these pages reflect in many ways a warmly treasured collaboration with Robert Scott, a masterful teacher and truly stimulating legal scholar.

CHARLES J. GOETZ

Charlottesville, Virginia
December, 1983

SUMMARY OF CONTENTS

*

TABLE OF CONTENTS

TABLE OF CONTENTS

TABLE OF CONTENTS

TABLE OF CONTENTS

TABLE OF CONTENTS

TABLE OF CASES

The principal cases are in Italic type. Cases cited or discussed are in Roman type. References are to Pages.

TABLE OF CASES

CASES AND MATERIALS
ON
LAW AND ECONOMICS

*

Chapter I

ANALYZING HUMAN CHOICE UNDER ALTERNATIVE RULES

There can be little doubt that one primary purpose of legal systems is to modify human behavior, to induce at least some people to act in ways that they would not choose but for the pressure of legal incentives or disincentives. If this behavior-modification or "channelling" function of law is truly important, then it also becomes imperative to understand the predictable behavioral implications of alternative legal doctrines and policies. When a particular rule change is enacted, exactly what will happen? Or, if we cannot predict "exactly" what will happen, can we make any useful generalizations at all about the results of a proposed modification in law? And if it is indeed impossible to make useful predictions about consequences, then on what grounds are institutional changes to be advocated?

These observations suggest that the study of Law can be thought of as having a close affinity to the social sciences. Jurisprudence is, after all, inevitably concerned with predicting and describing the behavior of human beings under alternative institutional arrangements. Increased awareness of this is precisely why the nexus between Law and traditional social sciences, especially Economics, has become the focus of intensified interest in recent years. Methodological tools and concepts of the social sciences are increasingly applied in legal scholarship because they provide insights about the interaction of human beings—judges, parties litigant, potential tortfeasors, etc.—as they confront alternative legal rules.

The use of economics in legal analysis is sometimes viewed with alarm and alleged to be infected with ideological connotations. Of course, any "approach" to legal analysis can be, and frequently is, bent to serve ideological purposes. Just bear in mind that economic analysis is no more and no less subject to this danger than many another tool of intellectual inquiry. Whatever the goals of its users, the power of economic analysis to predict and describe many facets of human behavior has no necessary link with value judgements about

1

what conduct or institutions should be classified as good, bad, or in-different. One can, after all, describe in essentially neutral fashion the objective implications of alternative rule systems without sitting in judgement on the results themselves. Occasionally, the mere lay-ing bare of policy implications seems to lead rather directly to value judgements, but this is not an inherent characteristic of the analysis itself; rather, it reflects what is frequently the natural reaction of an observer to any revelatory process.

Economists use special terms of art to distinguish descriptive-pre-dictive analysis from prescriptive-judgmental statements, labelling the two analytical modes as "positive economics" and "normative eco-nomics," respectively. Inevitably, objective economic analysis and subjective opinion tend to become intertangled in the hands of many practitioners. Nevertheless, an expert in positive social science anal-ysis does not, merely by virtue of his technical expertise, warrant having any greater-than-ordinary deference paid to whatever purely normative opinions he may from time to time intermingle with his analysis.

On the other hand, a reasonable ability to describe the implications of alternatives does seem to be a necessary precondition for compe-tent formation of value judgements, if forming value judgements is what one ultimately is interested in doing. After all, unless the ob-jective consequences of alternatives are first correctly understood, how can subjective value weightings be rationally and intelligently attached? One useful result of analysis therefore is to expose counterintuitive effects or ill-considered indirect consequences of a policy. Indeed, it is not uncommon to hear economic reasoning used to suggest that a legal policy adopted in pursuit of some goal is unin-tentionally counterproductive. Hence, although prediction is not it-self an inherently normative act, it serves as an essential input into the process wherein people ultimately arrive at reasoned value judge-ments about law—or any other public policies, for that matter. From this point of view, predictions about the economic consequences of legal decisions are a valid and useful part of the "means to ends" debate in a legislative or judicial proceeding. Of course, in an adver-sary process, it is perhaps unsurprising that the predictive inputs are frequently selective and self-serving. Still, such inputs are no more and no less than specialized and occasionally quite persuasive formal tools of legal argumentation. Potentially powerful tools of legal ar-gumentation can be ignored only at one's peril. In fact, the probabili-ty of having to deal with economic reasoning in law seems to be growing, whether in the form of affirmative arguments to be ad-vanced and supported or as allegations that someone else raises and which, therefore, must be probed, criticized, and rebutted.

Advocacy is not the only use of economic-type behavioral analysis, however. Sometimes the application is quite simply educative and explanatory, an attempt to understand something or reconcile it with apparently conflicting information. For instance, a pervasive concern in legal studies is the role of coercion. Behavioral strictures rise above the status of mere exhortations and become "laws" precisely because they are backed by a sanction or coercive force. Yet, in a democratic society, laws supposedly arise out of the consent of the governed. To many, this smacks of mystery, or at least paradox. Why would people consent to—and, presumably, benefit from—a system of coercion? Some of the early analysis in this chapter is directed precisely at the question of why self-imposed coercion is a plausible and voluntarily chosen response to a wide class of societal problems.

Behavioral analysis frequently reveals that results which appear to have been chosen freely and voluntarily are, on closer inspection, not so greatly desired as they superficially seem. This is a very important realization because the fact that a decisionmaker freely chooses an option is often offered as an allegedly persuasive empirical proof that the chosen option must be "better" than the other available choices. Otherwise, why did the person choose what he did rather than something else? [a] In fact, whereas there is indeed a kernel of truth in that somewhat Panglossian argument, it is at best a prima facie argument or presumption, subject to qualifications that are of great relevance in precisely the factual circumstances that typify many legal applications. Even in this initial chapter, we shall see that circumstances frequently induce people to choose results that they would certainly regard as "inferior" to other available results.

Another recognizable objective of economic analysis in Law is that of mere explanation. Under this rubric, one may hypothesize about why people did historically make a particular policy choice without also necessarily endorsing the values of the original decisionmakers. This involves a process of working backwards, of discovering a plausible rationale for observed behavior, of ferreting out what may have been the motivation for a law. One is then free to take the additional step of approving or disapproving what are perceived as the underlying objectives of those who actually made the choices. Becoming aware of an underlying systematic basis for some class of phenomena can powerfully assist one in learning a body of doctrine, manipulating it, appreciating its nuances, and even predicting its evolution in response to changing conditions.

This chapter introduces some elementary concepts that will be useful in reasoning about legal phenomena in terms of behavioral sci-

---

a. For a critical view of this, see Leff, "Economic Analysis of Law: Some Realism About Nominalism," 60 Va.L.Rev. 451, 456–459.

ence concepts. Initially, the behavioral science concepts employed are not notably "economic" in character. Although the vocabulary of the economist's conceptual bag of tools has become increasingly important in legal applications, the application of economic terminology should not imply any claim that the phenomena being analyzed are necessarily economic in the narrow sense of the term. In fact, it just happens that certain conceptual tools created by economists for the analysis of explicitly economic transactions can usefully be adapted to the legal environment. Legal issues frequently do have an explicitly economic component, of course. Nonetheless, if the methodology presented below is properly understood, it can legitimately be applied in many areas where mere economic motivation would be a gross oversimplification. In many cases, the language of economics represents merely the application of a specialized tool of formal logic, a deducing of conclusions from premises in a way somewhat akin to the still more abstract methods of symbolic logic and mathematics upon which, in turn, economic theory itself draws. It is perhaps true that the more formal and elegant a mode of analysis, the more an unwary person runs the risk of being overly dazzled. On the other hand, formal reasoning is valuable precisely because it permits a careful observer to scrutinize critically both the premises and the logical links that are alleged to justify certain conclusions.

Finally, one should be sensitive to the limits of economic argumentation in legal contexts, even when "economic" is construed in its most expansive and generous sense. In some circumstances, arguments based on economic reasoning will have undeniable relevance and potent persuasive force. In other situations, economic factors may be of relatively trivial weight as compared to amorphous—yet perfectly valid—ethical, moral or even viscerally instinctive notions of what is right and just. As with any other source of legal arguments, economic factors must ultimately be evaluated through each individual's own views of their relevance and weight. Economic analysis is not a single great searchlight that will penetrate and illuminate every nook and cranny of the law, but neither is any other "approach," whether it be rooted in ethics, sociology, legal history, or some other discipline that can be brought to bear on legal problems. Since this is a book about economic reasoning in law, practical constraints will impose what may occasionally resemble methodological tunnel vision. With only that caveat, the reader is credited with the good sense to integrate, where necessary, the narrowly focused materials that follow into a more fully articulated intellectual framework.

What follows is not intended to be elegant or highly technical economics. An attempt is made to develop and apply only that limited set of economic-type constructs that is most useful in legal reasoning. Even so, there is relatively short shrift given to many traditional economic topics that are adequately treated elsewhere, in standard economic textbooks at an elementary or intermediate level. The analytic concepts are introduced in a carefully phased process wherein the applications grow progressively more sophisticated. Considerable cohesiveness and intrinsic interest has been designed into these legal applications, since the intent is for this to be genuinely a law book rather than intermediate economic theory thinly cloaked with market-linked legal issues. But the reader should be warned that communication of an underlying set of analytic principles is the real goal and organizing principle of these pages. Accordingly, communication of economic content is frequently pursued in ways detrimental to a potentially more informative treatment of the substantive law involved.

Several of the first few concepts introduced below are originally drawn from game theory. Why give such a primacy of place to game theory? A standard dictionary definition of a game is: "a contest, physical or mental, according to set rules, undertaken for amusement or for a stake." Two elements of that definition should be especially noted. One is that games are explicitly defined as behavioral situations governed by *rules*. The second is that game theory deals neither exclusively nor even primarily with contests undertaken for amusement; rather, it analyzes the behavior of "players" in serious conflict situations, frequently for heavy stakes. Conflict within a set of rules is what a great deal of the law is really about. Some of the "games" affected are played out in a marketplace where buyers and sellers compete for resources subject to a set of property and trading rules. This is the traditional domain of economic analysis. Legal proceedings can themselves be conceptualized as games, governed by their own peculiar system of rules, entitlements, costs, etc. Many of the underlying conflict situations giving rise to legal proceedings can also be understood as games. In any case, students of the Law ought to be fundamentally interested in how the strategies of players change and how the predicted outcomes vary as the applicable rules of various law-related "games" are modified.

QUESTIONS

1. There are many situations in which some agenda of societal goals and the trade-offs between them has already been fully articulated and predetermined. A legal analyst's role, therefore, is merely to offer counsel to decisionmakers regarding the advisability of alternative laws as means to these ends.

a. What real-world jobs for a lawyer fit the above scenario? In what respects is predictive competence necessary?

b. Drug addicts are responsible for a large amount of crime. This crime is thought to be motivated by the addicts' eagerness to "earn" the income necessary to support an expensive drug habit. In 1973, the State of New York passed tough new mandatory sentencing provisions which increased the penalties for drug distribution. It is plausible to assume that the legislators were attempting to reduce the availability of drugs and the attendant crime problem. Are tougher drug laws an effective means to that end? Does your answer depend on empirical data?

c. Supply some specific examples wherein it can persuasively be argued that a statute or common law rule adopted as a means to an identifiable end is actually detrimental to that end. Can you supply another example of a law that has unintended "byproduct" consequences that substantially vitiate the benefits of what was originally viewed as its direct or primary objective?

2. You are a basketball fan. A proposal is made to penalize a team two points per inch or fraction thereof for the number of inches by which the average height of its players used in a game exceeds 76.

a. Could a basketball coach help you in describing what effect this rule change would have on how the game is played? What kinds of things would the "expert" be able to tell you that you couldn't figure out for yourself? Would you expect any surprises? (E.g., can you advance any argument that suggests that having one or more real giants on a team would become more important than ever before?)

b. Once he had expounded on the consequences to the game, to what extent would you be willing further to defer to the expert's opinion as to whether the resultant changes would make the game better or worse? If possible, provide an example of a sports rule wherein you suspect that the preferences of coaches and fans are antagonistic.

c. Are the "experts" always right in predicting consequences? NCAA rules allowed conferences to use several kinds of "experimental" basketball rules—such as the three-point shot and the time clock—for the first time during the 1982-83 college season. If you do not remember yourself, ask a friend who is a real fan. When are experts most likely to be right or to be wrong?

3. Richard Posner and others have argued that common law legal rules implement goals of "economic efficiency."

The rules assigning property rights and determining liability, the procedures for resolving legal disputes, the constraints on law enforcers, methods of computing damages and determining the availability of injunctive relief—these and other important elements of the legal system can best be understood as attempts, though rarely acknowledged as such, to promote an efficient allocation of resources.[b]

This position is, as might be imagined, a controversial one. In fact, the very sense in which the term economic efficiency should be understood is itself subject to some debate.

    a. Suppose that economic efficiency were defined as a situation in which potential economic gains were fully exploited or, what is pretty much the same thing, "wasteful" conduct were discouraged and avoided. How plausible does it seem to you that a large part of common law doctrines might be explicable in terms of economic efficiency goals?

    b. One seldom finds explicit use of economic analysis in judicial decisions, a fact which does not seem to support the assertion that economic considerations are determinants of judicial policy. The following remark by Prof. Neil Komesar may be interpreted as casting some doubt on the strength of that evidence:

> Traditional legal analysis teaches that the reasons articulated by the decisionmaker are seldom sufficient—and are sometimes irrelevant—as indicators of the actual determinants of decisions. Judicial opinions are more often observations to be explained than sources of explanation. They yield insights only to one who can approach them systematically.[c]

What do you think? To what extent are written opinions themselves probative as to the underlying motivation of judicial decisions?

    c. One objection to the efficiency hypothesis about common law formation is that many jurists never have and never will know very much about economics. To what extent would a Darwinian-type "survival of the fittest" explanation meet that objection?[d]

b. Posner, "The Economic Approach to Law," 53 Texas L.Rev. 757, 764 (1975) (footnotes omitted). See also, Posner, "Some Uses and Abuses of Economics in Law, 46 U.Chi.L.Rev. 281, 288-89 (1979). Other scholars have also advanced similar theories although they differ, and to some considerable extent disagree, among themselves with respect to methodology and details of the theory. These include: Rubin, "Why is the Common Law Efficient?," 6 J.Legal Stud. 51 (1977); Priest, "The Common Law Process and the Selection of Efficient Rules," 6 J.Legal Stud. 65 (1977); Goodman, "An Economic Theory of Evaluation of the Common Law," 7 J.Legal Stud. 393 (1978); and Priest, "Selective Characteristics of Litigation," 9 J.Legal

Stud. 399 (1980). A discussion of the difficulty of proving the efficiency hypothesis may be found in Kornhauser, "A Guide to the Perplexed Claims of Efficiency in the Law," 8 Hofstra L.Rev. 591, 610–21 (1980).

c. Komesar, In Search of a General Approach to Legal Analysis: A Comparative Institutional Approach," 79 Mich.L. Rev. 1350, 1354–55 (1981).

d. For instance, Rubin, supra, posits an evolutionary mechanism guided by the decisions of the litigants rather than the judges. The evolutionary approach is criticized in Cooter and Kornhauser, "Can Litigation Improve the Law Without the Help of Judges," 9 J.Legal Stud. 235 (1980).

  d. Assume that the common law efficiency hypothesis were persuasively established as a more or less accurate reflection of historical fact, but you are a Marxist and regard the pursuit of economic efficiency as a vicious capitalistic excuse for grinding the faces of the poor. Would knowing the economic efficiency implications of various legal rules have any value to you as a lawyer?

  4. The following rule is proposed: when property subject to a security interest is claimed by a creditor and sold, the debtor must be credited with the actual proceeds of the resale or the fair retail value, whichever is higher.

  a. What are the implications of such a rule if adopted? Are such implications likely to be important in determining the decision? If your answer would be different depending on the forum (court, legislature, regulatory commission, etc.), indicate why.

  b. Would you know how to cross-examine an economist testifying as to these implications? If the forum were a court, would expert testimony of that type be allowed?

THE PRISONER'S DILEMMA

  The following scenario illustrates a famous game-theoretic model that is attributed to the mathematician A. W. Tucker. Widely known as the "Prisoner's Dilemma," this situation, together with several closely related fact patterns, provides powerful insights into behavioral problems that have importance in the law.[e] The scenario presented here is embellished slightly for pedagogical purposes but, as the title suggests, closely follows Tucker's original anecdote.

  Imagine that you are an urban clerical worker who stops off in a downtown bar after working late one night. You encounter a kindred soul, hitherto a perfect stranger. In the course of having several drinks, the two of you commiserate over your mutual senses of extreme financial deprivation. One thing leads to another and, after suitably cautious circumlocutions, this new friend finally suggests that there might be a very nice gain indeed from knocking over a certain downtown jewelry store. In true Hollywood fashion, the fadeout of one scene depicts the larcenous proposal. Then, cut to the next scene wherein the two of you are braced against a building wall being frisked during an arrest by the Metropolitan Police. The jewelry store alarm bell is ringing and a few nice rope-of-gold necklaces are drooping accusingly out of your pocket.

  e. There is an extensive literature dealing with this famous game-theoretic concept. For general discussions at a reasonably accessible level, see R. Luce and H. Raiffa, Games and Decisions, 94–102 (1967); A Rapoport and A. Chammah, Prisoner's Dilemma (1965); A. Rapoport, N-Person Game Theory (1970).

The following scene is set in the interview room of the City Jail on the very next morning. Present is a grim, businesslike Assistant Prosecutor. With an admirably straight face, you are telling her how two other people broke into the store but, when the alarm bell started to clang, dropped some of the loot in an attempt to beat a hasty retreat." All my friend and I did was pick up a little of the overflow that they dropped," you protest indignantly.

"Yes, yes," she sighs. "Very imaginative. Only the umpteenth time this week I've heard almost the same fairytale. Face facts! At the very least we've got you for possession of stolen property, about a 9-month stretch in the workhouse I'd say. But maybe we can work something out."

"Work something out? . . ." you murmur encouragingly.

"Yeh. The Chief is taking a lot of flak about petty thieves always getting off with reduced charges in these cases. If you'll give us some good testimony—testimony that'll permit a heavy conviction against your accomplice—we'll dismiss any charges against you."

"Very nice, very nice," you respond. "But isn't there some catch to this?"

With an incongruously little-girlish grin she allows that "I never did say there *wasn't* a catch, did I now? To be perfectly honest, I'm about to make exactly the same offer to your partner-in-crime across the hall."

"But what happens if we *both* accept the deal and agree to testify?"

"Well now, you could hardly expect the People to make much of a concession to you in that case, could you? After all, if your accomplice is willing to sing, your own testimony isn't worth precious much. What we'd do then is to stick you both for breaking and entering, but only ask for a moderate sentence, like maybe about three years instead of the five allowable under the statute."

"_____ _____!", you screech. "I'll just keep my mouth shut! Whadda y'think I'm some kind of stupid chump?!!"

"Indeed we really do hope that you're *not*," the Assistant Prosecutor smirks knowingly as she signals to the guard to let her out. "We'd just like you to give a lot of thought to what happens if you keep silent and your great and good friend over there squeals: we go for the full five-year term. Have it your own way, though. The offer is open."

QUESTIONS

1. First a predictive question. If it were necessary to complete the "script" of the above scenario, what is a plausible ending to the story? How sure are you?

    a. First, assume that an agreement between the two prisoners not to testify is unenforceable by any sanction, whether legal or retributive. Would both prisoners testify? Neither one? How would they behave and why? How would *you* behave under similar circumstances? Does it matter whether or not the prisoners are allowed ample opportunity to communicate with each other?

    b. If an agreement not to talk is unenforceable legally, one or both parties may nonetheless attempt to convince the other that an agreement not to testify will be enforced by subsequent retribution against the party who "squeals." Assess the credibility of this threat. Would the prisoners be better off if they both belonged to the Mafia?

    c. Suppose that a court of law would provide traditional damage remedies for any agreement between the prisoners. Specifically, the prisoners could make a legally binding contract and the party who breached the contract would be held liable for damages suffered by the breachee. This possibility suggests another predictive question: Exactly what contract would you expect them to make?

    d. How can the prisoner's dilemma concept be applied more generally to the whole field of executory contracts? What relationship is there to the traditional legal concept of "reliance"? [f]

2. Now some "normative" considerations.

    a. "Should" such a contract between prisoners be enforceable? Why?

    b. A corollary question. Is it appropriate that prosecutors be permitted to place prisoners in conditions that produce a Prisoner's Dilemma?

3. Now a conceptualization. Assume that you are not able to use the above scenario as an illustration. How would you explain or define a Prisoner's Dilemma to someone else?

4. A policy application. It has sometimes been suggested that the same attorney should not be permitted to represent two co-defendants being tried in connection with the same criminal incident.[g]

---

f. See the application to the law of contract in Birmingham, "Legal and Moral Duty in Game Theory: Common Law Contract and Chinese Analogies," 18 Buffalo L.Rev. 99, 105–10 (1968–69).

g. See, for example, Geer, "Representation of Multiple Criminal Defendants: Conflicts of Interest and the Professional Responsibilities of the Defense Attorney," 62 Minn.L.Rev. 119 (1978); Gary T.

The thesis is that conflicts of interest inevitably arise between two defendants such that no common position can fairly represent the interests of both clients.

    a. What relevance does the Prisoner's Dilemma have to this proposed ban against joint representation? In the text above, a "dilemma" was created by the prosecutor's structuring of a possible deal. Does joint representation address difficulties that may arise merely out of the facts of the case and the applicable law?

    b. Prof. Gary Lowenthal observes the following:

> To the extent that counsel do not cooperate with each other, it reasonably can be inferred that the interests of the clients conflict. When clients have conflicting interests, one attorney representing all of the defendants can present a unified strategy only at the expense of prejudicing one or more of the clients.[h]

Do you agree?

    5. Finally, an attempt to generalize or analogize: describe some other fact situation wherein the participants seem to be confronted with a behavioral problem similar to the Prisoner's Dilemma.

THE STUDENT'S DILEMMA: UNIVERSITY v. EAGER

The following facts describe a situation that arose in a science course at a large state university:

    a. The University has a rule that penalizes cheating by dismissal and the notation "Dismissed for Cheating" on the offender's transcript.

    b. The mechanics of the examination process are such that it is very easy to cheat. There is a negligible risk of any penalty; the probability of being caught is very close to zero, but not zero.

    c. Grades are distributed strictly on a required curve: A to the highest 10%, B+ to the next 20%, etc.

    d. The course is a key subject required for pre-med students and is known to be an important consideration in the process of medical school admissions reviews. Hence, the benefits from high grades and the penalties for low ones are exceptionally great.

Lightning strikes! While the class is taking the final examination, the proctoring system manifests one of its rare, seemingly spasmodic

Lowenthal, "Joint Representation in Criminal Cases: A Critical Appraisal," 64 Va.L.Rev. 939 (1978).

h. Lowenthal, supra, at 986.

surges into action. Fourth-year student Edward L. Eager is caught *in flagrante delicto*. The evidence that he did in fact cheat is absolutely conclusive; consequently, Ed faces dismissal.

Chris Pensive, another student in the class, is troubled by Ed's predicament and was overheard to make the following comment.

> "Something is wrong, all out of proportion, with the way Ed is being treated. Maybe what he did wasn't right, but he's being punished almost as if he were a criminal. Under the circumstances, his behavior just doesn't seem that bad to me. Ed was almost under duress, almost compelled to do what he did. I don't blame him. I blame the school for holding exams like that."

Ed now faces an administrative hearing prior to the imposition of the penalty pursuant to University rules.

QUESTIONS

1. Is a Prisoner's Dilemma among the students involved here? Or is the situation "something like" a PD?

2. How would you defend Ed if assigned as his counsel at the hearing? Is the University arguably at fault? Is Ed subjected to an irresistible temptation? Is this a case of "self defense"?

3. Chris apparently finds the penalty disproportionate. How should an appropriate penalty ideally be determined?

4. Bribery of foreign officials by the agents of U. S. corporations operating abroad is subject to sanction under U. S. law. Does this bear any similarity to the Ed Eager scenario?

5. What are some real-world analogues of University v. Eager? What legal or policy issues are suggested?

THE PRISONER'S DILEMMA AS A MATRIX MODEL

The use of models is almost ubiquitous in social science. In one sense, the term "model" has almost its vernacular meaning of a representation. When used in a theoretical context, however, a model transcends mere representation; indeed, it may to some extent deliberately sacrifice accuracy of representation for a more abstract and general description that highlights the most important elements in the phenomenon being "modelled." Models may even be caricatures, having the same goal as a deft cartoonist who, with a few expertly chosen but highly oversimplified lines, seeks to convey a meaning more clearly than through a photographic likeness. It must already be apparent that the Prisoner's Dilemma is a conceptual model, a *paradigm* or pattern of potentially wide application that can be analogized to many other interesting situations. It is interesting to see, however, that the paradigm of the Prisoner's Dilemma can itself be modelled in several different ways, varying greatly in their degree of formality. One approach is the one just used: simply to tell the story, employing only ordinary English words similar to those used above. Alternative descriptions, or models, of the same situation may convey additional insights, or at least conceptualize the situation with greater clarity. This possibility will probably be apparent as we now construct a more formal and compact rendition of the same Prisoner's Dilemma conflict.

The Prisoner's Dilemma is frequently presented in the form of a *matrix model* of the type shown in Exhibit 1.1. In this simple form of model, the rows of the matrix represent the possible choices open to a particular prisoner: either Testify or Silence. The columns represent the exogenously controlled circumstances. Hence, the "other" prisoner will either have chosen Testify or Silence. In creating these matrix models, the same general convention is usually followed: choices or "strategies" under the decisionmaker's own control appear on the rows while the externally-controlled "state of nature" is represented by the columns. Each "cell" formed by the intersections of the rows and columns therefore corresponds to a unique combination of the individual's own decision and the external conditions imposed on him exogenously, in this case by the other person's choice.

EXHIBIT 1.1   PD Matrix Model

Your Own Behavior	Behavior by the Other Prisoner	
	SILENCE	TESTIFY
SILENCE	−0.75	−5.0
TESTIFY	0.0	−3.0

Do the row and column labels in Exhibit 1.1 encompass all of the relevant possibilities both for the choosing individual's own choice and the other individual's choice? If so, then the resulting four cells properly represent the four possible outcomes of the Prisoner's Dilemma. Such a representation of the possible choices and outcomes is an important first step in modelling. In more formal language, this process is frequently called identification of the "choice space" or "opportunity set."

Once the possible outcomes are thus identified, the implications of each outcome can also be indicated. In Exhibit 1.1, this is accomplished by placing a number in each cell to tell the outcome or "payoff" in terms of years spent in jail. Other kinds of numbers might be more appropriate for certain purposes. (Can you think of any draw-backs of using years as opposed to something else?)

In any event, the resulting matrix model does give a concise kind of "picture" of the situation faced by any decisionmaker. It is now easy to see that the Testify strategy has what game theorists call the quality of "dominance": no matter which column is assumed, the Testify strategy row always results in the best payoff, i.e., the lowest jail sentence. [Place a circle around the lowest jail sentence in each column of Exhibit 1.1.] In other words, dominance exists when, no matter what the external situation is (as represented by the columns), the "best" strategy for the decisionmaker is always the same row. This presence of dominance is why we might reasonably predict that a prisoner who understands the situation will choose to Testify.

But the other prisoner faces the same kind of matrix—a condition known as "symmetry" of the payoff matrix for the two individuals—and hence can also be predicted to Testify. That enables us to proceed a step further and hazard a prediction about the *particular* outcome of the game that we are most likely to see: because Testify is a dominant strategy for both players, the expected "solution" of the game will be the lower right-hand cell. This, of course, is precisely what the Prosecutor's office hopes for and is the reason why it has structured the "rules" of the game the way they are. A classical Prisoner's Dilemma, then, falls into the wider category of games with a predictable outcome or "solution." In economic models, such a solution will be called an "equilibrium" outcome.

Not all models have determinate solutions or equilibrium outcomes. [The "Chicken" game described later in this chapter will be one that does not.] Even when there does exist what seems to be a determinate theoretical solution, one should be wary of the fact that models are almost always abstractions and simplifications of reality. Still, within appropriate limits, models are powerful analytic tools because they help clarify what forces are at work and how these forces interact. Hence, it is properly cautious to think of models as formalized descriptions of "what tends to emerge" under specified behavioral conditions and factual assumptions.

As we have already seen, models may also be articulated in mere vernacular speech rather than through formal constructions. Lawyers, after all, traditionally pride themselves on their ability to distinguish, deduce, and generally massage and manipulate the English language during any process of legal analysis. One thesis of these pages, however, is that there is frequently some advantage in going through a more formal modelling process, of "writing down" the behavioral conditions in slightly more technical fashion. For instance, do you find that Exhibit 1.1 conveys the essence of the Prisoner's Dilemma game more clearly than mere words? Most, though not all, people feel that it does. The construction just used, the matrix model, is a relatively simple one. As subsequent situations are analyzed, the modelling will require many additional building-blocks of a conceptual type. These building-block concepts are labels and analytical devices that provide tools of thought in much the same way that having more brushes and colors enables an artist to paint better pictures. Equally important, many of the concepts are concise and convenient means of communicating about complex situations with others who "speak the language," just as terms such as negligence, consideration, and reliance are key concepts that facilitate communication among students of the law. That is why it is important to have the patience to learn a certain amount of behavioral science jargon and terminology.

At the same time, a caveat should be issued as we undertake to add to the arsenal of technical terms and concepts: beware of using technical jargon in an inappropriate forum. Economic jargon is frequently not only incommunicative but, worse yet, runs the risk of arousing negative reactions from those—including senior partners and powerful judges—who have not themselves assimilated the language. After working out the implications of a situation in more rigorous terms, therefore, the legal practitioner is often confronted by the necessity to translate arguments and conclusions into more traditional legal terms. Although the translation process may require care and sensitivity, what truly makes sense in one language ought to be susceptible to communication in another form, even if less elegantly. In sum, rigorous terms of art may be ideal in working out one's own personal analysis, but ultimately the language of argument and persuasion must be carefully adapted to its audience.

THE "PRISONER'S DILEMMA" DEFINED

Labelling various behavioral conflicts with names such as Prisoner's Dilemma is merely a technique of classifying situations in a way that may lead to generalizable insights; one should not take the strict requirements of the classic "models" or paradigms too seriously. Nevertheless, a significant advantage of formalizing definitions is that distinctions between otherwise similar situations become apparent. Note that, although we have used the concept and discussed it at some length, a Prisoner's Dilemma has not yet been formally defined. Although you may think that you more or less know what one is, could you really distinguish a classic PD-type situation from just a garden-variety "tough spot"? A rigorous formal definition should clarify just what are the important elements of the phenomenon being discussed. Once these elements of the definition are isolated, one can more easily recognize relevant distinctions among closely related phenomena. Looking ahead, a formal definition will suggest why it is worth distinguishing Prisoner's Dilemma from one of its close lineal descendants in the game theory family, the game of Chicken.

In order to construct an appropriate definition, the structure of the Prisoner's Dilemma game will once more be presented in its now-familiar matrix form. In Exhibit 1.2, the standard conventions are used whereby the rows designate the strategies, the things the player does control, while the columns reflect the "states of nature" that are externally controlled. "Cooperate" is the strategy that involves cooperation among the people in the Dilemma and "Defect" is any departure from this mutually beneficial behavior. By substituting abstract symbols for the numbers in the cells, however, a great deal of additional generality can be derived from the model. Hence, the algebraic symbols a, b, c, and d are now used to represent the payoffs associated with each box or "cell" of the matrix. Note that these symbols may still signify years in jail, as postulated in the original scenario. They are also consistent, however, with payoffs denominated in other kinds of units: money, an index of "satisfaction," etc. The payoff matrix is assumed to be "symmetric," that is the other player is looking at a payoff matrix that has the same structure.

Whereas we have previously described the Prisoner's Dilemma only in rather imprecise terms, use of symbols in the payoff matrix permits a formal definition that is quite generalizable. In order to qualify technically as a Prisoner's Dilemma, there must exist a particular set of relationships among the relative magnitudes of payoffs a, b, c, and d in Exhibit 1.3.

EXHIBIT 1.2   Matrix Model in Symbolic Form

	Other Cooperates	Other Defects
You Cooperate:	a >	c
You Defect:	b ≷	d

Specifically, the payoff matrix of any PD situation must satisfy these three conditions:

    1. $b>a$ and $d>c$, so that Defect is a "dominant" strategy, one which always leads to the highest payoff no matter what behavior is expected of others.

    2. $a>c$ and $b>d$, so that more cooperation by the other player always increases one's own payoff.

3. (a + a) exceeds the similar summation of the two players' payoffs for any other outcome, so that the cooperative solution is really "best" from the standpoint of the players.

The function of conditions 1 and 2 is probably easy to see: the former makes it advantageous for each party to defect, and the latter makes that defection costly to the other party. Condition 3 is a bit more subtle, and at this point its function need be indicated only briefly. Suppose that the sum of the payoffs in a Cooperate/Defect outcome were higher than in a Cooperate/Cooperate, i.e., that $(b+c)>(a+a)$. Assume, then, that a proposed "deal" involves one player being randomly selected to cooperate and the other to defect. Why might this proposed deal be regarded as possibly superior to a Cooperate/Cooperate solution? (If you don't see at least intuitively why, return to this question after the treatment of "expected values" in Chapter II below.) In short, condition 3 is there merely to avoid the possibility that Cooperate/Cooperate is not really the desired solution.

In addition, some social scientists attribute a behavioral significance to the within-column payoff variations $(b - a)$ and $(d - c)$. These are termed "temptation differentials" since they show the incentive to profit by abandoning a cooperative mode of behavior. The larger these are, the less cooperation is predicted, ceteris paribus. Similarly, the diagonal difference $(a - d)$ is called the "cooperation differential" since it is an index of the incentive to achieve the cooperative solution.

"CHICKEN" vs. PRISONER'S DILEMMA

One use of the formal PD definition just derived is to distinguish the prisoner's dilemma from other similar "dilemma"-type situations. For instance, another interesting game, called "Chicken," can be created by altering assumption 1 above so that if the other party is sufficiently uncooperative then cooperation becomes the optimal strategy. Specifically, assume $b > a$ but $d < c$. If you were sure that the other person were *not* going to cooperate, now it would actually be better to cooperate than to remain noncooperative. Since the other player would react similarly if convinced that you would not cooperate, the circumstances are such that it pays to convince the other party of one's stubbornness and obduracy. Note that b is the highest payoff achievable (you defect, other cooperates). This can be gained by successfully bluffing your opponent.

As will become apparent in subsequent sections, bluffing problems are frequently involved in situations of interest to lawyers and that is why Chicken is an important concept. A Chicken Game will be exemplified later in this chapter in the form of the Road Problem, dealing with negotiating agreement on road repair levels. After reflecting on the Road Problem in its purely verbal form, it will be profitable to fit the words into the sort of formal matrix model just laid out. With that forewarning about the role of the Chicken model, we shall develop some additional terminology and then turn to the factual scenario.

OTHER USEFUL JARGON: EXTERNALITIES

The Prisoner's Dilemma has been chosen as a starting point for several reasons. One is that—as will become clearer and clearer as the applications multiply—the situation is an interesting one per se; it has a more or less direct bearing on many interesting legal phenomena. A second reason, however, is that it helps to edge one into a whole set of terminology that is helpful in conceptualizing and distinguishing other situations.

A fundamental characteristic of the Prisoner's Dilemma situation is the presence of some act whose benefits exceed its costs (if any) for a single individual but whose aggregate costs to all affected parties exceed its benefits. Condition 3 in the definition of the PD given above implies that this is true; since the (a + a) aggregate payoffs to the two individuals at the Cooperate/Cooperate solution are larger than the summed payoffs at any other solution, then any defection from that solution necessarily involves a lesser magnitude of gain to the defector than the magnitude of loss to the other player. In pursuing their individual benefits, the players in the Prisoner's Dilemma game will tend to impose on each other what may be a very considerable amount of costs that overbalance any attendant benefits. It does not help the situation that each individual can recognize the ultimately unsatisfactory outcome, the mutually self-defeating nature of the behavior involved. This point deserves some emphasis. It is a simple but dismayingly common error to believe that the reciprocal nature of the damaging behavior either "cancels out," and can therefore be neglected, or that their own recognition of the reciprocity of the damages will cause the "players" to desist from the behavior.

The Prisoner's Dilemma anecdote sets the stage for some additional concepts dealing with costs and benefits. Specifically, there are several economic terms of art worth introducing at this point, both because they are useful in further articulating the Prisoner's Dilemma type of problem and also because they have important applications in other contexts. The terms in question deal with what economists call "externalities."

Economists classify the effects of any act as being "internal" to the extent that they are felt only by the actor and "external" to the extent that they affect third parties. Hence, the Prisoner's Dilemma falls in a class of situations where the internal benefits selfishly pursued by any individual are exceeded by the external costs imposed by others engaged in similar activity. The regulation of many types of external effects, both costs and benefits, will turn out to be a very pervasive theme in Law and Economics problems. Unfortunately, a variety of terminology is sometimes used to describe external effects. Sometimes they are referred to simply as "externalities" or "spillover" effects. Also, the words "private" and "social" are substituted for internal and external, respectively. These alternative sets of terminology are essentially interchangeable. The key question involved is whether the impact of an act is confined to the person who performs it and, if not, whether others are affected beneficially or detrimentally.

The Prisoner's Dilemma illustrates a situation where the external effect is a cost, a harmful effect. Consider what happens to the "other" prisoner if one prisoner decides to testify rather than remain silent: the second prisoner suffers an increase in the years that he will spend in jail. Thus, the testifying creates an *internal benefit* for the prisoner who squeals, but it levies an *external cost* on the second prisoner. The exact magnitude of the external cost depends on whether the second prisoner is already cooperating with the prosecution or not.

There is a rule of thumb about external effects that is worth remembering: activities that produce external costs tend to generate the perception of a "problem" involving "too much" of the activity in question. The PD game, of course, is a classical illustration of the imposition of heavy external costs because of (as viewed by the prisoners) "too much" testifying. We shall shortly be dealing with problems caused when the external effect is a benefit rather than a cost. Such a situation is generally regarded as producing a problem of exactly the opposite sort: a tendency for there to be "too little" of the activity that produces the external benefit.

QUESTIONS

1. Under the facts of the original PD scenario presented above, what are these magnitudes of external cost that the prisoners impose on one another? What are the associated internal benefits to the prisoner who squeals? (Answer as specifically as possible, e.g., in terms of years or some other quantity.)

2. Suppose that a prisoner who squealed were penalized by having to serve additional time equal to the external costs imposed on the other prisoner. What would the outcome be in terms of the amount of cooperation with the prosecution that you would then expect?

3. Now suppose that a prisoner had to compensate the other for any external costs suffered, but that the compensation could be in the form of a monetary payment. (This would be the equivalent of treating the squealing as a tort.) Would either prisoner testify? Indicate any additional factual assumptions necessary to answer this question. [Hint: Do we have to know anything about the money value of years of freedom to each prisoner?]

4. One of the first applications of the Prisoner's Dilemma model in the economic literature was in relation to the decisions of property owners whether or not to invest in maintenance and improvements. See Davis and Whinston, "Economics of Urban Renewal," 26 J.Law and Contemp.Prob. 105 (1961). Do such activities produce "externalities"? What would you guess was the structure and content of the PD matrix used by Davis and Whinston? Why would they apply this model to explain such things as building codes and "urban renewal" through government acquisition and redevelopment of large tracts?

ETHICAL AND OTHER EXTRALEGAL BEHAVIORAL REGULATIONS

The simple game-theoretic notions introduced above obviously provide one possible rationale for the coercive function of a legal system in removing individuals from predictably mutually-destructive "dilemmas." The role of "liability" or punishment in channelling behavior will be an important theme in much of the analysis below. One should not, however, suppose that extralegal institutions have an unimportant role in the social problems addressed by laws. Extralegal behavioral influences may supplement law in important ways or even obviate its need entirely. On the other hand, the breakdown of extralegal pressures may supply the impetus for creation of new or modified legal rules.

This general subject is, for instance, dealt with by ethician J.L. Mackie in terms of exactly the game-theoretic methodology introduced above. He analyzes the following anecdote as a variant of the Prisoners' Dilemma. [Ethics: Inventing Right and Wrong, 115–121 (1977)] Tom and Dan are soldiers assigned to adjacent fortified posts in the path of an enemy attack. If both remain at these posts, they have a reasonable chance of holding out until a relief column arrives, and so of both surviving. If they both desert their posts, the enemy will break through immediately and the chance of either of them surviving is markedly reduced. On the other hand, if one stays at his post while the other flees, the coward will have a much better chance of survival than if both soldiers remain. In this latter case, the one who stays will have a worse chance of survival than if they both deserted their posts.

Under the circumstances, it would be rational for both men to agree to be literally chained to their posts. Each soldier would benefit from this loss of his own freedom of choice, provided that his comrade's freedom was similarly constrained. An effective alternative would be some external discipline that confronted a deserter with the prospect of a sufficiently severe punishment, such as execution. But Mackie stresses that there can be psychological substitutes for physical chains and external penalties. Military traditions of honor and loyalty to comrades can serve as invisible chains, while the stigma of cowardice, with its attendant disgrace and shame, can substitute for external sanctions. Indeed, given the hypothetical situation, one would actually prefer to belong to a group whose members were encumbered with an appropriate set of psychological fetters.

Mackie also points out that if Tom and Dan have a general tradition of keeping agreements, they will be able to pledge that each will persevere at his post, and the agreement-keeping tradition will then tend to hold each man there. In practice, however, a general agreement-keeping tradition is likely to be rather less effective in situations of extreme stress (such as our hypothetical one) than more focussed, situation-specific mechanisms as exemplified by military traditions of honor and loyalty. On the other hand, a general ethic of agreement-keeping has the advantage of being more flexible and widely applicable than special-purpose ethical constraints. A tradition of observing agreements can support the making and keeping of all sorts of useful bargains. Thus, observes Mackie, Hume was quite right in saying that a man is the more useful, both to himself and to others, the greater degree of probity and honor he is endowed with.

The particular example used to illustrate this form of two-person game is both dramatic and realistic, but it has the disadvantage that it does not lend itself to repeated trials by the same two players. That is, it deals with a single-trial game rather than an "iterated" one. Hence, Mackie considers another example where even if Tom, say, comes off badly at the first trial he will still survive to play with Dan again. The following assumptions are made: (1) that each man has only a weak agreement-keeping tendency; (2) that neither can see, on any one occasion, whether the other is keeping the bargain until he himself is committed either to keeping it or to breaking it; (3) that if both men keep the agreement on one occasion, each is more likely to keep it next time, whereas if either or both men break the agreement on one occasion, each is less likely to keep it next time; (4) that all these tendencies are known to both men; and (5) that each time Tom and Dan play this game they know that they will have to play it again with one another.

These assumptions are said to alter the form of the game in the following way:

> [I]f, on any one occasion, Dan is going to keep the agreement, it will be to Tom's selfish advantage, with a view to the future, to do so too, though if Dan is going to break the agreement this time, it will be to Tom's advantage to break it. And of course the situation is still symmetrical. Self-interest no longer unambiguously urges each man to break the agreement on any one occasion: consequently only a fairly weak agreement-keeping tendency will be needed to tip the balance. Fairly obvious and natural assumptions lead to a similar conclusion if we extend the game in another direction as well, and assume that there are more than two players.[i]

Mackie also considers the possibility of outcomes that are not symmetrical for the parties involved:

> Even if Tom and Dan are initially placed alike, there may be several possible agreements between them, each of which is better for each man singly than the results of failure to agree or of failure to keep the agreement, but some of which are in various degrees more advantageous to Tom than to Dan, and vice versa. In these circumstances the man who is, or gives the appearance of being, the more reluctant to make, or to adhere to, an agreement is likely to get more advantageous terms. Though complete intransigence in either party is disastrous for both, incomplete relative intransigence is differentially advantageous to its possessor. This holds, as I have said, even if the initial situation is symmetrical; but if one party has less to lose by failure to agree, or less to gain from a stable agreement, further possibilities of unequal agreements arise.[j]

Finally, the conclusion of this ethician's section on "Game Theory" provides an appropriate combination both of endorsement of the game-theoretic conceptualization and of caveat about the limitations of any general model:

> There can be no doubt that many real-life situations contain, as at least part of their causally relevant structure, patterns of relationship of which various simple 'games' are an illuminating description. An international arms race is one obvious example: another is the situation where inflation can be slowed down only if different trade unions can agree to limit their demands for wage increases. One merit of such simplified analyses is that they show dramatically how the combined outcome of several intentional actions, even of well-informed and rational agents, may be

i. J.L. Mackie, Ethics: Inventing   j. Ibid., 118–19.
Right and Wrong, (1977) at 118.

something that no one of the agents involved has intended or would intend. * * * The main moral is the practical value of the notion of obligation, of an invisible and indeed fictitious tie or bond, whether this takes the form of a general requirement to keep whatever agreements one makes or of various specific duties like those of military honour or of loyalty to comrades or to an organization.

* * * The real weakness of the Hobbesian solution lies not in anything that the game theory models show, but in what, just by being models, they leave out. Real situations always incorporate, along with the skeletal structure of some fairly simple game, other forces and tendencies whose strength varies through time.[k]

QUESTIONS

1. Provide an illustration of a situation wherein an ethical, moral or other extralegal compulsion seems adequately to regulate a form of behavior that might otherwise necessitate some more formal sanction system. Exemplify, if possible, a situation wherein the progressive breakdown of a formerly effective extralegal behavioral convention has already caused, or seems likely to cause, recourse to a formal coercive regulation.

2. Exactly how does a factor such as "guilt" or "approbation" change the PD matrices? What changes in the facts of the original PD scenario in the text above would make it plausible that these factors would eliminate the dilemma for the prisoners?

3. What circumstances determine whether extralegal rules are preferable to formal legal sanctions? Are the most relevant considerations on the "cost" side or the "benefit" side? Are relative "flexibility" advantages of interest?

4. Even though there are fines for traffic infractions and legal liabilities imposed for driving-related torts, there is arguably a certain gaming aspect to careful driving, an activity that produces "external benefits." This exchange in *The Great Gatsby* is instructive:

"You're a rotten driver," I protested. "Either you ought to be more careful or you oughtn't to drive at all."

"I am careful."

"No, you're not."

"Well, other people are," she said lightly.

"What's that got to do with it?"

"They'll keep out of my way," she insisted. "It takes two to make an accident."

k. Ibid., 120.

"Suppose you met somebody just as careless as yourself."

"I hope I never will," she answered. "I hate careless people. That's why I like you." [l]

In your experience, do informal codes of "driving courtesy" differ substantially as one travels from place to place? If so, how and why? Would you expect their degree of observance or "strength" to vary predictably in accordance with any particular circumstances?

5. Re-read and critique the paragraph quoted above on the iterated game as played under Mackie's five assumptions. What is your own analysis of the difference it makes if the game is an iterated one rather than a single-play game?

6. Suppose that a Prisoners Dilemma game is to be played in iterated form, but the number of trials is known to be equal to n, where n is any positive number. What can you say about the results of this game? [m]

7. Do you understand the paragraph quoted in the text above that deals with asymmetrical results and the advantages of intransigence? If you do not understand it, return to this question after completing the "Road Problem" in the next section below.

EXTERNAL BENEFITS, EXCLUDABILITY AND "FREE RIDERS"

As indicated earlier, external effects may be produced in the form of benefits rather than the harms exemplified in the original Prisoner's Dilemma situation. We turn now to a specific consideration of such external benefit production. The "road problem" scenario provided below deals with external benefits and the difficulties that occur when such benefits are potentially available at no cost. In the original Prisoner's Dilemma presented above, it is at least arguable that the prisoners "should" be kept in their dilemma. Indeed, one function of Law may be to keep certain types of people in a dilemma-like environment because, although this is detrimental to the "prisoners," it is regarded as producing benefits to other parts of society. By contrast, in the road scenario below, the sympathy or normative feeling that one has for the players will be less ambiguous; most

---

l. F. Scott Fitzgerald, The Great Gatsby, (___ ed.), at 59.

m. Although logic may seem to suggest that repeated plays of the same game should not produce any change in behavior, a number of game theorists argue that altered behavior will in fact occur. See, e.g., R. Luce & H. Raiffa, Games and Decisions, at 102–04. A stronger case for unaltered behavior can be made when the number of iterations (the value n in the text) is known. The nth iteration becomes, in effect, a non-iterated game and the non-cooperative strategy is therefore clearly dominant. But, it is reasoned, if this is known, then there is no reason to cooperate on the (n–1)th play. A similar logic can then, of course, be extended backward without limit.

people would agree that the situation is somehow troubling and that the "players" should be removed from the dilemma if possible.

ROAD MAINTENANCE PROBLEM

Adams and Braun own lots A and B, respectively, of Section 236, bordering on State Route 116. The Adams lot is adjacent to the state road and the Braun lot is immediately behind it. Access to 236B is provided for in an easement under which the owner of 236A must allow free passage to occupants of all inner lots. Adams already has a house on lot A and has resided there for five years. Upon constructing the house, Adams also caused a road to be prepared, running from Route 116 to the back border of his lot. The road is not hard-surfaced, but is a type of "oiled gravel" surface common to private roads and driveways in rural areas. This kind of surface is subject to erosion and general deterioration over time. However, Pitts Gravel will come and provide any number of "doses" of road repair at a price of $25.

[This concept of a "dose" of an input is a pedagogical simplification that will be utilized a number of times below. It will be used when it is expositionally desireable to collapse a heterogeneous, multi-dimensional package of possible adjustments into a single dimension. Hence, "road repair" could be a mix of many different services in varying proportions, but no useful purpose is served by explicitly considering multidimensional adjustments. Through the simplification provided by the "dose" concept, we can focus on a straightforward quantitative adjustment.]

Fortunately, we just happen to be in possession of Adams' true subjective evaluations of how much different levels of road repair would be "worth" to him. Column 1 of Exhibit 1.3 shows the total value of the services received from the road, assuming different levels of maintenance, i.e., different qualities of road. Note that these values are "gross" of any costs incurred in actually purchasing the maintenance.

EXHIBIT 1.3 Benefits of Road Repair Levels

No. of Doses	Total Benefits	Marginal Benefits	Two-Person Marg. Ben.
0	$50	—NA—	—NA—
1	$90	40	80
2	$120	30	60
3	$140	20	40
4	$150	10	20
5	$150	0	0

QUESTIONS

1. Fill in Column 3 of Exhibit 1.3 with the incremental values that each dose of road repair adds to Adams' evaluation of the benefits from the road. In economists' jargon, these values are called "marginal" evaluations. [Strictly speaking, the word "marginal" should be associated only with infinitesimal changes, but it is commonly used loosely to refer, as in the present case, to discrete changes.]

2. If only Adams were on the scene, how much road repair do you predict would be purchased? Why? Try to explain your answer in terms of marginal benefits and marginal costs.

3. Suppose Braun now builds a house on lot B. Braun has, by remarkable coincidence, the same preferences about this road repair as does Adams. Enter in Column 4 the aggregate 2-person marginal benefits now that both Adams and Braun benefit in precisely the same way from each unit of road repair. (Since the frequency of their trips on the road is low, the possibility of detrimental mutual interference because of attempted simultaneous use can be regarded as negligible.)

4. How much road repair do you think will be purchased now? Who will pay what? Describe the negotiating process.

5. Enter Chernak, the owner of lot C. Mirabile dictu, Chernak also has the same preferences. What happens now? How do things change as Donatelli, Eglin, etc. also arrive on the scene?

6. In what sense might the people on the road regard the situation as "unsatisfactory"? Would they like to be coerced? To do what?

7. What difference, if any, did it make in this problem that the preferences of the individuals were assumed to be identical? That is, was it a mere "simplifying assumption"? Or did it affect the results in some significant way?

8. Can you explain this situation as due to a "defect in the applicable property rights"? Does the creation of patent rights fit this model in any way? Can you think of any other examples?

9. One way of providing roads would be for all roads to be privately-owned, excludable facilities, i.e., toll roads. Why is this not done? Is it because of the cost of exclusion? Other disadvantages? [n]

10. In practice, what policies does society adopt in response to the impracticality of providing roads that are privately (excludably) owned?

JOINTNESS AND EXCLUDABILITY AS ELEMENTS OF PROPERTY

The road scenario illustrates that the concepts of ownership and property are sometimes elusive. Because of the way the legal rights regarding road use are structured, nobody can effectively be excluded from the benefits of any road maintenance once it is provided. Economists apply the terms "excludability" and "appropriability" in this context. If a good lacks excludability, then the one who provides it cannot appropriate from its users a return on his investment in its provision; that is, the provider cannot charge for or sell what he provides. This may be true even if the provider nominally "owns" what he has provided.

"Jointness" in consumption is the characteristic whereby some goods, such as the road, can be consumed by many people at once. The road case was, for simplicity, presented as a case of perfect jointness in consumption, i.e., where the value of the good to any single user is the same regardless of how many co-consumers there are. In practice, this is seldom true outside of narrow limits. But the fact that a good "congests" and begins to degrade in value beyond a certain point does not radically alter the kind of problem epitomized in the road anecdote. [Ask yourself what difference it would have made to the analysis if each co-user resulted in, say, a 5% degradation of the road's prior value to the previous users.]

In combination, the characteristics of jointness and non-excludability present the opportunity for someone to be a "Free Rider," one who receives the external benefits of another's act and pays nothing

---

n. See McKean and Minasian, "On Achieving Pareto Optimality—Regardless of Cost!" 5 Western Econ.J. 14–23 (1966); Demsetz, "The Private Production of Public Goods," 13 J.Law and Econ. 293, 293–306 (1970).

in return. In the hypothetical presented above, there is the literal prospect of a free ride on the road, but the phenomenon is also widely generalized as the so-called "Free Rider Problem."

In the hypothetical, there was nothing inherently preventing the excludability of the private road, so that the underlying problem could be remedied by a reformulation of the legal rights. Thus, you should be sensitive to instances in which courts can attack such problems by "creating" excludability in the form of new kinds of property rights. Sometimes, however, a mere legal fiat is meaningless, either because the enforcement of the exclusion right is prohibitively expensive, because enforcement interferes with the flow of benefits, or for some other practical consideration. Can you think of examples of such cases?

In sum, the rectification of a property right "defect" may or may not suffice to cure a problem of the type outlined above. Alternatively, some form of direct mandate of a result may be adopted. For instance many types of goods having very high excludability costs and jointness in consumption are provided coercively by a government that dispenses the goods and then taxes individual beneficiaries for some share of the cost. Because jointly consumable, non-excludable goods are so commonly provided by governments, economists frequently refer to such goods as "public goods," using the terminology of a classic article by Paul Samuelson on the welfare economics of the public sector.[o] Samuelson derives "optimality" conditions for the level of so-called public good provision: *jointly consumable goods should be produced up to the point where the sum of the marginal evaluations of all potential consumers equals the marginal cost of the good.* The application of this "Samuelson Summation Condition" for public goods provision is, of course, exemplified in the road hypothetical where each resident is a potential beneficiary. Note, however, that excludability may exist in various degrees, so that private provision of "public" goods may be quite feasible. In some situations, considerable excludability can be enforced, even if not against all users. In other cases, a good or activity provides distinguishable types of benefits, some of which are excludable and some not. As long as *some* excludability is practical, private provision is a distinct possibility. The Samuelson Summation Condition can then be used as a benchmark to determine how close the expectable private level of

---

o. Samuelson, "The Pure Theory of Public Expenditure," 36 Rev. of Econ. & Stat. 387 (1954); or, in diagrammatic form, "Diagrammatic Exposition of a Theory of Public Expenditure," 37 Rev. of Econ. & Stat. 350 (1955). An early description of the difficulties of providing "public goods" through voluntary arrangements is Musgrave, "The Voluntary Exchange Theory of Public Economy," 53 Quarterly J. of Econ. 213 (1938). There is an enormous modern literature on "public goods theory," as the citations in any modern public finance treatise will indicate.

provision comes to the "optimal" level. (Remember, however, that optimal is defined in a special technical sense.) An important point is that the "public goods" terminology is somewhat of a misnomer because public provision for such goods is not the only, nor even necessarily the most desirable, institutional arrangement for the provision of such goods.

QUESTIONS

1. "The doctrine of adverse possession boils down to this: when, because of expiration of the statute of limitations, a landowner loses the right of excludability, he also loses title." Comment.

2. The legal right of excludability may be more apparent than real. Describe a situation in which an asset is protected by a damage or injunctive remedy for unauthorized use, but enforcement of this nominal excludability is impractical.

CHICKEN vs. PRISONER'S DILEMMA

Much of what we have been discussing above deals with the circumstances in which individuals are likely, absent some external impetus, to fail to engage in behavior that would ordinarily be termed cooperative or mutually beneficial. The failure to exploit available mutual gains is, roughly speaking, what economists mean by "inefficient" results. Failure to cooperate usually implies an inefficient result, but it does not necessarily mean that nothing will be done at all. The distinction between Prisoner's Dilemma and the closely related Chicken Game makes this apparent.

According to its original set of facts, the road scenario yields a Chicken game rather than a Prisoner's Dilemma. As an exercise, you should attempt to confirm this by filling in the cells of the matrix in Exhibit 1.4. This matrix is a little more complicated than the original ones constructed above. Those were (2 × 2) or 4-cell matrices because there were fewer possibilities. Now, the description of the opportunity set has to allow for varying levels of cooperation. Note, however, the implicit assumption that doses of road maintenance can only be bought in discrete units. Relaxation of this assumption will be a desirable feature of other types of models that we will develop shortly.

For each cell in Exhibit 1.4, consult the corresponding row and column headings in order to determine the total amount of road maintenance provided. That amount is the sum of the quantity provided by you (the row label) and the quantity provided by others (the column label). Then check Exhibit 1.3 to find out the total value of the road benefits at that level of maintenance. Remember, though, that

Exhibit 1.3 presents only gross benefits whereas the Exhibit 1.4 entries should be in *net* terms. Deduct your contribution (units you provided times their unit cost), if any, and enter the resulting net payoff in the appropriate cell of the matrix. There is no need to complete the entries for total provisions of more than 4 units of maintenance. (Why?)

In Exhibit 1.4, circle the cell that contains the best payoff in each column. Note that this circled cell corresponds to different row strategies, depending on what the "other" provision is. Do you think that there is a "dominant" strategy in this game? (Remember that dominance requires that there exist some best strategy regardless of what the other party is expected to do.) Is there a determinate or predictable outcome? In particular, how likely do you think it is that no road repairs will be undertaken, even if one is as pessimistic as possible about "cooperation"?

EXHIBIT 1.4   Road Problem As A "Chicken" Matrix

Doses Provided By You	Doses Provided By Others			
	3	2	1	0
3	XXXXX	XXXXX	75	65
2	XXXXX	100 ~~150~~	90	70
1	125	115	95	65
0	140	120	90	50

Now change the facts by assuming that a dose of road maintenance costs $55.00 rather than $25.00. Complete Exhibit 1.5 by using the same procedure as for Exhibit 1.4. The resultant matrix should satisfy the requirements of a classic Prisoner's Dilemma. Is cooperative behavior by one player likely in the absence of cooperative behavior by the other? Can you explain in "common-sense" terms why changing the cost alters the game from Chicken to Prisoner's Dilemma?

EXHIBIT 1.5   Road Problem As A Prisoner's Dilemma

Doses Provided By You	Doses Provided By Others			
	3	2	1	0
3	XXXXX	XXXXX	-15	-25
2	XXXXX	40	30	10
1	95	85	65	45
0	140	120	90	50

Although Chicken shares some of the same strategic characteristics as Prisoner's Dilemma, it dramatically demonstrates the potential importance of bluff and hold-out behavior when bargaining or trying to influence the behavior of others. By contrast, PD is not really a bluffing game, since the maximizing strategy is unaffected by what one's opponent does or is expected to do. A simple form of Chicken bluffing is merely to adopt a very stubborn, uncooperative stance, even if it seems to involve "cutting off your nose to spite your face." In the road example, for instance, Adams might threaten to provide no road maintenance, although Braun knows that Adams would find two units worthwhile even without any cost contribution from anyone else. But matters usually are much worse in the real world where, instead of the preferences of the parties being known, their respective valuations of the alternatives can only be guessed at or based on information interchange. Unfortunately, under these circumstances, there is a very real loss of ability of the bargainers to communicate with each other. The reason is that the parties have reason to offer false information to each other, to convince each other that there is less possibility for mutual gain than really exists. This is the essence of the bargaining bluff. Unfortunately, the parties then lose much of their ability to discriminate between "real" information and the kind of disinformation commonly produced as a self-interested bargaining ploy.

The production of misinformation during bargaining is easily understood if one contemplates the typical process of buying a used car. Assume that you have gone to the lot and see a car that fits your purposes and which, if necessary, you would be willing to acquire at a price as high as $1000. Unbeknownst to you, the used car dealer would be happy to sell at any price over $600. Since the car is worth $1000 and $600, respectively, to the potential buyer and seller, there is a range of "gains from trade" equal to $400. The bargaining is, in essence, about who gets what part of that $400 potential gain. During the bargaining process, each party can benefit by attempting to convince the other that his own "fallback position" or "best offer" is tougher than it really is. What kinds of things do the buyer and seller typically say to each other in an attempt to mislead about their willingness to sell? Is this deceptive process costly? And do you think that beneficial deals are sometimes lost because one party perceives the other party's real fallback as merely a tough bargaining position?

In sum, our earlier models reflected the implicit assumption that each party had "full information," i.e., substantially complete knowledge of the gains and losses attaching to the relevant alternatives, both for himself and also for the "opponent" in the game. That assumption is now relaxed since, unfortunately, many real world situations are characterized by so-called "limited information" about the implications of the alternatives. In such circumstances, the flow of information itself becomes part of the gaming process and is affected by strategic considerations.

GAMING ABOUT INFORMATION

Persons who have not engaged in tough bargaining are frequently naive about the possible benefits—sometimes even the outright necessity for survival—of what may euphemistically be called "dissimulation" during negotiating processes. The following story, based on a March, 1980 *Wall Street Journal* article, makes a sobering point.

AT HARVARD, TELLING LIES JUST A MATTER OF COURSE

* * *

UNTRUTHS CAN IMPROVE BUSINESS–SCHOOL GRADE; PEER PRESSURE CLASHES WITH ETHICS

BOSTON—A Harvard Business School student won the highest grade in part of his Competitive Decision Making course because "I was willing to lie to get a better score."

That reaction is just fine with Prof. Howard R. Raiffa, whose course is aimed at teaching would-be business executives to negotiate in the real world. Like it or not, Prof. Raiffa says, lying—or "strategic misrepresentation," as he calls it, is sometimes resorted to in business negotiations.

Each week, Prof. Raiffa and his students play a game. He pairs them off and assigns them roles in a negotiation. One week a big-city mayor and a police-union leader bargain over a contract. Another week, a plaintiff and an insurance company try to reach a settlement. Next time, one executive tries to buy a company from another. The students negotiate outside the classroom during the week, then report the results.

The results determine the grade. The mayor who held the police union to the smallest wage-and-benefit package gets the best grade among the mayors; the police union chief who negotiated with him gets the worst grade among the union leaders.

Students find that hiding certain facts, bluffing or even outright lying often gains them a better deal. But the objective isn't necessarily to teach them to lie. Rather, Prof. Raiffa says, it is to teach them they may be lied to. Raiffa thinks the students become "much more aware." "They're very naive when they start," he claims.

One-third of the course grade is based on success in the negotiating games. For ambitious, aggressive students, the pressure to win is intense, and the course evokes strong reactions. During one class discussion of a game, a woman burst into tears. She had discovered that the man she negotiated with, who repeatedly assured her he opposed any misrepresentation, had in fact lied blatantly. Another student, who has worked for Arabian American Oil Co. in Saudi Arabia negotiating construction contracts, said he found the students here less reasonable than the people he dealt with in the business world.

Raiffa doesn't tell his students how to negotiate in any particular game. The students develop their own strategies and methods as they go along. Part of the course is theoretical; students learn how to analyze competitive situations. But to Raiffa and most of his students, the actual negotiations are the heart of the course.

"You learn a lot about negotiating and a lot about yourself," says a lawyer who put in a year as counsel to a congressional subcommittee before taking the course.

Raiffa says he structures the negotiations so that in some of the early games, "the truth teller is at an extreme disadvantage" against someone who lies or bluffs. In later games, liars may lose a chance to reach a profitable settlement because their opponent is outraged and becomes more stubborn. "People have to learn to understand the nature of the game," Raiffa says, "and understand how they are vulnerable."

Many students are surprised at the amount of lying, claiming that while some people never misrepresent their position, others do it pathologically. Another student, who was a research assistant at Harvard before coming to the business school, says that attitudes toward lying changed during the semester. "There was a period when it seemed as if everyone was lying. It wasn't bluffing; it was outright lying," she says. "I did it too."

This student says the experience taught her that peer pressure can overcome personal ethics. Since she doesn't want to lie, she plans to avoid fields where she thinks dishonesty is commonplace.

Another member of the class, who had worked for the National Park Service, says she preserved her ethical standards, but only at the cost of losing in several negotiations with people who lied. Deeply disturbed, she went to Prof. Raiffa to discuss the course and her future in business. "I concluded there are businesses I'd better not go into," she says. "I'm not willing to compromise my principles to the point of baldfaced lying."

Some students say that lying in the course is acceptable while that lying outside isn't. But most students feel that the way they play the games does reflect what techniques they'll be using in their careers.

To what extent is misdirection during negotiation a mutually destructive process? Would all (or most?) parties be better off if only truthful information could be exchanged? Ask yourself whether any legal mechanisms seem to address these questions or, indeed, whether society attempts to provide extralegal "psychological" incentives not to dissimulate. Finally, bear in mind the possibility that dissimulation may not be an optimal long-term policy in an iterated or repetitious negotiating game, especially where parties have some control over who one "plays" with.

QUESTIONS

1. Do most *bilateral* negotiations or trades broadly fit the paradigm of the Chicken game? Illustrate your answer with respect to the used car sale example in the text above.

2. What application of the models in this chapter is there to negotiations designed to reach out-of-court settlements?

3. Do threats of suit frequently fall into the mold of the Chicken paradigm? Can you give some (other) examples from the legal environment?

4. Is it desirable to be able to "rely" on what someone else tells you? What costs are incurred if it is impossible to rely on information proffered? Are there any legal mechanisms designed to ensure the reliability of information used in arriving at bargains?

5. How do bargainers invest resources in making their bargaining stances credible (even when they are fundamentally untrue)? Is this an "unprofitable" process in some overall sense?

6. What is the distinction between what the Harvard professor called "strategic misrepresentation" and what the law calls fraud?

CHICKEN IN ACTION: LAND ASSEMBLY

Misinformation is not the only obstacle to bargaining. One should not become overly optimistic merely because the "real" payoffs to the parties are known. When the parties possess the relevant facts about the options available to them, the situation is termed by economists as involving "full information." One can debate whether the real world example supplied immediately below was literally one of full information, but it is certainly plausible that the parties are substantially informed about the respective benefits and costs and that dissimulation was not the major obstacle to the bargaining process. In order to further concretize the example, however, assume that the real estate developer could have made a gross profit of $11,000,000, before any deductions for land acquisition costs, if he could have assembled the entire tract as a casino site. Also, assume that each homeowner could move to a comparable house in another location and be just as well off with a compensation payment of anything over $30,000.

HOMEOWNER BICKERING ENDS $100,000 OFFER FOR HOUSES

[Adapted from newspaper stories appearing in mid-August 1979.]

ATLANTIC CITY, N.J., AUG. 23—An offer of $100,000 apiece for 72 homes in a Boardwalk neighborhood has fallen through because greedy residents ruined the deal, according to the real estate agent who tried to assemble the land.

The tract, which contains mostly small homes that sold for about $15,000 three years ago, is adjacent to Playboy's casino hotel, and was desired as a site for a proposed casino.

Many homeowners on the Boardwalk block between Bellevue and Texas avenues, reportedly are bitter over the attempt to assemble the building site.

"We went through a year of aggravation on this block. And for what? Nothing," said one disgruntled Bellevue Avenue homeowner. "Most of these people didn't come out with one red cent."

"I'm glad the whole stir is done with," said Sam Glaspert, a longtime Texas Avenue resident. "But next time, the people around here are going to be a lot more careful—money up front and the rest. If you didn't learn a lesson from this deal, you never will.

"The pressure was unbelievable. I had two neighbors come into my living room and pressure me. They wouldn't leave until I agreed to sell."

Thomas Blossom, the agent who last year offered $100,000 to each homeowner if all agreed to sell, says many owners "suddenly came back and argued their land was worth much more."

He said only 20 of the 68 homeowners who agreed to sell out in March were willing to close the deal in June.

"Getting the whole block in one shot was the only way we felt we could make the deal go," Blossom said. "Now some of these holdouts are in for an unpleasant surprise. If that block can't become a casino site immediately, their homes won't be worth even $30,000."

QUESTIONS

1. Suppose that the developer had managed to purchase 71 of the required 72 pieces of property for an average price of $50,000. If you owned the 72nd house, how much could you hope to get for it?

2. In a similar situation, it is proposed to use a contingent contract scheme. An offer is made to each homeowner at a price of $50,000. Acceptance by the homeowner is irrevocable, but the contract is subject to the condition that all 72 accept. Is this technique likely to produce the required amount of agreement?

3. Suppose the 72 landowners could be compelled to accept offers of $50,000 apiece. Would they find a mechanism for such coercion to be desirable?

4. What is the amount of the loss if no agreement is reached? Who loses and by how much? Would you characterize the loss as "waste"?

5. Does the land assembly bargaining problem fit the paradigm of either the Prisoner's Dilemma or the Chicken game?

The last several sections should serve to suggest that the kinds of formal models represented by Exhibits 1.4 and 1.5 above can be extended either exactly or by analogy to a wide range of situations, many of which have a rather obvious relationship to the legal system. Two specific comments about the generalization of these models should be made. One is that the models can handle more complex behavioral choices than the binary Cooperate-Defect types of decisions originally considered. But it is easy to see that matrix models become very cumbersome as the number of row and column alternatives increase. Indeed, even in the road maintenance case, the notion of an arbitrarily-sized "dose" of maintenance is an extreme simplification. What if it were possible to purchase half-doses, quarter-doses, etc.? Hence, it will come as no surprise that other techniques of modelling will be urgently required when the behavior adjustments are potentially very complex, even continuously variable.

Another conclusion is that Exhibits 1.4 and 1.5 can be applied to many-person situations as well as two-person games; the column headings are ambiguous as to whether the "other" provision comes from one or several persons. Therefore, the game concepts developed in the simple 2-person context have many-person analogues. The term of art for "large" games is "n-person game" where n stands for any number greater than two. In sum, the important insights gained from two-person, two-strategy games can be applied in more complicated real-world situations.

QUESTIONS

1. Is a coercive settlement better for people in a Prisoner's Dilemma, as opposed to letting them work things out for themselves? (Sometimes, always, or never?) Is your answer the same for parties caught in a Chicken game?

2. "If there is no impediment to enforceable contracts, then the 'dilemma' problem is not generally a valid rationale for externally imposed coercion in the two-person cases; in n-person cases, coercion may well be prescribed."

TRANSFERABILITY AS AN ELEMENT OF PROPERTY

When a good or activity is characterized by perfect jointness in consumption, multiple beneficiaries do not interfere with each other. Consequently, more than one person can truly and completely own the entire property and its stream of benefits—if not in the legal sense, at least in a more fundamental underlying sense. When jointness does not apply, persons cannot fully share "ownership" in precisely the same way. In our legal system there are many forms of what are commonly thought of as shared ownership: tenants in common; life tenant and remainderman; lessor and lessee; common stockholder with voting rights and non-voting stockholder; owner of fee simple and owner of mineral rights; etc. In general, these are really *divisions* of ownership rather than sharing, since in the absence of perfect jointness one interest bars a simultaneous participation in precisely the *same part* of the benefits flow. Thus, for non-joint goods, appropriability requires not only the minimal prerequisite of excludability, but also the potential assignment or transferral of part of the benefits to someone else.

In legalese, what one hopes to get in return for an assignment of benefits is a "consideration." Trade takes place because the original owner of property finds an opportunity to transfer away all or part of his rights for a consideration that is deemed more valuable than the rights given up. In contrast, the giver of the consideration, the purchaser, must regard the rights as more valuable than the consideration paid for them. In sum, for trade to be possible, the trading partners must *disagree* about the relative values of the things being exchanged. Because of this disagreement, both parties can benefit by converting a lesser-valued thing into a higher-valued thing.

What does this all have to do with property? Well, a bit of reflection should indicate that "ownership" without the privilege of transferability is only a limited form of ownership. The owner can use the good himself, but loses the possibility to exact a charge for what is at least potentially the even higher use-value that someone else applies to the good. This "appropriability" (i.e., ability to "make one's own") the benefits of something to a non-owner user may take place through transfer of full and permanent rights, as through conferral of fee simple title. Alternatively, the exercise of appropriability may involve transfer merely of an entitlement to some part of the fruits of the property, limited either in manner or in time, as by a lease, entitlement to a "share," etc. Legal rules occasionally inhibit or completely bar the transfer of certain kinds of property. The question is: Why?

Rather than deal with commonplace kinds of property, the following pages first examine the implications of excludability and transferability for some legal phenomena not commonly thought of as property. These phenomena involve actual or potential property rights in some aspect of legal process itself. Partially, this is done to drive home the fact that property is what the legal system makes it, by conferring or withholding excludability and transferability. Also, quite frankly, the notions of potential "property" about to be considered would be regarded by many traditional students of jurisprudence as somewhat bizarre. All the better! Some of the most insightful uses of formal analysis arise from being compelled to view familiar phenomena from an unaccustomed angle.

After dealing with somewhat unorthodox notions of property in legal process, we shall take up a line of more traditional "nuisance" cases.

By posing the questions in the next few sections, the intent is to engage in analytical exercises rather than to advocate policy changes. Inevitably, the factual or positive economics implications are likely to lead to normative judgments. Still, you should attempt to analyze the situations dispassionately without any visceral preconceptions. Whatever "bottom line" normative judgments that emerge in your own mind, be alert for objective implications that surprise or are counterintuitive. In particular, try to be sensitive to how, if at all, your normative views of the questions are influenced.

ASSIGNABILITY OF CAUSES OF ACTION

This section deals with legal causes of action as a species of intangible property. Preliminarily, we should note some general facts about the body of American law that governs the assignability of a cause of action by a plaintiff to a third party.[p] Although courts were originally hostile to assignment of virtually all causes of actions, many types of claims are now transferable. Claims arising out of contract are, in general, fully assignable and are, indeed, actively exchanged in commerce. Many tort claims, e.g., those for damage to property, nuisance, etc., are also generally assignable. We focus here, however, on personal injury claims, one type of cause of action that is normally *not* assignable. Although personal injury claims are not directly transferable, they may be *de facto* transferable, at least in part, through certain assignments of interests, perhaps most notably through subrogation by an insured to the insurance carrier.[q] Strangely, some jurisdictions have permitted assignment of the *proceeds* of personal injury claims although the assignment of the claim itself is barred.[r]

THE CASE OF NIKE v. LOBEL

Victoria Nike is a graduate student in aerospace engineering and, until a fateful day last Fall, an avid competitive runner for her local track club. On the day in question, Victoria was running on one of the streets adjacent to her university's campus. Suddenly her dreams of a medal-winning performance in the annual Lynchboro 10-Miler were rudely shattered by an "encounter of the worst kind" with an automobile driven by a local businessman, George Lobel. Lobel was cited by the investigating police officer for driving under the influence of alcohol. However, it has subsequently become apparent that, if Nike sues, Lobel's attorney will vigorously raise a defense of contributory negligence. Nike was, he will contend, running on a

p. See generally, Weinberg, "Tort Claims as Intangible Property: An Exploration from an Assignee's Perspective," 64 Ky.L.J. 49 (1975); Lytle, Personal Injuries: Creditors v. Victim, Claim and Award," 81 Dick.L.Rev. 82, 93–101 (1976); 6 Am.Jur.2d Assignments Secs. 34–45 (1963); Annot., 76 A.L.R.2d 1286 (1961).

q. Kimball and Davis, "The Extension of Insurance Subrogation," 60 Mich.L. Rev. 841, 858, 867–68 (1962); Reed, "Insurance Subrogation in Personal Injury Actions: The Silent Explosion," 12 Am. Bus.L.J. 111 (1974).

r. Although New York Statutory and common law both appeared to bar assignment of personal injury claims, in Richard v. National Transportation Co., 158 Misc. 324, 285 N.Y.S. 870 (1936) in injured party's assignment to a hospital of the proceeds from such a claim was held valid. But see Southern Farm Bureau Casualty Insurance Co v. Wright Oil Co., 248 Ark. 803, 454 S.W.2d 69 (1970) where the distinction between the cause of action and a contingent claim on proceeds is rejected.

heavily travelled street at dusk and failed to wear a reflective vest or any highly visible kind of clothing. Also, the damage calculations are likely to be the subject of fierce dispute since the extent and permanence of Nike's injuries are not perfectly clear. Specifically, Nike's ability to pursue her athletic career in the future is highly debatable.

Nike's roommate, Carla Konomos, is a first-year student in the economics Ph.D. program. Konomos has a low tolerance for Nike's frequent wailing about the painful uncertainties of her legal position. Indeed, Konomos has recently been heard to mutter under her breath: "Idiot! Why doesn't she just peddle her claim for a little up-front money?! Just sell out and avoid all the months and months of grief over this."

QUESTIONS

1. Suppose that Nike did want to sell her claim in exchange for some advance compensation. Under present law in the U.S., important restrictions exist as to her ability to transfer rights to a cause of action in exchange for financial or other consideration. Whom do you understand to be the intended beneficiary of these restrictions on transfer? Are there any general public policy purposes that the restrictions are designed to serve?

2. Absent any legal restraints, why might Nike want to sell her claim rather than litigate it herself? Enumerate as many conceptually distinguishable reasons as possible.

3. Suppose that Nike had a disability policy under which her insurance carrier will pay her immediately for various bodily injuries under a fixed-payment schedule. To what extent is it possible for an insurance company to recover from Lobel under Nike's personal injury claim?

4. What problems, if any, do you see with legal restrictions against free assignment of tort claims to third parties? Are there any areas in which you would be prepared to expand on the present degree of assignability?

5. Does membership in the bar constitute a good reason why a potential claim purchaser might not be permitted to engage in such transactions?[s]

Now assume the same basic facts as in the Nike situation described above, except that all legal restrictions on the assignability of legal claims have been abolished. After careful consideration of her situation, Nike feels, that compared to litigating the claim

---

s. For instance, New York law bars an attorney from acquiring an interest in any suit where the primary, and not merely incidental, purpose of the assignment is to bring a suit. See N.Y. Judiciary Law Sec. 488 (McKinney 1968).

herself, it would be preferable to sell the claim if she can get any price over $7200. Six lawyers have approached Nike and expressed an interest in buying her claim. Although Nike of course has no way of knowing it, the maximum bids that the lawyers are willing to pay are $6800, $7300, $7550, $7650, $7900, and $8200, respectively.

6. What would explain why the various parties place different values on Nike's claim?

7. What prediction would you make about the price that Nike is likely to receive?

8. Suppose that only lawyers #2 and #5 above exist. They realize that, by concerted action, they probably could get Nike to sell for $7201. What is the concerted action? Use a Prisoner's Dilemma analysis to assess the prospect of their being able to collude effectively against Nike. How would the presence of additional lawyers affect matters?

9. Back to all six lawyers again. In addition, assume that, by remarkable coincidence, there are four other cases exactly like Nike's. Each lawyer is only capable of handling at most one case. How would the existence of the four other cases affect the price that Nike could expect?

10. "Laymen tend to have a fundamental misconception about the behavior of markets. They believe that buyers compete against sellers and sellers against buyers. Actually, it is the buyers who are their own worst opponents, and likewise for the sellers." Comment on this statement.

SOME COMMENTS ON THE "ANSWERS"

WARNING: If you read this section without having first tried to work out the questions above, the author cannot take responsibility for resultant defects in your learning!

Here are a few thoughts on what you might have gotten out of the preceding questions. Not all of the items are dealt with, and you should work out the details of some of these general answers, if you have not already done so.

Most people initially feel that an underlying aim of the restrictions on transferability is protection of the unsophisticated victim from exploitation. One important lesson of the Nike hypothetical is the troubling case that it makes that the restrictions on assignability tend actually to disadvantage plaintiffs. The favored parties appear to be (a) defendants, who effectively buy the cause of action in what we call "settlement;" and (b) lawyers and insurance companies to whom a modified interest in the cause of action can be given through contingency fees and subrogation, respectively. These parties are not obliged to compete against possibly higher bids for claims that might otherwise be forthcoming from persons to whom full or partial assignment is legally impermissible.

The gain to defendants is perfectly clear. However, it might be objected that, if the number of lawyers or insurance companies is large, then competition will tend to eliminate any net gains to the lawyers and insurance companies: the consideration given for the contingency fee or subrogation will tend to equal the value of the interest surrendered by the victim. For instance, market pressure will force the price of insurance policies to be lowered by the prospective value of the insurance company's potential recovery under the subrogation privilege. Similarly, lawyers will have to give "value received" in services for the contingency fees they get. Thus, these "favored" parties would not really gain at the expense of the Nikes of the world. Is this argument correct? There is a subtle aspect to the answer that requires analytical results treated in Chapter II. By way of preview, the answer is: Yes and no; market pressure does guarantee some return to assignments of interests through the "back door" means of contingency fees and subrogations, but the value received in this way is likely to be less than it would be if the claims were capable of outright sale. Can you guess why at this point?

The small-scale competition among several would-be purchasers is designed to show something of the process whereby freer transferability might ensure the victim of receiving a fair value for the claim. Allowing a competitive market *generates information* about the claim's value. Unlike the two-person Chicken game analyzed above, bluffing and misinformation is not likely to work when the number of parties increases; one's bluff is likely to be in effect "called" by a competitor. Thus, Nike does not have to be a sophisticated evaluator of her own claim, so long as the potential purchasers are themselves sophisticated and are compelled to compete against one another.

The answer to the part of the problem dealing with price prediction is that the potential purchaser who places the highest value on the claim will get the claim. This bidder must at least outbid the second-highest valuation. Where between that minimum outbid and the maximum valuation will the actual payment made to Nike fall? That ultimate result is somewhat indeterminate, a product of the bargaining process between Nike and the high-value lawyer.

The key to the remainder of the question is this: if four claims are now to be (bought) sold instead of one, the price must be low enough to induce the fourth most reluctant buyer to buy and, at the same time, high enough to induce the fourth most reluctant seller to sell. What range of prices meets these criteria? The price predictions just suggested involved an area of indeterminacy, a bargaining range.

What do you think happens to the range of indeterminacy as the number of buyers and sellers increases? If you can work out the answers to these questions, you are well on your way to understanding the process of price formation in a competitive market.

An objection frequently raised against transferability is that it will result in cases being litigated that otherwise would have been settled. Now, it is not so clear that this would be such a bad thing even if true. Bias against plaintiffs may now cause cases not to be litigated that *should* be litigated. More surprisingly, it is not even so clear that the incidence of settlement would not be increased rather than decreased.

Cases tend to be settled when the opposing parties have similar estimates of the expected value of the recovery. For instance, suppose that plaintiff and defendant have identical estimates of the outcome of a case if it is litigated to final judgment: they both estimate that the prospect of judgment to the plaintiff is worth about $55,000. [In the next chapter, we will get a little bit more sophisticated about how prospects are evaluated when they are to any extent uncertain.] Suppose further that litigation costs are $4000 for plaintiff and $3000 for defendant. In total, the parties can save $7000 in costs by not going to trial. Hence, they will both be better off at any settlement figure between $51,000 and $58,000.

The above example can be generalized. Estimates of the outcome need not be identical in order for mutual gains from settlement to exist; the divergence in views must merely be less than the cost to both parties of proceeding to final judgment. Do you see why this is true?

Now for the relevance of assignability to all of this. A plausible argument might be that assignability would produce a more objective valuation of claims by people who are specialists in such evaluations. After all, if the present holder of a claim placed an unduly low value on it, there would be money to be made from detecting this fact and purchasing the claim for a figure closer to its real value. Indeed, a market-like valuation of one's claim might induce a downward revaluation by one who overvalues his cause of action. After all, if I see that nobody else values my asset as highly as I do, it may produce some reassessment in my mind as to the accuracy of my original subjective valuation. In sum, transferability might well produce more uniformity in the valuation of claims. If so, an increase rather than a decrease in pretrial settlement is a defensible prediction. Do you find this a persuasive argument? Why?

OTHER PROPERTY RIGHTS IN LEGAL PROCESS

Here are several shorter questions, again on the general topic of property rights in legal process, but drawing on elements from almost all of the preceding sections of the Chapter.

1. Mutuality of Estoppel

The doctrine of mutuality of estoppel traditionally maintained that one may not invoke a judgment in his own favor unless an adverse judgment could have been used against him. This rule has increasingly been subject to attack as possibly requiring wasteful use of resources in the repetitive relitigation of identical issues. To make matters even worse, this relitigation may also result in inconsistent resolutions of the issues involved.

a. Party A has been adjudged guilty of negligence in an accident that caused injuries to B. The same act that caused B's injuries also led to damages sustained by C. What legal considerations determine whether C can adversely invoke B's judgment against A?

b. Can mutuality of estoppel be defended as a response to a possible Free Rider problem? Or a Chicken problem? Or a Prisoner's Dilemma? Devices such as class actions and compulsory joinder are sometimes regarded as mechanisms to overcome Free Rider problems among litigants. How effective do you think they are? For an informative discussion of the legal devices to deal with multiparty actions, see McCoid, "A Single Package for Multiparty Disputes," 28 Stanford L.Rev. 707 (1976).

c. The rules restricting estoppel confer a species of excludability on a judgment, but they do not create full appropriability because a determination is not saleable. What would be wrong with making a determination transferable for consideration? For instance, multiple plaintiffs in an airline disaster could either "produce" proof of liability against the airline themselves or they could "purchase" the favorable judgment secured by an early litigant.

d. "One way of explaining the present situation is to say that the law treats 'precedents' differently, depending on whether they are precedents as to law or as to facts. We usually don't call the latter 'precedents,' but they are." What does the quoted statement mean? Is there any good reason why judgments as to facts ought to be treated differently from judgments as to law?

2. Discovery of Computerized Litigation Files

Presumably, the ideal behind the discovery process is to facilitate the uncovering of truth by making available as many facts and "investigative resources" as possible. A very real impediment to understanding certain complex cases is the overwhelming mass of documents and facts unearthed during discovery. At some point, the truth-seeking process almost grinds to a halt under the sheer weight of the accumulated evidence. Computerized litigation support systems are emerging as an important tool in coping with complex cases. Documents are coded, classified, summarized, and sometimes entered in "full text" form into computer-accessible files. The ability to quickly and accurately retrieve and process information is thought to be very useful by litigators. However, putting documents into computer-accessible form can be a very expensive process, often running into the hundreds of thousands of dollars.

Assume that there is a computer-readable file containing the full text of all documents discovered in a pending suit. The file has been prepared by litigant A at a cost of $350,000. The file contains nothing of what would ordinarily be called attorney work product; it consists only of the full text of the original documents, now reduced to computer-readable form. Litigant B seeks discovery of the computerized file.

    a. What are the pros and cons of permitting discovery by party B?

    b. The cost to A of duplicating the tapes for B is approximately $1000 dollars. If B is granted access to the file, what should B have to pay to A?

    c. What could A have done to improve the possibility that a computerized document file would be held non-discoverable? Is it fair to consider the extra cost of this as an investment in "staking a claim" to property?

BROADCAST MUSIC, INC. v. MOOR–LAW, INC.

United States District Court for the District of Delaware, 1981.
527 F.Supp. 758.

[Almost all licensing of U.S. performing rights to musical compositions is done by two large organizations, Broadcast Music, Inc. (BMI) and the American Society of Composers, Authors & Publishers (AS-CAP), each of whom represent thousands of individual copyright owners. Licensees fall into two categories: (1) broadcast licensees, who include television and radio stations or networks; and (2) non-broadcast licensees, who include hotels, concert halls, and "GLAs". GLAs are small establishments, such as nightclubs and bars, that provide live music under a blanket General Licensing Agreement. In 1977, BMI filed a copyright infringement action against Moor-Law, Inc., doing business as the Triple Nickel Saloon. Moor-Law raised the affirmative defense of copyright misuse and counterclaimed that BMI's licensing practices to GLAs violated Sections 1 and 2 of the Sherman Act and Section 3 of the Clayton Act.]

* * *

The relevant market in this case is the licensing of musical performing rights to GLA licensees. An examination of the characteristics of this unique market is essential to an evaluation of the Triple Nickel's antitrust and copyright misuse claims. Although the parties dispute the significance of some market characteristics, they are in basic agreement about many features of the market, including the applicability of the economic concepts of natural monopoly and public goods.

Both parties' experts agreed that this market has natural monopoly characteristics. Because there are thousands of individual copyright "sellers" seeking to deal with thousands of GLA buyers, the potential transaction costs are very high. Economies of scale exist as sellers band together to spread transaction costs of identical transactions over a larger group. Thus, some pooling of copyrights by individual copyright holders is a necessity in order to take advantage of the natural monopoly characteristics of the market.

In addition, both parties' experts agree that the goods in this market—the performing rights to the musical compositions—have the characteristics of "public goods". Public goods have two salient characteristics which operate in this market. First, unlike private goods (e.g. apples), one can use a public good without leaving any less for others to consume. Once a musical composition is created, the marginal cost of additional consumption is zero.[5] The second characteristic of public goods is that it is difficult to exclude persons who do not pay from using the good. The owners of private goods can withhold their goods from the market and release them only in return for payment; but, once a composer's song becomes known, he or she finds it difficult to prevent that good from being "stolen" by users. The enforcement problem resulting from this public good characteristic manifests itself in the GLA market through users who don't pay any licensing fee. During the course of this litigation, this has been labeled the "free rider" problem.

Because the high transaction costs derived from natural monopoly characteristics are increased by the public good enforcement problem,

5. See Cirace, CBS v. ASCAP: An Economic Analysis of a Political Problem, 47 Fordham L.Rev. 277, 282 (1978).

very large performing rights organizations, like BMI and ASCAP, in which individual copyright holders pool their rights are necessary to achieve efficiency. The larger the organization, the more efficient it will be in reducing transaction costs; indeed, Triple Nickel's expert, Dr. Cirace, advocated one combined licensing operation in this market. The necessity for these large licensing organizations makes competition in the sense of many sellers competing against each other in the GLA market unrealistic.

The parties are also in agreement that the nature of the GLA market makes some kind of blanket license a necessity. As the Supreme Court observed in *CBS IV:*

> Individual sales transactions in this industry are quite expensive, as would be individual monitoring and enforcement, especially in light of the resources of single composers. Indeed, as both the Court of Appeals and CBS recognize the costs are prohibitive for licenses with individual radio stations, nightclubs, and restaurants, * * * and it was in that milieu that the blanket license arose.

CBS IV, 441 U.S. at 20, 99 S.Ct. at 1562.

Moreover, the Supreme Court's recognition in the *CBS* case, Id. at 20, 99 S.Ct. at 1562, that most users want "unplanned, rapid and indemnified access" to a wide range of compositions, is particularly apt in the GLA market. Testimony at trial made clear that GLA users typically do not know in advance what compositions will be performed nightly in their establishments and yet want the right to perform them instantaneously. The blanket license provides instantaneous access to any composition desired.

A corollary of the conclusion that the blanket license is a necessity in the GLA market is that the alternatives required by BMI's consent decree of direct licensing with individual copyright owners or of per piece licensing are unfeasible in this market. Again, the parties seem to agree on this point. Unlike the situation in *CBS* where large networks were interested in a relatively small number of compositions known in advance of performance, GLAs like the Triple Nickel are small establishments which lack the resources or the advance notice to contract copyright owners individually on a large scale. Likewise, because GLA owners rarely know in advance of performance the songs a band intends to play and because GLA bands often take audience requests, a prospective per piece license is unrealistic.

Finally, although the parties disagree over appropriate methods of pricing, they seem to agree that the natural market forces of supply and demand do not operate normally on pricing in this market. Because of the public good characteristic that the marginal cost of using a musical composition is zero, normal cost-based pricing is not feasible. The parties seem to agree that some form of pricing based on benefit conferred is appropriate. But, since as a practical matter a GLA needs a license from both ASCAP and BMI, the normal constraint on benefit pricing—alternative supply—does not operate in this market.

Thus, although large performing rights organizations are a necessity in this market, the result in the current market is that BMI can exercise substantial monopoly power over price. This monopoly power of the seller is particularly strong in a negotiating situation where there is not corresponding power on the buyer's side. Unlike the television network market where buyers like CBS exercise some monopsony power of their own, the buyers in the GLA market are weak and diffuse.

While normal competitive forces do not operate in this market, it is not true that BMI's price for its GLA license is unconstrained. Testimony at trial convinced me that the free rider problem does provide a significant constraint on the price BMI charges. The higher the price it charges, the greater the resistance of GLA users is likely to be, and, conversely, the lower the price, the lower the resistance will be. Since the free rider problem tends to make BMI's enforcement costs high and can, indeed, cause increased costs to more than consume increased revenue from a higher price, BMI considers this problem when setting a price.

*   *   *

QUESTIONS

1. In the case excerpted above, the court is sympathetic, based on a free-rider argument, to a pricing arrangement that might otherwise be deemed a violation of the antitrust laws. Summarize in your own words how a free-rider situation is alleged to result and why the court might view this as bad. Are you persuaded by the argument? Can you suggest other industries that might plausibly make similar claims?

2. A free-rider argument may be made to explain certain restrictions on price competition imposed by manufacturers on their dealers. Briefly, this thesis suggests that manufacturers may want to induce dealers to substitute non-price competition—in the form of service, advertisement, parts availability, etc.—for price competition. In principle, the restrictions may be beneficial to all parties, i.e., manufacturer, dealers, and customers. Indicate how you think this argument might be developed and what might be the countervailing anti-trust risks.[t]

t. See Richard A. Posner, Antitrust Law, (1976) at 147–151; Telser, "Why Should Manufacturers Want Fair Trade?," 3 J.Law & Econ. 86 (1960). But see, Comanor, "Vertical Territorial and Customer Restrictions: White Motor and Its Aftermath," 81 Harv.L.Rev. 1419, 1425–33 (1968).

FONTAINEBLEAU HOTEL CORP. v. FORTY–FIVE TWENTY–FIVE, INC.

District Court of Appeals of Florida, Third District, 1959.
114 So.2d 357.

*   *   *   In this action, plaintiff-appellee sought to enjoin the defendants-appellants from proceeding with the construction of [an] addition to the Fontainebleau alleging that the construction would interfere with the light and air on the beach in front of the Eden Roc and cast a shadow of such size as to render the beach wholly unfitted for the use and enjoyment of its guests, to the irreparable injury of the plaintiff; further, that the construction of such addition on the north side of defendants' property, rather than the south side, was actuated by malice and ill will on the part of the defendants' president toward the plaintiff's president; and that the construction was in violation of a building ordinance requiring a 100-foot setback from the ocean. It was also alleged that the construction would interfere with the easements of light and air enjoyed by plaintiff and its predecessors in title for more than twenty years and "impliedly granted by virtue of the acts of the plaintiff's predecessors in title, as well as under the common law and the express recognition of such rights by virtue of Chapter 9837, Laws of Florida 1923. *   *   * " Some attempt was also made to allege an easement by implication in favor of the plaintiff's property, as the dominant, and against the defendants' property, as the servient, tenement.

*   *   *

The chancellor *   *   * entered a temporary injunction restraining the defendants from continuing with the construction of the addition. His reason for so doing was stated by him as follows:

*   *   * The ruling is not based on alleged presumptive title nor prescriptive right of the plaintiff to light and air nor is it based on any deed restrictions nor recorded plats in the title of the plaintiff nor of the defendant nor of any plat of record. It is not based on any zoning ordinance nor on any provision of the building code of the City of Miami Beach nor on the decision of any court, nisi pruis or appellate. It is based solely on the proposition that no one has a right to use his property to the injury of another and that the intended use by the Fontainebleau will materially damage the Eden Roc. There is evidence indicating that the construction of the proposed annex by the Fontainebleau is malicious or deliberate for the purpose of injuring the Eden Roc, but it is scarcely sufficient, standing alone, to afford a basis for equitable relief.

This is indeed a novel application of the maxim *sic utere tuo ut alienum non laedas*. This maxim does not mean that one must never use his own property in such a way as to do any injury to his neighbor. It means only that one must use his property so as not to injure the lawful *rights* of another. Cason v. Florida Power Co., 74 Fla. 1, 76 So. 535. In Reaver v. Martin Theatres (Fla.1951) 52 So.2d 682, 683, 25 A.L.R.2d 1451, under this maxim, it was stated that "it is well settled that a property owner may put his own property to any reasonable and lawful use, so long as he does not thereby deprive the adjoining landowner of any right of enjoyment of his property *which is recognized and protected by law, and so long as his use is not such a one as the law will pronounce a nuisance.*" [Emphasis supplied.]

No American decision has been cited, and independent research has revealed none, in which it has been held that—in the absence of some contractual or statutory obligation—a landowner has a legal right to the free flow of light and air across the adjoining land of his neighbor. Even at common law, the landowner had no legal right, in the absence of an easement or uninterrupted use and enjoyment for a period of 20 years, to unobstructed light and air from the adjoining land. Blumberg v. Weiss, (N.J.1941), 17 A.2d 823.

* * * There being, then, no legal right to the free flow of light and air from the adjoining land, it is universally held that where a structure serves a useful and beneficial purpose, it does not give rise to a cause of action, either for damages or for an injunction under the maxim *sic utere tuo ut alienum non laedas*, even though it causes injury to another by cutting off the light and air and interfering with the view that would otherwise be available over adjoining land in its natural state, regardless of the fact that the structure may have been erected partly for spite. See the cases collected in the annotation in 133 A.L.R. at pp. 701 et seq.; 1 Am.Jur., Adjoining Landowners, Sec. 54, p. 536. * * *

We see no reason for departing from this universal rule. If, as contended on behalf of plaintiff, public policy demands that a landowner in the Miami Beach area refrain from constructing buildings on his premises that will cast a shadow on the adjoining premises, an amendment of its comprehensive planning and zoning ordinance, applicable to the public as a whole, is the means by which such purpose should be achieved.

* * *

Since it affirmatively appears that the plaintiff has not established a cause of action against the defendants by reason of the structure here in question, the order granting a temporary injunction should be and it is hereby reversed with directions to dismiss the complaint.

QUESTIONS

1. If the Florida courts had ruled in favor of the Eden Roc owners, what do you think would subsequently have happened?

2. To whom do you think what are, in effect, the "solar property rights" were most valuable before the Fontainebleau commenced construction of the tower? If the law had at that time been known to be clearly against the highest-valued user, what option would have been available? Is the option a practical one?

3. "Solar rights constitute an area where the legal system need only define and enforce a clear system of rights through injunctive remedies. Then these property rights, like any other, can be efficiently reallocated via transfers, easements, etc." Comment.

4. Are the problems of allocating wind rights essentially the same as those involved with solar rights? What about aesthetic rights?

COASE AND COSTS, "OPPORTUNITY" AND OTHERWISE

The facts of the nuisance cases in this part of the chapter can be used to comment briefly on a disarmingly simple but extremely powerful proposition frequently applied in economic analysis of Law: the so-called "Coase Theorem." The Coase Theorem had its genesis in a classic article by Ronald Coase [u] in which the author discussed a series of specific fact situations that link common law tort and nuisance doctrines with the economic theory of externalities. Since Coase himself never indicated explicitly what generalizations were to be drawn from his specific examples, the so-called "Theorem" bearing his name has been the subject of slightly different formulations, but its general flavor can be gleaned from the situation faced by the Fontainebleau and Eden Roc Hotels. In determining whether blockage of the sunlight is actionable or not, what the court really does is to determine who "owns" the relevant aspect of the local environment. If the Eden Roc is denied any remedy against the blockage of the sunlight, then the Fontainebleau has effectively been declared the owner of a valuable right. If, conversely, the Fontainebleau is restrained by the law through the issuance of an injunction or damage remedies, then the Eden Roc owns the property right. Coase's insight was to point out that the story does not necessarily stop after this initial determination of ownership. Let us consider why.

u. Coase, "The Problem of Social Cost," 3 J. Law & Econ. 1 (1960).

Assume that the value of the right to put the new building in a position that blocks the Eden Roc's sunlight is worth $X to the Fountainebleau while the right to have the light unobstructed is worth $Y to the Eden Roc. If the law assigns the right to the Fountainebleau, how much does it cost the Fountainebleau to use that right? It is tempting to say that it costs nothing, but that answer is clearly wrong. While no *expenditure* is required in order for the Fountainebleau to use a right that it already owns, that use necessitates what legal scholars have traditionally called a "forebearance." In our present example, the Fountainebleau must turn down the offer of up to $Y that the Eden Roc would be willing to pay to acquire the right. Following a similar reasoning, modern economists correctly insist that the cost of something is what one gives up in order to have it, and there is a very relevant sense in which it makes no difference whether the lost opportunity derives from an outlay or a foresworn receipt. This doctrine is known as the "opportunity cost" concept, where the relevant opportunity is the highest-valued alternative that is lost.

The opportunity cost concept leads directly to the main thrust of what has come to be known as the "Coase Theorem." It suggests that, in order for any right to be "used" by a party, that party must place a higher value on the right than any other bidder. If this were not so, the owner would be exercising a right that is worth (to him) less than its opportunity cost. Hence, who ultimately winds up exercising the right will tend to be determined only by the relative magnitudes of the numbers that correspond to X and Y, i.e., the values of the alternative uses. Note that the same logic applies if we now shift our assumption and suppose that the court had been willing to enjoin the Fontainebleau, thus making the Eden Roc the initial owner of the legal entitlement.

In brief, the thesis is that *in an environment where there are no obstacles to transacting,* legal rights will tend ultimately to be allocated, through trade if necessary, to the party that values them most highly, regardless of their initial assignment. The emphasized proviso in the previous sentence is critically important. We already have reason to believe, for instance, that the proviso is not met if the transferability or excludability of rights is somehow defective, and other such situations will appear below. Subject to its very emphatic qualifier, however, the Coase Theorem still points out an important truth: to the extent that transactions can reasonably be counted upon to reallocate rights, if necessary, to the "highest valued" use, then courts need not worry about the "waste" that might occur if low-valued uses of rights impeded higher-valued ones.

In sum, the Coase Theorem may be interpreted as an identification of circumstances in which the assignment of legal rights "makes no difference" to the achievement of an efficient use of resources because bargaining will reallocate and correct any initial misassignment. But the theorem can easily be misinterpreted as saying additionally that there is no difference in a much wider sense. Plainly, that is not true. The initial allocation of rights ownership does make a difference because it affects the distribution of income, thus effectively making some people richer and some poorer. The Coase Theorem states only that no significant economic waste consequences are thereby implicated. Properly understood, it does not deny that the court's decision will make one party or the other better or worse off by the amounts that the relevant rights are "worth," but merely asserts that an initial ownership decision does not by itself mandate the final result as to how rights are used and by whom. The latter questions are still the focus of a cost-benefit calculus ultimately determined by the parties themselves.

The theorem has sometimes also been interpreted as claiming that the *same* allocation of resources will result regardless of the initial assignment. This claim is plainly erroneous, although perhaps precipitated by the misleadingly simple examples commonly used to describe the theorem. For instance, if X is greater than Y, then it is asserted that the Fontainebleau will also emerge as the end-user, whichever way the court initially decides. This thesis, however, fails to consider the possible effect of the rights assignment on the values that the parties attach to the rights after an initial allocation has been determined. In general, a so-called "wealth effect" causes people to attach higher or lower values to things—i.e., change the numbers corresponding to X and Y—when their wealth level varies. Thus, through its original assignment of the wealth represented by the transfer value of the right, a legal system may create an "income effect" on the magnitudes of X and Y, the values placed by different parties on some particular right people. Reversal of the relative magnitudes of X and Y perhaps requires what is usually an implausibly large wealth effect, but the point should be made that, where the valuations of the parties are close, even comparatively small wealth effects caused by legal assignments can tip the balance as to who will place the highest value on the right when post-assignment bargaining becomes possible. Under those conditions, altering the original assignment of rights does result in different final resource allocations (because the wealth effect actually determines who *is* the high-value user of the right) but those different final results are equally consistent with the Coase Theorem's key prediction that, regardless of the legal rule, final allocations will be highest-valued uses.

Of course, the optimistic prediction of the Coase Theorem will frequently be inapplicable because there are substantial impediments to the reallocation of rights through bargaining. In general, for instance, the Coase Theorem has greater applicability in Contracts where the parties are already involved in a rights-and-duties trading process than in Torts where the parties may even be unknown to each other before the precipitating event. Hence, great caution must be exercised to invoke the Coase Theorem only under appropriate fact circumstances.

Although it presented an important common-sense insight, the Coase Theorem can facilitate a certain brand of myopia in legal analysis if one over-concentrates on the environment of extremely low bargaining costs. Whatever the narrowness of vision of some of those who invoke his Theorem, Coase himself had an admirable perspective:

> I would not wish to conclude without observing that, while consideration of what would happen in a world of zero transactions costs can give us valuable insights, these insights are, in my view, without value except as steps on the way to analysis of the real world of positive transactions costs. We do not do well to devote ourselves to a detailed study of the world of zero transactions costs, like augurs divining the future by the minute inspection of the entrails of a goose.[v]

It has just been suggested that the famous Coase Theorem is really a straightforward corollary of the opportunity cost concept. Discussion of a few additional cost concepts will also be useful for purposes of possible application to legal reallocation. Legal process costs, including filing, preparation, litigation, etc., will be referred to as "process costs." Eventually, it will be useful for certain purposes to further subdivide transaction and process costs into other components such as "monitoring" and "precautionary" costs.

Finally, the notion of "error costs" should also be introduced. In brief, error costs are the foregone gains due to not achieving the "ideal" result, i.e., the costs of "getting it wrong." For example, in the road maintenance scenario above, it would be the increase in net benefits, if any, derivable by producing the optimal level of road repairs rather than the existing one. Paradoxically enough, error costs are a benchmark concept and do not necessarily represent "true" costs in the opportunity cost sense. For instance, it may not be technologically or practically possible to achieve the ideal results, in which case the "opportunity" to have perfection is not a real alternative. More importantly, however, the concept of error costs is used below to focus attention on the fact that it is seldom desirable in the real world to attempt to achieve "perfect" or "ideal" outcomes. In general, any reallocation yielding lower error costs can only be accomplished at the expense of additional transaction or process costs. It is the *sum* of these various costs that presumably should be mini-

v. Coase, "The Coase Theorem and the Empty Core: A Comment," 24 J. Law and Econ. 175 (1981) at 187.

mized, usually by trading off among categories. Frequently, therefore, it is sensible to accept substantial error costs because the transactions or processes available to bring about superior reallocations are not cost-effective. Zero error costs are the benchmark result that would hold only if there were an omniscient, omnipotent, and benevolent entity prepared to effectuate and enforce "optimal" results.

BOOMER v. ATLANTIC CEMENT CO.

Court of Appeals of New York, 1970.
26 N.Y.2d 219, 257 N.E.2d 870.

BERGAN, Judge. Defendant operates a large cement plant near Albany. These are actions for injunction and damages by neighboring land owners alleging injury to property from dirt, smoke and vibration emanating from the plant. A nuisance has been found after trial, temporary damages have been allowed; but an injunction has been denied.

*   *   *

The cement making operations of defendant have been found by the court at Special Term to have damaged the nearby properties of plaintiffs. That court, as it has been noted, accordingly found defendant maintained a nuisance and this has been affirmed at the Appellate Division. The total damage to plaintiffs' properties is, however, relatively small in comparison with the value of defendant's operation and with the consequences of the injunction which plaintiffs seek.

The ground for the denial of injunction, notwithstanding the finding both that there is a nuisance and that plaintiffs have been damaged substantially, is the large disparity in economic consequences of the nuisance and of the injunction. This theory cannot, however, be sustained without overruling a doctrine which has been consistently reaffirmed in several leading cases in this court and which has never been disavowed here, namely, that where a nuisance has been found and where there has been any substantial damage shown by the party complaining an injunction will be granted.

The rule in New York has been that such a nuisance will be enjoined although marked disparity be shown in economic consequence between the effect of the injunction and the effect of the nuisance.

The problem of disparity in economic consequence was sharply in focus in Whalen v. Union Bag & Paper Co., 208 N.Y. 1, 101 N.E. 805. A pulp mill entailing an investment of more than a million dollars polluted a stream in which plaintiff, who owned a farm, was "a lower riparian owner". The economic loss to plaintiff from this pollution was small. This court, reversing the Appellate Division, reinstated the injunction granted by the Special Term against the argument of the mill owner that in view of "the slight advantage to plaintiff and the great loss that will be inflicted on defendant" an injunction should not be granted (p. 2, 101 N.E. p. 805). "Such a balancing of injuries cannot be justified by the circumstances of this case", Judge Werner noted (p. 4, 101 N.E. p. 806). * * * The rule laid down in that case, then, is that whenever the damage resulting from a nuisance is found not "unsubstantial", viz., $100 a year, injunction would follow. This states a rule that had been followed in this court with marked consistency.

* * *

This result at Special Term and at the Appellate Division is [thus] a departure from a rule that has become settled; but to follow the rule literally in these cases would be to close down the plant at once. This court is fully agreed to avoid that immediately drastic remedy; the difference in view is how best to avoid it.

One alternative is to grant the injunction but postpone its effect to a specified future date to give opportunity for technical advances to permit defendant to eliminate the nuisance; another is to grant the injunction conditioned on the payment of permanent damages to plaintiffs which would compensate them for the total economic loss to their property present and future caused by defendant's operations. For reasons which will be developed, the court chooses the latter alternative.

If the injunction were to be granted unless within a short period— e.g., 18 months—the nuisance be abated by improved methods, there would be no assurance that any significant technical improvement would occur.

The parties could settle this private litigation at any time if defendant paid enough money and the imminent threat of closing the plant would build up the pressure on defendant. If there were no improved techniques found, there would inevitably be applications to the court at Special Term for extensions of time to perform on showing of good faith efforts to find such techniques. * * * Moreover, techniques to eliminate dust and other annoying by-products of cement making are unlikely to be developed by any research the defendant can undertake within any short period.

On the other hand, to grant the injunction unless defendant pays plaintiffs such permanent damages as may be fixed by the court seems to do justice between the contending parties. All of the attributions of economic loss to the properties on which plaintiffs' complaints are based will have been redressed.

The nuisance complained of by these plaintiffs may have other public or private consequences, but these particular parties are the only ones who have sought remedies and the judgment proposed will fully redress them. The limitation of relief granted is a limitation only within the four corners of these actions and does not foreclose public health or other public agencies from seeking proper relief in a proper court.

It seems reasonable to think that the risk of being required to pay permanent damages to injured property owners by cement plant owners would itself be a reasonably effective spur to research for improved techniques to minimize nuisance.

* * *

The orders should be reversed, without costs, and the cases remitted to Supreme Court, Albany County to grant an injunction which shall be vacated upon payment by defendant of such amounts of permanent damage to the respective plaintiffs as shall for this purpose be determined by the court.

JASEN, Judge (dissenting).

* * *

I see grave dangers in overruling our long-established rule of granting an injunction where a nuisance results in substantial continuing damage. In permitting the injunction to become inoperative upon the payment of permanent damages, the majority is, in effect, licensing a continuing wrong. It is the same as saying to the cement company, you may continue to do harm to your neighbors so long as you pay a fee for it. Furthermore, once such permanent damages are assessed and paid, the incentive to alleviate the wrong would be eliminated, thereby continuing air pollution of an area without abatement.

It is true that some courts have sanctioned the remedy here proposed by the majority in a number of cases, but none of the authorities relied upon by the majority are analogous to the situation before us. In those cases, the courts, in denying an injunction and awarding money damages, grounded their decision on a showing that the use to which the property was intended to be put was primarily for the public benefit. Here, on the other hand, it is clearly established that the cement company is creating a continuing air pollution nuisance primarily for its own private interest with no public benefit.

This kind of inverse condemnation (Ferguson v. Village of Hamburg, 272 N.Y. 234, 5 N.E.2d 801) may not be invoked by a private person or corporation for private gain or advantage. Inverse condemnation should only be permitted when the public is primarily served in the taking or impairment of property. The promotion of the interests of the polluting cement company has, in my opinion, no public use or benefit.

Nor is it constitutionally permissible to impose servitude on land, without consent of the owner, by payment of permanent damages where the continuing impairment of the land is for a private use. (See Fifth Ave. Coach Lines v. City of New York, 11 N.Y.2d 342, 347, 229 N.Y.S.2d 400, 403, 183 N.E.2d 684, 686; Walker v. City of Hutchinson, 352 U.S. 112, 77 S.Ct. 200, 1 L.Ed.2d 178.) This is made clear by the State Constitution (art. I, Section 7, subd. [a]) which provides that "[p]rivate property shall not be taken for *public use* without just compensation" (emphasis added). It is, of course, significant that the section makes no mention of taking for a *private* use.

In sum, then, by constitutional mandate as well as by judicial pronouncement, the permanent impairment of private property for private purposes is not authorized in the absence of clearly demonstrated public benefit and use.

I would enjoin the defendant cement company from continuing the discharge of dust particles upon its neighbors' properties unless, within 18 months, the cement company abated this nuisance.

* * *

Moreover, I believe it is incumbent upon the defendant to develop such devices [to abate the nuisance], since the cement company, at the time the plant commenced production (1962), was well aware of the plaintiffs' presence in the area, as well as the probable consequences of its contemplated operation. Yet, it still chose to build and operate the plant at this site.

* * *

Accordingly, the orders of the Appellate Division, insofar as they denied the injunction, should be reversed, and the actions remitted to Supreme Court, Albany County to grant an injunction to take effect 18 months hence, unless the nuisance is abated by improved techniques prior to said date.

* * *

QUESTIONS

Consider the following facts for the hypothetical case of Bomber et al. v. Particular Gypsum Co. Sections 38 and 39 are adjacent 100-acre parcels of land in the northwestern part of Clementine County. Section 38 is owned by the Particular Gypsum Co. and is the site of its main production plant. Section 39 has been subdivided into 100 one-acre lots, almost all of which contain owner-occupied residences. Plaintiff Bomber is one of a class of individual property owners in Section 39 and is seeking to enjoin Particular from emitting dust and other particulate matter whose airborne passage onto the property in Section 39 allegedly constitutes a nuisance.

Expert testimony establishes that the loss to Section 39 property values resulting from Particular's emissions are approximately $1,000 per acre. In turn, Particular offers unrebutted evidence that (1) it is not feasible to produce at all in the present location without causing an objectionable level of emissions and (2) relocation of the plant would result in a cost to it of $12,437,000.

1. Counsel for Particular suggests that the precedent of Boomer v. Atlantic Cement Co. be applied. Do you agree that the Boomer case should be interpreted as teaching the following rule: an injunction should not issue when it can be shown that the value of a nuisance greatly exceeds the damages that it is imposing? If not, what?

2. Would it make any difference to your treatment of the case if Section 39 were an apartment complex owned in its entirety by Bomber Development Corporation?

3. Suppose that the Particular plant long antedated the residential development. Particular's counsel urges that no damages are owed, that the homeowners have already been compensated: when they bought the land from the original developer, each parcel sold for $1000 less than it otherwise would have because the purchasers knew about the dust emissions and took this into consideration in establishing the market price of the property. What is your reaction to this argument?

4. Assume that a strong tradition of no damages for a party who "comes to the nuisance" exists in your jurisdiction. Also, time has been turned back so that neither the factory nor the housing development presently exist; the developmental conditions of the area are not yet really ripe for such activities. Will the "comes to the nuisance" rule affect the pace and pattern of development? Is there anything objectionable about the behavior potentially motivated by a comes to the nuisance rule? [Hint: The rule in question sets up a "race" for valuable legal rights. Is this race costless? Might society arguably be "better off" if the rights were allocated in some other way? When is it worth paying the costs of having the race?]

5. This case and several that follow involve the notion that property can be defined in terms of legal rules that have varying degrees of potency. It can make a great deal of difference whether the "ownership" of a right is protected by an injunctive remedy or a damages remedy. In the legal literature, the distinction was emphasized by Calabresi and Melamed in "Property Rules, Liability Rules, and Inalienability," 85 Harv.L.Rev. 1089 (1972). Do you understand the implications of using "property rules" rather than "liability rules"? For an extended discussion, see Polinsky, "Resolving Nuisance Disputes: The Simple Economics of Injunctive and Damage Remedies," 32 Stan.L.Rev. 1075 (1980).

J. WEINGARTEN, INC. v. NORTHGATE MALL, INC.

Supreme Court of Louisiana, 1981.
404 So.2d 896.

DENNIS, Justice.

We are called upon to decide whether, under the circumstances of this case, a court should specifically enforce a lease by ordering the destruction of the major part of a $4 million building which a shopping center developer erected in an area reserved to its tenant for customer parking. The trial court refused to order the building razed, but the court of appeal reversed, requiring that approximately 60% of the building be torn down and removed within six months of the effective date of its judgment.

*   *   *

The defendant, Northgate Mall, Inc., * * * developed an enclosed shopping mall on approximately 35 acres of land. In 1968, the defendant subleased space in the mall to the plaintiff, J. Weingarten, Inc., for the operation of a grocery store.

In early 1978, the defendant began planning to renovate and expand the mall to counter expected competition from a new mall to be built in Lafayette. * * * The defendant's right to expand was limited to roughly 40,000 square feet, but it proposed to add slightly over 100,000 square feet. Therefore, consent of both parties was necessary under the lease to permit * * * expansion. However, no written modification ever resulted from [the parties'] preliminary negotiations.

In February, 1979, the defendant erected a construction fence and began moving construction equipment and material onto the job site. The plaintiff alerted the defendant that it considered the defendant's activities a breach of contract and that injunctive relief would be sought if such activities did not cease. Last minute negotiations between the parties were unsuccessful, and the plaintiff filed suit on March 1, 1979 seeking preliminary and permanent injunctive relief.

Pursuant to plaintiff's petition, the trial court issued a temporary restraining order prohibiting further construction activities and continued the order until March 19, 1979 when a hearing was held on plaintiff's motion to dissolve the restraining order. The trial court denied the preliminary injunction and dissolved the temporary restraining order based on its finding that Weingarten failed to show that it would sustain irreparable damage without injunctive relief. * * * The trial on the merits of the petition for a permanent injunction was not held until October 25 and 26, 1979. By this time the $4 million expansion project was virtually complete and the new stores therein were open for business.

After the trial on the permanent injunction, the trial court reaffirmed its earlier finding that the plaintiff had not demonstrated that it would be irreparably harmed and could be adequately compensated monetarily. The court refused to enforce specifically a provision in the lease stipulating that an injunction to enforce Weingarten's rights to egress and passage over the parking area occupied by the new building could be obtained without the necessity of showing irreparable harm or the inadequacy of damages. The trial court concluded the agreed remedy provision was against public policy relying on Termplan Arabi, Inc. v. Carollo, 299 So.2d 831 (La.App. 4th Cir.).

The court of appeal reversed the trial court, holding that the plaintiff was entitled to permanent injunctive relief because the agreed remedy provision was valid and because the plaintiff was irreparably harmed. We granted defendant's application to consider the appropriateness of specific performance in this case.

Northgate agreed not to erect any additional buildings in the parking area of the shopping center except within the space shown on a plat attached to the lease designated as sites for future department store and a proposed theater. The defendant also promised to maintain a ratio of six car parking spaces for each 1,000 feet of floor space in the shopping center. It further agreed that its tenant, Weingarten, would have the right to an "irrevocable non-exclusive easement" over all parking areas shown on the plat attached to the lease. In connection with the "easement," the lease provides that Weingarten "shall have the right to obtain an injunction specifically enforcing such rights and interests without the necessity of proving inadequacy of legal remedies or irreparable harm."

We concur in the court of appeal's findings that Northgate breached each of the contractual provisions. * * * However, we disagree with the court of appeal finding that the plaintiff had shown that it would be irreparably injured by the breaches of contract. The evidence fully supports the trial judge's determination that plaintiff failed to demonstrate that its injury would be irreparable or insusceptible to adequate compensation.

The decisive issue presented by the breaches of contract is whether Weingarten is entitled to the substantive right of specific performance under the circumstances of this case. * * * Plaintiff Weingarten has asked specific performance of defendant Northgate's obligation not to do something—namely, not to infringe on plaintiff's contractual rights over areas reserved for parking by the lease. Civil Code articles 1926 through 1929 govern the enforcement of obligations to do, or not to do.

Articles 1926 through 1929 provide:

Art. 1926.   On the breach of any obligation to do, or not to do, the obligee is entitled either to damages, or, in cases which permit it, to a specific performance of the contract, at his option, or he may require the dissolution of the contract, and in all these cases damages may be given where they have accrued, according to the rules established in the following section.

Art. 1927.   In ordinary cases, the breach of such a contract entitles the party aggrieved only to damages, but where this would be an inadequate compensation, and the party has the power of performing the contract, he may be constrained to a specific performance by means prescribed in the laws which regulate the practice of the courts.

Art. 1928.   The obligee may require that any thing which has been done in violation of a contract, may be undone, if the nature of the cause will permit, and that things be restored to the situation in which they were before the act complained of was done, and the court may order this to be effected by its officers, or authorize the injured party to do it himself at the expense of the other, and may also add damages, if the justice of the case require it.

Art. 1929.   If the obligation be not to do, the obligee may also demand that the obligor be restrained from doing any thing in contravention of it, in cases where he proves an attempt to do the act covenanted against.

Since they are not models of clarity, the articles are susceptible to more than one reasonable interpretation.

A literal reading of the codal language may lead one to conclude that the general rule, i.e., the one to be applied in ordinary cases, is that the breach of a contract entitles the party aggrieved only to damages; and specific performance may only be obtained where damages would be an inadequate compensation.   Under this review, an obligee could only require a thing done in violation of the contract to be undone if the nature of the cause would permit, viz., in the exceptional case in which damages are an inadequate remedy.   Such an interpretation is suspect, however, because of its common law overtones.

Eminent Louisiana civilian commentators have argued persuasively to the contrary that these articles of the code were designed to enhance the rank of specific performance over damages as a remedy for the nonperformance of obligations to do or not to do in a manner not expressed in the comparable French articles.

We agree with the distinguished doctrinal writers that Articles 1926 through 1929 were intended to give first rank to the obligee's right to performance in specific form, consistently with other provisions of the Code. Therefore, we reject the common law view that the obligee must first clear the inadequacy of damage-irreparable injury hurdle before invoking the remedy.

A reading of the articles as a whole, however, implies that courts are empowered to withhold specific performance in some exceptional cases even when specific performance is possible. The phrases, "if the nature of the cause will permit" and "in ordinary cases," suggest a reference to a traditional civilian concept. The civil law systems, i.e., those descended from Roman law, have by and large proceeded on the premise that specific redress should be ordered whenever possible, unless disadvantages of the remedy outweigh its advantages. The main reservations have been for cases where specific relief is impossible, would involve disproportionate cost, would introduce compulsion into close personal relationships or compel the expression of special forms of artistic or intellectual creativity. Dawson, Specific Performance in France and Germany, 57 Mich.L.Rev. 495, 520 (1959). Professor Litvinoff has described the French jurisprudence as allowing courts to deny specific performance whenever the inconvenience of such forced execution would exceed the advantage, as when the cost of performing in kind is disproportionate to the actual damage caused, or when it would have a negative effect upon the interest of third parties.

For the foregoing reasons, we conclude that the legislative aim of the redactors of the code was to institute the right to specific performance as an obligee's remedy for breach of contract except when it is impossible, greatly disproportionate in cost to the actual damage caused, no longer in the creditor's interest, or of substantial negative effect upon the interests of third parties.[6] Applying this interpretation to the present case, we conclude that its nature will not permit specific performance.

The evidence clearly reflects that the cost of tearing down most of the $4 million building and doing incalculable damage to the remainder of the shopping center greatly outweighs any actual damage caused to the plaintiff. It is dubious that the devastation of such a building in a shopping center built with the hope of competing with a neighboring market complex is in Weingarten's real interest. It is evident that the third persons not party to the contract or to this lawsuit would be negatively affected. Shopping center tenants in the

---

6. Even when a valid agreed remedy provision such as stipulated damages is included in the parties' contract, the court retains some discretion to modify that provision when circumstances such as partial performance make the agreed remedy inappropriate or unjust.

new building would lose their store space and risk losing their investments. H.J. Wilson Company, which occupies over 63,000 square feet of the building, would be particularly disadvantaged. The owners of the land and John Hancock Mutual Life Insurance Company, whose long term loan is secured by a mortgage on the shopping center and pledges of the leases of the five major tenants, would suffer a substantial negative effect. Although perhaps not controlling, additional considerations weighing against specific performance and its consequent destruction of a major commercial building are the potential negative effects upon the community in the form of economic waste, energy dissipation, and possible urban blight.

Although the contractual provisions involved here cannot be specifically enforced under the circumstances of this case, we hold that they could have been under different conditions. Indeed, unless exceptional conditions prevail as in this case anything which has been done in violation of the contract may be undone, including the destruction of a building. Moreover, plaintiff is not without a remedy because it is entitled to be compensated fully in damages for any loss it sustains as a result of the breach of contract. Because the record presently does not provide an adequate basis for the assessment of damages, however, the case will be remanded to the trial court for that purpose.

Reversed and Remanded.

QUESTIONS

1. Assume that, in addition to Weingarten, there were originally 20 other lessees who held similar contractual rights. Could this case have been decided on the same principles as *Boomer?* Would your answer to this question change if the 20 others had all settled amicably through out of court negotiations before Weingarten filed suit?

2. Does the court's announced principle for resolving the case arguably result in bad behavioral incentives for future parties who are in the position of Northgate?

SPUR INDUSTRIES, INC. v. DEL E. WEBB DEVELOPMENT CO.

Supreme Court of Arizona, In Banc, 1972.
108 Ariz. 178, 494 P.2d 700.

CAMERON, Vice Chief Justice.

From a judgment permanently enjoining the defendant, Spur Industries, Inc. from operating a cattle feedlot near the plaintiff Del. E. Webb Development Company's Sun City, Spur appeals. Webb cross-appeals. Although numerous issues are raised, we feel that it is necessary to answer only two questions. They are:

1. Where the operation of a business, such as a cattle feedlot is lawful in the first instance, but becomes a nuisance by reason of a nearby residential area, may the feedlot operation be enjoined in an action brought by the developer of the residential area?

2. Assuming that the nuisance may be enjoined, may the developer of a completely new town or urban area in a previously agricultural area be required to indemnify the operator of the feedlot who must move or cease operation because of the presence of the residential area created by the developer?

[The area in question is located in Maricopa County, Arizona, 14 to 15 miles west of Phoenix, on Grand Avenue. About two miles south of Grand Avenue is Olive Avenue which runs east and west. Farming started in this area about 1911. By 1950, the only urban areas in the vicinity were agriculturally related communities. The retirement community of Youngstown, between Grand and Olive Avenues, was commenced in 1954.

In 1956 Spur's predecessors in interest developed feedlots about one half mile south of Olive Avenue. The area is well suited for cattle feeding, and in 1959, there were 25 cattle feeding pens within a 7 mile radius. In May of 1959 Del Webb began to plan the development of an urban area to be known as Sun City. The price which Del Webb paid for the land was considerably less than the price for land near Phoenix, and this price, along with the success of Youngstown, was a factor influencing the decision to purchase the property in question.

In 1960 Spur began a rebuilding and expansion program and by 1962 had extended its expansion north and south to encompass 114 acres. Del Webb offered its first homes in January 1960. The first unit to be completed was approximately 2.5 miles north of Spur. By May 1960, 450 to 500 houses were completed or under construction. At this time, Del Webb did not consider odors from the Spur feed pens a problem and continued to develop in a southerly direction, until sales resistance became so great that the parcels were difficult if not impossible to sell.

Del Webb filed its original complaint alleging that lots in the southwest portion were unfit for development for sale as residential lots because of the operation of the Spur feedlot. Del Webb's suit complained that the Spur feeding operation was a public nuisance because of the flies and odor. Despite the admittedly good feedlot management and good housekeeping practices by Spur, the odor and flies resulting from the huge amounts of wet manure produced an annoying if not unhealthy situation as far as the senior citizens of southern Sun City were concerned. Some were unable to enjoy the outdoor living which Del Webb had advertised, and Del Webb was faced with sales resistance from prospective purchasers as well as strong and persistent complaints from the people who had purchased homes in that area.

It is noted, however, that neither the citizens of Sun City nor Youngstown are represented in this lawsuit and the suit is solely between Del Webb and Spur Industries, Inc.]

The difference between a private nuisance and a public nuisance is generally one of degree. A private nuisance is one affecting a single individual or a definite small number of persons in the enjoyment of private rights not common to the public, while a public nuisance is one affecting the rights enjoyed by citizens as a part of the public. To constitute a public nuisance, the nuisance must affect a considerable number of people or an entire community or neighborhood. City of Phoenix v. Johnson, 51 Ariz. 115, 75 P.2d 30 (1938).

Where the injury is slight, the remedy for minor inconveniences lies in an action for damages rather than in one for an injunction. Kubby v. Hammond, 68 Ariz. 17, 198 P.2d 134 (1948). Moreover some courts have held, in the "balancing of conveniences" cases, that damages may be the sole remedy. See Boomer v. Atlantic Cement Co., 309 N.Y.S.2d 312 (1970), and annotation comments, 40 A.L.R.3d 601.

Thus, it would appear from the admittedly incomplete record as developed in the trial court, that, at most, residents of Youngstown would be entitled to damages rather than injunctive relief.

We have no difficulty, however, in agreeing with the conclusion of the trial court that Spur's operation was an enjoinable public nuisance as far as the people in the southern portion of Del Webb's Sun City were concerned.

* * *

In addition to protecting the public interest, however, courts of equity are concerned with protecting the operator of a lawfully, albeit noxious, business from the result of a knowing and willful encroachment by others near his business.

In the so-called "coming to the nuisance" cases, the courts have held that the residential landowner may not have relief if he knowingly came into a neighborhood reserved for industrial or agricultural endeavors and has been damaged thereby:

"Plaintiffs chose to live in an area uncontrolled by zoning laws or restrictive covenants and remote from urban development. In such an area plaintiffs cannot complain that legitimate agricultural pursuits are being carried on in the vicinity, nor can plaintiffs, having chosen to build in an agricultural area, complain that the agricultural pursuits carried on in the area depreciate the value of their homes. The area being *primarily agricultural*, any opinion reflecting the value of such property must take this factor into account. The standards affecting the value of residence property in an urban setting, subject to zoning controls and controlled planning techniques, cannot be the standards by which agricultural properties are judged." Dill v. Excel Packing Company, 183 Kan. 513, 525, 526, 331 P.2d 539, 548, 549 (1958).

And:

" * * * a party cannot justly call upon the law to make that place suitable for his residence which was not so when he selected it. * * *." Gilbert v. Showerman, 23 Mich. 448, 2 Brown 158 (1871).

Were Webb the only party injured, we would feel justified in holding that the doctrine of "coming to the nuisance" would have been a bar to the relief asked by Webb, and, on the other hand, had Spur located the feedlot near the outskirts of a city and had the city grown toward the feedlot, Spur would have to suffer the cost of abating the nuisance as to those people locating within the growth pattern of the expanding city:

"The case affords, perhaps, an example where a business established at a place remote from population is gradually surrounded and becomes part of a populous center, so that a business which formerly was not an interference with the rights of others has become so by the encroachment of the population * * *." City of Ft. Smith v. Western Hide & Fur Co., 153 Ark. 99, 103, 239 S.W. 724, 726 (1922).

We agree, however, with the Massachusetts court that:

"The law of nuisance affords no rigid rule to be applied in all instances. It is elastic. It undertakes to require only that which is fair and reasonable under all the circumstances. In a commonwealth like this, which depends for its material prosperity so largely on the continued growth and enlargement of manufacturing of diverse varieties, 'extreme rights' cannot be enforced. * * *." Stevens v. Rockport Granite Co., 216 Mass. 486, 488, 104 N.E. 371, 373 (1914).

There was no indication in the instant case at the time Spur and its predecessors located in western Maricopa County that a new city would spring up, full-blown, alongside the feeding operation and that the developer of that city would ask the court to order Spur to move because of the new city. Spur is required to move not because of any wrongdoing on the part of Spur, but because of a proper and legitimate regard of the courts for the rights and interests of the public.

Del Webb, on the other hand, is entitled to the relief prayed for (a permanent injunction), not because Webb is blameless, but because of the damage to the people who have been encouraged to purchase homes in Sun City. It does not equitably or legally follow, however, that Webb, being entitled to the injunction, is then free of any liability to Spur if Webb has in fact been the cause of the damage Spur has sustained. It does not seem harsh to require a developer, who has taken advantage of the lesser land values in a rural area as well as the availability of large tracts of land on which to build and develop a new town or city in the area, to indemnify those who are forced to leave as a result.

Having brought people to the nuisance to the foreseeable detriment of Spur, Webb must indemnify Spur for a reasonable amount of the cost of moving or shutting down. It should be noted that this relief to Spur is limited to a case wherein a developer has, with foreseeability, brought into a previously agricultural or industrial area the population which makes necessary the granting of an injunction against a lawful business and for which the business has no adequate relief.

It is therefore the decision of this court that the matter be remanded to the trial court for a hearing upon the damages sustained by the defendant Spur as a reasonable and direct result of the granting of the permanent injunction.

QUESTIONS

1. In the court's view, which party "owned" the relevant property right? Was that party deprived of the value of any part of its property through the court's ruling?

2. Why should Del Webb not have been required to bribe Spur to move away?

3. Suppose Del Webb had acquired its tract in 1954 and placed thereupon large signs announcing "Future Site of Sun City Residential Development." Would this have been likely to change the court's assessment of Del Webb's position? If not, what more would Del Webb have had to do in order to avoid risking future legal liability to Spur?

SPRECHER v. ADAMSON COMPANIES et al.

Supreme Court of California, In Bank, 1981.
30 Cal.3d 358, 178 Cal.Rptr. 783, 636 P.2d 1121.

[Respondent Adamson Companies is a joint owner of a 90-acre parcel of land in Malibu. Opposite the parcel are a number of homes, including that of appellant, Peter Sprecher. Respondents' tract contains part of an active landslide which extends seaward from the parcel for some 1,700 feet along Malibu Road and beyond the boundaries of respondent's property. In March 1978, heavy spring rains triggered a major movement of the slide which caused Sprecher's home to rotate and to press against the home of his neighbor, Gwendolyn Sexton. She filed an action against Sprecher, seeking to enjoin the encroachment of his home upon hers. Appellant cross-complained against Sexton, the County of Los Angeles and respondents. Specifically, appellant sought damages for the harm done to his home by the landslide, alleging that such damage proximately resulted from respondents' negligent failure to correct or control the landslide condition. Respondents successfully moved for summary judgment, arguing that a possessor of land has no duty to remedy a natural condition of the land in order to prevent harm to property outside his premises.]

* * * Under the common law, the major important limitation upon the responsibility of a possessor of land to those outside his premises concerned the natural condition of the land. (Prosser, Law of Torts (4th Ed. 1971) Sec. 57, p. 354.) While the possessor's liability for harm caused by artificial conditions was determined in accord with ordinary principles of negligence (id., at p. 355; see Rest. 2d Torts, Secs. 364–370), the common law gave him an absolute immunity from liability for harm caused by conditions considered natural in origin. (Prosser, supra, at p. 354; see Rest. 2d Torts, Sec. 363.) No matter how great the harm threatened to his neighbor, or to one passing by, and no matter how small the effort needed to eliminate it, a possessor of land had no duty to remedy conditions that were natural in origin.

This court has held that it will not depart from the fundamental concept that a person is liable for injuries caused "by his want of ordinary care * * * in the management of his property or person * * *" except when such a departure is "clearly supported by public policy." (Rowland v. Christian (1968) 69 Cal.2d 108, 112, 70 Cal. Rptr. 97, 443 P.2d 561.) Accordingly, common law distinctions resulting in wholesale immunities have been struck down when such distinctions could not withstand critical scrutiny. * * * In *Rowland*, this court stated that "[a] departure from [the] fundamental principle involves the balancing of a number of considerations[.] [T]he major ones are the foreseeability of harm to the plaintiff, the degree of certainty that the plaintiff suffered injury, the closeness of the connection between the defendant's conduct and the injury suffered, the moral blame attached to the defendant's conduct, the policy of preventing future harm, the extent of the burden to the defendant and [the] consequences to the community of imposing a duty to exercise care with resulting liability for breach and the availability, cost, and prevalence of insurance for the risk involved."

*   *   *

This progression of the law in California mirrors what appears to be a general trend toward rejecting the common law distinction between natural and artificial conditions. Instead, the courts are increasingly using ordinary negligence principles to determine a possessor's liability for harm caused by a condition of the land. The early case of Gibson v. Denton (1896) 4 A.D. 198, 38 N.Y.S. 554 was a precursor of this trend. In *Gibson*, the court held a possessor of land liable for damage caused when a decayed tree on her premises fell on the home of her neighbor during a storm. After noting that the defendant clearly would be liable for the fall of a dilapidated building, or artifical structure, the court observed that it could "see no good reason why she should not be responsible for the fall of a decayed tree, which she allowed to remain on her premises." (Id., at p. 555.) "[T]he tree was on her lot, and was her property. It was as much under her control as a pole or building in the same position would have been." (Ibid.) Thus, "[t]he defendant had no more right to keep, maintain, or suffer to remain on her premises an unsound tree * * * than she would have had to keep a dilapidated and unsafe building in the same position." (Id., at pp. 555–556.)

In more recent years, at least 13 other states and the District of Columbia have begun applying ordinary negligence principles in determining a possessor's liability for harm caused by a natural condition. * * * Not surprisingly, all these cases involved an injury caused by a fallen tree. However, the principles expressed by these courts are not so limited. For example, the court in Dudley v. Meadowbrook, Inc., supra, 166 A.2d 743, held that a possessor of land has a "duty of common prudence in maintaining his property, including trees thereon, in such a way as to prevent injury to his neighbor's property." (Id., at p. 744; see also Turner v. Ridley, supra, 144 A.2d at pp. 270–271 [same court; duty applied to automobile parked on public road].)

The courts are not simply creating an exception to the common law rule of nonliability for damage caused by trees and retaining the rule for other natural conditions of the land. Instead, the courts are moving toward jettisoning the common law rule in its entirety and replacing it with a single duty of reasonable care in the maintenance of property. This development is reflected in the Restatement Second of Torts, which now recognizes that a possessor of land may be subject to liability for harm caused not just by trees but by any natural condition of the land.

* * *

In rejecting the common law rule of nonliability for natural conditions, the courts have recognized the inherent injustice involved in a rule which states that a "landowner may escape all liability for serious damage to his neighbors [or those using a public highway], merely by allowing nature to take its course." (Prosser, supra, at p. 355.) As one commentator has observed: "[w]here a planted tree has become dangerous to persons on the highway or on adjoining land, and causes harm, the fault lies not in the planting of the tree but in permitting it to remain after it has become unsafe." (Noel, Nuisances from Land in Its Natural Condition (1943) 56 Harv.L.Rev. 772, 796–797.)

Historically, the consideration most frequently invoked to support the rule of nonliability for natural conditions was that it was merely an embodiment of the principle that one should not be obligated to undertake affirmative conduct to aid or protect others (Rest. 2d Torts, Sec. 314; see generally, James, Scope of Duty in Negligence Cases (1953) 47 Nw.U.L.Rev. 778, 800–809; Noel, Nuisances from Land in Its Natural Condition, supra, 56 Harv.L.Rev. at pp. 773, 796–797 and fn. 102; McCleary, The Possessors' Responsibilities as to Trees (1964) 29 Mo.L.Rev. 159; 2 Harper & James, The Law of Torts (1956) Sec. 27.19, pp. 1521–1522.) This doctrine rested on the common law distinction between the infliction of harm and the failure to prevent it, or misfeasance and nonfeasance. Misfeasance was determined to exist when a defendant played some part in the creation of a risk, even if his participation was innocent. Nonfeasance occurred when a defendant had merely failed to intervene in a plaintiff's behalf. (See generally, Weinrib, The Case for a Duty to Rescue (1980) 90 Yale L.J. 247, 251–258.) Liability for nonfeasance, or the failure to take affirmative action, was ordinarily imposed only where some special relationship between the plaintiff and defendant could be established. (Id., at p. 248 and fn. 7; Rest. 2d Torts, Sec. 314, com. a.)

Proponents of the rule of nonliability for natural conditions argued that a defendant's failure to prevent a natural condition from causing harm was mere nonfeasance. A natural condition of the land was by definition, they argued, one which no human being had played a part in creating. (See Noel, Nuisances from Land in Its Natural Condition, supra, 56 Harv.L.Rev., at p. 773.) Therefore, no basis for liability existed because a duty to exercise reasonable care could not arise out of possession alone. (Ibid.) Since there was no special relationship between the possessor of land and persons outside the premises, there could be no liability. (See Rest. 2d Torts, Sec. 314, com. f.) Conversely, a defendant's failure to prevent an artificial condition from causing harm constituted actionable misfeasance.

Whatever the rule may once have been, it is now clear that a duty to exercise due care can arise out of possession alone. One example is provided by modern cases dealing with the duty of a possessor of land to act affirmatively for the protection of individuals who come upon the premises. In days gone by, a possessor of land was deemed to owe such a duty of care only to invitees. That is, the duty to act affirmatively was grounded in the special relation between the possessor-invitor and the invitee. *Rowland* held that whether the individual coming upon the land was a trespasser, a licensee or an invitee made no difference as to the duty of reasonable care owed but was to be considered only as to the issue of whether the possessor had exercised reasonable care under all the circumstances.

Modern cases recognize that after *Rowland*, the duty to take affirmative action for the protection of individuals coming upon the land is grounded in the possession of the premises and the attendant right to control and manage the premises.

* * *

Thus, it becomes clear that the traditional characterization of a defendant's failure to take affirmative steps to prevent a natural condition from causing harm as nonactionable nonfeasance conflicts sharply with modern perceptions of the obligations which flow from the possession of land. Possession ordinarily brings with it the right of supervision and control. As Justice Mosk has aptly stated, the right of supervision and control "goes to the very heart of the ascription of tortious responsibility. * * *" (Connor v. Great Western Sav. & Loan Assn. (1968) 69 Cal.2d 850, 874, 73 Cal.Rptr. 369, 447 P.2d 609 [dis. opn. of Mosk, J.].)

Another deficiency of the historical justification of the rule of nonliability is simply that it proves too much. Under the traditional analysis, a possessor of land should be excused from any duty to prevent harm to persons outside his land whenever he has played no part in the creation of the condition which threatens the harm, be it artificial or natural. However, most courts recognize that the possessor is under an affirmative duty to act with regard to a dangerous artificial condition even though the condition was created solely by some predecessor in title or possession (Rest.2d Torts, Sec. 366; see e.g. Dye v. Burdick (1977) 262 Ark. 124, 553 S.W.2d 883, 836–837); or by the unauthorized conduct of some other third person (Rest.2d Torts, Sec. 364, subd. (c)). "To impose such a duty is to cross the line from misfeasance to nonfeasance" unless the present possessor somehow aggravates the danger. (See Weinrib, The Case for a Duty to Rescue, supra, 90 Yale L.J. at p. 257.)

Interestingly enough, in the cases holding that a possessor has an affirmative duty to prevent harm by a dangerous artificial condition created solely by another, the liability of the defendant has been predicated upon his possession and control of the artificial condition which caused the harm. (E.g., Dye v. Burdick, supra, 553 S.W.2d 833; cf. Pridgen v. Boston Housing Authority (1974) 364 Mass. 696, 308 N.E.2d 467, 475–478.) Thus, these cases confirm that mere possession with its attendant right to control conditions on the premises is a sufficient basis for the imposition of an affirmative duty to act. (See generally, 2 Harper & James, supra, at pp. 1523–1525.) In sum, the historical justification for the rule of nonliability for natural conditions has lost whatever validity it may once have had.

* * *

The trend in the law is in the direction of imposing a duty of reasonable care upon the possessor of land with regard to natural conditions of land. The erosion of the doctrinal underpinning of the rule of nonliability is evident from even a cursory review of the case law. Also evident is the lack of congruence between the old common law rule of nonliability and the relevant factors which should determine whether a duty exists. All this leads to but one conclusion. The distinction between artificial and natural conditions should be rejected. "A [person's] life or limb [or property] does not become less worthy of compensation under the law" because that person has been injured by a natural, as opposed to an artificial, condition.

It must also be emphasized that the liability imposed is for negligence. The question is whether in the management of his property, the possessor of land has acted as a reasonable person under all the circumstances. The likelihood of injury to plaintiff, the probable seriousness of such injury, the burden of reducing or avoiding the risk, the location of the land, and the possessor's degree of control over the risk-creating condition are among the factors to be considered by the trier of fact in evaluating the reasonableness of a defendant's conduct.

* * *

Construing appellant's evidence liberally and respondents' narrowly, as this court must, a rational inference can be drawn that effective measures for the control of the slide were within respondent's reach and that such measures would have entailed a substantial expense. Although the cost of implementing only slightly effective measures would not be justified by the benefit to appellant, it can be inferred that the cost of implementing effective measures might (or might not) be justified by the benefit to appellant and to respondents. Although the case is a close one, the evidence does not conclusively establish that no rational inference of negligence can be drawn under the circumstances of this case.

* * *

The judgment of the trial court is reversed and the cause remanded to the trial court for further proceedings consistent with the views expressed in this opinion.

QUESTIONS

1. "This case is a contest about the ownership of a bad rather than a good, a liability rather than an asset. The traditional rule is that the ownership of a bad rests upon the party whom Nature afflicts with its results." Comment.

2. What is the fundamental difference between the issue in Sprecher on the one hand and the nuisance cases of Boomer and Spur on the other? Is Sprecher analogous to the dispute between the Fontainebleau and Eden Roc?

3. Why does the court seem to find it necessary to overturn the traditional rule on natural immunities? Is its reasoning sound? How would you argue this case on behalf of Adamson Companies?

4. How do you think the rule of liability for mudslides should be formulated? Does your view in any way depend on factual questions? If you would not espouse the same rule for *all* natural hazards, explain why.

5. Suppose that the owner of a large tract became aware that a volcanic eruption, similar to Mt. St. Helens, was developing under his land. The prospect is that the eruption will cause $1 Billion worth of damages. The eruption can be "plugged" at the cost of $1 Million. Do you think that the Sprecher court would find a duty to plug?

Chapter II

BEHAVIOR INVOLVING UNCERTAINTY

Many human decisions are made at a point in time when all or many of their important consequences, whether costs or benefits, lie concealed in the mists of a future that can be known only in terms of probabilities. The dimension of time does not inevitably attach grave uncertainty to the consequences of a decision; there are some future events about which we can be quite confident. As a practical matter, however, intertemporal choices do almost always involve probability distributions of future results rather than the determinate, single-valued outcomes normally referred to as "certainty." For instance, even if one knows the costs of filing and litigating a case, the cost-benefit analysis of whether to go forward may require comparing a set of relatively predictable costs with the perhaps wildly variant values of the possible results when the case is ultimately decided by a judge or jury. In general, both the costs and benefits that will flow from a decision have at least some elements of uncertainty about them, but different aspects of a choice may implicate the uncertainty issue in different degrees.

How can decisionmaking in the face of uncertainty be dealt with? Specifically, how can whole constellations of possible results, each having different probability, be reduced to terms that are intelligible for analytic purposes? This chapter introduces simple models that explicitly involve time and uncertainty. By contrast, the situations dealt with in the last chapter were deliberately designed to make time and uncertainty either entirely irrelevant or at least not of major significance. Unfortunately, in many practical applications these factors loom as sufficiently important that their effects must be confronted squarely. Be aware, however, that we retain one important simplifying assumption in the present chapter: although prospective costs and benefits are adjusted for their uncertainty characteristics, no separate account is taken of *timing per se*, i.e., the distances into the future at which the events occur. Even at an intuitive level, it is apparent that a dollar of damages paid or received tomorrow is, in an important sense not at all the same magnitude as a dollar whose transfer takes place five years hence. Therefore, a separate issue is that of how costs and benefits that accrue at different points in time must, even after uncertainty has been taken into account, be adjusted to render them comparable for decisionmaking purposes. Dealing with time per se, as opposed to uncertainty, will be postponed to Chapter III where the "discounting" of intertemporal payments is treated initially in a non-risky environment. Finally, the two conceptually separable—but practically intertwined—notions of uncertainty and timing will be combined in an applications context.

PROSPECTS AND CERTAINTY EQUIVALENTS

In making present decisions, a person often confronts uncertain future consequences that may conveniently be termed "prospects." The prospects to be evaluated frequently consist of a range of alternative outcomes, perhaps differing very greatly in value or "payoff." Moreover, just as the potential consequences of a choice vary in their impact, they may also vary enormously in their likelihood; some may be of very high probability while others have almost negligible chances of occurring.

As we shall illustrate below, it is convenient to express the value of a stream of uncertain future prospects, whether costs or benefits, in terms of a concept called their "certainty equivalent." A certainty equivalent is the immediate (certain) payment that a person would regard as having a value equal to that of a particular uncertain set of prospects. In other words, a person given a choice should be indifferent between any prospect and its certainty equivalent.

For instance, suppose that your Fairy Godmother is about to toss a normal, six-sided die once. She will pay you $20 if a 2 turns up or $40 if a 4 turns up. You will lose $30 if a 6 turns up, and neither win nor lose if any other number results. Upon reflection about the "odds" involved and the possible payoffs, most people would regard this as an attractive prospect. But before she tosses the die, Gandalf the Wizard appears and asks what monetary payment you would accept and feel exactly compensated for the fact that he is about to make the Godmother forget her offer. (The wizard also puts you under a spell whereby you are constrained to give the truthful answer, rather than the exaggerated figure that avarice might otherwise suggest.) Your answer would then be the certainty equivalent of your lost prospect.

Of course, a prospect may also have a negative value. If it were the Wicked Witch of the East about to toss the die, the payoffs in the above example could be changed to all negative numbers. They would be alternative sums that she proposes to *take away* rather than give you. Now the magnitude that might interest Gandalf is what it is worth to you for him to drive the Witch away rather than permit you to be exposed to the risk of her extracting imposing costs on you. In either case, the essential nature of the exercise is really the same: the person facing the prospect formulates its certainty equivalent, whether it be a certain *loss* that is the equivalent of prospective costs or a certain *gain* that is the equivalent of uncertain benefits. Obviously, there is also the middle case where the prospects involve a mixture of benefits and costs. Depending on the net predominance of costs or benefits, the certainty value of the prospects will then be either negative or positive.

EXPECTED VALUES

Exactly how is a certainty equivalent actually derived from an underlying set of facts? Unfortunately, there are a number of different theories as to how people do this, and many of the theories are extremely complicated. What is presented below therefore is an admittedly oversimplified treatment which, however, will capture the flavor of more complex formulations. The reader interested in more sophisticated and technical theories of decisionmakng under uncertainty is invited to delve into the mass of sophisticated literature on decisionmaking under conditions of uncertainty and incomplete information. [See generally, Karl H. Borch, The Economics of Uncertainty, (Princeton Univ. Press, 1968); J. Hirshleifer and J. G. Reilly, "The Analytics of Uncertainty and Information—An Expository Survey," 17 J. of Econ. Literature 1375 (1979).]

One relatively simple and widely used method of computing a certainty equivalent is the concept of "mathematical expectation," perhaps more popularly called the "expected value." In essence, an expected value is the weighted average of all possible payoffs, where the weights used are the probabilities of the different results. Note that, because the probabilities of the events are used in the weighting process, an outcome is given an importance proportional to its likelihood as well as to the magnitude of its effect. For the die-tossing example given above, the expected value would be computed as indicated in Exhibit 2.1.

Observe that the expected value, a $5 gain, is not an actual outcome that would ever be possible in the retrospective or ex post sense; "Win $5" is not an outcome that can occur. The $5 payoff is "expected" only as an *average* value of the prospect considered ex ante, as opposed to a value that is particularly likely to be observed ex post.

EXHIBIT 2.1 Computing Expected Values

Outcome	Probability	Weighted Value
Win $20	$1/6$	$\$20 \times 1/6 = \$3.33$
Win $40	$1/6$	$\$40 \times 1/6 = \$6.67$
Lose $30	$1/6$	$-\$30 \times 1/6 = -\$5.00$
No Change	$3/6$	$\$0 \times 3/6 = \$0.00$

Expected Value $5.00

The example depicted in Exhibit 2.1 illustrates the general methodology for computing an expected value. The first column identifies all of the possible results and their associated payoffs. The second column is the probability of the outcome, commonly expressed as a decimal fraction but sometimes described as a percent or a common fraction. In any event, the sum of the probabilities in column 2 *must* be unity, or 100%, if all of the possibilities have indeed been accounted for. The third column is the product of the payoff times its associated probability. The method of computing this third column illustrates how the final results will depend equally on the size of an event's payoff and on the magnitude of its probability. Finally, adding up the third column yields the weighted average or "expected value."

The valuation of future prospects is sometimes depicted as if decisionmakers compared prospects exclusively in terms of their expected values. As a rough description, this practice is quite useful and has a considerable measure of plausibility. It does seem sensible, after all, that the alternative consequences should have "weights" approximately equal to their likelihoods. The actual process whereby individuals reduce prospects to certainty equivalents is nonetheless much more complicated. For instance, it is also plausible to think that such a decisionmaking process would pay some attention to the *dispersion* of the possible outcomes.

For instance, the same $5 expected value would result if the Fairy Godmother were about to flip a coin and give a person $50,010 for a head but extract $50,000 if a tail comes up:

$$1/2 \ \times \ +\$50,010 = +\$25,005$$
$$1/2 \ \times \ -\$50,000 = -\$25,000$$

Expected Value $=$ $ 5

The expected value computation above implies that this prospect is a "good" one, that it is worth $5. But would you pay $5 to have this prospect? Would you be indifferent between this prospect and the

Fairy Godmother's die-tossing prospect described above? (Remember, both of these prospects have the same $5 expected value.) Do you think that some people might even pay something to *not* be exposed to the prospect of flipping a coin for $1000? These questions, when answered in the way most people do, betray the fact that typical decisionmakers do not care only about the *average* results that the expected value describes; they are also concerned with some measure of the degree of inherent uncertainty, the range or dispersion of the results around that average. Since expected values depend exclusively upon an averaging concept and do not indicate the dispersion around that summary measure, it should be apparent that expected values are not perfectly satisfactory descriptions of the way most people compare uncertain prospects and convert them to certainty equivalents. Hence, we shall have to complicate the story a bit in order to formulate even a very simple theory of decisionmaking under uncertainty.

RISK PREFERENCE

When a decisionmaking entity cares about the *dispersion* of prospects in addition to their expected values, "risk preference" is said to be present. The existence of risk preference, its strength, and even its direction are a matter of each individual's subjective preferences. If a particular person really did not care about the inherent uncertainty or dispersion in his prospects, then expected values would be a totally accurate way of describing that person's assessment of prospects. Such a person, who would always rank different prospects in the exact order of their expected values, is called "risk neutral." Many of us, however, would be prepared at times to reject an opportunity that has a higher expected value in favor of one with a lower expected value, provided that the alternative with the higher expected value also had a sufficiently higher level of risk attached. Although higher expected value is a "good," additional risk in the form of result-dispersion is a "bad," and we are prepared to trade off losses of expected value in exchange for reductions of risk, at least to some extent. Thus, in arriving at certainty equivalents, one might want to "discount" a prospect's expected value in order to reflect dislike of its magnitude of risk. Individuals who attach such a negative value to risk are called "risk averse." [Do not risk provoking horselaughs from the cognoscenti by saying risk *ad*verse rather than risk averse; the proper sense of the term is aversion or avoidance, not opposition.] Finally, there are some people, epitomized by the "gambler" type, who may actually place a positive value on risk and who would adjust expected values upward to reflect a premium for risk. The latter are described as risk-seekers or "risk prone."

What accounts for the existence of different sets of risk preferences in individuals? One explanation derives from the fact that the
payoffs of prospects are commonly denominated in terms of things
like money rather than in units of satisfaction. Would a person's decline in satisfaction from a $1000 loss be exactly the same magnitude
as the increase in satisfaction from a $100 gift? Suppose that the
answer is "no," that the relevant numbers are a −100 and a +60,
respectively, as measured on a particular person's internal pleasure
meter. Economists call such satisfaction measures "utility" indexes.
For now, we shall assume that we are working with a utility index
that is "cardinal," i.e., whose numbers have a meaning analogous to
those on a thermometer, units of utility measuring satisfaction in the
same way that degrees on the thermometer measure quantities of
heat. (So-called "ordinal" utility indices, which measure directions of
preference change but not magnitudes, will be treated in the "indifference curve" models of Chapter IV.) Then, on the above facts,
where a $1000 loss implies a 100-unit utility reduction but a $100 gain
produces only a 60-unit utility increase, the coin-flip for $1000 is *not*
an attractive prospect in utility terms: $(-100 \times .5) + (+60 \times .5) =
(-50 + 30) = -20$. Even though the pecuniary expected value of the
prospect is zero, corresponding to what is sometimes called a "fair
bet," it would not be surprising if a person with the hypothesized
characteristics were willing to pay out a small sum of money rather
than be forced to play the coin-flip game for those stakes.

The operative principle in the above example is "diminishing marginal utility of money," i.e., each successive increment of money generates a smaller increase in satisfaction than the one before it. If
this condition is true, equal monetary prospects of gains and losses
do not counterbalance each other exactly; a dollar's worth of loss is
more important than a dollar's worth of gain. A rudimentary "utility
function" will make this clear. A utility function is just a mathematical way of describing the relationship between money (or some other
good or bad) and a person's utility index. Here is a simple example:

$$U = 100M^{1/2}$$

In words, this says that the utility index U rises proportionately to
one hundred times the square root of the quantity of money M that
the person has to spend. (A number raised to the $1/2$ power is a
square root.) In general, utility functions are hypothesized or "made
up" in order to exemplify some specific point in much the same way
that illustrative facts are supplied in law school hypothetical cases.
The example given above deliberately incorporates the principle of declining marginal utility of income. Based on the function specified,
one could construct a table that shows various income levels and their
resultant utility levels:

EXHIBIT 2.2 Money and Utility

Money	U.Index	Marg.U.
15	387.30	13.13
16	400.00	_____
17	412.31	_____
⋮	⋮	⋮
63	793.73	6.32
64	_____	_____
65	_____	_____
66	_____	_____
⋮	⋮	⋮
120	1095.45	4.57
121	_____	_____
122	_____	_____
123	_____	_____
⋮	⋮	⋮
143	1195.83	4.19
144	1200.00	4.17

Given the equation $U = 100M^{1/2}$ above, one should be able to fill in, if necessary, the value of U for any value of M, even for non-integer values of M. For instance, what are the missing entries in column two of Exhibit 2.2? Also, filling in the marginal or incremental utilities in column three confirms the existence of diminishing marginal utility of income.

As exemplified by the equation $U = 100M^{1/2}$ that we have been discussing, a "utility function" is an algebraic method of relating values of a satisfaction index to other values that describe different outcomes. Many times the equation used will be very much more complex than our present example, the reason being that the conditions to be illustrated are themselves more complex. Even the present example may be "generalized" by replacing the 100 and $1/2$, respectively, by the abstract parameters a and b; thus yielding $U = aM^b$. It is tempting to lose patience with these algebraic expressions, but their advantages become apparent if one compares the utility function to an alternative expression of similar information. Specifically, Exhibit 2.2 conveys some of the same information as is embodied in the utility function, but it does so only incompletely and rather inelegantly. It would, of course, be literally impossible to supply a table that indicates the utility index for all possible values of M, even just for all of the integer values. Yet this is exactly what the equation does in a very succinct fashion.

Diminishing marginal utility of income is generally regarded as one plausible rationale for the refusal of persons to be indifferent about prospects that have zero expected money values and even to reject prospects that have positive expected money values. But what would we say about someone who rejects a bet that has zero or positive expected value in *utility* terms? This phenomenon may be regarded as a form of "pure" risk aversion, the result of a cost being attached to risk per se. It implies that such a person will be willing to trade off some loss in the expected value of utility for a diminution in the dispersion of the possible results.

Risk-neutral behavior is often assumed for expository purposes, despite there being reason to believe that most people are at least slightly risk averse. The practical problem reflected here is that risk aversity is a subjective phenomenon which differs from person to person; although we know that high-dispersion prospects should probably be subject to some discount, we do not know exactly what magnitude that discount should be in any particular case. The relevant magnitude is likely to be highly idiosyncratic. Hence, the expected values are taken as a simple approximation. Any approximation inevitably introduces some bias and inaccuracy. For many purposes, the distortion costs of this simplification are dwarfed by its expository benefits. Occasionally, however, the existence of so-called "risk preference" must be explicitly taken into consideration because it is an important element in the behavior being modelled.

What is the bottom line here? Well, at minimum, one should be familiar with this terminology and with the way in which expected values are derived. Also, one should be sensitive to those instances in which the assumption of risk neutrality becomes something other than an expository simplification, but rather an element that arguably introduces significant changes in the results derived. Although such cases are the exception, it is worth being alert for them. You should also be aware that the "Expected Utility Model"—the assumption that a decisionmaker maximizes the expected value of his utility index—is a behavioral hypothesis that has many complications not discussed in the necessarily simple treatment provided in this book. For a critical survey of the literature on expected utility decisionmaking, see Schoemaker, "The Expected Utility Model: Its Variants, Purposes, Evidence and Limitations," 20 J. Econ. Literature 529 (1982).

QUESTIONS

Answer the following questions on the assumption that your utility function for money is accurately summarized by the simple square root function $U = 100M^{1/2}$ given in the text above. [Borrow a calculator from a friend in Engineering or Business, if necessary! If you are not disposed to calculate actual answers, at least think about how one would go about deriving an exact answer.]

1. Suppose that you already have 100 dollars. You are to be exposed to the prospect of a coin-flip with stakes of $19. Is this an attractive prospect or not? Why?

2. What would be the certainty equivalent of the prospect in the previous question? I.e., what sum would you pay out to avoid the prospect (or avoid losing the prospect, as the case may be).

3. What does the previous question have to do with determining insurance premiums, or the value of warranties?

4. How much would the probability of winning the $19 have to be in order to make the expected value be zero in utility terms? What would the expected value in money terms then be? Can the immediately preceding questions be addressed by solving the following equation for p?

$$100(100^{1/2}) = P[100(119^{1/2})] + (1-p)[100(89^{1/2})]$$

If that equation is used, what does it implicitly assume about the presence or absence of "pure" risk aversion? About risk aversion due to diminishing marginal utility of income?

LAW OF THE LEANING TREE

One of the disillusioning aspects of early legal studies is the dawning realization that the law is, alas, not always so certain. An example of this is the question of liability for the effects of a tree that falls and damages property underneath it, or even threatens to do so.

Abbott and Benson are neighbors. Close to their property line, but with its roots entirely located on Abbott's land, is a very large and imposing oak tree. Not long ago, a major windstorm almost blew the tree down. The tree now leans across the property line into Benson's air space, casting a threatening shadow upon a storage room attached to Benson's house. Now, it is by no means clear that a subsequent windstorm will blow the tree entirely down, but both Abbott and Benson privately assess the probability of a fall as being 60%.

Benson has approached Abbott with the view of having the tree cut down. "That's fine with me," says Abbott, "go right ahead and have it cut down."

"No, no. You don't understand," Benson replies. "The tree belongs to you and *you* have to cut it down."

"I understand very well that removing the tree will cost $385. If you want it down, do it yourself!"

In most U.S. jurisdictions, the law governing this situation is a bit muddy. There is little doubt that Benson, at his own expense, has the right to sever that portion of the tree intruding into his own airspace. What is less clear is (1) whether Benson can secure an injunction to have Abbott remove the tree or (2) who pays for the damages if the tree does fall on Benson's storage room, possibly damaging both the structure itself and the contents therein. In this problem, adopt the initial simplifying assumption that all parties are risk-neutral, basing their assessments of alternative prospects solely on the mathematical expected value. When you are done, reflect on what difference, if any, an assumption of risk aversion would have made.

QUESTIONS

1. Do you have any view on what the "right" legal rules should be about the two points described as unclear above? Describe the rationale for your position.

2. Suppose that, if the tree does fall, the damages incurred will be $750. "Should" the tree be cut down now, or would it be "better" to just accept the risk without any attempt at removing the potential danger? By how much would the probability of fall have to change in order for your answer to be different?

3. Assume that local law does not permit Benson to secure an injunction for the tree removal. It is unclear who would have to pay if the tree falls; no similar case has been litigated in this state's courts. Abbott and Benson have reason to believe that it is a "coin flip" as to liability. What will be done about the tree. Why?

4. Same facts as in the previous question, except that the two neighbors have formed conflicting views as to the likelihood of liability for Abbott. Abbott thinks the odds are 3 to 2 in his favor. Benson feels that the probability that a court will find against Abbott is 60%. What do you predict will happen under these circumstances?

5. Is the characteristic of clarity and certainty a desideratum for legal rules? Why?

6. Suppose that the clear rule in a jurisdiction is that Abbott would not be liable for a tree fall under the circumstances depicted. However, a poll of laymen indicates that 80% of them are under the impression that a person in Abbott's position would be responsible for the damages suffered by Benson. Does this information affect your assessment of the desirability of the rule itself?

THE CASE OF MRS. CRISPY'S CHICKEN

Mrs. Crispy is insured by the Faithless Fidelity Co. in the form of a policy with a $10,000 coverage limit. Crispy is sued for $100,000. Liability is disputed under conflicting legal theories and factual contentions. If liability is found, however, both Crispy and her insurance company agree that the judgment is likely to be exactly the $100,000 claimed by the plaintiff. Crispy thinks that the odds of being held liable are about fifty-fifty. The insurance company thinks that there is only a 40% chance of having to pay off if it spends $7,000 on Crispy's defense.

Plaintiff offers to settle for $10,500. Faithless Fidelity, ignoring Crispy's offer to chip in $1500 toward the required $10,500, refuses the settlement offer. The suit goes to final judgment and plaintiff is indeed awarded the full $100,000 sought. Mrs. Crispy is understandably miffed at Faithless Fidelity.

Once again, begin your analysis by adopting the simplifying assumption that the parties are risk-neutral, basing their assessments of alternative prospects solely on the mathematical expected value.

QUESTIONS

1. Show that the settlement offer was a lesser cost than the expected value of the cost to Faithless Fidelity from going to final judgment.

2. Can Faithless Fidelity's superficially uneconomic behavior be explained as a Chicken game against Mrs. Crispy? [Hint: What is Mrs. Crispy's exposure and what can she do about it if Faithless Fidelity refuses to settle?]

3. Even in the light of 20/20 hindsight, it can be argued that Faithless Fidelity's decision not to settle may have been in its long-term best interests. What is this argument? Does this argument suggest a systematic bargaining advantage to certain categories of litigants? [Hint: Is this a single-shot or an iterated game for Faithless Fidelity? For Mrs. Crispy? For the plaintiff in the original case?]

4. Suppose that the assumption of risk neutrality on the part of the parties were dropped. Could you make any kind of plausible speculation about the relative degrees of risk preference that the insurance company and Mrs. Crispy might have? Would this affect the results in any of the preceding questions?

5. What generic sorts of problems are involved in working out a settlement when at least some degree of joint liability may be involved? See "Settlement Devices with Joint Tort-Feasors," 25 U.Fla.

L.Rev. 762 (1973); "The Mary Carter Agreement—Solving Problems of Collusive Settlements in Joint Tort Actions," 47 S.Cal.L.Rev. 1393 (1974). For discussion of a similar problem regarding antitrust settlements, see Easterbrook, Posner & Landes, "Contribution Among Antitrust Defendants: A Legal and Economic Analysis," 23 J. Law & Econ. 331 (1980).

6. Suppose Crispy sues Faithless Fidelity for having negligently failed to settle. Here is a proposed rule:

> * * * It may not be unreasonable for an insured who purchases a policy with limits to believe that a sum of money equal to the limits is available and will be used so as to avoid liability on his part with regard to any covered accident. In view of such an expectation an insurer should not be permitted to further its own interests by rejecting opportunities to settle within the policy limits unless it is also willing to absorb losses which may result from its failure to settle.

Crisci v. Security Insurance Co., 66 Cal.2d 425, 58 Cal.Rptr. 13, 426 P.2d 173 (1967). Is this a desirable rule from the standpoint of insurance purchasers? Does the proposed rule change a potential insurance purchaser's ability to buy a "limited" coverage? Can you suggest a better rule for potential insurance purchasers?

EX ANTE ANALYSIS OF PUNISHMENTS

Social scientists tend to be stubbornly insistent that the behaviorally relevant aspect of rewards and punishments is how they are viewed "ex ante." After all, a decisionmaker is influenced only by subjective expectations of the good or bad consequences of an act; once the act has been done, its consequences may depart radically from the initial expectations. In more familiar legal language, one would discuss the same things as being evaluated "prospectively." This beforehand assessment is, of course, contrasted with retrospective or "ex post" analysis. The point of view that one adopts in analyzing awards and punishments can affect the results powerfully, especially when the events in question have small probabilities or probabilities that vary widely in a relative sense.

Read *Lynch* below from the stance of an Assistant Attorney General given the opportunity for reargument of the case on behalf of the State of California. Reflect on how a sensitivity to the probabilistic aspects of punishments might suggest useful rebuttals to the court's own language in the opinion.

IN RE JOHN LYNCH

Supreme Court of California, In Bank, 1972.
8 Cal.3d 410, 105 Cal.Rptr. 217, 503 P.2d 921.

MOSK, Justice.

One who commits an act of indecent exposure in California is guilty of a simple misdemeanor and can be punished by no more than a brief jail sentence or a small fine. If he commits the identical act a second time, however, the law declares him guilty of a felony and inflicts on him a punishment of imprisonment in the state prison for the indeterminate period of one year to life. We adjudicate here the question whether the aggravated penalty for second-offense indecent exposure provided by Penal Code Sec. 314 violates the prohibition of the California Constitution against cruel or unusual punishments. We conclude that the penalty offends the Constitution in the respect charged, and petitioner is therefore entitled to relief.

The issue is presented by John Lynch, a state prison inmate. In 1958 he was convicted of misdemeanor indecent exposure in violation of Penal Code Sec. 314. For this offense he spent two years on probation. In 1967 he was again convicted of indecent exposure. The court ruled he was not a mentally disordered sex offender, denied probation, and sentenced him to prison for the indeterminate term provided by Sec. 314 in the case of a second offense.

*   *   *

Petitioner urges that a life sentence *for indecent exposure* is cruel or unusual punishment under the California Constitution because it is grossly disproportionate to the offense. No California court has yet held a statutory penalty unconstitutional on the ground it is disproportionate to the crime committed. The rule has been recognized, however, in several opinions considering the constitutionality of the death penalty. Thus in In re Finley (1905) 1 Cal.App. 198, 202, 81 P. 1041, 1042, the court stated that a punishment may be denounced as unusual in the constitutional sense only when it "is out of all proportion to the offense, and is beyond question an extraordinary penalty for a crime of ordinary gravity, committed under ordinary circumstances."

A similar rule has evolved at the federal level in the interpretation of the cruel and unusual punishment clause of the Eighth Amendment. In O'Neil v. Vermont (1892) 144 U.S. 323, 12 S.Ct. 693, 36 L.Ed. 450, the defendant was convicted on multiple counts of unauthorized sale of liquor and sentenced to a fine of over $6,000 or, if he could not pay the fine, to hard labor for more than 54 years. A majority of the United States Supreme Court declined on federal-state grounds to consider whether this sentence constituted cruel and unusual punishment. Dissenting, Justice Field would have held the sentence to be "one which, in its severity, considering the offenses of which [the defendant] was convicted, may justly be termed both 'unusual and cruel.'" (Id. at 339.) He recognized that the cruel and unusual punishment clause was traditionally thought to prohibit physically torturous methods of punishment such as the rack and the screw, but explained: "The inhibition is directed, not only against punishments of the character mentioned, but against all punishments which by their excessive length or severity are greatly disproportioned to the offenses charged. The whole inhibition is against that which is excessive either in the bail required, or fine imposed, or punishment inflicted." (Id. at 339–340, 12 S.Ct. at p. 699.) Less than two decades later Justice Field's view became law in the landmark case of Weems v. United States (1910) supra, 217 U.S. 349, 30 S.Ct. 544, 54 L.Ed. 743.

* * * The principle was recently reaffirmed in Furman v. Georgia (1972) supra, 408 U.S. 238, 92 S.Ct. 2726, 33 L.Ed.2d 346, the United States Supreme Court decision holding the death penalty unconstitutional as applied. In the course of his separate opinion in support of the majority, Justice Brennan gave as his view that "Although the determination that a severe punishment is excessive may be grounded in a judgment that it is disproportionate to the crime, the more significant basis is that the punishment serves no penal purpose more effectively than a less severe punishment." (id. at 280, 92 S.Ct. at p. 2747.) In turn, Justice Marshall recognized that "a penalty may be cruel and unusual because it is excessive and serves no valid legislative purpose * * * The decisions [of the United States Supreme Court] are replete with assertions that one of the primary functions of the cruel and unusual punishments clause is to prevent excessive or unnecessary penalties [citations]; these punishments are unconstitutional even though popular sentiment may favor them." (Id. at 331, 92 S.Ct. at p. 2773.)

Finally, the highest courts of our sister states have repeatedly invoked the rule of proportionality in applying their equivalents of our cruel or unusual punishment clause.

* * *

Whether a particular punishment is disproportionate to the offense is, of course, a question of degree. The choice of fitting and proper penalties is not an exact science, but a legislative skill involving an appraisal of the evils to be corrected, the weighing of practical alternatives, consideration of relevant policy factors, and responsiveness to the public will; in appropriate cases, some leeway for experimentation may also be permissible. The judiciary, accordingly, should not interfere in this process unless a statute prescribes a penalty "out of all proportion to the offense" (Robinson v. California

(1962) supra, 370 U.S. 660, 676, 82 S.Ct. 1417, 1425, 8 L.Ed.2d 758 (concurring opinion of Douglas, J.); In re Finley (1905) supra, 1 Cal. App. 198, 202, 81 P. 1041, 1042), i.e., so severe in relation to the crime as to violate the prohibition against cruel or unusual punishment.

We conclude that in California a punishment may violate Article I, Sec. 6, of the Constitution if, although not cruel or unusual in its methods, it is so disproportionate to the crime for which it is inflicted that it shocks the conscience and offends fundamental notions of human dignity. * * * To aid in administering this rule, we point to certain techniques used in the decisions discussed herein.

First, a number of courts have examined the nature of the offense and/or the offender, with particular regard to the degree of danger both present to society. Thus in *Anderson* we spoke in this connection of excessive punishment for "ordinary offenses", and in *Finley* the court referred to an extraordinary penalty for "a crime of ordinary gravity committed under ordinary circumstances" (1 Cal.App. at p. 202, 81 P. at 1042).

The second technique used by the courts is to compare the challenged penalty with the punishments prescribed in the *same jurisdiction for different offenses* which, by the same test, must be deemed more serious. The underlying but unstated assumption appears to be that although isolated excessive penalties may occasionally be enacted, e.g., through "honest zeal" (Weems v. United States (1910), 217 U.S. 349, 373, 30 S.Ct. 544, 54 L.Ed. 793) generated in response to transitory public emotion, the Legislature may be depended upon to act with due and deliberate regard for constitutional restraints in prescribing the vast majority of punishments set forth in our statutes. The latter may therefore be deemed illustrative of constitutionally permissible degrees of severity; and if among them are found more serious crimes punished less severely than the offense in question, the challenged penalty is to that extent suspect.

Closely related to the foregoing is the third technique used in this inquiry, i.e., a comparison of the challenged penalty with the punishments prescribed for the *same offense in other jurisdictions* having an identical or similar constitutional provision. Here the assumption is that the vast majority of those jurisdictions will have prescribed punishments for this offense that are within the constitutional limit of severity; and if the challenged penalty is found to exceed the punishments decreed for the offense in a significant number of those jurisdictions, the disparity is a further measure of its excessiveness.

At common law indecent exposure was deemed to be no more than a public nuisance, and was punished by a misdemeanor. The penalties were generally a fine or a brief jail sentence. * * * In California a similar pattern prevailed until the present penalty was added in 1952.

The low-key approach of the common law is also that adopted by modern psychiatric science. Clinical studies "support and confirm the traditional legal provisions which have treated this behavior as a social nuisance, as disorderly conduct rather than an offense causing personal injury." (Gigeroff, Mohr, and Turner, Sex Offenders on Probation: The Exhibitionist (1968) 32 Fed.Prob. (No. 3) 17, 21, [hereinafter referred to as Gigeroff].)

Turning to the typical offender, we find a similar pattern of nonviolence. "The vast majority of exhibitionists are relatively harmless offenders; mostly they are public nuisances and sources of embarrassments" (Report of Karl M. Bowman, Medical Superintendent of the Langley Porter Clinic, in 2 Assem.J. (1951 Reg.Sess.) p. 2847 [hereinafter referred to as Bowman]). They are characterized as "generally passive, inoffensive people" with low self-esteem.

Finally, although indecent exposure is not a "victimless" crime, any harm it may cause appears to be minimal at most. As noted above, the nonviolence of the conduct ensures there is no danger of physical injury to the person who witnesses the exposure. Nor is there any convincing evidence that the person is likely to suffer either long-term or significant psychological damage. (See Mohr, Turner, and Jerry, Pedophilia and Exhibitionism (1964), p. 121.) Indeed, the statute itself defines the offense as exposure in public or in any place where there are persons who may merely be "offended or annoyed" thereby. Such an "annoyance" is not a sufficiently grave danger to society to warrant the heavy punishment of a life-maximum sentence.

These considerations make a persuasive case for a finding of unconstitutional disproportionality between the offense and the aggravated penalty prescribed by Sec. 314. The case is further strengthened by a comparison of this penalty with the punishments for other crimes in California which are undeniably of far greater seriousness. For example, is it rational to believe that second-offense indecent exposure is a more dangerous crime than the unlawful *killing* of a human being without malice but in the heat of passion? Yet the punishment for manslaughter (up to 15 years) is far less than the life maximum inflicted by Sec. 314. The same is true for such other violent crimes against the person as assault with intent to commit murder (1–14 years), kidnaping (1–25 years), mayhem (up to 14 years), assault with intent to commit mayhem or robbery (1–20 years), assault with caustic chemicals, with intent to injure or disfigure (1–14 years), and assault on a peace officer or fireman engaged in the performance of his duties (up to 2 years, or up to 1 year in jail).

* * *

We recognize, of course, that an important additional element must be taken into account: Sec. 314 prescribes a life-maximum sentence for indecent exposure only when the offender has previously been convicted of the same crime or of lewd and lascivious acts upon a child. We further recognize that the potential for recidivism is here very real: "exhibitionists are more likely to repeat their offense than other kinds of sex offenders." (Gigeroff, at 21; accord, Bowman, at 2847.) But this likelihood does not result in a pro tanto repeal of the cruel or unusual punishment clause. Petitioner does not challenge—nor do we consider—the validity of our general habitual criminal law or of any other recidivist statute. He is entitled, however, to question whether in the particular context of indecent exposure the phenomenon of recidivism constitutionally justifies the greatly enhanced punishment of Sec. 314. We hold that it does not.

* * *

Finally, we may profitably compare Sec. 314 with other California statutes which prescribe enhanced punishment for recidivism. First, however, we pause to note that in all but three of the above-listed dangerous crimes involving personal violence, sexual assaults, or harm to children, there is no statutory provision increasing the penalty for recidivism. In other words, a man may repeatedly commit manslaughter or mayhem, assault with intent to commit rape or sodomy, child-beating or felony drunk driving, and still be subject each time to a lighter penalty than one who twice exposes his private parts.

Second, of all the statutes which increase the punishment in the case of a second offense, only Sec. 314 and one other compel the enormous single leap from an ordinary misdemeanor to a life-maximum felony. In each of the remaining statutes there is a reasonable relationship between the punishments for the first and subsequent offenses. If the crime is of a minor nature, its enhanced penalty remains proportionately light; if the crime is more serious, its original penalty was proportionately heavy. The theory in each instance is that whatever the response appropriate to the factor of recidivism, the judgment of the Legislature as to the gravity of the act itself should remain relatively constant.

* * *

The last technique to be employed—a comparison of the challenged penalty with the punishments prescribed for the same offense in other jurisdictions—is no less revealing. A study of the indecent exposure statutes of each of our sister states and the District of Columbia reveals only two other states—Michigan and Oklahoma—which permit life-maximum sentences for second-offense exhibitionists. By contrast, 34 states and the District of Columbia do not enhance the punishment for any degree of recidivism; in each, indecent exposure remains a misdemeanor at all times.   *   *   *   Thus it is the virtually unanimous judgment of our sister states that indecent exposure, no matter how often it may recur, can be adequately and appropriately controlled by the imposition of a short jail sentence and/or a small fine.   In this setting the California penalty of a life-maximum sentence in state prison strikes a discordant note indeed.

*   *   *

Viewing the total disparity between the life-maximum sentence currently inflicted by Sec. 314 for second-offense indecent exposure and the far lighter penalties in force in California and elsewhere, we conclude with Justice McKenna in *Weems* that "this contrast shows more than different exercises of legislative judgment.   It exhibits a difference between unrestrained power and that which is exercised under the spirit of constitutional limitations formed to establish justice."   (217 U.S. at p. 381, 30 S.Ct. at p. 554.)

The question of relief remains.   If petitioner's offense is treated as a misdemeanor, he has long since served his time.   If it is treated as a felony, Sec. 314 no longer prescribes a valid punishment; and if no provision is made for punishment in a statute declaring a felony, the offense is "punishable by imprisonment in any of the state prisons, not exceeding five years" (Pen.Code, Section 18).   Petitioner has now served more than five years, and is therefore entitled to his freedom.

The writ is granted and petitioner is ordered discharged from custody   *   *   *

QUESTIONS

1.   In this context, what is the difference between the *prospect* of punishment and the actual punishment provided under the statute? Which of these is more relevant?

2.   What would your speculation be about the proportion of convictions to offenses for, respectively, the crimes of indecent exposure and aggravated assault?   What implications might a substantial difference in these proportions have for setting statutory penalties? Does it make a difference whether the objective is deterrence or "punishment"?

3.   If sentences were being adjusted for a "probability of getting away with it" factor, how might this affect the treatment of multiple offenders?   (Hint: Suppose one were worried about "overpunishing" a person who committed the crime only once?)

4. Suppose that you were defending the position of the State in this case. What portions of the court's opinion represent views that might be turned to your advantage?

5. What possible generalization is there of the Lynch case to other areas of law? For instance, do similar considerations explain the trebling of damages in antitrust law? If not, what does? [The antitrust damages issue is specifically dealt with by Elzinga and W. Breit, The Antitrust Penalties: A Study in Law and Economics, (New Haven, 1976) Ch. 7.] For a general discussion and bibliographical footnotes that provide a guide to applications in many different areas, see A. Polinsky and S. Shavell, "The Optimal Tradeoff Between the Probability and Magnitude of Fines," 69 Amer.Econ.Rev. 880 (1979).

CRAIG v. BOREN

Supreme Court of the United States, 1976.
429 U.S. 190, 97 S.Ct. 451, 50 L.Ed.2d 397.

Mr. Justice BRENNAN delivered the opinion of the Court.

The interaction of two sections of an Oklahoma statute prohibits the sale of "nonintoxicating" 3.2% beer to males under the age of 21 and to females under the age of 18. The question to be decided is whether such a gender-based differential constitutes a denial to males 18–20 years of age of the equal protection of the laws in violation of the Fourteenth Amendment.

* * *

* * * Clearly, the protection of public health and safety represents an important function of state and local governments. However, appellees' statistics in our view cannot support the conclusion that the gender-based distinction closely serves to achieve that objective and therefore the distinction cannot under *Reed* withstand equal protection challenge.

The appellees introduced a variety of statistical surveys. First, an analysis of arrest statistics for 1973 demonstrated that 18–20-year-old male arrests for "driving under the influence" and "drunkenness" substantially exceeded female arrests for that same age period. Similarly, youths aged 17–21 were found to be overrepresented among those killed or injured in traffic accidents, with males again numerically exceeding females in this regard. Third, a random roadside survey in Oklahoma City revealed that young males were more inclined to drive and drink beer than were their female counterparts. Fourth, Federal Bureau of Investigation nationwide statistics exhibited a notable increase in arrests for "driving under the influence." Finally, statistical evidence gathered in other jurisdictions, particularly Minnesota and Michigan, was offered to corroborate Oklahoma's experience by indicating the pervasiveness of youthful participation in motor vehicle accidents following the imbibing of alcohol. Conceding that "the case is not free from doubt," 399 F.Supp., at 1314, the District Court nonetheless concluded that this statistical showing substantiated "a rational basis for the legislative judgment underlying the challenged classification." Id., at 1307.

Even were this statistical evidence accepted as accurate, it nevertheless offers only a weak answer to the equal protection question presented here. The most focused and relevant of the statistical surveys, arrests of 18–20-year-olds for alcohol-related driving offenses, exemplifies the ultimate unpersuasiveness of this evidentiary record. Viewed in terms of the correlation between sex and the actual activity that Oklahoma seeks to regulate—driving while under the influence of alcohol—statistics broadly establish that .18% of females and 2% of males in that age group were arrested for that offense. While such a disparity is not trivial in a statistical sense, it hardly can form the basis for employment of a gender line as a classifying device. Certainly if maleness is to serve as a proxy for drinking and driving, a correlation of 2% must be considered an unduly tenuous "fit". Indeed, prior cases have consistently rejected the use of sex as a decisionmaking factor even though the statutes in question certainly rested on far more predictive empirical relationships than this.

Moreover, the statistics exhibit a variety of other shortcomings that seriously impugn their value to equal protection analysis. Setting aside the obvious methodological problems,[14] the surveys do not adequately justify the salient features of Oklahoma's gender-based traffic-safety law. None purports to measure the use and dangerousness of 3.2% beer as opposed to alcohol generally, a detail that is of particular importance since, in light of its low alcohol level, Oklahoma apparently considers the 3.2% beverage to be "nonintoxicating." Okla.Stat., Tit. 37, Sec. 163.1 (1958); see State ex rel. Springer v. Bliss, 199 Okla. 198, 185 P.2d 220 (1947). Moreover, many of the studies, while graphically documenting the unfortunate increase in driving while under the influence of alcohol, make no effort to relate their findings to age-sex differentials as involved here. Indeed, the only survey that explicitly centered its attention upon young drivers and their use of beer—albeit apparently not of the diluted 3.2% variety—reached results that hardly can be viewed as impressive in justifying either a gender or age classification.

14. The very social stereotypes that find reflection in age-differential laws, see Stanton v. Stanton, 421 U.S. 7, 14–15, 95 S.Ct. at 1378 (1975), are likely substantially to distort the accuracy of these comparative statistics. Hence "reckless" young men who drink and drive are transformed into arrest statistics, whereas their female counterparts are chivalrously escorted home. See, e.g. W. Reckless & B. Kay, The Female Offender 4, 7, 13, 14–17 (Report to Presidential Commission on Law Enforcement and Administration of Justice, 1967).

There is no reason to belabor this line of analysis. It is unrealistic to expect either members of the judiciary or state officials to be well versed in the rigors of experimental or statistical technique. But this merely illustrates that proving broad sociological propositions by statistics is a dubious business, and one that inevitably is in tension with the normative philosophy that underlies the Equal Protection Clause. Suffice to say that the showing offered by the appellees does not satisfy us that sex represents a legitimate, accurate proxy for the regulation of drinking and driving. In fact, when it is further recognized that Oklahoma's statute prohibits only the selling of 3.2% beer to young males and not their drinking the beverage once acquired (even after purchase by their 18–20-year-old female companions), the relationship between gender and traffic safety becomes far too tenuous to satisfy *Reed's* requirement that the gender-based difference be substantially related to achievement of the statutory objective.

We hold therefore, that under *Reed*, Oklahoma's 3.2% beer statute invidiously discriminates against males 18–20 years of age.

* * *

Mr. Justice REHNQUIST, dissenting.

The Court's disposition of this case is objectionable on two grounds. First is its conclusion that *men* challenging a gender-based statute which treats them less favorably than women may invoke a more stringent standard of judicial review than pertains to most other types of classifications. Second is the Court's enunciation of this standard, without citation to any source, as being that "classifications by gender must serve *important* governmental objectives and must be *substantially* related to achievement of those objectives." Ante, at 197 (emphasis added). * * * I think the Oklahoma statute challenged here need pass only the "rational basis" equal protection analysis expounded in cases such as McGowan v. Maryland, 366 U.S. 420, 81 S.Ct. 1101, 6 L.Ed.2d 393 (1961), and Williamson v. Lee Optical Co., 348 U.S. 483, 75 S.Ct. 461, 99 L.Ed. 563 (1955), and I believe that it is constitutional under that analysis.

* * *

Quite apart from * * * alleged methodological deficiencies in the statistical evidence, the Court appears to hold that that evidence, on its face, fails to support the distinction drawn in the statute. The Court notes that only 2% of males (as against .18% of females) in the age group were arrested for drunk driving, and that this very low figure establishes "an unduly tenuous 'fit' " between maleness and drunk driving in the 18–20-year-old group. On this point the court misconceives the nature of the equal protection inquiry.

The rationality of a statutory classification for equal protection purposes does not depend upon the statistical "fit" between the class

and the trait within the included class than in the excluded class to justify different treatment. Therefore the present equal protection challenge to this gender-based discrimination poses only the question whether the incidence of drunk driving among young men is sufficiently greater than among young women to justify differential treatment. Notwithstanding the Court's critique of the statistical evidence, that evidence suggests clear differences between the drinking and driving habits of young men and women. Those differences are grounds enough for the State reasonably to conclude that young males pose by far the greater drunk-driving hazard, both in terms of sheer numbers and in terms of hazard on a per-driver basis. The gender-based difference difference in treatment in this case is therefore not irrational.

The Court's argument that a 2% correlation between maleness and drunk driving is constitutionally insufficient therefore does not pose an equal protection issue concerning discrimination between males and females. The clearest demonstration of this is the fact that the precise argument made by the Court would be equally applicable to a flat bar on such purchases by *anyone*, male or female, in the 18–20 age group; in fact it would apply *a fortiori* in that cases given the even more "tenuous 'fit'" between drunk-driving arrests and femaleness. The statistics indicated that about 1% of the age group population as a whole is arrested. What the Court's argument is relevant to is not equal protection, but due process—whether there are enough persons in the category who drive while drunk to justify a bar against purchases by all members of the group.

Cast in those terms, the argument carries little weight, in light of our decisions indicating that such questions call for a balance of the State's interest against the harm resulting from any overinclusiveness or underinclusiveness. Vlandis v. Kline, 412 U.S. 441, 448–452, 93 S.Ct. 2230, 2234–2236, 37 L.Ed.2d 63 (1973). The personal interest harmed here is very minor—the present legislation implicates only the right to purchase 3.2% beer, certainly a far cry from the important personal interests which have on occasion supported this Court's invalidation of statutes on similar reasoning. Cleveland Board of Education v. LaFleur, 414 U.S. 632, 640, 94 S.Ct. 791, 796, 39 L.Ed.2d 52 (1974); Stanley v. Illinois, 405 U.S. 645, 651, 92 S.Ct. 1208, 1212, 31 L.Ed.2d 551 (1972). And the state interest involved is significant— the prevention of injury and death on the highways.

This is not a case where the classification can only be justified on grounds of administrative convenience. Vlandis v. Kline, supra, 412 U.S., at 451, 93 S.Ct., at 2236; Stanley v. Illinois, supra, 405 U.S., at 656, 92 S.Ct., at 1215. There being no apparent way to single out persons likely to drink and drive, it seems plain that the legislature was faced here with the not atypical legislative problem of legislating in terms of broad categories with regard to the purchase and consumption of alcohol. I trust, especially in light of the Twenty-first Amendment, that there would be no due process violation if no one in this age group were allowed to purchase 3.2% beer. Since males drink and drive at a higher rate than the age group as a whole, I fail to see how a statutory bar with regard only to them can create any due process problem.

The Oklahoma Legislature could have believed that 18–20-year-old males drive substantially more, and tend more often to be intoxicated than their female counterparts; that they prefer beer and admit to drinking and driving at a higher rate than females; and that they suffer traffic injuries out of proportion to the part they make up of the population. Under the appropriate rational-basis test for equal protection, it is neither irrational nor arbitrary to bar them from making purchases of 3.2% beer, which purchases might in many cases be made by a young man who immediately returns to his vehicle with the beverage in his possession. The record does not give any good indication of the true proportion of males in the age group who drink and drive (except that it is no doubt greater than the 2% who are arrested, but whatever it may be I cannot see that the mere purchase right involved could conceivably raise a due process question. There being no violation of either equal protection or due process, the statute should accordingly be upheld.

QUESTIONS

1. Compare this case to In re Lynch, supra (punishment of multiple offender for indecent exposure).

2. The majority finds the different offense rate for the two sexes to be *de minimis*. Do you find that position persuasive?

3. Explore the hypothesis that this law is in the best interests even of the young males who are "discriminated against." What are the costs and benefits to them? Are the benefits equal in every year? If not, does some sort of adjustment need to be made for the different time periods in which they accrue? (See Chapter III below.)

4. If it were to be concluded that the law *is* in the best interests even of young males, how do you explain the suit to overturn it?

THE HUNTING OF A TAKEOVER

A corporate executive generally cannot appropriate personally the full gains to the firm from good managerial decisions; only a part of the benefits will accrue to the manager in the form of higher salary, etc., while the remainder goes to stockholders. Normally, the cruel truth is that it is easier for managers, as for most other working people, to do a slipshod job than a very good job. Better management usually requires that the managers themselves shoulder certain personal costs in the form of overtime work, greater intensity of effort, confronting distasteful personal situations, risking embarrassment, etc. To the extent that the executive must bear internal costs that produce what are to him or her substantially external benefits, there exists an incentive to "shirk," to fail to make some cost-justified efforts that would improve the quality of managerial performance and increase net profitability. Losses—i.e., foregone profits—stemming from this conflict of interests between owners and their agents are frequently termed "agency costs." [a] The inherent conflict of interest itself, and the incentive response thereto, is explored in greater detail below, e.g., in the "Real Estate Agent" hypothetical. At this point, we shall be concerned with a specific application to the corporate environment.

One response to the existence of suboptimal agency efforts is *monitoring* by the principal. In the case of corporations, however, the principals are the frequently very numerous shareholders who are themselves implicated in an easily recognizable Free Rider problem: monitoring is a costly activity whose potential benefits are nonexcludible vis-a-vis the other stockholders. Moreover, the Free Rider problem is exacerbated by the necessity of any stockholder, once monitoring has detected a suboptimal performance, to persuade a majority of the other stockholders to authorize any disciplinary or remedial action.

One theory of capital markets holds that tender offers are an efficacious alternative method of monitoring the performance of corporate management. If management's performance is sufficiently suboptimal, the attention of a prospective bidder will tend to be attracted. The outsider who buys up a majority of the shares of such a corporation can install new management, improve the performance of the corporation, and benefit from the subsequent increase in share prices. In principle, all (ownership) parties gain from the takeover. The bidder profits from the increase in value of his purchased majority interest, nontendering shareholders receive a similar price increase, and tendering shareholders enjoy a higher selling price for their stock than if the tender offer had not occurred. Furthermore, the *threat* of such a takeover bid acts as a spur to managerial efficiency even in firms where a takeover bid never occurs.

The target company's managers frequently have a substantial personal interest in resisting such takeovers. Since managerial resistance is generally couched in terms of resisting an "inadequate offer"

---

a. The term was popularized by Johnson and Meckling, "Theory of the Firm: Managerial Behavior, Agency Costs and Ownership Structure," 3 J. Financial Econ. 305 (1976).

or "looking for a better offer," it seems difficult to distinguish good faith efforts by management to protect the stockholders' interests from mere defenses of well feathered nests by slothful birds. In any event, managerial resistance may facilitate an "auction" bidding market for the shares and a resultant higher price to the shareholders. Alternatively, it may defeat the takeover entirely. But this latter eventuality is not necessarily inconsistent with the stockholders' interests because any determined effort to extract the highest possible price runs the risk of obstructing quick, short-run sales.

When managerial resistance leads to the defeat of a takeover bid, suits by disappointed shareholders against management are sometimes filed. Such suits are almost always unsuccessful because, absent some clear showing of bad faith, the common law "business judgment" rule normally insulates the discretion of managers from judicial review. Assessing the merits of a tender offer is therefore within management's peculiar discretionary purview and, indeed, courts have held that directors have not only the right but the affirmative duty to resist tender offers deemed not to be in the best interests of shareholders.

NOTES AND QUESTIONS

In a recent article, Easterbrook and Fischel proffer the initially counterintuitive suggestion that the interests of stockholders would best be served by legal rules that restrict or prohibit entirely the ability of a target company's management to engage in defensive tactics in response to a tender offer, even if the purpose of the resistance is to trigger a bidding contest and higher price. [Easterbrook and Fischel, 94 Harvard L.Rev. 1161 (1981).] Here is a key section of their argument:

> * * * The value of any stock can be understood as the sum of two components: the price that will prevail in the market if there is no successful offer (multiplied by the probability that there will be none) and the price that will be paid in a future tender offer (multiplied by the likelihood that some offer will succeed). A shareholder's welfare is maximized by a legal rule that enables the sum of these two components to reach its highest value. [At 1184.]

1. Can the above paragraph be translated into the equation $V = (1 - p)M + pT$? What do the different symbols mean? Is V an "expected value"?

2. Elaborate on the quoted paragraph. What do you think is the rest of the authors' basic argument? Are "ex post" and "ex ante" distinctions relevant?

3.   If the authors' basic argument above is accepted, does it then also follow that V is maximized by a strategy of *no* resistance?

4.   On balance, does it seem in the best interests of stockholders as a class that courts impose an affirmative duty of resistance on management?   If so, how should that duty be defined?

5.   The Easterbrook and Fischel analysis that underlies this section is but one example in a now prolific literature that applies economic analysis to questions of legal governance for corporations and capital markets.   Pathbreaking efforts of this type is represented by Henry Manne's work: "Mergers and the Market for Corporate Control," 73 J.Pol.Econ. 110 (1965); Insider Trading and the Stock Market (1966); "Our Two Corporate Systems: Law and Economics," 53 Va.L.Rev. 259 (1967); "The Limits and Rationale of Corporate Altruism," 59 Va.L.Rev. 708 (1973).   Representative recent works include: Halpern, Trebilcock and Turnbull, "An Economic Analysis of Limited Liability in Corporation Law," 30 U. Toronto L.J. 117 (1980); Levmore, "Securities and Secrets: Insider Trading and the Law of Contracts," 68 Va.L.Rev. 117 (1982); Posner and Scott, Economics of Corporation Law and Securities Regulation (1980); and Prichard, Stanbury and Wilson, Canadian Competition Policy: Essays in Law and Economics (1979).

AGENT–PRINCIPAL CONFLICTS OF INTEREST

Real estate agents are nominally—and legally—in the employ of the potential seller of the property.   Their behavior is, of course, meant to be disciplined by the applicable laws of agency.   Nevertheless, the complaint is frequently voiced that real estate agents tend in actual practice to act in some ways that are detrimental to the seller and beneficial to the buyer.   For instance, an agent will hint to a potential buyer that the seller would really be willing to accept a bid lower than the asking price or will attempt to persuade the seller to accept a lower price than might be warranted.

Assume that the agent in the following problem is hired under a simplified version of the standard real estate listing contract.   The agent receives 6% of the sales price and bears all selling costs, such as advertising and showing.   The agent shows the property to prospective purchasers, each of whom makes a bid that must be reported to the seller.

A considerable amount is known about the market for the property in question.   Specifically, the "average" bid will be $50,000, but there is considerable dispersion of such bids among individuals who will like the property either more or less than the average amount. Neither the seller nor the agent are, of course, concerned with the below-average bidders, but the agent is being hired to, in effect, search out the above-average bidders. Bidders are distributed in the classical bell-shaped "Gaussian normal" curve centered around the $50,000 average. That is, the probability of a $50,000 bid is highest and the probabilities of other bids decline as variations from $50,000 increase. As higher and higher bids are found, it becomes more and more difficult to improve matters by searching more. This is true for two reasons: (1) bidders who will exceed the current bid become scarcer; and (2) once found, the probable amount by which a higher bidder exceeds the current bid becomes smaller. With the simplifying assumption that bids can only be made in multiples of $100, the market information can be summarized in Exhibit 2.3.

It costs the real estate agent $10 worth of transportation expense, time, trouble, etc. to bring about each additional "showing." Hence, this $10 is the relevant opportunity cost to the agent of searching for buyers. Once a bid is received, the agent's own cost-benefit calculus will determine whether he desires that the owner accept the bid or would prefer the opportunity to search for a higher bid. In sum, the problem is one of deciding whether to settle for the "bird in hand" or to expend additional resources in searching for the fatter bird still lurking in the bush.

QUESTIONS

1. Assume that this is an "exclusive listing" with the agent. At approximately what bid level does it behoove the agent to persuade the owner to accept? Why? (If you cannot derive an exact numerical answer, attempt to describe the logic behind the decision process.)

2. If the same agent were selling *his own* house, what would he think of advice to sell at the price he advised in the previous question? At approximately what price would he be disposed to sell?

3. What difference would it make if the agent's contract were not for an exclusive listing but involved co-listing with one or more other brokers?

4. How can the underlying cause of the conflict of interest between principal and agent be explained? Can you suggest a revision of the terms in the agent's contract such that the conflict would be mitigated? Why would it be unsatisfactory for the owner to pay the owner for the number of showings accomplished? Why don't the agent and seller agree on a sale price and a fixed fee, as opposed to the "sliding scale" of a commission based on an indeterminate price?

5. The facts assumed in this scenario are simplified in order to facilitate the analysis. In the real world, which of the factual assumptions would be unrealistic and to what extent? How much difference, if any, does this make to the results derived.

Goetz Law & Economics ACB—5

EXHIBIT 2.3   Real Estate Market Information

Current Bid	Probability of Higher Bid	Expected Gain From Higher Bid	Expected Value Of Add'l Showing
$50,000	.4760	$1,134	_____
$50,200	.4472	1,100	_____
$50,300	.4312	1,123	_____
$50,400	.3893	1,083	_____
$50,500	.3640	1,062	_____
$50,600	.3445	994	_____
$50,700	.3215	985	_____
$50,800	.3011	962	_____
$50,900	.2859	912	_____
$51,000	.2641	885	_____
$51,100	.2404	858	_____
$51,200	.2210	835	_____
$51,300	.1956	821	_____
$51,400	.1779	791	_____
$51,500	.1587	765	_____
$51,600	.1516	740	_____
$51,700	.1266	719	_____
$51,800	.1184	700	_____
$51,900	.1013	690	_____
$52,000	.0895	674	_____
$52,100	.0823	662	_____
$52,200	.0704	640	_____
$52,300	.0654	625	_____
$52,400	.0524	600	_____
$52,500	.0485	592	_____
$52,600	.0416	583	_____
$52,700	.0344	574	_____
$52,800	.0300	557	_____
$52,900	.0275	532	_____
$53,000	.0222	519	_____
$53,100	.0192	508	_____

NOTE: The above table is based on a probability distribution of bids that is approximately Gaussian Normal with a standard deviation of $1500. Figures have been rounded.

6. A seller files suit against his agent, claiming that the agent has shirked his duty to show and otherwise promote the sale of a house being marketed by the agent under an exclusive contract. Assuming that there is no difficulty in ascertaining any of the relevant facts, what is the standard of duty to which the agent should be held? How should "shirking" by the agent be understood?

7. If the law could lay some duty on agents to exert more efforts than the profit-maximizing amount for them in each transaction, would agents be worse off? If the answer depends on the nature of the duty, explain what extra duty, if any, might be preferred by agents? Would this be good or bad for principals?

8. Suppose that the "shirking" by an agent can neither be eliminated by monitoring nor shown to be a legally *provable* breach of contract. (What difficulties would be involved in either of those remedies?) The principal is then "stuck" with less-than-satisfactory performance. One possibility is that a sophisticated principal will have anticipated the problem and adjusted downward his return promise or fee in consideration of the lower level of expected performance. More naive principals may, however, suffer a lesser performance than they thought they bargained for.

To what extent will extralegal market sanctions penalize shirking? Will the word "get around" that Shirke Realty represents a seller's interests poorly, so that sellers will either not deal with them or require a "discounted" fee? Does the nature of the "product" make a difference? (Specifically, is real estate a likely or unlikely market environment for this reputational effect?) See Klein and Leffler, "The Role of Market Forces in Assuring Contractual Performance," 89 J. of Polit.Econ. 615 (1981).

9. "Sharecropping" is an arrangement wherein a tenant farmer receives the use of farmland in exchange for a rental payment calibrated in terms of a share of the crop. Is this analogous to the real estate agent situation? What problems would you predict and how, if at all, can they be mitigated? See Cheung, "Private Property Rights and Sharecropping," 76 J.Law and Econ. 1107 (1968); Hsiao, "The Theory of Share Tenancy Revisited," 83 J.Pol.Econ. 1023 (1975).

"CURVE" MODELS: MARGINAL AND TOTAL EFFECTS

In the last chapter, we used a matrix model to translate the Prisoner's dilemma from words to a possibly more useful form for analytical purposes. Up to this point, we have been modelling the uncertainty problems in tabular form, as exemplified by the real estate agent situation just discussed. In the next section, we shall once again perform a translation from words into a more formal model, this time introducing the type of "curve" diagrammatic model that is almost ubiquitous in economic analysis. First, however, it will be useful to review certain fundamentals about the kinds of relationships that will appear in these diagrammatic models.

Not surprisingly, many of our models will be concerned with the effect that a particular variable has on something else. Think for a moment of the causal factor as an "input" and the thing that it affects as an "output." Exhibit 2.4 depicts a hypothetical relationship between an "input" whose quantity is designated by X on the horizontal axis and the resultant "output" of Y as measured on the vertical axis. In the example at hand, Y may be interpreted as the recovery from a lawsuit, measured in dollars, while X is the input of doses of "effort." Obviously, X and Y may be suitably redefined to fit other similar situations; e.g., X may be units of care and Y reductions in the expected harm from a dangerous activity. Exhibit 2.4 is drawn according to the usual assumptions about the shape of such a relationship: the total output climbs steeply at first, but then the ascent "flattens out" as more and more units of X are employed. The slowing of the rate of increase in the curve indicates that successive marginal units of X have less and less efficacy in producing additional Y. You may be interested to know that the actual relationship used for the example in the Exhibits is $Y = 100X^{1/2}$, the same "functional relationship" that was used for the utility function example earlier in this chapter. (See Exhibit 2.2 above.)

If we examine any level of input X along the horizontal axis, the rate at which a small adjustment in X will affect Y is the *slope* of the output curve directly above. (Readers who have a little knowledge of calculus will recognize the marginal curve as the "first derivative" of the total curve. What is its exact algebraic form in the example?) For instance, for adjustments in the neighborhood of X_a the slope is taken at point *A* directly above it. At the greater level of input, X_b, the corresponding slope is less. In words, these slopes are the marginal effects of X. If Y were a benefit, then the marginal effect in question would more precisely be termed the marginal benefit at the associated level of X, and similar reinterpretations would exist if Y were utility level and X income, if Y were cost and X some production level, etc.

Economic analysis usually employs marginal curves similar to Exhibit 2.5, rather than total curves such as Exhibit 2.4. The marginal curve in effect plots the slopes of its associated total curve for all possible values of X. (Usually the vertical scale is appropriately adjusted since the total levels are much larger magnitudes than the marginal ones.) As a rough approximation, one can think of constructing a series of rectangular columns, the area of each corresponding to the increase in total output for some arbitrarily defined "dose" of input X.

EXHIBIT 2.4

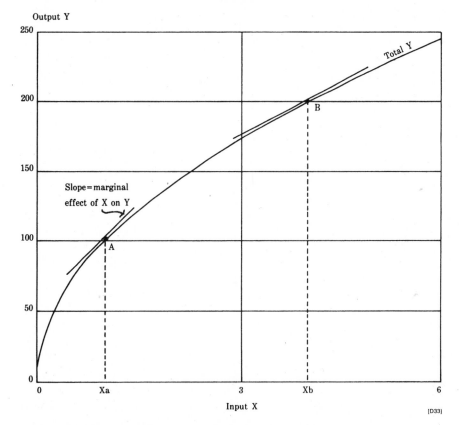

In Exhibit 2.5, the assumed sizes of doses are one-unit increments. Thus, the effect of the first dose is the first rectangular area, a height of 100 times a width of one. By a similar process, the effects of the second and successive doses are representable as the area of the second rectangle, the third rectangle, etc. Then, it is easy to see that the total output for any level of input is the sum of the incremental dose effects up to the current level of X. In Exhibit 2.5, the rectangles overlap the actual marginal curve drawn on the same diagram. This is only true, however, because we have been showing discrete, one-unit adjustments.   Technically, a marginal curve presupposes a series of *infinitesimal* adjustments of X.   Accordingly, imagine the width of the doses in Exhibit 2.5 getting smaller and smaller, skinnier and skinnier.   If we redrew Exhibit 2.5 for smaller and smaller dose sizes, it would start to look like we were shading in the area under the curve with vertical lines.   The smaller the width of the dose rectangles, the less the "overlapping the curve" problem.   On reflection, you should be able to see that the sum of the dose increments would, in the limit when the doses approach infinitesimal size, become equal to the *area under the marginal curve.*

The importance of this is that we can, in effect, work backwards from marginal curves and depict the *total* effects as the area under the marginal curve.   Thus, if Y is a measure of benefits, then the gross benefits from X_b units of input is the shaded area under the marginal cost curve between the zero output and the relevant output X_b.   Frequently, the areas under *two* marginal curves will be of interest; e.g., if the area under a marginal benefits curve is gross benefits

EXHIBIT 2.5

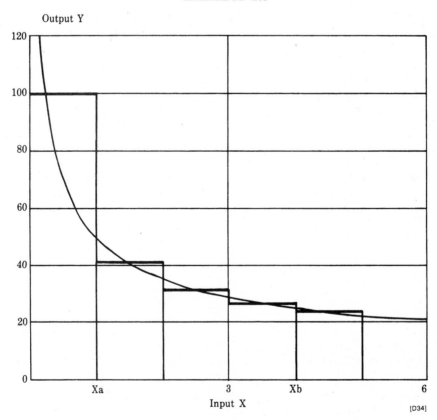

[D34]

and the area under a marginal cost curve is total costs, then the *difference* between those two areas will be equivalent to net benefits. In applying economic analysis to legal problems, you may find it convenient to "shade in" such areas to depict in visible form the magnitude of some gain or loss.

We will now apply this simple diagrammatic technique to the situation of a lawyer working under a contingency fee. You should recognize that this situation closely parallels the real estate problem just discussed. Be alert, however, for the ways in which the diagrammatic analysis arguably improves on the tabular model. For instance, one obvious methodological improvement is that it does away with the arbitrarily-sized discrete "dose" used in our previous discussions, now allowing continuous variation in the level of the activities being analyzed. See how many other possible advantages you can identify.

ATTORNEY–CLIENT RELATIONSHIPS

Vic Timm, a widower suing for damages in the alleged wrongful death of his wife Clara, has retained a well known personal injury litigator, Kate Advo, as his attorney. Timm and Advo have agreed to a contingency fee arrangement under which Advo is to receive $33\frac{1}{3}\%$ of any recovery ultimately awarded to Timm.

Since Advo is a highly successful trial attorney, she is frequently compelled to turn down cases because of constraints on her available time. Defendant's insurance company is engaged in vigorous attempts to negotiate a settlement of the case. In turn, Advo has done sufficient preparation of Timm's case to have formed an estimate of the chances of success and expected recoveries. These probable outcomes vary depending on the "effort" expended by her in carrying forward the litigation. For simplicity, assume that there is a "dose" of such effort definable in some standard form such as a mix of attorney time, paralegal time, etc.

QUESTIONS

1. Construct a diagram in which "Expected Value of Recovery" is measured on the vertical axis and "Doses of Effort" on the horizontal axis. Unlike some of our previous discussions, effort is adjustable in other than discrete doses; indeed, its quantity is continuously adjustable in gradations as small as desired. Draw a curve that you think might be a plausible representation of the relationship between effort level and the expected recovery. Explain briefly the reasons why the curve has the particular shape given to it. How, if at all, does it differ from Exhibit 2.4 above?

2. The curve that you just drew is in terms of *total* recovery. Draw a new curve that shows the relationship between effort levels

and *marginal* recovery from the defendant. On the same diagram, add a curve that shows Advo's expected returns as a function of her effort inputs. (Be sure that the latter curve is drawn in approximately the correct scale to the former one.) Finally, assume that the marginal cost to Advo of additional doses of effort is constant and add a curve that plausibly represents these marginal costs. What analogy is there between the diagram just created and Exhibit 1.3 in the previous chapter?

3. Using the diagram just completed, explain (a) what level of effort will maximize Advo's personal returns from the case; (b) what effort level would be preferred by Timm; and (c) what level seems to you to be optimal or cost-justified in some objective sense.

4. What are the "error costs" if the optimal result of (3) above is not achieved? What area in your diagram represents these costs? Who bears the error costs?

5. Advo might well be expected to want to "hold back" or shirk somewhat on her effort inputs to the case. In the real world, in what kinds of behavior might Advo's desire be manifested? What mechanisms can be used to mitigate the problem? In your view, are they effective?

6. What "should" be the level of effort legally or ethically demanded of an attorney in the above situation? Why? Who gains or loses from your proposed rule?

7. Consider the arrangement wherein client and attorney each bore the same share of costs that they enjoy of the benefits. For instance, the attorney's contingency fee might be reduced to 25% of the judgment but the client bears 75% of the costs of litigating the claim. First, explain why *in theory* this arrangement would produce an optimal amount of effort by the attorney. What practical considerations make this arrangement less attractive than it appears in theory?

HEINZMAN v. FINE, FINE, LEGUM & FINE

Supreme Court of Virginia, 1977.
217 Va. 958, 234 S.E.2d 282.

[Heinzman, a plaintiff in a personal injury suit, engaged Legum's law firm of Fine, Fine, Legum & Fine to represent him in a suit against defendant Mouser. Heinzman signed a written "power of attorney" promising Legum a fee of "1/3 of the gross amount recovered" by way of "compromise," "trial," or "appeal." About three months later, Heinzman discharged Legum and retained attorney Anninos who, on the day before trial, settled the case for $10,000. Upon suit by Legum against Heinzman, the trial court found that Legum was entitled to $3,333.33 in satisfaction for breach of the contingency fee agreement. Heinzman appealed.]

* * * The question remains whether, as Legum contends, an attorney employed under a contingent fee contract and discharged without just cause is entitled to recover from the proceeds of a later settlement the full amount of the contractual fee.

Courts which make no distinction between contracts for legal services and other contracts answer this question in the affirmative. The decisions rest upon various rationales: courts cannot convert bilateral contracts into unilateral contracts and relieve one of the parties of the burdens of his bargain, Friedman v. Mindlin, 91 Misc. 473, 155 N.Y.S. 295 (1915); a client "who has wrongfully broken a contract should not be permitted to reap advantage from his own wrong," Dolph v. Speckart, 94 Or. 550, 186 P. 32, 35 (1920); when the client wrongfully frustrates performance, the attorney is entitled to the presumption that he would have performed, McElhinney v. Kline, 6 Mo.App. 94 (1878).

We reject such rationales, for we believe the premise upon which they rest is wrong. Contracts for legal services are not the same as other contracts.

"[I]t is a misconception to attempt to force an agreement between an attorney and his client into the conventional modes of commercial contracts. While such a contract may have similar attributes, the agreement is, essentially, in a classification peculiar to itself. Such an agreement is permeated with the paramount relationship of attorney and client which necessarily affects the rights and duties of each." Krippner v. Matz, 205 Minn. 497, 506, 287 N.W. 19, 24 (1939).

Seldom does a client stand on an equal footing with an attorney in the bargaining process. Necessarily, the layman must rely upon the knowledge, experience, skill, and good faith of the professional. Only the attorney can make an informed judgement as to the merit of the client's legal rights and obligations, the prospects of success or failure, and the value of the time and talent which he must invest in the undertaking. Once fairly negotiated, the contract creates a relationship unique in the law. The attorney-client relationship is founded upon trust and confidence, and when the foundation fails, the relationship may be, indeed should be, terminated.

* * *

Legum does not dispute the fact that a client has an absolute right to discharge his attorney. He contends, however, that when the discharge is without just cause, the act constitutes a breach of contract and that the measure of damages is the fee fixed in the contract. We agree with the courts that hold otherwise.

"That the client may at any time for any reason discharge his attorney is a firmly established rule * * *. [T]he attorney may recover the reasonable value of the services which he has rendered but he cannot recover for damages for the breach of contract. The discharge of the attorney by his client does not constitute a breach of the contract because it is a term of such contract, implied from the peculiar relationship which the contract calls into existence, that the client may terminate the contract at any time with or without cause." Martin v. Camp, 219 N.Y. 170, 174, 114 N.E. 46, 48 (1916).

Overruling its prior decisions, the court in Fracasse v. Brent, 6 Cal.3d 784, 789–90, 100 Cal.Rptr. 385, 388–89, 494 P.2d 9, 12–13 (1972), applied the same rule and explained the reasons for the rule:

"The right to discharge is of little value if the client must risk paying the full contract price for services not rendered upon a determination by a court that the discharge was without legal cause. The client may frequently be forced to choose between continuing the employment of an attorney in which he has lost faith, or risking the payment of double contingent fees equal to the greater portion of any account eventually recovered. * * * Unless a rule is adopted allowing an attorney as full compensation the reasonable value of services rendered to the time of discharge, clients will often feel required to continue in their service attorneys in whose integrity, judgement or capacity they have lost confidence."

We share the conclusion that *quantum meruit* is the most functional and equitable measure of recovery. The law does not favor recoveries based upon conjecture. In awarding the contractual fee, the trial court presupposed that Legum, had he not been discharged, would have achieved a recovery exactly equivalent to that achieved by Anninos. But this is entirely speculative. Legum might have effected a greater settlement or won a larger verdict; considering the vagaries of trial, he might have recovered nothing.

Having in mind the special nature of a contract for legal services, we hold that when, as here, an attorney employed under a contingent fee contract is discharged without just cause and the client employs another attorney who effects a recovery, the discharged attorney is entitled to a fee based upon *quantum meruit* for services rendered prior to discharge and, as security for such fee, to the lien granted by Code 54–70.

QUESTIONS

1. The court applies a special treatment to contracts for legal services as opposed to contracts for other goods and services. Might the rationale of this special treatment have anything to do with agency costs, shirking, and monitoring?

2. Are lawyers better off in states that, unlike Virginia, treat attorney-client relationships as "ordinary" contracts? Does your answer to this question depend in any way on whether the typical client *knows* about this special rule governing contracts with lawyers?

3. Even if the attorney is discharged without cause and in a manner that normally would constitute a breach by the client, the remedy awarded in Heinzman is "only" quantum meruit rather than the usual contractual measure of damages, which would be the lawyer's lost profits. Under what circumstances could the recovery of damages based on quantum meruit actually amount to *more* than the lost profits awarded under an expectation theory of damages? What do you think a court would say if these circumstances were shown to hold under facts otherwise similar to Heinzman?

BLOOMER v. LIBERTY MUTUAL INSURANCE CO.

Supreme Court of the United States, 1980.
445 U.S. 78, 100 S.Ct. 925, 63 L.Ed.2d 215.

Mr. Justice MARSHALL delivered the opinion of the Court.

Under the Longshoremen's and Harbor Workers' Compensation Act, a longshoreman is entitled to receive compensation payments from his stevedore for disability or death resulting from an injury occurring on the navigable waters of the United States. If the longshoreman believes that his injuries warrant a recovery in excess of the compensation provided under the Act, he may also bring a negligence action against the owner of the vessel on which the injury occurred. The longshoreman's recovery from the shipowner is subject to the stevedore's lien in the amount of the compensation payment. The question for decision is whether the stevedore's lien must be reduced by a proportionate share of the longshoreman's expenses in obtaining recovery from the shipowner, or whether the stevedore is instead entitled to be reimbursed for the full amount of the compensation payment.

*   *   *

* * * The Court of Appeals concluded that a stevedore should not be required to pay a share of the longshoreman's legal expenses in a suit brought against the shipowner. We granted certiorari to resolve this recurring question, on which the courts of appeals have been divided. * * * We affirm.

Petitioner's argument amounts to an appeal to the equitable principle that when a third person benefits from litigation instituted by another, that person may be required to bear a portion of the expenses of suit.

The Act provides a comprehensive scheme governing an injured longshoreman's rights against the stevedore and shipowner. The longshoreman is not required to make an election between the receipt of compensation and a damage action against a third person. After receiving a compensation award from the stevedore, the longshoreman is given six months within which to bring suit against the third party. If he fails to seek relief within that period, the acceptance of the compensation award operates as an assignment to the stevedore of the longshoreman's rights against the third party. The Act makes explicit provision for the distribution of any amount obtained by the stevedore in a suit brought pursuant to the assignment. The stevedore is entitled to reimbursement of all compensation benefits paid the employee, and its costs, including attorney's fees. Of the remainder, four-fifths is distributed to the longshoreman, and one-fifth "shall belong to the employer."

The Act does not provide for the distribution of amounts recovered in a suit brought by the longshoreman. The unambiguous provision that the stevedore shall be reimbursed for all of his legal expenses if he obtains the recovery does, however, speak with considerable force against requiring him to bear a part of the longshoreman's costs when the longshoreman recovers on his own. * * * Petitioner asserts, however, that in the absence of an explicit statutory resolution, the recovery against the shipowner represents a common fund for whose creation the stevedore may properly be charged.

* * *

In 1972 Congress enacted more extensive amendments to the Act, * * * designed to reduce litigation and to ensure that stevedores would have sufficient funds to pay the additional compensation. First, Congress abolished the unseaworthiness remedy for longshoremen, * * *. Second, Congress eliminated the third-party action by the shipowner against the stevedore, * * *. The elimination of the shipowner's cause of action against the stevedore was intended to reduce litigation, immunize stevedores and their insurers from liability in third-party actions, and assure conservation of stevedore resources for compensation awards to longshoremen.

* * *

Petitioner argues that the 1972 amendments so altered the equities as to compel a holding that a stevedore must pay a proportionate share of the longshoreman's expenses in a third-party action brought against the shipowner. He observes that before the amendments, the longshoreman and the stevedore had adverse interests in the third-party action: if the longshoreman were successful in that suit, the shipowner frequently would attempt to require the stevedore to make payment of amounts due the longshoreman. With the abolition of the shipowner's cause of action, the stevedore and the longshoreman had a common interest in the longshoreman's recovery against the shipowner. Petitioner concludes that the common fund doctrine should be available to permit the employee to recover from the stevedore a proportionate share of the expenses of suit.

In light of the Act and its legislative history, however, we are unable to accept petitioner's argument. It is of course true that the stevedore and longshoreman now have a common interest in the longshoreman's recovery against the shipowner, but it does not follow that the stevedore should be required to pay a share of the longshoreman's legal expenses.

[W]e are unwilling to attribute to Congress an intention to allow creation of a new liability irreconcilable with its general desire to reduce litigation and to ensure conservation of the legal expenses of stevedores and their insurers.

Finally, we return to the original basis for the rule that a stevedore would not be required to pay a portion of the longshoreman's expenses in his suit against the shipowner. The compensation award was intended to be an immediate and readily available payment to the injured longshoreman. By receiving this payment, the longshoreman was not foreclosed from pursuing an action against the shipowner. At the same time he was not entitled to double recovery, and the stevedore would be reimbursed in full for his compensation payment. The result we reach enables the longshoreman to recover an amount no less than that which he would receive through an ordinary negligence action, and also immunized the stevedore from liability in connection with the third-party action. If we were to accept petitioner's view, an injured longshoreman would ultimately receive a sum equal to the full amount of his recovery against the shipowner and, in addition, a supplement consisting of the stevedore's contribution to the longshoreman's legal expenses. This supplement would represent a windfall in excess of what the longshoreman received as compensation for the injuries he has suffered. The stevedore would not obtain reimbursement for the full amount of its compensation payment, but would instead have that amount reduced by a possibly substantial legal fee. This result would be contrary to the allocation of attorney's fees expressly provided by Congress for suits brought by the stevedore pursuant to an assignment from the longshoreman.   In these circumstances we do not believe that the Act and its legislative history can fairly be read to support the distribution proposed by petitioner.

The judgment of the Court of Appeals is Affirmed.

Mr. Justice BLACKMUN, dissenting.

The Court's approach in this case strikes me as somewhat crabbed.   By tilting with the specter of "double recovery," the Court adopts a construction of the Longshoremen's and Harbor Workers' Compensation Act, * * * that relegates the injured longshoreman's welfare to secondary status, well behind the interest of his stevedore-employer in conserving resources.

Under the Court's rule, the stevedore has everything to gain and nothing to lose.   The longshoreman takes the risk and the worry of the litigation and, if he gains enough, the stevedore is home free. This result does not seem to me to square with the Court's recent recognition that the Act should be construed with the beneficent purpose of worker protection foremost in mind. * * * Nor does it entirely square with the modern concept that the costs of industrial accidents are expenses to be borne by the industrial enterprise and not by the injured workman.   It also fails to do equity where equity is due.

*   *   *

* * * [T]he Court errs when it implies that the case law presented a settled judicial construction of the Act for Congress to approve.   Indeed, the situation was even more complicated * * *, since the various rationales employed by the courts led them into disarray over the handling of attorney's fees in cases where the third-party recovery was insufficient to satisfy both the fees and the stevedore's compensation lien in their entirety.

As a result, I think that the Court informs congressional inaction with the wrong meaning, and that it draws an analogy to the statutory allocation of stevedore-initiated recoveries where none, in fact, exists. * * * I view the absence of action in this case as a clear signal that Congress regarded the allocation of a recovery in a suit by a longshoreman as a more fluid and complicated matter than allocation in a suit by a stevedore, and that it left the courts free to balance the equities instead of commanding adherence to a strict "arithmetic ranking" of liens.

* * * [T]he analogy to the division of a recovery under Sec. 933(e) itself is flawed.   When the stevedore brings the lawsuit, its own recovery comes first after expenses and costs of litigation have been paid;   the longshoreman, as nonparticipating beneficiary, re-

ceives only a portion of the remainder. In contrast, under the Court's ruling, the longshoreman who brings suit must wait in line until the nonparticipating stevedore's interests have been satisfied in full. Under the statute, then, the party who takes the risk of loss receives priority of treatment. Under the Court's ruling, he does not.

 *   *   * Thus, it is now clear from the outset of each longshoreman's suit that the attorney's efforts serve the interests of the stevedore as well as those of the longshoreman. If the action is successful, the stevedore obtains recoupment of the compensation benefits it has paid, without risk, without the jeopardy to customer relations that might arise if the stevedore or its insurer brought the suit, and without adjustment for the possibility that the stevedore itself is partly responsible for the injury. The amount of the stevedore's recoupment ordinarily depends directly on the lawyer's skill in proving both the shipowner's negligence and damages. This direct pecuniary interest in the outcome of the litigation justifies, in my view, an equitable allocation of the costs of bringing suit in proportion to recovery from the common fund. See Sprague v. Ticonic National Bank, 307 U.S. 161, 166–167, 59 S.Ct. 777, 779–780, 83 L.Ed. 1184 (1939). Without that allocation, the longshoreman must bear all the risk for only a limited part of the benefit.

In addition to eliminating the only sound reason for refusing an allocation on equitable grounds, the 1972 Amendments also show clearly that congressional concern was primarily for the workman and not for the stevedore-employer or for the shipowner. The chief purpose of the Amendments was to benefit the longshoreman. *   *   * When, for example, Congress eliminated the litigation merry-go-round produced by the indemnity and unseaworthiness actions *   *   *, it did so *   *   * because this layering of recoveries failed to produce "a real increase in actual benefits for injured workers." S.Rep. No. 92–1125, p. 4 (1972), *   *   *.

The Court also makes much of the putative "windfall" a longshoreman would receive if petitioner prevailed. The longshoreman would receive no windfall. Any costs or fees he must pay reduce his net recovery below the amount of his adjudicated injuries. This deficit would be alleviated, but never exceeded, if the stevedore were charged with a proportionate share of the attorney's fees. The longshoreman, of course, would be better off than if he had to depend either on the statutory compensation or on the negligence suit alone. But Congress long ago eliminated the necessity of electing a remedy, and an increase in total recovery accomplished by resort to both methods of redress is fully consistent with the statutory scheme. So long as the longshoreman's total compensation remains less than his actual damages, there is no true "double recovery."

* * * Where the recovery against the shipowner is less than the stevedore's lien and the expenses of the suit, * * * it is to be hoped that the injured longshoreman will not be required to disgorge part of his compensation payments. Yet such disgorgement would not be inconsistent with the gloss on congressional priorities that the Court imposes today.

QUESTIONS

1. The common fund doctrine requires a third person (the stevedore) who benefits from litigation instituted by another (the longshoreman) to bear a portion of the expenses of suit. Justice Marshall refers to this doctrine as an "equitable principle" and rejects its application in this case. Is the common fund doctrine based solely on considerations of "fairness"?

2. If the longshoreman had elected to bring suit against the shipowner and forego the compensation payment from the stevedore, the longshoreman would clearly bear all the expenses of his suit. Should the situation be different when the longshoreman first receives compensation from the stevedore and then repays that amount after recovering from the shipowner? Consider Justice Marshall's comment: "It is of course true that the stevedore and longshoreman now have a common interest in the longshoreman's recovery against the shipowner, but it does not follow that the stevedore should be required to pay a share of the longshoreman's legal expenses." Translate this "common interest" into a marginal benefit curve.

3. What factors determine the likelihood of a longshoreman bringing suit against the shipowner? How are these factors affected by a rule which requires the longshoreman to bear all the expenses of the suit and satisfy the stevedore's lien out of the recovery? Although the stevedore in *Bloomer* apparently benefits from the decision, what is the prospective impact likely to be? Is it clear whether stevedores in the future will be helped or harmed by the decision. Why?

4. If the potential recovery from the shipowner were $20,000, the stevedore's lien amounted to $10,000, and the marginal cost of bringing the suit were $5,000, would the longshoreman bring suit against the shipowner? Why or why not?

5. If the longshoreman fails to bring suit against the shipowner within six months after receiving a compensation award from the stevedore, his acceptance of the compensation award operates as an assignment to the stevedore of the longshoreman's rights against the shipowner. According to the provisions of the Longshoremen's and Harbor Workers' Compensation Act, how is the stevedore's recovery pursuant to this assignment distributed between the stevedore and

the longshoreman? Are the stevedore's incentives to bring suit against the shipowner the same as the longshoreman's? (See #4). Why or why not? How could you change the provision for distribution of the stevedore's recovery to reduce the probability that suit will be brought against the shipowner?

According to Justice Marshall, the 1972 amendments to the Act were "designed to reduce litigation and to insure the stevedores would have sufficient funds to pay the additional compensation." Is this goal satisfied? How? Is the result what Congress intended?

7. What is meant by Justice Blackmun's comment: "Under the statute, then, the party who takes the risk of loss receives priority of treatment. Under the court's ruling, he does not"?

8. Do the majority and dissenting opinions, taken together, provide a clear articulation of what you see as the underlying issues of the case? Are the issues more or less complex than they initially seem?

SHOULD SUBROGEES KEEP "EXCESS" RECOVERIES?

Although obviously not a common occurrence, it sometimes happens that there is a "windfall gain" to be distributed between an insurance company and its insured. In the case of The Livingstone, 130 F. 746 (2d Cir. 1904), the owner of a ship which sank in a collision with The Livingstone was paid $25,000 by his insurer under the terms of a fixed-recovery "valued policy." The insurance company, as subrogee, promptly recovered $37,500 from the tortfeasor. Both insurer and insured claimed the extra $12,500. Victory to the insured.

In another leading case, however, an insurance company paid its insured in full for loss due to a building deliberately destroyed by an arsonist. The company subsequently recovered not only compensatory but also substantial punitive damages from the parties responsible. The insurance company was permitted to keep the excess recovery. Urban Industries Inc. v. Thevis, No. c 75–0342 L(A) (W.D.Ky., 1978).

The basic issue here is whether a subrogee should be permitted to recover a net gain over what he pays out to the subrogor. That is, who "owns" the excess recovery?

QUESTIONS

1. Putting aside for a moment any distributional implications (fat, wealthy insurance companies versus impecunious orphans and crippled personal injury victims), is there any economic argument as to what the rule should be here?

2. In connection with the Victoria Nike scenario in Chapter I above, it was suggested that potential holders of legal claims may not receive the full expected value of that claim when the rights to it are transferred in the form of a contingency fee interest. What relationship is there between this conclusion and the present question about the rights to "windfall" gains under subrogation?

3. Now let's confront the distributional issue. Taking "insureds" as one class and "insurors" as another, who benefits or loses from a rule requiring insurance companies to turn back any "excess" recovery? Does *anyone* benefit?

LEAST–COST RISK BEARING

Following the seminal work of Guido Calabresi,[b] scholarly articles in the Law and an increasing number of judicial opinions now commonly invoke the concept of the "least-cost risk-bearer." The meaning of this term can be clarified by considering the series of questions supplied below. In each case, there will be a least cost risk-bearer, but the *reason* for the existence of such a party will differ.

By design, it is possible to derive a precise numerical answer to many of the questions. Those who are modestly competent with high school algebra can "solve" some of the questions by expressing the problems in the form of equations. Even if you cannot remember enough algebra to solve the equations for actual numbers, it will be profitable to try and formulate some of the problems conceptually in this manner. In this age of the pocket calculator, the truly innumerate can even just "plug in" some numbers and search for an approximate numerical answer.

If you are able to see how one would go about getting actual numerical answers, your effort will be repaid by enhanced understanding of the underlying concepts. Fumbling with algebraic formulations is not absolutely necessary, however, if one seriously reflects on the underlying problem in each situation. Minimally, you should try to answer the questions before reading the brief explanation of the three conceptually distinct sources of optimal risk-bearing. See whether you can identify the force[s] involved in each scenario. Of course, in the real world, these conceptually distinct factors might all

b. The Costs of Accidents (1970). See also, Calabresi, "The Decision for Accidents: An Approach to Non-fault Allocation of Costs," 78 Harv.L.R. 713 (1965); Calabresi and Bass, "Right Approach, Wrong Implications: A Critique of McKean on Products Liability," 38 U.Chi. L.R. 74 (1970); Calabresi and Hirshkoff, "Toward a Test for Strict Liability in Torts," 81 Yale L.J. 1055 (1972); Calabresi, "Optimal Deterrence and Accidents," 84 Yale L.J. 656 (1975). Although he focused primarily on torts, Calabresi applied essentially the same ideas to other areas of law in "Some Thoughts on Risk Distribution and the Law of Torts," 70 Yale L.J. 499 (1961) at 534–53.

be operating at the same time, even in ways that are mutually counteractive.

QUESTIONS

1. Assume two individuals who have the same square root utility functions as indicated in the text earlier in this chapter: $U = 100M^{1/2}$. (Remember that raising any number to the 1/2 power means taking its square root, to the 1/3 power its cube root, etc.) Sehler is about to sell a Whizbang to Beyer. The agreed price is $100. After payment of the $100, Beyer would have $1000 and Sehler $500. Whizbangs are purchased in the hope that they will whiz, but there is a 50% chance that they will bang instead. When they do bang, they cause $250 worth of damage to the holder, in this case Beyer. Whizbangs cannot be made any safer by exercising more care; they are sold in their natural state, just as they are found by trained swine rooting underneath poplar trees by the light of a full moon. The existing law on whizbang damages is caveat emptor: tough luck, Beyer. Nothing, however, prevents Beyer and Sehler from voluntarily entering into an agreement whereby the risk of whizbang malfunction is reallocated from Beyer to Sehler.

a. Beyer suggests that Sehler guarantee the product, accepting the liability to pay all damages if the whizbang bangs instead of whizzes. In exchange for this contractual modification, Beyer will agree to negotiate some additional consideration above and beyond the $100. First, see whether you can confirm that Beyer will pay at most $129.48 to get rid of the risk he now bears and that Sehler would need a minimum of $132.82 in order to take on the risk. What can you say about the likely outcome of the suggestion that a guarantee be sold? Why is one person more willing than the other to bear the risk? In what sense do we mean "willing"?

b. Now change Sehler's utility function by placing a 1000 in front of the M on the right-hand side instead of a 100:

$$U = 1000M^{1/2}.$$

Thus, at every level of money, changes in income have ten times as much impact on Sehler's welfare as before. Re-answer the previous question in the light of this new fact situation. What explains the change in result, or lack thereof?

c. Assume that, after the payment of the $100 original price, both parties would have $500 left. Would Beyer be willing to pay as much as $135.72 for a guarantee? What are the possibilities for a change in the original risk allocations now?

d. Finally, make Sehler's utility function a cube root, rather than a square root, function. Would $135.72 be enough to compensate Sehler for taking on the risk? Who will predictably wind up bearing the risk of a bang and why?

e. What is the nature of the "error cost" if the law does not allow the risk to be transferred, if necessary, to the least-cost risk bearer? (Use specific numbers from the above questions as illustrations.)

f. Assuming that the law does not prevent risk reallocation between the parties, does it make any difference where the law initially assigns the liability for the risk?

2. Suppose that Beyer is the predictable bearer of the risk, either because he is least-cost as compared to his possible vendors or because the law prevents reassignment of this particular risk. Nobody ever buys more than one whizbang in a lifetime. The good news is that whizbangs have become a lot safer than before; the probability of a bang is only 10% now. Remember that, by any of the utility functions attributed to him, Beyer places negative value on the dispersion of his risks.

a. If Beyer bears his risk "as is," what is the expected value of his loss? What is the expected range or average dispersion of his loss?

b. Someone shows Beyer the attached Exhibit 2.6, which is a portion of a binomial distribution table from a mathematical handbook. They explain to him that the columns show the probability of loss assumed for a single "trial" of any experiment. The row headings indicate the number of losses that might conceivably be observed. Finally, the entries in the cells are the probabilities of observing a particular number of losses, given the single-loss probability at the column head. Beyer runs out and finds 19 other whizbang purchasers and induces them to join with him in a mutual loss-sharing arrangement, each bearing 1/20th of any losses occurring within the group. Does this reduce the expected value of Beyer's risk? Why does he find this "risk spreading" or "pooling" arrangement attractive?

c. Suppose that Beyer found 100 fellow whizbang consumers with whom to share the risk. What do you think the analogue of Exhibit 2.6 would say about the probability distribution of different losses? What general principle is at work here as the number of possible risk-sharers goes up to 1,000,000, then 2,000,000 etc.?

d. Beyer is a consumer of whizbangs. Do you think that it would be costly for him to organize this risk-sharing scheme? Who is likely to be a cheaper organizer, consumers or sellers? Why?

EXHIBIT 2.6 Binomial Distribution

Probability of a Single Loss

p

n^{**}	$x\dagger$	.05	.10	.15	.20	.25	.30	.35	.40	.45	.50
19	0	.3774	.1351	.0456	.0144	.0042	.0011	.0003	.0001	.0000	.0000
	1	.3774	.2852	.1529	.0685	.0268	.0093	.0029	.0008	.0002	.0000
	2	.1787	.2852	.2428	.1540	.0803	.0358	.0138	.0046	.0013	.0003
	3	.0533	.1796	.2428	.2182	.1517	.0869	.0422	.0175	.0062	.0018
	4	.0112	.0798	.1714	.2182	.2023	.1491	.0909	.0467	.0203	.0074
	5	.0018	.0266	.0907	.1636	.2023	.1916	.1468	.0933	.0497	.0222
	6	.0002	.0069	.0374	.0955	.1574	.1916	.1844	.1451	.0949	.0518
	7	.0000	.0014	.0122	.0443	.0974	.1525	.1844	.1797	.1443	.0961
	8	.0000	.0002	.0032	.0166	.0487	.0981	.1489	.1797	.1771	.1442
	9	.0000	.0000	.0007	.0051	.0198	.0514	.0980	.1464	.1771	.1762
	10	.0000	.0000	.0001	.0013	.0066	.0220	.0528	.0976	.1449	.1762
	11	.0000	.0000	.0000	.0003	.0018	.0077	.0233	.0532	.0970	.1442
	12	.0000	.0000	.0000	.0000	.0004	.0022	.0083	.0237	.0529	.0961
	13	.0000	.0000	.0000	.0000	.0001	.0005	.0024	.0085	.0233	.0518
	14	.0000	.0000	.0000	.0000	.0000	.0001	.0006	.0024	.0082	.0222
	15	.0000	.0000	.0000	.0000	.0000	.0000	.0001	.0005	.0022	.0074
	16	.0000	.0000	.0000	.0000	.0000	.0000	.0000	.0001	.0005	.0018
	17	.0000	.0000	.0000	.0000	.0000	.0000	.0000	.0000	.0001	.0003
	18	.0000	.0000	.0000	.0000	.0000	.0000	.0000	.0000	.0000	.0000
	19	.0000	.0000	.0000	.0000	.0000	.0000	.0000	.0000	.0000	.0000
20	0	.3585	.1216	.0388	.0115	.0032	.0008	.0002	.0000	.0000	.0000
	1	.3774	.2702	.1368	.0576	.0211	.0068	.0020	.0005	.0001	.0000
	2	.1887	.2852	.2293	.1369	.0669	.0278	.0100	.0031	.0008	.0002
	3	.0596	.1901	.2428	.2054	.1339	.0716	.0323	.0123	.0040	.0011
	4	.0133	.0898	.1821	.2182	.1897	.1304	.0738	.0350	.0139	.0046
	5	.0022	.0319	.1028	.1746	.2023	.1789	.1272	.0746	.0365	.0148
	6	.0003	.0089	.0454	.1091	.1686	.1916	.1712	.1244	.0746	.0370
	7	.0000	.0020	.0160	.0545	.1124	.1643	.1844	.1659	.1221	.0739
	8	.0000	.0004	.0046	.0222	.0609	.1144	.1614	.1797	.1623	.1201
	9	.0000	.0001	.0011	.0074	.0271	.0654	.1158	.1597	.1771	.1602

EXHIBIT 2.6   Binomial Distribution—Continued

		Probability of a Single Loss p									
n^{**}	$x^{\dagger}$	.05	.10	.15	.20	.25	.30	.35	.40	.45	.50
	10	.0000	.0000	.0002	.0020	.0099	.0308	.0686	.1171	.1593	.1762
	11	.0000	.0000	.0000	.0005	.0030	.0120	.0336	.0710	.1185	.1602
	12	.0000	.0000	.0000	.0001	.0008	.0039	.0136	.0355	.0727	.1201
	13	.0000	.0000	.0000	.0000	.0002	.0010	.0045	.0146	.0366	.0739
	14	.0000	.0000	.0000	.0000	.0000	.0002	.0012	.0049	.0150	.0370
	15	.0000	.0000	.0000	.0000	.0000	.0000	.0003	.0013	.0049	.0148
	16	.0000	.0000	.0000	.0000	.0000	.0000	.0000	.0003	.0013	.0046
	17	.0000	.0000	.0000	.0000	.0000	.0000	.0000	.0000	.0002	.0011
	18	.0000	.0000	.0000	.0000	.0000	.0000	.0000	.0000	.0000	.0002
	19	.0000	.0000	.0000	.0000	.0000	.0000	.0000	.0000	.0000	.0000
	20	.0000	.0000	.0000	.0000	.0000	.0000	.0000	.0000	.0000	.0000

** n = Number of Trials.

† x = Number of Losses.

e. How is all of the above changed if whizbangs cause different damages for different consumers? Is there a "Gresham's Law" of insurance, i.e., that bad risks tend to drive out good risks? [c] Explain. What relationship does this have to what is sometimes termed "adverse selection"? In a world of full information, would there be a tendency for risk pooling arrangements to consist of relatively homogeneous risks?

3. Assume that both Sehler and Beyer are risk neutral; they care about the expected value of the loss but not the dispersion. It is discovered that specially trained swine can discriminate between bang-prone whizbangs and a safer variety, but only if special precautions are taken at the time the whizbangs are first found in the wild. Specifically, the specially trained swine can filter out half of the

c. Gresham's Law was originally coined (pun intended) in the days when more than one type of coinage,—e.g., both silver-based and gold-based—was put into circulation. As the values of the underlying precious metals fluctuated, one type of money would tend to become relatively overvalued in respect to its nominal rate of conversion to the other type of money. Hence, the original form of the adage, that "Bad money drives out good" because the "good" money would be hoarded and the "bad" money used for exchange.

bang-prone whizbangs, thus reducing the probability of loss from the original 10%.

    a.   The extra cost of using the trained pigs instead of ordinary swine comes to $X per whizbang found. What is the highest value that X can have in order for you to predict that Sehler will assume the liability for "safer" whizbangs? Explain your answer.

    b.   Suppose that the cost of using the trained pigs is greater than the $X computed above, but the law places a non-reassignable strict liability on the seller. Will the trained pigs be used?

    c.   The cost of the pigs is still greater than $X —$X + 1, to be exact—but the seller is legally liable only when he fails to mitigate expected damages by using trained pigs to preselect the whizbangs that he offers. What will happen? Who, if anyone, will be better or worse off?

SOURCES OF LEAST COST RISK–BEARING

The three sets of questions above deal with three distinct ways of reducing risk. The first scenario considers party-to-party transfers that can reallocate who bears the consequences of a risk. Such transfers reduce risk only in a purely subjective sense. They depend upon differences in the risk preferences of the two persons, i.e., the way in which they subjectively assess the certainty equivalent of what is objectively precisely the same risk. If there is a difference in the certainty equivalents, then one can predict who will wind up bearing the risk when the parties are permitted to trade money for risk assumption: the risk will tend to be borne by the person who places the lowest money cost on it. If the risk is not already allocated to the least-cost bearer, then a transfer to that party, together with at least a compensatory payment to the risk-bearer, will be mutually advantageous. One caveat, however, is that the transactions costs of actually effecting the transfer may diminish or even overcome the potential gain. Risk *transferral* thus reduces risk costs when an otherwise unchanged risk is reallocated to a person who, merely for psychological reasons, attaches a lower certainty equivalent to the risk.

If the underlying utility functions of the two individuals are different, then the possibility for a determinate least cost bearer seems greater because the individuals will evaluate the risks in variant ways. But the specific fact situations imbedded in the questions should demonstrate that different utility functions do not *guarantee* a difference in risk preference. For instance, when the difference in the utility functions is merely by some multiplicative factor, e.g., 1000 instead of 100, the *relative* rankings of different outcomes remains unchanged; replacing the 100 by a 1000 makes the impact of both gains and losses ten times greater. Similarly, identical utility functions do not preclude diverse evaluations of a risk; if the two people are assessing movements from different starting positions on those identical functions, then their assessments of the same risk will not be the same. This latter phenomenon pops up in many different economic contexts as an "income effect" or "wealth effect," i.e., a behavioral impact based on income level rather than underlying preferences. Finally, you should also see from the first set of questions that it is not true that the person who would feel the greatest utility loss from the risk will necessarily be the least-cost bearer. A person who feels losses very intensely may also feel gains very intensely! It is the relative *difference* in the intensity of feeling gains and losses that produces risk preference.

It is very important to perceive that reduction in the subjective cost of risk is nonetheless a very *real* reduction in costs. Many extremely significant economic costs are essentially subjective in origin. The fact that people are willing to pay real things, money or other advantages, in order to avoid subjective costs is a dramatic proof of the potential "objectification" of subjective costs.

The second process of cost reduction is also mainly personal or subjective in its operation, although there is some objective change in the form in which the risk is borne. What is involved is an alteration in the *distribution* of an unchanged set of risks, a process sometimes called risk "spreading" or pooling. Each of the mutual risk-bearers now faces a different, more complex set of objective risks than before. The expected value of the loss is exactly the same, but the accompanying amount of dispersion falls. Note, however, that the aggregate amount of risk facing "the world" is not altered in any way, although the prospect facing each individual is improved. Because the individuals are assumed to be risk averse, the reduction in dispersion due to the pooling arrangement translates into a reduction in the subjective cost to each of the mutual riskbearers. As more and more sharers get together, the "law of large numbers" works, and *in the limit* each person is faced by an almost-certainty of the expected value of the loss. It is only an "almost-certainty" because the dispersion never falls to zero, but does grow narrower and narrower.

A diagrammatic illustration is sometimes helpful in seeing the effects of risk pooling. The accompanying Exhibits 2.7, 2.8, and 2.9 assume that the probability of loss associated with any single risk is 40% and the magnitude of a single loss equals $1. The histograms in each Exhibit illustrate the changing shapes of the probability distributions of the possible losses for any individual when 5, 10, and 20 people bear their $1 risks by "pooling." The plotted shapes of these

EXHIBIT 2.7   Pool of 5 Shared $1 Risks

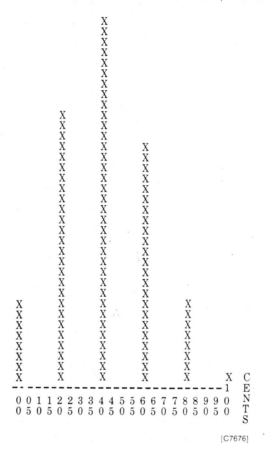

[C7676]

EXHIBIT 2.8   Pool of 10 Shared $1 Risks

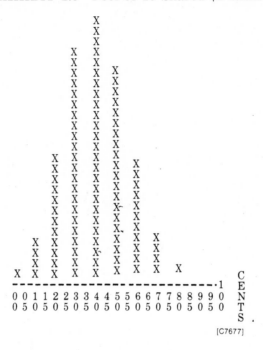

[C7677]

EXHIBIT 2.9   Pool of 20 Shared $1 Risks

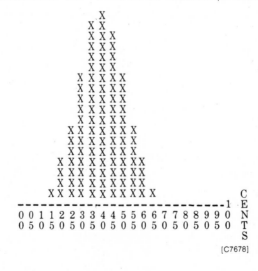

[C7678]

distributions can be related to the table of probabilities provided above in Exhibit 2.6.

Pooling involves summing the losses, if any, from each separate risk and then sharing these losses in pro rata fashion among the participants in the pool. Hence the 20 cents column of Exhibit 2.7 represents an outcome consisting of one $1 loss shared among 5 people ($1/5 = 20 cents) whereas the same column of Exhibit 2.8 represents the occurrence of two losses out of ten risks ($2/10 = 20 cents). Each X in a column of the histogram corresponds to approximately one percent of probability, although the sum of X's in each histogram may not add to 100 because of rounding. The probabilities plotted in the Exhibits can be found in any standard table of probabilities for the so-called "binomial distribution" and correspond to the results indicated in Exhibit 2.6.

The third set of questions deals with a situation in which one party or the other can act in a way that alters the objective amount of risk created in the world. When such actions are cost-beneficial, there is a potential social gain from seeing to it that they are undertaken. In this third factor, we are dealing with purely objective considerations, perhaps best thought of as the "technology of risk variation."

In the next few sections, we shall illustrate optimal risk-bearing principles in several different legal contexts.

QUESTIONS

1. Note that the questions were constructed so as to carefully separate these three conceptually distinct factors. Can you think of situations where more than one such factor is present? Where the directionality of the factors may be at cross purposes among the parties?

2. Can you supply an example of a situation wherein the placement of a legal liability is allegedly based upon consideration of who is the least-cost riskbearer?

3. An argument may be made that pharmaceutical companies, rather than their customers, are the least-cost bearers of risks from consuming the product. What is the argument based on, and how persuasive do you find it? Is the pharmaceutical company an obviously superior bearer of the kinds of "generic" risk involved when, despite all proper precautions in research and testing, a drug turns out years later to have extremely harmful side effects? What about the risk, that, notwithstanding all proper efforts at quality control in production, every now and then a "batch" of improperly produced drugs causes harm to users?

PORTFOLIO ANALYSIS AND THE PRUDENCE STANDARD

Professional investment managers are held by the law to standards of both prudence and competence in regard to the handling of their clients' accounts. The manager is expected to abstain from speculation, to sell off unsuitable assets, to maintain productivity, and to "diversify" a client's account.[d] Unfortunately, such duties are stated in broad terms and their precise content is susceptible to considerable variation in interpretation.

Although neither the federal nor the common law restrictions on "speculation" provide very precise definitions of the term, the legal system's understanding of speculation seems to place important weight on the existence of exceptional risk both of gain and loss. On this basis, some specific types of investment media have been condemned as unsuitable for purchase by trustees: junior mortgages on property, unsecured loans, new issues, etc.[e] Whatever the risks of any single investment, the risk-pooling effect described above can be recognized as relevant to the duty to "diversify." If the risks associated with different investments are random, then a large "portfolio" of such investments may have little risk, even though the individual components of that portfolio seem to involve heavy risk.

Why would one be willing to put very risky investments, i.e., those with a high variance in their possible results, into a portfolio at all? Some of our earlier discussion suggests the answer: an investor may be willing to "trade off" between rate of return and risk, that is, accept greater variability of results if the expected value of the return is higher. Conversely, the "sellers" of such risks would plausibly be willing to offer a higher return when the variability is great. If "risky" investments are barred from portfolios, opportunities for higher return may be lost.

The legal system might still have an understandable solicitude for the construction of portfolios with "too many" risky components when the actual bearer of the risks is not competent to understand or evaluate what his investment manager is doing. "After all," it may be argued, "pooling only reduces risks. The overall portfolio would always have less risk if, in a choice between two investments, the one with the lower variability were added to the portfolio." Right? No. Modern portfolio theory suggests that overall risk can actually be *reduced* by adding more risk!

d. See Restatement (Second) of Trusts, Secs. 227, 230, 181, 228. The general topic covered in this section is treated at length in Bines, "Modern Portfolio Analysis," 76 Colum.L.Rev. 721 (1976).

e. Restatement of Trusts, Sec. 227, comments, f–1 (1935).

The trick is that the added risk must be of the right kind. In our previous discussions of pooling, we implicitly assumed that the risks were random and uncorrelated. Hence, the pooling arrangement really just gave us the benefit of the "law of large numbers" or the ability to in effect count on something close to an "average" result. Suppose, however, that we could find two risks, A and B, that are correlated, that tend to move in a predictable relationship to one another. When risks vary in this way, investment theorists refer to them as having significant "covariance." If the returns on A and B are closely related in the sense that, when the return on A is known, one can make a good prediction about the return on B, the risks are highly covariant.

Covariance can be either negative or positive. When it is positive, the returns move together: if A is a loser, so is B. Negative covariance, on the other hand, implies that when A is up, B will tend to be down, and vice versa. Positive covariance among the investments in a portfolio exacerbates the swings and increases the risks, but negative covariance permits a swing in one direction to *counterbalance* a swing in the other direction.

In Trustees of Hanover College v. Donaldson, Lufkin & Jenrette, Inc.,[f] plaintiffs sued an investment manager, alleging that certain specific securities purchases were unsuitable. In their motion to dismiss, defendants alleged, inter alia, that the commitments in question were not objectionable when judged in light of the performance of the portfolio as a whole. The court refused to adopt a full portfolio approach in judging the manager's performance and the parties settled before final judgment.

QUESTIONS

1. What is the policy argument to be made against the court's refusal to adopt the overall portfolio approach? How persuasive is this argument? Are there counterbalancing considerations?

2. Obviously, the judge in Hanover College was not impressed with the policy argument in the form it was actually made. How would you try to communicate the argument to the judge? Would you use an expert witness, your own oral argument, briefs, homely examples? Be as specific as possible.

3. If the portfolio approach were to be implemented, who should have the burden of proof as to the effect of a security? How could

f. Civil No. 71–C686 (S.D.Ind.1971). Although the case is unreported, it is summarized in Belliveau, Discretion or Indiscretion, 16 Instit. Invest. 65 (August 1972).

that burden be met? Should the traditional classifications of "risky" investments play any role?[g]

4. Merger of businesses that have no apparent commercial or productive relationships are sometimes criticized as sterile financial exercises. Does the portfolio approach suggest any other explanation for such combinations?

OPTIMAL INSURANCE AND RISK ADJUSTMENT

[The material in this section is based upon the analysis in Section II of Goetz & Scott, "Liquidated Damages, Penalties, and the Just Compensation Principle: Some Notes on an Enforcement Model and a Theory of Efficient Breach," 77 Colum.L.Rev. 554 (1977).]

Martin Wurrier, IV, a graduate of his state's major law school, is a wealthy senior partner in a prosperous land development firm and, even more importantly, a truly fanatical fan of the State University's basketball team. After years as an also-ran in its highly competitive conference, State University produced a conference championship basketball team that has advanced to the regional finals of the NCAA championship tournament. Never one to pinch a penny in following his beloved State U. hoopsters, Wurrier acquired twenty-five tickets to the regional championship game in a metropolis 250 miles away. He then entered into contract negotiations with the Reliable Charter Service, Inc. to arrange for a bus to transport himself and twenty-four good buddies, also loyal State U. alumni, to the site of the Big Game. The standard price for a bus charter of this type is $500.

Wurrier considered his attendance at the game to be of supreme importance and began to suffer many anxieties over whether the bus might break down and deprive him of witnessing State U.'s moment of glory. He was eager to quiet his fears by securing adequate compensatory "insurance" to salve his feelings in case Reliable failed to perform. Ordinarily, damages for non-performance of a contract in effect provide this insurance by paying the disappointed breachee compensatory damages. Wurrier realizes, however, that the $11,000 sum required to compensate him for not seeing the game would be so large as to be deemed "fanciful" by a court and, therefore, not legally cognizable as breach of contract damages. Wurrier would expect only about $1,000 in damages to be legally recoverable.

Under such circumstances, what can a worried promisee do to insure against the $10,000 of unprotected potential losses from breach?

g. For a more progressive view than Hanover, see In re Bank of New York, 35 N.Y.2d 512, 364 N.Y.S.2d 164, 323 N.E.2d 700 (1974). Here, the court acknowledged that each investment was not in "its own watertight compartment" but retained an individual security focus, subject to the weighing of other factors including the entire portfolio.

One option is to attempt to insure with a third party (Lloyd's of London, for example). For instance, adding the proceeds of a $10,000 policy to the award of $1,000 legally cognizable expectation damages would provide Wurrier with full insurance of losses resulting from breach by Reliable.

Alternatively, Wurrier could negotiate for direct insurance from Reliable. He might propose to pay Reliable $500 above the usual price for the charter service if, in return for the additional premium, Reliable would agree to a penal sanction of $10,000 upon failure of performance. The stipulated sum of $10,000 would represent that amount at which Wurrier would be indifferent between performance and breach. Unfortunately, insurance purchased directly from the promisor, Reliable, is not a real alternative; the mere labeling of the idiosyncratic damages as pursuant to an "insurance" contract is unlikely to prevent a perceptive court from recognizing that such payments are de facto equivalent to a "penalty" and are therefore legally unenforceable under the penalty doctrine. Hence, legally collectible insurance for losses not otherwise recoverable as breach damages is in practice obtainable only from third parties.

As between the third-party insurance company and the promisor, which would be able to bear the risk at least cost? Identifying the efficient insurer requires an analysis of the costs of providing insurance. Perhaps the overwhelming element in the cost of this insurance would be the expected value of the underwriting loss to the insurer. Algebraically, this expected value can be defined as the product pR, where p is the probability of non-performance and R is the recovery payable to the insured. In addition, an insurer will also have other transactions costs, such as the costs of ascertaining the true probability p and the costs of negotiation and communication with the insured. These transaction costs will be subsumed in the portmanteau variable T, so that the total cost C of a policy paying R on the occurrence of an event with probability p can be summarized as $C = pR + T$. If the services in question are marketed competitively, the cost of breach insurance to Wurrier will be $(1 + a) C$ where a is the competitive rate of return or profit for the insurer. The question, then, is whether C would differ between the bus company and the third-party insurer.

One focal point of interest is the transaction cost element T. Here, it is tempting to argue that the advantage lies with the bus company. In the first place, the bus company is in a superior position to know the breakdown probability p. Secondly, many of the other transactions costs normally incident to customer communication may be negligible when communication is already being undertaken relative to the carriage service itself. Hence, T may be lower for the bus company and thus so would C and the offering price of the insurance to Wurrier.

Actually, however, the transaction cost element is not the strongest argument in favor of the bus company as the most efficient insurer. The bus company's main advantage derives from its power to exercise some control over the breakdown probability p. This can be illustrated by examining how the rational enterprise will make the maintenance and repair decisions which affect the breakdown probability.

Exhibit 2.10 reflects the fact that there is an inverse relationship between the probability of breakdown and the level of maintenance. ("Maintenance" is used as a summary term for all bus company activities that potentially affect the breakdown probability.) Each upward adjustment of the level of maintenance reduces p, presumably by smaller and smaller amounts as the level increases.

In Exhibit 2.11, the technological facts of Exhibit 2.10 are converted into their investment implications. If D is the damage liability upon non-performance (here $10,000), the *expected* damages decline as increasing maintenance decreases the probability of breakdown. Since these expected damages are pD, the saving in expected damage costs attributable to a marginal unit of maintenance is rD where r is the marginal reduction in p brought about by the maintenance increase. Hence, the "marginal damage reduction" curve in Exhibit 2.11 is simply a schedule of the value rD for alternative maintenance levels. This is an inverse relationship, as it is closely related to the curve in Exhibit 2.10. As the maintenance level grows (from q_0 to q_1), the marginal damage reduction decreases, eventually tending to zero, a point where increased maintenance does not reduce the probability of breakdown at all.

The "marginal cost" curve is, in turn, a reflection of the incremental costs incurred as the maintenance level is varied. In Exhibit 2.11, this marginal cost is a constant; i.e., each additional unit of maintenance has the same cost. If it seeks to maximize its own net benefits, the bus company will maintain up to the point where the last or marginal unit of maintenance is "just worth it," the quantity q_0 at which the marginal damage reduction curve intersects the marginal cost curve. If the company spent another unit of maintenance beyond q_0, any such unit would cost C_m but reduce the expected damage liability by a lesser amount. Note that this predicted decision of q_0 maintenance also determines the Exhibit 2.10 probability p_0, the probability of breakdown when the bus company has completed its maintenance and the bus actually sets out.

EXHIBITS 2.10 and 2.11

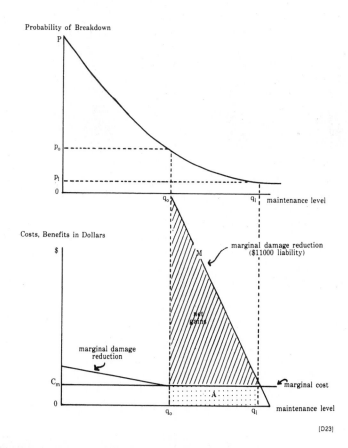

[D23]

Absent any specially arranged damage provision, the bus company anticipates that D will embody only the standard objective damage recovery of $1,000 for the Wurrier bus trip. This anticipation underlies the marginal damage reduction curve in Exhibit 2.11 and is the ultimate basis for the p_o breakdown probability. In computing the expected underwriting loss, a third party insurance company will therefore arrive at a value ($p_o \cdot$ $10,000).

Suppose, however, that the bus company can offer the same insurance. The expected value of damages is now based, not on a D of $1,000, but on a D composed of $1,000 actual provable damages plus the $10,000 insurance recovery. Therefore, the new marginal damage reduction curve (M) for maintenance will be exactly eleven times higher than the original one. The company will expend additional maintenance costs A, equivalent to the shaded area in Exhibit 2.11 or $C_m (q_1 - q_2)$, and the breakdown probability will consequently decline to p_1.

What are the implications of these adjustments on cost? For the bus company, the insurance cost must now be modified to reflect the net benefits of possible risk-avoidance efforts. Hence, the appropriate cost function for the provision by the bus company of $10,000 coverage is $C = (p_o \cdot \$10,000) - [\$11,000 (p_o - p_1) - A] + T$ where the terms in the square bracket are net gains from adjusting maintenance levels $+ (p_o - p_1)$ is the change in breakdown probability, its product with $11,000 is the expected damage reduction, and A is the added cost of maintenance.[h] Furthermore, we know: (1) that these net gains are positive; and (2) that they would not be achieved when the third-party insurance is purchased. Hence, even where the transaction cost component T is identical for the alternative insurers, the bus company has a cost advantage equal to the square-bracketed term in the equation above. (Graphically, this quantity is represented in Exhibit 2.11 by the crosshatched triangular area of net gains above the shaded area of incremental costs A and below the new marginal benefits curve M.)

The preceding argument has been that non-enforcement of liquidated damages provisions has the result of inducing individuals to protect against otherwise non-recoverable losses through special third-party insurance. This is likely to be an inferior alternative since strong economic arguments suggest that the vendor himself would be the lowest-cost insurer against his own non-performance. Although this argument has been illustrated in terms of a bus company, a similar conclusion may be generalized to all cases in which the vendor has some control over the probability of externally caused non-performance.

In sum, many people may not want to make deals unless they can shift to others the risk that they will suffer idiosyncratic harm or otherwise uncompensated damages. To the extent that the law altogether prevents such shifts from being made or reduces their number

h. Note that the relevant cost function for the bus company is the expected loss *due to the provision of the insurance*. The present expected loss to the bus company is $C_1 = (\$11,000 \cdot p_1) + A + T$. In computing the insurance premium, the pre-insurance expected loss of $C_o = \$1,000 \cdot p_o$ (provable damages upon breach multiplied by probability of breach) must be deducted. The cost function is thus $C_1 - C_o = (\$11,000 \cdot p_1) - (\$1,000 \cdot p_o) + A + T$.

The equation in the text is equivalent to this one. It is presented in a more complicated form to demonstrate the relationship between the bus company's insurance and the third party's. The first term is equal to the cost function of the insurance company $(p_o \cdot \$10,000)$. The bracketed term, which is positive, is then subtracted, thus indicating that the bus company's insurance is less expensive by this amount than the third-party insurance.

by unnecessarily high costs, it creates efficiency losses; that is, it prevents some welfare-increasing deals from being achieved.

QUESTIONS

1. Notwithstanding the argument in the text, is it possible that a third-party insuror could bear the risk at lesser cost? Why?

2. Suppose that the conduct of the insured also affected in some way the expected value of the risk. In Wurrier's case, you may hypothesize that a boozy, raucous party on the way to the game might distract the driver. Better yet, you may change the facts to generate a more important or plausible real-world example. A care-reduction response by the insured is commonly known by the term "moral hazard." How can the same diagrammatic models used for the insurer be adapted to analyze moral hazard.

3. What kind of contractual arrangements might be used to minimize the effects of moral hazard? [For discussions by economists, see Arrow, "Insurance, Risk and Resource Allocation," in Essays in the Theory of Risk Bearing (Chicago: Markham, 1971); Pauly, "The Economics of Moral Hazard: Comment," 58 Amer.Econ.Rev. 531 (1968); Shavell, "On Moral Hazard and Insurance," 93 Quarterly J. of Econ. 541 (1979).]

4. One important purpose of legal liability presumably is to channel the behavior of people. Yet, insurance against many forms of legal liability (e.g., for automobile accidents) seems to take away the very incentives that the imposition of liability supposedly creates. Then why is such insurance allowed?

AFTER–THE–FACT INDEMNIFICATION: REALLY INSURANCE?

We are accustomed to thinking of insurance as provision against the consequences of events that have not already happened, and perhaps never will. Although major examples are rather unusual, it is not impossible to find instances wherein the "risk" against which protection is sought seems to be one that is no longer a mere prospect, but already has materialized. Once such case stirred at least a minor controversy, as is described in the following excerpt, representative of the press coverage at the time.

PLAN FOR MGM FIRE INSURANCE BLASTED

A consortium of insurance companies plans to "insure" retroactively liabilities stemming from the November 1980 fire at the MGM Grand Hotel in Las Vegas in which 84 persons were killed.

Retroactive insurance of $170 million above the existing coverage of $30 million is being purchased to cover claims from the fire. The premium for the coverage is an estimated 37.5 million.

Frank B. Hall, Inc., the brokerage firm handling the insurance package, is spreading the coverage among insurers here and abroad. Those firms, in turn, will reinsure portions of the coverage to spread the risk broadly.

The National Consumer Insurance Organization has criticized these plans, contending that the added cost of providing such retroactive "insurance" may fall on small policyholders and the tax-paying public.

J. Robert Hunter, president of NCIO, argues that "all the problems associated with this unusual deal stem from the fact that this is simply not insurance. * * * Insurers have always said that you can't insure a burning a house, but when the client is big enough, apparently you can insure one that's already burnt."

Hunter claims that one result of this "non-insurance" could be higher rates for "true insurance policyholders".

John F. McCaffrey, executive vice-president of the Hall firm, feels that uncertainty about the ultimate amounts of the claims settlements makes it a valid form of insurance.

"It's not like property insurance where a building is insured for x-dollars and it burns down—then you're covered for the amount of insurance. In liability, we don't know what the costs will be until all the claims are settled. Therefore, you have risk, so you also have something that's insurable."

Don Heath, Nevada Insurance Commissioner, sided with Hunter on the issue of whether the coverage is truly "insurance".

"My chief concern throughout the whole thing is determining what it is," Hunter stated. "If it's not insurance, maybe it's simply a reserving program. But I'm not going to speak to that until I have all the facts before me."

QUESTIONS

1. Why do some people think that this is not legitimate insurance? What argument is there that the arrangement really is insurance? What is your own opinion?

2. Assuming that this is insurance, why would the insurance consortium be a better bearer of the risk than MGM? (If insurance companies enjoy no superiority over MGM, then why are the parties agreeing to "transfer" the risk for valuable consideration?)

3. Arrangements of this type *are* unusual. Why do you think they are not more frequently seen? For instance, why do we not observe insurance companies agreeing to after-the-fact indemnification of uninsured motorists who find themselves in the same predicament as the driver who hit Victoria Nike in Chapter I?

4. Commentators have attempted to identify the characteristics of a risk that make it "insurable" in practice. For instance, it is said [i] that an insurable risk must possess the following characteristics: (1) it must entail a real loss; (2) the loss must be of significant magnitude; (3) the amount and circumstances (cause, time, place, etc.) must be accurately ascertainable; (4) the cost must not be excessive; and (5) the magnitude and probability of the loss must be susceptible of accurate calculation by the insurer. Why would each factor on the list arguably be important? Are there any that you think might be of lesser importance, or even not necessary at all? How do the listed factors apply to the MGM situation?

NATIONAL STEEL SERVICE CENTER v. GIBBONS

Supreme Court of Iowa, 1982.
319 N.W.2d 269.

McCORMICK, Justice.

The United States Court of Appeals for the Eighth Circuit has certified the following question to us: "Does the theory of strict liability for abnormally dangerous activities apply to a common carrier under the circumstances of this case?" We answer the question affirmatively.

The court of appeals recited the facts it deemed relevant to the certified question:

> This is a civil action brought by National Steel against William Gibbons, the bankruptcy trustee of the Chicago, Rock Island and Pacific Railroad Company (Rock Island) for damages resulting from a train accident on September 1, 1975. On that date, the Rock Island operated a train along its right-of-way which consisted in part of eleven tank cars loaded with propane gas. The train derailed and four tank cars exploded, resulting in extensive damage to a warehouse owned by National Steel. National Steel sought recovery under theories of *res ipsa loquitur*, specific negligence, and strict liability.

> At trial, the jury ruled in favor of the defendant on the *res ipsa loquitur* claim. The district court directed a verdict for the defendant on the specific negligence theory. The court entered a

---

i. See R. Riegel, J. Miller, & C. Williams, Insurance Principles and Practices: Property and Liability 4–6 (6th ed. 1976) at 16–17.

directed verdict for the plaintiff on the strict liability claim. In a special interrogatory, the jury found that National Steel suffered $443,623 in damages as a result of the explosion, and judgment was entered accordingly.

The certification was in response to a motion by the Rock Island asking the court of appeals to certify to this court the question of whether the theory of strict liability was properly applied in the federal action.

*   *   *

The doctrine is incorporated in Restatement (Second) of Torts Sec. 519 (1977):

> (1) One who carries on an abnormally dangerous activity is subject to liability for harm to the person, land or chattels of another resulting from the activity, although he has exercised the utmost care to prevent the harm.

> (2) This strict liability is limited to the kind of harm, the possibility of which makes the activity abnormally dangerous.

The reason for the rule is explained in Comment d:

> The liability arises out of the abnormal danger of the activity itself, and the risk that it creates, of harm to those in the vicinity. It is founded upon a policy of the law that imposes upon anyone who for his own purposes creates an abnormal risk of harm to his neighbors, the responsibility of relieving against that harm when it does in fact occur. The defendant's enterprise, in other words, is required to pay its way by compensating for the harm it causes, because of its special, abnormal and dangerous character.

Rock Island appears to concede that the strict liability doctrine would apply in this case if it were not a common carrier. *   *   * The determinative issue presented by the certified question is whether this court will adopt the common carrier exception to the strict liability rule. In making that choice we are confronted with two lines of authority.

One line holds that a common carrier that is required to carry abnormally dangerous cargo offered to it for carriage should not be held strictly liable. The leading case for this view is Actiesselskabet Ingrid v. Central Railroad Co., 216 F. 72 (2nd Cir.), cert. denied, 238 U.S. 615, 35 S.Ct. 284, 59 L.Ed. 1490 (1914):

> We think there can be no doubt, so far as a common carrier is concerned, that such danger as necessarily results to others from the performance of its duty, without negligence, must be borne by them as an unavoidable incident of the lawful performance of legitimate business. *   *   * It certainly would be an extraordinary doctrine for courts of justice to promulgate to say that a com-

mon carrier is under legal obligation to transport dynamite and is an insurer against any damage which may result in the course of transportation, even though it has been guilty of no negligence which occasioned the explosion which caused the injury. It is impossible to find any adequate reason for such a principle.

Id. at 78; [other citations omitted].

The second line of authority, shorter but more recent, does not recognize the common carrier exception. The leading case for this view is Chavez v. Southern Pacific Transportation Co., 413 F.Supp. 1203 (E.D.Cal.1976), where the court found that the common carrier exception would not be recognized in California. The court based its decision on the California Supreme Court's use of risk distribution analysis in imposing strict liability in tort in such cases as Greenman v. Yuba Power Product, Inc., 59 Cal.2d 57, 27 Cal.Rptr. 697, 377 P.2d 897 (1963). The *Chavez* court reasoned that the common carrier or "public duty" exception is based only on a consideration that it is unfair to impose liability on a carrier for engaging in an activity required by the public. It added:

> But, there is no logical reason for creating a "public duty" exception when the rationale for subjecting the carrier to absolute liability is the Carrier's ability to distribute the loss to the public. Whether the carrier is free to reject or bound to take the explosive cargo, the plaintiffs are equally defenseless. Bound or not, Southern Pacific is in a position to pass along the loss to the public. Bound or not, the social and economic benefits which are ordinarily derived from imposing strict liability are achieved. Those which benefit from the dangerous activity bear the inherent costs. The harsh impact of inevitable disasters is softened by spreading the cost among a greater population and over a larger time period. A more efficient allocation of resources results. Thus, the reasonable inference to be drawn from the adoption of the risk distribution rationale in Smith v. Lockheed Propulsion Co. is that California would follow the path of the Supreme Court of Washington in Siegler v. Kuhlman, supra, and find that carriers engaged in ultrahazardous activity are subject to strict liability.

413 F.Supp. at 1214. Strict liability was also imposed in Siegler v. Kuhlman, and the *Chavez* rationale was endorsed and applied in Indiana Harbor Belt Railroad Co. v. American Cyanamid Co., 517 F.Supp. 314 (N.D.Ill.1981), a suit against a manufacturer.

Rock Island contends this court has already recognized the common carrier exception, and since it is the better view, should adhere to that position. We do not believe, however, that the issue has been answered in prior cases, and we believe, in any event, that the *Chavez* line of authority represents the better view.

* * *

In arguing that the common carrier exception represents the better view, Rock Island attacks risk distribution analysis as applied to common carriers generally and as applied in the circumstances of this case. It also points out that the exception has been adopted by the American Law Institute in Restatement (Second) of Torts section 521.

In attacking risk distribution analysis as applied to carriers generally, Rock Island asserts carriers cannot raise their tariffs to cover past losses. The fallacy in this argument, however, is that risk of liability is a factor to be considered in determining tariffs. See Akron, Canton & Youngstown Railroad Company v. Interstate Commerce Commission, 611 F.2d 1162, 1170 (6th Cir. 1979), cert. denied, 449 U.S. 830, 101 S.Ct. 97, 66 L.Ed.2d 34 (1980) ("A question of possible liability for damage resulting from carriage of a commodity is therefore within the Commission's jurisdiction as the regulator of the economics of interstate rail transport.") Thus, assuming tariffs cannot be increased to cover past losses, they can be adjusted to cover potential liability. Moreover, tariffs may be set at a level to assure "a reasonable and economic profit or return (or both) on capital employed in the business." 49 U.S.C. Sec. 10704(a)(2). Rock Island cites Consolidated Rail Corporation v. Interstate Commerce Commission, 646 F.2d 642 (D.C.Cir.), cert. denied, ___ U.S. ___, 102 S.Ct. 587, 70 L.Ed.2d 488 as contrary authority. The court in that case, however, merely held that the Commission did not act illegally in rejecting certain tariffs as unreasonable when they included amounts for a safety measure that the Commission determined was unnecessary.

In challenging application of risk distribution analysis in the circumstances of this case, Rock Island points out that it is bankrupt and that, in contrast, the corporate plaintiff was insured for all but $5,000 of its loss. We decline, however, to decide the issue of a carrier's liability for abnormally dangerous activities on the basis of the parties' relative abilities to spread the risk of loss in a particular case. To achieve a measure of uniformity and predictability, we prefer to adopt a rule for general application. We believe it is more likely in the generality of cases that a carrier will be better able to bear the loss than the party whose property is damaged. Moreover, the carrier is in a position to spread the risk of liability among the beneficiaries of its services. As in Lubin v. Iowa City, 257 at 391, 131 N.W.2d at 770, we think "they should bear the loss and not the unfortunate individual whose property is damaged without fault of his own." Although tort liability should not always be determined on the basis of which party can ordinarily best stand or distribute the loss, that basis is appropriate in this kind of case. See id. at 392, 131 N.W.2d at 771.

Here we have two parties without fault. One of them, the carrier, engaged in an abnormally dangerous activity under compulsion of public duty. The other, who was injured, was wholly innocent. The carrier was part of the dangerous enterprise, and the victim was not. The carrier was in a better position to investigate and identify the cause of the accident. When an accident destroys the evidence of causation, it is fairer for the carrier to bear the cost of that fortuity. Apart from the risk distribution concept, the carrier is also in a better position than the ordinary victim to evaluate and guard against the risk financially.

Furthermore, the carrier is in a superior position to develop safety technology to prevent such accidents, and assessment of accident costs is one means of inducing such developments:

> In some cases it may be reasonably clear that only injurers, or only victims, can be looked to for advances in safety technology or other adjustments that might minimize accident costs * * *.
>
> This analysis might explain the major pockets of strict liability in the law. These include liability for damage caused by "ultrahazardous" activities * * *. All are cases where the potential victims of the injury are not in a good position to make adjustments that might in the long run reduce or eliminate the risk of injury. It is difficult to imagine the development of cost-justifiable technologies that would * * * enable a traveler at a railroad crossing to supervise the selection and monitoring of the railroad's crew.

R. Posner, Economic Analysis of Law at 140–41 (2d ed. 1977).

We conclude that the doctrine of strict liability for abnormally dangerous activities should be applied in the circumstances of this case. In so holding we do not overlook the Restatement position. We note, however, that we are committed to a broader application of the strict liability doctrine of Rylands v. Fletcher than is reflected in the Restatement. We do not limit it to "ultrahazardous activity." See, e.g., Healey v. Citizens' Gas & Electric Co., 199 Iowa 82, 201 N.W. 118 (1924); cf. W. Prosser, The Law of Torts, supra, at 512 ("The Restatement of Torts has accepted the principle of Rylands v. Fletcher, but has limited it to an 'ultrahazardous activity' of the defendant. * * *"). Nor have we limited risk distribution analysis to the products liability field. See, e.g., Lubin, 257 Iowa at 391, 131 N.W.2d at 770. For the reasons expressed in this opinion, we decline to adopt the common carrier exception in Restatement (Second) of Torts, supra, section 521. Other Restatement provisions affecting the strict liability doctrine are not at issue here, and we do not pass on them.

We answer the certified question in the affirmative.

All Justices concur except ALLBEE and SCHULTZ, JJ., who dissent, and UHLENHOPP, J., who takes no part.

ALBEE, Justice (dissenting).

I dissent because I believe that the court should adopt as our own rule the common carrier exception to the strict liability rules for abnormally dangerous activities embraced by the American Law Institute in the Restatement (Second) of Torts (1977), to wit:

> § 521. Abnormally Dangerous Activity Carried on in Pursuance of a Public Duty
>
> The rules as to strict liability for abnormally dangerous activities do not apply if the activity is carried on in pursuance of a public officer or employee or as a common carrier.

This exception is explained by Comment *a* to section 521, which states in pertinent part:

> [A] common carrier, in so far as it is required to carry such explosives as are offered to it for carriage, is not liable for harm done by their explosion, unless it has failed to take that care in their carriage which their dangerous character requires.

The considered view of the American Law Institute seems to me to be more authoritative and to carry much greater weight than the reasoning of the single district judge in Chavez v. Southern Pacific Transportation Co., the decision this court builds upon to reach its ultimate rationale.

QUESTIONS

1. Who are the *potential* bearers of the risk under alternative assumptions as to the liability rule, regulatory reaction, etc.?

2. What do you understand to be the rationale of the traditional "common carrier exception"? In what sense, if at all, is it a "fairness" approach? [You may wish to re-answer this question after considering the material on Justice and Fairness below.]

3. The Court notes that "assuming tariffs cannot be increased to cover past losses, they can be adjusted to cover potential liability." If past liabilities are not provided for, to what extent will this affect the behavior of a business enterprise? Aren't bygones bygones? Under the opportunity cost doctrine, how would past liability affect the cost of remaining in the business in the future? What difference does it make whether the liabilities imposed on railroads can be "passed on" to users of the railroad?

4. What sources of least-cost risk-bearing seem to play a part in the Court's reasoning? Cite the passages in the opinion that support, either implicitly or explicitly, your view. Is there any doubt in your mind as to whether the court's assumption about who constitutes the least-cost risk-bearer is empirically sound?

5. Does the majority opinion address the rationale underlying the common carrier exception that it rejects? Does the dissenting opinion address the majority's rationale for the rejection?

6. Who would you personally prefer to see saddled with the cost of the explosion risk? If the court did not adopt that ideal solution, why do you think it did not do so?

JUSTICE AS FAIRNESS

"Justice" is a slippery concept which, like beauty, often shifts with the eye of the beholder. One persistent strain in the historical efforts to objectify norms for justice is that of ex ante fairness, the opportunity to enjoy fair and attractive prospects which, considered ex post, may or may not yield ultimately happy results. A contractarian analysis of social institutions falls within this genre because the social contract is, just as any garden-variety commercial contract, an agreement that is entered into precisely because it offers attractive prospects but which in any particular case may nevertheless retrospectively generate considerable regret and disillusionment for some parties. Contracts allocate risks of losses, presumably in exchange for prospectively more attractive chances for gains. Yet, things sometimes turn out badly for one party to a contract. As the ancient cliche puts it, one pursuing some potential benefit may have to "take the bitter with the better" and bear some downside risk. In legal terms, ex ante approaches correspond most closely to process fairness rather than to a requirement of substantive fairness in the ultimate results.

Along these lines, recent work by philosopher John Rawls has been the subject of vigorous discussion by legal scholars and social scientists alike. [See his A Theory of Justice, 1971. Many of the same basic ideas are contained in Rawls' earlier article "Justice As Fairness," 57 Philosophical Rev. 164–94 (1958).] One major theme in Rawls' writings is that basic agreements are made "too late," by which he means a time at which individuals already know their social positions, abilities, and those other characteristics that enable a person to predict the impact of social institutions on his own narrow self interests. This knowledge distorts the process of rendering justice because it induces self-serving choices among institutional alternatives.

In an effort to remedy the problem of self-interested choice, the notion of an "original position" is introduced. In this original position, individuals know generally the consequences of alternatives, but they do not know their own personal positions in the different outcomes. For instance, a similar situation would exist if a person were looking down at Earth, understanding a great deal about how any particular body observed below will fare under each of a set of policy alternatives, realizing also that his own being is about to be infused into a body, but not knowing anything about *which* body will be his own. Subject to certain other conditions, it is contended that choices made in this situation are likely to be "fair" and confirm to a Rawlsian conception of social justice. This lack of "morally irrelevant" information about personal consequences is sometimes called the "behind the veil [of ignorance]" assumption.

Decisionmaking "behind the veil" may be illustrated by a simple matrix model. The rows labelled S1, S2, and S3 represent three different sets of social institutions, differing in their constitutional guarantees, economic regulations, systems of property rights, etc. Following the usual conventions for these matrix models, the row states are what the decisionmaker gets to choose, whereas the columns are the circumstances that external forces impose. In this case, the uncontrolled conditions represented by the columns will be the status of the decisionmaker in society, designated by the letter A for an Alpha class individual and B for a Beta type. In our example, there will be equal numbers of Alphas and Betas in society. By the "behind the veil" assumption, the decisionmaker does not know who he will be, whether an Alpha or a Beta. Suppose that the numbers in the cells of the Exhibit 2.12 matrix are the utility or satisfaction payoffs of the various alternatives. Which set of social institutions would the person choose?

The certainty equivalent techniques discussed earlier in the chapter may be applied to this situation. Since the probabilities of A and B are each .5, the expected values of states S1, S2 and S3 are 50, 45, and 40, respectively. Hence, a risk-neutral chooser would rank the alternative social states in the same order as they are listed in the matrix. Mild risk aversion might result in S2 being ranked first because it achieves considerably less dispersion of the results at relatively small cost in terms of decreased expected value. Strong risk aversion might cause S3 to be highest-ranked, however, if the better average results under the other two states were deemed not "worth it" because of their higher risk cost.

EXHIBIT 2.12 Social Choice Matrix

Social State	Individual's Status	
	A	**B**
S1	100	0
S2	60	30
S3	40	40

The behind the veil methodology allegedly leads to disinterested choice and, in effect, results closely allied to those predictable under other well known ethical principles, e.g., the Biblical "Golden Rule" of doing unto others as you would have done unto yourself and the Kantian categorical imperative. Since the chooser does not know how to serve his own selfish interests, he will presumably be led to give equal weight to the interests of each person affected by the policies chosen.

One fact deserves special emphasis here: the insight embodied in the "behind the veil" approach is not unique to Rawls. Indeed, this general approach of impersonal ex ante decisionmaking is quite consistent with the prescriptions of extreme Utilitarians, who would maximize the aggregate welfare of society, thus producing the highest possible expected value or "average" result. However, the extreme Utilitarian approach seems to imply risk neutrality, since it attaches no importance to the dispersion of individual results around the average. Thus, extreme Utilitarianism is analogous to a policy of maximizing per capita national income without giving any thought to possible extreme disparities in the way that income is distributed among individuals.

While extreme Utilitarianism stands at the one polar position imposing no distributional norms whatever, Rawls is representative of approaches at the other polar extreme where rather inflexible distributional norms are superimposed upon the behind the veil decision process. Specifically, one of Rawls' additional normative requirements is the so-called "difference principle" which requires that choices always be made so as to maximize the prospects for the "least favored" person or group in society. This principle dictates what in game theory is known as a "maximin strategy" wherein the decisionmaker assumes that the worst will happen and therefore maximizes the minimum possible payoff. For instance, in Exhibit 2.12, the worst result under each rule set is column B and S3 would therefore be chosen because it leads to the largest minimum (max-imin) expectation. Such a strategy is, of course, an example of extreme risk aversion.

Exhibit 2.13 has been suggested as a device to demonstrate the difficulties with Rawls' difference principle. [See D. Mueller, R. Tollison and T. Willett, "The Utilitarian Contract: A Generalization of Rawls' Theory of Justice," Theory and Decision 345–347, at 348.] Assuming that n is some number greater than or equal to 1, rule S5 is mandated by the difference principle because the "underdog" Bs are always better off under that system (1/n is better than 0 for the "least advantaged" group). On the other hand, the expected value or average prospect under S4 is always higher. Specifically, the expected value of S4 is .5n + .5(0) = .5n whereas the expected value of S5 is .5(1) + .5(1/n) = .5(1 + 1/n). By letting the value of n start at one and then take on increasingly bigger values, one can make the prospective advantage of S4 grow larger and larger because the expected value of S4 approaches infinity at half the rate of n while the prospect of S5 quickly shrinks toward the limit of .5 as 1/n approaches a value of zero. The purpose of the Exhibit 2.13 construction is therefore to dramatize the question of whether, at some sufficiently high value for n, even a fairly strong proponent of egalitarian distributional principles would not willingly trade off the modest distributional superiority of S5 for the far higher average results under S4. In sum, the Exhibit is an attempted *reductio ad absurdum* suggesting that, while distributional goals are one plausible choice criterion, few people regard them as absolutely inflexible when they can be met only at an exorbitant cost in terms of other desiderata.

EXHIBIT 2.13 Maxi-Min Social Choice Matrix

Social State	Individual's Status	
	A	**B**
S4	n	0
S5	1	1/n

As a practical matter, the Utilitarians and strong distributional advocates such as Rawls would opt for similar policies under a great many circumstances, especially where distributional consequences are reasonably neutral. It is, for instance, difficult to maintain that the question of whether to observe the rule of Hadley v. Baxendale has any very powerful distributional implications. In any particular application, such a rule will of course have distributional ramifications for the parties involved, but the rule's application over the generality of cases does not seem likely to generate any systematic redistributive trends. Indeed, rules that have apparently clear distributional consequences are frequently seen, upon careful economic analysis, to have more diffuse or unexpected results than first impressions suggested. (Consider, for example, the rule determining the rights of subrogors versus those of subrogees in the distribution of "excess" recoveries, a question discussed earlier in this chapter.) Where the distributional implications are, for one reason or another, unimportant, a Rawlsian and an extreme Utilitarian stand revealed as very close methodological kinfolk, both depending crucially on an ex ante analysis of prospects.

Whatever its limitations, the criterion of ex ante fairness as a test of justice is an intellectually intriguing notion. The following question sections are designed to reflect how ex ante fairness may be applied in different contexts and, incidentally, how tricky the impression of fairness may be: in each of the scenarios presented, the application of a rigorous formal analysis raises hidden problems, demonstrating that the notion of justice and fairness is not as simple or intuitively clear as it may first seem.

FAIR DIVISION SCHEMES: DIVIDE AND CHOOSE

Mrs. Bupporpington is an extemely wealthy widow who knows that she is suffering from a terminal illness. She wishes to divide the large and extremely heterogeneous stock of assets in her estate between her two daughters, Doris and Cloris. The daughters are known to be extremely antipathetic to each other; past treatment at their mother's hands, however equitable in both intent and practice, has produced frequent bouts of jealousy and animosity. Nonetheless, Mrs. Bupporpington loves both daughters dearly and wishes to distribute the estate in a manner that will minimize eventual recriminations about their respective legacies.

Dividing the cash and other liquid assets of the estate presents no problem. As both sisters are aware, however, the division of certain real property, heirlooms, family jewelry, artwork, etc. involves subjective valuations which are highly variant from person to person. The sisters, not unexpectedly, each have considerable knowledge about each other's tastes and preferences for various items that are included in the estate. Although one possible solution would be to liquidate all assets and divide the proceeds equally, Mrs. Bupporpington regards the diffusion of many family assets to "outsiders" to be highly objectionable and wants the division of the estate to be physical or in kind—i.e., each daughter is to receive a fair share of the land and other personal property.

The troubled woman has previously sought the advice of a "fair division" expert who suggests that Doris be empowered to divide the physical assets into two shares from which her sister Cloris will then be entitled to choose whichever one she wants. Doris, of course, would receive the share not chosen by Cloris.

You are the trusted old family attorney for the Bupporpington family. The mother contacts you and asks for a will to be drafted that incorporates the expert's proposed fair division scheme. Assume that there are no strictly legal objections to the process proposed. However, she also solicits your opinion as to whether the scheme will achieve the desired result, that is, a division that both sisters will acknowledge as fair.

QUESTIONS

1. In a dazzling exhibition of the cunning of the legally trained mind, you impress the bejabbers out of the old woman by coming up with an explanation of how the process is arguably quite unfair to one of the sisters. Who is placed at a disadvantage, and why?

2. Assume that Mrs. B. nevertheless has her will written according to the original divide-and-choose scheme. When the mother dies, daughter Doris is notified by the executor that she is to be the Divider. The process of dividing is carried out and the moment comes when Cloris is entitled to choose between the divisions of the estate that Doris has made. Just as Cloris is about to choose, the executor rushes in and informs the sisters that a terrible error has been made: due to a misreading of the will, the roles of the sisters have been reversed. Why does Cloris now rejoice, expecting to improve her position as she takes over the role of Divider? (Note that this scenario lays the basis for a generalization and "proof" of the answer to #1 above.)

3. Parents commonly use a similar scheme to divide a piece of cake between two children. How does this situation differ from the Doris-Cloris scenario?

4. Dividing cake among the children in a larger family requires a more complex process. Suppose there is a rectangular layer cake to be divided among more than two children. A parent proposes to pass a knife over the cake from left to right. At any moment, any child can say "I'll take it." A cut is made at the current position of the knife and the child who spoke out gets the piece to the left of the knife. The last child, of course, gets the residual piece. Do you think that this is a fair scheme?

5. Some asset or collection of assets is required to be divided up among n people. It is proposed to create exactly n shares with random—and possibly quite disparate—composition. Slips of paper with

n numbers corresponding to each of the shares are placed in an urn and each beneficiary assigned a share by random selection of a slip. Is this a "fair" scheme? In what sense might it be argued that it is *not* fair?

EQUITABLE DISTRIBUTION OF VOTING POWER

In a majority-rule voting system, it might be contended that a voter exercises "power" only when the casting of his vote turns a non-winning coalition into a winning one. In other words, a voter has power only when the casting of his vote tips the result in a direction it would not otherwise have taken. In several articles, John Banzhaf has proposed that this concept of voting power be used as a benchmark in assessing the equity and constitutionality of various representation schemes, such as multi-member districts and weighted voting. [See J. Banzhaf, "Weighted Voting Doesn't Work: A Mathematical Analysis," 19 Rutgers L.Rev. 317 (1965); "Multi-member Electoral Districts—Do They Violate the 'One Man, One Vote' Principle," 75 Yale L.J. 1309 (1966).] Banzhaf suggests that, since the ways in which coalitions of voters will form cannot be predicted a priori, all possible coalitions should be regarded as equally likely. Then, a voter's power will be measured by the number of winning coalitions in which he is "necessary" divided by the number of all possible coalitions. Basically, this "power index" can be interpreted as the probability that a vote will "matter" as far as the ultimate result is concerned. In turn, a single vote will make a difference to the result when the other voters have divided themselves into two equal-sized coalitions such that the casting of the last vote will break a tie and determine which alternative will win.

QUESTIONS

1. In a system of representative delegations, the power of different delegations ought presumably to be proportional to the populations of their respective constituencies. I.e., the power of a delegation from a district of 300,000 ought to be three times that of one having a population of 100,000. In practice, political "weights" may be attached to districts of different sizes either by actual weighted votes cast by a single member or by multimember delegations. Consider a four-district legislature with district populations of 300,000, 500,000, 700,000, and 900,000. Each district has a representative for every 100,000 constituents. For simplicity, assume that the representatives of each particular district always bloc vote. Is the power of each delegation proportional to its population? [Hint: There are 16 different possible ways the delegations can vote. In how many of these does a particular delegation "make the difference" in forming a

winning coalition?] See Morris v. Board of Supervisors of Herkimer County, 50 Misc.2d 929, 273 N.Y.S.2d 929 (1966) in which the Banzhaf analysis is cited as a basis for striking down a weighted representation scheme.

2. Assume that the relative power of each delegation is properly proportional to its constituency size. The next question is the amount of power that any *individual voter* has over deciding the nature of the delegation. Again, for simplicity assume that each delegation is elected as a "slate." There are two competing slates running in each district. In a district that has $n+1$ voters, it can be argued that a voter has power in those cases in which all other voters divide up into two coalitions of identical $n/2$ size, thus permitting a single voter to break the tie. Banzhaf shows that the proportion of such "tie" combinations is approximately equal to one divided by the square root of two times Pi times n. [Banzhaf, "Multimember Districts * * *", n. 28] Thus, the probability of being a tie-breaker is not inversely proportional to n, but rather to the *square root* of n; i.e., an individual's power over his delegation declines less than proportionally as the size of the constituency increases. What is the implication of this result for the fairness of the allocation of power among voters in different-sized districts? What remedy does it suggest about the size of district delegations?

3. Note that the definition of power being used above implies that, in the real world, *no* voter exercises power in any except a very small fraction of elections: those decided by a one-vote margin. Do you think that there is something wrong with this concept of power? Why or why not?

STATE OF IOWA v. HENRY PARRISH

Supreme Court of Iowa, 1975.
232 N.W.2d 511.

HARRIS, Justice.

Henry Parrish (defendant) was involved in a fight on August 17, 1974 with Leslie Ford, during which he struck Ford over the head with a beer bottle. Ford has since married defendant's sister. At the time of sentence defendant's counsel said the fight occurred as the result of defendant's feeling Ford was attempting to make defendant's sister "into what's called a dealer's woman." Defendant also believed Ford had gotten his sister pregnant.

On August 30, 1974 defendant appeared with counsel in district court before Judge Lewis C. Schultz. Following arraignment defendant entered a plea of guilty to the charge. The proceedings included the following:

"THE COURT: Are you ready at this time to enter a plea? DEFENDANT: Yes.

"THE COURT: And what is that plea? DEFENDANT: I guess I'm going to plead guilty to the charge.

"THE COURT: Do you wish to plead guilty? DEFENDANT: Yes.

"THE COURT: Now is this the result of a plea bargain, Mr. County Attorney? MR. HORAN: Yes, Your Honor. We have agreed that on a plea of guilty we would recommend that the defendant be sentenced to one year in the county jail and be given credit for time served.

"THE COURT: How long has he served? MR. MONROE: Since August 13th, I believe, Your Honor.

"THE COURT: Did you understand that, that this is the recommendation of the County Attorney and the Court would be free to pass whatever sentence the Court would determine would be necessary? DEFENDANT: I believe so.

"THE COURT: I am going to have to ask you some questions, Mr. Parrish, which I do on any plea of guilty, to determine the voluntariness of the plea and determine whether or not you understand it, and also whether or not you understand the rights you are about to give up. The sentence under 694.6 is imprisonment in the county jail not to exceed one year or by a fine not exceeding $500, or by imprisonment in the penitentiary not exceeding one year. Any one of those things. Do you understand that? DEFENDANT: I believe so.

* * *

"THE COURT: By your plea of guilty you in fact admit that the State can prove the necessary elements of the crime. You are entitled to have a jury trial, and the jury would have to find beyond a reasonable doubt that you were guilty of the following elements: That on or about August 17, 1974, in Linn County, you did willfully and unlawfully assault one Leslie Gene Ford with intent to inflict upon him great bodily injury. 'Willfully' means intentionally. 'Assault' means to put another person in fear or threaten their body, and this assault must be with intent to inflict great bodily injury. By pleading guilty you are admitting the State can prove these elements beyond a reasonable doubt. You understand that? DEFENDANT: Yes.

* * *

"THE COURT: By your plea of guilty you also give up your right to a jury trial, to confront the witnesses against you, they must testify in open court before you, and you have the right to cross examine them and to have an attorney assist you. If you don't have funds to hire an attorney one will be appointed at county expense. You have the right to call witnesses on your behalf, you have the right to testify yourself, or you have the privilege against self-incrimination, which means you don't have to testify or admit anything, and if you would request it, the jury would be told that your failure to take the stand was done as a matter of right. By a plea of guilty you give these rights up. Do you understand that? DEFENDANT: Yes.

*   *   *

"THE COURT: And you understand that the Court is the one that passes punishment and that I can disregard the County Attorney's recommendation of one year in the county jail, I can pass a lesser sentence or fine you, or I could pass a sentence to the Men's Reformatory. DEFENDANT: Yes.

"THE COURT: You have never been convicted of a felony previously, have you? DEFENDANT: I have been convicted of a felony and received a bench parole.

"THE COURT: But you have never been to the reformatory? DEFENDANT: No.

"THE COURT: You understand the Court is the one that passes judgment and that I am not bound by your agreement with the County Attorney? DEFENDANT: What you are saying is that the Court here, the judge, is the one that says what happens, that the people I have talked to out here can't tell me what will happen, they can only make recommendations.

"THE COURT: That is exactly right. You said it better than I can. DEFENDANT: Yes, I understand.

"THE COURT: And what is your plea? DEFENDANT: A plea of guilty, Your Honor.

On the same date, August 30, 1974, Judge Schultz also ruled "an actual basis" existed for the plea and that the plea had been voluntarily made with knowledge and understanding of the charge, plea, and consequences of such plea. A presentence investigation was ordered.

Defendant appeared with counsel in district court for sentencing before Judge James H. Carter on September 25, 1974. At this time the State again noted it had entered into a plea bargain with defendant and stated the terms thereof. At this time the State recommended "*   *   * the defendant be sentenced to a six month term in the Linn County jail and that he be credited for time served." Judge Carter never advised defendant he had a right to withdraw his guilty plea or that the county attorney's proposal was not binding on the trial court. Judge Carter ignored both recommendations of the county attorney. Defendant was sentenced to one year in the state reformatory at Anamosa with the recommendation he be transferred to the security medical facility for psychiatric evaluation and treatment.

*   *   *

In the two recent opinions we have considered the obligation of a trial court which rejects the terms of a plea bargain after accepting a guilty plea. State v. Fisher, 223 N.W.2d 243 (Iowa 1974); State v. Runge, 228 N.W.2d 35 (Iowa 1975). Defendant relies on language in our opinion in *Fisher:*

"*   *   * [P]rior to entry of judgment, trial court, having elected not to honor the aforesaid plea bargain, neither so advised defendant nor accorded him related opportunity to stand on his guilty plea or move to withdraw same. Upon the record here made we cannot say defendant's guilty plea was voluntarily entered." 223 N.W.2d at 246.

In *Runge* the trial court had actual knowledge of a plea bargain and made no record of the fact. In reversing for failing to allow the plea to be withdrawn we explained:

"Briefly stated, defendant's guilty plea was not shown of record to have been free from inducement flowing from the county attorney's pre-plea concessions. Thus the controverted plea was not knowingly and voluntarily entered. See United States v. Mancusi, [275 F.Supp. 508, 515–519 (E.D.N.Y.1967)]; State v. Fisher, 223 N.W. 2d 243, 244–246 (Iowa 1974), and citations." 228 N.W.2d at 37.

We believe the facts in the instant case fall outside the situations outlined in *Fisher* and *Runge*. The record now before us clearly shows there was no taint of false inducement of the plea by the judge accepting it. The trial court clearly renounced any willingness to grant a sentence concession on the basis of the bargain. Defendant noted his understanding the judge would not be bound by any recommendations in his own words: "What you are saying is the Court here, the judge, is the one that says what happens, that the people I have talked to out here can't tell me what will happen, they can only make recommendations."

Our holdings in *Fisher* and *Runge* do not render all guilty pleas tentative and subject to withdrawal as a matter of defendant's right where there has been a plea bargain. The court is not bound to allow withdrawal of the plea where each of the following conditions is met: (1) the court renounces participation in the bargain, (2) denies any inclination to be bound thereby, (3) such renunciation and denial are made known to the defendant, and (4) the defendant thereafter enters or (as in this case) affirms his plea of guilty. All four conditions are established in the record before us.

Accordingly the question is governed by our cases which grant a trial court discretion in deciding whether to allow withdrawal of a guilty plea under Section 777.15, The Code. As stated in State v. Vantrump, 170 N.W.2d 453, 454 (Iowa 1969) (quoting from State v. Vantrump, 163 N.W.2d 899, 902 (Iowa 1969)): "A defendant should not be permitted to enter a guilty plea, gamble on the sentence and then move to withdraw the plea if he is disappointed with the severity of the sentence imposed. [Authority]."

Affirmed.

* * *

McCORMICK, Justice (concurring specially).

I agree with the dissent by Rawlings, J., that the procedure in this case did not comport with ABA Standards, The Function of the Trial Judge, Section 4.1(c) (1972), approved unanimously by the court in State v. Fisher, 223 N.W.2d 243 (Iowa 1974), and again in State v. Runge, 228 N.W.2d 35 (Iowa 1975). The standard does not authorize denial of a motion to withdraw a guilty plea when the judge has forewarned the defendant he will not be bound by the prosecutor's recommendation. It requires the judge in any case in which he decides in fact not to follow the prosecutor's recommendation, whether he has forewarned the defendant or not, to notify the defendant he will not do so and accord the defendant the opportunity at that time to withdraw his plea. United States ex. rel. Culbreath v. Rundle, 466 F.2d 730 (3 Cir. 1972); Commonwealth v. Wilson, 335 A.2d 777 (Pa.Super. 1975); Quintana v. Robinson, 31 Conn.Sup. 22, 319 A.2d 515 (1973).

The ABA standard approved by the court in Fisher does not depend for its applicability upon proof the defendant entered his plea from a belief the court would follow the prosecutor's recommendation. As the commentary to the rule makes clear, the standard is preventive. It seeks to avoid false inducement in some cases by removing the occasion for false inducement in all cases. ABA Standards, The Function of the Trial Judge, supra, commentary at 57 ("Even though the judge has said nothing to the defendant * * * except that he need not follow the prosecutor's recommendations, there nevertheless remains at least the taint of false inducement.").

I concur in the result because this guilty plea and sentencing proceeding antedated the decision of this court in Fisher, and defendant's guilty plea has not been shown to have been the result of unlawful inducement under standards then applicable. The sentencing occurred here September 25, 1974, and Fisher was decided November 13, 1974.

* * *

QUESTIONS

1.　In both the majority opinion and concurring opinion, concern is raised with "false inducement." What is meant by this? Is it a "fairness" issue? From the defendant's perspective, does it matter whether some probability p of non-performance by the State is due to false inducement or to bona fide disapproval by a judge who regards the plea bargain as not being in the public interest?

2.　Assume that the possibility of false inducement can be ignored because of other safeguards. Does the inability of the defendant to withdraw his plea then seem unfair to you?

3.　Consider whether inability to withdraw the plea is a poor rule on other grounds. Specifically, who gains or loses from the rule in future cases? How will defendants and prosecutors alter their bargaining behavior? (In answering these questions, you may wish to give specific attention to the treatment of risk by defendants and the prosecutor's office, respectively.)

"PATERNALISM" IN THE LAW

Paternalism—or maternalism, if you will—is not necessarily a factor to be excluded from a system of justice. One problem if course, is that rules which protect may also hinder valuable personal freedoms.

The decision in Williams v. Walker-Thomas Furniture Co., 121 U.S. App.D.C. 315, 350 F.2d 445 (1965) is based on a rather narrow procedural ruling as to the possibility under D.C. law of offering an unconscionability defense for contract breach; the appellate court does not actually consider the merits of the allegation of unconscionable acts by the seller. It is not hard to find in the full text of the opinion, however, a certain interstitial sense of uneasiness about any vendor who would sell, under seemingly very onerous terms, a very expensive stereo set to an impecunious person subsisting on welfare payments. (For comparative purposes, it may be instructive to note that the 1962 price of the stereo set would be the equivalent in real purchasing power terms to over $1600 in 1983 dollars.)

Unconscionability is ordinarily defined in terms of the conditions of the bargaining process, either absence of "meaningful choice" by one of the parties or unreasonably imbalanced contractual terms. But suppose that the Williams court had gone the whole distance and ruled that, notwithstanding otherwise acceptable terms and bargaining conditions, it is unconscionable to sell to a person who is recognizable to any prudent seller as one who later will almost certainly regret making the contract. One prediction as to the effect of such a rule is, of course, that a welfare mother, such as Mrs. Williams, would thereafter experience considerable difficulty in buying an expensive stereo on credit.

What is being suggested here is the possibility of examining not only the conditions of the bargaining process but also the capacities of the participants. Arguably, such an approach is already codified in the Wisconsin Consumer Act, Sec. 425.107(3), which allows courts to consider the following, *inter alia*, as possible indices of unconscionable practice:

> (a) That the practice unfairly takes advantage of the lack of knowledge, ability, experience, or capacity of customers;

> (b) That those engaging in the practice know of the inability of customers to receive benefits properly anticipated from the goods or services involved.

Subsection (b) above might be interpreted as dealing with the case of easily foreseeable mistake.

QUESTIONS

1. Is a preference-inference role of the type suggested in the Williams dictum or the Wisconsin statute justifiable within the context of an ex ante theory of "behind the veil" justice (Rawls, the Utilitarians, etc.)? How *can* it be defended, if at all?

2. What are likely to be the arguments offered against a rule of the type in question?

3. How do you personally assess the balance of the arguments? Would it make any difference if you were told that an empirical study showed that, in a random sample of 100 welfare mothers who bought similar stereo sets for over $1500, 92% responded that they "regretted having spent my money on this item" when surveyed six months after the purchase?

4. Can the Wisconsin statute reasonably be stretched to cover a situation of the Williams type? Is this an appropriate area for "judge-made law" or is it only a legislative concern?

5. What are some actual statutes or legal doctrines that you believe to be plainly motivated by paternalistic objectives? Why is this whole line of inquiry indulged in a section on "uncertainty"?

6. It is easy to muddle a relevant distinction between paternalistic and *self-protective* rules. You may even have done so in thinking about some of the preceding questions. Consider, for instance, the "cooling off period" for door-to-door sales contracts or the waiting period traditionally required for a marriage license. How do these rules differ from prescription drug restrictions, the special provisions affecting minors, or an arguably "foolish" buyer such as Mrs. Williams?

Chapter III

INTERTEMPORAL ADJUSTMENTS OF
COSTS AND BENEFITS

INTEREST RATES AND "PRESENT VALUES"

In deriving an expected value, one converts a possibly very complex set of possibilities into a single value, the certainty equivalent of the prospect being considered. An analogous computation in temporal problems is the conversion of one or more future payments, perhaps differing greatly in timing and magnitude, into a single-valued sum that is the equivalent of the future payments. This time-adjusted equivalent is typically expressed in terms of a lump sum payment transferred immediately, i.e., a "present value." The application of this concept would be exemplified by a settlement negotiation wherein defendant offers either $800,000 paid in two annual installments beginning one year from now or 24 monthly payments of $40,000 beginning one month from now. Which is a better offer? In order to make the two rather different flows comparable, the most common procedure is to convert each individual future payment to its present lump sum equivalent, i.e., "discount" the future payments to their "present values." By summing the present values of the future payments called for in alternative streams, a decisionmaker reduces the information to intelligible and comparable terms. Although less frequently encountered, the reverse procedure may also be performed, i.e., computation of the flow of payments that can be achieved over a certain period by converting a lump sum to an equivalent stream of future receipts.

The following section explains very briefly the logic behind the use of interest rates to determine the comparability of different time streams of payments. Much more elaborate discussions may be found in elementary economics and business texts, but the treatment herein should suffice to deal with the subsequent legal application problems. Notwithstanding any attempt to render the principles involved in as simple a "commonsense" fashion as possible and to pro-

157

vide a variety of examples, the material of this chapter is inevitably somewhat quantitative and may be offputting to some. Nevertheless, one should be prepared to face the reality that there is no short-cut substitute for performing calculations when a quantity must be expressed as its equivalent at a different time period; the answer will not leap out of the page at you, even if the principles involved are thoroughly understood. Fortunately the growing accessibility of calculators and computers to lawyers will obviate any real computational drudgery. Still, one must take the time and have the diligence to ask even a computer the correct questions.

DISCOUNTING AND COMPOUNDING

Most people have very little difficulty in understanding how a present sum of money grows into a larger sum in the future. The holder of money can invest his original principal and earn interest during each period. The interest from the first period then becomes available as an addition to investible capital and, in turn, itself becomes a source of interest accumulation. Assuming a $1.00 initial sum and a 10% interest rate per period, the following numerical example could be developed. After one period, the original $1.00 would have grown to:

$$\$1.00 \ (110\%) = \$1.10$$

After the second period, the growth would have attained the level:

$$[\$1.00 \ (110\%)] \ (110\%) = \$1.21$$

where the square-bracketed term represents the new principal available after the first period's growth. At the end of three periods, the original $1.00 would be:

$$\{ \ [\$1.00 \ (110\%)] \ (110\%) \ \} \ (110\%) = \$1.33$$

where the numbers in the curley brackets indicate the reinvestible sum available from the previous two periods of growth.

Just a glance at the numerical example suggests a way of creating a general formula. For each period, we are just multiplying the original principal by 110% one more time. Hence, we could just as easily say that the three-period result is equal to $\$1.00 \ (110\%)^3$. Even better, the same reasoning supports the assertion that, after any arbitrary number of periods symbolized by the variable n, the value of a $1.00 invested at 10% compound interest will be $1.00 $(1.10)^n$. A full generalization occurs when we substitute symbols for all of the relevant parameters, not just the number of periods. This substitution yields the standard compound interest formula:

$$F = V(1+r)^n$$

where F is the future value at the end of n periods, V is the present or starting value and r is the periodic interest rate expressed as a decimal.

Note that the standard compound interest formula really tells us how a present sum V *transforms* into a future sum F. The formula answers the question: "If I have V dollars now and invest it at a compound interest of r per period, how much will I have after n periods?" In a relevant sense, F and V are "equivalents," assuming a passage of n periods and an earning rate of r. This "compounding" of interest and growth of the original capital is familiar to anyone who has a savings account.

A less familiar, but conceptually linked, question is: "If I need F dollars in the future, how much would I need to invest now in order to reach my goal?" A slight manipulation of the compound interest formula given above produces an equation that "solves" for the present value V rather than the future value F:

$$V = F/(1+r)^n$$

If I were originally entitled to receive F dollars at a time n periods from today, the formula suggests that I would presumably be indifferent to receiving the lesser sum V now, since it would grow to exactly the same sum by the appointed date. For similar reasons, I would presumably be indifferent as to whether I had to *pay* F in the future or V right now. "Discounting" a future sum to its "present value" equivalent involves dividing it by $(1+r)^n$ or, what amounts to the same thing, multiplying it by a "discount factor" equal to $1/(1+r)^n$.

The two tables provided below are very closely related. Exhibit 3.1 is a table of values of $(1+r)^n$ for various values of n and r. It may be used either for the compound interest formula (as a multiplicative "growth factor" applied to V) or for the present value formula (as the divisor applied to F). In essence, the entries in this table can be interpreted as the number of dollars to which one dollar will have grown when invested at the interest rate indicated on the column heading and for the number of periods indicated in the row heading. Exhibit 3.2 is a table of the *reciprocals* of the values in Exhibit 3.1, i.e., $1/(1+r)^n$. These are the multiplicative form of the "discount factors" that, when multiplied by the relevant future value F, will yield the present value equivalent V. The multiplicative factors table is perhaps more suggestive and easier to understand for discounting purposes because the numbers have an appealing commonsense interpretation as the cents-per-dollar that a future payment is worth in present value terms. The entries in both of the tables have been rounded and should not be regarded as exact.

At times, it is necessary to convert a stream of many future sums, each received at different times, into a single present value equivalent. The method for this is straightforward enough. Each of the individual future payments is separately discounted to its present value and then the present values are summed. The method is the same whether one is discounting future costs or future benefits.

There is a special formula that simplifies the computation of the value of a stream of payments when the payments are the same in each future period. Such a stream is called an "annuity" and its present value is:

$$V = A\,[1-(1+r)^{-n}]/r$$

where A is the amount of each periodic payment. Although the general annuity formula is complex to derive and difficult to remember accurately, it is worth committing to memory the special case of an annuity that goes on forever, i.e., a so-called "perpetuity." The present discounted value of $A per period received forever is simply:

$$V = A/r$$

Although the perpetuity may seem to have little real-world applicability, it is actually quite useful as a quick "rule of thumb" way of estimating the value of a stream. Remember that the value of a perpetuity of $A always constitutes an upper bound on how much a shorter stream could be worth. In fact, for annuities of any considerable length, the degree of overestimate is surprisingly small, especially for higher interest rates: for instance, at a 10% rate a 30-year annuity of $1 is worth $9.48 as compared to a perpetuity's $10; at a 20% rate it is worth $4.98 compared to $5.00 for a perpetuity.

The interest rate itself is, of course, the transformation rate between present and future money or, quite simply, the price of having money earlier in time. Lenders will require a higher-than-ordinary interest rate to the extent that they must bear certain risks regarding repayment. One of these is the risk of outright non-payment or default by the borrower. Thus, poor risks must generally pay higher interest rates because the "cost" of lending to them is in effect higher. Another risk borne by lenders is that the money returned on their investment will have depreciated in terms of purchasing power because of the impact of inflation. For this reason, expectations about inflation tend to cause the market interest rate to fluctuate in order to maintain an adequate "real" rate of interest.

QUESTIONS

1. Construct a rough graph with dollar values on the vertical axis and time on the horizontal axis. Draw a curve that you think reflects the "growth path" of $1 invested at 5% compound interest and

also at 10% interest. Check your results against Exhibit 3.1. Make sure that you understand why the curves have the shape that they do.

2.   Construct another similar graph and plot a curve that shows the present discounted value of $1.00 received at varying times in the future. Do this for 10% and 20% interest rates. How do your rough plots compare with the values in Exhibit 3.2? Is there any relationship between the shapes of the present curves and the curves in the previous question?

3.   Suppose that you had an 18-year old client who has been seriously injured in an accident. The tortfeasor's insurance company offers $100,000 per year for life to the victim in lieu of the $1,000,000 lump-sum judgment (net of litigation costs) that would be certainly achievable by going through to final judgment. Your client finds the offer attractive. What is your advice? (If the answer depends on facts not given, say what they are.)

4.   Look at the general formula for an annuity in the text above. Can you see why the formula for a perpetuity is so much simpler? What is the common sense of why the perpetuity formula is a close approximation of the true annuity value at reasonably long terms? And why is it an even closer approximation when the interest rates get higher?

EXHIBIT 3.1 Compound Interest Growth Factors

(Values of $(1+r)^n$)

Inter. Rates:	.01	.015	.02	.025	.05	.10	.12	.15	.20
n = 1	1.01	1.01	1.02	1.02	1.05	1.10	1.12	1.15	1.20
2	1.02	1.03	1.04	1.05	1.10	1.21	1.25	1.32	1.44
3	1.03	1.05	1.06	1.08	1.16	1.33	1.40	1.52	1.73
4	1.04	1.06	1.08	1.10	1.22	1.46	1.57	1.75	2.07
5	1.05	1.08	1.10	1.13	1.28	1.61	1.76	2.01	2.49
6	1.06	1.09	1.13	1.16	1.34	1.77	1.97	2.31	2.99
7	1.07	1.11	1.15	1.19	1.41	1.95	2.21	2.66	3.58
8	1.08	1.13	1.17	1.22	1.48	2.14	2.48	3.06	4.30
9	1.09	1.14	1.20	1.25	1.55	2.36	2.77	3.52	5.16
10	1.10	1.16	1.22	1.28	1.63	2.59	3.11	4.05	6.19
11	1.12	1.18	1.24	1.31	1.71	2.85	3.48	4.65	7.43
12	1.13	1.20	1.27	1.34	1.80	3.14	3.90	5.35	8.92
13	1.14	1.21	1.29	1.38	1.89	3.45	4.36	6.15	10.70
14	1.15	1.23	1.32	1.41	1.98	3.80	4.89	7.08	12.84
15	1.16	1.25	1.35	1.45	2.08	4.18	5.47	8.14	15.41
16	1.17	1.27	1.37	1.48	2.18	4.59	6.13	9.36	18.49
17	1.18	1.29	1.40	1.52	2.29	5.05	6.87	10.76	22.19
18	1.20	1.31	1.43	1.56	2.41	5.56	7.69	12.38	26.62
19	1.21	1.33	1.46	1.60	2.53	6.12	8.61	14.23	31.95
20	1.22	1.35	1.49	1.64	2.65	6.73	9.65	16.37	38.34
21	1.23	1.37	1.52	1.68	2.79	7.40	10.80	18.82	46.01

EXHIBIT 3.1 Compound Interest Growth Factors—Continued

(Values of $(1+r)^n$)

Inter. Rates:		.01	.015	.02	.025	.05	.10	.12	.15	.20
	22	1.24	1.39	1.55	1.72	2.93	8.14	12.10	21.64	55.21
	23	1.26	1.41	1.58	1.76	3.07	8.95	13.55	24.89	66.25
	24	1.27	1.43	1.61	1.81	3.23	9.85	15.18	28.63	79.50
	25	1.28	1.45	1.64	1.85	3.39	10.83	17.00	32.92	95.40
	26	1.30	1.47	1.67	1.90	3.56	11.92	19.04	37.86	114.48
	27	1.31	1.49	1.71	1.95	3.73	13.11	21.32	43.54	137.37
	28	1.32	1.52	1.74	2.00	3.92	14.42	23.88	50.07	164.84
	29	1.33	1.54	1.78	2.05	4.12	15.86	26.75	57.58	197.81
	30	1.35	1.56	1.81	2.10	4.32	17.45	29.96	66.21	237.38
	31	1.36	1.59	1.85	2.15	4.54	19.19	33.56	76.14	284.85
	32	1.37	1.61	1.88	2.20	4.76	21.11	37.58	87.57	341.82
	33	1.39	1.63	1.92	2.26	5.00	23.23	42.09	100.70	410.19
	34	1.40	1.66	1.96	2.32	5.25	25.55	47.14	115.80	492.22
	35	1.42	1.68	2.00	2.37	5.52	28.10	52.80	133.18	590.67
	36	1.43	1.71	2.04	2.43	5.79	30.91	59.14	153.15	708.80
	37	1.45	1.73	2.08	2.49	6.08	34.00	66.23	176.12	850.56
	38	1.46	1.76	2.12	2.56	6.39	37.40	74.18	202.54	1020.67
	39	1.47	1.79	2.16	2.62	6.70	41.14	83.08	232.92	1224.81
	40	1.49	1.81	2.21	2.69	7.04	45.26	93.05	267.86	1469.77
	50	1.64	2.11	2.69	3.44	11.47	117.39	289.00	1083.66	9100.44
	75	2.11	3.05	4.42	6.37	38.83	1271.90	4913.06	35672.87	868147
	99	2.68	4.37	7.10	11.53	125.24	12527.83	74573.45	1021142	69014980

EXHIBIT 3.2 Discount Factors

(Values of $1/(1+r)^n$)

Inter. Rates:		.01	.015	.02	.025	.05	.10	.12	.15	.20
n =	1	0.99	0.99	0.98	0.98	0.95	0.91	0.89	0.87	0.83
	2	0.98	0.97	0.96	0.95	0.91	0.83	0.80	0.76	0.69
	3	0.97	0.96	0.94	0.93	0.86	0.75	0.71	0.66	0.58
	4	0.96	0.94	0.92	0.91	0.82	0.68	0.64	0.57	0.48
	5	0.95	0.93	0.91	0.88	0.78	0.62	0.57	0.50	0.40
	6	0.94	0.91	0.89	0.86	0.75	0.56	0.51	0.43	0.33
	7	0.93	0.90	0.87	0.84	0.71	0.51	0.45	0.38	0.28
	8	0.92	0.89	0.85	0.82	0.68	0.47	0.40	0.33	0.23
	9	0.91	0.87	0.84	0.80	0.64	0.42	0.36	0.28	0.19
	10	0.91	0.86	0.82	0.78	0.61	0.39	0.32	0.25	0.16
	11	0.90	0.85	0.80	0.76	0.58	0.35	0.29	0.21	0.13
	12	0.89	0.84	0.79	0.74	0.56	0.32	0.26	0.19	0.11
	13	0.88	0.82	0.77	0.73	0.53	0.29	0.23	0.16	0.09
	14	0.87	0.81	0.76	0.71	0.51	0.26	0.20	0.14	0.08
	15	0.86	0.80	0.74	0.69	0.48	0.24	0.18	0.12	0.06
	16	0.85	0.79	0.73	0.67	0.46	0.22	0.16	0.11	0.05
	17	0.84	0.78	0.71	0.66	0.44	0.20	0.15	0.09	0.05
	18	0.84	0.76	0.70	0.64	0.42	0.18	0.13	0.08	0.04
	19	0.83	0.75	0.69	0.63	0.40	0.16	0.12	0.07	0.03
	20	0.82	0.74	0.67	0.61	0.38	0.15	0.10	0.06	0.03

EXHIBIT 3.2 Discount Factors—Continued

(Values of $1/(1+r)^n$)

Inter. Rates:	.01	.015	.02	.025	.05	.10	.12	.15	.20
21	0.81	0.73	0.66	0.60	0.36	0.14	0.09	0.05	0.02
22	0.80	0.72	0.65	0.58	0.34	0.12	0.08	0.05	0.02
23	0.80	0.71	0.63	0.57	0.33	0.11	0.07	0.04	0.02
24	0.79	0.70	0.62	0.55	0.31	0.10	0.07	0.03	0.01
25	0.78	0.69	0.61	0.54	0.30	0.09	0.06	0.03	0.01
26	0.77	0.68	0.60	0.53	0.28	0.08	0.05	0.03	0.01
27	0.76	0.67	0.59	0.51	0.27	0.08	0.05	0.02	0.01
28	0.76	0.66	0.57	0.50	0.26	0.07	0.04	0.02	0.01
29	0.75	0.65	0.56	0.49	0.24	0.06	0.04	0.02	0.01
30	0.74	0.64	0.55	0.48	0.23	0.06	0.03	0.02	.0042
31	0.73	0.63	0.54	0.47	0.22	0.05	0.03	0.01	.0035
32	0.73	0.62	0.53	0.45	0.21	0.05	0.03	0.01	.0029
33	0.72	0.61	0.52	0.44	0.20	0.04	0.02	0.01	.0024
34	0.71	0.60	0.51	0.43	0.19	0.04	0.02	0.01	.0020
35	0.71	0.59	0.50	0.42	0.18	0.04	0.02	0.01	.0016
36	0.70	0.59	0.49	0.41	0.17	0.03	0.02	0.01	.0014
37	0.69	0.58	0.48	0.40	0.16	0.03	0.02	0.01	.0011
38	0.69	0.57	0.47	0.39	0.16	0.03	0.01	.0049	.0009
39	0.68	0.56	0.46	0.38	0.15	0.02	0.01	.0042	.0008
40	0.67	0.55	0.45	0.37	0.14	0.02	0.01	.0037	.0006
50	0.61	0.48	0.37	0.29	0.09	0.01	.0034	.0009	.0001
75	0.47	0.33	0.23	0.16	0.03	.0078	.0002	.00003	.000001
99	0.37	0.23	0.14	0.09	0.01	.00008	.00001	.000001	.000000

DETERMINING THE VALUE OF A LEASEHOLD

In eminent domain condemnations, the taking of land under long-term lease frequently causes confusion as to the allocation of damages between the owner of the fee simple and the lessee. In the following segment of Kentucky Department of Highways v. Sherrod, 367 S.W.2d 844, at 850 (Ky.1963), the Commissioner quite properly is troubled by the damage calculation procedure adopted in another case:

As related to the leased parcel, and the determination of the respective damages of the landowners and the lessees, the evidence in this case was directed in a loose way towards application of the method outlined in City of Ashland v. Price, Ky., 318 S.W.2d 861. The key to this method is "to ascertain the present fair rental value, compare it with the rent stipulated in the contract and allow the aggregate difference for the period of the unexpired term of the lease" (318 S.W.2d 863).

Aside from the fact that the foregoing method furnishes no criterion or basis for determining the lessee's damages where only *part* and *not all* of the leased property is taken, we have come to the conclusion that the method is completely unsound, unfair, and unworkable.

Let us use an illustration that is not far from the actual facts of this case: The property as whole, if sold free and clear of the lease, would have a value of $100,000. The fair rental value would be $12,000 per year (there is testimony in this case that 12% rent is fair for commercial property). The lessees have contracted to pay only $6,000 per year. Their lease has 20 years to run. The state condemns the entire tract. By applying the method outlined in the Ashland case, the lessees would be damaged $120,000 ($6,000 per year for 20 years) or $20,000 more than the whole property was worth. This is so patently absurd as to establish beyond any question the fallaciousness of the method. The foregoing illustration is not at all inappropriate because in the instant case the lessees were paying $7,200 a year rent; they said the fair rental was $14,400 a year; their lease had 15 years to run; therefore their damage was $108,000. Yet they testified that the leased property as a whole was worth only $120,000 (one said it was worth only $105,000) and the state took less than one-fourth of the area and none of the structures.

QUESTIONS

1. Is the approach in City of Ashland v. Price "completely unsound and unworkable"? What is really wrong with the procedure?

2. Assume that the state took the entire property (and leasehold). On the other facts of the above case, about how much should have been awarded to the lessees as compensatory damages?

VALUING A PROPERTY ENCUMBERED BY A LEASE

Raines Land Co. is the owner of 70 acres of commercially zoned land on the outskirts of a small Virginia city. Fashion Shopping Centers, Inc. has entered into negotiations with Raines for a 99-year lease on the 70 acres. Under the proposed lease, Fashion will construct $30,000,000 worth of buildings and other permanent improvements on the property. Title to all such improvements vests in Raines immediately, but Fashion has full use and certain other specified rights, including that of subletting, during the term of the lease. Financial arrangements are that Fashion makes an $800,000 lump sum payment immediately, followed by monthly payments of $16,667 for the period of the lease. Fashion bears all normal expenses of ownership (e.g., maintenance of buildings, etc.) except for payment of any applicable local real property taxes, the latter being the responsibility of the landowner. The reversion value of the land and improvements 99 years hence is estimated at $3,000,000.

Local real estate taxes are levied at the rate of 2% of the assessed value of land and improvements. In turn, state statutes require assessed value to be based on "fair market value." State courts have construed fair market value to be the price that would be paid in an arms-length transaction by "a willing buyer and a willing seller."

Raines has other current offers to sell the land for $40,000 per acre. It believes that it could secure a long-term return of 10% on any investments made currently. If you believe that other relevant facts have been omitted, please make plausible assumptions.

QUESTIONS

1. Briefly relate the common sense of why the market value of any asset, such as the title to a land parcel, can be expected to be approximately equal to the present discounted value of the future flow of net receipts derivable from owning the asset. Net receipts should be understood as gross receipts (rental payments, etc.) minus any costs attributable to the owner (taxes, operating costs, etc.)

2. If Raines executes the lease, collects the $800,000, and then attempts to sell the property, what is your estimate of how much it could be sold for? Why?

3. The county tax assessor expects to bill Raines for $650,000 on an assessed valuation of $32,500,000 for the land and improvements. As Raines' attorney, would you advise him that he is liable for this full amount? Why?

4. Is Fashion liable for any part of the real estate taxes? Assume that the relevant state statute reads as follows:

*   *   *   For purposes of this chapter, and other provisions of law relating to the assessment of real estate for taxation, the term "taxable real estate" shall include a leasehold interest in every case in which the land or improvement, or both, as the case may be, are exempt from assessment or taxation to the owner. [Va. Code § 58–758.]

Except for the above section, the state code appears to make no provision for the taxation of a leasehold interest.

5. The "Bottom Line." What do you think of the proposed lease overall? Is it a good deal for Raines? For Fashion?

6. Should the value of a leasehold be taxable as real estate? What are the consequences of taxing or not taxing it?

PREJUDGMENT INTEREST ON DAMAGES

Since damages that would in principle accrue only in the future are subjected to "discounting" to present values, the awarding of interest on damages that ought in principle to have been paid at some past date may seem logically symmetrical. Nonetheless, the law has traditionally been hostile to the award of prejudgment interest on damages, especially when the claim is "unliquidated" or the cause of action sounds in tort rather than contract. The case of Busik v. Levine below represents a trend by state courts to award prejudgment interest on damages more liberally than heretofore.

BUSIK v. LEVINE

Supreme Court of New Jersey, 1973.
63 N.J. 351, 307 A.2d 571.

WEINTRAUB, C.J.

These cases involve the validity of R. 4:42–11(b), adopted on December 21, 1972, which authorizes prejudgment interest in tort actions.

* * *

Although it is said with respect to interest on claims that "in this country interest is generally of statutory origin," Consolidated Police and Firemen's Pension Fund Commission v. City of Passaic, 23 N.J. 645, 653, 130 A.2d 377, 382 (1957), the contrary is true in our State. The Legislature has dealt with usury; that is, it has fixed the upper limit of the interest for which an ordinary loan may be made, see N.J. S.A. 31:1–1, but there is no statute dealing with interest upon other obligations or claims or with interest upon judgments. The controlling rules have always been and remain judge-made.

And, briefly, these are the rules which the courts of this State developed: As to interest upon judgments, the practice permitted collection at the "legal" rate, that is, at the rate permitted to be contracted under the usury statute to which we have referred. With respect to prejudgment interest, our courts of law assessed interest, if the demand was liquidated, at the same "legal" rate on the assumption that the creditor could have earned such interest if his obligor had paid him what was due, see Jersey City v. O'Callaghan, supra, 41 N.J.L. at 354, but declined to allow interest on claims that were unliquidated. The justice of that limitation has been questioned, as we will develop in a moment. Our courts of equity allowed or withheld interest or fixed the rate as justice dictated. [Citations omitted.]

In this setting we adopted R.4:42–11 which reads:

"*Interest: Rate on Judgments; in Tort Actions.*

(a) *Rate.* Judgments, awards and orders for the payment of money and taxed costs shall bear interest at 6% per annum from the date of entry, except as otherwise ordered by the court.

(b) *Tort Actions.* In tort actions, including products liability actions, the court shall include in the judgment interest at 6% per annum on the amount of the award from the date of the institution of the action or from a date 6 months after the date of the tort, whichever is later. The contingent fee of an attorney shall not be computed on the interest so included in the judgment."
*   *   *

We turn then to the merits. Interest is not punitive, Wilentz v. Hendrickson, 135 N.J.Eq. 244, 255–257, 38 A.2d 199 (E. & A.1944); here it is compensatory, to indemnify the claimant for the loss of what the moneys due him would presumably have earned if payment had not been delayed. We mentioned earlier the judge-made limitation that interest should not be allowed if the claim was unliquidated. That limitation apparently rested upon the view that a defendant should not be deemed in default when the amount of his liability has not been adjudged. But interest is payable on a liquidated claim when liability itself is denied, even in good faith, Kamens v. Fortugno, 108 N.J.Super. 544, 552–553, 262 A.2d 11 (Ch.Div.1970). The fact remains that in both situations the defendant has had the use, and the plaintiff has not, of moneys which the judgment finds was the damage plaintiff suffered. This is true whether the contested liability is for a liquidated or for an unliquidated sum. For that reason, the concept of a "liquidated" sum has often been strained to find a basis for an award of interest.

It is said there is now, in general, a willingness to allow interest on unliquidated claims as justice may dictate. 22 Am.Jur.2d, Damages, Section 181, pp. 259–260. In upholding the retrospective application of a New York statute providing for interest in contract actions upon unliquidated damages, the United States Supreme Court observed that "The statutory allowance is for purpose of securing a more adequate compensation by adding an amount commonly viewed as a reasonable measure of the loss sustained through delay in payment," and that "It has been recognized that a distinction, in this respect, simply as between cases of liquidated and unliquidated damages, is not a sound one." Funkhouser v. J.B. Preston Co., 290 U.S. 163, 168, 54 S.Ct. 134, 136, 78 L.Ed.2d 243, 246 (1933).

So also, a refusal to allow interest in tort matters has been criticized. See Moore-McCormack Lines v. Amirault, 202 F.2d 893 (1 Cir. 1953). It is questioned whether justice is thereby done as between parties to the suit. But beyond their interest, there is also a public stake in the controversy, for tort litigation is a major demand upon the judicial system. Delay in the disposition of those cases has an impact upon other litigants who wait for their turn, and upon the taxpayers who support the system. And here there is a special inducement for delay, since generally the claims are covered by liability insurance, and when payment is delayed, the carrier receives income from a portion of the premiums on hand set aside as a reserve for pending claims. See In re Insurance Rating Board, 55 N.J. 19, 258 A.2d 892 (1969). Hence prejudgment interest will hopefully induce prompt defense consideration of settlement possibilities. In that meaningful way, prejudgment interest bears directly upon the judicial machinery and the problems of judicial management. It is this facet, added to the consideration of justice between the litigants, which warrants our holding that prejudgment interest be payable in these matters.

The proposition we thus accept is not uniquely ours. There are a number of States which so provide by statute. [Citations omitted.] We add, parenthetically, that it is of no moment that there the principle was established by Legislature. As we have already noted, the subject of interest on claims rests wholly in case law in our State, and, assuming as we do for the moment that the issue is one of substantive law, the power and responsibility of the judiciary to deal with the subject in the absence of a statute cannot be questioned.

We see no strength in the assertion that the allowance of interest duplicates some element of damage or constitutes a payment with respect to damages not yet experienced. The jury is not instructed to add interest to its verdict in tort cases. In any event an instruction to the jury can obviate the risk. And with respect to the criticism that a verdict may embrace losses not yet suffered, the answer is that a verdict necessarily anticipates future experience, and the interest factor simply covers the value of the award for the period during which the defendants had the use of the moneys to which plaintiffs are found to be entitled. We think the equities are met when the date for the commencement of liability for interest is fixed as set forth in paragraph (b) of R.4:42–11 (the rule here under attack).

* * *

Finally we add that we see no merit in the proposition advanced by the intervenor, that the usual insurance policy, which provides for payment of interest upon a judgment, does not cover prejudgment interest and therefore we should not impose such liability. It is enough to say the carrier's obligation to pay the judgment plainly includes the obligation to pay the constituent elements of damage incorporated in that judgment, among which, of course, is the item of prejudgment interest.

* * *

The final question is whether the rule denies equal protection because it is limited to tort actions.

We see no serious issue. To begin with, tort actions are a distinctive class of litigation having a special impact upon the administration of the judicial system in terms of volume. They are distinctive too insofar as overall there is insurance coverage permitting to invest for gain portions of the premiums allocated to the reserve for pending claims. Further, problems of this kind may be met in stages or on the basis of intensity. Hence it is no solid objection that a rule, whether announced in a judicial opinion or in a rule of court, does not go as far as it might. See New Jersey Chapter, American Institute of Planners v. New Jersey State Board of Professional Planners, 48 N.J. 581, 601–603, 227 A.2d 313 (1967), appeal dismissed, 389 U.S. 8, 88 S.Ct. 70, 19 L.Ed.2d 8 (1967). Finally the adoption of the rule does not foreclose holders of other liquidated claims from contending the circumstances which attend their scene are so like the circumstances here involved that interest should also be allowed to them.

* * *

The judgments are affirmed.

CONFORD, P.J.A.D., Temporarily Assigned, dissenting.

* * *

* * * Were it necessary to decide whether the substance of the rule should be embraced judicially by the Court as a matter of substantive law, I would conclude in the negative, at least as to the rule as drawn. The primary objection to it is its mandatory nature. There would be no serious objection to the principle of prejudgment interest if its application were subject to the discretion of the trial court in the particular case, as it continues to be the rule on interest in equity and in relation to unliquidated damages in contract cases. See Small v. Schuncke, 42 N.J. 407, 415–416, 201 A.2d 56 (1964); Consolidated Police &c., Pension Fund Commn. v. Passaic, supra, 23 N.J. at 655, 130 A.2d 377. The justice of making the defendant pay the claimant for the use of the money declared due during the pendency of the action is as pertinent to the contract or equitable obligor as to the tort obligor. Yet the sanction of interest remains discretionary in the former instances. And for good reason! Experience teaches that in many situations the winner of a money award is nevertheless denied costs by the court because of equities the other way. Why disarm the trial judge of discretion to deny, or to allow only partial prejudgment interest in tort cases when a comparable balance of equities points in that direction?

As one of numerous illustrations which might be afforded, there might be intervening appeals between institution of action and final judgment, inordinately protracting the interest-payment period under the rule, yet where the occasion for the appeal was not attributable to acts of the defendant but to those of the trial court or the plaintiff. Defendant may even have prevailed on such appeals. Must interest be nevertheless inexorably awarded the plaintiff for the entirety of the intervening period before final judgment without the tempering discretion of the judge? Or suppose the defendant tenders at the outset a settlement offer which the plaintiff unreasonably refuses. Under the rule as framed this is irrelevant to the accrual of the interest. Cf. R.4:58–3.

The main rationale advanced for the rule is that it merely transfers to the plaintiff interest which defendant or his insurer was drawing on money which theoretically was due the plaintiff the moment the tort took place or the action instituted. But not all tort defendants are insured; many are insured for substantially less than the trial award; and many, who are not insured at all or are insufficiently insured, may be relatively impecunious. Torts encompass not only automobile and product liability cases, but defamation, malicious prosecution, interference with economic opportunity, household negligence and miscellaneous other causes of action where insurance may well be non-existent, spotty or inadequate, and where defenses may be advanced in good faith. In such instances the defendant may not have actually earned interest on the award during the intervening period, or on the total amount of the award, and allowance of prejudgment interest on the whole award could well operate oppressively or unfairly. Surely discretion should be reposed in the trial court in all cases to control the matter.

It is difficult to resist the impression that the impelling motivation for adoption of the rule was clearance of trial dockets in automobile and kindred insured-tort situations by imposing coercive pressure on insurance companies to settle cases early. But beyond the observation above that others than insurers may be penalized by the rule, it does not seem fair to assume, as does the rule, that only defendants or their insurers are responsible for unreasonable failures of litigants to arrive at pretrial settlements. The rule may well operate to encourage unreasonable recalcitrance on the part of some plaintiffs. It is a blunderbuss which strikes its objects indiscriminately and without necessary regard to the justice of its effect in particular cases. In my view it does not, as drawn, calendar control in a justifiable manner.

* * *

QUESTIONS

1. If a claim is unliquidated, it is alleged, the defendant does not know how much is owed. Compare the situation of a liquidated claim and uncertain liability to that of certain liability but uncertain magnitude of damages. Specifically, Defendant A knows that, if he is found liable, the damages payable are a liquidated claim of exactly $100,000, but it is a "coin flip" as to whether liability will be found. In another case, Defendant B has no doubt that he is liable for some sum, but there are equal probabilities that the judgement against him will be $50,000 or $150,000. Is there any relevant distinction with respect to the equities of charging prejudgement interest?

2. What effect, if any, would the giving of prejudgement interest have on the incentive to settle cases out of court?

3. The dissent makes the point that the defendant may not have been earning money on the funds. First of all, is this correct? If it *is* correct, does it matter?

"BACK DOOR" PREJUDGEMENT INTEREST?

In many jurisdictions, an attorney may confront a statute that appears to bar interest on past damages. All is not necessarily lost, however, as the following case demonstrates. As you read this case, reflect on what legal advice might be useful to a client as a similar situation enters its very early, pre-litigation stages.

UNITED TELECOMMUNICATIONS, INC. v. AMERICAN TELE-VISION AND COMMUNICATIONS CORP.

United States Court of Appeals, Tenth Circuit, 1976.
536 F.2d 1310.

[Telephone company which exchanged its interest in a cable television company for shares of defendant corporation brought action for breach of contract and breach of warranty in that defendant failed to use its best efforts to register its shares. Plaintiff was therefore unable to sell the shares and was deprived of the use of the business capital that would have been secured from the anticipated sale. The U.S. District Court for the District of Colorado entered judgment for plaintiff and defendant appealed. Among other allegations of error, defendant alleged that it was error for the court to charge the jury that United was entitled to recover interest costs or borrowing costs paid as a result of ATC's breach of the agreement.]

WILLIAM E. DOYLE, Circuit Judge.

This is a diversity action in which the appellant was defendant in the trial court and suffered the award of a judgment based on a jury verdict in the amount of $2,021,500. The action brought by plaintiff-appellee was for a breach of contract and breach of warranty. The case was filed December 5, 1973 and was tried in March 1975.

* * *

At the trial United presented testimony which showed the amount of its borrowing and the nexus between these costs and the breach of ATC. United also presented testimony showing that ATC was aware before entering into the agreement that United had planned to convert the ATC stock to cash and would use that cash to reduce its short-term debts. Evidence was also offered to show that parties were aware that registration was necessary in order to have a successful public sale of the stock and that they were also aware that a private sale could be obtained only at a significant discount. For this element of damage United claimed the sum of $1.6 million.

The trial court explained to the jury that the plaintiff was claiming that it suffered an additional direct loss "by being unable to reduce its short term debt by the amount of money which it would have received on the sale to the public of the registered shares of ATC stock." The trial court also explained that the claim was that the cost of continued borrowing was a part of actual damages from the breach. The court then continued:

> "As to this claim, you must find from a preponderance of the evidence that this was a natural and probable consequence of the claimed breach of contract by the defendant and also that at the time the parties entered into the contract, the defendant reasonably could have anticipated from the facts and circumstances which it then knew or should have known, that these damages would probably be incurred by the plaintiff if the defendant breached the contract."

ATC claims that this instruction was erroneous. Its argument is that the instruction allowed United to recover prejudgement interest, and that applicable Colorado law bars such interest. United responds that this is not prejudgement interest in that it is not the kind of interest contemplated by the Colorado statutes and, instead, it is, according to United, borrowing costs that are recoverable like any other element of contract damage.

In general, we agree with the United argument and with the position taken by the trial court that interest as an item of damages or loss related to the substantive claim differs from interest measured by a percentage of the judgement. In our view the kind of interest that was here awarded is not barred or limited by the Colorado interest Statute and the Colorado cases. Here our concern is with United's borrowing costs and expenses. The Colorado statute does not deal with interest charges which arise from an independent debt owed by the plaintiff to a third party. So even on the assumption that the law of Colorado governs, it would not be the Hays v. Arbuckle [72 Colo. 328, 211 P. 101 (1922)] line of cases together with the interest statute that apply.

Had United claimed damages of $8 million for lost market value stemming from the stock not being registered together with interest measured by a percentage of that loss, the claim would have been one for prejudgement interest subject to the limitations of the Colorado law. When United claims, however, that it is entitled to recover from ATC expenses which resulted from interest which it was obligated to pay on money which it was required to borrow as a result of ATC's unwarranted delays and manipulations, a wholly different theory is presented. This latter type of interest is not regulated by the Colorado interest statute.

So, having determined that the substantive rights here asserted by United are governed by general damage principles, we need not pursue the Hays v. Arbuckle doctrine as to the choice of law in the area of prejudgement interest. Contractual rights such as we are here considering are under Colorado law governed by the place where the contract was made and the place designated by the parties as governing. See Western Enterprises, Inc. v. Robo Sales, Inc., 28 Colo.App. 157, 470 P.2d 931 (1970). In this case, that is North Carolina.

Finally, we consider whether the North Carolina court would allow recovery of borrowing costs and expenses as an element of damages. We conclude that it would and does. North Carolina recognizes that a party injured by a breach of contract has a right to be compensated "insofar as this can be done by money." Also, "he is entitled to be placed in the same position he would have occupied if the contract had been performed." Perfecting Service Co. v. Produce Dev. & Sales Co., 259 N.C. 400, 131 S.E.2d 9, 21 (1963). Accord, Tillis v. Calvine Cotton Mills, Inc., 251 N.C. 359, 111 S.E.2d 606 (1959). Indeed, North Carolina has specifically endorsed the doctrine of Hadley v. Baxendale, 9 Ex. 341 (1854). See Perkins v. Langdon, 237 N.C. 159, 74 S.E.2d 634, 643 (1953), holding that a defendant is liable for damages based upon proximate cause and foreseeability, including damages flowing from "special circumstances known and communicated." See Perkins, supra, 237 NC. at 170, 74 S.E.2d at 643; *Tillis*, supra; Chesson v. Kieckhefer Container Co., 215 N.C. 112, 1 S.E.2d 357 (1939); Industrial Circuits Co. v. Terminal Comm., Inc., 26 N.C. App. 536, 216 S.E.2d 919 (1975). The instruction given by the court in which foreseeability is the guide is in accord with North Carolina law on the subject. None of the cases cited are closely analogous to the present case with the possible exception of Gulf States Creosoting Co. v. Loving, 120 F.2d 195 (4th Cir. 1941).

Cases from other jurisdictions do give credence to the proposition here approved. See New Amsterdam Cas. Co. v. Mitchell, 325 F.2d 474 (5th Cir. 1963) (additional interest on construction loan because of builder's delay); Thompson v. Hanson, 6 Wash.App. 1, 491 P.2d 1065 (1971) (semble); Herbert & Brooner Construction Co. v. Golden, 499 S.W.2d 541 (Mo.App.1973) (semble); Repinski v. Clintonville Federal S & L Ass'n, 49 Wis.2d 53, 181 N.W.2d 351 (1970) (recovery of additional interest charge because of S & L's promise to loan money at favorable rates.)

* * *

We disagree with ATC's contention that in its instruction on damages the court gave the jury a license to speculate. It is well settled that the difficulties in assessing damages do not preclude an injured party from recovering compensation. See Bigelow v. RKO Radio Pictures, Inc., 327 U.S. 251, 265, 66 S.Ct. 574, 90 L.Ed. 652 (1945).

The judgment of the district court is affirmed.

QUESTIONS

1. Suppose that United admitted that, had it received the funds on time, it still would have borrowed the same amount of money. E.g., suppose that they would have declared it as dividends to stockholders. Logically, should that make any difference to their damage claim?

2. As a practical matter, what does the court's view suggest as to how a potential plaintiff should act when a cause of action for some loss arises? Are courts equally likely to recognize outlays and "opportunity costs" (foregone returns) as damages?

PREJUDGEMENT INTEREST ON PENALTIES

As the above cases suggest, the old rules against prejudgement interest on compensatory damages in civil cases are gradually breaking down in most jurisdictions. By contrast, the right to moratory interest on penalties—or other sums whose purpose is clearly punitive—receives surprisingly little attention. The general rule in federal cases derives from Rodgers v. United States, 332 U.S. 371, at 373–74, 68 S.Ct. 5, at 6–7, 92 L.Ed. 3 (1947):

> As our prior cases show, a persuasive consideration in determining whether such obligations shall bear interest is the relative equities between the beneficiaries of the obligation and those upon

whom it has been imposed. And this Court has generally weighed these relative equities in accordance with the historic judicial principle that one for whose financial advantage an obligation was assumed or imposed and who has suffered actual money damages by another's breach of that obligation, should be fairly compensated for the loss thereby sustained. See, e.g., Brooklyn Savings Bank v. O'Neil, supra; United States v. North Carolina, 136 U.S. 211, 216, 10 S.Ct. 920, 922, 34 L.Ed. 336; Funkhouser v. J.B. Preston Co., 290 U.S. 163, 168, 54 S.Ct. 134, 136, 78 L.Ed. 243.

The contention is hardly supportable that the Federal Government suffers money damages or loss, in the common law sense, to be compensated by interest, when one convicted of a crime fails promptly to pay a money fine assessed against him. The underlying theory of that penalty is that it is a punishment or deterrent and not a revenue-raising device; unlike a tax, it does not rest on the basic necessity of the Government to collect a carefully estimated sum of money by a particular date in order to meet its anticipated expenditures. For the foregoing reasons, this Court's holding that a criminal penalty does not bear interest, Pierce v. United States, 255 U.S. 398, 405, 406, 41 S.Ct. 365, 367, 368, 65 L.Ed. 697, is consistent with its holding that the Government does suffer recoverable damages if a taxpayer fails to pay taxes when due and is therefore equitably entitled to interest. Billings v. United States, supra. Furthermore, denial of interest on criminal penalties might well be rested on judicial unwillingness to expand punishment fixed for a criminal act beyond that which the plain language of the statute authorizes.

QUESTIONS

1. The language of the Court suggests that legislatures may have set penalties as deterrents. If interest is not added to penalties, does the amount of deterrent (or retributive punishment) associated with the same *nominal* fine change with circumstances?

2. Treble damages under the antitrust statutes provide an interesting mixed case of compensatory and "other" damages. Clearly, the single damages are compensatory. Various hypotheses exist as to the motivation of Congress with respect to the other two-thirds of the damage assessment. It has been suggested, for instance, that the additional damages are deterrent in nature and/or that they operate as an incentive "bounty" to plaintiffs who provide what are in effect private enforcement services. Federal courts have been generally unsympathetic to the award of prejudgement interest in antitrust

cases. In addition to the *Rodgers* rule, many courts seem to feel that interest would result in excessive recovery:

> Interest should not be allowed in antitrust actions where the statute provides for punitive damages. Treble damages compensate a plaintiff handsomely for all his losses, including the loss of the use of money rightfully his. [Trans World Airlines, Inc. v. Hughes, 308 F.Supp. 679, 696 (S.D.N.Y.1969).]

What is your own analysis of whether pre-judgement interest should be granted in antitrust actions?

2. Plaintiff alleges that it was deprived of profits amounting to $2,000,000 during fiscal 1981. If prejudgement interest were permitted on any part of the damages, would 17% presumptively be the proper rate if plaintiff had contracted $2,000,000 or more of medium term indebtedness at that rate during 1981?

3. If plaintiff files for and recovers the full $2,000,000 trebled, what is the latest year in which it can receive the damages (after litigation, possible appeal, etc.) and still be fully compensated for its loss if no prejudgement interest is awarded?

4. Assume that defendant has the same rate of return on capital as plaintiff. In contemplating the original offense, defendant had reason to believe that the odds against its being successfully prosecuted and fined were three to two (three out of five). Would a change in the rule on prejudgement interest be likely to affect its conduct?

5. Under what circumstances might the interest rates of plaintiff and defendant differ materially? In such cases, which rate should be used if prejudgement interest were given?

6. Describe the possible rationale for a "bounty" to antitrust plaintiffs in terms of an externalities or "public goods" effect of bringing such suits.

EVALUATING LOST FUTURE INCOME AS DAMAGES

Exhibits 3.3 and 3.4 represent the types of damage calculations sometimes presented by forensic economists in wrongful death or personal injury cases wherein an important component of damages is the lost future income of the victim. It is instructive to consider the types of predictive input that underly such calculations and the legitimate bases for argument about the conclusions reached.

Column (3) reflects a projection of future income in terms of dollars of current purchasing power. Such constant purchasing power measures of income are frequently called "real" income, as opposed to "nominal" income measured in dollars that may be depreciated in value due to future inflation. Both Exhibits assume a base year in-

come of $20,000 and project future gains in real income at a rate of
1% compounded annually. This rate of increase is presumably an estimate of gains in the individual's productivity, the scarcity of his
skills, etc.

Column (4) is a key difference between the two sets of calculations. The actual dollars earned in any future year will to some extent be determined by the rate of overall inflation in prices in the
economy. Hence, column (4) adjusts the constant purchasing power
income upward by an additional growth factor to account for the influence of inflation. Exhibit 3.3 assumes a 7% rate of inflation while
Exhibit 3.4 assumes a higher rate of 10%. In effect, nominal income
grows by 8% annually (1% real and 7% inflation) in Exhibit 3.3 and
11% (1% real and 10% inflation) in Exhibit 3.4. Note that the alternative assumptions about inflation rates produce substantially different
damage calculations.

EXHIBIT 3.3 Lost Income Damages

Real Income Growth = 1.0%   Inflation Rate = 7.0%

(1) Future Year	(2) Age	(3) Constant $ Income	(4) Inflated Income	(5) Investment Yield %	(6) Discount Factor	(7) Present Value	(8) Cumulative PV Sum	Age
1	60	20200.00	21600.00	10.50	.90497738	19547.51	19547.51	60
2	61	20402.00	23328.00	11.10	.81016202	18899.46	38446.97	61
3	62	20606.02	25194.24	12.37	.70477235	17756.20	56203.17	62
4	63	20812.08	27209.78	13.47	.60322007	16413.48	72616.66	63
5	64	21020.20	29386.56	14.00	.51936866	15262.46	87879.11	64
6	65	21230.40	31737.49	14.00	.45558655	14459.17	102338.29	65
7	66	21442.71	34276.49	14.00	.39963732	13698.16	116036.45	66
8	67	21657.13	37018.60	14.00	.35055906	12977.21	129013.66	67
9	68	21873.71	39980.09	14.00	.30750794	12294.20	141307.86	68
10	69	22092.44	43178.50	14.00	.26974381	11647.13	152954.99	69
11	70	22313.37	46632.78	14.00	.23661738	11034.13	163989.12	70
12	71	22536.50	50363.40	14.00	.20755910	10453.38	174442.50	71
13	72	22761.87	54392.47	14.00	.18206939	9903.20	184345.70	72
14	73	22989.48	58743.87	14.00	.15970999	9381.98	193727.69	73
15	74	23219.38	63443.38	14.00	.14009648	8888.19	202615.88	74
16	75	23451.57	68518.85	14.00	.12289165	8420.39	211036.28	75
17	76	23686.09	74000.36	14.00	.10779969	7977.22	219013.49	76
18	77	23922.95	79920.39	14.00	.09456114	7557.36	226570.85	77
19	78	24162.18	86314.02	14.00	.08294836	7159.61	233730.46	78
20	79	24403.80	93219.14	14.00	.07276172	6782.79	240513.25	79

Columns (5), (6), and (7) reflect the process of "discounting" the
lost future income (in nominal dollars) to its present value equivalent.
Thus, if r stands for the decimal equivalent of the column (5) term
interest rate available in a year n years in the future, as indicated by
column (1), then column (6) is the appropriate discount factor $1/(1 + r)^n$ for the nth period. Next, column (7) is calculated as the product

of the column (6) discount factor times the lost income from column (4).

Finally, column (8) aggregates the present values of the damages for each future year. If it were known, for instance, that the victim had been deprived of exactly 13 years worth of future income, then the relevant damage total as computed in Exhibit 3.3 would be $184,345.70. By contrast, the higher rate of inflation assumed in Exhibit 3.4 yields damages of $219,579.13.

EXHIBIT 3.4 Lost Income Damages

Real Income Growth = 1.00%   Inflation Rate = 10.0%

(1)	(2)	(3)	(4)	(5)	(6)	(7)	(8)	
Future Year	Age	Con-stant $ Income	Inflated Income	Investment Yield %	Discount Factor	Present Value	Cumulative PV Sum	Age
1	60	20200.00	22200.00	10.50	.90497738	20090.50	20090.50	60
2	61	20402.00	24642.00	11.10	.81016202	19964.01	40054.51	61
3	62	20606.02	27352.62	12.37	.70477235	19277.37	59331.88	62
4	63	20812.08	30361.41	13.47	.60322007	18314.61	77646.49	63
5	64	21020.20	33701.16	14.00	.51936866	17503.33	95149.82	64
6	65	21230.40	37408.29	14.00	.45558655	17042.71	112192.53	65
7	66	21442.71	41523.20	14.00	.39963732	16594.22	128786.76	66
8	67	21657.13	46090.76	14.00	.35055906	16157.53	144944.29	67
9	68	21873.71	51160.74	14.00	.30750794	15732.33	160676.62	68
10	69	22092.44	56788.42	14.00	.26974381	15318.32	175994.95	69
11	70	22313.37	63035.15	14.00	.23661738	14915.21	190910.16	70
12	71	22536.50	69969.01	14.00	.20755910	14522.71	205432.86	71
13	72	22761.87	77665.60	14.00	.18206939	14140.53	219573.39	72
14	73	22989.48	86208.82	14.00	.15970999	13768.41	233341.80	73
15	74	23219.38	95691.79	14.00	.14009648	13406.08	246747.88	74
16	75	23451.57	106217.89	14.00	.12289165	13053.29	259801.17	75
17	76	23686.09	117901.85	14.00	.10779969	12709.78	272510.96	76
18	77	23922.95	130871.06	14.00	.09456114	12375.32	284886.27	77
19	78	24162.18	145266.87	14.00	.08294836	12049.65	296935.92	78
20	79	24403.80	161246.23	14.00	.07276172	11732.55	308668.48	79

As might be imagined, the presentation of such damage calculations is frequently disputed quite vigorously at trial. Before reading further, you should reflect on how differences in the combinations of assumptions underlying the calculations will affect the ultimate damage figure. Also, it is worth attempting to determine exactly how exhibits such as Exhibits 3.3 and 3.4 are computed. If you have access to a calculator, check a few of the entries in each Exhibit in order to test your understanding of the underlying calculations.

QUESTIONS

1. What evidence is available to suggest how many years of future income have been lost? How controversial is the use of such evidence likely to be?

2. On what basis can any assumption about real income growth be supported? What kind of expert would be best qualified to do this projection, and what facts would he be relying upon?

3. How does one know what interest rates to use in the discounting process? The exhibits provided above use the "term" rates for each relevant maturity interval. Is that correct? Should a "risk free" rate, such as that on government securities, be used even if the plaintiff would predictably choose to invest in securities that impose some additional risk in exchange for a higher rate of return?

4. Would an economic expert be able to predict the future rate of inflation? With what accuracy? Would different experts be likely to disagree greatly on the future rate of inflation?

5. Compare the relative reliability of the different assumptions underlying tables such as Exhibits 3.3 and 3.4.

6. Under all of the other assumptions of Exhibit 3.3, how would the damages change if the rate of growth in real income were assumed to be 4% instead of 1%? [No calculations will be necessary here if you carefully compare Exhibits 3.3 and 3.4.]

BEAULIEU v. ELLIOTT

Supreme Court of Alaska, 1967.
434 P.2d 665.

DIMOND, Justice.

As a result of an automobile accident on April 13, 1963, James Elliott suffered a fracture dislocation of his right ankle. He brought this action for damages against Richard Beaulieu, and the issue of damages was termed by the court without a jury. The trial court filed findings of fact and conclusions of law and entered judgment awarding Elliott $169,937.25 compensatory damages, costs of $82.40, and attorney's fees in the amount of $13,870.29.

*   *   *

The trial court did not reduce the amount it found as damages for future impairment of earning capacity to present value. Instead, the court stated that "The interest rate reduction and decline in purchasing power of the dollar is off-set by pay increases plaintiff could have expected in the future from his military service." Beaulieu contends that the failure to reduce the damages to present value was prejudicial error.

The general principle underlying the assessment of damages in tort cases is that an injured person is entitled to be replaced as nearly as possible in the position he would have occupied had it not been for the defendant's tort.[10] In the case of impairment of future earning capacity, it is reasoned that a failure to reduce damage to present value would be to place the injured person in a better position than he would have occupied except for the defendant's tort, because the injured person would get all of his future wages long in advance and would be able to invest the lump sum and realize earnings on such investment during the intervening period.[11] For this reason—that money has the power to earn money—it has become the generally accepted rule that damages awarded for future loss of earnings should be reduced to present worth.[12]

In applying the general rule, the Supreme Court of Washington has stated a formula for reducing awards of future earnings to present value which involves the "rate of interest (which) could fairly be expected from safe investments which a person of ordinary prudence, but without particular financial experience or skill, could make in that locality." Wentz v. T.E. Connolly, Inc., 273 P.2d at 492. This formula, although empirical at best, is probably as definite as any that has been devised. But we believe that the rule for reducing awards, including the formula applied by the Washington court, ignores facts which should not be ignored. Annual inflation at a varying rate is and has been with us for many years. There is no reason to expect that it will not be with us in the future. This rate of depreciation offsets the interest that could be earned on government bonds and many other "safe" investments. As a result the plaintiff, who through no fault of his own is given his future earnings reduced to present value must, in order to realize his full earnings and not be penalized by reduction of future earnings to present value, invest his money in enterprises, other than those which are considered "safe" investments, which promise a return in interest or dividends greater than the offsetting rate of annual inflation. But ours is a competitive economy. By their very nature some enterprises backed by inves-

---

10. Hill v. Varner, 4 Utah 2d 166, 290 P.2d 448, 449 (1955); Restatement, Torts, Section 924 comment d, at 634–35 (1939); McCormick, Damages, Section 86, at 304 (1935). Accord United States v. Hatahley, 257 F.2d 920, 923 (10th Cir. 1958); Hughett v. Caldwell County, 313 Ky. 85, 96, 230 S.W.2d 92 (1950).

11. McCormick, Damages, Section 86, at 304 (1935).

12. Wentz v. T.E. Connolly, Inc., 45 Wash.2d 127, 273 P.2d 485, 491 (1954); Borcherding v. Eklund, 156 Neb. 196, 55 N.W.2d 643, 650 (1952); Daughtry v. Cline, 224 N.C. 381, 30 S.E.2d 322, 324 (1944); Rigley v. Prior, 290 Mo. 10, 233 S.W. 828, 832 (1921); Restatement, Torts, Section 924 comment d, at 634–35 (1939); McCormick, Damages, Section 86, at 304 (1935); Annots., 77 A.L.R. 1439, 1446 (1932) 154 A.L.R. 796, 797 (1945).

tors' money are going to fail with resulting loss to individuals. Thus, instead of being assured of earnings at rates greater than the annual rate of inflation, the injured plaintiff stands a chance of entirely losing his future earnings by unlucky or unwise investments. Since the plaintiff, through the defendant's fault and not his own, has been placed in the position of having no assurance that his award of future earnings, reduced to present value, can be utilized so that he will ultimately realize his full earnings, we believe that justice will best be served by permitting the trier of fact to compute loss of future earnings without reduction to present value. The plaintiff is more likely to be restored to his original condition under the rule we adopt than under the prevailing rule which calls for a discounting of the award for future earnings.

Our conclusion is fortified by another factor which also may not be ignored. This is the factor, relied upon by the trial judge, which involves wage increases that the injured plaintiff might have expected to receive in the future had he not been injured. It is a matter of common experience that as one progresses in his chosen occupation or profession he is likely to increase his earnings as the years pass by. In nearly any occupation a wage earner can reasonably expect to receive wage increases from time to time. This factor is generally not taken into account when loss of future wages is determined, because there is no definite way of determining at the time of trial what wage increases the plaintiff may expect to receive in the years to come. However, this factor may be taken into account to some extent when considered to be an offsetting factor to the result reached when future earnings are not reduced to present value. Thus, if there is any fear that failure to reduce the present value will give the plaintiff more than he is entitled to because of the possibility of his making successful investments of the sum awarded at returns greater than the annual rate of inflation, such fear is obviated by the fact that the award may well be deficient in that it does not take into account probable wage increases that the plaintiff would ordinarily be expected to receive in the future.

Elliott testified that he would receive disability retirement pay from the Air Force in the amount of $191.00 a month for the remainder of his life. Beaulieu contends that the trial judge committed prejudicial error in refusing to deduct the net present value of future retirement pay from the award for future loss of earnings. Beaulieu's argument is that to allow Elliott damages for future wage loss, in addition to his retirement pay, is to unjustly enrich Elliott by allowing him double compensation for his injuries.

The general principle underlying the assessment of damages in tort cases is that an injured person is entitled to be replaced as nearly possible in the position he would have occupied had it not been for the defendant's tort. Elliott has been in the Air Force for about 18 years at the time of his discharge and he testified that he had intended to remain the service for at least 20 years. If he had not been injured, Elliott could have continued to earn to his full capacity and, in addition, after 20 years' service, would have been entitled to retire and draw retirement pay. By reason of his injuries, Elliott was entitled under law to be retired early for disability and draw retirement pay in lieu of retirement on a regular basis after completion of 20 years' service. The award of damages for impaired earning capacity has the effect of putting Elliott in the same position he would have occupied had it not been for the injury, because the damages represent what Elliott could have earned had he not been injured and the disability retirement pay represents that which Elliott had earned and become entitled to under law by reason of his years of service in the Air Force. In other words, Elliott now receives an amount representing wages he could have earned were it not for the injury, plus retirement pay; had he not been injured, he would have received the full wages he could have earned during his remaining work life, in addition to receiving the retirement pay to which he would become entitled by reason of his years of service in the Air Force. Thus, Elliott, under the court's award, is getting no more than he would have gotten had he not been injured. The disability retirement pay Elliott is receiving should not be used to mitigate damages and reduce the award for loss of future earnings.

Beaulieu argues that the trial judge erred in failing to deduct from the damages awarded for impairment of future earning capacity an amount representing income taxes that Elliott would have had to pay on future income.

The courts are divided on this question. It is the more general view, supported by a majority of American decisions, that an amount representing future income taxes should not be deducted from the award. Annot., 63 A.L.R.2d 1393, 1396 (1959). As was stated by the Supreme Court of Rhode Island:

> This view has been adopted by the various courts on diverse grounds but primarily on the ground that the quantum of such taxation is of necessity in the realm of conjecture.

Oddo v. Cardi, 218 A.2d 373, 377 (R.I.1966). [Other citations omitted.]

We adopt the majority rule. Income tax rates, provisions relating to deductions and exemptions, and other aspects of income tax laws and regulations are so subject to change in the future that we believe that a court cannot predict with sufficient certainty just what amounts of money a plaintiff would be obliged to pay in federal and state income taxes on income that he would have earned in the future had it not been for a defendant's tortious conduct. We hold that a damage award for impairment of earning should not be reduced by an estimated amount representing income taxes that the injured party may be required to pay on future income. In awarding damages to Elliott for impaired earning capacity, the court did not err in failing to take income tax consequences into consideration.

The rule we adopt has no application, however, as to the court's award of past wages in the amount of $10,000. The reason for the rule—inability to predict with sufficient certainty what taxes would have to be paid—does not exist here, because taxes on income earned prior to trial can be easily calculated based on income tax laws and regulations as they existed at the time the wages would have been earned. The court erred in failing to deduct from the award for past loss of wages the income taxes Elliott would have had to pay had he earned the amount awarded prior to the trial.

Elliott testified that he had not lost any military pay or allowances between the date of the accident in April 1963 and the date of his military discharge in January 1966. During that period of time Elliott was either hospitalized or on leave, except for the period January to August, 1964, when he was on duty status. The trial court awarded $10,752.85 for a partial past wage loss covering the period from the date of the accident to the day of Elliott's discharge from the Air Force, but excepting the period between January and August, 1964, when Elliott was on duty status.

Beaulieu contends that this award for past wages was error. His argument in essence is that the general principle underlying the assessment of damages in tort cases is that the injured person is entitled to be replaced as nearly as possible in the position he would have occupied had it not been for the defendant's tort, and that since Elliott suffered no loss of wages during the period involved he should be awarded none.

In arguing that the award should be sustained, Elliott urges the adoption of the collateral source rule, which provides that damages may not be diminished or mitigated on account of payments received by plaintiff from a source other than the defendant. Bell v. Primeau, 104 N.H. 227, 183 A.2d 729, 730 (1962). The collateral source rule is followed in most jurisdictions. Annot., 7 A.L.R.3d 516, 520 (1966). We applied this rule as to workmen's compensation benefits in Ridgeway v. North Star Terminal & Stevedoring Co., 378 P.2d 647, 650 (Alaska 1963). We apply the rule in this instance. By entering the military service, Elliott in effect agreed to perform certain duties and functions in exchange for certain benefits to be given him by the government. One of those benefits was that he was to receive military pay and allowances during periods of physical incapacity from performing his duties. This was in the nature of a contractual arrangement between Elliott and the government when he became a member of the armed forces, and which he may have paid for by accepting wages lower than those he might have obtained from the performance of like duties in civilian life. The income that Elliott received from the government is not the result of earnings, but of such previous contractual arrangement.

Such a contractual arrangement was made for Elliott's own benefit, and not for the benefit of a tort feasor, such as Beaulieu. The latter has no right to claim the benefit of such an arrangement by having the damages awarded against him reduced by the amount that Elliott was paid by the government during the period of his disability. The trial court did not err in awarding damages for loss of wages during the period of Elliott's disability while he was still in the military service.

The court awarded Elliott $71,244 for pain and suffering that he would experience for the remainder of his life. Beaulieu contends that the evidence does not justify such an award. * * * We agree with the foregoing. As we stated in Patrick v. Sedwick, 413 P.2d 169, 176 n. 21 (Alaska 1966), there is no fixed measure of compensation in awarding damages for pain and suffering, and such an award necessarily rests in the good sense and deliberate judgment of the tribunal assigned by law to ascertain what is just compensation. We can see nothing manifestly unfair or unjust about the method used by the trial court in assessing damages for future pain and suffering. In fact, as we suggested in the dissenting opinion in the Kansas case of Caylor v. Atchison, Topeka & Santa Fe Ry. Co., 190 Kan. 261, 374 P.2d 53, 64 (1962), it appears to be a fair argument and a rational approach to treat damages for pain the way it is endured—day by day, month by month, year by year. Ultimately, however, the question for decision is whether the total sum is reasonable or not, regardless of how it was arrived at. We find no error in the method used by the trial court in awarding damages for future pain and suffering.

* * *

Beaulieu contends that the total sum awarded is unreasonable and is grossly excessive. We shall not set aside an award on a claim of excessiveness unless it is so large as to strike us that it is manifestly unjust, such as being the result of passion or prejudice or a disregard of the evidence or rules of law. Considering the evidence of permanent damage to Elliott's ankle, the osteomyelitis, and the pain and suffering that he is likely to endure for the remainder of his life, it is our opinion that the award for future pain and suffering was not manifestly unjust. And Beaulieu did not contend in his brief or in oral argument that the trial court acted through passion or prejudice.

Beaulieu contends that the court erred in not reducing the future pain and suffering award to present value. He relies principally on the case of Affett v. Milwaukee & Suburban Transp. Corp., 11 Wis.2d 604, 106 N.W.2d 274, 279 (1960), where the court, after disapproving of the use of a mathematical formula for computing damages for pain and suffering, said: "Logically, if this method were followed, the gross amount arrived at should be discounted to its present worth."

If an award for future pain and suffering must be reduced to present value when a mathematical formula is used, it must be for the same reason that an award for future earnings is discounted under the prevailing rule—i.e., because the plaintiff receives his damages for the future long in advance and is able to invest the sum awarded and realize earnings during the intervening period. But we have held that as to impairment of future earning capacity, the award should not be reduced to present value. The same reasoning applies here as to an award for future pain and suffering. Because of the annual rate of inflation offsetting dividends or interest that may be expected on "safe" investments, and of the risk of loss involved in making other investments, a plaintiff is more likely to be restored to his original condition had defendant not committed his tort by allowing the plaintiff his award for future pain and suffering without reduction to present worth.

[At this point, the court commenced a long discussion of factual findings which, it determined, were not adequate to permit a clear understanding by the reviewing court as to the basis for some aspects of the disability calculus. Hence, the case was remanded to superior court for purposes of clarifying certain specific factual issues.]

DOCA v. MARINA MERCANTE NICARAGUENSE, S.A.

United States Court of Appeals, Second Circuit, 1980.
634 F.2d 30.

* * * The final and most significant question raised by this appeal is whether and to what extent an award for lost future wages should be adjusted because of inflation. If an adjustment for inflation is to be made, two approaches are available. Under the first method the projection of current wages is increased to reflect the fact that the employee would have received cost of living increases to keep pace with inflation. The sum of those increased annual wage figures is then discounted to present value by the prevailing interest rate. See United States v. English, 521 F.2d 63, 75 (9th Cir. 1975). Under the second method the discount rate is decreased below the prevailing interest rate to reflect the estimated rate of inflation.

This reduced discount rate is then applied to the sum of the current wages projected to continue for each of the years for which wages will be lost. See Feldman v. Allegheny Airlines, Inc., 382 F.Supp. 1271 (D.Conn.1974), aff'd, 524 F.2d 384, 387–88 (2d Cir. 1975). If the same estimated inflation rate is used, the "outcome of the calculation under either approach would be very nearly identical," *Feldman*, supra, 524 F.2d at 391 (Friendly, J., concurring).

In this case the District Court took inflation into account, to an unspecified extent, apparently by using the second approach and adjusting for future inflation by decreasing the present value discount. The Court did not provide a computation for its award for loss of future earnings; however, Judge Duffy stated that he had reached his result by "considering both probability of continued inflation and a discount to present value." Doca infers that Judge Duffy used a discount factor of 1%.[4] Defendants object to this computation for lack of evidence to support an estimate of future inflation and, more fundamentally, on the ground that any adjustment for inflation is impermissible. Since the significance of inflation on damage awards for lost future wages seems to be as persistent a problem as inflation itself, the matter merits some examination.

In this Circuit, the issue has been considered but not resolved. In McWeeney v. New York, New Haven, & Hartford R.R. Co., 282 F.2d 34 (2d Cir.) cert. denied, 364 U.S. 870, 81 S.Ct. 115, 5 L.Ed.2d 93 (1960), the issue was whether the calculation of lost future wages should be made on the basis of gross wages or net wages after deduction for income taxes. In rejecting a deduction for taxes, but see Norfolk and Western Railway v. Liepelt, 444 U.S. 490, 100 S.Ct. 755, 62 L.Ed.2d 689 (1980), this Court noted that whatever benefit this gives to plaintiffs is partially offset by the absence of an upward adjustment for inflation. A decade later in Yodice v. Koninklijke Nederlandsche Stoomboot Maatschappij, 443 F.2d 76 (2d Cir. 1971), a damage award for lost wages was reversed for reasons that included the failure to apply any discount for present value. Judge Friendly presciently noted that "if inflation should continue at its present

---

4. Doca derives this 1% discount rate in the following manner. The difference between the award for lost wages, $352,560, and Doca's projection of future lost wages, $394,861, is $42,301. This difference represents approximately 1% of $352,560, multiplied by the 12 years for which future wages will be lost. Expressed as a formula, the computation would have been $x + (12i)x = w$, where x is the discounted value, i is the interest rate, and w is the projection of total future wages. If the District Court applied a 1% rate in this fashion (and we cannot be certain if the award for lost future wages was determined on this basis), the discount factor was incorrectly applied. The correct method is to apply to the future wages for each year a discount factor of $1/(1 + i)^n$, where i is the interest rate and n is the year for which present value of income is sought. See Dullard v. Berkeley Associates Co., 606 F.2d 890 at 895 n. 4. The discounted amounts for each year are then added together to determine the total award.

pace, courts may have to reconsider the propriety of the long recognized charge with respect to discount." Id. at 79.

More recently this Court, in a diversity case, approved District Judge Blumenfeld's use of an " 'inflation-adjusted discount rate' " of 1.5%. Feldman v. Allegheny Airlines, Inc., supra, 524 F.2d at 387. This rate was determined by subtracting the average annual change in the consumer price index over each of several periods of years from the effective annual interest on government bonds held during each of the same periods, and then selecting the average of the rates resulting from these subtractions. Feldman v. Allegheny Airlines, Inc., supra, 382 F.Supp. at 1306–12. The purpose of this method was to determine the " 'real yield' " of money, the portion of interest charged on virtually risk-free investments that represents only the real cost of the money and not the additional cost the lender exacts as a hedge against future inflation. Id. at 1293. Judge Friendly concurred *dubitante*, noting that the decision represented a prediction as to unsettled state law and not "a precedent on the inflation problem in a case arising under federal law." 524 F.2d at 390, 393. In another diversity case, Dullard v. Berkeley Associates Co., 606 F.2d 890, 896 (2d Cir. 1979), this Court was willing to assume the propriety of an inflation-adjusted discount rate only for purposes of ruling that even with such an adjustment applicable to lost future wages, the total award in question was excessive. Most recently, the Court, in a Federal Tort Claims Act case, approved use of a present value discount rate that had been reduced to 5% from the prevailing interest rate to reflect future inflation. Espana v. United States, 616 F.2d 41 (2d Cir. 1980).

Among other courts, there has been a growing recognition that inflation should be taken into account in damage calculations. At least four federal Courts of Appeals have explicitly so ruled, see Steckler v. United States, 549 F.2d 1375–78 (10th Cir. 1977); United States v. English, supra, 521 F.2d at 72–76; Riha v. Jasper Blackburn Corp., 516 F.2d 840, 843–45 (8th Cir. 1975); Bach v. Penn Central Transportation Co., 502 F.2d 1112, 1122 (6th Cir. 1974), as have a number of state courts, see e.g., Beaulieu v. Elliott, 434 P.2d 665 (Alaska 1967); Schnebly v. Baker, 217 N.W.2d 708 (Iowa 1974); Halliburton Co. v. Olivas, 517 S.W.2d 349 (Tex.Civ.App.1974). In addition, the commentators generally favor this position. See Dennis, Sirmon & Drinkwater, "Wrongful Death Damages," 47 Miss.L.J. 173 (1976); Formuzis & O'Donnell, "Inflation and the Valuation of Future Economic Losses," 38 Mont.L.Rev. 297 (1977); Henderson, "The Consideration of Increased Productivity and the Discounting of Future Earnings to Present Value," 20 S.D.L.Rev. 307 (1975); Hopkins, "Economics and Impaired Earning Capacity in Personal Injury Cases," 44

Wash.L.Rev. 351 (1969); Note, "Future Inflation, Prospective Damages, and the Circuit Courts," 63 Va.L.Rev. 105 (1977).

Though the Supreme Court has yet to rule definitively on the issue, it clearly indicated its approval of including inflation estimates in future wage loss awards in Norfolk and Western Railway v. Liepelt, supra. The issue in that case was whether wage loss should be estimated without deduction for estimated income taxes. The Court ruled that such a reduction should be made. The opinion is instructive on the issue of inflation for two reasons. First, the Court noted that the plaintiff's economic expert had estimated that the lost future earnings would have increased by five percent a year until the wage-earner's retirement. More significantly, the Court rejected the argument that reduction for future income taxes would be too speculative by noting that other aspects of a damage award computation, specifically including "future inflation," are also matters of "estimate and prediction." 100 S.Ct. 758. Thus, the Court not only noted that the award included an estimate for inflation, but also used the reasonableness of making such an estimate as support for similar estimates of future taxes. See also Grunenthal v. Long Island R. Co., 393 U.S. 156, 89 S.Ct. 331, 21 L.Ed.2d 309 (1968), in which the Court approved a damage award based upon anticipated wage increases attributable to inflation.

Although the view that inflation should be considered is clearly on the increase, several federal courts including three Courts of Appeals, have prohibited the adjustment of awards for future wages to account for inflation. See Johnson v. Penrod Drilling Co., 510 F.2d 234 (5th Cir. 1975) (en banc); Magill v. Westinghouse Electric Corp., 464 F.2d 294, 299–301 (3d Cir. 1972); Williams v. United States, 435 F.2d 804 (1st Cir. 1970). The principal rationale for these decisions is that estimates of future inflation are too speculative to serve as a basis for calculating damages.

We believe that the developing majority view is sound and that inflation should be considered in estimating the present value of lost future wages. According to the figures computed by the United States Department of Labor, inflation has become a constant feature of our modern economy. The Consumer Price Index, perhaps the leading indicator of inflation has increased in all but two years since the beginning of World War II, and in every year since 1955. This increase was particularly pronounced during the past decade, when the Index increased by five times as much as it had during the previous decade. In 1979, the year in which the District Court decided this case, the average annual Consumer Price Index was 217.4, compared to 100 in 1967, the base year, and 72.1 in 1950.[7] * * * In short,

7. Thus, if Doca had received a damage award for twelve years' future
wages in 1967, fully discounted to present value at then prevailing interest

courts cannot fail to recognize that inflation is a dominant factor on the current economic scene and, despite episodic recessions, is likely to be so for the foreseeable future.

To be sure, the idea that a person's future income will increase in dollar amount is a prediction, one based largely on our inductive assumption that the future will resemble the past. But using inductive inferences about economic conditions to adjust the value of an award for lost future income is hardly novel. In fact, it underlies the practice of discounting future lost wages to the present value of the right to receive such wages. This practice, first required by the Supreme Court in 1916, *Chesapeake & Ohio Ry. v. Kelly*, 241 U.S. 485, 36 S.Ct. 630, 60 L.Ed. 1117 (1916), and routinely followed by courts throughout the nation ever since, rests on the inductive inference that interest rates will continue at their present value. If interest rates decline after the lump sum award is received, the plaintiff will normally fail to realize the full dollar amount of the lost future wages.[8] If it is permissible, indeed required by *Kelly*, to make a prediction about interest rates, it seems as reasonable to make a prediction about inflation as well. See *Steckler*, supra, 549 F.2d at 1377.

In fact, as Judge Blumenfeld demonstrates by the data collected in *Feldman*, there is a fairly constant relationship between interest and inflation rates, so that it is more reasonable to make a prediction about the relationship of both rates than about the level of interest rates alone. Discounting without regard to inflation charges the plaintiff for that portion of the prevailing cost of money that represents the lenders' anticipation of inflation without allowing the plaintiff an offsetting addition for inflation, either by increasing the sum to be discounted or reducing the discount rate. Or, to put in another way, discounting necessarily includes a prediction about inflation (the

rates, and had invested this award at those prevailing interest rates with the intention of drawing out one-twelfth each year, his yearly amount, despite the interest, would have declined steadily in purchasing power. For the final year, 1979, the money would have been worth only 42% of what it was worth when the award was made.

8. At a minimum the plaintiff will earn compound interest only at the reduced prevailing interest rate. If the plaintiff invests his lump-sum award (plus earned interest) annually, he will also suffer a decrease of simple interest because of the reduced rates. It is possible for the plaintiff to avoid this latter reduction by investing his lump-sum award in long-term bonds, corresponding to the length of time for which the wages are lost. Yet if the plaintiff makes that type of investment, he takes the risk that if interest rates increase, the market value of his bonds will decrease, and he will suffer a loss each time he sells a bond to meet current needs. One way to avoid that risk is to purchase a series of bonds ranging in maturities from one year up to the number of years for which the wages were lost. That assures that each year's needs will be met from the proceeds of a maturing bond, without the risk of selling a bond at a discount. However, the average rate of such a series of short, medium, and long-term bonds will most likely be less than the rate on long-term bonds, which was used to discount the future wages to present value.

prediction made by those who determine the interest rate), and it is neither reasonable nor fair to use that prediction only to reduce an award instead of endeavoring to determine an award that approximates the present value of what the future wages would have been. Economics should not be an instrument for the undercompensation of plaintiffs. It should be used to achieve a realistic estimate of future conditions, so that an injured plaintiff can be compensated for his loss as fairly and completely as possible.[9]

The principal argument advanced against taking inflation into account is that it is too speculative. There can be no doubt that predicting next year's inflation rate is at least as hazardous a task as forecasting next year's weather. This concern about speculation persuades us to be rather cautious in determining the way in which inflation should be taken into account, but, for three reasons, is not sufficient to preclude any adjustment for inflation. First, the law of damages frequently recognizes the need to make some predictions about the future, despite the uncertainties of doing so. Estimates of lost future profits are an obvious example. See Autowest, Inc. v. Peugeot, Inc., 434 F.2d 556, 564–67 (2d Cir. 1970). Second, since discounting future lost wages to present value uses an interest rate that reflects inflation, the issue is not whether inflation is too speculative to be considered at all; it is whether inflation, as a component of interest rates, should be considered for the defendant (by discounting at the prevailing interest rate) but ignored for the plaintiff (by rejecting any compensating adjustment for inflation). Finally, and most important, as *Feldman* illustrates, it is entirely feasible to take inflation into account without making any prediction as to the specific level of future inflation rates. All that is needed is a prediction that in the future inflation rates will bear approximately the same relationship to long-term interest rates that they have in the past. Essentially the only premise for that prediction is that over the course of years investors in long-term bonds will demand returns that reflect the prospects of future inflation. They may guess wrong in some years and accept rates that fail to keep pace with inflation. "Yet common sense suggests," as Judge Friendly has pointed out, "that investors will not tolerate such a situation indefinitely." *Feldman,* supra, 524 F.2d at 392. These considerations persuade us that inflation is not too speculative to be taken into account in determining

---

9. It is worth noting that when the Supreme Court declared its present value discount rule in 1916, it was able to look back on an era when prices, though fluctuating, were not generally increasing. The estimated Consumer Price Index for 1916 stood at 32.7, having varied between 25 and 51 during the course of the previous century. Looking backward over the past four decades from 1980, rather than 1916, reveals an entirely different economic landscape, in which prices have increased almost every year, often at an accelerating rate.

awards for future lost wages. See Norfolk and Western Railway v. Liepelt, supra.

The next question is how inflation should be considered. Courts have favored various methods, which can generally be divided into two basic categories. In the first category are those methods that submit the question of the inflation rate to the factfinder, so that a separate determination is made in each case. In this category, one method treats the rate of future inflation as a fact to be proved by evidence, presumably expert opinion. See, e.g., United States v. English, supra, 521 F.2d at 75–76. Another method forbids evidence, but permits the fact-finder to apply his own knowledge and prediction in estimating a future inflation rate. See, e.g., Bach v. Penn Central Transportation Co., supra, 502 F.2d at 1122–23. A third method permits the fact-finder to apply his own knowledge but also permits expert testimony. See, e.g., Riha v. Jasper Blackburn Corp., supra, 516 F.2d at 845. In the other basic category are methods that remove the issue from the fact-finder and instead adopt a rule of law that focuses on a constant relationship between inflation and interest rates. Using this approach, the Alaska Supreme Court held that the inflation rate will be assumed to equal the interest rate, thereby eliminating any discount for present value. See Beaulieu v. Elliott, supra. A somewhat different technique was used in *Feldman*, where it was observed that over a period of years the inflation rate bore a relatively constant relationship to the interest rate, averaging 1.5% less; the Court used this 1.5% rate as a discount rate, reflecting the true cost of money with the effect of inflation removed.

Having considered these alternatives, we are not prepared to require any one particular method by which inflation should be taken into account in estimating lost future wages. Predictive techniques are constantly being refined, as are methods of correctly assessing the immediate past. If litigants prefer to offer evidence as to future rates of both inflation and interest, they are entitled to do so. We note, however, that one virtue of the *Feldman* approach is that it lessens trial disputes concerning the future impact of inflation. The average accident trial should not be converted into a graduate seminar on economic forecasting. The adjusted discount rate approach of *Feldman* avoids all predictions about the level of future inflation, and focuses instead only on the relationship between the inflation rate and the interest rate. Since that relationship is relatively constant in periods of stable inflation, as the historical data set forth in *Feldman* reveal, it may frequently be possible for litigants to agree on an adjusted discount rate, derived from that type of historical data. Without requiring a particular adjusted rate, we suggest that a 2% discount rate would normally be fair to both sides.

A 2% discount rate appears to be the estimate of the true cost of money appropriate for use in a computation whose purpose is to determine the present value of lost future wages. As Judge Blumenfeld recognized in *Feldman*, 2% is the real yield normally attainable during periods of low, stable rates of inflation. *Feldman*, supra, 383 F.Supp. at 1239, 1310 (Table A–II). It is also a figure that lies within the narrow range bracketed by many economists as representing the true yield of money.[10] *Feldman* used the slightly lower rate of 1.5% to allow "a margin of error to compensate for unexpected increases in the rate of inflation which may depress long term real yields." Id. at 1294 (footnote omitted). It may well be that during periods of unusually high inflation rates, interest rates will lag somewhat behind the inflation rate, at least temporarily, with the result that the interest return on a discounted lump sum award will not fully keep pace with inflation. But in such periods of high inflation, wages too will not keep pace with inflation.

In the only three years since 1947 when the rate of the annual increase in the Consumer Price Index (CPI) exceeded 8%, the annual rate of wage increases (non-farm weekly earnings) has been less than the annual rate of CPI increases by at least 3 percentage points; in all other years since 1947, wages have increased at a rate greater than the rate of increase within 1 percentage point of the CPI percentage increase. Thus, since there is little reason to expect that injured plaintiffs would have received wage increases sufficient to keep pace with unusually high rates of inflation, a present value discount rate normally need not be reduced below 2% just to compensate for unusually high inflation. To do so would ignore the basic objective of

10. Although economists disagree over the validity of the assumption that the real rate of interest is constant and consequently independent of inflation, cf. Fama, Interest Rates and Inflation: The Message in the Entrails, 67 Amer.Econ. Rev. 487 (1977) (real estate constant) with Carlson, Short-Term Interest Rates as Predictors of Inflation: A Comment, 67 Amer.Econ.Rev. 469 (1977) (real estate varies), there is substantial opinion that during periods of stable rates of inflation, the real yield of money, whether constant or slightly fluctuating, is approximately 2%, as estimated in *Feldman*. As Sharpe has suggested, an appropriate period for determining investor expectations of inflation and real rates of return is 1959–1972, when actual real returns may have been fairly close to expected real returns. W. Sharpe, Investments 170 (1978). For this period the *Feldman* calculation approximates 2%. Moreover, studies by economists, though taking different positions concerning the relation between the real rate and expectations about inflation, have estimated that the real rate of interest was between 1.5% and 3% for a similar time frame. See, e.g., Carlson, supra at 471 (expected real rate fluctuates around 2.5% during 1953–1975); Elliott, Measuring the Expected Real Rate of Interest: An Exploration of Macroeconomic Alternatives, 67 Amer.Econ.Rev. 429, 440 (1977) (mean expected real rate 1.44% for 1960–1974); Gibson, Interest Rates and Inflationary Expectations: New Evidence, 62 Amer. Econ.Rev. 854, 856 (1972) (real rate between 2% and 3% during 1952–1970); But cf. W. Sharpe, supra, at 170 (extrapolating from 1976 study by Ibbotson & Sinquefield, average actual real rate 1.2% for 1959–1972).

selecting a present sum of money that will replace what the future wages would have been.

We emphasize that we are not requiring the use of an adjusted discount rate, nor specifying that when such a rate is used, it must be set at 2%. Litigants are free to account for inflation in other ways, or, if they use the adjusted discount rate approach, to offer evidence of a rate more appropriate than 2%. But in the hope that disputes about the appropriate rate may be minimized, we simply suggest the 2% rate as one that would normally be fair for the parties to agree upon, and we authorize district judges to use such a rate if the parties elect not to offer any evidence on the subject of either inflation or present value discount.

Obviously, in this case the District Judge could not have been expected to anticipate this opinion. Nevertheless, his calculation of an award for lost future wages must be reconsidered for two reasons. First, if we assume, as the plaintiff urges, that a 1% discount rate was used, there is nothing in the evidence to support a reduction of the discount rate from prevailing interest rates all the way down to 1%. As indicated, the lowest discount rate we are willing to approve, in the absence of historical data justifying a different rate, is 2%. Second, the District Court to some extent gave duplicate consideration to the impact of inflation. In estimating what Doca's future wages would have been, the Court took into account a post-trial wage increase of 80¢ an hour, specified in Doca's union contract to take effect on October 1, 1970. Having based future lost wages on this cost of living increase, the Court then further reflected the impact of inflation by reducing the discount rate to 1%. When a discount rate is adjusted to reflect inflation, it must be applied to a stream of earnings calculated without regard to inflation, even to a cost of living increase already scheduled to occur. The certainty of such an increase does not lessen the fact that it reflects inflation, which is already accounted for by the reduced discount rate.

We therefore vacate the damage award and remand to the District Court for recomputation of the award for lost future wages in accordance with this opinion.

QUESTIONS

1. What are the courts in Beaulieu and Doca trying to do? Compare the approaches in the two cases. Which is more likely to be "right" in the sense of giving the most nearly correct quantum of damages? Is there any possible counterargument that the less exact approach is, all things considered, preferable? [For a review of recent cases on this general subject, see Note, "Inflation, Productivity,

and the Total Offset Method of Calculating Damages for Lost Future Earnings," 49 U.Chi.L.Rev. 1003 (1982).]

2. For purposes of discounting damages, what is the appropriate interest rate? At any moment of time, there are a host of different interest rates varying with the degree of risk of the creditor and the term of the loan or investment. Why is a "riskless" rate, such as the government bond rate usually used, rather than some higher rate?

3. Can you generate any argument that, regardless of the term of years by which the lump sum award anticipates future damages, the discount rate should be based upon short or intermediate-term interest rates rather than the (usually higher) long-term interest rates? What relevance does this have to the 2% discount rule suggested in Doca?

4. In Norfolk and Western Railway Co. v. Liepelt, 444 U.S. 490, 100 S.Ct. 755, 62 L.Ed.2d 689 (1980), the Supreme Court gave its approval to the consideration of the effect of taxes on the lost future income for which compensation is being given. Heretofore, damages have traditionally been calculated by discounting the stream of *before-tax* income to its present value. Suppose that the full effect of taxation were reflected in damage awards. Is it possible to say whether awards would be higher or lower than under the method where taxes are not considered? How difficult would it be to make the requisite adjustments? We return to this topic later in the present chapter, but it is worth forming a tentative opinion at this time.

CULVER v. SLATER BOAT CO.

United States Court of Appeals, Fifth Circuit, 1982.
688 F.2d 280.

JOHN R. BROWN, Circuit Judge:

This case comes before us on rehearing en banc to consider whether the holding of this Court in Johnson v. Penrod Drilling Co., 510 F.2d 234 (5th Cir. 1975) (en banc), that neither proof, nor argument, nor jury instructions concerning inflationary factors may be considered or used in maritime, Jones Act and FELA personal injury and wrongful death actions, should be overruled. After careful consideration of this singular issue, we overrule *Penrod* and remand this case to the District Court.

* * *

We agree with the critics that *Penrod* represents an idea whose time has passed. In an era of inflation, which has been with us for over forty years, it is quite clear that plaintiffs are unfairly penalized by their absolute inability to present evidence of a historical fact—inflation. The likely effect of inflationary trends upon future wages is forbidden even though *Penrod* allows evidence from defendants regarding the applicable discount rate which has been increased by the very inflation so roundly excluded.

However, we are less than satisfied with the so-called Alaska Rule, which by assuming that the discount rate and the inflation rate are virtually identical, unnecessarily penalizes defendants because * * * interest rates on relatively safe investments will typically ride several percentage points above the rate of inflation. In addition, tied as it is to changes in the Consumer Price Index (CPI), the result would unfairly award the plaintiff the difference between the changes in the CPI and the actual or average increase in wages.

We are much impressed with, but certainly not willing to embrace uncritically, *Feldman's* approval of an inflation-adjusted discount rate in the neighborhood of 1.5.%. This view represents a compromise between the Alaska rule's penalizing of defendants and *Penrod's* penalizing of plaintiffs. However, fixing the inflation-adjusted discount rate at 1.5%, or even 2% or 3%, would subject this Court to criticisms not unlike those aimed at *Penrod* and even the Alaska Rule. In the dynamic and ever-changing world of finance and economics, we as judges cannot rule out that the interest rate on risk-fee investments might equal the inflation rate during a certain period such that the Alaska Rule is vindicated. Indeed, the logic behind the Alaska Rule is that in an economy of ups and downs, "it will all come out in the wash"—the interest rate and the inflation rate being, on the average, roughly equivalent. However, any standard which is inflexible in a dynamic economy will likely be unable to cope with the problem of preventing windfalls either to plaintiff or defendant. Although a perfect method may never be found, we must attempt to create standards that are fair to both sides of the controversy, with the trier of fact being allowed to receive and act upon credible evidence of the economic facts bearing, pro and con, on the competing theories.

* * *

Various methods are available that allow the plaintiff to ensure consideration of the effects of future inflation on lost wages. We have already discussed the inflation-adjusted discounted rate (or real rate of interest) used in *Feldman*. Although we find such an approach acceptable, and certainly superior to the *Penrod* or Alaska Rule approach, we must emphasize that defendants must be permitted to demonstrate the likelihood that the plaintiff's wages have not kept up with inflation. Given this additional factor, the *Feldman* approach becomes less simple. Another approach * * * allows the plaintiff to present evidence of average annual national, local or occupational wage increases over the past several decades, and thereby to present an average annual increase in wages due to merit, productivity, promotion, or cost of living increases. This may, in some cases, be a simpler approach. Other approaches will likewise be found acceptable, insofar as they permit the plaintiff to show likely wage increases, due to inflation or any other reason, and at the same time allow defendants to present evidence of relatively risk-free investments in the economy that would allow a plaintiff to replace lost income in future years.

Jury Instructions

Where the case is tried to a jury, instructions are required. Without attempting to write or construct a suggested charge, we point out that the instructions may take several different forms depending on the permissible methodology used.

If the *Feldman* approach is used with its inflation-adjusted discount rate (real rate of interest), the jury must make three separate determinations. First, they must consider and determine all of the future income losses on the basis of the plaintiff's present income and, in addition, any increases that the plaintiff would likely have received due to merit, productivity, or promotion, but *not* inflation. In determining future merit raises or promotions, it should be made clear to the jury that any portion of such increases due to inflation or cost of living raises should not be added into the aggregate sum. Second, the jury must determine, on the basis of the evidence presented to them, the likely increase in the CPI (the acceptable inflation indicator under *Feldman*). Third, the rate of interest available on some safe investment must be determined. On the basis of the second and third findings, the trial judge will then be in a position to determine the inflation-adjusted discount rate (real rate of interest) by subtracting the projected change in the CPI from the investment interest rate. The result is the discount rate to be applied to reduce the lost future income to its present value to determine the amount of the award.

On the other hand, if the plaintiff shows *all* likely wage increases due to inflation and other factors (as in the hypothetical above where a 5.12% annual increase was used), which allows the defendant to show what amount of money is necessary, using a relatively risk-free investment, to ensure that the plaintiff will receive those projected future wage losses, the jury should be instructed to answer two basic questions. First, the amount of lost future earnings must be determined and must include all likely increases due to inflationary factors such as cost of living increases as well as non-inflationary factors such as merit or promotion raises. It must be made clear that the jury is to project only those increases that the plaintiff would actually have received, with reasonable likelihood. All projected future lost earnings are then aggregated by the jury without considering any discount to present value. Second, the jury must determine the likely earning capacity of an invested award. The answer to this question may take two forms: (1) Where the parties have introduced evidence of the probable availability of particular interest rates, or rates of return, on reasonably safe investments, the jury should find and fix the particular rate of interest available to the plaintiff. This finding would then serve as the discount rate to be applied by the judge to the aggregated lost earnings to reduce that sum to its present value. (2) If the parties wish to show, instead of an interest rate, an amount of dollars that, if invested in government bonds or some other safe investment, would fully compensate the plaintiff for all projected lost future wages, then the jury should consider that evidence and find a particular amount of money that they believe could produce the aggregate lost earnings, which they previously determined. It would then be possible for the judge to determine the amount to be awarded by either (1) applying the discount rate found by the jury to the aggregate lost earnings to reduce that amount to its present value, or (2) adopting the jury's finding as to the amount of money which, if invested, would produce in future years the plaintiff's projected lost earnings.

In the jury instructions, and, of course, in the final arguments, it should be clear that the purpose of the award for future lost wages is not to protect the plaintiff from future inflation. The goal is simply to replace for future wages actually lost. If the plaintiff's income in future years will be greater due to likely cost of living increases, then the plaintiff is entitled to those increases. But if the plaintiff's wages are likely to increase at a rate less than inflation (cost of living) the plaintiff is only entitled to such wage increases and not an increase based on the rate of inflation. Jurors are thus entitled to consider and determine the actual likely wages that the plaintiff would have received but for the disabling event.

*   *   *

Summary and Conclusions

Our goal in this opinion is to formulate a simple principle, without being simplistic, that will permit the determination of damages caused by future loss of wages such that neither the plaintiff nor the defendant is penalized (or given a windfall) by economic theory or reality. To begin with, we reject the suggestion that the discount rate, based upon safe investments, is roughly equal to the wage increases that an individual will receive. On any weekday in trial courts throughout the nation, a discount rate can be established using government securities or savings certificates, as examples of safe investments, for any amount of damages. However, the average wage increases for a particular plaintiff can be specified for a particular occupation and, if appropriate, in a particular area of the country. Thus it would be unfair and unreasonable to rule as a legal matter in advance that the discount rate equals wage increases, or, likewise, to say as a legal matter that the wage increases of a particular plaintiff are equal to the rise in the consumer price index or the average economy-wide wage increases for all workers. Our first conclusion, therefore, is that parties should be allowed, in future earnings damages cases, to present evidence not only of the interest rates available on safe investments, but also the likely wage increases that would have been obtained by the particular plaintiff in his occupation, whether these likely increases are due to cost of living, promotions, merit raises or productivity.[44] Significantly, this is only part of the solution, because the more difficult question is how the likely wage increases are to be established or determined.

We have discussed several acceptable methods that are useful in the consideration of the likely effect of inflation on future wages in a case involving total and permanent disability. Two may be summarized. In the first, the present-day value of the earnings that the plaintiff would likely have received may be calculated in three steps:

(1) Using the average annual rate of increase in the plaintiff's own salary in the years prior to the incapacitating event, or in the alternative, using the average wage increase of workers nationally or in the decedent's occupation and geographic area over, for example, the ten years prior to his injury, the parties can project the annual earnings for the remainder of the plaintiff's estimated income-generating years. A lump sum of likely lifetime earnings is the result of these calculations. This total would include wage increases due to cost of living increases, merit, or productivity, as they are received by the average worker or, if the plaintiff's own past wages are used, by the plaintiff.[46]

(2) The above lifetime earnings are converted to an average annual income by dividing the lump sum by the number of income-generating years.

44. "Of course, one cannot *predict* accurately the work-life earnings of each deceased but one can with great precision *project* the earnings of the statistical group to whom he or she had belonged. Specificity to this extent provides better, more reasonable awards than are available to one who uses a simplified procedure of applying aggregative type data." Coyne, Present Value of Future Earnings: A Sensible Alternative to Simplistic Methodologies, Insurance Counsel Journal, Jan. 1982, at 28.

46. This method is most useful where a plaintiff's annual income will likely increase at a somewhat regular rate. If on the other hand, the plaintiff would likely have experienced several large promotions during his/her work-life expectancy, then the plaintiff may prove up his/her projected earnings on the basis of those promotions, and not some average annual percentage rate of increase. The goal, however, remains the same: the plaintiff should show the grand total of his/her projected lifetime earnings including all increases due to promotions, cost of living raises, as they would likely be received during the remainder of his/her expected work-life.

(3) The present value of the plaintiff's average income is then computed by determining how much money must be invested at the present time to yield each year the average income for the remaining income-generating years. This calculation can take the form of applying a traditional discount rate, and it will be based upon relatively safe investments such as Treasury Bills or bonds, or similar instruments.

A second approach is the *Feldman* inflation-adjusted discount rate, which is based upon the real rate of interest. The steps followed in *Feldman* to ensure that the plaintiff was compensated for future wage losses due to inflation are as follows:

(1) Using historical economical data, the court establishes the effective annual interest rate payable on some safe investment for each year during a particular period of years, e.g. 1940–1980.

(2) For each of the years during that period, the average annual percentage change in the CPI is established.

(3) The average annual percentage change in the CPI for each year is subtracted from the effective annual interest rate on the chosen investment for that same year, thus establishing a series of real rates of interest, or the inflation-adjusted discount rates.

(4) All of the real rates of interest are averaged, and the resulting percentage rate represents the inflation-adjusted discount rate to be applied to the plaintiff's lump-sum award.

(5) In computing the lump-sum total, the plaintiff is permitted to show all likely future wage increases due to promotions, merit or productivity raises, or any other *non-inflationary* factor. If promotions are likely, then the annual salary of a worker *presently in that promoted position* should be used to compute the plaintiff's projected income for the years he/she will be in the promoted position. If the plaintiff can show no likely promotions or raises, then in the number of years remaining in his/her work-life expectancy, the plaintiff's present income is assumed as the projected salary for each year.

(6) The inflation-adjusted discount rate is then applied to reduce each projected annual salary to its present value, and the total of these future discounted annual salaries is the amount to be awarded.

The above methodologies are only suggested approaches, and not strait-jackets, for courts to use in determining future earnings. The methodologies do illustrate, however, the issues upon which evidence may be presented in this Circuit now that *Penrod* is overruled. In response to the plaintiff's evidence on inflation, defendants will continue to be permitted to introduce evidence of the interest rate available on risk-free investments, and plaintiffs will continue to be able to rebut that evidence. Plaintiffs will now also be able to introduce evidence, not only on inflation, but more importantly on the likely wage increases in the decedent's or injured party's occupation, basing their calculation on past average wage increases and future inflation, with all parties and trial courts keeping in mind that wage increases are influenced by, but not necessarily dependent upon or identical to, inflation.

Postlude

Having devoted substantial consideration to the economic problems inherent in properly taking inflation into account, we now emphasize that in most cases the apparent difficulties should not arise. As complicated as this subject appears to be, it is a place for vigorous pre-trial discussion and handling between the trial judge and the attorneys. In the great majority of cases, we believe, the parties can and will be able to stipulate to the methodology, discount rate, inflation rate the admissibility of economic data, tables, etc. and other technical aspects, as well as to any particular issues of fact underlying the calculations. In a jury trial, this should include, to the maximum extent possible agreement as to specific issues, the form and manner of their submission, appropriate jury instructions and interrogatories and any objections thereto.

And, to the extent complete stipulation is not reasonably possible the formalized pre-trial effort should assure that the areas of dispute are considerably reduced and certainly well defined.

If the trial court can bring the parties together in this fashion, economic technicalities should not trouble the jury and, we fervently hope, the issues, if any for appellate review will be sharply presented on an adequate evidentiary record preserving identifiably distinct legal problems.

* * *

On the basis of the above analysis, we overrule *Penrod*, and remand the present controversy to the District Court on the issue of damages. The panel opinion is adopted in all other respects.

Reversed and Remanded

[One partially dissenting and four dissenting opinions were produced in this case. The substance of the longest dissent is reproduced below.]

FRANK M. JOHNSON, Jr., Circuit Judge, dissenting:

I dissent. I find unacceptable the majority's proposals for incorporating the effects of future inflation into damage awards. Those proposals are founded upon a delusive belief in the ability of any court, jury, or expert to avoid utter speculation in attempting to predict future rates of inflation. Today's holding will inflict upon the district courts burdens that are both complex and time consuming.

Those burdens will serve no useful purpose because they will result in estimates of the damages due a plaintiff no fairer or more accurate than other, simpler methods would permit.

I do recognize that the courts must somehow deal with inflation in setting damage awards. I advocate adopting an approach that, as a matter of law, treats the inflation rate as totally offsetting the rate at which an award is discounted and that therefore considers neither rate in computing an award. Since an approach, which the majority calls the "Alaska Rule," is simple to apply and in my judgment more accurate than the formulae the majority advances for dealing with inflation.

The majority, although noting that other methods might be acceptable, presents and endorses two specific proposals for negating inflation's effect on damage awards.[2] The approach that it deems most desirable, in a bare summary, would increase an award by the likely increase in a plaintiff's wages resulting from all causes, including inflation, and then would discount the award at a rate reflecting the return on a relatively safe investment.[3] A second approach would follow what the majority conceives to be the rule announced in Feldman v. Allegheny Airlines, 524 F.2d 384 (2d Cir. 1975). The majority's treatment of the *Feldman* Rule is inconsistent[4] and may betray a misunderstanding of the Second Circuit approach.[5] Essential-

2. The majority informs us neither of who has the prerogative of choosing a particular method nor of which method should be used under particular sets of circumstances. It may intimate that the choice is that of the plaintiffs.

3. The majority opinion writes solely in terms of wage increases. For convenience I write in similar terms. I note, however, that inflation would affect components of a damage award other than wages, such as future costs of medical care. I can conceive of no reason to limit consideration of inflation solely to its effect on future wages.

4. There are at least two areas of confusion in the majority opinion. First, at times the Court correctly interprets *Feldman* as establishing a real rate of return on capital from past interest and discount rates and endorses use of that approach. At other times the majority interprets the *Feldman* approach as establishing a real rate of return from projected *future* increases in prices and from returns on safe investments (also presumably based on projections). Second, at times the majority refers to the court as establishing the factors relevant to the real rate of re-

turn, while at other times it refers to the *jury* as setting the factors from which a real rate of return could be determined. It would be wise for the majority at least to give a coherent presentation of the proposals it endorses in order to guide the trial courts.

5. The majority does not seem to realize that the "real rate of return" on capital as used in *Feldman* means the return on investments over the long term assuming no inflation and disregarding short term fluctuations. The majority suggests that the *Feldman* approach is defective because short term variations "[i]n the dynamic and ever changing world of finance and economics" will render any real rate of return erroneous. There will indeed be such short term fluctuations, but they would not affect the validity of a long term rate. The *Feldman* district court in fact averaged the short term fluctuations in order to derive a long term rate. Moreover, if there is a constant real rate of return, it can be established by relying on prior years' evidence. There would be no need, contrary to what the majority at times suggests, for projections of future inflation. The

ly, however, the majority would compute the difference between inflation and the discount rates. After consideration of any possibility that the rate of yearly increase in the plaintiff's wages would differ from the rate of inflation, the award for each future year of plaintiff's expected life would then be discounted by that difference.[6] These proposals, the majority asserts, best ensure that a plaintiff receives no more nor less than is his due in a damage award.

I agree that the paramount concern of a court should be ensuring that a damage award is as accurate and fair as is practically possible. I disagree, however, with the majority's notion that its proposals will ensure that a plaintiff will receive neither more nor less than is his due. The majority's analysis is curiously limited: it involves only computational precision, the determination of which formulae most accurately eliminate the effect of future inflation on a damage award *once the rate of inflation is known.* I note that even considered on such limited terms the majority's preferred approach is not beyond objection: simplifications that the majority introduces into its calculations will overstate an award to a plaintiff. I also think it unfortunate that the majority was unable to decide on one specific proposal to mandate. Since the two formulae that the majority endorses will produce different results even if using the same data, the amount of an award will depend arbitrarily on the method of computation chosen. Such concerns, however, are not critical to my dissent. The fundamental weakness of the majority's holding is its failure to consider at all the sheer speculation involved in any prediction of future inflation rates. The majority's willingness to consider only computational precision in gauging the effects of inflation creates a mere illusion of accuracy because the underlying data that the formulae would use are themselves unreliable.

I do firmly maintain that it is quite evident that economic theory cannot predict future inflation rates with any degree of certainty. A survey of the general literature for the past several years illustrates the sorry tale of the repeated confusion, contradictions, and uncertainties of economic forecasts. [citations omitted]. Moreover, these

---

ability to avoid speculation about future inflation is, in fact, one of the prime advantages of the approach in *Feldman.*

6. The majority indicates, at least at times, that a *Feldman*-type approach should establish a real rate of return as a matter of fact. Other courts have interpreted *Feldman* as being applicable as a matter of law. See *Doca, supra* 634 F.2d at 39 (although elsewhere suggesting that parties could dispute real rate of return); Freeport Sulphur Co. v. S/S Hermosa, 526 F.2d 300, 310–11 (5th Cir. 1976) (Wisdom, J. specially concurring); see also Note, "Future Inflation, Damages, and the Circuit Courts," 63 Va. L.Rev. 105, 130–31 (1977). Since a real rate of return could be established, as it was in *Feldman*, from statistics of prior years and should not vary with each case, there seems no reason to require finding a real rate of return as a matter of fact and not of law. I discuss adopting such an approach as a matter of law infra.

complaints about economic forecasting generally concern short term forecasts. Over a longer term, events as diverse—and unpredictable—as spending to finance a southeast Asian war, an oil embargo, or world agricultural shortfalls could have a profound impact on future inflation. [citations omitted]. To attempt to predict the course of inflation for decades into the future is to attempt the impossible, given our present economic knowledge.

* * *

The inability of the majority's proposals adequately to deal with inflation in computing damage awards is not the only sin of those proposals. The majority's holdings, both in the proposals adopted and in the procedures used for carrying out those proposals, are complex and extremely time consuming. Elaborate expert testimony will be necessary.[14] And this testimony will not be limited to future inflation and future returns on investments. A court must also allow evidence of whether a plaintiff's wages would keep up or would increase at a rate faster than the inflation rate. By extension it appears that a court must allow separate expert testimony on whether any other component of an award that might be affected by inflation, such as an award for future medical expenses, would increase at a rate greater or less than the inflation rate. * * *

* * *

Having taken the position that there is no way to predict inflation without undue speculation, there remains for me the task of establishing some fair and practicable approach for estimating damage awards. * * * Faced with the need to find some alternative method for dealing with the pernicious effects of inflation, I believe that the most desirable approach would be to offset, as a matter of law, the inflation rate with the discount rates.

The adoption of such a rule would have several advantages over the majority's plan. It would be simple to apply and would require no time consuming expert testimony. Speculation about future inflation would be unnecessary. Since the inflation rate and discount rate are covariant in opposite directions, the rule would be relatively accurate, certainly much more accurate in my opinion than the majority's proposals.[19] Finally, the effects of inflation would be considered uni-

---

14. The majority acknowledges that some courts have allowed a factfinder to use its common experience as well as expert testimony in determining the rate of future inflation, Riha v. Jasper Blackburn Corp., 516 F.2d 840, 845 (8th Cir. 1975), but it never indicates to the district courts whether it approves of reliance on common experience. Given its repeated references to the use of expert testimo-ny, however, the majority seems implicitly to disapprove of such reliance.

19. A court should, of course, still consider non-inflationary increases in wages. It could do so by considering the wages commensurate at the time of the award with the increases the plaintiff could be expected to receive in the future due to, for example, promotions or higher productivity.

formly and consistently for all damage awards. Since the inflation affecting awards will not vary in cases decided at similar times and compensating injuries over similar time periods, such uniform treatment is fairer than an approach in which estimates of inflation vary with each case.

Having espoused the adoption of an approach that would deal with inflation as a matter of law, I must resolve one further issue, which of two variants of such an approach is preferable. One variant would establish a positive real rate of return on capital, that is, the rate of return that would exist on a relatively safe investment if there were no inflation. Such an approach would mirror that of Feldman v. Allegheny Airlines, 524 F.2d 384 (2d Cir. 1975) (1.5% real return); see also Doca v. Marina Mercante Nicaraguense, 634 F.2d 30 (2d Cir. 1979) (suggesting using 2% real rate of return), cert. denied, 451 U.S. 971, 101 S.Ct. 2049, 68 L.Ed.2d 351 (1981). A second variant, the Alaska Rule disparaged by the majority, would treat the inflation and discount rates as offsetting each other totally and therefore cancelling each other out. Such an approach has been advocated or adopted by several courts. E.g., Freeport Sulphur Co. v. S/S Hermosa, 526 F.2d 300, 308–13 (5th Cir. 1976) (Wisdom, J., specially concurring); Pfeiffer v. Jones & Laughlin Steel Corp., 678 F.2d 453 (3d Cir. 1982); Beaulieu v. Elliott, 434 P.2d 665 (Alaska 1967); Resner v. N.Pac.Ry., 161 Mont. 177, 505 P.2d 86 (1973); Kaczkowski v. Bolubasz, 491 Pa. 561, 421 A.2d 1027 (1980).

I find a *Feldman*-type approach tempting since theoretically it may be preferable to the Alaska Rule. Ultimately, however, I, like Judge Wisdom in his specially concurring opinion in *Freeport Sulphur,* supra would adopt the Alaska Rule. A rule establishing a positive real rate of return in practice involves as much guesswork as ruling that the inflation and discount rates offset each other completely—as an examination of the data that the district court in *Feldman* used in setting a 1.5% real rate will establish. Moreover, according to some economists, at least in an inflationary period the inflation component in the discount rate will fail fully to take into account the actual rate of inflation because the future depreciation in the value of money is not entirely foreseen. E.g., I. Fisher, The Theory of Interest 43 (1930); See also *Freeport Sulphur Co.,* supra 526 F.2d at 310 & n. 7 (Wisdom, J., specially concurring). Such an effect would offset at least partially any positive real rate of return on capital. Even the assumption that there is some constant real rate of return is open to question; some economists have suggested that the real rate of return will vary with the inflation rate. J. Keynes, The General Theory of Employment, Interest, and Money 142–43 (1936); Carlson, "Short-Term Interest Rates as Predictors of Inflation: A Comment," 67 Am.Econ.Rev. 469 (1977); Steindl, "Price Expectations and Interest Rates," 5 J. Money, Credit & Banking, 939, 948 (1973). Given the uncertainty described above in setting any positive real rate of return, I firmly believe a court should err, if it errs at all, in favor of the plaintiff, the non-culpable party, by establishing a total offset of the inflation and discount rates.

To summarize, I believe that the majority has sunk into its own Serbonian bog in adopting cumbersome, complicated, apparently illegal (in disregarding Fed.R.Civ.P. 49(a)), and time consuming procedures for the district courts to follow in incorporating the effects of inflation into damage awards. Those procedures cannot be justified by their precision in offsetting the effects of inflation because the data the procedures would use would be the product of pure speculation. A better procedure than that proposed by the majority and far simpler to apply, would, as a matter of law, treat the discount and inflation rates as totally offsetting each other.

QUESTIONS

1. The majority is accused in the dissent of misunderstanding the real interest rate approach. Is this true? Do the jury instructions suggested by the majority effectively remove the potential advantages of the approach?

2. Judge Johnson's dissent claims that "simplifications that the majority introduces into its calculations will overstate an award to a plaintiff." He is alluding to the suggested procedure of basing the damage award on the *average* future income, described in the majority opinion, text following fn. 46. Do you agree with the criticism?

3. In its "Postlude," the majority opinion suggests that litigants would be able to resolve or narrow the issues considerably through pretrial conference and stipulation. How plausible do you find this?

4. Johnson's dissent recognizes that the real rate of interest approach "theoretically . . . may be preferable" to the Alaska Rule, but rejects the approach because "establishing a real rate of return in practice involves as much guesswork as ruling that the inflation and discount rates offset each other completely." Is this persuasive? What is the best rejoinder that an advocate of the real rate of interest rule could give?

5. Establishing any single "rule of thumb" procedure as a matter of law would greatly simplify things procedurally. In many cases, however, such a rule would give incorrect results. What are the pros and cons of a clearcut but oversimple rule? Would it be better to adopt a rule as a rebuttable *presumption?* Give some examples of how similar problems are dealt with in other areas of law.

6. If you have reflected carefully on the preceding materials in this chapter, you now know as much or more about the issues as most judges. (Perhaps that is a doleful thought.) The 5th Circuit's *Culver* decision runs 44 pages in its full text and obviously represents a great deal of time and reflection by members of the court. Is the resolution satisfactory? What would be your own opinion? In later sections of this chapter, we shall return again to the question of future damages—and muddy the waters still further.

COMBINED UNCERTAINTY AND DISCOUNTING

In most of the previous applications, the facts of the situations allowed uncertainty and present value adjustments to be considered separately. The following set of exercises is designed to demonstrate a few important considerations when uncertainty and present value factors are presented in virtually inseparable fashion. One issue that is raised is the extent to which it is proper, either analytically or in equity, to rely on "average" values. These questions are designed to lead into a difficult set of real world policy issues implicating the "fairness"—or lack thereof—of recognizing certain alleged empirical differences between the sexes, races, or other distinctive sub-sets of persons.

QUESTIONS

I. On the planet of Tintd, all citizens may be distinguished by the color of their fur. Only three pelt shades exist: mauve, fuschia, and calico. All workers are entitled to an annual retirement pension of 10,000 dize. Each worker must retire on the birthday marking its 42nd Tintd year and may then collect a 10,000 dize pension payment on each succeeding birthday. The life spans of Tintdians are much more predictable than that of humans, but vary systematically with fur color. All Tintdians die at precisely 27:00 hours on one of their birthdates. Exhibit 3.5 indicates the probability that a Tintdian of a particular color will live until various birthdays.

EXHIBIT 3.5 Data on Tintdian Pensions

Year	Mauve	Fuschia	Calico	P.V. at 10%
43	1.000	1.000	1.000	9090.91
44	1.000	1.000	1.000	8264.46
45	0.500	1.000	1.000	7513.15
46	0.500	0.667	1.000	6830.13
47	0.000	0.333	0.000	6209.21
48	0.000	0.000	0.000	6544.74

The last column of the table indicates the discounted present value of the pension payment in the corresponding year, assuming that the valuation is being done at the retirement date and that the ruling interest rate is 10% compounded annually.

1. What are the average lengths of time (in Tintdian years) that the Mauves, Fuschias and Calicos, respectively, will collect their pensions? [Note: Half of the Mauves must die on their 44th birthday because the table indicates that, whereas all live to 44, only half are left at the 45th birthday; the rest die on their 46th birthday because the tables says that no Mauves will make it to 47. Apply a similar logic to the other types of Tintdians.]

2. Tintdian law allows pensioners to assign their life pension proceeds to third parties. Duration of the pension is, of course, determined by the lifespan of the assignor, not the assignee. If you were a Calico and wished to sell your pension rights on the day of retirement, about how much do you think you could get if the interest rate were 10%. How does this compare to the prices that Mauves and Fuschias could expect?

3. What explains the difference in the values of the Fuschia and Calico pensions?

4. How would the ratios of the three different pension values change if the interest rate were 20% instead of 10%?

5. Each worker also receives a free 20,000-dize life insurance policy. If the rights to this policy can likewise be assigned, how much are they worth in the three relevant cases?

––––––––––

II. Assume that a $10,000 annual annuity is available to be paid in equal daily payments (of about $27.40) during each year and that any time length is possible. The interest rate is 15%. Draw a diagram that has time in years on its horizontal axis and the present value of the $10,000 annual-rate annuity for various time terms on the vertical axis. Finally, draw a curve that you think approximately reflects the shape of a function that relates the annuity's length to its discounted present value. (The diagram does not have to be precise, but think about what the shape of the curve should be, at least roughly.)

1. Select a point on the curve corresponding to an annuity of 10-year term. Draw a horizontal dotted line out to the vertical axis, such that the present value of the 10-year annuity is shown. Repeat the same operation for 5-year and 15-year annuities, respectively.

2. On the same diagram, indicate the value of the certainty equivalent of a lottery in which, depending on whether a flipped coin comes up heads or tails, you win an annuity of either 5 or 15 years.

(Assume risk neutrality.) Is this lottery worth more or less than the certainty of a 10-year annuity? Why?

3. How would the diagram, and the conclusions derived from it, change if the interest rate assumed were either higher or lower?

4. What analogy exists between the analysis in the preceding questions and the discussion in Chapter II above of the existence of risk aversion due to declining marginal utility of money?

––––––

III. A parcel of land has been condemned by the State and a hearing is being held by the Commissioners to award compensatory payments to those having interests in the land. A widow, under dower rights, enjoys a life tenancy on the land, whose annual rental value is presently estimated at $5,500. The Commissioners, after consulting standard mortality tables, find that the average remaining life span of a woman the widow's age is 22 years. Hence, it is proposed to award her the present discounted value of a $5,500 stream for 22 years. The relevant interest rate is approximately 10%. The market value of the land in question, unencumbered by the life tenancy, has been set at $180,000. This sum, minus the computed value of the life tenancy, is to be given to the remainderman.

1. If you represented the remainderman, what argument would you raise to modify the proposed procedure for determining the respective compensatory payments to the life tenant and remainderman?

2. If you represented the life tenant, could you advance any argument to suggest that the proposed procedure will undercompensate your client? [Hint: Does there seem to be any inconsistency between the rental and the land value figures that have been proposed?]

3. The widow's attorney proposes to introduce evidence that the woman in question is of exceptionally long-lived genetic stock and is in exceptional physical condition for a woman of her age. He contends that expert testimony will support a finding of an expected life span of 30 years for this particular woman. What considerations militate for and against hearing such evidence? Assess the "marginal benefits" versus the "marginal costs" of hearing such evidence. Are the issues in any way similar to *Culver* above?

AVERAGE vs. EXPECTED LIFESPAN

Exhibit 3.6 below provides a specific numerical example of a common error in computing lost future income damages, e.g., in wrongful death or disability cases. Under the incorrect procedure, the expected value of the victim's remaining lifespan is first estimated, then

EXHIBIT 3.6 Expected Value of Future Income

Starting Age................... 60
Starting Salary $20000
Real Income Growth % 1.0
Inflation Rate % 7.0

(1) Period	(2) Age	(3) Income	(4) Infl.Adj.	(5) Int.Rate	(6) Disc.	(7) Pres.Val.	(8) ← Cumul.	(9) Mort.	(10) Alive	(11) Ex.Value	(12) ← Cumul.	Age
1	60	20200.00	21600.00	10.50	.9049774	19547.51	19547.51	19.1	.9809000	19174.15	19174.15	60
2	61	20402.00	23328.00	11.10	.8101620	18889.46	38446.97	21.1	.9602030	18147.32	37321.47	61
3	62	20606.02	25194.24	12.37	.7047724	17756.20	56203.17	22.2	.9388865	16671.06	53992.53	62
4	63	20812.08	27209.78	13.47	.6032201	16413.48	72616.66	25.0	.9154143	15025.14	69017.67	63
5	64	21020.20	29386.56	14.00	.5193687	15262.46	87879.12	26.9	.8907897	13595.64	82613.31	64
6	65	21230.40	31737.49	14.00	.4555865	14459.17	102338.3	28.8	.8651350	12509.13	95122.45	65
7	66	21442.71	34276.49	14.00	.3996373	13698.16	116036.5	30.8	.8384888	11485.76	106608.21	66
8	67	21657.13	37018.60	14.00	.3505591	12977.21	129013.7	33.2	.8106510	10519.99	117128.25	67
9	68	21873.71	39980.09	14.00	.3075079	12294.20	141307.9	36.0	.7814675	9607.52	126735.7	68
10	69	22092.44	43178.50	14.00	.2697438	11647.13	152955.0	39.2	.7508340	8745.06	135480.8	69
11	70	22313.37	46682.78	14.00	.2366174	11034.13	163989.1	42.6	.7188485	7931.86	143412.6	70
12	71	22536.50	50363.40	14.00	.2075591	10453.38	174442.5	46.3	.6855658	7166.48	150579.1	71
13	72	22761.87	54392.47	14.00	.1820694	9903.20	184345.7	50.3	.6510818	6447.80	157026.9	72
14	73	22989.48	58743.87	14.00	.1597100	9381.98	193727.7	54.8	.6154025	5773.70	162800.6	73
15	74	23219.38	63443.38	14.00	.1400965	8888.19	202615.9	59.8	.5786015	5142.72	167943.3	74
16	75	23451.57	68518.85	14.00	.1228917	8420.39	211036.3	65.3	.5408188	4553.91	172497.2	75
17	76	23686.09	74000.36	14.00	.1077997	7977.22	219013.5	71.1	.5023666	4007.49	176504.7	76
18	77	23922.95	79920.39	14.00	.0945611	7557.36	226570.9	77.4	.4634834	3502.71	180007.4	77
19	78	24162.18	86314.02	14.00	.0829484	7159.61	233730.5	84.4	.4243654	3038.29	183045.7	78
20	79	24403.80	93219.14	14.00	.0727617	6782.79	240513.2	91.0	.3857482	2616.45	185662.2	79
21	80	24647.84	100676.7	14.00	.0638261	6425.80	246939.0	98.3	.3478291	2235.08	187897.3	80
22	81	24894.32	108730.8	14.00	.0559878	6087.60	253026.6	105.9	.3109940	1893.21	189790.5	81
23	82	25143.26	117429.3	14.00	.0491121	5767.20	258793.8	113.7	.2756340	1589.64	191380.1	82
24	83	25394.69	126823.6	14.00	.0430808	5463.66	264257.5	121.3	.2421996	1323.30	192703.4	83
25	84	25648.64	136969.5	14.00	.0377902	5176.10	269433.6	128.4	.2111012	1092.68	193796.1	84
26	85	25905.13	147927.1	14.00	.0331493	4903.67	274387.3	136.0	.1823914	894.39	194690.5	85
27	86	26164.18	159761.2	14.00	.0290783	4645.58	278982.9	144.0	.1561179	725.26	195415.7	86
28	87	26425.82	172542.1	14.00	.0255073	4401.08	283383.9	152.6	.1322981	582.25	195998.0	87
29	88	26690.08	186345.5	14.00	.0225748	4169.44	287553.4	161.6	.1109178	462.47	196460.4	88
30	89	26956.98	201253.1	14.00	.0196270	3950.90	291503.4	171.2	.0919317	363.13	196823.6	89
31	90	27226.55	217353.4	14.00	.0172167	3742.11	295245.5	181.3	.0752641	281.65	197105.2	90
32	91	27498.81	234741.7	14.00	.0151024	3545.15	298790.6	192.0	.0608107	215.58	197320.8	91
33	92	27773.80	253521.0	14.00	.0132477	3358.57	302149.2	203.4	.0484416	162.69	197483.5	92
34	93	28051.54	273802.7	14.00	.0116208	3181.80	305331.0	215.4	.0380053	120.93	197604.4	93
35	94	28332.06	295706.9	14.00	.0101937	3014.34	308345.3	228.2	.0293327	88.42	197692.8	94

the present discounted value of that income is computed and attributed to the victim. For instance, suppose that standard mortality tables indicate that for a 60 year old male the average number of years remaining is 17. It is then assumed as a certainty that the victim would have lived for precisely this average lifespan, neither more nor less. Then the projected annual income for each individual year within that period is discounted to its present value and cumulated. This procedure, corresponding to the leftmost eight columns of Exhibit 3.6 (and similar to Exhibits 3.3 and 3.4 earlier in the chapter), indicates that the appropriate damage figure for a person who would have lived 17 years longer is approximately $219,013. (See the column 8 entry for the seventeenth year, or age 76.)

An alternative procedure is to recognize that the victim might have died either much earlier or later than the average time for a man his age. The probability of dying at each age can be found in standard mortality tables in the form of a "mortality rate" per thousand. These mortality rates have been entered as column 9 of Exhibit 3.6. Remember that, since the rates are in thousands, their further use requires that the decimal points be moved leftward three places, i.e., 19.9/1000 = .0199, 21.1/100 = .0211, etc. At each year, the cohort of current 60 year olds will be reduced by the proportion that dies. Hence, at age 61 the fraction (1.00 − .0199) = .98090 will still be alive, and that is the probability that a sixty year old will live to earn the full income from his 60th year. During the next year, the fraction .0211 of the .98090 still alive will die, yielding the .98090 (1 − .0211) =.9602 of the original cohort of 60 year-olds alive to reap the second year's income. These fractions left alive, as listed in column 10, are interpretable as the probabilities that the 60 year old victim would actually be alive to receive income in any particular year.

The next step is to use the probability for each year to "weight" its corresponding income figure from column 7. In effect, this method "credits" a person with a proportion of potential income that appropriately reflects the probability that the income will indeed be received. Of course, this probability-weighted figure is really what Chapter II identified as the "expected value" of the income in that year. We are interested in the expected value of the income for the victim's *lifetime*, rather than for any single year. Therefore the expected values for each year, as listed in column 11, are cumulated in column 12. In principle, we should keep summing up until the column 11 figure becomes zero, but the reader can see that, because both the present value discounting and death factor operate so strongly in later years, little change in the "bottom line" number would occur if the table were carried out for additional periods. Hence, we can see that the expected value of the victim's income stream is really less than $200,000. Contrast this result with the much higher figure achieved by using the average life expectancy.

In a real-world application, the income for each year should be weighted by realization probabilities much lower than those shown in the same. Obviously, being alive is a necessary but not a sufficient condition that income will be earned. A further adjustment should be

made for the probability that a live individual is still an active participant in the workforce (i.e., not retired) and, if active, is not unemployed. Unemployment rates and labor force participation rates by
age and sex are available to analysts, so that the appropriate *joint*
probability of being alive, participating, and employed can be computed. Inclusion of these factors would make Exhibit 3.6 become somewhat more complicated, but the principle is the same.

There is no doubt that the expected value method is conceptually
superior to the average life expectancy method and, as illustrated,
the methods give rather different results. The specific numbers in
Exhibit 3.6 and some of the queries in the last question block above
should help you be able to explain in commonsense terms what the
fallacy is in the average life expectancy method.

RISK SELECTION AND RISK COMPENSATION

Kay Glehn owns and manages a number of apartment units in a
city which is the site of a large university. Most of her tenants are
students and she has been plagued by a midyear "skipping" problem
at around the end of first semester. Typically, about six percent of
her tenants default after making only five monthly payments toward
an annual lease. Of those remaining, four percent default after one
additional payment. The rest stay through the year and fulfill their
entire contractual obligation. Because of the seasonal nature of the
rental market, a midyear default has the practical implication that an
apartment will remain empty for the entire defaulted period. Although it is in theory possible to obtain a judgement for the lost rent,
that alternative is impractical because of a combination of legal expenses and the low probability of recovery against persons who have
left the jurisdiction, are impecunious, etc. Hence, although she attempts to create an impression otherwise, her actual policy is merely
to absorb the loss from any default.

Since rental housing is essentially a competitive market, Kay's
rental schedule of $500 per month presumably suffices to give her a
reasonable rate of return on invested capital and operating costs.
Hence, she (and other landlords in the market) are "charging" rent-
ers for the default risk that landlords must bear. This charge, of
course, manifests itself in the form of a contract rent that is slightly
higher than it would otherwise be.

Experience suggests to Kay that the tenants are composed of
three types: Alphas, who are sure that they will perform on the entire lease; Betas who regard themselves as sure "skippers" at midyear; and Gammas, who regard the probability of performance as a
fifty-fifty proposition. Unfortunately, she cannot tell in advance
which prospective renter belongs to which category. A worksheet
similar to Exhibit 3.7 can be found in Kay's files.

EXHIBIT 3.7 Analysis of Rental Income Flows

Payment #	DiscFac	PresVal	◄— Cumul.	%Default	%OK	Ex. Val.	◄—Cumul.
1	1.0	500.00	500.00	0.00	100.00	500.00	500.00
2	.9900990	495.05	995.05	0.00	100.00	495.05	995.05
3	.9802960	490.15	1485.20	0.00	100.00	490.15	1485.20
4	.9705901	485.30	1970.49	0.00	100.00	485.30	1970.49
5	.9609803	480.49	2450.98	0.00	100.00	480.49	2450.98
6	.9514657	475.73	2926.72	4.00	96.00	456.70	2907.69
7	.9420452	471.02	3397.74	6.00	90.24	425.05	3332.74
8	.9327181	466.36	3864.10	0.00	90.24	420.84	3753.58
9	.9234832	461.74	4325.84	0.00	90.24	416.68	4170.26
10	.9143398	457.17	4783.01	0.00	90.24	412.55	4582.81
11	.9052870	452.64	5235.65	0.00	90.24	408.47	4991.27
12	.8963237	448.16	5683.81	0.00	90.24	404.42	5395.69

QUESTIONS

1.   If the landlord *could* determine in advance who were Alphas, Betas, and Gammas, how might the rental terms to each group differ?

2.   Since, under the facts of this hypothetical, the groups are not identifiable in advance, the rental terms offered to all prospective tenants would presumably have to be identical.   If you were an Alpha, would you feel as though you were being "overcharged"?   By approximately what dollar amount?

3.   Given that the three classes of risks cannot be determined in advance, how can the terms of Ms. Glehn's leases be manipulated so as to "smoke out" the bad-risk Betas?   (If there is more than one way of doing this, explain the relative merits of each.)   How would the Gammas react to such manipulations?   Of what relevance is "least cost risk bearing"?

4.   Obviously, finding a way to discriminate among the three classes of risk alters the relative welfare of the Alphas, Betas and Gammas.   Do these effects merely cancel out?   If you were behind the Rawlsian "veil of ignorance," not knowing whether you were to be an Alpha, Beta or Gamma, what system of charging would you prefer?

5.   People try to find proxy variables to discriminate between good and bad risks in their transactions.   For instance, the seller of an almost-new used car may find a certain market resistance because buyers feel that the car is a "lemon."   [See Akerloff, "The Market for 'Lemons': Quality Uncertainty and the Market Mechanism," 84 Q.J.Econ. 488 (1970)]   Are certain classes of buyers discriminated against because they are suspected of being "lemons" in some economic sense?   Is this fair or not?   In what ways can people give qual-

ity assurance when they are incorrectly impacted by the "lemon effect"?

6.   Can the issues in any of the above questions be couched in the "externality" terminology introduced in Chapter I?

DEFAULT COST UNDER "BACKDOOR" INTEREST SCHEMES

If the market rate of interest for a particular class of creditor exceeds the legal maximum under a state usury statute, the continued availability of credit to that class may depend upon some way of circumventing the interest rate ceiling imposed by law. One way of doing this is by establishing a "cash price" and a higher "time price," such that the latter embodies an *implicit* charge for credit in order to supplement the legally imposed interest. In jurisdictions where the time price subterfuge is not permitted by the courts, some sellers may establish a single inflated price and then make credit available at the legal rate of interest. Other sellers will charge a lower price but will decline to extend credit. Of course, purchasers who do not desire credit would be foolish to purchase at the establishments that offer the credit, since that would involve being implicitly charged for *part* of the price of credit that is not received. In any event, sellers will generally find a way to make credit available by adjusting price in one of the ways described.

Exhibit 3.8 describes in some detail exactly how the "time price" subterfuge works. Suppose that the cash price of the goods would normally be $1000. The maximum legal rate is 18% (1.5% per month), but the market rate for the risk class in question is 30% (2.5% per month). The market rate of 2.5% is the rate at which the vendor will discount the stream of payments made for the goods, but he—at least nominally—can only charge explicit interest at the rate of 1.5% per month on outstanding balances.

When the vendor provides $1000 worth of goods to the credit buyer, the unalterable reality is that the "real" extension of credit is only $1000. Setting a time price of $1225.74 essentially involves the creation of a fictional $225.74 worth of credit such that the stream of $36.01 payments on the fictional loan at the below-market nominal interest rate of 18% (1.5% monthly) is also adequate to amortize the "real" loan of $1000 at the market rate of 30% (2.5% monthly).

Check Exhibit 3.8 to confirm that an "inflation" of the real $1000 credit extension by $225.74 is exactly the right amount to accomplish the desired purpose. If the goods are sold for $1225.74, columns (2), (3), and (4) of Exhibit 3.8 show that 48 monthly payments of $36.01 will amortize the "time price" loan and reduce the balance to zero. Note that accrued interest on each month's opening balance at the nominal 1.5% is first subtracted from the monthly payment, then any

EXHIBIT 3.8 Backdoor Interest Via Time Price

Terms: 48 monthly payments of $36.01. ($1728.29 aggregate)

Max. Legal Rate: 1.5% per mo.   Market Rate: 2.5% per mo.
Cash Price: $1000.00   Time Price: $1225.74

(1)	(2)	(3)	(4)	(5)	(6)	(7)	(8)
Loan Period	Nominal Interest	Principal Reduction	Nominal Balance	"True" Interest	Principal Reduction	"True" Balance	"Excess" Balance
1	$18.39	$17.62	1208.12	$25.00	$11.01	$988.99	$219.12
2	18.12	17.88	1190.23	24.72	11.28	977.71	212.52
3	17.85	18.15	1172.08	24.44	11.56	966.15	205.93
4	17.58	18.42	1153.65	24.15	11.85	954.30	199.36
5	17.30	18.70	1134.95	23.86	12.15	942.15	192.80
6	17.02	18.98	1115.97	23.55	12.45	929.70	186.27
7	16.74	19.27	1096.71	23.24	12.76	916.93	179.77
8	16.45	19.56	1077.15	22.92	13.08	903.85	173.30
9	16.16	19.85	1057.30	22.60	13.41	890.44	166.86
10	15.86	20.15	1037.15	22.26	13.74	876.70	160.46
11	15.56	20.45	1016.71	21.92	14.09	862.61	154.10
12	15.25	20.76	995.95	21.57	14.44	848.17	147.78
13	14.94	21.07	974.88	21.20	14.80	833.36	141.52
14	14.62	21.38	953.50	20.83	15.17	818.19	135.31
15	14.30	21.70	931.80	20.45	15.55	802.64	129.16
16	13.98	22.03	909.77	20.07	15.94	786.70	123.07
17	13.65	22.36	887.41	19.67	16.34	770.36	117.05
18	13.31	22.69	864.71	19.26	16.75	753.62	111.10
19	12.97	23.04	841.68	18.84	17.17	736.45	105.23
20	12.63	23.38	818.30	18.41	17.59	718.86	99.44
21	12.27	23.73	794.57	17.97	18.03	700.82	93.75
22	11.92	24.09	770.48	17.52	18.49	682.34	88.14
23	11.56	24.45	746.03	17.06	18.95	663.39	82.64
24	11.19	24.82	721.21	16.58	19.42	643.97	77.25
25	10.82	25.19	696.03	16.10	19.91	624.06	71.97
26	10.44	25.57	670.46	15.60	20.40	603.66	66.81
27	10.06	25.95	644.51	15.09	20.91	582.74	61.77
28	9.67	26.34	618.17	14.57	21.44	561.30	56.87
29	9.27	26.73	591.44	14.03	21.97	539.33	52.11
30	8.87	27.13	564.31	13.48	22.52	516.81	47.50
31	8.46	27.54	536.76	12.92	23.09	493.72	43.04
32	8.05	27.95	508.81	12.34	23.66	470.06	38.75
33	7.63	28.37	480.44	11.75	24.25	445.80	34.63
34	7.21	28.80	451.64	11.15	24.86	420.94	30.69
35	6.77	29.23	422.41	10.52	25.48	395.46	26.95
36	6.34	29.67	392.74	9.89	26.12	369.34	23.39
37	5.89	30.11	362.62	9.23	26.77	342.57	20.05
38	5.44	30.57	332.05	8.56	27.44	315.13	16.93

excess is applied to reduce the balance itself. Now examine columns (5), (6), and (7). These columns show what would be happening if the same monthly periodic payments of $36.01 were to be applied as amortization of the "true" loan of $1000 at the 2.5% monthly rate. In both cases, the "time price" loan and the real loan, the last payment is exactly enough to pay the accrued interest and reduce the outstanding balance to zero.

The repayment arrangement depicted in the example is a standard loan amortization procedure. The exact size of the equal periodic payments necessary to amortize any sum over any number of periods can be found by using a somewhat imposing-looking formula:

$$A = V \{r/[1 - (1 + r)^{-n}]\}$$

where A is the periodic payment to be found, V is the value to be amortized, n is the number of payments, and r is the periodic interest rate. (Note well that r is the *periodic* interest rate, i.e., the rate as adjusted for the relevant period, not the annual interest rate.) For notational simplicity, we shall rename the collection of terms within the curly brackets of the formula as Z; that is, $Z = \{r/[1 - (1 + r)^{-n}]\}$. The calculation of an actual value for Z, which depends on the values assumed for the interest rate and the number of periods, would be tedious if done by hand. Not so long ago, people therefore kept books of tables that, in effect, provided values for Z under many alternative assumptions about the values of r and n, thus permitting the earlier formula for A to be solved conveniently. Now, the same information is quickly accessible to anyone who knows the formula and has a pocket calculator.

How does one then calculate the correct value, in this case $225.74, for the time price surcharge? The method is easy to follow if the underlying reality of the distinction between the real and fictional credit extensions is borne in mind. First, solve for the necessary payment A, using the real (i.e., market) rate of interest and the actual credit extension of $1000. This reveals what the periodic payment A must be in order to satisfy the seller under the realities of the marketplace, ignoring the legal constraints.

The next question is to ask what fictional credit extension would imply the very same repayment scheme if the artificial interest rate were the applicable one. Since the formula above told us that A = VZ, a bit of inference from 9th grade algebra reveals that V = A/Z. In other words, just as one can find the periodic payment flow necessary to amortize any given sum, it is equally possible to work backwards from the payment stream to the implied sum being amortized. There is only one trick to the present application: the value of Z to be plugged into the equation V = A/Z is now the value based on the

Loan Period	Nominal Interest	Principal Reduction	Nominal Balance	"True" Interest	Principal Reduction	"True" Balance	"Excess" Balance
39	4.98	31.03	301.03	7.88	28.13	287.00	14.03
40	4.52	31.49	269.54	7.17	28.83	258.17	11.37
41	4.04	31.96	237.58	6.45	29.55	228.62	8.96
42	3.56	32.44	205.13	5.72	30.29	198.33	6.81
43	3.08	32.93	172.20	4.96	31.05	167.28	4.93
44	2.58	33.42	138.78	4.18	31.82	135.45	3.33
45	2.08	33.92	104.86	3.39	32.62	102.83	2.02
46	1.57	34.43	70.42	2.57	33.44	69.40	1.02
47	1.06	34.95	35.47	1.73	34.27	35.13	0.35
48	0.53	35.47	0.00	0.88	35.13	0.00	0.00

legal rate rather than the real rate, since the legal rate is the interest rate being nominally applied to the time price transaction.

QUESTIONS

1. Explain the first four columns of the exhibit. At what interest rate is the interest being accrued for purposes of column (2)? Check the exhibit's calculations for at least the first two payments.

2. Why is column (8) labelled an "Excess Balance"? Why does the amount of the overstatement vary over time as it does?

3. Suppose a purchaser were to make two years worth of payments and then default. What is the amount of the judgement that a vendor would be able to secure? Is this result arguably inequitable? [See Allen and Staaf, "The Nexus Between Usury, 'Time Price' and Unconscionability in Installment Sales," 14 Uniform Commercial Code L.J. 219 (1982). Suppose that you had to defend the position that the result *is* equitable, or at least desirable on other public policy grounds. What argument(s) might support this position?

4. Let V and Z stand for the values defined in the text above on the assumption that the "real" values of the credit extension and interest rates are used. Similarly, let V' and Z' stand for the analogous values when the time price and the legal rate of interest are involved. Can you show that the time price can be computed directly by the formula $V' = V (Z/Z')$? (Note that Z/Z' would then be interpretable as a "blowup factor" to be applied to the original cash price V.)

5. In comparing the advantages of paying cash versus buying on credit, one national "consumer buying advice" magazine habitually compares the cash price to the sum of the monthly payments. In this example, for instance, one would be advised that he will have to pay $1728.29 for the merchandise rather than $1000. Why is this somewhat misleading? In your opinion, is such advice on balance more deceptive or more informative?

We return now to the nagging problem of computing the lump sum equivalent of a stream of uncertain future damages. Earlier sections on this topic focussed principally on discount rates and adjustments for the contingent nature of the income flows being replaced. The *Liepelt* decision, which allowed tax consequences to be considered in calculating lump sum damages, was only alluded to in passing. The following case raises the tax issue squarely and directly.

For many types of damage awards—such as personal injury and wrongful death—the lump-sum damage award does not become part of taxable income to the recipient, thus seemingly providing a tax benefit to the extent that the income being replaced would have been subject to taxation. On the other hand, as the *DeLucca* opinion below recognizes, the interest rates used to discount future earnings are not generally reflective of the fact that earnings on the original lump sum are taxable and therefore do not constitute a *net* rate of return to the recipient. In other words, using the market interest rates *over*discounts future earnings. Note, however, that the tax exemption on the original lump sum and the overdiscounting are counterbalancing in the direction of their effects.

DeLUCCA v. UNITED STATES

United States Court of Appeals, Ninth Circuit, 1982.
670 F.2d 843.

SKOPIL, Circuit Judge:

The United States conceded liability in the death of plaintiff's decedent. The court below awarded the wife of the deceased $483,380 for loss of her husband's earnings and support. This amount was calculated as follows:

Projected earnings for 1980	$21,468
Less federal income tax	-3,099
Less state income tax	-1,073
After tax income	$17,296
Less 30% for decedent's consumption	-5,189
Annual Loss of Support	$12,107

The court then found that the rate of wage increases and the discount factor would "essentially balance off each other," so it simply multiplied the $12,107 by 30.5 (the expected work life of the deceased). The award for loss of support came to $369,263.50. To this the court added $21,793 (loss of support from accident to date of trial) for a total of $391,056.50.

The district court then added an amount to compensate for income taxes on the investment earnings of the lump sum award. It is this part of the calculation the government challenges. The district court stated:

> Since it is assumed that plaintiff wife will invest her award, a full compensation for loss of future support should also take into account the fact that income taxes must be paid on her investment earnings. Norfolk and Western Ry. Co. v. Liepelt, [444 U.S. 490] 100 S.Ct. 755 [62 L.Ed.2d 689] (February 1980). Cf. Sauers v. Alaska Barge, 600 F.2d 238, 247 (9th Cir. 1979). To provide plaintiff wife an income of $12,107.00 after paying state and federal income taxes reasonably approximated at a 20% effective rate, she must be given $15,134.00 ($15,134.00 × 80% = $12,107.00). To compensate for loss of support over 30.5 years, she should therefore receive $462,587.00 (30.5 × $15,134.00) as the present value of loss of support.

The total loss of support to plaintiff was therefore increased to $483,380.00 and judgment was entered accordingly.

The district court provided for interest on the total damage award at 4% per annum "from the date of judgment November 4, 1980, until this judgment is satisfied."

The issues presented on appeal are:

> (1) whether the district court erred in adding to the lump sum damage award an amount to compensate for taxes on income that will be earned by investing the award; and

> (2) whether the district court erred in specifying that post-judgment interest must be paid beginning on the date of entry of the judgment until the judgment is satisfied.

Damages to be awarded under the Federal Tort Claims Act ("FTCA") are governed by the law of the place of the wrongful act, but are limited to compensatory damages. 28 U.S.C. § 2674. California law, applicable in this case, also limits damages to compensatory damages. In re Paris Air Crash, 622 F.2d 1315 (9th Cir.), cert. denied 449 U.S. 976, 101 S.Ct. 387, 66 L.Ed.2d 237 (1980); Cal.Civ.Proc.Code § 377.

In United States v. English, 521 F.2d 63 (9th Cir. 1975), this court set specific guidelines for calculating wrongful death damages under the FTCA: (1) calculate the future earnings the decedent could have expected over his life work expectancy; (2) deduct taxes and other amounts the decedent would or could not have contributed; and (3) discount this amount to its present value. Id. at 76.

In Sauers v. Alaska Barge, 600 F.2d 238 (9th Cir. 1979), the plaintiff argued that the district court erred in "failing to increase the lump sum awarded to account for the fact that the interest earned when that sum is invested would be taxable." Id. at 247. The *Sauers* court rejected this contention. The court stated that

> "[m]athematically, the plaintiff is right. Had the judgment called for the defendant to make deferred payments rather than a lump sum award, the funding of such an award would have required either an investment large enough to allow for any income tax on the interest yield of the fund or management of the investment in a manner that would either eliminate, or compensate for, the income tax on its yield."

Id. The court, notwithstanding the mathematical correctness of the plaintiff's argument held that the plaintiff was not entitled to this increasing factor.

Shortly thereafter, the Supreme Court indicated that this tax on the income generated by the lump sum award should be included in the calculation. Norfolk and Western Ry. Co. v. Liepelt, 444 U.S. 490, 495, 100 S.Ct. 755, 758, 62 L.Ed.2d 689 (1980). In *Liepelt*, the plaintiff had contended that the decedent's income taxes on his future earnings should not be deducted from the lump sum award. The court rejected this contention and noted that since the income taxes on the decedent's future earnings should be deducted, properly offered estimates of the income taxes on the earnings generated by the lump sum damage award should correspondingly be added:

> "Logically, it would certainly seem correct that [the income to be earned by the damage award] should be estimated on an after-tax basis. But the fact that such an after-tax estimate, if offered in proper form, would also be admissible does not persuade us that it is wrong to use after-tax figures instead of gross earnings in projecting what the decedent's financial contributions to his survivors would have been had this tragic accident not occurred."

Id. This statement by the Supreme Court indicates the Court finds that a lump sum damage award should be increased by the amount of income tax that would have to be paid on the earnings of the award.

After *Liepelt*, this Circuit again addressed the identical issue in Hollinger v. United States, 651 F.2d 636 (9th Cir. 1981). This court, in remanding for a recalculation of damages, followed *Liepelt* and required the district court to adjust the lump sum award for the income taxes on the income generated by the award:

> "The interest that Hollinger will earn on the discounted principal in a safe investment, however, will also be taxable. The effective interest rate for an investor is equal to the stated interest rate reduced by the product of the stated interest rate and the investor's tax rate. The principal amount necessary to produce a given after tax yield per month is the principal amount that would be necessary to produce that amount if there were no tax divided

by the percentage of his income that the investor retains after taxes. Thus an award of $600,000, not taking the tax on interest into
effect, would be increased to $1,000,000 for a 40% tax bracket re-
cipient. Clearly, then, the possible adjustments involved in taking
this aspect of taxes into account are significant. Although we
have found no cases in our court where such a calculation was
made, other courts have properly made such an adjustment.
McWeeney v. New York, N.H. & H. R.R. Co., 282 F.2d 34, 37 (2d
Cir. 1960). This Supreme Court has also recently suggested that
the tax on the discounted principal might properly be considered.
Norfolk & Western Ry. Co. v. Liepelt, 444 U.S. 490, 495 [100 S.Ct.
755, 758, 62 L.Ed.2d 689] (1980)."

Id. at 642.

The government argues that the statement in *Liepelt* was dicta,
and therefore is not controlling in this court. However, the *Liepelt*
statement gives a clear indication of how the Supreme Court feels
damage awards should be calculated. Even if the statement was not
essential to its decision in *Liepelt*, the direction given by the Supreme
Court should be followed by this Circuit. This Circuit in *Hollinger*
expressly considered the *Leipelt* statement and followed it.

The government offers some calculations to show that even if
plaintiff was awarded the amount of lost earnings *without* the addition of the disputed tax factor, this amount invested at 7% would
yield $27,000 the first year. Since the plaintiff lost only $12,000 this
year, the government thus claims that even with this smaller award
the plaintiff would be awarded more than her annual loss of support.
This calculation is misleading and erroneous. The government neglects to explain that the lump sum award has been discounted to present value, which means that a large portion of her earnings in the
early years must be reinvested in order to generate enough income in
the later years to keep up with the inflation and wage increases that
will have occurred.

The government argues that the possibility of the plaintiff investing the award in tax-free bonds negates the addition of a factor for
income taxes on the earnings generated by the award. However, the
district court, to discount the award to present value, assumed that
plaintiff would invest her award in a secure investment. Tax-free
bonds yield a lower interest rate than other secure investments available in the market and thus are most advantageous to persons in a
high tax bracket because the higher the tax bracket the more the
savings in taxes. An awardee not in a high tax bracket who invested
in tax-free bonds would receive less of a return than if he invested in
a secure taxable investment, and thus the return would fail to be sufficient to yield the yearly amounts determined by the district court
before discounting to present value. The district courts should not

be prevented from estimating the effects of taxes of earnings from awards simply because the method plaintiff will use to invest her award is speculative; "so are most predictions courts make about future incomes [and] expenses." United States v. English, supra at 75. There was sufficient expert testimony about the effect of taxes and tax-free investments on the plaintiff's award such that the district court's finding cannot be said to be clearly erroneous. In this situation, where investment in tax-free bonds would not be advantageous, the possibility that plaintiff would invest in tax-free bonds is low and should not negate the increase of her award for the amount of income taxes on the earnings generated.

In light of the direction given by the Supreme Court in *Leipelt*, and followed by this Circuit in *Hollinger*, we affirm the district court.

* * *

QUESTIONS

1. For many years, courts have tended to hear evidence as to what the victim's before-tax income would have been, then discount that back to a present value without any allowance for taxes. This procedure is implicit in the examples supplied earlier in the chapter. An alternative technique is to estimate the lost income on an after-tax basis, then provide a lump-sum whose proceeds—the return on which is taxable—will yield a flow equal to the lost after-tax income. How hard would it be to do the latter in a substantially accurate manner? [Harder than you might imagine. Think carefully.] See Brady, Brookshire & Cobb, "Calculating the Effects of Income Taxes on Lost Earnings," 18 Trial 65 (1982)

2. How would a court cope with probabilistic factors that might have a material effect on one's future tax liability, e.g., children, marital status, charitable giving, place of residence, etc.?

3. Although it is far too complicated to demonstrate rigorously here (as your reflections on question one above may have caused you to suspect), computer simulations for representative taxpayers show that the tax benefits from the non-taxability of the original lump sum tend to be dominated by the taxability of the proceeds, provided that the time period involved is more than a few years. In short, neglecting the tax consequences does lead to a slight under-recovery by plaintiffs, all other things being equal. You may obtain some intuitive grasp of why this is so by reflecting on the possible analogy with the loan amortization table earlier in the chapter as Exhibit 3.8. In the present context, the lump sum damage award is the principal amount of an initial asset (rather than liability) and the lost after-tax income to be replaced represents a withdrawal (rather than a payment). Accrued interest adds to the principal, but the IRS takes a

bite of this, thus reducing the effective interest rate. To the extent that withdrawals for consumption come out of reduction in the original ("tax free") principal, however, the beneficiary enjoys a species of tax shelter. The net effect is, as suggested above, generally a slight disadvantage to the victim or his beneficiary, varying directly with the interest rates. Can you see at least roughly why this might be? How small would the inaccuracy have to be before you would be inclined to ignore it? Why are there arguably counterbalancing inaccuracies?

LOS ANGELES DEPARTMENT OF WATER AND POWER v. MANHART

Supreme Court of the United States, 1978.
435 U.S. 702, 98 S.Ct. 1370, 55 L.Ed.2d 657.

Mr. Justice STEVENS delivered the opinion of the Court.

As a class, women live longer than men. For this reason, the Los Angeles Department of Water and Power required its female employees to make larger contributions to its pension fund than its male employees. We granted certiorari to decide whether this practice discriminated against individual female employees because of their sex in violation of § 703(a)(1) of the Civil Rights Act of 1964, as amended.

For many years the Department has administered retirement, disability, and death-benefit programs for its employees. Upon retirement each employee is eligible for a monthly retirement benefit computed as a fraction of his or her salary multiplied by years of service. The monthly benefits for men and women of the same age, seniority, and salary are equal. Benefits are funded entirely by contributions from the employees and the Department, augmented by the income earned on those contributions. No private insurance company is involved in the administration or payment of benefits.

Based on a study of mortality tables and its own experience, the Department determined that its 2,000 female employees, on the average, will live a few years longer than its 10,000 male employees. The cost of a pension for the average retired female is greater than for the average male retiree because more monthly payments must be made to the average woman. The Department therefore required female employees to make monthly contributions to the fund which were 14.84% higher than the contributions required of comparable male employees. Because employee contributions were withheld from paychecks, a female employee took home less pay then a male employee earning the same salary.

* * *

It is now well recognized that employment decisions cannot be predicated on mere "stereotyped" impressions about the characteristics of males or females. Myths and purely habitual assumptions about a woman's inability to perform certain kinds of work are no longer acceptable reasons for refusing to employ qualified individuals, or for paying them less. This case does not, however, involve a fictional difference between men and women. It involves a generalization that the parties accept as unquestionably true: Women, as a class, do live longer than men. The Department treated its women employees differently from its men employees because the two classes are in fact different. It is equally true, however, that all individuals in the respective classes do not share the characteristic that differentiates the average class representatives. Many women do not live as long as the average man and many men outlive the average woman. The question, therefore, is whether the existence or nonexistence of "discrimination" is to be determined by comparison of class characteristics or individual characteristics. * * *

The statute makes it unlawful "to discriminate against any individual with respect to his compensation, terms, conditions, or privileges of employment, because of such individual's race, color, religion, sex, or national origin." 42 U.S.C. § 2000e–2(a)(1). The statute's focus on the individual is unambiguous * * *. Even a true generalization about the class is an insufficient reason for disqualifying an individual to whom the generalization does not apply.

That proposition is of critical importance in this case because there is no assurance that any individual woman working for the Department will actually fit the generalization on which the Department's policy is based.

* * *

It is true, of course, that while contributions are being collected from the employees, the Department cannot know which individuals will predecease the average woman. Therefore, unless women as a class are assessed an extra charge, they will be subsidized, to some extent, by the class of male employees. It follows, according to the Department, that fairness to its class of male employees justifies the extra assessment against all of its female employees.

But the question of fairness to various classes affected by the statute is essentially a matter of policy for the legisature to address. Congress has decided that classifications based on sex, like those based on national origin or race, are unlawful. * * *

Even if the statutory language were less clear, the basic policy of the statute requires that we focus on fairness to individuals rather than fairness to classes. * * *

Finally, there is no reason to believe that Congress intended a special definition of discrimination in the context of employee group insurance coverage. It is true that insurance is concerned with events that are individually unpredictable, but that is characteristic of many employment decisions. Individual risks, like individual performance, may not be predicted by resort to classifications proscribed by Title VII. Indeed, the fact that this case involves a group insurance program highlights a basic flaw in the Department's fairness argument. For when insurance risks are grouped, the better risks always subsidize the poorer risks. * * * Treating different classes of risks as though they were the same for purposes of group insurance is a common practice that has never been considered inherently unfair. To insure the flabby and the fit as though they were equivalent risks may be more common than treating men and women alike; but nothing more than habit makes one "subsidy" seem less fair than the other.

An employment practice that requires 2,000 individuals to contribute more money into a fund than 10,000 other employees simply because each of them is a woman, rather than a man, is in direct conflict with both the language and the policy of the Act. Such a practice does not pass the simple test of whether the evidence shows "treatment of a person in a manner which but for that person's sex would be different." It constitutes discrimination and is unlawful unless exempted by the Equal Pay Act of 1963 or some other affirmative justification.

* * *

The Department argues that the different contributions exacted from men and women were based on the factor of longevity rather than sex. It is plain, however, that any individual's life expectancy is based on a number of factors, of which sex is only one. * * *

* * *

In essence, the Department is arguing that the prima facie showing of discrimination based on evidence of different contributions for the respective sexes is rebutted by its demonstration that there is a like difference in the cost of providing benefits for the respective classes. That argument might prevail if Title VII contained a cost-justification defense comparable to the affirmative defense available in a price discrimination suit. But neither Congress nor the courts have recognized such a defense under Title VII.

Although we conclude that the Department's practice violated Title VII, we do not suggest that the statute was intended to revolutionize the insurance and pension industries. All that is at issue today is a requirement that men and women make unequal contributions to an employer-operated pension fund. Nothing in our holding implies that it would be unlawful for an employer to set aside equal retirement contributions for each employee and let each retiree purchase the largest benefit which his or her accumulated contributions could command in the open market. Nor does it call into question the insurance industry practice of considering the composition of an employer's work force in determining the probable cost of a retirement or death benefit plan.

* * *

* * * [A]lthough we agree with the Court of Appeals' analysis of the statute, we vacate its judgment and remand the case for further proceedings consistent with this opinion.

It is so ordered.

* * *

Mr. Chief Justice BURGER, with whom Mr. Justice REHNQUIST joins, concurring in part and dissenting in part.

* * *

Gender-based actuarial tables have been in use since at least 1843, and their statistical validity has been repeatedly verified. The vast life insurance, annuity, and pension plan industry is based on these tables. As the Court recognizes, * * * it is a fact that "women, as a class, do live longer than men." It is equally true that employers cannot know in advance when individual members of the class will die. * * * Yet, if they are to operate economically workable group pension programs, it is only rational to permit them to rely on statistically sound and proved disparities in longevity between men and women. Indeed, it seems to me irrational to assume Congress intended to outlaw use of the fact that, for whatever reasons or combination of reasons, women as a class outlive men.

* * *

The reality of differences in human mortality is what mortality experience tables reflect. The difference is the added longevity of women. All the reasons why women statistically outlive men are not clear. But categorizing people on the basis of sex, the one acknowledged immutable difference between men and women, is to take into account all of the unknown reasons, whether biologically or culturally based, or both, which give women a significantly greater life expectancy than men. It is therefore true as the Court says, "that any individual's life expectancy is based on a number of factors, of which sex is only one." * * * But it is not true that by seizing upon the only constant, "measurable" factor, no others were taken into account. All other factors, whether known but variable—or unknown—are the elements which automatically account for the actuarial disparity. And all are accounted for when the constant factor is used as a basis for determining the costs and benefits of a group pension plan.

* * * [S]ex is the umbrella-constant under which all of the elements leading to differences in longevity are grouped and assimilated, and the only objective feature upon which an employer—or anyone else, including insurance companies—reliably base a cost differential for the "risk" being insured.

This is in no sense a failure to treat women as "individuals" in violation of the statute, as the Court holds. It is to treat them as individually as it is possible to do in the face of the unknowable length of each individual life. Individually, every woman has the same statistical possibility of outliving men. This is the essence of basing decisions on reliable statistics when individual determinations are infeasible or, as here, impossible.

* * *

I find it anomalous, if not contradictory, that the Court's opinion tells us, in effect, * * * that the holding is not really a barrier to responding to the complaints of men employees, as a group. The Court states that employers may give their employees precisely the same dollar amount and require them to secure their own annuities directly from an insurer, who of course, is under no compulsion to ignore 135 years of accumulated, recorded longevity experience.

QUESTIONS

1. Judge Kilkenny, dissenting in the Circuit court decision of *Manhart*, comments, *"Unless and until* unisex tables are developed, an employer, to comply with the EEOC regulations on equal benefits, may not charge any additional amount to his female employees. In thus forcing the employer himself to cover the added amount necessary to assure equal benefits, this makes the employment of females economically unattractive, a result clearly at odds with the thrust of Title VII." 553 F.2d 581, 598 (9th Cir. 1976). Is this a valid argument? How might an employer react to the *Manhart* rule in making his hiring decisions? Does the rule benefit women employees in the manner intended by the Court?

2. The majority opinion states that "unless women as a class are assessed an extra charge, they will be subsidized, to some extent, by the class of male employees," yet "when insurance risks are grouped, the better risks always subsidize the poorer risk." What is the likely impact of this "subsidy" on the attitudes and employment decisions of male and female employees? Would the *Manhart* rule lead to a well-balanced composition of male and female employees in one particular company? What pressures might there be on the salaries paid to men and women?

3. "Nothing in our holding implies that it would be unlawful for an employer to set aside equal retirement contributions for each employee and let each retiree purchase the largest benefit which his or her accumulated contributions could command in the open market." The dissent claims that this statement by the majority is "anomalous, if not contradictory". Is there a valid distinction between employer-funded pension plans and those funded by third parties? Is there a difference between (a) equal contributions by employees and unequal benefits and (b) unequal contributions and equal benefits?

4. Some large employers are starting to create "flexible" benefits programs. Each employee is allotted a particular number of "points" that may be used to "purchase" various types of benefits from a "menu" of alternative group plan coverages. The menu may involve selecting various levels of medical coverage, retirement annuities, life insurance, child care, etc. The "points" of course are in effect shadow prices with some monetary equivalent and, by choosing to allocate them in different ways, individual employees can potentially end up with dramatically different benefit packages. The companies typically set the point prices of alternative benefit coverages in proportion to the cost incurred by the companies to support each type of group benefit. What would you predict would happen under such plans? Is this desirable or not? Why? Do you see any potential legal problems?

5. If the benefits from a pension plan could be assigned to third parties, a true market value of their worth could be arrived at. Should we attempt to determine the level of contributions required by an "assignment" concept? Or are there other considerations besides true market value?

CONSTRUING THE AGE DISCRIMINATION IN EMPLOYMENT ACT

The Department of Labor has interpreted the Age Discrimination in Employment Act (ADEA) to mean that workers in the protected 40–69 age group cannot be denied benefits extended to younger workers unless higher costs of providing the benefit to the older workers can be demonstrated actuarially and, perhaps most importantly, the modification of the benefits is "not a subterfuge" to evade the purposes of the statute. 29 CFR 860.120. Disputes have recently arisen with respect to the meaning of the ADEA as it applies to the group insurance benefits provided by certain employers. Consider the situation of a hypothetical employer, Beekins Manufacturing, Inc.

Under the group insurance plan provided by Beekins, life insurance proceeds are paid to the employee's beneficiary at death but, in the event of Permanent Total Disability (PTD), the insured employee can elect to receive what would have been the death benefit in monthly installments. The same level of life insurance protection is provided to employees of all ages but, beginning at age 60, PTD coverage ceases. Many other firms are likely to be in the same position as Beekins. A study of benefits plans shows that, when disability coverage is linked to life insurance, the common practice is to drop disability coverage at age 60 or 65. See, Blostin, "Is Employer-Sponsored Life Insurance Declining Relative to Other Benefits," Monthly Labor Rev., 3–13 (Sept. 1981).

Nobody contests the fact that disability insurance is more expensive for the older workers. But, suppose that the Equal Employment Opportunity Commission (EEOC) takes the position that the ADEA should be construed as forbidding the complete elimination of any benefit type to an age class. Specifically, it is argued that if a benefit—e.g., coverage against a distinct risk such as PTD—is provided to any employees at all, then any cost differential may be used only to justify a *reduction* but not an abolition of protection against that same risk for older workers.

QUESTIONS

1. Disabling health problems do increase in frequency with advancing age, and this factor alone would create higher costs of providing PTD benefits for older workers. In addition, there is also a "moral hazard" problem that becomes increasingly significant. What is the moral hazard and what is its significance in this context?

2. Why do the facts suggest that, under the Beekins plan, the older workers are "overbenefitted" relative to younger workers in terms of life insurance coverage? Is it plausible to think that the "overbenefit" on the value of the mortality coverage might roughly compensate for the "underbenefit" from loss of PTD coverage? If not, should an age-related differential in the value of the *total* benefits package be regarded as a violation of the purposes of the Act?

3. If the EEOC view prevails, why would you predict that employers would reduce life insurance coverage to older workers in order to counterbalance the mandated increase in PTD coverage?

4. If you were writing an *amicus* brief for the Golden Age Workers Association, what position would be in the best interests of your clients?

5. The scene is a meeting of house counsels for other similarly situated employers. Another attendee says:

"Look, what are we worrying about? The Act probably requires us to spend roughly the same amount on benefits for all age groups anyway. Why should we care how our payments are allocated as long as their total amount isn't going up?"

You blurt out "Idiot! . . ." And what do you say after that?

6. How would you decide this issue as a federal judge trying to implement what you think was Congressional intent? (You may assume that there is no legislative history that is dispositive on this point.)

Chapter IV

MAPPINGS AND "DEMAND" DECISIONS

In previous chapters, several different kinds of diagrammatic models were used. One advantage of diagrammatic models is their ability to depict the results of continuous adjustment of some variable such as quantity of road repairs, "effort" in litigation, level of care, etc. Those quantity adjustments, usually measured along the horizontal axis of the diagram, are then translated into a causative impact on benefits, costs, a probability of some happening, etc. The "result" variable is generally measured along the vertical scale of the diagram and the interaction between the two variables is captured in a "curve" that depicts the functional relationship between them. Note, however, that the number of variables involved is only two: one cause and one effect, corresponding to the horizontal and vertical dimensions of the diagram. Cause and effect relationships in the real world are frequently much more complex; for instance, two or more causes may act jointly to produce a particular effect. How can these more complex situations be modelled?

One response, of course, is to employ mathematical models. Professional economists frequently do employ mathematical models and such models are the most elegant and generalized method of dealing with many problems. But economists also have developed graphical models that retain the expository attractiveness of the "picture" approach while permitting at least a limited analysis of interactive causes. As we shall now see, certain widely used three-variable economic models (typically involving one effect and two interactive causes) are in essence topographic maps where the "height" dimension measures effect and the "longitude" and "latitude" dimensions measure the causes. This type of model will first be introduced in the context of an ordinary topographic map of real estate holdings where the questions dealt with are facially unrelated to economics. Nonetheless, the reasoning involved in interpreting such a map—which is familiar to most laymen—has almost exact analogues in economic models. Anyone who can understand the more familiar form of map should, with a modest amount of application, be able to make the transferral to the more abstract context of the economic models.

As a prefatory matter, it should perhaps be indicated that the models dealt with in this chapter are related most closely to what is known as "demand" economics. In the next chapter, very similar constructs will be reinterpreted as "production function" models that are useful in areas of law such as theories of tort liability.

TOPOGRAPHICAL MAP READING

The topographical map in the accompanying Exhibit 4.1 shows land currently being subdivided and sold off by the Bomber Land Company. Although most of this tract is still held by the developer, two lots have already been sold, to McNabb and Zepp, respectively. The boundaries of the lots and the siting of the houses thereupon are as indicated on the attached map.

Bomber Land Company has entered into certain covenants with the purchasers of lots in this tract. One is that the company will, at its own expense, construct a community TV antenna. The agreement is that the antenna tower must be placed at the highest point within an area demarcated by the following:

(1) a straight line connecting boundary markers 249–59 and 249–60;

(2) a straight line due southeast from marker 249–60; and

(3) a line running straight east from boundary marker 249–59.

The agreement calls for an antenna not less than 40 nor more than 60 feet in height, construction to be completed within 8 months after sale of the fourth lot in the development.

Bomber is also prepared to enter into other individualized agreements with subsets of property owners. One such agreement has already been completed. It involves an easement for a water pumping facility to be used jointly by the Zepp and McNabb families. Tentatively, the agreement entitles them to construct the pump at the point indicated on the map. However, the two property owners also have 12 months in which to agree upon and designate any other mutually agreeable site within Bomber Development's holdings.

QUESTIONS

1. Prospective purchasers of other lots in this development would reasonably be concerned with the precise location of the TV tower.

  a. Draw the boundaries of the area within which the TV antenna must be placed.

EXHIBIT 4.1

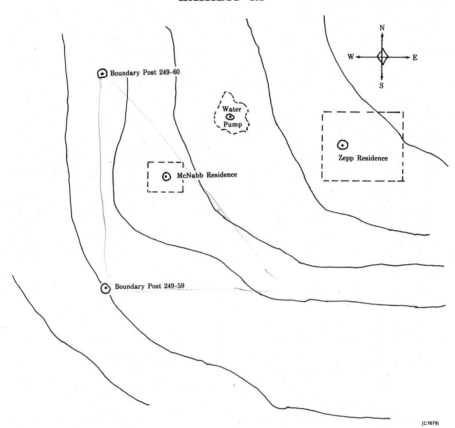

[C7679]

b. Does the information on the topographical map permit you to say approximately where the antenna must be placed? Indicate on the map your best estimate of the antenna site.

c. A colleague sees your map work and exclaims: "Idiot! You have the whole business just backwards. You're indicating one of the *lowest* sites in that tract, rather than the highest!" Can you prove her wrong?

2. In connection with the water pump easement, you may assume that McNabb and Zepp each wish to minimize the distance of the pump from their residences. The reason for this, of course, is the high cost of piping from the pump to the residences, which must be borne by each party individually. Other than distance, the two parties have no preferences as to the location of the pump.

a. Prove that the tentative site designation is not an "efficient" one for the parties, i.e., that there are other sites that are mutually preferable.

b. What can you predict about the location of the alternative site that will be designated? What conditions must be met in order for the designated choice to be "efficient," i.e., undominated by yet another site that is better for both parties?

INDIFFERENCE CURVE MODELS

In familiar topographic maps of land such as Exhibit 4.1, the "contour lines" on the map show points of equal height. Given a set of "coordinates" in terms of horizontal and vertical positioning, one can identify points on the map and say something about their height. Why is height important? In question one above, the best site for an antenna is presumably the highest one. Hence, any two points on the same contour line are, assuming that height alone is considered, equally good sites for an antenna. One would nonetheless prefer to be as high as possible on the "hill" or "mountain" depicted. The deed restrictions, however, constrain the choice of an antenna site to that subset of the land contained within well defined permissible boundaries. Except in the special case where there is a "peak" somewhere within the permissible boundaries, the highest achievable site will usually be found on one of the boundaries themselves, i.e., that on the "uphill" side.

Exhibit 4.2 is an analogous economic model. Now, the horizontal and vertical axes represent not distances but quantities of goods X and Y, respectively. Point a has "coordinates" of 8Y and 10X, thus identifying it as a "bundle" of goods containing eight units of Y and ten units of X. The contour lines on this topographic map indicate equal levels of preference; a "higher" bundle will be preferred to a "lower" one. Since bundles on the same contour line, such as a and b, are equally high, the preference relation between them is one of indifference and the contour lines are therefore commonly called "indifference curves." [Building on the Greek prefix "iso" meaning equal, the terms iso-utility or iso-preference curves are sometimes also encountered.] Hence, an "indifference curve model" is really a topographic map of an individual's preferences expressed in terms of quantities of two "goods." If allowed to do so, an individual will choose the bundle that is as high as possible on his or her "preference surface" or satisfaction mountain.

The "constraints" involved in the first problem were property rights, presumably enforced in terms of a penalty for trespassing or some other sanction that makes location of the antenna outside of the designated boundaries impractical. In an economic model, the constraints on choices may be legal rather than narrowly economic. For instance, legal prohibitions on the use or possession of controlled drugs inhibit their consumption. [Also, see Matthews v. Massell and

EXHIBIT 4.2

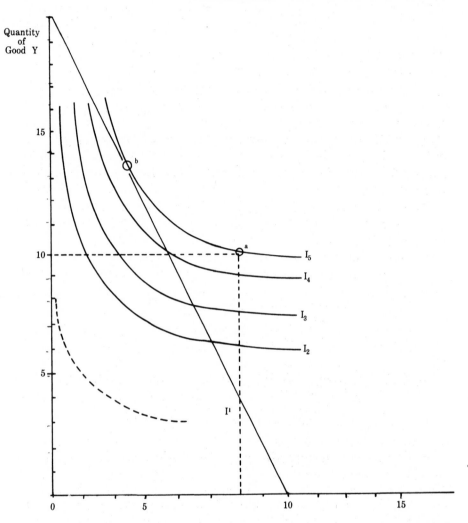

[D25]

Tilton v. Richardson later in this chapter.] The legal limitation may not be absolute, however, as exemplified by wartime "ration" allowances restricting consumers to certain maximum quantities of regulated commodities. Hence, it is quite appropriate to incorporate fundamentally legal constraints into economic-type decision models. The special form of constraint traditionally treated by economists is nonetheless based on narrowly economic parameters, namely prices and income.

Suppose Beyer has $100 and the prices of goods Y and X are $5 and $10 per unit, respectively. Is it possible for Beyer to purchase bundles a or b in Exhibit 4.2? What about any of the other possible bundles? It would be useful if we could partition the map, sometimes called a "commodity space", into two areas, that containing bundles that Beyer does have enough money to buy and that containing other bundles whose purchase is impossible because it would require more money than is available. The area of real possibilities, from which Beyer must choose, is called the "opportunity set" to distinguish it from the set of other theoretically possible bundles that do not represent real possibilities under the assumed circumstances of income and prices.

It is worth suffering the pain of a little simple algebra to achieve some generalizable results. Let M stand for the money available, X and Y for the quantities of the two goods, and P_x and P_y the respective prices of the goods. Then the combinations of X and Y purchases that exhaust all of the money are those that satisfy the equation

$$P_xX + P_yY = M$$

where the left-hand side is the summation of the money (price times quantity) spent on X and on Y and the right hand side is the money available to be spent. Rearranging the terms just a little bit yields the following form of the same basic "budget equation" above:

$$Y = (M/P_y) - (P_x/P_y)X$$

The above is the equation of the so-called "budget line" that forms the outer boundary of an individual's opportunity set when constrained only by income and prices. The appropriate line is drawn in Exhibit 4.2 for the assumed $100 income and the $5 and $10 prices for the two goods. Bundles on the budget line or within the triangular shaped opportunity set are possible choices; those to the right of the budget line exceed Beyer's resources. Note that the budget line is a straight line whose form corresponds to the algebraic equation above: if X were 0, then Y would be (M/P_y) or $(100/5)$, the height of the "intercept" of the straight line where it cuts the vertical axis. For each unit increase in the purchase of X, the amount of Y must fall by

(P_x/P_y) or (10/5), this magnitude corresponding to the downward "slope" of the budget line.

Economists traditionally eschew any analysis of why preference *maps* themselves change, i.e., why a set of indifference curves may shift. (That analysis is generally considered the domain of the sociologist or behavioral psychologist.) Rather, economic models concentrate on explaining observed changes in choices as due to *shifts in constraints*, such as the so-called budget line derived above. Exactly how the budget line shifts and what are the behavioral implications can have interesting legal ramifications.

The sections immediately following this introductory material provide illustrations of the use of indifference curve models in legal applications such as group decisionmaking, the theory of "efficient" contract breach and the analysis of promissory reliance. The group decisionmaking analysis builds on the same principles as developed above for the location of an optimal location for the well. That analysis is a rather special case of the trading model called the Edgeworth Box by economists. The contract breach model is a more traditional and straightforward application of the same Edgeworth Box trading analysis. The promissory reliance model depicts a promise as knowledge that shifts a budget line. The next few problems deal with alternative forms of governmental grants. When you read the grant cases, attempt to relate the facts to shifts in budget lines. In order to do so, you may wish to refer explicitly to the equation above, reflecting on which of the parameters M, P_x and P_y have changed and what that implies in terms of a budget line shift.

GROUP DECISIONS UNDER MAJORITY RULE

Majority rule voting processes are mechanisms designed to take individuals' preferences and aggregate them into a "group preference" in a reasonable way. Although earlier scholars had also pointed out some of the inherent peculiarities of voting as a rational decisionmaking process, Kenneth Arrow's 1951 book on *Social Choice and Individual Values* effectively marked the birth of a new subdiscipline of the social sciences dedicated to the study of "public choice" and, specifically, the implications of alternative voting institutions. In many respects, only some of which will be exemplified in the problems below, the results of the public choice scholarship [a] have been quite disturbing because they call into question the reasonable-

a. The public choice literature in the years between 1951 and 1976 is reviewed in Mueller, "Public Choice: A Survey," 14 J.Econ.Literature 395 (1976). A discussion of voting theory in a form accessible to a lay reader appears in Musgrave and Musgrave, Public Finance in Theory and Practice, 102–26 (2nd ed. 1976).

ness of results achieved under any conceivable set of voting institutions.

What do we mean by a reasonable or rational group decision process? Two widely accepted desiderata for a rational collective decisionmaking process are what may be termed "consistency" and "path-irrelevance." That is, there ought not to be anything inconsistent about the way in which different alternatives are ranked, nor ought the conclusion ultimately reached depend on the way in which the options are presented (i.e., the "path" a group follows in reaching the decision). Unfortunately, the mechanics of majority rule decision processes seem to have certain inherent weaknesses. The demonstrations of this fact originally were couched in terms of the political process itself, but the results are applicable to all voting bodies. Consider why the models and questions presented below can be said to raise qualms about possible inherent inconsistency and arbitrariness in some familiar legal mechanisms that involve voting.

Two types of voting models are presented below. The first is a variant of the trading model developed above to deal with the possibility of a mutually agreeable relocation of the well site. Then, a similar situation is modelled in the "matrix" format that has been used several times in the preceding chapters. As will become apparent, each type of model has its own particular advantages.

TOPOGRAPHIC MODELLING OF VOTING DECISIONS

A certain three-person local government commission has the authority to levy taxes up to 2% of assessed value on local real estate. Any funds raised through such taxation can then be allocated between use A and use B. Majority rule is used in making all decisions of the commission.

Each commissioner has different preferences about budgetary mix, as illustrated by Exhibit 4.3 below which shows the "ideal" outcomes of commissioners 1, 2, and 3 as points E_1, E_2, and E_3, respectively. Of course, no single commissioner is in a position to impose any result unless the acquiescence of at least one other commissioner is also secured.

QUESTIONS

1. Suppose that each commissioner regards all solutions equidistant from his ideal in Exhibit 4.3 as equally preferable; i.e., the relative preference ordering of different outcomes for any commissioner is inversely related to its distance from that commissioner's ideal outcome E_1. Select one of the commissioners, then convert Exhibit 4.3 to a topographic map that shows at least three of the "contour lines" (i.e., the indifference curves) around that commissioner's "peak."

EXHIBIT 4.3 Majority Rule Decision Model

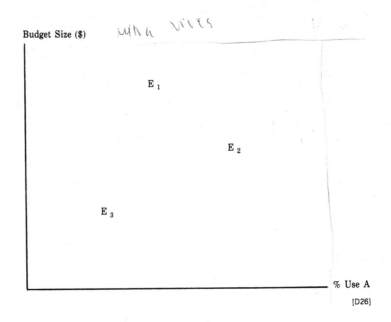

[D26]

2. On the topographic map just created, select a point vertically above ("north" of) the peak and label it X. If result X is not ranked as "high" as the result at the peak, why is that true? Doesn't result X correspond to more of *both* use A and use B? Then why isn't it better? Similarly, pick a point horizontally to the right of the peak and explain why the commissioner in question finds it inferior to the peak solution.

3. Now superimpose the preference maps of the other two commissioners on the same Exhibit. The interplay among these preferences will presumably determine the ultimate majority rule decision that emerges. Are there, however, any solutions shown on the map that are not possible choices for the commission? If so, indicate in some manner what constraint affects the possible choices. (If you believe that the information given is not sufficient, make a plausible assumption.)

4. Suppose that commissioners 1 and 2 were to form a majority coalition against commissioner 3. Show that all of the plausible "deals" involving a coalition between commissioners 1 and 2 ought to involve moving to some point along a line—commonly called the "con-

tract curve"—connecting their two "peaks." [What in the assumed facts causes this contract curve to be a *straight* line? What would determine its shape if that assumption were relaxed?] Pick a possible result from the coalition and label it A. What determines *where* along the contract curve for commissioners 1 and 2 that A will fall?

5. After result A has been reached through the operation of a coalition consisting of 1 and 2, commissioner 3 approaches 2 in hopes of creating a counter-coalition. Can 3 and 2 find any "improvements" on the tentative decision A such that they both would be better off? Identify these possibilities by using Exhibit 4.3, adding to it, if necessary, any other relevant curves or constructions.

6. Obviously, a majority coalition between any two voters is possible. If there are no procedural rules that limit counteroffers or the formation of alternative coalitions, what can be said about the final "majority choice" that will emerge from the voting process?

7. Assume that budget size and budget mix must be determined in separate decisions, i.e., first a vote is taken on the vertical adjustment of Exhibit 4.3, then a vote is taken on the horizontal adjustment. Does this specification of the procedural rules affect the answer to the previous question?

8. What in the original facts above required that the contour lines be perfect circles? Is this a plausible assumption? Why? Do any of the results in the questions above depend on the simplification embodied in the perfect circles?

9. The model developed here is a mere three-voter application. Can the same analytical tools be applied to more complex voting bodies? Give some thought to how the Exhibit 4.3 type of model would be used for the next step in generalization, a five-voter body. For an excellent and highly accessible discussion of this type of model, see Tullock, Toward a Mathematics of Politics (1967), Ch. II, esp. 33–36.

A MATRIX MODEL OF VOTE TRADING

A three-voter body is empowered to make a decision in which subresults A and B either may or may not be included in any combination. The three voters' preferences about A and B and the four alternative outcomes involving possible combinations of them are summarized in Exhibit 4.4. The numbers can be understood as evaluations of the results in terms of dollars, utility, or any other index that you find appealing.

EXHIBIT 4.4 Alternative Outcomes

Voter	A Only	B Only	A and B	Neither
1	+100	−1	+99	0
2	−1	−2	−3	0
3	−1	+100	+99	0

(handwritten above columns: C over "A and B", D over "Neither"; handwritten totals below: 98, 97, 195, 0)

QUESTIONS

1. How do the numerical entries in the last two columns of Exhibit 4.4 relate to the entries in the other columns?

2. If the inclusion of A and B were voted upon separately, e.g., as in a popular referendum, what result would be predictable?

3. Assume now that the result consisting of both A and B were offered directly. Does this command a majority over the result predicted in the previous answer?

4. "A result such as both A and B is achievable through either implicit or explicit logrolling that allows the intensities, and not just the directions, of the preferences on issues to count." Explain. In light of this, what would you say about the desirability of logrolling? What is meant by "implicit" logrolling?

5. Suppose that, in a different context, one of these voters were given an opportunity to choose between single pieces of different kinds of fruit presented in a pairwise fashion. First, a Coconut is chosen over a Date. Then, the opportunity is taken to replace the Coconut with a Banana. Finally, the Banana is surrendered in favor of an Apple. At this point, the possibility emerges of reoffering the same person a Date in exchange for the Apple. What would you predict as to whether the Date would be accepted? Why? What would you say if, upon actual presentation of the choice, the person acted contrary to your prediction?

6. Relabel the last columns of the Exhibit 4.4 as options C and D, respectively. Let the symbol ">" represent the words "is preferred to." Explain why the majority rule preferences of this voting body can then be summarized by the following relation:

$$A > B > C > D > A$$

What is bizarre about this result? What relation is there to #5 above?

7. Suppose that A, B, C, and D in the table above represented amendments to a main motion. Roberts' Rules of Order dictate that the last amendment introduced is the first to be voted upon. Is this likely to make a difference in the final result? Would you like your

(handwritten in left margin: "C D ↓ C B ↓ B A ↓ ? A D" and "cyclical majority")

amendment to be first or last? How can these results be applied to the question of whether control of the agenda also controls the ultimate result? See the legal applications in Levine and Plott, "Agenda Influence and Its Implications," 63 Va.L.Rev. 561 (1977).

8. Suppose that there are three voters who have the following sets of preference orderings over four alternatives A, B, C, and D: for Voter 1, C>B>A>D; for Voter 2, B>A>D>C; and for Voter 3, A>D>C>B. Assume that the alternatives are voted upon pairwise: first A against B, the winner of that first pairing against C, then the winner of the next pairing against D. Satisfy yourself that D will come out the final winner. In addition to being an arbitrary result of the order of the voting (as the previous question suggests), what *else* seems unsatisfactory about this result?

9. How do the above models and series of questions apply to an appellate court panel or a regulatory agency such as the Federal Communications Commission? [See Spitzer, "Multicriteria Choice Processes: An Application of Public Choice Theory to Bakke, the FCC, and the Courts," 88 Yale L.J. 717 (1979).] Does your answer to question 4 above depend on whether a court, an agency, or a legislature is involved? Why?

10. How can the "topographic map" trading model of the commissioners voting on a budget size and mix be interpreted as a *generalization* of this present matrix model? Explain. What would the preference maps of the individual voters have to look like in order for the problems reflected in the questions above not to arise?

CONSISTENCY IN THE COURTS

The question sets in the immediately preceding section were designed to highlight inherent problems in decisions that are made by voting. If the voting process is unconstrained, so that results previously rejected may be re-raised, there generally will be no "final" decision because there is no result that commands a majority against *all* possible alternatives. This is called the "cyclical majority" problem. Typically, procedural rules of some kind are used to constrain the process such that majority cycles are avoided. For instance, Roberts' Rules require a special procedure to "reconsider" a motion that has already been defeated. In the courts, a similar effect is exerted by the doctrine of *stare decisis*, which precludes the reassertion of arguments rejected in an earlier consideration. Any such limiting rule, however, produces "path dependence" wherein the ultimate results depend on seemingly arbitrary factors such as the order of consideration, the number and identity of other options considered at each stage, etc. In short, neatness and consistency can be imposed, but at the price of arbitrariness. For an interesting recent application of these notions to the decisions of the Supreme Court, see Easterbrook, "Ways of Criticizing the Court," 95 Harv.L.Rev. 802 (1982).

The previous problem set only hinted, however, at the issues raised by the possibility of vote-trading and strategic voting by judicial panels, juries, regulatory panels, etc. Once one understands the workings of voting processes, it becomes apparent that there are frequently practical gains to be had from voting for results that are, at least in part, strongly disfavored. There is, in fact, no possibility of designing a voting system that will not be subject to manipulation by strategic voting.[b]

Read the following criminal cases for possible practical applications of logrolling, strategic voting, or any of the other theoretical problems inherent in voting processes.

STATE OF MISSOURI v. BARTON

Missouri Court of Appeals, Eastern District, Division Three, 1980.
602 S.W.2d 479.

CRIST, Judge.

Defendant was charged by information with assault with the intent to kill *with malice aforethought,* but was convicted by the jury of a lesser included offense of assault with intent to do great bodily harm *without malice.* Under the Second Offender Act, his punishment was assessed at five years imprisonment. We affirm.

We are obliged to review the evidence, together with all reasonable inferences to be drawn therefrom, in a light most favorable to the state. State v. Winters, 579 S.W.2d 715, 717 (Mo.App.1979). Evidence or inferences to the contrary must be disregarded. State v. Arnold, 574 S.W.2d 1, 3 (Mo.App.1978). So viewed, the evidence appears as follows:

[Here the court briefly recounted the events leading up to the shotgun shooting by the defendant of the victim, Thomas Wells, outside a tavern where the two men had quarreled earlier in the evening.]

At first blush, defendant's "Point Relied On" is somewhat misleading, but a perusal of his argument indicated he believes the evidence was insufficient to support a conviction under the original charge, to-wit: assault with intent to kill with malice aforethought. Accordingly, he reasons that the trial court committed error when it failed to sustain his motion for acquittal and to dismiss the case in its entirety at the close of all the evidence. Defendant also argues that

b. See generally, Feldman, "Manipulating Voting Procedures," 17 Econ.Inquiry 452.

the court committed contiguous error in that it permitted the jury to be instructed as to the original charge.

Defendant's argument points to evidence which indicates that defendant was some 25–30 feet from the victim when he fired. Defendant states that had he actually intended to shoot Wells, from such a distance he would have inflicted considerably more damage than the victim actually suffered. Defendant relies on State v. Harty, 569 S.W.2d 783 (Mo.App.1978) which requires proof of intent in order to convict a defendant with either assault with intent to kill with malice aforethought or assault to do great bodily harm without malice. Defendant feels that without the requisite demonstration of intent, he is guilty of no more than common assault.

In our view, defendant erroneously equates intent with ability, or perhaps more aptly, with results. As so sagely pointed out in his brief, the jury might well have concluded that the defendant was, "* * * so drunk or ignorant that he missed * * *" Tom Wells, or at least, almost missed.

Contrary to defendant's ill-conceived supposition, it is not prejudicial error to submit the greater offense for the jury's consideration, even where the facts would not support a conviction therefor, when the verdict was for the lesser offense and that verdict is sustained by the evidence. State v. Brooks, 567 S.W.2d 348, 352 (Mo.App.1978). And, we specifically note that the charge of assault with intent to kill with malice aforethought did not expire from lack of evidence, but rather, from lack of a jury verdict.

Our foregoing, particularized recitation of the evidence purveys an adequate factual basis for defendant's conviction in that there was substantial evidence that defendant shot at Wells. We cannot oblige defendant by ignoring the evidence adduced by the state or in re-weighing the testimony. State v. Arnold, supra.

Judgment affirmed.

HARRIS v. RIVERA

Supreme Court of the United States, 1981.
454 U.S. 339, 102 S.Ct. 460, 70 L.Ed.2d 530.

PER CURIAM.

The questions presented by the certiorari petition concern the constitutionality of inconsistent verdicts in a nonjury criminal trial. Certiorari is granted and the judgment of the United States Court of Appeals for the Second Circuit is reversed.

* * *

Inconsistency in a verdict is not a sufficient reason for setting it aside. We have so held with respect to inconsistency between verdicts on separate charges against one defendant, Dunn v. United States, 284 U.S. 390, 52 S.Ct. 189, 76 L.Ed. 356, and also with respect to verdicts that treat codefendants in a joint trial inconsistently, United States v. Dotterweich, 320 U.S. 270, 279, 64 S.Ct. 134, 135, 88 L.Ed. 48.[14] Those cases, however, involved jury trials; as the Court of Appeals correctly recognized, both of those opinions stressed the unreviewable power of a jury to return a verdict of not guilty for impermissible reasons.[15] It is argued that a different rule should be applied to cases in which a judge is the factfinder.

* * *

We are not persuaded that an apparent inconsistency in a trial judge's verdict gives rise to an inference of irregularity in his finding of guilt that is sufficiently strong to overcome the well-established presumption that the judge adhered to basic rules of procedure.

* * *

The question that respondent has standing to raise is whether his trial was fairly conducted. The trial judge, the New York appellate courts, the Federal District Court, and the United States Court of Appeals all agreed that the record contains adequate evidence of his guilt.[20] These courts also agreed that the proceedings leading up to respondent's conviction were conducted fairly. Apart from the acquittal of Robinson, this record discloses no constitutional error. Even assuming that this acquittal was logically inconsistent with the conviction of respondent, respondent, who was found guilty beyond a

14. "Equally baseless is the claim of Dotterweich that, having failed to find the corporation guilty, the jury could not find him guilty. Whether the jury's verdict was the result of carelessness or compromise or a belief that the responsible individual should suffer the penalty instead of merely increasing, as it were, the cost of running the business of the corporation, is immaterial. Juries may indulge in precisely such motives or vagaries. Dunn v. United States, 284 U.S. 390 [52 S.Ct. 189, 76 L.Ed. 356]."

15. Justice Holmes' opinion in *Dunn,* his last for the Court, characteristically was brief and to the point. He quoted the following passage from Steckler v. United States, 7 F.2d 59, 60 (CA2 1925):

" 'The most that can be said in such cases is that the verdict shows that either in the acquittal or the conviction the jury did not speak their real conclusions, but that does not show that they were not convinced of the defendant's guilt. We interpret the acquittal as no more than their assumption of a power which they had no right to exercise,

but to which they were disposed through lenity.' " Dunn v. United States, 284 U.S. 390, 393, 52 S.Ct. 189, 190, 76 L.Ed. 356.

After citing Horning v. District of Columbia, 254 U.S. 135, he added:

"That the verdict may have been the result of compromise, or of a mistake on the part of the jury, is possible. But verdicts cannot be upset by speculation or inquiry into such matters." 284 U.S., at 393–394, 52 S.Ct., at 190–191.

20. "The question whether the evidence is constitutionally sufficient is of course wholly unrelated to the question of how rationally the verdict was actually reached. Just as the standard announced today does not permit a court to make its own subjective determination of guilt or innocence, it does not require scrutiny of the reasoning process actually used by the factfinder—if known." Jackson v. Virginia, 443 U.S. 307, 319 n. 13, 99 S.Ct. 2781, 2790, 61 L.Ed.2d 560.

reasonable doubt after a fair trial, has no constitutional ground to complain that Robinson was acquitted.

QUESTIONS

1. The court in Missouri v. Barton held that it was not prejudicial error to submit a greater offense for the jury's consideration, even where the facts would not support a conviction on this offense, when the verdict was for the lesser offense and that verdict was sustained by the evidence. One interpretation is that the court is saying that, even conceding arguendo that the submission of the more serious charge was error, the error was obviously harmless because the jury rejected the impermissible result. Is that a fair interpretation, or do you think that something else was meant? Assuming that the interpretation is correct, do you agree with the inference as to the harmlessness of the error?

2. Harris v. Rivera was not a jury trial, If it had been, what *additional* explanations of the "inconsistent" verdict (besides those potentially attributable to a judge) would be possible?

3. As a general matter, would defendants be better off if inconsistent verdicts were impermissible? From the perspective of society as a whole, "should" inconsistent verdicts be acceptable? [Note that, in the excerpted case, the Supreme Court does not directly decide this normative issue. Its holding is the more limited one that an inconsistent verdict does not *ipso facto* violate constitutional guarantees of a fair trial.]

EDGEWORTH BOX ANALYSIS OF CONTRACTS

Earlier sections of this chapter involved applications of "mapping" models to explore possibilities of trade and adjustment: the well-relocation problem in the map-reading section and the budgetary coalition-formation model at the beginning of the voting materials. Very similar trading models may be constructed for a host of other legal applications such as out-of-court settlement, plea bargaining, etc. Although the models can thus be applied in contexts that seemingly have little or no relationship to market-type transactions, the general class of mapping-based trade model used above is nonetheless closely related to the "Edgeworth Box" model used widely in traditional economic applications wherein "goods" are being traded for money. It will be useful at this point to present the Edgeworth Box model explicitly and exemplify its application in a market-like trading context.

One area of legal analysis that—like traditional economics—deals with goods-for-money transactions is contract law. Hence, it should not be surprising that the Edgeworth Box model can be used for contract analysis in more or less its original form, as it might appear in an economics textbook. Two examples of the application of an Edgeworth Box to contract analysis are therefore provided in the sections that follow. The first is an excerpt from what is probably the earliest explicit use of an Edgeworth Box model in legal literature: Birmingham's "Damages Measures and Economic Rationality: The Geometry of Contract Law," 1969 Duke L.J. 49 (1969). This excerpt lays out the Edgeworth Box model along the same lines as it has traditionally been used in economic analyses. The next section is adapted from Goetz and Scott, "Liquidated Damages, Penalties and the Just Compensation Principle: Some Notes on an Enforcement Model and a Theory of Efficient Breach," 77 Col.L.Rev. 554, 563–565 (1977). In this context, the same Edgeworth Box construction is used to address the problem of why the law sometimes seems to encourage breach of contract (together with payment of damages) rather than honoring of the original contractual obligation.

THE "CONTRACT CURVE" AND PARETO OPTIMALITY

[Excerpted from Birmingham, "Damage Measures and Economic Rationality: The Geometry of Contract Law," 1969 Duke L.J. 49, 53–58.]

The basis of contract, i.e. the possibility of individual benefit through exchange, may be simply demonstrated. Plot quantities of two goods, e.g. eggs and butter, along the horizontal and vertical axes in figure 1. Then any point within either quadrant or along an axis will denote a unique combination of the two goods. Associate each quadrant with an individual. Offered a choice between combinations of goods represented by any two points within this quadrant, an individual will either prefer one to the other or be indifferent as to which he obtains. The locus of all combinations of goods from which he derives equal satisfaction is called an indifference curve. Assuming infinite divisibility of both goods, each point along or between the axes will be on an indifference curve. Such a curve will usually be convex to the origin because acquisition of increasing quantities of an item will normally render it less valuable in terms of other goods possessed in unchanging amounts.

In figure 1 three indifference curves are drawn for each of two potential traders, X and Y. Assume that prior to exchange both are located at point a so that X possesses an amount O_xa of eggs and no butter while Y has no eggs but an amount O_ya of butter. They will be on indifference curves X_1 and Y_1 respectively. If the possibility of satiation is disregarded, the welfare of each individual can be increased through movement to an indifference curve with a higher subscript; such a shift can make available more of one good without reducing the supply of the other.

FIGURE 1

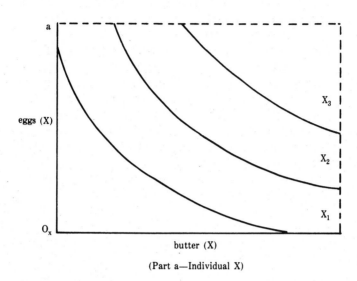

(Part a—Individual X)

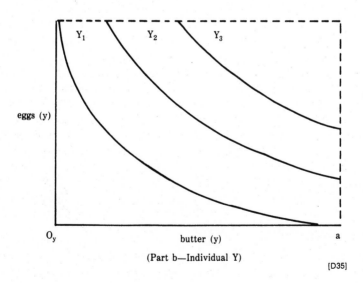

(Part b—Individual Y)

[D35]

Prospective advantage from exchange can be demonstrated by a combination of the two parts of figure 1. In figure 2, part (b) of figure 1 has been rotated 180 degrees and superimposed on part (a). The dimensions of the resulting rectangle, known as an Edgeworth box, are the combined endowments of the two individuals. Before trade occurs both remain at point a, the northwest corner; their welfare levels are those associated with indifference curves X_1 and Y_1 respectively. Through exchange the parties may move from point a to any point within the rectangle or along its edges. A shift to any position between X_1 and Y_1 will benefit each individual through placing him on a higher indifference curve: If point b is selected, for example, the welfare levels of the traders are increased to those associated with indifference curves X_2 and Y_2.

A position is Pareto optimal when movement from it cannot benefit one individual without injuring another. Disregard the impact of the actions of the potential traders on other members of the community. Then in figure 2 only points along the line $O_x cbc'O_y$, connecting all tangencies between the two sets of indifference curves satisfy this condition. The nonoptimality of positions not on this line, called a contract curve, is demonstrated in figure 3. Here a point e not on contract curve $O_x dd'O_y$ has been arbitrarily selected; the indifference curves on which it lies, X_e and Y_e, have been drawn in. X will benefit if the shift resulting from trade moves him to an indifference curve located northeast of X_e, while Y will gain if exchange causes movement to the southwest of Y_e. The shaded area between the two indif-

FIGURE 2

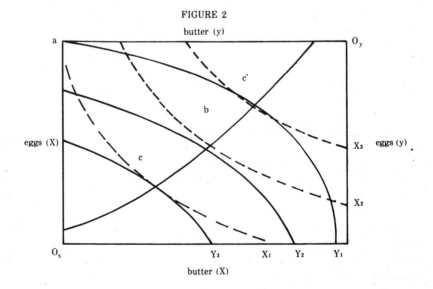

ference curves, lying to the northeast of X_e and to the southwest of Y_e, is a region of profit to both individuals. Such an area will exist for all points not on $O_x dd'O_y'$.

Assuming absence of transaction costs, knowledgeable pursuit by the parties of their own interests will dictate movement through trade from point a in figure 2 to a position on the segment of the contract curve bounded by c and c'. Shifts to points southwest of X_1 or northeast of Y_1 are precluded to the extent that neither individual can be expected voluntarily to lower his own welfare; equilibrium off the contract curve (e.g., at e in figure 3) implies either imperfect information or irrational behavior, since both individuals could gain through further adjustment.

FIGURE 3

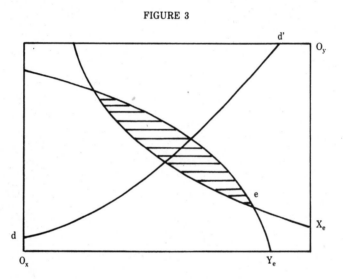

The ratio at which goods are exchanged is indicated by the slope of a straight line (called a price line) from point a through the point the parties have reached by trade. Given a competitive market, equilibrium in figure 2 is possible only at b, the single point where indifference curves are simultaneously tangent to each other and to a price line. A price line drawn through any other point on the contract curve would cut the indifference curves through that point. A price yielding such a line would not clear the market, since equilibrium would require one individual to exchange beyond his preferred position and the other suboptimally to restrict his transactions. In figure 4, for example, assume the market price given by the line from a through c. Individual X will then wish to trade only to point, on indifference curve X_f, while Y will consider point f' on indifference curve Y_f, ideal. At the established price, preferences dictate an excess demand for the first good equal to the vertical distance between f and f' and an excess supply of the second good equal to the horizontal distance between f and f'. The resulting imbalances will induce a corrective shift in price, increasing the cost of the first good in terms of the second. Adjustment will continue until the price ratio associated with the line from a through b in figure 2 is reached. Here f becomes identical with f' and the supply of each good equals its demand.

FIGURE 4

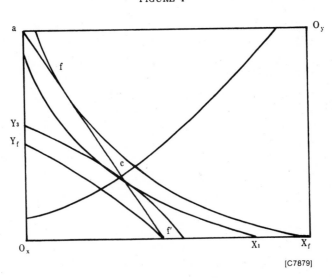

[C7879]

Under competitive conditions there is no incentive to either individual to accept a smaller gain from exchange than that yielded in figure 2, since by the definition of competition, alternative opportunities for trade with others along line ab would allow each to reach this position even if his prospective partner proves uncooperative. When each individual must remain at a if agreement is not reached, however, distribution of the potential joint gain from contract formation is a function of relative bargaining strengths: Equilibrium may be reached at any point on the contract curve from c to c' consistent with the most advantageous exchange ratio the stronger party is able to demand. There remains a continuum of situations between the polar cases of perfect competition and bilateral monopoly, where the availability of alternative transactions guarantees one or both parties a minimum level of welfare beyond that associated with point *a* but is insufficient to preclude joint loss from failure to contract.

QUESTIONS

1. This section introduces for the first time the concept of "Pareto Optimality," an important notion in welfare economics. How is Pareto Optimal defined?

2. Are all points on the "contract curve" Pareto Optimal? Pick a point in figure 2 that is *not* on the contract curve and label it *z*. "Optimal" usually means that the optimal thing is better than a non-optimal one. Are all points on the contract curve unambiguously "better" than point *z?* Why?

3. "If the existing solution is not Pareto Optimal, there always exists some alternative that is unambiguously preferable to the status quo." Comment.

4. The shaded area in figure 3 is sometimes called a "trading area" with respect to the starting point *a*. Moving to any point in that trading area will qualify as a "Pareto Move." How do you think that the term is defined? Does the concept of a Pareto Move clarify any of the preceding questions?

5. "If the starting point is at point *a*, then the only prediction that can be made about the outcome of a bilateral trading situation is that the parties will move to some point on the contract curve between c and c'." Explain.

6. What relationship do the "price ratio" lines in this excerpt have to the "budget lines" in Exhibit 4.2 above?

CONTRACTUAL REALLOCATION THROUGH "EFFICIENT BREACH"

Important elements of the rationale underlying modern contract theory can usefully be articulated in terms of the "indifference curve" analysis commonly used in economic theory. Basically, indifference curve maps may be thought of as mapping a "preferredness mountain" wherein higher "elevations" represent the greater preferredness of outcomes. The points in any single indifference curve constitute outcomes having equal preferredness, i.e., results among which the individual in question would profess indifference or a state of equal satisfaction. When indifference curves are used in mapping a preference "mountain," their significance is exactly analogous to the equal-elevation "contour lines" on a standard topographical map. The indifference curve labelled I_{b1} is a plausibly drawn contour line for B because his more preferred results (closer to his mountain's "peak") are presumably in the northeast direction where B's stocks of money and goods are increasing. Exactly the opposite reasoning applies for S, whose "peak" of preferredness is approached by moving toward the southwest, where S's money and goods stocks are maximized. Conceptually, an indifference curve can be drawn through any point on the map of possible results in an Edgeworth box. However, in order to avoid excessive clutter of the diagrams, it is customary to provide only the indifference curve segments actually necessary to understand the general contours of the individual's preferences about outcome. In this application, it will be necessary to remember only that:

> (1) for B, any point southwest of his indifference curve I_{b1} is inferior to the promised performance of R_c; and

> (2) for S, any point southwest of his indifference curve I_{s1} through R_c is preferred to performance while any point northwest is inferior.

Exhibit 4.5 is an adaptation of the economic trading model familiarly known as the "Edgeworth Box." The potential trade partners, B and S, are assumed to have started with money holdings of $80,000 and $20,000 respectively, for an aggregate of $100,000. Also, B is assumed to have a zero stock of "goods," the product being traded, while S has 100,000 units of goods. By measuring B's holdings from an origin at the southwest corner of the box and S's holdings from the northwest corner, we can represent, as a *point* in the box, any possible division of the aggregates of money and goods between B and S. For instance, the initial situation (which is sometimes called an "endowment point") is represented by R_0, where B has 0 goods (bottom scale) and $80,000 (left-hand scale).[35]

A contract between B and S would be representable as an agreement on some particular movement from the original endowment point or status quo ante result R_0 to a point such as R_c. The motivation for breach will ordinarily be that the perceived advantages of an agreement at the time of contract have been modified by changed conditions. Hence, if a potential breach is to be analyzed, we should expect to find that one of the parties now "regrets" his promise to move from R_0 to R_c.

As Exhibit 4.5 is drawn, changed conditions have shifted the seller's indifference curve (I_{s2}) back toward the northeast origin.[36] The seller now perceives the agreed upon post-performance result (R_c) as

---

35. Note that if we look at the situation in terms of S, the point R_0 is unchanged. It represents S's holding of $20,000 and 100,000 units of goods.

36. It should be emphasized that conditions inducing breach need not always be represented by a "shiftback" in seller's indifference curve. It could equally occur where the buyer's curve shifted. The essential condition to breach is that the changed circumstances indicate that the parties' indifference curves are no longer tangent at the contract point (R_c).

EXHIBIT 4.5

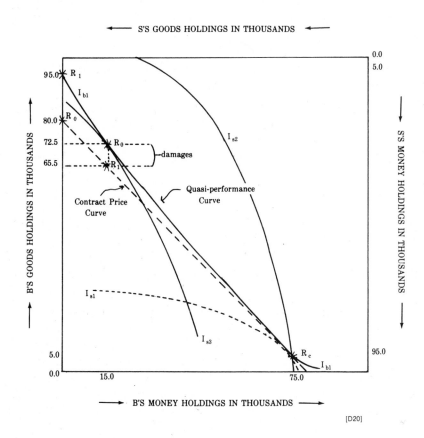

S'S GOODS HOLDINGS IN THOUSANDS

[D20]

B'S MONEY HOLDINGS IN THOUSANDS

an inferior outcome when compared to the status quo ante (R_0) and thus an incentive to breach exists.[37] In terms of Exhibit 4.5, the just compensation principle of modern contract theory is representable by B's indifference curve I_{b1}. This curve not only indicates solutions equivalent (equally preferred by B) to full performance at R_c, but also identifies end results southwest of I_{b1} which would fail to provide the buyer with an outcome meeting his original "expectations" of performance at R_c. Since I_{b1} does identify results which are, from B's standpoint, interchangeable with full performance (R_c), this important indifference contour will be termed the "quasi-performance" curve. The concept of quasi-performance expresses the fact that any point

---

37. The movement from R_0 to R_c is a movement down the preferredness surface for the seller. It places S on an in-difference curve (I_{s2}) which is northwest of R_0 and thus inferior to R_0 in S's eyes.

on the curve places the buyer in the same preferredness situation *as if* performance had taken place.

As Exhibit 4.5 is drawn, full breach by the seller would require that S pay B $15,000 in damages in order to move the buyer from the non-performance solution R_0 to the appropriate point R_f on the quasi-performance curve. Point R_f is the appropriate solution precisely because it supplies B with the equivalent of performance when no goods at all are delivered. Exhibit 4.5 is also drawn to reflect the fact that S can do even better by tendering partial performance of 15,000 units, thus creating the post-compensation result of R_b. Result R_b, permitting the seller to move to a new higher indifference curve I_{s3}, is preferable to both R_c and R_f. It is the most preferred available to S since the law guarantees to B at least some point on the quasi-performance curve. Not only is solution R_b unambiguously superior to performance at R_c, but it also represents an "efficient" end result in the sense that there is no movement from R_b possible without making at least one party worse off.[38] In reaching R_b, the seller would collect the original contract price of $1 per unit for the 15,000 unit partial performance, but would then be required to remit to the buyer $7,500 in damages in order to provide B with his quasi-performance expectation at R_b rather than the no compensation result R_i.

This efficient damage model indicates that upon total or partial non-performance the seller's obligation is to provide "just compensation" sufficient to place the buyer on his quasi-performance curve. Since the points along this curve represent the buyer's *subjective* preferences between performance and compensation, "just compensation" may require consideration of nonobjectifiable elements in determining appropriate compensation to the non-breaching buyer.

QUESTIONS

1. What is meant by an "efficient breach" or an "efficient contract"? What are the "error costs" if an efficient breach is prevented? Does the term "inefficient," as used in this context, mean about the same thing as "wasteful"?

2. The analysis in the text should suggest to you that the law actually encourages promisors not to perform their promises under certain circumstances. Explain why, under the standard contract rules of compensatory damages, the breacher gets *all* of the so-called efficiency gains when an inefficient contract is not performed.

38. The point R_b is superior as Exhibit 4.5 is drawn because it makes the seller better off by putting him on indifference curve I_{s3} while retaining the buyer on his indifference plateau I_{b1}. The result is also "optimal" in the sense that any movement away from R_b would necessarily produce an inferior result for one of the parties.

3. Think about some of the alternatives to the standard system of contract damages. For instance, compare the normal system of compensation for "expectation" damages to one wherein the promisee had the right to specific performance. Would the latter result in the performance of inefficient contracts? How about a system wherein the breacher and breachee "split" the gains fifty-fifty? Why do you think the standard legal rule is for compensatory damages rather than any of these other possible rules?

4. As the example was developed in the text, it was the breacher's indifference curves that shifted, representing a post-contract change in his assessment of the relative values of goods and money. Suppose that the breachee's preferences had also shifted. Would the quasi-contract curve for "expectation" damages be based on the "old" indifference curve running through R_c or on the "new" indifference curve existing at the time of breach? Explain.

CONSUMER CHOICE: MODELLING PROMISSORY RELIANCE

In the initial "map-reading" section, one question dealt with the mutually agreeable relocation of a well site. That part of the problem involved what should now be recognizable as a variation of the Edgeworth Box trading model, several additional examples of which have been provided in the intervening sections. The other part of the map-reading section, however, involved a somewhat different type of model, one that traditional economics would label a "constrained maximization" model of consumer choice. In such models, the focus is on the adjustment of a single decisionmaker to the opportunities confronting him, rather than two-party trade. In the antenna application, the constraint facing the decisionmaker was a legal one, the boundaries within which the antenna could be placed, and the "maximand" (thing to be maximized) was the height of the ground as mapped by the contour lines. Almost identical constructions are used in traditional economics to model consumer choice. In most traditional applications, the constraints or boundaries are determined by the individual's income and the rate at which the things open to choice must be substituted for one another in order to remain within the "budget constraint." The maximand is the level of utility or "preferredness" as represented by the indifference curve map. This type of indifference curve model of consumer choice was explained briefly as Exhibit 4.2 above and will now be the focus of the next few application sections.

Indifference curve models of consumer choice have a great many legal applications. The following examples involve constructions that might be used in any undergraduate economic theory course, since they explicitly cast the analysis in terms of income and prices. Bear in mind, however, that the "goods" chosen do not have to be standard economic entities nor does the opportunity set open to the chooser have to be defined in terms of income and prices. In short, the antenna-location application is just as legitimate a use of the model as these more standard applications that follow.

[Excerpted and adapted from: Goetz and Scott, "Enforcing Promises: An Examination of the Basis of Contract," 89 Yale L.J. 1261 (1980).]

A. *The Function of Promises: Adaptation by the Promisee*

In analyzing the promisee's reaction to a promise, it is critically important to bear in mind the conceptual distinction between the promise itself and the future benefit that it foretells. By communicating a promise, the promisor informs the promisee about the proposed future receipt of a benefit. The promise itself is merely the production of a piece of information about the future. Normally, advance knowledge of a future transfer will increase the benefit to the promisee because he can more perfectly adapt his consumption decisions to the impending change in wealth. For instance, a person informed of a $25,000 bequest to be made one year hence may revise some of the plans that he otherwise would have followed in the intervening twelve months. Because of the revisions in his plans, the individual can achieve a higher level of satisfaction than if the wealth were transferred without any advance notice. Such adaptive gain from the information embodied in a promise may appropriately be termed "beneficial reliance." The problem occurs, however, when the transfer foretold by the promise is not actually performed. In this case, the information conveyed by the promise turns out to have been misleading and the promisee's induced adaptation in behavior makes him worse off than he would have been without the erroneous expectation of a future benefit. Losses incurred by ill-premised adaptive behavior are commonly termed "detrimental reliance." Because the role of promises as units of information is so fundamental to the entire analysis developed below, we will use an economic indifference curve model to give more rigorous content to such key legal concepts as reliance and the reasonableness of the promisee's adaptation process.

1. *Reliance Reactions of a Promisee*

Exhibit 4.6 will be utilized to develop a very simple intertemporal allocation model, one in which a person must allocate his income between two periods, present and future. *A*, the potential promisee, begins with $100, which he can divide between consumption now and consumption in the future. In Exhibit 4.6, his possible choices are represented by the straight line budget constraint indicating all combinations of present and future consumption that sum to $100. His preferences about alternative combinations of present and future consumption are summarized by the indifference curves, which define a kind of topographic map of the desirability of different present-future consumption patterns. On these assumptions, the highest preference level consistent with the scarce resources is point e_1, where indifference curve I_1 is tangent to the budget constraint. This consumption allocation involves spending $50 now together with a planned expenditure of $50 in the future.

Suppose now that B promises A a transfer of $50 to be made in the future period and that A believes the promise. Even neglecting the possibility of borrowing against his future wealth, A's budget constraint will shift out to the dotted line in Exhibit 4.6.[24] The new constraint indicates that, although no more than $100 can be spent in the present, the two-period consumption levels may now total $150 rather than $100. Based on the new information, A's best two-period plan would be point e_2. A is thus led to revise his current consumption upward to $75 and to project $75 worth of future consumption.[25]

Because detrimental reliance is widely regarded as a basis for damage computation, an advantage of the Exhibit 4.6 model is that it clearly illustrates why it is a mistake to use A's observable action in reliance on a promise as the measure of his damages. Under the facts assumed, A's observable reliance is the $25 extra he spends in period 1. If, however, he were awarded this $25 as damages for breach, his ultimate position would be at e_5 on indifference curve I_5. He would have spent $75 in the first period and, including the $25 damages, would have available $50 for the final period. But since return to the status quo ante requires only that indifference curve I_1 be achieved, the true reliance damages are equal only to the lesser amount indicated by the horizontal distance between e_3 and e_6 in Exhibit 4.6. The common-sense explanation for this, of course, is that detrimental adaptation in behavior is usually only a partial rather than a total loss. In this case, A did get some benefit from the excessive $25 consumption even though not as much as he would have if the consumption had been postponed to the optimal time. Reliance is, simply, the opportunity cost of the broken promise. Thus, true damages are measured by the difference between the value of the stream

---

24. For simplicity, we assume that the interest rate on money is zero in order to produce a one-to-one tradeoff between present and future consumption. The introduction of interest is irrelevant to this analysis because it merely alters the rate of tradeoff, reflected in the slopes of the budget lines.

25. The promisee's consumption of all goods with nonzero income elasticities will be modified. [See the section on "elasticity" measures later in this chapter.] His intertemporal consumption stream will be adjusted to the higher wealth level created by the gift.

EXHIBIT 4.6

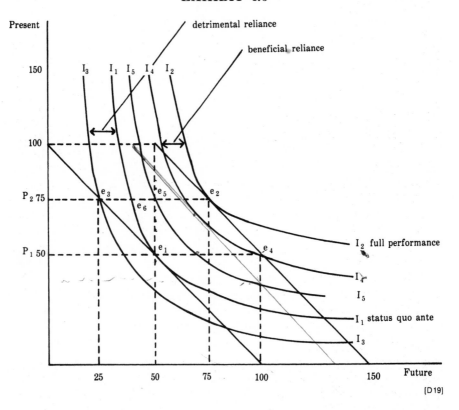

[D 19]

of consumption choices not taken—indifference curve I_1—and those choices induced by the promise—indifference curve I_3. Because it is important to distinguish compensation based on observable reliance from true reliance damages, we shall refer to the former as "reimbursement damages."

Even where the precise meaning is imperfectly captured, the notion of detrimental reliance tends to be better understood than that of beneficial reliance. This is unfortunate because the production of beneficial reliance is perhaps the principal social rationale of promising; the risk of detrimental reliance is merely the unavoidable concomitant cost. Exhibit 4.6 aptly illustrates the beneficial consequences of promising when the promise is performed. Assume, for instance, that the $50 in our hypothetical is merely transferred to A in period two without any advance warning. Not knowing about the wealth increase, A will have committed himself to plan e_1. When period two arrives, A will unexpectedly find himself with $100 to spend. At this point, the best available choice is at e_4, which is on a lower indifference curve than e_2, the point that would have been achievable had *A* obtained advance knowledge of the transfer. In common-sense terms, the difference between I_2 and I_4 illustrates the benefits to *A* of being able to adjust, because of the promise, to revised expectations about the future.

QUESTIONS

1. How is an indifference curve defined? Why are indifference curves useful devices in analyzing damages that have a *restitutio ad integrum* or compensatory purpose?

2. Draw an additional budget constraint, with the same slope as the other two, such that it is tangent to indifference curve I_4. Explain the relevance of that line to the following problem:

> I had intended to give *A* $100, but was unable to tell him about it in advance so that he could rely on it. Now I find it possible to inform him of my intent and give assurances of my performance. But it occurs to me that I can now make a promise of somewhat less than the originally intended $100 and achieve the same effect. How much less can I give?

Does this suggest to you that the promisor as well as the promisee may benefit from having promises be enforceable? See Posner, "Gratuitous Promises in Economics and Law," 6 J.Leg.Studies 411 (1977).

3. Suppose the promisee thought that there were only a 50% chance that the promise would be performed. He would have to pick his position on the vertical axis on the assumption that one of two possible budget lines would determine his eventual position on the horizontal axis. Why? The exact solution to this choice problem is difficult to derive graphically from an indifference curve model (although an analogous mathematical model handles it quite easily). Consider the problem in an approximate way, however, and take a guess at what decision the promisee would make. Why is this inevitably a "compromise" decision that is always somewhat "wrong" as viewed *ex post?* And what is the loss from not knowing whether the promise is completely reliable or not?

MATHEWS et al. v. MASSELL

United States District Court, N.D. Georgia, Atlantic Division, 1973.
356 F.Supp. 291.

RICHARD C. FREEMAN, District Judge.

This is an action brought by plaintiffs, citizens and taxpayers of the City of Atlanta on behalf of themselves and all others similarly situated against defendants, the mayor and members of the Board of Aldermen of the City of Atlanta. Plaintiffs challenge the way in which defendants have utilized a portion of the funds received by the City pursuant to the "State and Local Fiscal Assistance Act of 1972" popularly known as the Revenue Sharing Act.

On February 22, 1973, a hearing was held on plaintiffs' motion for preliminary injunction. A stipulation of the relevant facts was entered into by the parties prior to the hearing.

* * *

The relevant facts as stipulated by the parties are here summarized. Pursuant to the Revenue Sharing Act, which went into effect on October 20, 1972, the City of Atlanta received approximately $5,962,169 in revenue sharing funds for the year 1972. It has been anticipated that the City will receive approximately an additional $1.5 million in Revenue Sharing funds per quarter for the first three quarters of 1973.

* * *

The effect of the * * * ordinances [being challenged in this case] is as follows: The Revenue Sharing funds received for 1972 are to be utilized to raise firemen's salaries, an approved use under the Revenue Sharing Act. The $4.5 million in Revenue Sharing funds anticipated for the first three quarters of 1973 is likewise designated as being used to pay firemen's salaries, thereby relieving the general fund of this obligation. The $4.5 million from the general fund originally slated for the payment of firemen's salaries is then to be transferred to the City's Water/Sewer Fund to reimburse it for the $4.5 million reduction in the Water/Sewer Fund resulting from the rebate conferred upon firms and individuals having water accounts with the City. It is the Revenue Sharing Funds anticipated for the first three quarters of 1973 (a total of $4.5 million) which are to be used to release the $4.5 million in general funds which defendants propose to disburse in the form of a water/sewer rebate.

In his State of the City Annual Message, delivered on Tuesday, January 2, 1973, defendant [Mayor] Massell stated that he intended to return directly to the citizenry of Atlanta a portion of the Revenue Sharing funds in the amount of $4.5 million. On February 12, 1973, in a news release, defendant Massell announced that he was going to use the Revenue Sharing funds at least in part to "create some relief for the monthly budget of the average Atlanta householder * * * [T]his has made it possible for us to reduce the water/sewer rates on over 1,000,000 accounts by $4 per month per meter * * * a total benefit to the public of $4.5 million." Affidavits from three defendants, members of the Board of Aldermen, state that the series of ordinances described above was designed to carry out a plan to return $4.5 million of Federal Revenue Sharing funds to firms and individuals having active water/sewer accounts with the City of Atlanta.

Plaintiffs claim that the actions of the defendants, as set forth above, constitute a violation of Sec. 103(a) of the Revenue Sharing Act, which provides as follows:

(a) In general Funds received by units of local government under this sub[title] may be used only for priority expenditures. For purposes of this [title], the term "priority expenditures" means only—

(1) ordinary and necessary maintenance and operating expenses for—

(A) public safety (including law enforcement, fire protection, and building code enforcement)

(B) environmental protection (including sewage disposal, sanitation, and pollution abatement)

(C) public transportation (including transit systems and streets and roads)

(D) health

(E) recreation

(F) libraries

(G) social services for the poor or aged, and

(H) financial administration; and

(2) ordinary and necessary capital expenditures authorized by law.

It is plaintiffs' contention that defendants have violated the Act by, in effect, spending $4.5 million for water sewer rebates, which is not one of the priority uses set forth in Sec. 103(a).

* * *

The requisite financial harm to the taxpayers of the City of Atlanta is found in the Revenue Sharing Act itself. Section 123(a) of the Act provides * * * for a return of any Revenue Sharing funds spent in violation of the priority use requirements set forth in Sec. 103(a), plus a penalty of 10%. If defendants were to carry out their proposed plan to rebate $4.5 million of the Revenue Sharing funds and if, as plaintiffs allege, such use is in violation of Sec. 103(a), the City would be liable to the Secretary of the Treasury for $4.5 million plus 10%, a total of $4.95 million.

* * *

The court must now proceed to a consideration of the merits of plaintiffs' claim that the proposed plan of defendants to distribute a water/sewer rebate is in violation of Sec. 103(a) of the Revenue Sharing Act. It is clear from Sec. 103(a), and defendants do not contend otherwise, that the defendants could not have directly used any portion of the Revenue Sharing funds to make a rebate to those with

Goetz Law & Economics ACB—10

water sewer accounts. A water/sewer rebate does not fall within one of the "priority" uses permitted by Sec. 103(a).

Defendants do contend, however, that they have fully satisfied their duties under the Act by placing the Revenue Sharing funds in a trust account for the payment of firemen's salaries, a priority use. It is their position that the Revenue Sharing Act imposes restrictions only on the specific funds which are received by operation of the Act. They contend that the Act imposes no restrictions upon the City's general funds which are freed up by the influx of Revenue Sharing funds. Thus in the present case they state that $10.5 million of general funds would have been used for the payment of firemen's salaries but for the receipt of the Revenue Sharing funds. Defendants contend that use of the Revenue Sharing funds for firemen's salaries allows them to make any use whatsoever of the general funds which would otherwise have been put to such use.

It is true that the Revenue Sharing Act does not specifically impose any restrictions upon the use of legitimately freed-up funds. Thus the Act seems clearly to have contemplated that the infusion of Revenue Sharing funds into state and local governments would permit future tax relief to the hard-pressed taxpayers of those governments. Further, there is no requirement that a local government maintain at pre-Revenue Sharing levels its spending on "priority expenditures." There is a clear difference, however, between funds which are legitimately freed up by the designation of federal Revenue Sharing funds to provide municipal services which otherwise would have to have been paid for out of general City funds, and funds which are transferred from one account to another simply to avoid the restrictions imposed by Sec. 103(a) of the Act. The actions of defendants, the public statements made by defendant Mayor Massell and the affidavits of three of the defendant members of the Board of Aldermen, show clearly that the steps taken by defendants were designed to carry out a plan to return $4.5 million in Revenue Sharing funds to certain taxpayers, the defendants having decided to confer such tax relief by way of rebates on the water/sewer accounts.

Such an attempt to avoid the clear restrictions of federal statute cannot be accepted. While there is as yet no case law on the Revenue Sharing Act, in the interpretation of federal statutes generally, the courts have long made it clear that Congressional intent cannot be overridden by sham transactions. In the areas of federal income taxation, securities law, and antitrust statutes, the courts have consistently refused to exalt artifice over reality or to ignore the actual substance of a particular set of transactions. Thus the court must recognize that the defendants have merely transferred funds from one account to another in an effort to disguise the fact that they plan to distribute $4.5 million of Revenue Sharing funds to the holders of water/sewer accounts.

Defendants would seem to argue, however, that their proposed plan does not conflict with Congressional intent. Defendants, while recognizing the restrictions set forth in Sec. 103(a), contend that such restrictions were not meant to have any force and that thus defendants' proposal to circumvent those provisions would not actually run counter to the intent of Congress. Defendants' contention that Congress intended no effective restrictions on the funds is clearly belied by an examination of the legislative history of the Act.

* * *

One final argument by defendants is that Sec. 103(a) has no effect because it is so difficult to enforce. They draw support for this argument from the Senate report on the Senate version of the bill in which the committee justified the Senate's deletion of the restrictions on a local government's use of the funds by the argument that enforcement of the restrictions would be impossible and that therefore any restrictions would be illusory. And facially this argument is persuasive, but * * * it was in effect overruled by the action of the House-Senate conference and by the passage of the Act in its present form by both houses of Congress. Moreover, the Act itself provides an enforcement mechanism by requiring the Secretary of the Treasury to establish accounting and auditing procedures (Sec. 123c) and also by providing for imposition of a penalty if funds are spent in violation of Sec. 103(a).

Defendants seek support from a recent article on Revenue Sharing published in the Harvard Journal on Legislation. "The Revenue Sharing Act of 1972: Untied and Untraceable Dollars from Washington", 10 Harv.J.Legis. 276 (1973). In discussing the priority expenditures provision of the Act, the article makes the point that violations of Sec. 103(a) will be extremely difficult to discover and prove, for Revenue Sharing funds will be commingled in fact with other local funds, even if the books of account are kept separately. Such problems of proof will undoubtedly arise: however, in the present case the use of Revenue Sharing funds in violation of Sec. 103(a) has been clearly proved by plaintiffs in large part by the statements of defendants themselves.

In conclusion then, the court has looked to the substance of defendants' actions and determined that defendants' proposed plan would entail the expenditure of Federal Revenue Sharing funds for other than one of the priority expenditures set forth in Sec. 103(a). In light of this determination the court need not consider plaintiffs' other claims.

Accordingly, judgment is hereby entered for the plaintiffs. Defendants, their agents, employees, successors in office and attorneys are hereby permanently, enjoined from utilizing $4.5 million in Revenue Sharing funds in the manner proposed, that is, to make a reduction in water/sewer rates or to give a rebate to all those with active water/sewer accounts.

It is so ordered.

QUESTIONS

1. Assume that a grantee government has a set of preferences representable as a set of indifference curves. [The section above on group decisionmaking under majority rule should suggest that this assumption about the existence of a well ordered preference mapping for a voting group (in this case, the City Council) is a debatable simplification. Do you understand why? When you have completed this current question set, ask yourself to what extent the making of the assumption alters the points being discussed in the present exercise.] Construct a model showing quantity of Priority Expenditure goods on the horizontal axis and quantity of "Other" goods on the vertical axis. Show a pre-grant budget constraint and a hypothetical set of indifference curves.

2. After the receipt of the revenue-sharing grant, the grantee government's new economic constraint will lie to the right of and parallel to the original budget constraint. Why?

3. On this same model, use a distinctive line to distinguish the set of permissible choices under Sec. 103(a) from those which would violate the Act. This line should, in effect, represent the proverbial "bright yellow line" that separates legal and illegal budgetary decisions. If you think there is more than one possible interpretation of where this legal constraint lies, indicate each possible answer and explain the underlying reasoning.

4. On completion of the last question, you should have what is really just a variant of the standard consumer choice model, except that it has *two* constraints, one economic and one legal. What is the "price" for violating the statutory constraint? Is that price probabilistic (i.e., a "prospect")? Have you incorporated this element in your model?

5. Defendants in this case allegedly supplied the proof against themselves. Absent such admissions, what possible evidence would permit an inference that the funds had been used improperly? For a discussion of the "tracing" problem, see Comment, "The Revenue Sharing Act of 1972: Untied and Untraceable Dollars from Washington," 10 Harv.J.Legis. 276 (1973). An empirical analysis of the extent to which funds were used for substitutional purposes rather than

new spending can be found in Nathan, "The Uses of Shared Revenue," 30 J.Finance 557 (1975).

TILTON v. RICHARDSON

Supreme Court of the United States, 1971.
403 U.S. 672, 91 S.Ct. 2091, 29 L.Ed.2d 790.

[Mr. Chief Justice Burger.]

This appeal presents important constitutional questions as to federal aid for church-related colleges and universities under Title I of the Higher Education Facilities Act of 1963, 77 Stat. 364, as amended, 20 USC Secs. 711–721 (1964 ed. and Supp. V), which provides construction grants for buildings and facilities used exclusively for secular educational purposes. We must determine first whether the Act authorizes aid to such church-related institutions and, if so, whether the Act violates either the Establishment or Free Exercise Clauses of the First Amendment.

* * *

* * * The Act authorizes federal grants and loans to "institutions of higher education" for the construction of a wide variety of "academic facilities." But Sec. 751(a)(2) (1964 ed., Supp. V) expressly excludes "any facility used or to be used for sectarian instruction or as a place for religious worship, or * * * any facility which * * * is used or to be used primarily in connection with any part of the program of a school or department of divinity * * *."

* * *

We are satisfied that Congress intended the Act to include all colleges and universities regardless of any affiliation with or sponsorship by a religious body. Congress defined "institutions of higher education," which are eligible to receive aid under the Act, in broad and inclusive terms. Certain institutions, for example, institutions that are neither public nor nonprofit, are expressly excluded, and the Act expressly prohibits use of the facilities for religious purposes. But the Act makes no reference to religious affiliation or nonaffiliation. Under these circumstances "institutions of higher education" must be taken to include church-related colleges and universities.

* * *

Numerous cases considered by the Court have noted the internal tension in the First Amendment between the Establishment Clause and the Free Exercise Clause. Walz v. Tax Comm'n, 397 U.S. 664, 90 S.Ct. 1409, 25 L.Ed.2d 697 (1970), is the most recent decision seeking to define the boundaries of the neutral area between these two provisions within which the legislature may legitimately act. There, as in other decisions, the Court treated the three main concerns against which the Establishment Clause sought to protect: "sponsorship, financial support, and active involvement of the sovereign in religious activity." Id., at 668, 90 S.Ct., at 1411.

* * *

* * * [W]e consider four questions: First, does the Act reflect a secular legislative purpose? Second, is the primary effect of the Act to advance or inhibit religion? Third, does the Administration of the Act foster an excessive government entanglement with religion? Fourth, does the implementation of the Act inhibit the free exercise of religion?

The stated legislative purpose appears in the preamble where Congress found and declared that "the security and welfare of the United States require that this and future generations of American youth be afforded ample opportunity for the fullest development of their intellectual capacities, and that this opportunity will be jeopardized unless the Nation's colleges and universities are encouraged and assisted in their efforts to accommodate rapidly growing numbers of youth who aspire to a higher education." 20 USC Sec. 701. This expresses a legitimate secular objective entirely appropriate for governmental action.

The simplistic argument that every form of financial aid to church-sponsored activity violates the Religion Clause was rejected long ago in Bradfield v. Roberts, 175 U.S. 291, 20 S.Ct. 121, 44 L.Ed. 168 (1899). There a federal construction grant to a hospital operated by a religious order was upheld. Here the Act is challenged on the ground that its primary effect is to aid the religious purposes of church-related colleges and universities. Construction grants surely aid these institutions in the sense that the construction of buildings will assist them to perform their various functions. But bus transportation, textbooks, and tax exemptions all gave aid in the sense that religious bodies would otherwise have been forced to find other sources from which to finance these services. Yet all of these forms of governmental assistance have been upheld. [Citations omitted.] The crucial question is not whether some benefit accrues to a religious institution as a consequence of the legislative program, but whether its principal or primary effect advances religion.

* * *

The Act itself was carefully drafted to ensure that the federally subsidized facilities would be devoted to the secular and not the religious function of the recipient institutions. It authorizes grants and loans only for academic facilities that will be used for defined secular purposes and expressly prohibits their use for religious instruction, training, or worship. These restrictions have been enforced in the Act's actual administration, and the record shows that some church-related institutions have been required to disgorge benefits for failure to obey them.

* * *

Appellants * * * rely on the argument that government may not subsidize any activities of an institution of higher learning that in some of its programs teaches religious doctrines. This argument rests on Everson where the majority stated that the Establishment Clause barred any "tax * * * levied to support any religious * * * institutions * * * whatever form they may adopt to teach or practice religion." 330 U.S. at 16, 67 S.Ct. at 511. In Allen, however, it was recognized that the Court had fashioned criteria under which an analysis of a statute's purpose and effect was determinative as to whether religion was being advanced by government action. 392 U.S. at 243, 88 S.Ct., at 1926, 20 L.Ed.2d at 1065; Abington School District v. Schempp, 374 U.S. 203, 222, 83 S.Ct. 1560, 1571, 10 L.Ed.2d 844 (1963).

Under this concept appellants' position depends on the validity of the proposition that religion so permeates the secular education provided by church-related colleges and universities that their religious and secular functions are in fact inseparable. The argument that government grants would thus inevitably advance religion did not escape the notice of Congress. It was carefully and thoughtfully debated, 109 Cong.Rec. 19474–19475, but was found unpersuasive. It was also considered by this Court in Allen. There the Court refused to assume that religiosity in parochial elementary and secondary schools necessarily permeates the secular education that they provide.

The record, similarly, provides no basis for any such assumptions here. * * * There is no evidence that religion creeps into the use of any of these facilities.

* * *

We next turn to the question of whether excessive entanglements characterize the relationship between government and church under the Act. Walz v. Tax Comm'n, supra, at 674–676, 90 S.Ct., at 1414–1415. Our decision today in Lemon v. Kurtzman and Robinson v. DiCenso has discussed and applied this independent measure of constitutionality under the Religion Clauses. There we concluded that excessive entanglements between government and religion were fostered by Pennsylvania and Rhode Island statutory programs under which state aid was provided to parochial elementary and secondary schools. Here, however, three factors substantially diminish the extent and the potential danger of the entanglement.

* * *

There are generally significant differences between the religious aspects of church-related institutions of higher learning and parochial elementary and secondary schools. The "affirmative if not dominant policy" of the instruction in pre-college church schools is "to assure future adherents to a particular faith by having total control of their education at an early age." Walz v. Tax Comm'n, supra, at 671, 90 S.Ct., at 1412. There is substance to the contention that college students are less impressionable and less susceptible to religious indoctrination. Common observation would seem to support that view, and Congress may well have entertained it. The skepticism of the college student is not an inconsiderable barrier to any attempt or tendency to subvert the congressional objectives and limitations. Furthermore, by their very nature, college and postgraduate courses tend to limit the opportunities for sectarian influence by virtue of their own internal disciplines. Many church-related colleges and universities are characterized by a high degree of academic freedom and seek to evoke free and critical responses from their students.

Since religious indoctrination is not a substantial purpose or activity of these church-related colleges and universities, there is less likelihood than in primary and secondary schools that religion will permeate the area of secular education. This reduces the risk that government aid will in fact serve to support religious activities. Correspondingly, the necessity for intensive government surveillance is diminished and the resulting entanglements between government and religion lessened. Such inspection as may be necessary to ascertain that the facilities are devoted to secular education is minimal and indeed hardly more than the inspections that States impose over all private schools within the reach of compulsory education laws.

The entanglement between church and state is also lessened here by the nonideological character of the aid that the Government provides. Our cases from Everson to Allen have permitted church-related schools to receive government aid in the form of secular, neutral, or nonideological services, facilities, or materials that are supplied to all students regardless of the affiliation of the school that they attend. In Lemon and DiCenso, however, the state progams subsidized teachers, either directly or indirectly. Since teachers are not necessarily religiously neutral, greater governmental surveillance would be required to guarantee that state salary aid would not in fact subsidize religious instruction. There we found the resulting entanglement excessive. Here, on the other hand, the Government provides facilities that are themselves religiously neutral. The risks of Government aid to religion and the corresponding need for surveillance are therefore reduced.

Finally, government entanglements with religion are reduced by the circumstance that, unlike the direct and continuing payments under the Pennsylvania program, and all the incidents of regulation and surveillance, the Government aid here is a one-time, single-purpose construction grant. There are no continuing financial relationships or dependencies, no annual audits, and no government analysis of an institution's expenditures on secular as distinguished from religious activity. Inspection as to use is a minimal contact.

No one of these three factors standing alone is necessarily controlling; cumulatively all of them shape a narrow and limited relationship with government which involves fewer and less significant contacts than the two state schemes before us in Lemon and DiCenso. The relationship therefore has less potential for realizing the substantive evils against which the Religion Clauses were intended to protect.

We think that cumulatively these three factors also substantially lessen the potential for divisive religious fragmentation in the political arena. This conclusion is admittedly difficult to document, but neither have appellants pointed to any continuing religious aggravation on this matter in the political processes. Possibly this can be explained by the character and diversity of the recipient colleges and universities and the absence of any intimate continuing relationship or dependency between government and religiously affiliated institutions. The potential for divisiveness inherent in the essentially local problems of primary and secondary schools is significantly less with respect to a college or university whose student constituency is not local but diverse and widely dispersed.

Finally, we must consider whether the implementation of the Act inhibits the free exercise of religion in violation of the First Amendment. Appellants claim that the Free Exercise Clause is violated because they are compelled to pay taxes, the proceeds of which in part finance grants under the Act. Appellants, however, are unable to identify any coercion directed at the practice or exercise of their religious beliefs. Board of Education v. Allen, supra, 392 U.S., at 248–249, 88 S.Ct., at 1929, 20 L.Ed.2d 1060. Their share of the cost of the grants under the Act is not fundamentally distinguishable from the impact of the tax exemption sustained in Walz or the provision of textbooks upheld in Allen.

We conclude that the Act does not violate the Religion Clauses of the First Amendment except that of Sec. 754(b)(2) providing a 20-year limitation on the religious use restrictions contained in Sec. 751(a)(2). We remand to the District Court with directions to enter a judgment consistent with this opinion.

Vacated and remanded.

Mr. Justice DOUGLAS, with whom Mr. Justice BLACK and Mr. Justice MARSHALL concur, dissenting in part.

*   *   *

*   *   * The fact that money is *   *   * given once at the beginning of a program rather than apportioned annually as in Lemon and DiCenso is without constitutional significance *   *   *. Thus it is hardly impressive that rather than giving a smaller amount of money annually over a long period of years, Congress instead gives a large amount all at once. The plurality's distinction is in effect that small violations of the First Amendment over a period of years are unconstitutional (see Lemon and DiCenso) while a huge violation occurring only once is de minimis. I cannot agree with such sophistry.

What I have said in Lemon and in the DiCenso cases decided today is relevant here. The facilities financed by taxpayers' funds are not to be used for "sectarian" purposes. Religious teaching and secular teaching are so enmeshed in parochial school that only the strictest supervision and surveillance would insure compliance with the condition. Parochial schools may require religious exercises, even in the classroom. A parochial school operates on one budget. Money not spent for one purpose becomes available for other purposes. Thus the fact that there are no religious observances in federally financed facilities is not controlling because required religious observances will take place in other buildings. Our decision in Engel v. Vitale, 370 U.S. 421, 82 S.Ct. 1261, 8 L.Ed.2d 601, 86 A.L.R.2d 1285, held that a requirement of a prayer in public schools violated the Establishment Clause. Once these schools become federally funded they become bound by federal standards [Ivanhoe Irrig. Dist. v. McCracken, 357 U.S. 275, 296, 78 S.Ct. 1174, 1186, 2 L.Ed.2d 1313, 1328; Rosado v. Wyman, 397 U.S. 397, 427, 90 S.Ct. 1207, 25 L.Ed.2d 442, 464 (concurring opinion): Simkins v. Moses H. Cone Memorial Hosp., 4 Cir., 323 F.2d 959] and accordingly adherence to Engel would require an end to required religious exercises. That kind of surveillance and control will certainly be obnoxious to the church authorities and if done will radically change the character of the parochial school. Yet if that surveillance is not searching and continuous, this federal financing is obnoxious under the Establishment and Free Exercise Clauses for the reasons stated in the companion cases.

In other words, surveillance creates an entanglement of government and religion which the First Amendment was designed to avoid. Yet after today's decision there will be a requirement of surveillance which will last for the useful life of the building and as we have previously noted, "[it] is hardly lack of due process for the Government to regulate that which it subsidizes." Wickard v. Filburn, 317 U.S. 111, 131, 63 S.Ct. 82, 92, 87 L.Ed. 122, 138. The price of the subsidy under the Act is violation of the Free Exercise Clause. Could a course in the History of Methodism be taught in a federally financed building? Would a religiously slanted version of the Reformation of Quebec politics under Duplessis be permissible? How can the Government know what is taught in the federally financed building without a continuous auditing of classroom instruction? Yet both the Free Exercise Clause and academic freedom are violated when the Government agent must be present to determine whether the course content is satisfactory.

As I said in the Lemon and DiCenso cases, a parochial school is a unitary institution with subtle blending of sectarian and secular instruction. Thus the practices of religious schools are in no way affected by the minimal requirement that the government financed facility may not "be used for sectarian instruction or as a place for religious worship." Money saved from one item in the budget is free to be used elsewhere. By conducting religious services in another building, the school has—rent free—a building for nonsectarian use. This is not called Establishment simply because the government retains a continuing interest in the building for its useful life, even though the religious schools need never pay a cent for the use of the building.

* * *

I would reverse the judgment below.

QUESTIONS

1. Create a model similar to the one used for Mathews v. Massel above. Place quantities of "Secular Buildings" and "Religious Uses" on the vertical and horizontal axes, respectively. Assume that the federal grant program paid for exactly 50% of the cost of secular buildings. What are the pre- and post-grant economic constraints faced by a church-related university? Why is the shift in the budget constraint not a parallel shift as illustrated by the revenue sharing grants?

2. If the grant moves the church-related institution onto a higher "indifference curve," is that fact relevant for an anlysis of the Act's constitutionality? Will such a movement to a higher indifference curve always take place?

3. "The proper constitutional test for this program is whether it has the predictable effect of increasing, or stimulating, the religious activities of the grantee." On your indifference curve model, depict in some appropriate manner the implicit constitutional constraint represented by the quoted statement. Do you agree with the quote? If not, depict the constitutional constraint implied by the test you deem proper. Explain your answer.

4.   Does one's attitude towards the issues in Tilton v. Richardson depend on empirical data or can the problem be framed adequately in theoretical terms?

5.   Viewing both Mathews v. Massell and Tilton v. Richardson against the background of the indifference curve models, what comments do you have on the decisions? If any grant is given at all, is some degree of unintended effect inevitable? Does the magnitude of the unintended effects depend on the form of the grant?

6.   By the year 1995, the previously upper middle-class penchant for quiche and white wine has made deep inroads into the traditional American preference for pizza and beer. Nowhere is this more apparent than in federal procurement contracts for the military services, where wine consumption has recently outstripped beer in mess halls and enlisted personnel's recreational clubs.

Low bidder on a recent government contract for military forces wine supply was the Christian Friars Vinery, a west-coast wine producer run by a religious order that devotes all of the profits from its wine sales to subsidize the religiously-oriented secondary schools in which its members teach. A ruling of the General Services Administration required that the Department of Defense reject the Vinery's bid and award the contract to the next lowest qualified bidder, reasoning that the transaction with the Christian Friars would involve a constitutionally impermissible relationship between church and state. The Friars have filed suit in federal court alleging that the refusal to accept its bid is an unconstitutional discrimination on the basis of religion. "Religion shouldn't be any part of this," the Brother Vintmaster, stated in a press conference. "The government wants wine and we have wine to sell. What difference does it make how we use our profits?"

On what principles should this case be decided? Does it make a difference if the labels of the wine bottles bear a trademark consisting of a Friar pausing to meditate while he harvests a basket of wine grapes? To what extent is the position of the Christian Friars Vinery analogous to that of Albertus Magnus College in the Tilton case?

BRIBES VERSUS THREATS

If one takes seriously the notion of opportunity cost, there is a dismaying similarity between the impact of bribes and threats: a bribe foregone is as much a cost as a tax or penalty paid out. To the extent that certain activities are deemed to be protected from interference by the State, the issue may arise as to whether the State may achieve with the carrot what it would be forbidden to achieve via the stick or, alternatively, to achieve by the back door what it cannot at the front. The next few real cases and hypotheticals should be read with at least two major questions in mind. One is the distinction, if any, between using bribes or threats to modify behavior. The other is whether the "bribe" given by the State is real or in some sense only apparent.

UNITED STATES v. BUTLER

Supreme Court of the United States, 1936.
297 U.S. 1, 56 S.Ct. 312, 80 L.Ed. 477.

[The Agricultural Adjustment Act of 1933, in order to raise farm prices by reducing production, authorized the secretary of agriculture to contract with farmers to reduce productive acreage. Payments were made out of the revenues of a processing tax exacted from the processors of the agricultural products. A cotton processor challenged the tax as beyond Congress' constitutional authority.]

Mr. Justice ROBERTS delivered the opinion of the Court.

The Government asserts that * * * Article I, Section 8 of the Constitution authorizes the contemplated expenditure of the funds raised by the tax. This contention presents the great and the controlling question in the case.

* * *

The clause thought to authorize the legislation, the first, confers upon the Congress power "to lay and collect Taxes, Duties, Imposts and Excises, to pay the Debts and provide for the common Defense and general Welfare of the United States. * * *" It is not contended that this provision grants power to regulate agricultural production upon the theory that such legislation would promote the general welfare. The Government concedes that the phrase "to provide for the general welfare" qualifies the power to "to lay and collect taxes." The view that the clause grants power to provide for the general welfare, independently of the taxing power, has never been authoritatively accepted. Mr. Justice Story points out that if it were adopted "it is obvious that under color of the generality of the words, 'to provide for the common defence and general welfare,' the government of the United States is, in reality, a government of general and unlimited powers, notwithstanding the subsequent enumeration of specific powers." The true construction undoubtedly is that the only thing granted is the power to tax for the purpose of providing funds for payment of the nation's debts and making provision for the general welfare. ·

* * *

We are not now required to ascertain the scope of the phrase "general welfare of the United States" or to determine whether an appropriation in aid of agriculture falls within it. Wholly apart from that question, another principle embedded in our Constitution prohibits the enforcement of the Agricultural Adjustment Act. The act invades the reserved rights of the states. It is a statutory plan to regulate and control agricultural production, a matter beyond the powers delegated to the federal government. The tax, the appropriation of the funds raised, and the direction for their disbursement, are but parts of the plan. They are but means to an unconstitutional end.

From the accepted doctrine that the United States is a government of delegated powers, it follows that those not expressly granted, or reasonably to be implied from such as are conferred, are reserved to the states or to the people. To forestall any suggestion to the contrary, the Tenth Amendment was adopted. The same proposition, otherwise stated, is that powers not granted are prohibited. None to regulate agricultural production is given, and therefore legislation by Congress for that purpose is forbidden.

It is an established principle that the attainment of a prohibited end may not be accomplished under the pretext of the exertion of powers which are granted.

*   *   *

The power of taxation, which is expressly granted, may, of course, be adopted as a means to carry into operation another power also expressly granted. But resort to the taxing power to effectuate an end which is not legitimate, not within the scope of the Constitution, is obviously inadmissible.

*   *   *

*   *   * If the taxing power may not be used as the instrument to enforce a regulation of matters of state concern with respect to which the Congress has no authority to interfere, may it, as in the present case, be employed to raise the money necessary to purchase a compliance which the Congress is powerless to command? The Government asserts that whatever might be said against the validity of the plan if compulsory, it is constitutionally sound because the end is accomplished by voluntary cooperation. There are two sufficient answers to the contention. The regulation is not in fact voluntary. The farmer, of course, may refuse to comply, but the price of such refusal is the loss of benefits. The amount offered is intended to be sufficient to exert pressure on him to agree to the proposed regulation.[19]

19. U.S. Dept. of Agriculture, Agriculture Adjustment, p. 9. "Experience of cooperative associations and other groups has shown that without such Government support, the efforts of the farmers to band together to control the amount of their product sent to market are nearly always brought to nothing. Almost always, under such circumstances, there has been a noncooperating minority, which, refusing to go along with the rest, has stayed on the outside and tried to benefit from the sacrifices the majority has made. *   *   * It is to keep this noncooperating minority in line, or at least prevent it from doing harm to the majority, that the power of the Government has been marshaled behind the adjustment.

The power to confer or withhold unlimited benefits is the power to coerce or destroy. If the cotton grower elects not to accept the benefits, he will receive less for his crops; those who receive payments will be able to undersell him. The result may well be financial ruin.
* * *

* * *

But if the plan were one for purely voluntary co-operation it would stand no better so far as federal power is concerned. At best it is a scheme for purchasing with federal funds submission to federal regulation of a subject reserved to the states.

It is said that Congress has the undoubted right to appropriate money to executive officers for expenditure under contracts between the government and individuals; that much of the total expenditures is so made. But appropriations and expenditures under contracts for proper governmental purposes cannot justify contracts which are not within federal power. And contracts for the reduction of acreage and the control of production are outside the range of that power. An appropriation to be expended by the United States under contracts calling for violation of a state law clearly would offend the Constitution. Is a statute less objectionable which authorizes expenditure of federal moneys to induce action in a field in which the United States has no power to intermeddle? The Congress cannot invade state jurisdiction to compel individual action; no more can it purchase such action.

* * *

Since, as we have pointed out, there was no power in the Congress to impose the contested exaction, it could not lawfully ratify or confirm what an executive officer had done in that regard. Consequently the Act of 1935 does not affect the rights of the parties.

The judgment is affirmed.

Mr. Justice STONE, dissenting.

I think the judgement should be reversed.

* * *

* * * Here regulation, if any there be, is accomplished not by the tax but by the method by which its proceeds are expended, and would equally be accomplished by any like use of public funds, regardless of their source.

The method may be simply stated. Out of the available fund payments are made to such farmers as are willing to curtail their productive acreage, who in fact do so and who in advance have filed their written undertaking to do so with the Secretary of Agriculture.   In saying that this method of spending public moneys is an invasion of the reserved powers of the states, the Court does not assert that the expenditure of public funds to promote the general welfare is not a substantive power specifically delegated to the national government, as Hamilton and Story pronounced it to be.   It does not deny that the expenditure of funds for the benefit of farmers and in aid of a program of curtailment of production of agricultural products, and thus of a supposedly better ordered national economy, is within the specifically granted power.   But it is declared that state power is nevertheless infringed by the expenditure of the proceeds of the tax to compensate farmers for the curtailment of their cotton acreage. Although the farmer is placed under no legal compulsion to reduce acreage, it is said that the mere offer of compensation for so doing is a species of economic coercion which operates with the same legal force and effect as though the curtailment were made mandatory by Act of Congress.   In any event it is insisted that even though not coercive the expenditure of public funds to induce the recipients to curtail production is itself an infringement of state power, since the federal government cannot invade the domain of the states by the "purchase" of performance of acts which it has no power to compel.

Of the assertion that the payments to farmers are coercive, it is enough to say that no such contention is pressed by the taxpayer, and no such consequences were to be anticipated or appear to have resulted from the administration of the Act.   The suggestion of coercion finds no support in the record or in any data showing the actual operation of the Act.   Threat of loss, not hope of gain, is the essence of economic coercion.   Members of a long depressed industry have undoubtedly been tempted to curtail acreage by the hope of resulting better prices and by the proffered opportunity to obtain needed ready money.   But there is nothing to indicate that those who accepted benefits were impelled by fear of lower prices if they did not accept, or that at any stage in the operation of the plan a farmer could say whether, apart from the certainty of cash payments at specified times, the advantage would lie with curtailment of production plus compensation, rather than with the same or increased acreage plus the expected rise in prices which actually occurred.

* * *

The Constitution requires that public funds shall be spent for a defined purpose, the promotion of the general welfare.   Their expenditure usually involves payment on terms which will insure use by the selected recipients within the limits of the constitutional purpose. Expenditures would fail of their purpose and thus lose their constitutional sanction if the terms of payment were not such that by their influence on the action of the recipients the permitted end would be attained. The power of Congress to spend is inseparable from persuasion to action over which Congress has no legislative control. Congress may not command that the science of agriculture be taught in state universities. But if it would aid the teaching of that science by grants to state institutions, it is appropriate, if not necessary, that the grant be on the condition, incorporated in the Morrill Act, 12 Stat. 503, 26 Stat. 417, that it be used for the intended purpose. Similarly it would seem to be compliance with the Constitution, not violation of it, for the government to take and the university to give a contract that the grant would be so used. It makes no difference that there is a promise to do an act which the condition is calculated to induce. Condition and promise are alike valid since both are in furtherance of the national purpose for which the money is appropriated.

*   *   *

The limitation now sanctioned must lead to absurd consequences. The government may give seeds to farmers, but may not condition the gift upon their being planted in places where they are most needed or even planted at all. The government may give money to the unemployed, but may not ask that those who get it shall give labor in return, or even use it to support their families. It may give money to sufferers from earthquake, fire, tornado, pestilence or flood, but may not impose conditions—health precautions designed to prevent the spread of disease, or induce the movement of population to safer or more sanitary areas. All that, because it is purchased regulation infringing state powers, must be left for the states, who are unable or unwilling to supply the necessary relief. The government may spend its money for vocational rehabilitation, 48 Stat. 389, but it may not, with the consent of all concerned, supervise the process which it undertakes to aid. It may spend its money for the suppression of the boll weevil, but may not compensate the farmers for suspending the growth of cotton in the infected areas. It may aid state reforestation and forest fire prevention agencies, 43 Stat. 653, but may not be permitted to supervise their conduct. It may support rural schools, 39 Stat. 929, 45 Stat. 1151, 48 Stat. 792, but may not condition its grant by the requirement that certain standards be maintained. It may appropriate moneys to be expended by the Reconstruction Finance Corporation "to aid in financing agriculture, commerce, and industry," and to facilitate "the exportation of agricultural and other products." Do all its activities collapse because, in order to effect the permissible purpose, in myriad ways the money is paid out upon terms and conditions which influence action of the recipients with the states, which Congress cannot command? The answer would seem plain. If the expenditure is for a national public purpose, that purpose will not be thwarted because payment is on condition which will advance that purpose. The action which Congress induces by payments of money to promote the general welfare, but which it does not command or coerce, is but an incident to a specifically granted power, but a permissible means to a legitimate end. If appropriation in aid of a program of curtailment of agricultural production is constitutional, and it is not denied that it is, payment to farmers on condition that they reduce their crop acreage is constitutional. It is not any the less so because the farmer at his own option promises to fulfill the condition.

STEWARD MACHINE CO. v. DAVIS

Supreme Court of the United States, 1937.
301 U.S. 548, 57 S.Ct. 883, 81 L.Ed. 1279.

[A tax was imposed on employers, based on their employees' wages. The proceeds went into general fund revenues and were not earmarked for any purpose; however, a credit of up to 90 percent of the federal tax was allowed to the extent the employer contributed to a state unemployment fund that met detailed statutory requirements and was also approved by the Social Security Board.]

The excise is not void as involving the coercion of the States in contravention of the Tenth Amendment or of restrictions implicit in our federal form of government.

*   *   *

[Petitioner argues] that the tax and the credit in combination are weapons of coercion, destroying or impairing the autonomy of the states. *   *   * Who then is coerced through the operation of this statute? Not the taxpayer. He pays in fulfillment of the mandate of the local legislature. Not the state. *   *   * For all that appears she is satisfied with her choice, and would be sorely disappointed if it were to be annulled. *   *   * [E]very rebate from a tax when conditioned upon conduct is in some measure a temptation. But to hold that *   *   * temptation is equivalent to coercion is to plunge the law in endless difficulties. The outcome of such a doctrine is the acceptance of a philosophical determinism by which choice becomes impossible. Till now the law has been guided by a robust common sense which assumes the freedom of the will as a working hypothesis in the solution of its problems. The wisdom of the hypothesis has illustration in this case. Nothing in the case suggests the exertion of a power akin to undue influence, if we assume that such a concept can ever be applied with fitness to the relations between state and nation. *   *   * We cannot say that [Alabama] was acting, not of her unfettered will, but under the strain of a persuasion equivalent to undue influence, when she chose to have relief administered under laws of her own making, by agents of her own selection, instead of under federal laws, administered by federal officers, with all the en-

suing evils, at least to many minds, of federal patronage and power.
*   *   *

In ruling as we do, we leave many questions open. We do not say
that a tax is valid, when imposed by act of Congress, if it is laid upon
the condition that a state may escape its operation through the adoption of a statute unrelated in subject matter to activities fairly within
the scope of national policy and power. No such question is before
us. In the tender of this credit Congress does not intrude upon fields
foreign to its function.   *   *   *

United States v. Butler is cited by petitioner as a decision to the
contrary.   *   *   *   The decision was by a divided court, a minority
taking the view that the objections were untenable. None of them is
applicable to the situation here developed.

(a) The proceeds of the tax in controversy are not earmarked for a
special group.

(b) The unemployment compensation law which is a condition of
the credit has had the approval of the state and could not be a law
without it.

(c) The condition is not linked to an irrevocable agreement, for the
state at its pleasure may repeal its unemployment law, terminate the
credit, and place itself where it was before the credit was accepted.

(d) The condition is not directed to the attainment of an unlawful
end, but to an end, the relief of unemployment, for which nation and
state may lawfully cooperate.

The statute does not call for a surrender by the state of powers
essential to their quasi-sovereign existence.

*   *   *   A wide range of judgement is given to the several states
as to the particular type of statute to be spread upon their books.
*   *   *   What they may not do, if they would earn the credit, is to
depart from those standards which in the judgment of Congress must
have the benefit of a fair margin of discretion. One cannot say with
reason that this margin has been exceeded, or that the basic standards have been determined in any arbitrary fashion.   *   *   *

We are to keep in mind steadily that the conditions to be approved
by the Board as the basis for a credit are not provisions of a contract,
but terms of a statute, which may be altered or repealed.   *   *   *
The state does not bind itself to keep the law in force. It does not
even bind itself that the moneys paid into the federal fund will be
kept there indefinitely or for any stated time. On the contrary, the
Secretary of the Treasury will honor a requisition for the whole or
any part of the deposit in the fund whenever one is made by the appropriate officials.   *   *   *

CARROTS vs. STICKS

The underlying theme of the above two cases continues to arise in varying contexts many decades later.[c] For instance, the salient issue in Brown v. Environmental Protection Agency, 521 F.2d 827 (9th Cir. 1975) was whether the Administrator of EPA may, as part of a State Implementation Plan issued pursuant to the Clean Air Amendments of 1970, direct the State of California to undertake certain air-improvement programs under penalty of fines or other civil sanctions. The D.C. Circuit held that the State might decline to undertake the EPA-mandated programs without becoming liable to sanctions. However, it noted that

> Our interpretation is in no way inconsistent with the recognition that Congress has the power to authorize the Administrator to obtain the consent of a reluctant state by conditioning certain federal expenditures within that state on the granting of such consent.

In this connection, the Court cited Steward Machine Co. v. Davis, 301 U.S. 548, 57 S.Ct. 883, 81 L.Ed. 1279 (1937) in favor of the "conditioning" position. But the *Steward* decision might well be compared with the seemingly contrary view in United States v. Butler, 297 U.S. 1, 56 S.Ct. 312, 80 L.Ed. 477 (1936). Which of the lines of argument is most valid?

In cases such as National League of Cities v. Usery, 426 U.S. 833, 96 S.Ct. 2465, 49 L.Ed.2d 245 (1976), the Supreme Court continues to show a concern for the Federal system by limiting the power of the national government over state-local governments. On the other hand, the growing importance of conditional grants may be viewed as a *de facto* erosion of the states' independent spheres of authority. This position is expounded trenchantly in a recent law review note:

> When tested against a standard of uninfluenced decisionmaking, state acceptance of grants whose conditions invade state powers fails. In practice, state legislatures often go beyond allowing national grants to influence their decisions on such policy matters. The states, in effect, cede the responsibility for making some decisions to the national government by accepting conditions that are subject to subsequent determination and revision by national

---

c. The following are examples of the numerous recent cases in which courts have held that a state's action was voluntary because it could have rejected a national grant that imposed obligations on the state: Florida Department of Health and Rehabilitative Service v. Califano, 449 F.Supp. 274, 284 (N.D.Fla.1978), affirmed per curiam on opinion of court below, 585 F.2d 150 (5th Cir.), certiorari denied 441 U.S. 931, 99 S.Ct. 2051, 60 L.Ed. 659 (1979); Walker Field, Colorado, Public Airport Authority v. Adams, 606 F.2d 290, 297–98 (10th Cir. 1979); Oklahoma v. Harris, 480 F.Supp. 581, 588 (D.D.C. 1979).

agencies.   *   *   *   Such an abdication is a dangerous threat to Federalism and should be found unconstitutional.

Note, "Taking Federalism Seriously: Limiting State Acceptance of National Grants," 90 Yale L.J. 1694, 1713 (1981) [footnotes omitted]. But would not an outright ban on all such "deals" between governmental units risk losing mutually advantageous "gains from trade"? Is a principled distinction possible?

Finally, consider the hypothetical question involving interpretation of the United World League Charter in the year 2053. The charter contains a provision which forbids any member state from "making any agreements or taking any actions which infringe the sovereign powers of any other nation." Middleclasia proposes a treaty which offers to pay 50% of the annual GNP of Lesser Developia to the latter's Treasury in return for the right to enact and enforce "public health laws," specifically including compulsory sterilization programs and environmental regulations, in Lesser Developia. Since both nations are UWL member states, the Global Court is asked to construe the charter on this point. The justices of that august body issue the following opinion, 597 G.C. 214, at 223 (2053):

> *   *   *   [Through this treaty] Middleclasia confronts Lesser Developia with a situation which, while it retains the trappings of a consensual arrangement, is nonetheless recognizable as one devoid of any meaningful choice. When the illusory veil of voluntariness is pierced, the impact on Lesser Developia's sovereignty can be adjudged just as predictable and irresistible as a threat of armed attack. In the last century, behavioral scientists were already cognizant of the essential symmetry between bribes and threats. We therefore hold that the proposed treaty is inconsistent with Article 24 of the UWL charter.

By way of brief historical digression only, it may be worth noting that the reaction of Middleclasia was then to switch to a strategy of nuclear threat, with the comment "Well, it sure is a whole lot cheaper—and apparently not any more contrary to the UWL charter—than our illegal and invalidated treaty."

QUESTIONS

1. What is the theoretical argument that the impact of bribes and threats is symmetrical? Of what relevance are such economic concepts as opportunity cost, budget line slopes, etc.? Sketch out, if possible, the opportunity sets of the taxpayers or other relevant economic units before and after the programs being considered by the courts in the above cases.

2.   Are there any important distinctions among the *Brown, Butler*, and *Middleclasia* cases?   Or do they each embody essentially the same situation?

3.   In your opinion, what is the "right" ruling on the three cases? Can you suggest any useful compromises between strict constitutional logic as to "noninterference" and the demands of practicality?   Or does such a conflict not even really exist?

4.   Briefly, suggest one or two other real world contexts where the issues embodied in the above section on "bribes" might be raised in the same or closely related forms.

MEASURING RESPONSIVENESS: ELASTICITIES

In many legal applications, it is of great interest to know the sensitivity of response on the part of decisionmakers to changes in key economic parameters.   Often, these key parameters are changes in the costs (prices) of goods or activities or in the expendable resources (income) available to the decisionmaker.   Why this may be important is illustrated by the *Mathews* and *Tilton* cases above.

In *Mathews*, the economic impact of the block grant is equivalent to an income increase, a parallel outward shift of the recipient's budget constraint.   The grantor is—if the language of the statute is taken at face value—interested in stimulating "Priority Expenditures" and not those other things upon which the grant recipient may prefer to spend the money.   Although this intent of the grantor is manifested in the form of a nominal legal constraint, our analysis of the *Mathews* case should have suggested that proof of a violation of the legal constraint will, barring highly exceptional circumstances, be difficult to establish.   In sum, the legal constraint is of little or no practical consequence as an influence on the results attributable to the grant. Hence, a realistic appraisal of the grant's impact would focus on the grant being, in effect, a mere income transfer to the recipient government.   Then, we might ask with what sensitivity the quantities of the Priority Expenditure goods will vary as the municipal budgetary authorities perceive their unit as being "richer" after the grant is received.   The exact response of any municipality depends partially on its own preferences, i.e., the configuration of its particular indifference curve map for public goods.   But Congress would presumably still be interested in what is expected to be the typical or average responsiveness to the revenue sharing grants.

One straightforward way of measuring responsiveness would be with a simple rate of change concept:

$$\text{Rate of Change} = \frac{\text{Change in Quantity Chosen}}{\text{Change in Income}}$$

For some purposes, this simple concept might be suitable, but it generally has been objected to as being ambiguous, especially if the quantity responsiveness rates of two different goods are to be compared. In short, the problem is that the actual number yielded by the formula above *depends on the units of measurement chosen* for both the quantity and the income changes. For instance, the quantity of roads may be measured in feet or yards, linearly or areally, while income changes may be measured in dollars, cents, thousands of dollars, etc. Hence, as a sensitivity index the simple rate of change concept is in a fundamental sense arbitrary and of limited use for comparative purposes.

The economist's response is to use an "elasticity" concept rather than rates of change. For an income change, the relevant elasticity formula is the "income elasticity":

$$\text{Income Elasticity} = \frac{\text{Change in Quantity Chosen}}{\text{Change in Income}} \times \frac{\text{Income}}{\text{Quantity}}$$

or, by rearranging the terms,

$$\text{Income Elasticity} = \frac{\text{Change in Quantity Chosen}}{\text{Quantity}} \times \frac{\text{Income}}{\text{Change in Income}}$$

where income and quantity are the starting income and quantity. Because the "rate of change" term is multiplied by a new term, income divided by quantity, any change in the units that affects the numerator of one of the fractional terms will similarly affect the denominator, thus negating any effect on the size of the elasticity index. Hence, a group of economists might discuss a *Mathews*-type block grant in terms of the expected income elasticity that recipient governments would have for the quantities of priority and non-priority goods. The grantor presumably would like to see a highly positive income elasticity for the priority goods. To the extent that the *non-priority* goods had a highly positive income elasticity, an unintended "diversion" of the grant funds would occur.

In *Tilton*, the grant program is a so-called "matching" grant scheme wherein the effective price of one category of goods is lowered while the cost of other goods remains the same. Here, a "price elasticity" rather than an income elasticity is relevant. What is usually meant by a price elasticity is the index measuring the responsiveness of a good's quantity to a change in its *own* price:

$$\text{Own Price Elasticity} = \frac{\text{Change in Quantity Chosen}}{\text{Change in Own Price}} \times \frac{\text{Price}}{\text{Quantity}}$$

An own-price elasticity is always expected to have negative algebraic sign because any change in price produces a change in quantity of opposite sign (i.e., price increases stimulate quantity reductions, and vice versa).

In addition to its own price, the quantity of a good chosen may also be influenced by the price of another good to which it is "related." The relevant index of sensitivity is called a "cross elasticity":

$$\text{Cross Elasticity of A and B} = \frac{\text{Change in Quantity A}}{\text{Change in Price of B}} \times \frac{\text{Price of B}}{\text{Quantity of A}}$$

where A and B are two different goods. The absolute magnitude (i.e., size without regard to algebraic sign) of the cross elasticity between two goods tells to what extent they are "related." If goods are related, the terms on which one good is offered will affect the quantity purchased of the other. The *kind* of relationship between the goods is indicated by the algebraic sign of their cross elasticity: positive sign indicates substitutes and negative sign is evidence of complements. Examine the first term of the cross-elasticity formula above to see why it makes sense to interpret the sign of the cross elasticity as evidence about substitutability or complementarity.

There are many legal applications of cross elasticities. For instance, courts examine the cross elasticities among sets of goods to determine which should be grouped as forming part of the same "market" for antitrust analysis. In the *Tilton* case, the concept of "entanglement" between religious and secular expenditures of colleges may be expressed in term of cross elasticities. Examine the abortion case immediately following with a view to the possibility of expressing the issue in terms of cross elasticities.

HARRIS v. McRAE

Supreme Court of the United States, 1980.
448 U.S. 297, 100 S.Ct. 2701, 65 L.Ed.2d 831.

[The majority opinion, by Justice Stewart, held that a state that participates in medicaid is not obligated under Title XIX of the Social Security Act to continue to fund medically necessary abortions nor are the funding restrictions of the Hyde Amendment itself in violation of either the Fifth Amendment or the establishment clause of the First Amendment.]

Mr. Justice BRENNAN, with whom Mr. Justice MARSHALL and Mr. Justice BLACKMUN join, dissenting.

I agree entirely with my Brother Stevens that the State's interest in protecting the potential life of the fetus cannot justify the exclusion of financially and medically needy women from the benefits to which they would otherwise be entitled solely because the treatment that a doctor has concluded is medically necessary involves an abortion. I write separately to express my continuing disagreement with the Court's mischaracterization of the nature of the fundamental right recognized in Roe v. Wade, 410 U.S. 113, 93 S.Ct. 705, 35 L.Ed. 2d 147 (1973), and its misconception of the manner in which that right is infringed by federal and state legislation withdrawing all funding for medically necessary abortions.

Roe v. Wade held that the constitutional right to personal privacy encompasses a woman's decision whether or not to terminate her pregnancy. *Roe* and its progeny established that the pregnant woman has a right to be free from state interference with her choice to have an abortion—a right which, at least prior to the end of the first trimester, absolutely prohibits any governmental regulation of that highly personal decision.[3] The proposition for which these cases stand thus is not that the State is under an affirmative obligation to ensure access to abortions for all who may desire them; it is that the State must refrain from wielding its enormous power and influence in a manner that might burden the pregnant woman's freedom to choose whether to have an abortion. The Hyde Amendment's denial of public funds for medically necessary abortions plainly intrudes upon this constitutionally protected decision, for both by design and in effect it serves to coerce indigent women to bear children that they otherwise would elect not to have.[4]

3. After the first trimester, the State, in promoting its interest in the mother's health may regulate the abortion *procedure* in ways that are reasonably related to that end. And even after the point of viability is reached, State regulation in furtherance of its interest in the potentiality of human life may not go so far as to proscribe abortions that are necessary to preserve the life or health of the mother. See Roe v. Wade, 410 U.S. 113, 164–165, 93 S.Ct. 705, 732–733, 35 L.Ed. 2d 147 (1973).

4. My focus throughout this opinion is upon the coercive impact of the congressional decision to fund one outcome of pregnancy—childbirth—while not funding the other—abortion. Because I believe this alone renders the Hyde Amendment unconstitutional, I do not dwell upon the other disparities that the Amendment produces in the treatment of rich and poor, pregnant and non-

pregnant. I concur completely, however, in my Brother Stevens' discussion of those disparities. Specifically, I agree that the congressional decision to fund all medically necessary procedures except for those that require an abortion is entirely irrational either as a means of allocating health-care resources or otherwise serving legitimate social welfare goals. And that irrationality in turn exposes the Amendment for what it really is—a deliberate effort to discourage the exercise of a constitutionally protected right.

It is important to put this congressional decision in human terms. Nonpregnant women may be reimbursed for all medically necessary treatments. Pregnant women with analogous ailments, however, will be reimbursed only if the treatment involved does not happen to include an abortion. Since the refusal to fund will in some significant number

When viewed in the context of the Medicaid program to which it is appended, it is obvious that the Hyde Amendment is nothing less than an attempt by Congress to circumvent the dictates of the Constitution and achieve indirectly what Roe v. Wade said it could not do directly. * * * Though it may not be this Court's mission "to decide whether the balance of competing interests reflected in the Hyde Amendment is wise social policy," it most assuredly is our responsibility to vindicate the pregnant woman's constitutional right to decide to bear children free from governmental intrusion.

UNITED STATES v. E. I. DU PONT DE NEMOURS & CO.

Supreme Court of the United States, 1956.
351 U.S. 377, 76 S.Ct. 994, 100 L.Ed. 1264.

In a civil action under Sec. 4 of the Sherman Act, the Government charged that appellee had monopolized interstate commerce in cellophane in violation of Sec. 2 of the Act. During the relevant period, appellee produced almost 75% of the cellophane sold in the United States; but cellophane constituted less than 20% of all flexible packaging materials sold in the United States. The trial court found that the relevant market for determining the extent of appellee's market control was the market for flexible packaging materials and that competition from other materials in that market prevented appellee from possessing monopoly powers in its sales of cellophane. Accordingly, it dismissed the complaint.

The Government contends that, by so dominating cellophane production, du Pont monopolized a "part of the trade or commerce" in violation of Sec. 2. Respondent agrees that cellophane is a product which constitutes "a 'part' of commerce within the meaning of Section 2." Du Pont brief, pp. 16, 79. But it contends that the prohibition of Sec. 2 against monopolization is not violated because it does not have the power to control the price of cellophane or to exclude

of cases force the patient to forego medical assistance, the result is to refuse treatment for some genuine maladies not because they need not be treated, cannot be treated, or are too expensive to treat, and not because they relate to a deliberate choice to abort a pregnancy, but merely because treating them would as a practical matter require termination of that pregnancy. Even were one of the view that legislative hostility to abortions could justify a decision to fund obstetrics and child delivery services while refusing to fund nontherapeutic abortions, the present statutory scheme could not be saved. For here, that hostility has gone a good deal farther. Its consequence is to leave indigent sick women without treatment simply because of the medical fortuity that their illness cannot be treated unless their pregnancy is terminated. Antipathy to abortion, in short, has been permitted not only to ride roughshod over a woman's constitutional right to terminate her pregnancy in the fashion she chooses, but also to distort our Nation's health care programs. As a means of delivering health services, then, the Hyde Amendment is completely irrational. As a means of preventing abortions, it is concededly rational—brutally so. But this latter goal is constitutionally forbidden.

competitors from the market in which cellophane is sold. The court below found that the "relevant market for determining the extent of du Pont's market control is the market for flexible packaging materials," and that competition from those other materials prevented du Pont from possessing monopoly powers in its sales of cellophane. Finding 37.

The Government asserts that cellophane and other wrapping materials are neither substantially fungible nor like priced. For these reasons, it argues that the market for other wrappings is distinct from the market for cellophane and that the competition afforded cellophane and that the competition afforded cellophane by other wrappings is not strong enough to be considered in determining whether du Pont has monopoly powers. Market delimitation is necessary under du Pont's theory to determine whether an alleged monopolist violates Sec. 2. The ultimate consideration in such a determination is whether the defendants control the price and competition in the market for such part of trade or commerce as they are charged with monopolizing. Every manufacturer is the sole producer of the particular commodity it makes but its control in the above sense of the relevant market depends upon the availability of alternative commodities for buyers: *i.e.,* whether there is a cross-elasticity of demand between cellophane and the other wrappings. This interchangeability is largely gauged by the purchase of competing products for similar uses considering the price characteristics and adaptability of the competing commodities. The court below found that the flexibile wrappings afforded such alternatives. This Court must determine whether the trial court erred in its estimate of the competition afforded cellophane by other materials.

* * *

If cellophane is the "market" that du Pont is found to dominate, it may be assumed it does not have monopoly power to control prices or exclude competition. It seems apparent that du Pont's power to set the price of cellophane has been limited only by the competition afforded by other flexible packaging materials. Moreover, it may be practically impossible for anyone to commence manufacturing cellophane without full access to du Pont's technique. However, du Pont has no power to prevent competition from other wrapping materials. The trial court consequently had to determine whether competition from the other wrappings prevented du Pont from possessing monopoly power in violation of Sec. 2. Price and competition are so intimately entwined that any discussion of theory must treat them as one. It is inconceivable that price could be controlled without power over competition or vice versa. This approach to the determination of monopoly power is strengthened by this Court's conclusion in prior cases that, when an alleged monopolist has power over price and competition, an intention to monopolize in a proper case may be assumed.[19]

If a large number of buyers and sellers deal freely in a standardized product, such as salt or wheat, we have complete or pure competition. Patents, on the other hand, furnish the most familiar type of classic monopoly. As the producers of a standardized product bring about significant differentiations of quality, design, or packaging in the product that permit differences of use, competition becomes to a greater or less degree incomplete and the producer's power over price and competition greater over his article and its use, according to the differentiation he is able to create and maintain. A retail seller may have in one sense a monopoly on certain trade because of location, as an isolated country store or filling station, or because no one else makes a product of just the quality or attractiveness of his product, as for example in cigarettes. Thus one can theorize that we have monopolistic competition in every nonstandardized commodity with each manufacturer having power over the price and production of his own product. However, this power that, let us say, automobile or soft-drink manufacturers have over their trademarked products is not the power that makes an illegal monopoly. Illegal power must be appraised in terms of the competitive market for the product.

*   *   *

IV. *The Relevant Market.*—When a product is controlled by one interest, without substitutes available in the market, there is monopoly power. Because most products have possible substitutes, we cannot, as we said in Times-Picayune Co. v. United States, 345 U.S. 594, 612, 73 S.Ct. 872, 882, give "that infinite range" to the definition of substitutes. Nor is it a proper interpretation of the Sherman Act to require that products be fungible to be considered in the relevant market.

The Government argues:

"We do not here urge that in no circumstances may competition of substitutes negative possession of monopolistic power over trade in a product. The decisions make it clear at the least that the courts will not consider substitutes other than those which are substantially fungible with the monopolized product and sell at substantially the same price."

But where there are market alternatives that buyers may readily use for their purposes, illegal monopoly does not exist merely because the product said to be monopolistic differs from others. If it

19. United States v. Columbia Steel Co., 334 U.S. 495, 525, 68 S.Ct. 1107, 1123, 72 L.Ed. 1533; United States v. Paramount Pictures, 334 U.S. 131, 173, 68 S.Ct. 915, 936, 92 L.Ed. 1260; Apex Hosiery Co. v. Leader, 310 U.S. 469, 501, 60 S.Ct. 982, 996, 84 L.Ed. 1311; cf. Rostow, 43 Ill.L.Rev. 745, 753–763; Oppenheim, Federal Antitrust Legislation, 50 Mich.L.Rev. 1139, 1193.

were not so, only physically identical products would be a part of the market. To accept the Government's argument, we would have to conclude that the manufacturers of plain as well as moistureproof cellophane were monopolists, and so with films such a Pliofilm, foil, glassine, polyethylene, and Saran, for each of these wrapping materials is distinguishable. These were all exhibits in the case. New wrappings appear, generally similar to cellophane: is each a monopoly? What is called for is an appraisal of the "cross-elasticity" of demand in the trade. See Note, 54 Col.L.Rev. 580.

*   *   *

An element for consideration as to cross-elasticity of demand between products is the responsiveness of the sales of one product to price changes of the other. If a slight decrease in the price of cellophane causes a considerable number of customers of other flexible wrappings to switch to cellophane, it would be an indication that a high cross-elasticity of demand exists between them; that the products compete in the same market. The court below held that the "[g]reat sensitivity of customers in the flexible packaging markets to price or quality changes" prevented du Pont from possessing monopoly control over price. 118 F.Supp., at 207. The record sustains these findings. See references made by the trial court in Findings 123–149.

We conclude that cellophane's interchangeability with the other materials mentioned suffices to make it a part of the flexible packaging material market.

*   *   *

QUESTIONS

1. In this case, "flexible packaging material" would include products that have necessarily similar physical characteristics. Suppose that the issue involved the definition of a market for the provision of "off-hours theft protection" to business establishments. Some alternative approaches would involve watchmen, guard dogs, local alarms, alarms connected to a central response station, special locks, etc. Would all of these be part of the same market? See United States v. Grinnell Corp., 384 U.S. 563, 86 S.Ct. 1698, 16 L.Ed.2d 778 (1966).

2. The Court's use of the cross elasticity measure in this case is generally regarded by economists as a case of erroneous inference. Can you tell why? [Hint: Will the cross elasticity among products be the same at all prices?]

LEGAL APPLICATIONS FROM DEMAND THEORY

1.   "Elasticities" are the economist's measures for the responsiveness of choices to changes in economic variables such as income, prices, etc. The magnitudes of elasticities may be important for various types of legal analysis.

   a.   "One view of constitutional protections is this: the State must exercise great caution when it affects the choices that have high cross-elasticities with protected goods or activities." Explain what you think is meant by the quoted statement. Do you agree?

   b.   A recent New York State statute provided for heavy mandatory penalties on drug pushers. By raising the cost of purchasing drugs, the statute was intended indirectly to curb the type of street crime and burglary that is commonly engaged in by addicts seeking to support a drug habit. How does the rationale of this law depend on an implicit premise about the [own price] elasticity of demand for illegal drugs? Do you regard this premise as plausible?

2.   Your client, Zenavox Corp., manufactures consumer electronics equipment including television receivers. Suit has been filed against Zenavox by a group of its own retailers seeking treble damages under the Sherman Antitrust Act. The conduct alleged is, inter alia, that the corporation conspired with a group of "favored" retailers to monopolize sales of Zenavox TV sets in the southern part of the State of North Dakolina. The time period is 1969.

   a.   Your economic consultant advises that a study be conducted to determine the cross elasticity of demand between Zenavox TVs and other brands. Normally, what results would you be looking for? Why? (This part is easy.)

   b.   Plaintiffs also allege that Zenavox's semi-annual factory sales of TV sets to its own employees make it a retailer. If the court so holds, Zenavox's Fair Trade agreements with its franchisees would not be protected by the Miller-Tydings amendment to Section 1 of the Sherman Act. In this time period (1969), the Miller-Tydings provision protected "vertical" price-fixing agreements among entities competing at the same market level but not "horizontal" agreements as, for example, among several retailers. Unless so protected, price-fixing agreements would be per se illegal, i.e., not subject to any defense such as lack of market power. Under these circumstances, does it still seem prudent to generate evidence that there is a high cross elasticity of demand between Zenavox products and those of competing brands? [Hint: Under

this type of resale price maintenance agreement, dealers were required to charge no less than certain minimum prices. What kind of
damage does a retailer suffer by not being able to lower his price?]

Chapter V

CHANNELLING BEHAVIOR THROUGH LEGAL INCENTIVES

LIABILITY AND BEHAVIOR REVISTED

The notion of legal rules as behavioral modifiers is hardly a new one in these pages. Indeed, that role of the legal system was introduced in the very first part of Chapter I and formed one of several main themes of that chapter. Initially, the focus was primarily in the context of "property": how it is defined and protected, transferred, and affected by rules that discourage what might be termed "wasteful" use or infringement. In subsequent chapters, the use of legal liabilities, penalties, prohibitions, etc., has continued to be an underlying theme in many applications, ranging over a wide spectrum of legal phenomena. In this chapter, however, we take a much more focussed look at some important liability rules and their behavioral implications.

Although other areas of law are also implicated, the bulk of the applications that follow are from the mainstream of tort and contract law. In both of these branches of law, there is a "wrongful" party (the tortfeasor or breacher) and a "wronged" party (the victim or breachee). One purpose of assessing what the law calls "damages" is to compensate the injured party for the wrong or breach of duty that has occurred. Little will be said herein about the compensatory purpose of damages, not because this purpose is in any way unimportant, but mainly because the compensatory aspects of damage payments tend to be relatively obvious. Instead, primary emphasis will be placed on explicating the much less obvious implications of damage rules on the *conduct* of the parties who pay or receive the damages. One major goal is merely to explore how conduct might vary under the different rules, and we shall see that the effects are not always as straightforward as is generally believed. Once the behavioral variations under different rules are understood, one can better address the issue of how what may be deemed "desirable" or "undesirable" behavioral incentives might be "traded off" against various normative goals. One of these goals is, of course, compensation, and it will be instructive to see how, if at all, compensatory goals conflict with other plausible desiderata that are principally behavioral.

The discussion leads off with familiar notions from tort theory. A second major goal of the chapter is, however, to apply our conceptual tools to an interweaving of tort liability rules with the similar or contrasting elements of contractual liability. Although only a few of the aspects of the torts-contracts nexus can be pursued, some provocative questions nevertheless do emerge.

TORT LIABILITY STANDARDS

A finding of negligence on the part of a person who accidently injures another has for almost two centuries been the most important standard that triggers civil liability in tort. But exactly what is meant by the term "negligence"? Perhaps the most famous attempt to give exact content to the concept was that of Judge Learned Hand in United States v. Carroll Towing Co., 159 F.2d 169 (2d Cir. 1947). Hand stated that the factfinder must consider three factors: the magnitude of the loss if the accident should occur, the probability of occurrence, and the cost of taking precautions that would avert it. The product of the first two factors—what an economist might term the expected value of the harm—should be balanced against the cost of precautions, with failure to engage in cost-effective precautions constituting negligence. This formulation is widely known as the Learned Hand Rule.

Obviously, the Learned Hand Rule has an economic flavor to it, but economists tend to criticize the original formulation as ambiguous or at least imprecise. The complaint is that the original formulation does not make it sufficiently clear that the rule must, in order to convey the sense that Hand almost certainly intended, be interpreted as applying to *marginal adjustments* of care and not to the *total* amount of care exercised. In most situations, many different levels of care are possible, each of which yield different answers for the three factors that Hand emphasized.

Recall, for instance, Exhibit 2.10 above where the bus company could, by engaging in different levels of preventive maintenance, alter the probability that Wurrier would not be delivered to the Big Game on time. In the bus hypothetical, we implicitly assumed that the magnitude of harm caused was invariant, that only its probability could be adjusted. Even under the facts of that hypothetical, however, it might have been argued that various short delays (i.e., flat tire, running out of gas) would likely cause Wurrier only partial loss of the game, whereas graver faults (no oil in the crankcase, malfunctioning windshield wipers on a rainy night) would result in full damages. Similar statements can be made about investments in order to reduce the prospects of harm resulting from an accidental tort rather than an accidental contract breach. Except perhaps for classificatory purposes, it is unimportant for the Hand approach whether precautions affect the probability of harm, the magnitude of the harm if it occurs, or both. At base, what is really involved is reduction of the expected value of the harm. Remember also that "care" is a convenient summary or portmanteau term; in general, care consists of heterogeneous activities rather than adjustment of any single dimension of activity.

What Hand presumably wants potential tortfeasors to do is to act in much the same fashion as our bus company in Chapter II above. The marginal benefits of each "dose" of additional care (these benefits being composed of reductions in the expected value of harm) should be compared to the marginal cost of taking the precautions. Exhibit 5.1 depicts such a marginal analysis. The vertical axis is used to measure costs and benefits in dollars, while the variable T on the horizontal axis represents levels of care taken by the tortfeasor. For simplicity, the marginal cost of precautions is represented as constant, but increasing or decreasing marginal cost would not materially affect the analysis. Also for simplicity, the "injurer" in the remainder of this chapter will generally be referred to loosely and somewhat inaccurately as the "tortfeasor" even when his conduct conforms to the legal standard so that technically the injury is not a "tort."

QUESTIONS

1. In Exhibit 5.1, draw a line (bright yellow if you have it!) perpendicular to the horizontal axis such that levels of care to the left would be negligent under the Learned Hand Rule. On the horizontal axis, label the level of care that just satisfies the rule as T^*.

2. Absent any legal rule, what level of T would you expect the tortfeasor to pick? Why? If a tortfeasor must compensate the victim only when negligent, what level of T would be predictable? Why? (Assume, for the moment, that courts always apply the standard with accuracy and precision. This assumption will be relaxed later.)

EXHIBIT 5.1

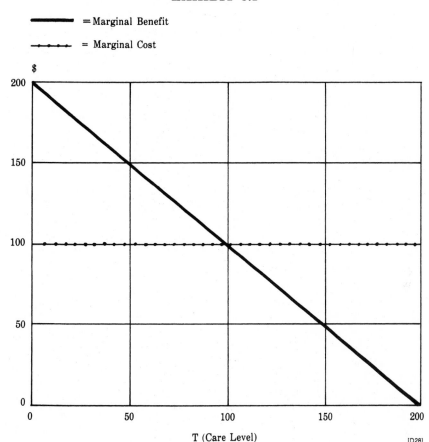

T (Care Level)

[D28]

3. It is sometimes said that legal liabilities are used to "internalize" external costs. What is meant by that assertion? And of what relevance is it to the negligence standard?

4. Assume that all potential tortfeasors adopt care level T*. Some positive level of expected costs will be imposed by the class of potential tortfeasors on the class of potential victims. How can you tell that from Exhibit 5.1? Does Exhibit 5.1 permit you to say what the magnitude of those costs would be?

5. Suppose that liability could be escaped only if "all possible effective precautions" were exercised. Label that level of care T′ in Exhibit 5.1. Assume that T′ were adopted by all potential tortfeasors. In what way would that assumption affect what is said in question 4 immediately preceding?

6. You were just asked to *assume* a precaution level of T′. Under the liability rule posited, is precaution level T′ the behavior that you would predict?

7. What do you understand to be meant by the standard of "strict liability." Explain, in terms of Exhibit 5.1, the level of T that would be likely under that standard. How is question 4 above affected if recast to apply to the strict liability rule?

8. From a normative perspective, do you find anything particularly attractive about the negligence standard? If not, can you articulate what might be the position of its adherents?

"ERRORS" IN ASSESSMENT OF DAMAGES

Careful completion of the question set immediately preceding should have led you to what is to many persons a surprising and counterintuitive conclusion: under a perfect adjudication system, the level of care taken by a potential tortfeasor is the same under a strict liability system as under a negligence rule. The reason why this is so, and why the conclusion changes when there are "errors" in the adjudication system, can be further explored with some additional simple models.

In order to make the illustrations more concrete, the diagrammatic models provided as Exhibits 5.1 through 5.4 in the beginning of this chapter are all based upon a specific numerical example. This example assumes that the cost of a unit of care, T, is $100. A specific assumption is also made about the efficacy of care; namely, that the expected value of the harm, H, from a dangerous activity varies according to the formula:

$$H = 22000 - [200T - .5T^2] \qquad T < 200$$

where T is the level of precautionary care taken by the tortfeasor and the square-bracketed term indicates the *reduction* in harm that has taken place as a result of the care exercised. Hence, if no care is taken, the level of harm will be $22,000. Thereafter, the value of H declines as T increases within the range from zero to 200. At the 200 level, additional care will have no further effect, as the "side condition" to the right of the formula indicates by constraining T to values of less than 200. By inference from the formula for the total level of H, the *marginal* effect of T in reducing harm can be expressed by the formula 200 − T; that is, the first dose of T reduces H at a rate of almost 200, but the efficacy of care declines and reaches zero when 200 units of care have been applied. (Readers who have had a little calculus will recognize 200 − T as the first derivative of the formula given above for H, i.e., the value of dH/dT.) Note that the marginal benefits curve in Exhibit 5.1 above follows the factual assumptions just laid out: it incorporates (1) a marginal benefits curve for care having an intercept of 200 and a negative slope of one and (2) a marginal cost curve of care which is constant at the level 100.

Although economic models usually focus almost exclusively on marginal effects, the present topic provides an instance when it may be helpful to one's understanding to see the problem in total terms. Exhibit 5.2 plots out the total magnitudes underlying the problem presented in marginal terms in Exhibit 5.1. The straight line is the total cost of care taken. If we symbolize the total cost of care as C, then Exhibit 5.2 shows the relationship

$$C = 100T$$

as a straight line. The "harm reduction" curve is the square-bracketed term in the formula for H above. It is, in essence, the "total benefits" curve from the societal standpoint. Note that the greatest excess of benefits over costs occurs at the 100 level of T, just as the marginal analysis in Exhibit 5.1 suggested. Indeed, the *slope* of any total curve is diagrammatically equivalent to the marginal effect.

EXHIBIT 5.2

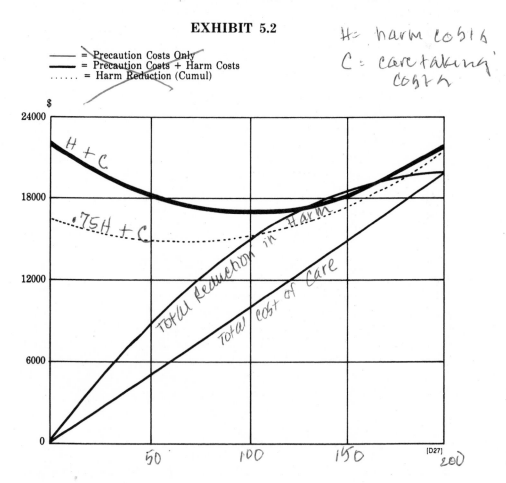

——— = Precaution Costs Only
━━━ = Precaution Costs + Harm Costs
…… = Harm Reduction (Cumul)

H = harm costs
C = caretaking costs

Verify the optimality of the 100 level by constructing the tangent to the harm reduction curve of Exhibit 5.2 at the 100 level. Since the tangent indicates the slope of a curve at the point where it touches, the slope should be the same as the straight line that represents total costs. Do you see the common-sense of the result that one should stop incurring costs at the point where benefits begin to rise more slowly (i.e., have a lesser slope) than the associated rate of increase in costs? Finally, the heavy top curve shows the *net result* at different levels of care, i.e., the value H $+$ C. Note that the minimum point of this curve lies, as expected, at the 100 level of T, but the absolute height of the curve is quite high; H has not been reduced to zero, even in the range that clearly meets the negligence standard. Take a colored pencil and trace out a potential tortfeasor's costs for different levels of care under a perfectly administered negligence standard. It follows the top curve up to the point where T = 100, then "jumps" down to the straight C curve. Do you see why? By contrast, what curve or curves are relevant under strict liability? Why is the expected conduct the same?

Thus far, the results from Exhibit 5.2 are just a different way of expressing the analysis of Exhibit 5.1. Let us now, however, begin to introduce "errors" into the adjudication system. Specifically, let us start by assuming that courts will correctly set the negligence standard at 100 units of care, but will underassess damages, setting them at only 75% of H. Under the alternative rule of strict liability, the tortfeasor will always have to pay damages, but the same degree of underassessment will occur. This form of error will, of course, undercompensate victims and may also be expected to affect behavior with respect to the level of care taken.

In effect, the form of error just hypothesized converts the original formula for H into:

$$H = .75 \{(22000 - [200T - .5T^2])\} \qquad T < 200$$

where only .75 of the true harm is "charged" to the tortfeasor.

QUESTIONS

1. Which curves in Exhibits 5.1 and 5.2 are based on H? Is it true that these curves now lie exactly three-fourths as high as they did originally? Draw them in on your copies of the respective exhibits.

2. The dotted curve in Exhibit 5.2 is the new "net result" or H $+$ C curve. About where does its minimum point lie? Is this the same level of T as suggested by the marginal analysis in Figure 5.1?

3. Imagine that you were a potential tortfeasor. If the standard were one of negligence, it would be rational for you still to invest in

100 units of care. Why? What is your cost-minimizing level of care under strict liability? What explains the difference?

4. Suppose that the error took the form of an overassessment of damages by 25%, rather than an underassessment. How are the results affected?

5. If T = 100 is the desired behavior under the Learned Hand Rule, then the preceding analysis suggests that the negligence standard is "robust" in that damage miscalculations—even of high relative magnitude—may not distort the desired behavior. What would the degree of misassessment have to be to affect the results under the conditions hypothesized in Exhibits 5.1 and 5.2? How could the facts of the hypothetical have been chosen so as to weaken the finding of no behavioral effect?

6. Would most people regard the results developed above as counterintuitive or contrary to expectation? If so, are they the result of any "sleight of hand" or are they a fair representation of reality? (You may wish to defer a final judgement on this question until after the completion of this chapter.)

7. Robert Cooter developed models almost identical to those in this section in his interesting analysis of the rationale for punitive damages. See Cooter, "Economic Analysis of Punitive Damages," 56 S.Cal.L.Rev. 79 (1982). Cooter suggests that most injurers are at fault only "unintentionally" in the sense of what economists would regard as mistaken or "disequilibrium" behavior. Gross fault, he argues, is likely to be intentional and attributable to an idiosyncratic cost or returns function possessed by the individual. Punitive damages would then be necessary to secure the individual's compliance with a normal standard. Would a persistent pattern of modest fault fit his hypothesis equally well?

"ERRORS" IN THE LIABILITY STANDARD

In contrast to the last section, let us now assume that damages are assessed correctly (equal to H) when liability is found, but that judges and juries sometimes set the standard of care either above or below the 100 level called for by a precise Learned Hand Rule application. Figure 5.3 shows a familiar bell-shaped Gaussian or "Normal" curve centered on the "correct" level of 100, but dispersed for a considerable range around this midpoint. (For those really interested, the "standard deviation" of the probability distribution assumed in Exhibits 5.3 and 5.4 is 15.) The height of the bell-shaped curve indicates the relative probability that a court will find that a particular level of T fails to satisfy the minimum requirements of the negligence standard. Hence there is almost no chance that a court would accept a level as low as 55 or demand one as high as 145, but the intervening values are all possible. The area around 100 is, as the diagram suggests, the most likely standard to be adopted by a judge or jury.

The heavier curve of cumulative probabilities is derived from the bell-shaped one. Note that the area under the bell-shaped curve must account for 100% of the probabilities. The heavy downward sloping curve is the fraction of the area under the bell-shaped curve that, at any level of T, lies to the right. Therefore, it can be interpreted as telling us the probability that a court would set its liability standard higher than any given level of T, thus finding the tortfeasor who chooses that level of care to be negligent.

EXHIBIT 5.3

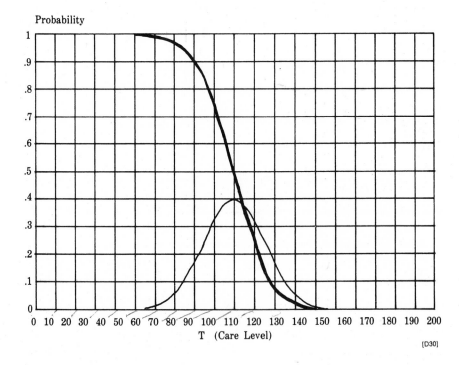

For expository simplicity, assume that a potential tortfeasor is risk-neutral, so that he wishes to minimize the expected value of his costs. Under the circumstances posited, the sum of the costs under the negligence system may be expressed as:

$$L = pH + C$$

EXHIBIT 5.4

— = Marginal Harm Reduction
_ = Marginal Liability Reduction
····· = Partial Marg. H Reduction

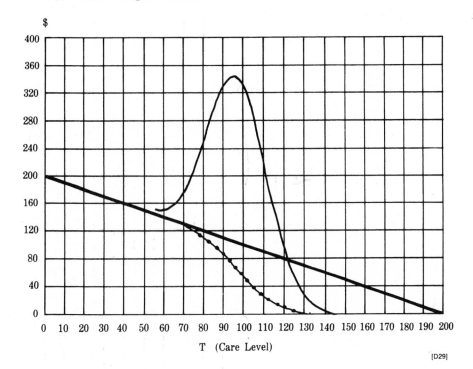

T (Care Level)

[D29]

where L signifies the costs in question, p is the probability of being held liable, H is the damages (assumed now to be accurately levied as compensatory damages), and C is the cost of the care taken. In the specific numerial example being used in these sections

$$L = p\ \{22000 - [200T + .5T^2]\} + 100T.$$

The care level T appears explicitly in part of this formula, but it also is involved implicitly as a determinant of the value taken on by p. (See Exhibit 5.3.)

An orthodox marginal adjustment model can be constructed by examining the effect of this situation on marginal benefits and costs from increasing care. In general terms, the marginal effect of T on the expected value of the damages to be paid will be:

[p(marginal harm reduction)] +[(marginal reduction of p)H]

Readers who have had calculus will recognize the words above as the first derivative of pH with respect to T, i.e., $d(pH)/dT = p\ dH/dT +$

dp/dT H. The "common sense" of the formulation may, in any event, be perceived by giving a practical interpretation to its components. The first square-bracketed term above is what we shall call the "harm reduction effect," since it measures the amount by which one's costs will be reduced due to the necessity to pay smaller damages upon any judgment of liability. By contrast, the second square-bracketed term is the "liability risk reduction effect," since it measures the impact on costs of a diminished probability that one will indeed be held liable at all.

Whenever p is less than one, the harm reduction effect is, of course, attenuated because the *ex ante* prospect is that one will be held somewhat less than fully responsible for any harm done. Thus, in Exhibit 5.4, the heavy straight line shows the true marginal harm reduction effect (when p = 1.00) while the curve below it indicates how the importance of harm reduction is attenuated when the probability of liability begins to fall below 1.00, starting at about 55 on the care axis. The liability risk reduction effect from the second part of the formula works in the opposite direction. It has the effect of making care adjustments have a *greater* impact to the extent that they produce a change in p. Under plausible conditions, this latter effect greatly overbalances the attenuation factor, producing a net change (sum of both effects) that distorts the true marginal benefits curve upward in the manner indicated by the humped curve in Exhibit 5.4. Under the assumptions of our specific numerical example, the formula for that net curve is:

$$p (200 - T) + \Delta p (22000 - 200T + .5T^2)$$

where Δp is the reduction in p that occurs as a result of a marginal increase in T. Values for p and Δp can be inferred approximately from Exhibit 5.3 or looked up more precisely in a reference book containing tables of values for the Gaussian Normal probability distribution. One can, however, merely inspect the formula and see that even relatively small values for Δp, the *change* occurring in p, will cause the second part of the formula to have a value sufficiently high to overbalance the effect of a small value of p in otherwise diminishing the marginal benefit curve from its "true" value of (200 - T).

Add the appropriate marginal *cost* of care curve to Exhibit 5.4. Then find the interesection point that identifies the level of T at which the marginal costs of care and the marginal effect on legal exposure are properly balanced so that the tortfeasor's prospective costs are minimized in the face of this inaccurately applied negligence standard. How does this compare with what would happen under a strict liability rule?

QUESTIONS

1. Explain in as non-technical terms as possible why high—and arguably "excessive"—levels of care might be very cost-effective for tortfeasors in the context just laid out. Why do the symmetric errors of the courts (equal incidence of too-strict and too-lenient standards) not just "cancel out" in terms of behavioral incentives?

2. How could the facts of the example in the text be altered to change the results? Under what circumstances would strict liability produce higher levels of care than negligence?

3. What do you think the shapes of the actual probability distributions of standard-setting errors look like? Why do the shapes matter?

4. Suppose that the liability standard were perfectly applied in all cases. Draw a graph that shows the level of p as a function of the level of T. If T* is the level of care that satisfies the negligence standard, what value does Δp have when T* care is taken? This exercise may improve your understanding of the analysis in the previous section, where it was suggested that the levels of care under negligence standards may not be much affected by incorrect calibration of the damages. Try to explain that earlier result in terms of the factors introduced in this present section.

5. What if the level of care actually chosen either exceeds or falls short of that called for in the Learned Hand Rule? Who is better or worse off? Why should we care?

6. "The negligence rule, properly understood, is really a right of private eminent domain given to performers of dangerous acts. What's more, it doesn't even require them to pay full compensation." Comment.

MULTI–PARTY HARM PRODUCTION FUNCTIONS

Up to this point, all of the discussion in this chapter has been couched in terms of the impact that the tortfeasor's conduct has on the probability and magnitude of an accident. But a very large proportion of potential torts involve situations in which the conduct of the victim can influence either the probability or magnitude of the harm. Indeed, this fact is recognized in the legal doctrine of contributory negligence, which imposes upon the victim a duty to take cost-effective precautions in a manner similar to that which we have just discussed for the tortfeasor. If the victim is found contributorily negligent, he cannot recover damages even if the injurer is found negligent.

When both parties have a duty to take care, and both parties have an impact on the result, the analysis becomes a bit more complicated.

This can be illustrated by an example in which we shall retain, insofar as is possible, the terminology developed earlier in the chapter. Hence, let H once again represent the expected value of the harm and T the level of care taken by the tortfeasor. In addition, we must now create a new variable, V, to denote the level of care taken by the victim. Then H might be expressed as a function of *both* T and V such as:

$$H = 22000 - 100 \, V^{1/3} T^{1/2}$$

In this case, the marginal effect of T on H (i.e., dH/dT) will be:

$$50V^{1/3} T^{-1/2} \quad \text{or} \quad \frac{50V^{1/3}}{T^{1/2}}$$

Note that, for any value of T, its marginal effect will always be greater if the level of V is higher. A similar statement is true about the marginal effect of victim precautions V on H:

$$33.33V^{-2/3} T^{1/2} \quad \text{or} \quad \frac{33.33T^{1/2}}{V^{2/3}}$$

Our specific numerical example merely reflects a common empirical relationship, that the effect of the victim's and the tortfeasor's care is complementary, the efficacy of each party's acts depending to some extent on what the other party does. When this is true, one cannot draw the kind of marginal benefits curve used in Exhibit 5.1 without first knowing the level of care that will be taken by the other party; the other party's care will shift the marginal benefits curve up and down.

From the discussion of the Learned Hand Rule above, it may fairly be hypothesized that the combination of the negligence and contributory negligence doctrines is designed to create incentives for parties to minimize harms in the most cost-effective way possible. We can adapt the "mapping" tools employed in Chapter IV to a consideration of this interaction between the "inputs" of care by the two parties and the resultant "output" of a level of social cost. The model yielded is similar to "production function" models in more traditional economics.

In its more abstract and generalizable form, a two-party production function for harm could be written as H = H(V,T) where the H (V,T) is understood as some mathematical function that has V and T as two of its variables. Similarly, cost could be written abstractly as C = C(V,T), where C(V,T) simply says that the total cost of care is determined in some way by the levels of V and T. If one were interested in minimizing the net social cost attributable to the dangerous activity in question, then the goal could be formalized as one of minimizing S where

$$S = H(V,T) + C(V,T)$$

Exhibit 5.5 is an example of what a "map" of the production function of S might look like.[a] Think of it as a topographic map of a valley or "bowl" where the contour lines show equal levels of S. Social cost is minimized by getting to the bottom of the bowl, point a in Exhibit 5.5. As one moves around on the map, by varying the levels of V and T, H and C undergo changes in opposite directions.

EXHIBIT 5.5

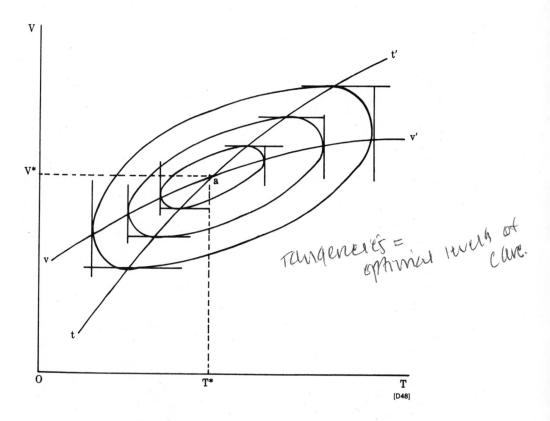

[D48]

Exhibit 5.5 also shows two lines that are clearly distinguishable from the contour lines. These are "lines of optima" that denote the S-minimizing reaction level of each party to any level of the other party's care. Follow line tt' to where it intersects the middle contour line. Now draw in a horizontal line at that point. When referred to the vertical axis, the horizontal line can be interpreted as a fixed or predetermined level of V. The tortfeasor can move back and forth along this line, because he controls the value of T, but he cannot move up or down in a vertical direction since V is controlled by the

a. A pathbreaking use of a "map" approach in tort analysis is Brown, "Toward An Economic Theory of Tort Liability," 2 J.Leg.Stud. 323 (1973).

other party. Where, then, is the "optimal" response of the tortfeasor
in terms of a level of T that achieves the lowest achievable level of S?
It is at the tangency point with the contour line. Do you see why?
You should satisfy yourself that every point on the tt' line is the "optimal" S-minimizing response of the tortfeasor on the assumption
that V has been fixed at the corresponding level of the vertical axis.
Line vv' is, of course, an analogous construct showing the optimal
cost-minimizing response of the victim on alternative assumptions as
to the care taken by the tortfeasor.

QUESTIONS

1.   What relationship does a point on tt' in Exhibit 5.5 have to the
marginal analysis in Exhibit 5.1? Can Exhibit 5.2 be interpreted as a
"slice" of Exhibit 5.5?

2.   To what extent is it accurate to interpret tt' and vv' as, respectively, conceptualizations of the negligence and contributory negligence standards?

3.   Absent any legally imposed incentives, does minimizing S represent the best result for the tortfeasor? For the victim? If not, to
what location on the "map" would you expect the parties to adjust if
there were no legal system at all?

4.   Do the relevant legal doctrines give the parties incentives that
will lead to a solution at point a, the minimum level of S? Why?

5.   In the absence of the contributory negligence doctrine, what
solution would you predict?

6.   What kinds of changes in the facts of the world would cause
the "topography" represented by the map to shift?

COMPARATIVE NEGLIGENCE

The doctrine of comparative negligence is now applied in many jurisdictions in lieu of a strict rule of no recovery when the victim is
contributorily negligent. Perhaps the increasing popularity of comparative negligence reflects a sense that there exists a certain harsh-
ness and apparent injustice when, although both parties fail in their
duties of care, the consequences are borne solely by the contributorily negligent victim.

Exactly what does comparative negligence mean? Loosely speaking, nobody seems to have any difficulty with the notion that comparative negligence involves allocating the damages between the negligent tortfeasor and the contributorily negligent victim in a manner
proportional to their relative degrees of negligence. Surprisingly enough, however, the concept is somewhat ambiguous if one at-

tempts to give it more precise operational content. This ambiguity can be illustrated effectively with a mapping model.

Exhibit 5.6 is another production function model similar to that introduced in the previous section as Exhibit 5.5. The contours of these two harm production function maps are dissimilar because they represent two different activities or products, each of which involves its own unique "technology" of harm reduction and diverse costs of care. Otherwise, the contour lines and lines of optima have the same significance as we have already discussed.

EXHIBIT 5.6

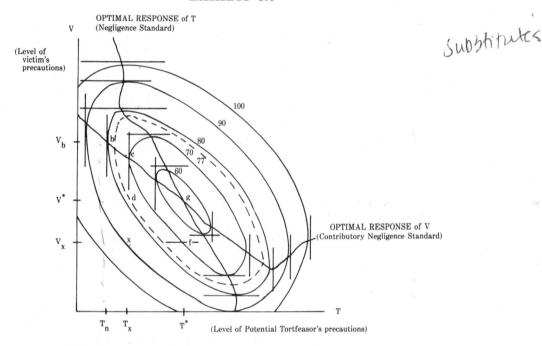

If both parties complied with the negligence standard, the tort-feasor would supply T^* of care and the victim V^*, thus achieving the global minimum of social cost S at point a, the "bottom of the bowl." At that optimal result, the level of social costs (the cost of the harm plus the cost of the care taken to minimize the harm) would be only 50. Assume, however, that tortfeasor takes only T_x of care and victim V_x of care, so that the actual result is at point x. Exhibit 5.6 tells us exactly what the shortfalls of care are by both parties and exactly what the consequences of those shortfalls are; we have none of the uncertainties or measurement problems of the real world. Consequently, it is a fair question to ask how the exact degrees of comparative negligence should be determined in light of the full information available.

The actual result x is on a contour line labelled 90, thus indicating that there are 90 dollars (or hundred or thousands or millions of dollars, if you prefer) in social costs to be allocated between the two parties. One plausible approach would be to look to the shortfalls in *inputs* of care as the basis for measuring relative degrees of negligence. The victim's shortfall in care inputs is equal to $(V^* - V_x)$ and the tortfeasor's to $(T^* - T_x)$. If those two shortfalls are somehow added together, we would have an index of total negligence and could express each party's negligence as a proportion of the total. A threshold problem is that V and T are not necessarily the same kinds of care; i.e., T may be a pedestrian's care in looking carefully before crossing the street and V the restraint with which an automobile is driven. One way (perhaps not the only or the best way) of making the inputs comparable for aggregation purposes is to measure them in *cost* terms. For expository simplicity, assume that the prices of each kind of care input are identical, so that we can avoid the necessity to weight the physical units by their costs. Then we can allocate the victim's share of the social costs as

$$(V^* - V_x)/[(V^* - V_x) + (T^* - T_x)]$$

and the tortfeasor's as

$$(T^* - T_x)/[(V^* - V_x) + (T^* - T_x)]$$

The following values for the relevant variables are consistent with Exhibit 5.6: $T^* = 48$; $T_x = 22$; $V^* = 50$; and $V_x = 30$. (You may wish to measure the axes to confirm that the relevant distances are indeed in the proportions indicated by the numbers just suggested.) By inserting the numbers in the formulas, the comparative negligence of the tortfeasor will be computed as 56.5% and that of the victim as 43.5%. Those percentages would be used to apportion the damages.

The method just described may be termed the "inputs approach," since it focuses on the inputs of care. An alternative, however, is to focus on the *impact* of the care shortfalls. The latter is the "outputs approach" and proceeds as follows. The optimal result at point a would have involved costs of 50. If only the tortfeasor had been negligent, the "difference" from the optimal result would have been the increase in cost between point a and point d. Point d is on a contour line labelled 77, so this impact of negligence by the tortfeasor alone is (77 – 50) or 27. Analogously, contributory negligence alone would have moved the result from a to f where the contour line indicates a level of 70. Thus, the output differences caused by each party's shortfall of care might be measured as 27 and 20 for the tortfeasor and victim respectively. On the basis of this outputs approach, the tortfeasor would find that, instead of 56.5%, his comparative negligence would be based on the proportion $27/(27+20)$ or 57.0% Only a small difference, to be sure.

Now, consider the fact that the dotted contour line with point d on it might be relabelled with any number between 70 and 80. This relabelling would correspond to a change in the "steepness" of the topography in that band of the production function map, a change whose economic significance is that the efficacy of care inputs in that range has been raised or lowered. Using a value of 71, the tortfeasor's comparative negligence would be $21/(21+20)$ or 51.2%, while assuming a level of 79 for d's contour would yield $29/(29+20)$ or 59.2%. The perceptive reader will soon see the trick: if the "bowl" has unequal degrees of steepness in different parts of the map, then the effect on output will not necessarily be proportional to the relative sizes of the input shortfalls.

QUESTIONS

1. The text demonstrates that different results can be achieved through the inputs approach and the outputs approach. Therefore, they cannot both be right. What are the arguments for and against each approach? Which is to be preferred? If you were a judge, how would you charge a jury on this question?

2. Just to muddy the waters further, one of the parties claims that the procedure of the outputs approach computation as described in the text above is exactly backwards. "You are asking the wrong question in starting from point a. You should start from point x and ask what difference it would have made if each party had *not* been negligent. For the tortfeasor, the relevant difference is between the result at x and the result at f, while for the victim it is the difference between x and d." Which party would benefit from adopting this approach rather than the one in the text above? Which is more correct?

3. Note that the map was originally defined in terms of social cost S, which includes the cost of care taken by each party. In discussing the comparative negligence standard, should a map of only the harm H been used? If so, the contour lines of a map of H could have been superimposed on the map of S. Which, if any, of the difficulties discussed in the text above would have been affected?

4. Now that you have been put in the mood, can you think of any other defensible interpretations of how comparative negligence should be measured? See also, Schwartz, "Contributory and Comparative Negligence: A Reappraisal," 87 Yale L.J. 697 (1978).

5. In Exhibit 5.6, the lines of optimal response indicate a "substitutional" relationship between the care inputs of the two parties. That is, the lower the level of V the higher T should be in order to minimize social cost S, and vice versa. How do you account for the lines of optimal response in Exhibit 5.5? Is one of these exhibits constructed unreasonably? If not, give examples of real activities or

products that you believe might be exemplified by the different forms of production function. What relationship, if any, is there to the type of marginal analysis done in Exhibit 5.1?

6. The text in this section suggests that comparative negligence is not a very precise legal concept, a thesis that may be buttressed by the cases and other material below. Whatever its meaning, however, comparative negligence means that each of the negligent parties will bear only *partial* responsibility for the damages. On these grounds, the doctrine has been criticized as not providing the proper incentives for the parties to take care. Elaborate on the form that you think the criticism might take. Is the criticism persuasive?

BENTZLER v. BRAUN

Supreme Court of Wisconsin, 1967.
34 Wisc.2d 362, 149 N.W.2d 626.

The question, therefore, is not whether the guest's negligence contributed to the cause of the accident, but, rather, whether it contributed to the injuries. In view of the Wisconsin statutes that the legislative mandate in regard to seat belts applies merely to installation and not to use, the failure to use available seat belts is a question for determination by the jury as in the case of any ordinary negligence, i.e., was the conduct a substantial factor in producing a result.

We therefore conclude that, in those cases where seat belts are available and there is evidence before the jury indicating causal relationship between the injuries sustained and the failure to use seat belts, it is proper and necessary to instruct the jury in that regard. A jury in such case could conclude that an occupant of an automobile is negligent in failing to use seat belts. In the instant case, however, because of the lack of any evidence of causation, the trial judge properly refused the requested instruction. There was proof that seat belts were available and were not used, but that fact alone does not prove causation, for the driver of the vehicle also failed to use the available seat belts, but his injuries were minimal. In motions after verdict the trial judge stated that there was a complete failure of proof in that regard:

> "There is no evidence, by expert witnesses or otherwise, that Janet Bentzler's injuries would have been reduced or minimized had she been wearing a seat belt. The jury could only speculate as to whether her injuries would have been less severe."

The only witness offered was an orthopedic surgeon, who, although qualified in his chosen profession, did not purport to be able to testify what effect the use of seat belts might have had in this particular case. The record supports the trial court's determination that there was no proof whatsoever to show that Janet Bentzler's injuries were caused or aggravated by the failure to use the seat belts. In the absence of credible evidence by one qualified to express the opinion of how the use or nonuse of seat belts would have affected the particular injuries, it is improper for the court to permit the jury to speculate on the effect that seat belts would have had.

While in this case there was evidence that could have sustained the court's finding that Janet Bentzler was negligent in failing to wear the seat belts, that negligence could only have been related to her negligence in using ordinary care to protect herself from injuries and could not have been negligence that was a factor in producing the crash. In the absence of any proof of causation, the court properly refused the requested instruction on the question of Janet Bentzler's negligence in the use of seat belts.

VICTOR SCHWARTZ, COMPARATIVE NEGLIGENCE, p. 297

The process is *not* allocation of physical causation, which could be scientifically apportioned, but rather of allocating *fault*, which cannot be scientifically measured. For example, suppose an intoxicated motorcyclist speeds at eighty miles an hour down a highway with a 55 mile speed limit. He loses control of his vehicle and crosses over into the opposite lane where he collides with a large truck traveling 65 miles per hour. The point of collision is the left fender of the truck. As a result of the impact, the motorcyclist is killed and his vehicle is a total loss. The truck, however, is only slightly damaged and the truckdriver is not hurt at all.

In terms of pure physical causation, perhaps an expert could testify that the truck supplied 95% of the force that killed the motorcyclist, based on formulae combining the relative weights, speeds and directions of the vehicles. Even without expert assistance, the jurors might, by instinct, regard the truck as the more substantial cause. Nevertheless, the jury's line of inquiry under comparative negligence does not focus on physical causation; rather, it considers and weighs culpability. In Nebraska and South Dakota, the question is whether plaintiff's negligence was "slight" and defendant's "gross" in comparison. In many other states, the jury must determine the percentage of fault to be allocated to the plaintiff when the accident is considered as a whole.

STATE v. KAATZ

Supreme Court of Alaska, 1977.
572 P.2d. 775.

* * * What is to be compared to negligence—conduct, fault, culpability—not causation, either physical or legal. Pan-Alaska Fisheries, Inc. v. Marine Const. & Design Co., 402 F.Supp. 1187 (W.D. Wash.1975); V. Schwartz, Comparative Negligence, Section 17.1 at 276 (1974). There is no requirement that the party who is negligent in more ways, or for whom a greater number of individual negligent acts can be found, must be assigned the higher percentage. [Citations omitted].

Briefly summarized, the facts indicating Kaatz' negligence are these: The Mitkof Highway was icy and very slippery, which condition was apparent to the casual observer. Kaatz had driven the section of the Mitkof Highway in question shortly before riding in the loader. Loaders are not designed for travel on a highway, but they are often driven over highways under their own power. Kaatz was familiar with the characteristics of the loader. He also knew the condition of the road. The loader is designed to carry only a driver, not a passenger, and the policy of Kaatz' employer forbade riding on loaders, with exceptions not relevant to this case. Kaatz was not the first person to ride as a passenger on a loader in violation of policy. On previous trips, Kaatz had ridden in a pickup truck instead of on the loader. In those circumstances, Kaatz was negligent in riding in the loader on the Mitkof Highway.

The facts from which the state was held negligent in brief, are: The state highway department had a standard operating procedure that called for sanding of roads in inclement weather, even in outlying areas and even if it required overtime or night work. Cecil Donohue, the state maintenance foreman in the Petersburg sector, knew of the slippery condition of the Mitkof Highway before the accident occurred. His sanding machine did not work, but repairs were being undertaken. His stockpile of sand was frozen and covered with snow. He drove the stretch of road in question a few hours before the accident but decided not to sand it until the next morning, because he thought it might snow and cover the sand, even though he thought the road probably needed sanding that evening. Later that evening, after the accident, he and his men sanded the road. In those circumstances, the state was negligent in failing to sand the road in the late afternoon.

The state's foreman testified that the road needed sanding for regular traffic, not for front-end loaders. Two nearby residents testified the road was worse that evening than they had ever seen it before. If he had considered only the testimony of Mr. Schouweiler, one of these nearby residents, the trial judge said he would have found Kaatz at least fifty percent negligent. On the other hand, he pointed out, other witnesses testified that they had negotiated the highway without inordinate difficulty. Kaatz himself drove the highway in a pickup truck without apparent incident shortly before riding the loader. Kaatz suggests another aggravating factor concerning the state's negligence: it exposed large numbers of persons—everyone who traveled the highway—to danger, whereas Kaatz' negligence had the potential to harm no one but himself.

Kaatz and the driver of the loader were killed when the loader slipped off the road and plummetted down an embankment.

QUESTIONS

1. How would you fit the facts of the above cases into the production function paradigm? Is the court in *Bentzler* rejecting the "fault" criterion advocated in Schwartz's treatise? In State v. Kaatz, how does it seem to be contemplated that one would compare the state's negligence or fault with that of Mr. Kaatz?

2. In Butand v. Suburban Marine & Sport Goods Inc. the Alaska Supreme Court applied its version of comparative negligence to a strict liability case. Consider the concurrence by Justice Rabinowitz:

> RABINOWITZ, Justice (concurring).
>
> I generally agree with the court's treatment of the issues which arise in the situation where a plaintiff who is himself negligent asserts a claim founded upon strict liability. Perhaps it is only a semantic difference rather than reflective of a true functional distinction but I prefer adoption of a comparative causation analysis in strict liability cases. Thus, I would require the trier of fact to compare the harm caused by the product's defect with the harm caused by the claimant's own negligence. See Solet v. M/V Capt. H.V. Dufrene, 303 F.Supp. 980, 986 (E.D.La.1969). Adoption of a comparative causation approach would avoid the theoretical problems inherent in any attempt to compare relative degrees of fault where the defendant's negligence, or fault, is determined by principles of strict liability. 555 P.2d. 42 (1976) at 47.

Can what Justice Rabinowitz seems to have in mind be translated into the production function approach? Are there any ambiguities in what he seems to be saying?

3. If you are still wondering what courts "really" have in mind, consider the statement made by the Wisconsin Supreme Court in Kohler v. Dumke, 13 Wisc.2d 211, 108 N.W.2d 581 (1961):

> * * * This court has never attempted to lay down any formula for determining how much weight is to be accorded to the element of negligence and how much to that of causation in comparing causal negligence. Neither do we think it advisable to attempt to do so. This is something that had best be left to the common sense of juries.

Do you think that, given differing arguments from counsel, the typical jury might come up with wildly variant results in the face of precisely the same facts? Indeed, what is your own—presumably sophisticated—view of the best "common sense" treatment of these issues?

THE "LEVEL" OR QUANTITATIVE PROBLEM

One way to understand liability rules is to hypothesize that they are designed to allow the balancing of the benefits and harms from potentially injurious activities. This is the "marginal cost vs. marginal benefits" theme that has been present in the preceding sections. To the extent that this hypothesis is true, however, it means that there are two conceptually distinct dimensions to the balancing. One is that the "quality" of a potentially injurious act should be properly adjusted in the sense that all cost-beneficial care should be exercised in connection with any act taken. In addition, the "quantity" of acts must also be adjusted such that only acts whose benefits exceed their costs are taken. Our discussion thus far has not been very explicit about those distinct dimensions, but the perspective has in fact been principally from the qualitative or "caretaking" perspective. It is now time to complete the picture.

As Chapter I suggested, individuals have the proper incentives to engage in maximization behavior in the light of their own internal costs and benefits. The problem arises when there are third-party effects,—i.e., "externalities"—associated with an act. Unless legal liabilities are imposed to alter the incentives, a person will engage in what is arguably a "wrong" quantity and/or quality of the act in question. Since we have already discussed the quality-adjusting implications of liability rules at some length, let us now elaborate some simple models in which the quantitative adjustment is the focus.

Absent legal liability of any kind, the individual's cost-benefit calculus might be represented as:

[1] $\Delta B(Q) = \Delta K(Q)$

where $B(Q)$ is a benefit function that presumably rises monotonically as the quantity Q of the act increases, $K(Q)$ is whatever private costs there are to the activity, and the symbol Δ indicates that we are dealing with the *marginal* changes as Q is adjusted. In a no-liability world, the individual would choose a value of Q that satisfies equation [1].

Now let us go to the other extreme and describe an "ideal" incentive system that balances all relevant costs and benefits, including those to third parties. The notation and terminology of earlier sections in this chapter will be modified only slightly. Care levels T^* and V^* are the tortfeasor and victim responses that satisfy the "qualitative" considerations discussed above, while $C_t(Q,T^*)$ and $Cv(Q,V^*)$ are the respective costs of achieving those care levels for activity level Q. The "harm function" now also explicitly has Q added to it in addition to T and V. Then the ideal marginal balance is where the following condition is satisfied:

[2] $\Delta B(Q) = \Delta K + \Delta C_t(Q,T^*) + \Delta C_v(Q,V^*) + \Delta H(Q,T^*,V^*)$

The last two terms in [2] are the externalities or third party effects that do not appear in [1] above because their consequences are ignored by the potential injurer. Similarly, $\Delta C_t(Q,T^*)$ did not appear in [1] because there would be no incentive for the injurer to incur care costs when no compensatory benefits accrue.

It will now be of interest to produce equations that represent the behavorial incentives under each of several major liability principles. The terms of the individual equation are written with the same positions and spacing as equation [2] in order to facilitate comparison. Assuming (in line with the discussion earlier in the chapter) that potential injurers will rationally choose to adopt care level T^*, negligence may be represented as

[3] $\Delta B(Q) = \Delta K + \Delta C_t(Q,T^*)$. ✓

In words, the marginal cost of additional quantity is increased only by the incremental cost of engaging in that quantity of activity non-negligently; the injurer's choice of activity level is not deterred by actual harm occurrence. By contrast, strict liability involves the condition

[4] $\Delta B(Q) = \Delta K + \Delta C_t(Q,T^*) \qquad\qquad + \Delta H(Q,T^*,V^*)$

if contributory negligence is permitted as a defense, but

[5] $\Delta B(Q) = \Delta K + \Delta C_t(Q,T') + \qquad\qquad + \Delta H(Q,T^*,V')$

when contributory negligence is not a defense and the victim will engage in some unknown level of self-defensive care V'. (The value of V' will normally be less than V^* and may be zero.) If the victim is not at V^*, then the tortfeasor may find it advantageous to adjust his behavior to T', a care level different from the optimal T^*.

Conditions [3] and [4] seem plainly to suggest underdeterrence and an excessive level of Q, since one or more of the elements of external cost are not imposed on the injurer. Condition [5] is ambiguous with respect to the optimal level Q^*: the victim's care costs (if any) are omitted, but the marginal legal liability $\Delta H(Q,T^*,V)$ may be excessive due to the victim's presumptive failure to exercise V^* of care and the consequent upward bias introduced into the resultant damages. Once raised explicitly, this "level problem" emerges as an extremely thorny barrier to the construction of simple liability rules that have all of the ideal behavior-adusting characteristics. The reader may, however, also wish to reflect on whether any of the equation formulations are arguably too simplistic. For instance, should the definition of "negligence" include the choice of Q as well as T?

There is a very noteworthy special class of situations that affect the conclusions drawn from the simple models just discussed. Suppose that an activity results in a substantial amount of *reciprocal* externalities being imposed by persons who engage in it. For instance, when a person drives, he imposes costs on other motorists, both in the form of victim avoidance costs $C_v(V)$ and possible uncompensated harms. But the other motorists, in turn, may impose roughly comparable costs on him. What implications does this have for the level problem? Are these implications compensatory or behavioral?

QUESTIONS

1. Create a diagrammatic exhibit that illustrates the potential tortfeasor's marginal choice calculus under the different situations of equations [1] through [5], labelling the quantities as Q_1 through Q_5. By shading or other markings, indicate the magnitude of what might be regarded as the social "error costs" in each situation.

2. Is there a possible "level problem" in defining contributory negligence?

3. The text of this section was implicitly based upon a situation in which the rules of liability are accurately applied. Earlier in the chapter, the influence of various types of adjudication errors was discussed. How do those types of errors affect the results in this section? And, equally important, how are the earlier results affected by the necessity to consider the level problem?

GREENLAWN NEIGHBORHOOD ASSOCIATION v. FIRST GUARANTY BANK

The president of the First Guaranty Bank likes to fly helicopters, perhaps because his license to drive automobiles has been revoked upon conviction for excessive vehicular violations. When a new building was constructed for the bank, a rooftop helicopter pad was incorporated into the design. The bank uses the helicopter to transport its checks to a Federal Reserve clearinghouse about 75 miles away, thus avoiding an additional day's "float" on the checks being presented for collection. The alternative would be to transport the checks to an airport about 8 minutes away by automobile and then to use a fixed-wing aircraft. Fixed-wing aircraft have much better accident rates than helicopters.

QUESTIONS

1. If an accident occurs, what should be the standard of negligence? Is it just the appropriately careful operation of the helicopter? Or does a comparison with *alternative* transport modes have to be factored into the calculus called for under the Learned Hand rule?

2. What difference might it make if the applicable standard were one of strict liability rather than negligence?

3. The bank is in an area, Greenlawn Heights, which is now quite congested. Does it make any difference if the accident involves a

crash into an area that did not develop until after the bank had instituted a regular practice of using the helicopter?

4. What are some other activities or scenarios that are analogous to the helicopter case?

5. If a strict liability standard is used, what are the arguments for and against coupling it with a contributory negligence defense?

TAKING COST–MINIMIZATION SERIOUSLY(?)

The cost-minimization principles that seemingly underly the negligence and contributory negligence doctrines have at least a defensible—if not outright attractive—rationale. Pushing a principle to what are apparently its logical implications nevertheless often poses interesting questions. This is, of course, the classical method of *reductio ad absurdum.* Arguably, the following scenarios push cost-minimization to an unacceptable extreme. Or are they so "absurd" after all???

THE CASE OF INNOCENTE v. VINHO

Innocente lives in a house about 50 yards from a sharp turn on a mountain road. He has observed that Vinho makes a regular practice of getting drunk after work on paydays, which occur on alternate Fridays. Vinho then drives down the mountain in a dangerous manner and appears likely, sooner or later, to be incapable of negotiating the curve in the road. The most convenient place for Innocente to park his car is on the curving driveway in front of his house. Unfortunately, the driveway is in the likely path of Vinho's vehicle if it leaves the road. At the cost of some modest inconvenience, Innocente could park his car on the utility driveway at the side of the house, thus avoiding all prospect of damage due to Vinho's binges, except for the insubstantial matter of possible tire tracks across the lawn. Assume that Innocente nonetheless continues to park his car in front of the house, Vinho smashes into it, and the damage to the Innocente automobile is estimated at $8500.

In answering the following questions, you may wish to utilize the model incorporated in Exhibit 5.6 above. Vinho's predicted level of care would be the level indicated as T_n in Exhibit 5.6. Normally, Innocente would be held only to the V^* level of care, on the assumption that Vinho is non-negligent.

QUESTIONS

1. If you were counsel for Vinho, how would you try to argue that Innocente should not collect $8500?

2. If you were the attorney for Innocente, how would you respond to the arguments made? *incentive effects - going forward.*

3. Would it make any difference in the previous two questions if Innocente were able, at a time when he still had time to move his car, to look 5 miles up the mountain and see the Vinho vehicle approaching in a manner that made an accident seem almost certain? *iterated conduct vs one time shot.*

4. What does the doctrine of "Last Clear Chance" require? Does it *always* apply to one who has "last chance" to avoid a harm? Why?

5. On these facts, how do you think a real court would find? What do you think is the "right" rule? Why?

6. Assume that the jurisdiction in question employs a comparative negligence liability rule. Does this affect your answer to any of the first three questions above? *one unusual incident -*

7. Suppose that Innocente came to you before the accident, described the situation, and asked whether he had to move his car. What advice would you have given? *but why hold victim responsible?*

* * *

The above hypothetical was created purely to dramatize a pedagogical point and was first used in the author's classes in 1977. Many students may have regarded it as infected with more than a hint of unreality. It is impossible to resist, therefore, the inclusion of the following item based on press accounts in August 1982.

DRUNKS WON'T LET THE PREACHER ALONE

Chattanooga, Tenn.—A Baptist preacher says he's fed up with the flying bodies and flaming cars of drunken drivers who repeatedly crash into his house.

He's so angry he's threatening to erect a brick wall in his front yard even though "it's going to kill everybody who hits it."

"If the city doesn't put up a guardrail, we're going to put up a brick wall," the Rev. Martin Pinion said Wednesday. "It's either deflect them with a guardrail or kill them with a brick wall."

"I'm not real concerned about the motorists because they're just about always drunk. It's just like war," he said.

Seven drivers in the past six years have slammed into the house after careening off the busy highway that curves past.

"They're always drinking," said Pinion's wife, Debra. "It seems like they always hit in the middle of the night when you're sleeping. Then it's up to us to go out and pull them out of their burning cars."

"These wrecks move the whole house," Mrs. Pinion said. "Things get shifted around, pushed one way and the other. After an accident the doors won't close and the cabinets are crooked. Everything in the house is out of keel."

Once again, Nature verifies even the most outlandish hypothetical!

THE FIREMAN'S RULE

The so-called "fireman's rule" has traditionally provided what may be viewed alternatively as a bar to certain plaintiffs' recovery or a defense to a certain class of tortfeasors. This recent case represents a reexamination of the wisdom of the rule. Implicitly, the case may seem to involve an "assumption of risk" argument. Ask yourself whether you *really* know what that familiar term means or "ought" to mean. Is assumption of risk a contract or a tort concept? Does it have anything to do with optimal riskbearing as discussed in Chapter II above?

WALTERS v. SLOAN

Supreme Court of California, In Bank, 1977.
20 Cal.3d 199, 142 Cal.Rptr. 152, 571 P.2d 609.

CLARKE, Justice.

Plaintiff appeals from judgment of dismissal entered after demurrer to the second amended complaint was sustained without leave to amend.

The second amended complaint is summarized as follows: Robert and Madylon Sloan left their home in the charge of their 16-year old daughter, Helen. Acting with their knowledge, and as their agent, Helen hosted a party attended by 200 people, many of whom were minors. She provided her guests, including a named minor, with alcoholic beverages. Marijuana and dangerous drugs were also available at the party. Helen knew, or should have known, that those invited would become disruptive and a danger to others if they consumed the liquor and drugs in the quantities available.

Disorder developed. Plaintiff, in the course of his duties as a police officer was sent to the Sloan residence. When plaintiff attempted to arrest the named minor and fictitiously named defendants for being drunk in public they attacked him causing personal injury and property damage. The attack was a proximate result of Helen's unlawful serving of alcoholic beverages. Rejecting claims that the venerable fireman's rule should be abolished, we reaffirm the rule and conclude that it precludes recovery in this case.

The fireman's rule provides that negligence in causing a fire furnishes no basis for liability to a professional fireman injured fighting the fire. Firemen, "whose occupation by its very nature exposes them to particular risks of harm, 'cannot complain of negligence in the creation of the very occasion for [their] engagement.' " Solgaard v. Guy F. Atkinson Co. (1971) 6 Cal.3d 361, 369, 99 Cal.Rptr. 29, 33, 491 P.2d 821, 825. While denominated the fireman's rule, the rule is applicable to policeman as well. (Giorgi v. Pacific Gas Elec. Co. (1968) 266 Cal.App.2d 355, 357, 72 Cal.Rptr. 119.)

The rule was born almost a century ago, earning nearly unanimous acceptance. [Citations omitted.] In recent years, the rule has been repeatedly attacked as being "behind the times," based on outdated concepts of tort liability. However, the courts in this and other jurisdiction have answered the attacks, pointing out the rule is premised on sound public policy and is in accord with—if not compelled by—modern tort liability principles.

*   *   *

*   *   * [T]he fireman's rule is based on a principle as fundamental to our law today as it was centuries ago. The principle is not unique to landowner cases but is applicable to our entire system of justice—one who has knowingly and voluntarily confronted a hazard cannot recover for injuries sustained thereby. We have consistently applied this concept in our recent pronouncements in other cases of basic tort doctrine. These include cases dealing with product liability (Luque v. McLean (1972) 8 Cal.3d 136, 145, 104 Cal.Rptr. 443, 501 P.2d 1163), comparative fault (Li v. Yellow Cab Co. (1975), 13 Cal.3d 804, 824–825, 119 Cal.Rptr. 858, 532 P.2d 1226), and employee negligence (Gyerman v. United States Lines Co. (1972) 7 Cal.3d 488, 500 et seq., 102 Cal.Rptr. 795, 498 P.2d 1043; see Spencer v. G. A. MacDonald Constr. Co. (1976) 63 Cal.App.3d 836, 861–865, 134 Cal.Rptr. 78).

The principle denying recovery to those voluntarily undertaking the hazard causing injury is fundamental in a number of doctrines, including nullification of the duty of care, satisfaction of the duty to warn because the hazard is known, contributory negligence, and assumption of risk, as well as in the fireman's rule. (See Prosser, Torts (4th ed. 1971) p. 439 et seq.; Chesapeake and Ohio Railway Company v. Crouch, supra, 208 Va. 602, 159 S.E.2d 650, 653.) It is unnecessary to attempt to separate the legal theories or to catalog their limitations. The rule finds its clearest application in situations like that before us—a person who, fully aware of the hazard created by the defendant's negligence, voluntarily confronts the risk for compensation.

A second reason underlying the fireman's rule does not have a significant historical background, but rather is a modern one of public policy, adopted by progressive courts and based on fundamental concepts of justice. As succinctly stated in Solgaard v. Guy F. Atkinson Co., supra, 6 Cal.3d 361, 369, 99 Cal.Rptr. 29, 33, 491 P.2d 821, 825, firemen "cannot complain of negligence in the creation of the very occasion for [their] engagement." (Giorgi v. Pacific Gas Electric Co., 266 Cal.App.2d 355, 72 Cal.Rptr. 119.)"

Former Chief Justice Weintraub of the Supreme Court of New Jersey explained the principle. "The question is ultimately one of public policy, and the answer must be distilled from the relevant factors involved upon an inquiry into what is fair and just * * * [I]t is the fireman's business to deal with that very hazard [the fire] and hence, perhaps by analogy to the contractor engaged as an expert to remedy dangerous situations, he cannot complain of negligence in the creation of the very occasion for his engagement. In terms of duty, it may be said there is none owed the fireman to exercise care so as not to require the special services for which he is trained and paid. Probably most fires are attributable to negligence, and in the final analysis the policy decision is that it would be too burdensome to charge all who carelessly cause or fail to prevent fires with the injuries suffered by the expert retained with public funds to deal with those inevitable, although negligently created, occurrences. Hence, for that risk, the fireman should receive appropriate compensation from the public he serves, both in pay which reflects the hazard and in workmen's compensation benefits for the consequences of the inherent risks of the calling." (Krauth v. Geller, supra, 31 N.J. 270, 157 A.2d 129, 130–131.)

California is not insensitive to its obligation to compensate public safety officers for hazards faced or for injuries received. Firemen and policemen are paid for the work they perform including preparation for facing the hazards of their professions and dealing with perils when they arise. When injury occurs liberal compensation is provided. In addition to the usual medical and disability benefits ordinarily provided all employees covered by the Workers' Compensation Act, firemen and policemen are provided special benefits.

* * *

Additionally, abolition of the fireman's rule would burden our courts with litigation among the employer public agency, the retirement system, and the negligence insurer. Whether the employee is ultimately compensated with money derived from taxes or from insurance, the public pays the bill.

It is asserted that the fireman's rule should not apply where negligence is predicated on a violation of statute such as Business and Professions Code section 25658, subdivision (a) (furnishing alcoholic beverages to persons under the age of 21), because the Legislature has established a public policy which courts should promote in negligence per se doctrine as now codified in Evidence Code section 669. Under the doctrine, violation of a statute gives rise to a presumption of negligence in the absence of justification or excuse, provided that the "person suffering * * * the injury * * * was one of the class of persons for whose protection the statute *   *   * was adopted." (Evid. Code, Section 669, subd. (a)(4); Vesely v. Sager (1971) 5 Cal.3d 153, 164–165, 95 Cal.Rptr. 623, 486 P.2d 151; 4 Witkin, Summary of Cal. Law (8th ed. 1974) pp. 2810–2811.)

Ordinarily, a criminal statute is enacted not to protect policemen from injury while investigating or terminating the prohibited conduct but rather to protect the public. Enforcement of any criminal statute causes policemen to confront persons violating the statute, thereby imposing a confrontation and risk to the officer where none existed before. An officer called to enforce a criminal statute is thus not one of the class of persons for whose protection the criminal statute is adopted.

The negligence causing injury alleged against defendants Sloan is furnishing alcoholic beverages to persons under 21 resulting in their becoming drunk. The same negligence occasioned summoning the police. Based on sound legal theory and solid public policy, the fireman's rule has served us well. We reaffirm it and conclude that it bars this action.

The judgment is affirmed.

TOBRINER, Acting Chief Justice, dissenting.

I dissent.

*   *   * Relying upon the "fireman's rule" which, inter alia, precludes a fireman who is injured by a fire from recovering against one whose negligence caused the fire, the majority hold that a policeman is similarly barred from maintaining a cause of action against an individual whose negligence occasioned the officer's exposure to danger. Although I doubt that policemen can be distinguished from firemen for purposes of the fireman's rule as plaintiff urges, I believe that plaintiff's suit is not barred on this theory for a more basic reason. In my view, the fireman's rule itself, representing an unwarranted exception to the generally applicable duty of care tort standard, should not be followed in California.

In evaluating the present validity of the fireman's rule we must place it in perspective by reviewing it against the background of legal principles that generally govern an employee's right to recover for injuries sustained in the course of employment as a proximate result of a third party's negligence. A leading textwriter has summarized the general rule in this state as follows: "An employee who sustains injury arising out of and in the course of his employment because of the negligence of a third party, not his employer, may bring a civil action for damages against such third party in the same manner as though his injury were not work-connected. As a matter of fact, the employee's right against the negligent third party is precisely the same as if the injury had occurred outside the employer-employee relationship *   *   * [A]n employee's claim against a third party may properly arise from any situation where occupational injury or death arises from the latter's fault." (2 Hanna, Cal. Law of Employee Injuries and Workmen's Compensation, Sections 23.01, 23.02, pp. 23–2, 23–5; [other citations omitted.]

Applying this general rule, California courts have permitted injured employees to maintain traditional tort actions against third parties for virtually all negligently inflicted injuries, allowing, for example, highway workers to recover for injuries suffered as the result of a third party's negligent driving, employees of a subcontractor to recover for injuries suffered on a construction job as a result of the general contractor's or owner's negligence, and mechanics to obtain recovery for job-related injuries proximately caused by a customer or his agent. [Citations omitted.] So long as the negligent tortfeasor is not the plaintiff's employer, tort recovery has not been barred simply because the plaintiff was injured while performing his job.

Firemen—and, to some extent, policemen—have, however, traditionally found it more difficult than other employees to obtain recovery for negligently-inflicted injuries incurred in the course of their employment. To a large extent, the explanation for this "second class" treatment lies in the historical vagaries of early common law property doctrine, which drew distinctions between a landowner's duties to "invitees" and to "licensees." (See, e.g., 2 Harper James, The Law of Torts (1956) 1501–1505.)

Most employees who entered a landowner's premises during the course of their employment fell into the category of "business invitees" to whom the landowner owed a general duty of exercising reasonable care for their protection. Because firemen and policemen had the right to enter the landowner's consent, however, the early common law decisions regularly refused to categorize firemen and policemen as "invitees" and most often classified them as "mere licensees" to whom the landowner or occupier owed a much lesser standard of care. (See, e.g., Pennebaker v. San Joaquin etc. Co. (1910) 158 Cal. 579, 587–588, 112 P. 459; Nastasio v. Cinnamon (Mo. 1956) 295 S.W.2d 117, 119. See generally Note (1966) 19 Vand.L.Rev. 407; annot. (1921) 13 A.L.R. 637.)

In light of this "licensee" classification, firemen and policemen could recover for injuries sustained as a result of a dangerous condition of the premises only if they could prove that the occupier had actual knowledge of the danger and had failed to take appropriate precautions, whereas other employees could generally recover so long as the occupier should reasonably have discovered the defect and repaired it. (See, e.g., Prosser, Law of Torts (4th ed. 1971) pp. 376–398.) Moreover, given the general rule that an occupier bore no duty to protect a licensee from an obvious or patent danger on his premises, courts frequently reasoned that the occupier could not be held liable for the injuries which a fireman sustained as a result of the obvious danger of a fire, even if the fire had been proximately caused by the occupier's negligence. (See, e.g., Buckeye Cotton Oil Co. v. Campagna (1922) 146 Tenn. 389, 242 S.W. 646.) Thus, even though one who negligently caused a fire would normally be liable under the "rescue doctrine" for injuries sustained by those who attempted to avert the danger of the fire (see, e.g., Haverstick v. Southern Pac. Co. (1934) 1 Cal.App.2d 605, 37 P.2d 146), firemen traditionally had been excluded from such protection.

In Rowland v. Christian (1968) 69 Cal.2d 108, 70 Cal.Rptr. 97, 443 P.2d 561, of course, this court reviewed at some length the common law distinctions that had been drawn between invitees, licensees and trespassers, and concluded that with respect to all injured persons "[t]he proper test to be applied to the liability of the possessor of land * * * is whether in the management of his property he has acted as a reasonable man in view of the probability of injury to others * * *." (69 Cal.2d p. 119, 70 Cal.Rptr. at p. 104, 443 P.2d at p. 568.) Defendants, and the majority, concede that in light of *Rowland* the historical "invitee-licensee" distinction can no longer justify the retention of a fireman's rule which places special disabilities on firemen or policemen.

Defendants assert, however, that while *Rowland* may permit a fireman to sue a possessor of land for injuries sustained while fighting a fire as a result of a defective or dangerous condition of the premises (accord Bartholomew v. Klingler Co. (1975) 53 Cal.App.3d 975, 126 Cal.Rptr. 191), our *Rowland* decision does not affect the fireman's rule insofar as that rule precludes a fireman from recovering from one who negligently caused the fire in the first place. Pointing out that a person who negligently causes a fire may not necessarily be either a landowner or land occupier, defendants maintain that this separate prong of the fireman's rule, barring a fireman's cause of action against an individual who negligently causes a fire, survives our *Rowland* decision. As defendants suggest, the two California appellate court decisions which have endorsed the fireman's rule have applied the rule only in this limited context. (See Giorgi v. Pacific Gas Electric Co., supra, 266 Cal.App.2d 355, 357, 72 Cal.Rptr. 119.) Defendants contend that this limited doctrine of nonliability applies to policemen as well as to firemen, and bars plaintiff's recovery in the instant case because defendants' negligence, if any, simply created the occasion or need for plaintiff's normal employment services.

This contention, while properly noting that liability in the instant case does not necessarily turn on defendants' status as landowners, fails to meet the fundamental question as to why an injured fireman or a policeman should be precluded from recovering damages from *any* third party tortfeasor whose negligence proximately causes his injuries. A tortfeasor who negligently causes a fire is, of course, generally liable for all injuries sustained by rescuers who attempt to mitigate the damage which an uncontrolled fire might work. In light of the general duty of care imposed by Civil Code section 1714, the burden remains on defendants to demonstrate that overriding policy considerations, if any, justify a rule that bars recovery by a fireman or policeman under circumstances in which all other individuals may recover for their injuries. (See Rowland v. Christian, supra, 69 Cal.2d at p. 112, 70 Cal.Rptr. 97, 443 P.2d 561.)

Defendants point to a number of policy considerations which courts have relied on in the past in barring a fireman's recovery from one who negligently causes a fire. Defendants emphasize that a fireman is trained, and paid, to confront and extinguish fires, that a fireman knows that his occupation will subject him to dangers, and that a negligently caused fire often poses no greater hazards than one that is accidently set. Defendants also suggest that public policy dictates that the risk of damages for injuries from fires be spread to the public generally, rather than placed upon those who negligently cause fires. Finally, defendants assert that because the determination of the cause of a fire is often an onerous burden, considerations of efficient judicial administration support the preservation of the fireman's rule. As I explain, none of these reasons suffice to overcome the general common law principle that one is responsible for an injury to another caused by the tortfeasor's want of ordinary care.

Proponents of the fireman's rule argue most frequently that it is the fireman's job to extinguish fires and the policeman's job to make arrests. They conclude that a fireman or a policeman can base no tort claim upon damage caused by the very risk that he is paid to encounter and with which he is trained to cope. The argument, in essence, is that the fireman or policeman, in accepting the salary and fringe benefits offered for his job, assumes all normal risks inherent in his employment as a matter of law, and thus may not recover from one who negligently creates such a risk. (See, e.g., Maltman v. Sauer (1975) 84 Wash.2d 975, 530 P.2d 254, 257; Buren v. Midwest Industries, Inc. (Ky.1964) 380 S.W.2d 96, 98–99.)

The fallacy in this argument is simply that it proves too much. Under this analysis, an employee would routinely be barred from bringing a tort action whenever an injury he suffers at the hand of a negligent tortfeasor could be characterized as a normal inherent risk of his employment. Yet, as noted above, past California cases have regularly permitted highway workers whose jobs obviously subject them to the "inherent risk" of being injured by a negligent driver—to recover for damages inflicted by such third party negligence (see, e.g., Mecham v. Crump, supra, 137 Cal.App. 200, 30 P.2d 568), and have permitted construction workers—whose employment poses numerous risks of injury at the hands of another—to recover tort damages for work-related injuries so long as the negligent tortfeasor is not their employer. (See, e.g., Woodcock v. Fontana Scaffolding and Equip. Co., supra, 69 Cal.2d 452, 72 Cal.Rptr. 217, 445 P.2d 881.)

As these and countless other cases demonstrate, while policemen and firemen regularly face substantial hazards in the course of their employment and are, theoretically at least, compensated for such risks, a host of other employees—highway repairmen, high rise construction workers, utility repairmen and the like—frequently encounter comparable risks in performing their jobs and, again theoretically, also receive compensation for such risks. California decisions have never perceived such theoretical compensation as a sufficient basis for barring the employee's cause of action against a negligent tortfeasor.

* * *

Accordingly, neither the fact that the injury in the instant case may have resulted from a reasonably foreseeable risk of plaintiff's employment nor the fact that defendants' negligence created the need for plaintiff's services is sufficient under past authorities to bar this action.

Some courts which have nevertheless upheld the fireman's rule have alternatively emphasized that a negligently caused fire frequently poses no greater danger to a fireman than a fire that results from nonnegligent causes. (See, e.g., Romedy v. Johnston, supra, 193 So.2d 487, 491; Aravanis v. Eisenberg (1965) 237 Md. 242, 206 A.2d 148, 153.) Since a fireman cannot recover damages for injuries sustained in a nonnegligently caused fire, these decisions reason that he should not be allowed recovery based on the "fortuity" that a particular fire was negligently caused. This "reasoning" is simply a non sequitur. In all negligence actions, of course, a plaintiff's recovery rests on the "fortuity" of his being injured by negligent conduct; if he suffered similar injuries in the absence of negligence, recovery would generally be precluded. Thus, this explanation cannot justify a departure from normal tort principles.

A related contention is that because both negligently caused and nonnegligently caused fires create similar hazards for firemen, a fireman really incurs no extra or special risk at the hands of a tortfeasor who negligently causes a fire. Firemen, of course, receive their normal wage whether or not fires actually occur, but whenever a fire is negligently set a fireman is required to encounter an added substantial risk that he would *not* have faced in the absence of the tortfeasor's negligence. In this respect, the fireman is no different than any other person injured as a result of negligent conduct.

QUESTIONS

1. Assumption of risk is sometimes used by courts in a way that confuses it with gross contributory negligence. There is, however, a

sense of the term that is more consonant with Chapter II's discussion of least-cost risk-bearing. How would this apply to the employer-employee relationship in which the doctrine of assumption of risk first arose historically? Wouldn't employees have feared a moral hazard problem from a nonliable employer? Why would employees be the least-cost bearers of the risk? [Hint: Suppose that all parties already have fairly good incentives to be careful. Would they have any incentive to want to avoid litigation and disputes over responsibility?]

2. From whom has the fireman "accepted" the risk? Is it a party in the same position as in most other assumption of risk applications?

3. Does the dissent fully rebut the arguments in the majority opinion? If not, why not?

4. Even if the dissent were fully correct in everything it says, can you think of any rationale for why there might be a special rule of non-liability toward certain public servants?

PROMISE–BREAKING ANALYZED AS A TORT

Review, if necessary, the indifference curve model in Chapter V above where the concepts of beneficial and detrimental reliance were illustrated. To the extent that a broken promise has created detrimental reliance, the promisee has suffered a harm caused by the promisor. An extraterrestrial visitor upon first encountering our legal system might inquire what is the difference between the treatment of a harm that is labelled as a contract breach and one that carries the name of a "tort."

The extraterrestrial might well be puzzled as to why the harms flowing from some broken promises are penalized—or, if you prefer, are the subject of compensation—while others are ignored as being the product of "naked" or "gratuitous" promises. The uncompensated breaches, he might argue, appear to the otherworldly eye to be no less than unrestrained torts. On the other hand, if a promise is enforceable because it is for some reason classified as a "contract," then we seem to go to the opposite extreme of over-restraining; after all, the only true social loss is the detrimental reliance and not the full value of the expectation interest usually given as contract damages.

The analysis that follows is worked out more thoroughly in Goetz and Scott, "Enforcing Promises: An Examination of the Basis of Contract," 89 Yale L.J. 1261, 1273–1286 (1980). This edited excerpt, however, may suggest how one would approach the enforcement of promises from a perspective very similar to tort theory. You may find that, with due allowance for practical considerations, the principles governing the enforcement of torts and contracts are quite congruent.

*   *   *

*   *   *   When a promise is made in good faith, the promisor presumably believes that he is likely to perform. Still, many good-faith promisors would acknowledge the possibility that events may arise that cause them to regret having made the promise. Thereafter, if it were costless to do so, they would indeed breach the promise. Such contingencies may involve a wide range of factors, from changes in personal conditions to disappointment about external considerations that orginally made the promise seem desirable. The term "regret contingency" will be used to denote the future occurrence of a condition that would motivate breach if breach were a costless option for the promisor. Assuming any reliance, the occurrence of a regret contingency necessarily implies that either the promisor or promisee must bear a cost.

When a regret contingency arises, the promisor's options are either to bear the loss attributable to performance, which now costs more than it is worth, or to breach and accept the cost of any corresponding sanction. Presumably the promisor would adopt the cheaper of these regret costs. In any event, someone will suffer a net loss whenever a regret contingency arises, whether in the form of regret costs to the promisor, uncompensated detrimental reliance to the promisee, or both.

By what means does the promisor adapt to the prospective costs of promising? The promisor can substantially influence the probability of a regret contingency, and thus its prospective costs, by adjusting his behavior ex ante. One means of mitigating potential costs is by altering the form of the promise. For instance, the promisor may condition performance on the proviso that certain circumstances—potential regret contingencies—not arise. Alterations in the form of the promise will generally entail a cost to the promisor either in terms of direct resource cost—time and trouble—or in the possibility that the benefit of the promise-making to the promisor will be diminished. The second means of avoiding regret costs is simply to make fewer promises. The costs of this option are forgone benefits from unmade promises.

The costs that result from restrictions in the scope or number of one's promises can be termed "precautionary costs." It is useful to distinguish these further as either quality precautions or quantity precautions. Quality precautions involve adjustments restricting the scope of promises and impose a cost of decreased reliability. Quantity precautions, which consist of reductions in the number of promises made, result in a loss of benefits from promising. A rational promisor will pursue precautionary adjustments up to the point at which marginal precautionary costs are exactly balanced by marginal reductions in regret costs.

Precautionary adjustments by the promisor decrease the value of the promise. Conversely, when the promise is worth more to the promisor than its prospective cost, the promisor may engage in "reassurance." Reassurance includes such actions as the offer of guarantees, verbal persuasions, and the development of a reliable reputation, designed to convince the promisee that the promise is valuable. Reassurances increase the value of the promise to the promisee. Indeed, promisees may regard voluntary reassurance measures as substitutes for sanctions. Reassurance usually entails some cost to the promisor and, hence, will be pursued up to the point at which marginal reassurance costs are exactly balanced by increases in resulting benefits to the promisor.

Precautionary and reassurance reactions by promisors are triggered by variations in the cost of promising. It should be apparent, therefore, that an additional legal sanction will raise prospective costs, thereby precipitating adjustments of the scope and volume of promises.

Optimizing Promisor-Promisee Interaction

To what extent do legal sanctions optimize the interactions between promisor and promisee? In the present context, optimization is defined as maximizing the net social benefits of promissory activity—that is, the benefits of promises minus their costs. This approach is equivalent to the balancing of prospective costs and benefits under the widely accepted Learned Hand test for the required duty of care in potential tort-producing activities. Indeed, there are strong theoretical parallels between the production of dangerous, but useful, products and the making of promises.

The role of damages or sanctions in generating socially optimal behavior can be focused more sharply by observing the distinction between internal and external effects. Because self-interested maximizing behavior entails consideration of only internal costs and benefits, unfettered individual behavior is incompatible with social optimization in circumstances in which significant external costs or benefits are present. Individuals will oversupply activities with external costs and undersupply those with external benefits. By imposing costs and creating incentives, the law can cause individuals to consider external effects in their decisionmaking and thus "internalize" them.

Inducing optimal promise-making therefore requires that the promisor's costs of promising be adjusted to reflect any external effects on the promisee. But this adjustment process is complex. Changes in the costs and benefits of promising are highly interactive in two senses. First, an individual's adjustments may substitute one category of his costs for another. Second, the actions of one party may produce reactions by the other and, in turn, feedback responses to the first party.

1. *Nonreciprocal Promises*

Consider the case of a gratuitous promisor who has adjusted his promise-making to an arbitrarily assumed level of extra-legal sanction so that he cannot further improve his situation. In addition, assume that social considerations effectively prevent the promisee from influencing the promisor's calculations through bargaining. Under these conditions, when does the intervention of the law lead to optimal results?

The effect of a decision to enforce legally any particular class of nonreciprocal promises depends upon the nature of the sanction imposed for breach. Promisors will respond to higher levels of sanction by increasing their qualitative and quantitative precautions, reducing both the reliability of a given volume of promises and the number of promises actually made.

A necessary starting point in determining an optimal damage rule is to specify the external effects of a nonreciprocal promise as the supply of such promises is increased by one marginal unit. The external effects are the prospective detrimental reliance incurred if the promise is broken and the prospective beneficial reliance enjoyed if the promise is performed. Proper reflection of external effects therefore requires not only that the promisor be charged for the harm expected from broken promises, but also that he be rewarded for the prospective benefits of performance. It is helpful to state this condition symbolically. Let p be the promisor's reasonable, subjective assessment of the probability that he will perform a promise under an existing legal rule calling for damages of D in the event of breach. For the damage rule to deter all promises with net social costs and encourage those with net benefits, the amount of damages awarded must satisfy the following equation:

$$(1 - p)\text{D} = (1 - p)\text{R} - p\text{B}$$

where R and B are the values of detrimental and beneficial reliances, respectively. Assuming that all broken promises are litigated, the left-hand side of the equation represents the expected value of the prospective legal sanction. Because only broken promises are affected by the law, the probability $(1-p)$ of the promise being broken is used to "discount" the damages D. The values for R and B on the right-hand side of the equation should be understood as those resulting from optimal self-protection by the promisee. Thus, promisees will appropriately minimize the value of the right-hand term, which is the net social cost of the promise. In calculating this prospective net reliance, the magnitudes of the potential detrimental and beneficial reliances are each discounted by their probabilities. When the equation is satisfied through the imposition of optimal damages D, the promisor's internal cost-benefit calculus will reflect the external effects of his promise-making. If the external effects are thus accounted for, the promisor's maximization of his internal net benefits is consistent with supply of the socially optimal quantity and quality of promises. We call this damage rule the "prospective net reliance" formulation.

In some cases, the prospective beneficial reliance from a promise will exceed its prospective detrimental reliance. Because the net external effect of such a promise is beneficial, it would be optimal to reward the making of such promises. However, in the nonreciprocal setting no practical legal mechanism exists for rewarding promises. This limitation renders true optimization impossible; the situation is necessarily second-best. At minimum, promises with prospects of net beneficial reliance should not be the subject of damages if breached. Only promises with prospective net detrimental external effects should be enforceable.

The prospective net reliance formulation developed above can be used to analyze the optimal level of enforcement. By dividing both sides of the original equation by the probability of breach $(1 - p)$, the following damage rule emerges:

$$D = R - \left[\frac{p}{(1 - p)} \right] B.$$

The optimal damage rule thus subtracts from the promisee's reliance cost a fraction of his potential beneficial reliance. This fraction is the ratio of the ex ante subjective probability of performance to that of nonperformance. It determines the extent to which the prospect of beneficial reliance when the promise was made is credited against the promisee's prospective detrimental reliance. Because this ratio may be thought of as an index of the promisor's good faith, we call it the "good-faith ratio." A damage offset based on the good-faith ratio and on the amount of potential beneficial reliance will encourage the optimal quantity and quality of promises by reflecting in the promisor's decision calculus both the harmful and beneficial effects of his promise-making. This optimal legal sanction is likely to be unattainable in an environment of costly legal process and imperfect information. But specifying an optimal sanction permits more rigorous evaluation of the error produced by any practical adjustment attributable to process costs.

The rule suggested by the formula above will admittedly result in a large quantity of uncompensated damages from broken nonreciprocal promises. Although greater damages would deter many injurious transactions, a stricter standard also would deter beneficial transactions in even greater magnitudes. Viewing an already-broken promise, the affected promisee would always prefer the highest possible damage award. But from the ex ante standpoint, a promisee would not wish to discourage a promise that creates a prospect of gain outweighing the risk of uncompensated loss. Such promises are "good bets" for the promisee over the long run, even though some of the promises will result in uncompensated harm. The penalty formulation developed above awards damages both to protect promisees from "bad bet" promises and to avoid deterrence of promises that are "good bets."

Under this prospective net reliance damage formula, the gratuitous promisor also has an incentive to undertake cost-effective qualitative precautions to modify prospective reliance induced by any promise actually made. A properly calibrated legal sanction will induce the promisor to convey to the promisee socially beneficial information about the risk of regret contingencies. In essence, such a promisor is encouraged to make cost-effective adjustments in both the quality and the quantity of his promises because the legal rule converts social benefits into savings for him. If, in addition, the law recognizes only the amount of damages that constitutes a "reasonable"—i.e., cost-effective—reliance by the promisee, then the promisee will also have an incentive to minimize net social costs. Thus, the rule penalizes each party for failing to take cost-effective steps to minimize the social costs of promising. Damages exceeding those described above will tend to induce the promisor to invest too much in precautionary adjustments. This phenomenon is analogous to the excessive level of prudence anticipated if tort victims were awarded a multiple of their true damages.

2. *Reciprocal Promises*

Promising is reciprocal when the parties can adjust interactively to the nature and amount of promise-making. The prospective net reliance formulation is equally applicable to reciprocal as well as to nonreciprocal promises. But the net reliance damage rule seems in sharp conflict with accepted legal doctrine in the reciprocal promise context, in which damages for breach are typically based on the promisee's full-performance expectation rather than on his detrimental reliance. Upon analysis, the apparent conflict can be dissipated; moreover, reciprocal promises are easier than nonreciprocal promises for the law to address.

This conclusion is buttressed by two independent lines of argument. First, in the case of reciprocal promises, a plausible empirical generalization is that a promisee's acceptance of one promise frequently requires his foregoing a potential substitute promise. The forgone value of the best substitute promise available—the opportunity cost—is key in determining the promisee's detrimental reliance when an accepted promise is subsequently broken. In a well-organized market, alternative promises will be close, if not perfect, substitutes. In that case, detrimental reliance is equal to the full performance value of the breached promise. Similarly, beneficial reliance will be small, because the promisor's pledge, even if performed, will not constitute a very substantial improvement over the potential beneficial reliance from substitute promises. This empirical generalization implies that, in the damage formula developed above, full performance expectation E can be substituted for detrimental reliance R because $E \approx R$. Furthermore, because $B \approx 0$, the term of $\left[\dfrac{1-p}{p} \right]$ B drops out. We are left with $D \approx E$; thus, expectation damages are a good proxy for the prospective net reliance damage formulation developed above. Nothing in the logic of this argument limits its applicability to reciprocal promises. Although the argument's empirical premise tends to have greater validity with respect to bargained-for promises, classes of nonreciprocal promises may exist for which forgone substitute promises also yield a close convergence between reliance and expectation.

Second, a fundamental theoretical difference exists between reciprocal and nonreciprocal promises. In the case of a reciprocal promise, the principal objective of a promisor is to obtain consideration in the form of a return promise. The value of the return promise elicited is the main element of the promisor's benefit. Therefore, changes in the qualitative aspects of the promise are reflected in commensurate shifts of benefits to the promisor; a higher quality promise motivates a more valuable return promise, and vice versa. In contrast to the case of nonreciprocal promises, qualitative adjustments are internalized in the promisor's cost-benefit calculus by generating a more or less valuable consideration for his promise. Hence, the bargaining process accomplishes an important part of the behavioral regulation that, for nonreciprocal promises, must be performed by the legal system.

Furthermore, the bargaining process, not available by definition in the nonreciprocal context, can facilitate the optimal allocation of risk for reciprocal promises. Precautionary action is subject to a test of the ability of the promisee to bribe the promisor to make an unconditioned promise. Within any scheme of enforcement, then, the parties can reallocate the risks of regretted promises by buying or selling protection through the terms of their agreement. The least-cost bearer of any risk will presumably agree to absorb that risk in exchange for an enhanced return promise.

For much the same reasons, the consequences of excessive damages for breaching reciprocal promises are also mitigated, as long as the rule providing for excessive damages is understood in advance. The parties can always bargain out from the rule, for instance by a limited damages agreement. Thus, when transactions costs are zero, the particular damage rule selected for reciprocal promises is irrelevant. Although the existence of transactions costs renders bargaining over damage rules costly in practice, the feedback adjustment of the return promise markedly reduces the potentially inefficient effects of legal rules. While in the nonreciprocal case, excessive damages overdeter the promisor from promissory activity, in the reciprocal relationship, the promisee will regard the excessive damages as a quality improvement and will offer an enhanced return promise. The enhanced return promise will tend to offset the deterrence effect of the damages. However, some inefficiencies remain. Legally mandated "overinsurance" induces a moral hazard because the promisee will not exercise optimal self-protection. Furthermore, there is a cheaper allocation of risk than the legally mandated level of reassurance provided to—and paid for by—the promisee.

The result may be even more costly, however, when the law provides a suboptimal level of enforcement. The extreme case of a complete refusal to enforce reciprocal promises provides an instructive illustration. The initial impact of the rule, which is to underdeter promisors, will be counterbalanced by reductions in the value of return promises. Promisors may then substitute extra-legal forms of reassurance for legal sanctions. Creating adequate extra-legal enforcement mechanisms is likely to be less efficient than legally sanctioned reassurance. If so, the inefficiency consequences of under-enforcement may be more serious than those of overenforcement.

In sum, the theoretical damages principles developed in connection with nonreciprocal promises apply to reciprocal promises as well. The difference in their legal treatment may be due to a close empirical identity of reliance and expectation in reciprocal promises. However, modification of the return promise is a powerful additional adjustment mechanism, which exists, by definition, only for reciprocal promises. By internalizing many of the promissory interactions among contracting parties, the return promise reduces the stress placed on legal rules for optimally influencing the behavior of promisors and promisees.

QUESTIONS

1. In what respect was the present section concerned with what was discussed earlier as a "level problem"? Why is the problem more complicated here?

2. Under what circumstances would promisees prefer that a certain class of promise not be enforced?

3. "In the realm of bargained-for promises, the breach damages can be considered as a form of 'insurance policy' that each party sells to the other as protection against his own breach." Explain. Does

this perspective suggest that parties would never want more than reliance damages?

4. Suppose that the law mandates higher damages than the parties themselves would prefer. Why is this less troublesome with bargained-for promises than with gratuitous ones? In what form do the resultant "error costs" occur?

5. Buyer contracts with Seller for the delivery of one gadjett at a price of $200. Seller is the exclusive source of gadjetts and can produce a single gadjett per period at a cost of $150. Buyer's potential benefits from the gadjett depend on how many hours of gadjett-using instructions he takes at a cost of $10 per hour: $230 of gross benefits with one hour of instruction, $242 with 2 hours of instruction, $258 with three hours of instruction. Since gadjett expertise is quickly forgotten, any hours of instruction purchased by Buyer will be worthless if the promised gadjett is not delivered at the agreed time. Both Buyer and Seller know that there is one chance in three that Otherbody will, at the time set for delivery, also desire a gadjett and, if so, would bid $260 for it. No matter which of the common contract remedies is assumed, Otherbody will probably wind up with the gadjett. Why? Would a reliance measure of damages cause Buyer to over-rely? Does the same answer apply in the case of expectation damages?

6. To what extent is "reasonable reliance" in contract analogous to the contributory negligence doctrine in tort?

7. If contract damages are in any sense similar to insurance payments, does it make sense to distinguish between exogenous risks not controllable by either party and endogenous risks that are subject to a significant degree of control? What kinds of things would fit into each category? [If this question is not clear at this point, return to it after the section on relational contracting below.]

SEC. 90, RESTATEMENT OF CONTRACTS

Section 90 of the Restatement of Contracts is one basis upon which gratuitous promises have traditionally been enforced. The original wording of Sec. 90 was altered in Restatement (Second) by deleting the bracketed phrase below and adding the underlined sentence.

A promise which the promisor should reasonably expect to induce action or forbearance [of a definite and substantial character] on the part of the promisee and which does induce such action or forbearance is binding if injustice can be avoided only by enforcement of the promise. The remedy granted for breach may be limited as justice requires.

QUESTIONS

1. What reasoning might account for the deletion of the requirement for reliance to be "definite and substantial"?

2. What factors would justify a limitation of the remedy?

3. Why are the words "if injustice can be avoided only by enforcement of the promise" included in Section 90? After all, are there any circumstances when an uncompensated detrimental reliance would *not* imply an "injustice"?

4. Which version of Section 90 do you find preferable? Why?

CENCO, INC. v. SEIDMAN & SEIDMAN

United States Court of Appeals, Seventh Circuit, 1982.
686 F.2d 449.

[Between 1970 and 1975, managerial employees of Cenco, Inc. engaged in a massive fraud which Cenco's independent auditor throughout the period, the accounting firm of Seidman & Seidman, either never discovered or, if it did, failed to report. The fraud involved the inflating of inventories far above their actual value, thus exaggerating the profitability of Cenco and leading to a higher market price for its stock. The unmasking of this practice, followed by a 75% fall in the price of Cenco stock, led to the filing of a class action in federal district court against Cenco, its corrupt managers, and Seidman & Seidman. The class was composed of purchasers of Cenco stock during the period of the fraud, when the stock price was inflated. Cenco filed a cross-claim against Seidman & Seidman for having failed to prevent the fraud by Cenco's managers. Seidman then filed its own cross-claim against Cenco, alleging that Seidman had been one of the victims of Cenco's fraud and was thus entitled to damages from Cenco. Cenco's and Seidman's cross-claims against each other were set for trial together. Several aspects of the cross claims were settled by directed verdict or dismissal. The case went to the jury, however, on three counts in Cenco's cross-claim, alleging respectively breach of contract, professional malpractice (negligence), and fraud. Cenco's evidence claimed to show that in the early stages of the fraud Seidman had been careless in checking Cenco's inventory figures and its carelessness had prevented the fraud from being nipped in the bud. Seidman's evidence attempted to show that Seidman had diligently attempted to follow up all signs of fraud but had been thwarted by the efforts of the large group of managers at all levels of Cenco who collaborated to prevent Seidman from learning about the fraud. The jury found for Seidman on all three counts. Cenco appeals from the judgment, contending that the jury's verdict was based on erroneous instructions.]

POSNER, Circuit Judge.

This brings us to the main issue in the case—whether the district judge gave erroneous instructions to the jury. The challenged instructions relate to the question whether Seidman was entitled to use the wrongdoing of Cenco's managers as a defense against the charges of breach of contract, professional malpractice, and fraud. Despite the plurality of charges it is one question because breach of contract, negligence, and fraud, when committed by auditors, are a single form of wrongdoing under different names. The contract in question here * * * consists of the letters between Seidman and Cenco outlining the terms of Seidman's annual retention to audit Cenco's books. The material part of the letters is the incorporation by reference of general accounting standards which require the auditor to use his professional skill to follow up any signs of fraud that he discovers in the audit. The tort of negligence in the context of auditing is likewise a failure to use professional care and skill in carrying out an audit. And if such care and skill are not used, then the audit reports to the client will contain misrepresentations, either negligent or, if the auditor knows that the representations in the reports are untruthful or is indifferent to whether or not they are truthful, fraudulent.

Because these theories of auditors' misconduct are so alike, the defenses based on misconduct of the audited firm or its employees are also alike, though verbalized differently. A breach of contract is excused if the promisee's hindrance or failure to cooperate prevented the promisor from performing the contract. See Restatement (Second) of Contracts Sec. 245 (1979). The corresponding defense in the case of negligence is, of course, contributory negligence.

Negligence is not a defense to an intentional tort such as fraud. E.g. Mother Earth, Ltd. v. Strawberry Camel, Ltd., 72 Ill.App.3d 37, 52, 28 Ill.Dec. 226, 238, 390 N.E.2d 393, 405 (1979). But a participant in a fraud cannot also be a victim entitled to recover damages, for he cannot have relied on the truth of the fraudulent representations, and such reliance is an essential element in a case of fraud. See, e.g. Broberg v. Mann, 66 Ill.App.2d 134, 139, 213 N.E.2d 89, 92–93 (1965). If the misrepresentation is negligent rather than intentional, contributory negligence plays the same role it would play in an ordinary negligence case. See Prosser, supra, at 706.

The jury instructions in this case stated these defenses accurately, but Cenco contends that the instructions should not have been given, because they related not to Cenco's conduct but to that of its managers. The judge was aware of the distinction but instructed the jury that the acts of a corporation's employees are the acts of the corporation itself if the employees were acting on the corporation's behalf. If this instruction was correct, then the instructions which allowed the jury to consider Cenco's misconduct as a defense to Seidman's alleged wrongdoing were proper.

To determine the correctness of the instruction requires us to decide in what circumstances, if any, fraud by corporate employees is a defense in a suit by the corporation against its auditors for failure to prevent the fraud. Illinois precedent allows us to reject one extreme position on this question, which is that the employee's fraud is always attributed to the corporation by the principle of respondeat superior. This position *   *   * was rejected in Cereal Byproducts Co. v. Hall, 8 Ill.App.2d 331, 132 N.E.2d 27 (1956), where a company's independent auditors were held liable for negligently failing to detect embezzlement by the company's bookkeeper. Auditors are not detectives hired to ferret out fraud, but if they chance on signs of fraud they may not avert their eyes—they must investigate. The references to keeping an eye out for fraud that appear in the accounting standards incorporated (by reference) in the retention letters between Cenco and Seidman would have little point if not interpreted to impose a duty on auditors to follow up any signs of fraud that come to their attention.

But this does not tell us what the result should be if the fraud permeates the top management of the company and if, moreover, the managers are not stealing from the company—that is, from its current stockholders—but instead are turning the company into an engine of theft against outsiders—creditors, prospective stockholders, insurers, etc. On this question the Illinois cases on auditors' liability provide no guidance. In fact, to our knowledge the question has never been the subject of a reported case. Leeds Estate, Bldg. & Inv. Co. v. Shepherd, 36 (L.R.) Ch. D. 787, 802, 809 (1887), described by Cenco in its main brief as "the one squarely applicable common law decision on accountants' liability," is nothing of the sort. The auditor in that case had failed to discover that the company's manager, by misrepresenting the profits of the company, had caused the company to pay out dividends, directors' fees, and bonuses for himself—all in violation of the charter—as a result of which the company went broke. This was stealing from, not for, the company.

In predicting how the Illinois courts might decide the present case, we assume they would be guided by the underlying objectives of tort liability. Those objectives are to compensate the victims of wrongdoing and to deter future wrongdoing. With regard to the first, we must refine our earlier statement that the "victim" of Seidman's alleged laxity was Cenco Incorporated. A corporation is a legal fiction. The people who will receive the benefits of any judgment rendered in favor of Cenco on its cross-claim against Seidman are Cenco's stockholders, comprising people who bought stock in Cenco before the fraud began, people who bought during the fraud period and either sold afterwards when the stock price fell or continue to hold the stock at a loss, and people who bought after the fraud was unmasked. A judgment in favor of Cenco on its claim against Seidman would not differentiate among these classes, but would benefit every stockholder as of the date of the judgment (or the date when a judgment was anticipated with some precision) in proportion to the number of shares he owned.

Once the real beneficiaries of any judgment in favor of Cenco are identified, it is apparent that such a judgment would be perverse from the standpoint of compensating the victims of wrongdoing. Among the people who bought stock in Cenco before the fraud began are the corrupt officers themselves. To the extent they are still stockholders in the company, they would benefit pro rata from a judgment in favor of Cenco. The other stockholders in this class are innocent in a sense, but of course it is they who elected the board of directors that managed Cenco during the fraud. The people who bought during the fraud period and either sold at a loss or continue to hold at a loss are the plaintiffs in the recently settled class action in which both Cenco and Seidman were defendants. Seidman has already paid $3.5 million to them. Those who continue to own stock in Cenco (as distinct from those who sold at a loss) would receive additional compensation if Cenco prevailed in this action against Seidman. This is not to say they would be overcompensated; but it seems odd that the same shareholders should be able to recover damages from Seidman twice for the same wrong—once directly and once, in this suit, indirectly. Finally, the shareholders who bought after the fraud was unmasked lost nothing. The unmasking of the fraud caused the price of Cenco's stock to be bid down to reflect not only the true value of its inventories but also any anticipated injury to the company as a result of the fraud.

Because of shareholder turnover, there is always a potential mismatch between the recovery of damages by a corporation and the compensation of the shareholders actually injured by the wrong for which the damages were awarded. It is simply a more dramatic mismatch in this case than usual.

From the standpoint of deterrence, the question is whether the type of fraud that engulfed Cenco between 1970 and 1975 will be deterred more effectively if Cenco can shift the entire cost of the fraud from itself (which is to say, from its stockholders' pockets) to the independent auditor who failed to prevent the fraud. We think not. Cenco's owners—the stockholders—hired managers (directly, in the case of the president and chairman, who were both members of the board of directors, indirectly in the case of the others) who turned out to be thoroughly corrupt and to corrupt the corporation so thoroughly that it caused widespread harm to outsiders. If Seidman had been a more diligent auditor, conceivably if it had been a more honest auditor, the fraud might have been nipped in the bud; and liability to

Cenco will make Seidman, and firms like it, more diligent and honest in the future. But if the owners of the corrupt enterprise are allowed to shift the costs of its wrongdoing entirely to the auditor, their incentives to hire honest managers and monitor their behavior will be reduced. While it is true that in a publicly held corporation such as Cenco most shareholders do not have a large enough stake to want to play an active role in hiring and supervising managers, the shareholders delegate this role to a board of directors, which in this case failed in its responsibility. And not all of Cenco's shareholders were "little people." During the period of the fraud Curtiss-Wright Corporation owned between 5 and 16 percent of Cenco's common stock and had its own accounting firm conduct a study of Cenco's operations—without discovering the fraud.

Thus, not only were some of Cenco's owners dishonest * * *, but the honest owners, and their delegates * * * were slipshod in their oversight and so share responsibility for the fraud that Seidman also failed to detect. In addition, the scale of the fraud—the number and high rank of the managers involved—both complicated the task of discovery for Seidman and makes the failure of oversight by Cenco's shareholders and board of directors harder to condone.

* * * [I]f Cenco may be divorced from its corrupt managers, so may Seidman from the members and employees of the firm who suspected the fraud. If Seidman failed to police its people, Cenco failed as or more dramatically to police its own.

Furthermore, we must assume that Cenco's corrupt managers were acting for the benefit of the company, not against it as in the Cereal Byproducts case. The jury was instructed that it could attribute the fraud of Cenco's managers to Cenco only if it found that the managers had been acting on Cenco's behalf, and the verdict for Seidman implies that the jury either so found or found that Seidman had not even committed a prima facie breach of duty to Cenco. The former assumption is more favorable to Cenco.

Fraud on behalf of a corporation is not the same thing as fraud against it. Fraud against the corporation usually hurts just the corporation; the stockholders are the principal if not only victims, their equities vis-a-vis a careless or reckless auditor are therefore strong. But the stockholders of a corporation whose officers commit fraud for the benefit of the corporation are beneficiaries of the fraud. Maybe not net beneficiaries, after the fraud is unmasked and the corporation is sued—that is a question of damages, and is not before us. But the primary costs of a fraud on the corporation's behalf are borne not by the stockholders but by outsiders to the corporation, and the stockholders should not be allowed to escape all responsibility for such a fraud, as they are trying to do in this case.

We need not go so far as to predict that the Illinois courts would hold that in any action by a corporation against its auditors an employee's fraud intended to benefit the company rather than the employee at the company's expense will be attributed to the corporation, however lowly the employee. It is true that the lower down the employee is in the company hierarchy, the less likely he is to commit fraud for rather than against the company. But there are overzealous employees at every level—many a corporation has paid heavy damages for antitrust violations committed by low-level sales managers who thought they were acting in the company's best interests as well as their own—and we think it premature as well as unnecessary to decide that an auditor is never liable for the frauds of loyal but misguided company employees that he could have prevented by taking care. But here the uncontested facts show fraud permeating the top management of Cenco. In such a case the corporation should not be allowed to shift the entire responsibility for the fraud to its auditors.

Hence the challenged jury instruction was proper in the circumstances * * *

HYPOTHETICAL: PERILS OF A TAXJACQUES

Marie Taxjacques is a 1973 graduate of Prestige University Law School with degrees earned through the joint MBA/JD program. Her undergraduate major was in accounting and she has since qualified as a CPA. Presently, she is a partner in the firm of Taxjacques and Lehgerscan, a medium-sized company that provides a broad range of legal and financial services on a contract basis.

a. Last year, Taxjacques' services were much in demand as an advisor on certain arcane tax shelters arising out of the latest revisions in the tax code. Unfortunately, Taxjacques tendered advice that now appears clearly to have been not only erroneous but the result of professional negligence on her part. In addition to her own direct clients who relied to their detriment on her advice, two other groups of plaintiffs have also filed suit against Taxjacques.

The first of these are clients of a local branch of S.N. Arbloch, a local financial advisor who, in turn, had retained Taxjacques as his own source of expert information to be passed on to his clients. It has been established that Arbloch was not in any way himself negligent and he is, in any event, not possessed of financial resources adequate to cover the claimed damages of his clients. Consequently, Arbloch's clients are seeking to recover against Taxjacques, the "real source" of the incorrect advice.

A second group of suits has been filed against Taxjacques by friends of Edith M. Goodolgal. It seems that Goodolgal sought

Taxjacques' advice on her own behalf but also passed on this advice to her wealthy friends at the next local meeting of the Dames of the American Insurrection.

Should Taxjacques' be liable to any of these "third party" plaintiffs who have been injured as a result of her negligence? Why? If the answer depends in part on facts that are not specified, say what they are and why they are relevant.

b.   It has truly not been a good year for Taxjacques.   She was also the principal in a longstanding contract to perform the annual audits of the books of the Pseudo Corporation.   It now turns out that for the past three years the officers of the Pseudo Corp. had been engaging in sham accounting transactions designed to overstate the company's profits.   The emergence of the truth has now seriously damaged the company in the financial markets.   A stockholders suit was filed against Taxjacques on the grounds that she negligently failed to discover the financial manipulations during her periodic audits.

You represent the stockholders.   A colleague has just informed you, albeit somewhat sketchily, of the gist of a recent Federal Appeals Court opinion (by Judge Richard Posner of Law and Economics fame) that holds the stockholders primarily responsible for monitoring the management that they have, after all, themselves selected and perpetuated in office.   Fortunately, the opinion in question is not binding precedent in your District, but another judge may be persuaded by similar reasoning.   Do you have any good counterargument(s)?

PERFORMANCE DEFINITION AND RELATIONAL CONTRACTING

At first glance, it seems as if another difference between contract and tort law is the way in which the obligations of parties are defined.   In contracts, the promisee's obligation is frequently defined in rather precise terms, and the nature of this obligation does not vary with external circumstances such as the cost of performance; there is usually the rough equivalent of what in tort would be strict liability. By contrast, tort law frequently depends on a broad "standard" of behavior.   This is exemplified by the negligence rule, which calls for a level of care that depends upon what is in essence a highly circumstantial cost-benefit analysis.   On further reflection, however, it is not difficult to cite many tort duties that are defined in rather specific and absolute terms, as well as to understand why these departures from the ordinary rule occur.   Less well understood is the phenomenon of contracts wherein the rules are defined in extraordinarily general ways.   We therefore now turn our attention to contracts wherein the standard of liability may be expressed in terms of a standard or other variable obligation rather than a fixed performance.

The class of contracts wherein flexible standards of performance are most likely to be found is that of so-called "relational contracts." This section and the one that follows are adapted from Goetz and Scott, "Principles of Relational Contracts," 67 Va.L.Rev. 1089 (1981) where the themes presented below are developed in further detail and related to other legal literature.

* * *

Many private contracts deviate significantly from the presuppositions of classical legal analysis. One reason for this deviation is the pivotal role played in conventional legal theory by the concept of the complete contingent contract (or a "fully specified" contract). Parties in a bargaining situation are presumed able, at minimal cost, to allocate explicitly the risks that future contingencies may cause one or the other to regret the agreement. Under these conditions, contract rules serve as standard or common risk allocations that can be varied by the individual agreement of particular parties, thus saving most bargainers the cost of negotiating a tailor-made arrangement. If the basic risk allocation provided by a legal rule fails to suit the purposes of particular parties, then bargainers are free to negotiate an alternative allocation of risks. All relevant risks can thus be optimally assigned—either by legal rule or through individualized agreement—because future contingencies are not only known and understood at the time the bargain is struck, but can also be addressed by contractual responses that are efficacious in coping with the risks presented by the future contingencies.

In a complex society, parties frequently enter into continuing, highly interactive contractual arrangements where a complete contingent contract may not be feasible. When future contingencies are peculiarly intricate or uncertain, practical difficulties arise that impede the contracting parties from allocating all risks at the time of contracting. Not surprisingly, therefore, parties who enter into such exchange relationships seek specially adapted contractual devices. The resulting "relational contracts" encompass most generic agency relationships, including distributorships, franchises, joint ventures, and employment contracts.

Although a certain ambiguity has always existed, there has been a tendency to equate the term "relational contract" with long term contractual involvements. The discussion below adopts a very specific construction of the term based more explicitly on the characteristics that distinguish the relational contract from the classical contingent contract. A contract is relational to the extent that the parties are incapable of reducing important terms of the arrangement to well defined obligations. Such definitive obligations may be impractical because of inability to identify uncertain future conditions or because of inability adequately to characterize complex adaptations even when the contingencies themselves can be identified in advance. As the discussion below illustrates, long term contracts are more likely than short term agreements to fit this conceptualization, but temporal extension *per se* is not the defining characteristic. Most actual contracts are, of course, neither perfectly contingent nor entirely relational. Legal theory has merely tended to focus on agreements that fall close to the one polar extreme. The focus in the following analysis is deliberately directed toward the other, relatively neglected, end of the continuum.

A key step in sharing the benefits of contractual exchange involves specifying the performance standard of each party and then selecting a mechanism to ensure compliance with the agreed-upon standard. In conventional contracts, the parties are generally able to reduce performance standards to rather specific obligations. By contrast, relational contracts create unique, interdependent relationships, wherein unknown contingencies or the intricacy of the required responses may prevent the specification of precise performance standards. Complexity and uncertainty each play conceptually distinct roles, although they frequently operate in combination. An example of this is provided if one thinks of attempting to write a contract providing for the care of a fine home garden during a summer out of town. Uncertainty is represented by the difficulty of determining in advance the climatic conditions, incursions of the gypsy moth, windborne powdery mildew, etc. Quite another level of difficulty is involved in specifying to the gardener exactly what responses should be made in each case: how much to spend on sprays, whether to water, when a diseased plant should be cut down to prevent infection of adjacent ones.

A typical response to this problem of complexity and uncertainty is to define the performance standard in unusually general terms. Some responses involving generalized performance standards have already been hinted at in earlier chapters: these include the ethical standards of attorneys, brokers and other agents; and the implied fiduciary obligation that attaches to certain special classes of transactions. As the Bloor v. Falstaff case below indicates, another common response to the articulation of performance obligations in relational contexts is the "best efforts" clause.

Because these standards are typically described in general terms, it is difficult to apply them in any specific context. Relational contracts therefore require more creative control mechanisms than do conventional contingent contracts. In any cooperative contract where performance obligations remain imprecise, there are inevitable costs in insuring that any particular level of performance is achieved. Parties will bear this cost in a number of ways. They may grant the principal the right to monitor the agent's efforts. Performance can thus be controlled by direct supervision or by indirect incentive systems designed to encourage the agent to consider fully the principal's interests. Alternatively, in cases where monitoring is relatively costly, the agent may seek to reassure the principal by a "bonding" agreement. Liquidated damages provisions, covenants not to compete, and unilateral termination clauses are common examples of agent bonding. Ideally, the parties will select that combination of monitoring and bonding arrangements that optimizes the costs of governing the standard of performance.

Parties will enmesh themselves in the inevitable vagaries of relational contracts only after considering alternative methods of achieving their objectives. One obvious alternative is vertical integration of potentially separable activities, such as manufacturing and distribution, into a single firm. An integrated firm would presumably take all the relevant cost and benefit interactions of the two activities into consideration and would provide the optimal level of manufacturing and distribution inputs such that overall profits are maximized. The vertically integrated firm thus provides a benchmark against which various alternative contractual arrangements can be measured. Vertical integration will be the preferred mechanism if the cost of performing the activity *within* the firm is less than the costs of accomplishing the same goal by "contracting out" the function. Part of the cost of contracting out a function is, unfortunately, the imperfection of the contractual mechanisms available to the parties. Consider, for example, an industry in which manufacturing and distribution are specialized activities and are, at least potentially, much more efficiently performed by separate firms. Where a single integrated firm is no longer the exclusive decisionmaker, the respective parties need to engage in a form of explicit agreement in order to ensure that the interactions between the manufacturing and distributing activities will be properly considered. How, then can the parties trade in order to exploit the potential technical efficiencies of separate firms while preserving an optimal level of combined efforts analogous to that achieved by the integrated firm?

An analysis of this question can usefully begin by identifying some conditions that produce variations in the nature and form of contracting. For the sake of concreteness and ease of exposition, the discussion will be carried on in terms of a "manufacturer" and a "distributor." These are merely convenient labels to describe relative positions of the parties in a production chain. In any particular real world situation the appropriate terminology may vary: e.g., franchiser-franchisee, supplier-fabricator, client-broker.

Consider the common situation where one party is the distributor of a product supplied, at least in part, by the manufacturer. As a simple hypothetical case, assume that adjustments in distribution efforts are the only dimension of production influencing output on the margin and that "distribution efforts" can be regarded as units of product distributed. (Although product volume provides us with a straightforward concretization, the same analysis would apply if efforts were reinterpreted in the form of any other volume or quantitative adjustment, including, for example, quality level, advertising, or any other activity that affects joint profits.) The parties are assumed each to know their own costs (but not necessarily the other party's costs) and to know the external market conditions during the effective period of the proposed contract.

In Exhibit 5.7, IMC represents the aggregate of the marginal costs of "manufacturing" (MM) and of the marginal "distributing" costs (the vertical distance between IMV and MM) where a firm carries on both manufacturing and distribution as an integrated process. If MR is the marginal revenue curve, then the intersection of MR and IMC at Q represents the output volume that maximizes profits. In other words, Q and its associated profit level is the best that the integrated firm can do by both manufacturing and distributing. The agent presumably enters the picture because he enjoys a productive advantage over the manufacturer, such as, lower marginal distribution costs as exemplified by MD in Exhibit 5.7. The joint marginal cost curve JMC would result if the parties were able to treat their separate costs as a single entity.

The potential savings from separate performance of their respective functions now provide manufacturer and distributor with an economic incentive to enter into a distributorship agreement. Two predictions can be made as to the terms of an agreement designed to exploit that potential. First, as Exhibit 5.7 suggests, the parties will not have exploited all of the potential gains from trade in the situation unless their agreement somehow calls for the manufacture and distribution of quantity Q^* in Exhibit 5.7, where the sum of the marginal costs to the joint producers equals the marginal revenues from sales. From any output other than Q^*, a movement to Q^* will increase the combined profits of the parties. If, therefore, there are no special impediments in the form of bargaining or other transaction costs, one would expect to find contract terms facilitating this "joint maximization" quantity outcome.

Second, certain limits can be placed on the minimum and maximum amounts that the distributor will pay to the manufacturer for the predicted Q^* units of the product. Each party must be at least as well off under the contractual arrangement as it would have been

EXHIBIT 5.7

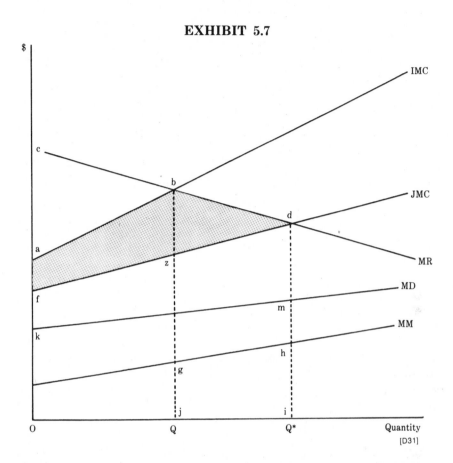

[D31]

otherwise. Consequently, the manufacturer must receive at least its additional manufacturing costs under the higher-volume distributorship agreement plus the "go-it-alone" profits that it would otherwise earn as an integrated firm. Graphically, these sums correspond, respectively, to area ghij and triangle abc in Exhibit 5.7. The distributor would, in turn, be willing to pay a maximum of the total revenues from sales minus its distribution costs (area kcdm). A range of indeterminancy exists because the gains from trade (cost saving fabz + profits on expanded output zbd) must be divided through bargaining between the parties. These potential net gains from the distributorship arrangement are represented by the shaded area in Exhibit 5.7.

On the bare facts presented above, one would not predict a best efforts term or another flexible performance standard in the contract. There simply is no need for it. Where the optimal output Q * can be predetermined, a fixed quantity term would be a direct and perfectly suitable mechanism for specifying volume. Furthermore, fixed quantity terms and other precisely stated contractual obligations are generally the most efficient instruments for measuring subsequent performance. Thus, under these assumed conditions, the parties will predictably require the manufacturer to provide and the distributor to sell Q^* units of production. Suppose, however, that the curves depicted in Exhibit 5.7 are known only probabilistically at the time of contract formation. How is the parties' behavior altered when they are uncertain as to future conditions?

Fixed-Quantity Terms. Even under uncertain conditions there is still a determinate output Q^* that optimizes the parties' contractual relationship based on essentially the same considerations discussed above. Assume, however, that this output must now be calculated with future cost and revenue information known only imperfectly by the parties at the time of contract formation. One approach would be to retain the fixed-quantity term in the contract, specifying the volume that maximizes the expected value of the joint profits based on an ex ante calculation of the risks and their associated probabilities. Such a determinate volume will, however, always turn out to be "wrong" at the time set for performance.

In Exhibit 5.8, for example, a distribution contract is negotiated in the context of but a single contingency—the future imposition of a particular governmental regulation. Assuming that governmental regulation increases costs and that the probabilities of imposition and non-imposition are equal, quantity E will represent the fixed quantity term that maximizes the expected value of the exchange at the time of contracting. Nevertheless, output E will always be inferior to some other output level. If the regulation *is* imposed, quantity Q_1 will be the optimal output and the actual profits will diverge from the optimal profits by the shaded area A in Exhibit 5.8. On the other hand, if the regulation is *not* imposed, optimal profits at volume Q_2 will exceed actual profits by the amount represented by area B. The foregone profits constitute "error costs." Under any conditions of uncertainty, an obligation designed in advance to be optimal on average will tend always be wrong in the particular situation that ultimately pertains. In either case, therefore, the difference between actual and optimal profits is the error cost incurred by the parties from couching their agreement in terms of a fixed contractual quantity.

Of course, the parties are not required to set a single output term. In Exhibit 5.8, if the uncertainties about costs and revenues are tied to a set of objectively verifiable contingencies that are few in number, the volume called for in the contract may be "keyed" to those uncertain future events. Thus, the parties can agree to quantity Q_1 if the regulation is imposed and, in the alternative, specify quantity Q_2 in the absence of regulation. However, any increase in the complexity of the risk factors or any greater uncertainty about the future will substantially increase the risk that any fixed volume contract will specify the "wrong" output. Such contingent volume agreements

EXHIBIT 5.8

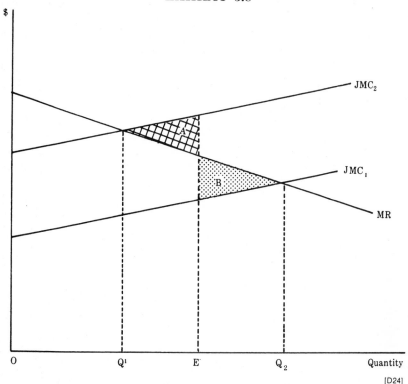

[D24]

thus represent an intermediate point between the complete contingent contract and more complex forms of relational exchange.

Sequential Contingent Contracts: Responses to Strategic Behavior. One response to increasing levels of complexity or uncertainty is to limit the temporal scope of the contract. By negotiating a series of recurring contingent contracts, the parties can reduce the error costs of specifying fixed obligations. But in many cases the performance of the initial agreement will produce specialized, idiosyncratic skills. Assume, for example, that the parties agree to a one-year distribution contract for a determinate quantity of the manufactured product. Once the distributor learns the skills peculiar to the distribution of the manufactured product in the market area, he enjoys a comparative advantage over the market of unskilled agents. The distributor then has an incentive, when the contract is renegotiated the following year, to secure a larger compensation for similar efforts in order to exploit the advantage gained by his "on the job" training. On the other hand, his newly acquired skills can be fully exploited only if he remains as the manufacturer's representative. Thus, as specialization occurs, each party becomes more vulnerable to strategic demands from the other. When the contract is renegotiated, the bargaining stakes are greater and both have incentives to use strategic or opportunistic behavior in order to secure a larger slice of the enhanced contractual "pie." The essence of the problem here is that, even where perfectly substitutable trading parties are initially available in a competitive market, the increasing specialization of the parties vis-a-vis each other produces a species of bilateral monopoly. Continuance of the original relationship becomes increasingly desirable in order to exploit the accrued specialization advantages, but the division of those gains must be bargained out in a non-competitive environment.

Requirements Contracts. As another alternative, the parties may enter into a requirements contract, thus confronting the problem of strategic behavior by encouraging competition in the market for manufacturers and distributors. The manufacturer is obligated to supply each distributor with the product quantity it "requires" but does not offer any particular distributor the *exclusive* right to a marketing area. The requirements contract permits marginal adjustments in distribution effects by the distributors since the quantity "required" will vary as conditions change over time. The advantage of this arrangement lies in the use of a competitive distribution market to monitor any individual distributor's "requirements." The availability of close market substitutes for any particular distribution contract prevents a distributor from using contractually-based discretion to extort special advantages. In addition, where there are substitutes for the manufacturer's product, the ability of distributors to switch products may curtail strategic behavior by the manufacturer.

Exclusive Dealing Arrangements. Frequently, however, the profit-maximizing level of distribution activity cannot be achieved in an unrestrainedly competitive market. The conditions that characterize a natural monopoly—substantial fixed costs coupled with relatively modest marginal costs, or restricted market size—occur in many relational contexts, especially when the distribution takes place in spatially limited sub-markets. When classical natural monopoly conditions arise, the economies of scale associated with an activity are not fully exploited unless the number of firms is limited, possibly even to a single distributor. Under these conditions, ordinary requirements contracts are inefficient as well as unstable. The manufacturer will examine the market and conclude, either because economies of scale are large or market size is limited, that a single distributor is the most profitable arrangement. If he licenses more than one distributor, the potential returns from the distribution arrangement will be diminished because competition among distributors will produce an inefficient investment in distribution activities.

As an alternative, the parties may agree to an "exclusive dealing" contract in which the manufacturer will offer the distributor the exclusive rights within a defined market. The exclusivity of these rights creates a relationship of dependence and vulnerability for the manufacturer during the life of the contract. In response, the manufacturer will generally attempt to limit his vulnerability from the exclusive arrangement by securing the agent's promise to use his "best efforts" to promote sales. The tensions inherent in such a situation are obvious. If a sequential contingent contract is negotiated, the parties once again expose themselves to future strategic demands for increased compensation. Alternatively, if the compensation agreement extends for the life of the relationship, the parties must either specify an "erroneous" fixed-volume term or the manufacturer will be vulnerable to a failure by the distributor to extend those "best efforts" that were paid for in the original compensation agreement.

In the simple model described above, where a manufacturer licenses a single distributor, the exclusive licensing agreement is adequate to induce an optimal investment in distribution activities. More typically, however, the manufacturer will license a number of distributors, granting each a form of access to a limited sub-market. Once a network is established, the parties face a second-order "free rider" problem. Optimal distribution activity will frequently include pre-sales advertising and promotion. Yet, any individual distributor will be reluctant to invest in such services where the prospective customers can learn about the product through one distributor's promotion efforts and then purchase the product from another distributor. To protect the integrity of the distribution network, therefore, parties to an exclusive dealings arrangement will typically bargain for territorial restrictions on the market each distributor is entitled to serve. These restrictions serve to prevent a distributor from "poaching" on either the customers or the distribution efforts of other distributors in the network.

Indirect Monitoring Mechanisms: Price Adjustments. As we have suggested above, contractually fixed quantity terms are not always effective means of achieving joint profit maximization in an uncertain environment; some system of monitoring the level of effort undertaken by the distributor or agent is needed. Direct monitoring is feasible in contexts such as franchising where operating procedures are standardized and one agent's efforts can be compared to those of similar agents. Indeed, franchisors may retain vertically integrated distributional outlets in representative locations in order to provide benchmarks against which franchisee operations can be compared. Such direct forms of monitoring may not always be practical. In such circumstances, joint profit maximization will be better achieved by indirect means.

One indirect instrument for adapting volume to uncertain future conditions is the proper calibration of the marginal price between the manufacturer and the distributor. Since the distributor has *de facto* control of the maximum volume sold by the parties, the objective should be to set pricing terms that will induce the distributor always to choose a close approximation of the optimal quantity Q^* even when he is nominally free to choose any volume level at all. Marginal cost to the distributor is the sum of his own marginal distribution costs plus the marginal contractual price payable to the manufacturer. In practice, this "price" will typically be termed a royalty, license fee, franchise fee, or some other term appropriate to the business context. Since the distributor will choose the output that equates marginal cost with marginal revenue (MC = MR) in order to maximize his own profits, a proper calibration of price by the manufacturer can induce the Q^* optimal output to be chosen. The optimal output will be chosen voluntarily by the distributor only if his marginal costs can be made to approximate the aggregate marginal costs of distribution and manufacturing (MD + MM), i.e., what we have above termed the joint marginal costs.

One useful scheme is for the contract to call for sales to the distributor at marginal manufacturing costs (MM), but pay over to the manufacturer some share (K) of the distributor's net profits in the form of a franchise fee, license, or royalty. Marginal cost to the distributor then becomes

$$MC = MD + MM + K\,[MR - (MD + MM)\,]$$

and automatically leads to the selection of Q^*. This result will obtain because the distributor's own profit maximization calculus will lead him to expand volume until

$$(i{-}K)\,[MR - (MD + MM)\,] = 0$$

where the term in square brackets is the increment in joint profits and $(i{-}K)$ is the fractional share of those joint profits that the distributor gets to keep. Indeed, $(i{-}K)$ may be reinterpreted as a fractional "commission" payment paid over to the distributor or agent out of the proceeds of any sales. The above formulation directly reflects the common sense purpose of this pricing scheme, because it shows how the distributor cannot maximize his own profits without also fully exploiting any opportunities for joint profits as represented by the square-bracketed term. In addition, a simple algebraic manipulation demonstrates that the formulation implicitly yields a result wherein MR = MD + MM, which is the underlying general condition for joint profit maximization: marginal revenue equals marginal cost where both costs and revenues are summed over all affected parties.

Unfortunately, there are numerous practical drawbacks to the implementation of a profit-sharing arrangement such as that just described. One limitation is that the pricing scheme requires information on marginal costs of the manufacturer. Since accurate incremental cost information is much harder to acquire than total cost information, the parties may not wish to tie the contract to magnitudes that are costly to ascertain or otherwise impractical to monitor. This limitation is less important when marginal manufacturing costs are either insignificant in magnitude or closely approximated by average cost, a more readily ascertainable value. For instance, marginal "manufacturing" costs are frequently negligible when the "manufacturer" is providing only a license rather than some actual product.

Even though the distributor's costs and revenue need—at least in theory—to be measured only in totals in order to arrive at the profits figure upon which the contractual payments are based, the distributor's treatment of costs may create problems. The divergence between accounting costs and economic costs may confuse profit measurement. One example of this is the exclusion of "fixed" costs as economic costs. Perhaps most important is the problem of monitoring and segregating costs and revenues within multi-product firms where it becomes increasingly difficult to monitor the allocation of joint costs—overhead, etc.—which may be shifted strategically among various contracts. A multi-product distributor has an incentive to impute as many costs as possible to those activities where his share of net profits is lowest.

Similarly, the distributor may "pad" costs, disguising his own returns and denying profits to the manufacturer. For instance, the distributor may provide himself with unnecessary amenities such as a "company car" or place relatives on the payroll at unwarranted salaries. Gross abuses will, of course, be easy to detect, but cost padding can take a variety of subtle forms that are extremely difficult to discover and perhaps impractical to prove.

Given the increased monitoring burdens of profit-based pricing, it is not surprising that relational contractors frequently choose alternative pricing arrangements. Commonly observed, for example, are initial flat fee payments coupled with royalty payments tied to a percentage of gross sales. These arrangements reduce the costs of monitoring the distributor's expenditures but, in turn, also reduce the congruence of interests concerning optimal output between the manufacturer and the distributor. Once the distributor's return is reflected in a sales-based pricing mechanism, there is an inherent conflict of interests between the contracting parties over profit-maximizing output: the distributor's self-interest will induce him to produce a lesser quantity than the manufacturer's interests would demand. Thus, these more common pricing arrangements reduce the burden of monitoring the agent's costs and revenues but increase the burden of controlling the agent's level of effort. Presumably, firms choose sales-based pricing because the cost of monitoring the level of effort is perceived as less than the cost of monitoring operating expenditures.

BEST EFFORTS PROVISIONS

The previous section on the general problems of relational contracting provides a background to consideration of what is perhaps the most poorly understood class of relational contracts: that involving agreements wherein one party explicitly, or even implicitly, undertakes the contractual duty of using its "best efforts" to carry on an activity beneficial to the other. Notwithstanding the frequency with which such terms are observed empirically, the precise legal meaning to be attached to a best efforts requirement is not at all clear, either from a consideration of the case law or from theoretical discussions in standard legal scholarship. Nevertheless, there appears to be a relatively straightforward and persuasive definition that emerges from the preceding economic conceptualization of the problem faced by two parties who are attempting to set a contractual volume in which they have joint interests.

Best efforts cases hinge on two factors: strategic adaptation to the conflict of interest between the parties and the problem of managerial incompetence. These elements may, of course, coexist in a single case. Since the courts appear not to have sharply distinguished the factors, it is not surprising that existing case law has been unhelpful in working out a consensus about the meaning of the legal rule.

Exhibit 5.9 illustrates a contract in which the distributor faces a marginal cost curve MC composed of his own marginal distribution costs MD plus the marginal "price" R negotiated with the manufacturer. In addition, it is assumed that the payment takes the form of a 50% royalty on gross sales. Absent any other information, one might expect that the distributor would then be legally entitled to choose volume Q where his marginal costs ($MC = MD + R$) are equal to marginal revenues (MR). This is the point at which the distributor's own profits are maximized. If he were required to sell an additional quantity beyond Q, the distributor's profits would be reduced, as exemplified by the shaded triangle A in Exhibit 5.9. Suppose, however, there were some way in which he could oblige himself to adjust to the joint maximization output that we have previously identified at Q^*. In exchange for such an undertaking, which at the time it is accepted represents a loss to the distributor, the manufacturer should be willing to agree in advance to a compensatory contractual concession through which the two parties can split the additional profits generated by the higher volume. These profits are represented by the cross-hatched triangle B in Exhibit 5.9.

Optimal Volume Definition. The obligation to produce at the joint maximization volume is the meaning that is proposed here for the best efforts term in commercial contracts. This interpretation of the best efforts provision has a great deal of theoretical attractiveness since, absent the specification of an alternative construction by the parties, it directs the outcome that maximizes the net gains that parties could achieve from their contractual relationship. It is a plausible means of identifying a goal presumably desired by most parties, albeit not always well articulated.

In addition, the definition suggested above is consistent with a "fairness" obligation as might be formulated by distributive justice theorists. The distributor is required, under this conception, to treat the manufacturer "fairly," giving the manufacturer's interests (profits) equal weight with his own when output decisions are made. Moreover, such special consideration has presumably been anticipatorily paid for by the manufacturer in the form of some compensatory concession.

EXHIBIT 5.9

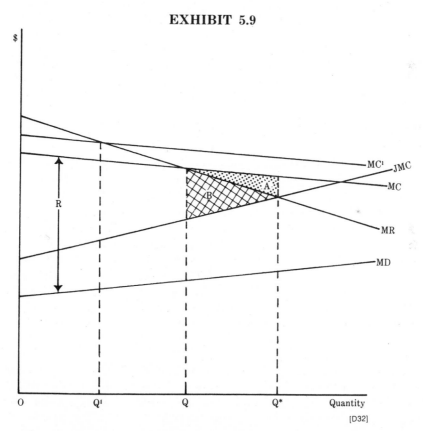

[D32]

Unfortunately, a best efforts obligation, as defined above, inherently implies a serious monitoring problem. This is illustrated in Exhibit 5.9 where shaded triangle A represents the reduction in profits suffered by the distributor because he is obligated to produce at Q* rather than Q. Hence, the best efforts promisor will generally have a strong economic incentive to "chisel" on the obligation. In a world of cost-free information, such breaches of the best efforts requirement would be easily detected, and the behavior restrained through the legal damages imposed for breach of contract. In a real-world situation, however, the requisite information for proof of liability or quantification of damages may be chillingly costly to obtain, especially when the plaintiff bears the burden of such proof. Hence the standard legal mechanism may not be a viable one for enforcement of this type of contract provision.

Where recourse to the courts is not an attractive option, these economic considerations suggest that a best efforts promisee—such as the manufacturer—will attempt to contract for other means of controlling the standard of performance. Presumably, the self interest of both contracting parties will induce them to seek out that combination of monitoring or bonding arrangements that represents the optimal tradeoff between expected costs of contractual governance and profits foregone because the ideal output Q^* is not perfectly enforced. As the cost of contract-specific monitoring strategies increases, the price of contracting to the best efforts promisor similarly increases. The best efforts promisor has an incentive, therefore, to propose cost-effective bonding agreements which, by reducing the costs of contractual control, reduce the contract "price" paid by him. The "price" reductions might take the form of a reduction in the initial license payment required by the manufacturer, or a reduction in the royalty paid to the manufacturer on the contractual product or, indeed, any other adjustment in contract terms favorable to the distributor.

A commonly observed form of bonding is a termination privilege that could be invoked by the manufacturer if he detects a breach of the best efforts obligation. Moreover, the parties might be expected to negotiate a termination clause that granted the manufacturer considerable discretion as to the circumstances under which termination would be permitted. If, instead, the termination clause were only triggered by specific events, any attempt to exercise it might create precisely those problems of proof that the clause was originally designed to circumvent. A limited right of termination, by reducing the value to the manufacturer of the reassurance of contractual performance, would presumably induce some compensatory increase in the contract "price" paid by the distributor. A discretionary termination clause is not an ideal safeguard. Considering the available alternatives, however, it frequently permits a mutually beneficial adaptation to the inevitable conflict of interest generated by a best efforts agreement.

While the best efforts result Q^* is in theory a clearly optimal result for the parties, the realities of enforcement, especially coupled with the inherent chiseling incentive, may dim the practical attractiveness of such agreements. On the other hand, the problems arising in legal regulation of such agreements should not be viewed as dispositive. Many contractual provisions are honored even where there is no effective legal sanction for their breach. In some circumstances this is due to the existence of informal, extra-legal sanctions, including a sense of commercial ethics. Notwithstanding practical difficulties of securing legal enforcement, therefore, a contractual provision also has value as a mere communication of understanding between the parties as to their mutual rights and duties. Hence, the inclusion of a best efforts term may, at a minimum, serve as a signal alerting good faith bargainers that the proposed contractual relationship is one in which special concerns are to be considered.

Where courts are compelled to attach a meaning to otherwise ambiguous terms of agreements, it makes sense to look to the likely intent of the parties or the goal the parties might reasonably be deemed to have sought. The "joint-maximization" definition of best efforts is, we argue, the single most plausible interpretation of the underlying economic motivations involved. This proposed meaning of best efforts need not be seen as describing in any particular case what the contracting parties actually intended. Rather, it is designed to offer a plausible way in which the legal rule can allocate unknown risks in advance of individual bargaining, thus reducing the uncertainty costs of an imprecise legal standard.

Best Efforts as Diligence Insurance. Although the joint-maximization output interpretation may be the single most persuasive meaning for best efforts, one alternative plausible definition merits discussion: best efforts requires the exercise of due diligence and ordinary business prudence. Under this alternative conception, a breach of the best efforts obligation would exist where the distributor's efforts diverge from the standard of diligent or reasonably prudent business conduct.

In terms of Exhibit 5.9, our previous analysis has focused on the losses from a shortfall between the joint maximization volume Q^* and the distributor's profit-maximizing output Q. However, it is interesting to consider in addition the case where the distributor chooses an even lower output than Q, for example Q_1 in Exhibit 5.9.

Why would the distributor ever choose an output of less than Q if, under the cost and revenue conditions for the product he sells, the quantity Q represents the point of maximum profitability? One of the simplest explanations is to reinterpret Exhibit 5.9 as containing "objective" cost and revenue curves as they would exist for a typical distributor. The cost and revenue functions underlying the actual output calculus of any particular distributor may diverge greatly from the objective, either because of truly subjective elements such as misapprehension of the market or due to more concrete factors such as carelessness or incompetence in restraining production costs.

The distributor, either through misapprehension or incompetence in restraining costs, perceives marginal cost to be MC' and selects volume Q_1. Whatever the reason for the distributor's failure to serve even his own interests competently, the manufacturer will understandably be distressed if the original agreement was predicated on his perfectly reasonable expectation that the objective circumstances experienced "should" have motivated a volume of *at least* Q.

For at least two distinct reasons, it makes good economic sense that the distributor would be the efficient bearer of the risk of both his own and the manufacturer's lost profits from sales foregone due to business mistakes on the part of the distributor. First, the distributor is the party who has effective control of his own level of care invested in undertaking business activities and, hence, the opportunity to adjust that level of care to the cost-effective extent. Second, the distributor is in a better position to assess ex ante his own capability to achieve the ordinary or expectable level of business performance. Consequently, inclusion of the best efforts term might be construed as an explicit allocation of all risks from the possible business blunders of the party who promises his "best" efforts.

For expository ease, we shall refer to this interpretation of best efforts as the "diligence insurance" definition. Such a conception of the meaning of best efforts is not an unattractive one and provides at least a minimal standard for the term. One can argue persuasively, however, that the diligence standard is properly subsumed within the joint-maximization output definition. This result is suggested when one attempts to give rigorous content to the question of precisely *how much* diligence is required. The response is that the obligation is to use a cost-effective amount, to, in lay terms, "do the prudent thing, taking into account the interests of both parties" in a manner similar to that mandated by the negligence standard in tort law. But this is only another way of expressing the original fundamental insight that the parties can mutually benefit when the distributor acts as a joint maximizer.

Once it is granted that the parties are motivated by a concern to maximize the joint contractual product, it seems odd to restrict that type of reasoning to a single aspect of the business relationship. One can be diligent and produce an "erroneous" or nonoptimal output such as the distributor's profit-maximizing quantity Q. On the other hand, the obligation to produce the jointly optimal output is easily understood as an all-encompassing optimality condition, directly mandating the "correct" result in objective terms. Since the two interpretations spring from essentially the same underlying principles, the one with greater generality seems preferable.

HYPOTHETICAL: INTERWOOD v. FORREST LUMBER

In July 1969, Interwood Products and Forrest Lumber Co. entered into a joint venture, the Forinter Corporation. As its name suggests, Interwood Products is a large, vertically integrated wood products company with interests extending from raw lumber production and wholesale wood supply to the fabrication of finished wood products such as office furniture, parquet flooring, etc. Forrest Lumber Co. has traditionally operated in the "wood farming" business. It plants and cultivates forests suitable for commercial wood production. Forrest also is well known for engaging in research and development of highly innovative techniques of wood production, ranging from experimental tree varieties to new methods of planting and cultivation.

The Forinter joint venture was conceived of as harnessing Forrest's greater expertise in the raw product end of the business with Interwood's marketing ability and superior access to business capital. Forrest has filed suit against Interwood for losses arising from alleged abuse of the fiduciary relationship created by their joint venture. The existence of a fiduciary relationship between joint venturers is widely acknowledged:

> "The relationship between joint venturers, like that existing between partners is fiduciary in character and imposes on all the participants the obligation of loyalty to the joint concern and of the utmost good faith, fairness and honesty in their dealings with each other with respect to matters pertaining to the enterprise." 46 Am.Jur.2d 69.

Forrest cites three specific examples of conduct by which Interwood is thought to have breached its fiduciary duty.

1. In 1970, Forinter agreed to a supply contract with Interwood whereby Forinter undertook to furnish the raw wood components for a future delivery contract between Interwood and Maxim Construction Co. Under this contract, Maxim Construction Co. acquired an option on a large quantity of oak paneling to be delivered by Interwood in 1973. The agreed price to Forinter under this contract was $2,220,000. Forinter delivered the required raw oak to Interwood's fabrication division in early 1973, although the current market price of the wood was at that time $3,020,000. It has subsequently been conceded, however, that Interwood waived a 6-month prepayment provision in its contract with Maxim, due to Maxim's "tight cash position such that it would otherwise have been unable to exercise its option on the paneling." Forrest contends that Interwood should not have waived the prepayment provision.

2. Interwood outbid Forinter on a valuable forestland property, the Brush Mountain Tract. Forrest asserts that the value of

the Brush Mountain Tract was recognized by Interwood only because of information and expertise developed through its Forinter joint venture.

3. Interwood outbid Forinter on another valuable tract, the Cleve Valley Property. Interwood's willingness to outbid Forinter was based on its own large new orders for finished wood products, which it knew would tend to drive up the value of all wood resources. Forrest asserts that this special knowledge should have been shared with Forinter, thus placing Forinter in an equal bidding position.

Consider yourself to be a member of a state appellate court panel. There are no directly pertinent precedents in your state. How would you decide the case? In preparing your opinion, you would presumably have to cover each of the following points, even if the considerations in (b) below did not appear explicitly in the opinion. (You may wish to reflect on whether or not they *should* appear.)

QUESTIONS

(a) Which, if any, of the examples of conduct by Interwood should be actionable? What are the underlying reasons for your conclusions with respect to each charge? (If you need to assume additional facts, do so, but develop a clear rationale as to why the additional facts are relevant and necessary.) [Hint: In the author's opinion, one of the charges should fairly plainly be actionable, one should not, and another is uncertain.]

(b) What are the implications for *future* contractual relations of the precedents that you would create? Specifically, what would be the likely alternative effects of a decision either restricting or expanding the scope of the duty owed to a joint venturer? How would you predict future contracting parties would adjust their behavior to any specific resolution of the legal issues confronted in this case?

BLOOR v. FALSTAFF BREWING CO.

United States District Court, S.D. New York, 1978.
454 F.Supp. 258.

[The following is perhaps the leading recent case dealing with an important term of contractual liability, the obligation to use "best efforts." Before reading the case, try to define rigorously your own understanding of that common legal term of art.]

BRIEANT, District Judge.

This action was filed July 21, 1976 to recover monetary damages for breach of contract. Plaintiff James Bloor is the Reorganization Trustee of Balco Properties Corporation, formerly named P. Ballantine & Sons ("Ballantine"). Defendant is the Falstaff Brewing Corporation ("Falstaff"), which on March 31, 1972 bought from Investors Funding Corporation ("IFC") the Ballantine brewing labels, trademarks, accounts receivable, distribution systems and other property, excepting only the Ballantine brewery.

The purchase agreement called for an immediate payment to Ballantine of $4,000,000 and royalty payments thereafter of $.50 to be paid on each barrel (31 gallons) of the Ballantine brands sold between April 1, 1972 and March 31, 1978. The contract contained a liquidated damages clause, calling for payments of $1,100,000 a year which were to be made in the event Falstaff "substantially discontinue[d] the distribution of beer under the brand name 'Ballantine'." The contract also required that Falstaff "use its best efforts to promote and maintain a high volume of sales" of the Ballantine brands.

This action arises out of defendant's alleged breach of these covenants by its substantial discontinuance of the Ballantine brands or its failure to use best efforts in their promotion, and also by its failure to pay any royalties whatsoever on sales of those brands after December 1975 and by its alleged underpayment of royalties before that date.

* * *

By contract dated March 3, 1972, Falstaff acquired Ballantine's assets. The closing took place on March 31, 1972. At that time Falstaff was the fifth ranking brewer in the United States but had failed to acquire a substantial foothold in New York, New Jersey and Pennsylvania, the highest beer consuming region in the country. Its purchase of Ballantine was apparently prompted by the desire to acquire a ready-made distribution system in the New York area, and by its need to utilize the excess capacity of its own breweries. Falstaff did not buy the Ballantine brewery in Newark, New Jersey. At some undetermined date during its ownership of Ballantine, Falstaff began using its own beer, without formula alteration, to fill Ballantine Beer containers. At the present time, the only difference between Ballantine and Falstaff Beer is the label. Falstaff was also motivated in its purchase by the fact that Ballantine Beer was (and is) a "price" beer in the Northeast and would in the normal course of events not compete with Falstaff's own so-called "premium" beer.

Shortly after acquiring the Ballantine assets, Falstaff moved the "retail" distribution operation from Newark, New Jersey (the location of the Ballantine brewery) to North Bergen, New Jersey, where it continued until 1975 to service generally the same accounts. Between 1972 and 1975, Falstaff also continued the former policy of substantial advertising of Ballantine products, spending more than $1 Million a year for that purpose. Falstaff continued in every way the former pricing policies used by IFC, including substantial "post-offs" from listed prices. During this period, Falstaff claims to have lost $22 Million in its Ballantine brands operations.

A very significant change in the *modus operandi* of Falstaff-Ballantine took place in 1975. In March of that year, Mr. Paul Kalmanovitz, an entrepreneur with 40 years experience in the brewing industry who had owned a small position in Falstaff stock prior to that time, advanced $3 million to Falstaff to enable it to meet its payroll and other pressing debts then due. On March 10, 1975, in return for some $10 million cash advanced, and additional loan guaranties, Mr. Kalmanovitz was issued new convertible preferred shares in amounts equal to about 35% of the company's outstanding shares. A voting trust arrangement was made to give him control of the Board of Directors. The shareholders of Falstaff approved the agreement on April 28, 1975. At present, Mr. Kalmanovitz is Chairman of the Board of Falstaff.

* * *

Since Mr. Kalmanovitz's assumption of control of Falstaff the advertising budget for Ballantine products has decreased from about $1 Million a year to a point near non-existence (about $115,000 since the beginning of 1976). Substantial cuts have also been made in sales and management personnel. In late 1975 four of the six "retail" distribution centers, including the North Bergen depot, were substantially closed or phased out. The North Bergen depot was replaced by two independent distributors who together service substantially fewer accounts. In mid-1976 Mr. Kalmanovitz also discontinued the price cutting policies of former management, ordering that no beer was to be "given away" in the future.

Concomitant with these changes, and plaintiff argues, causally related to them, there has been a precipitous decline in the sales of Ballantine products, and a slightly less precipitous diminution in the sale of Falstaff products. In December 1975, Falstaff unilaterally discontinued royalty payments on sales of Ballantine products.

* * *

Plaintiff's Claims Pleaded

Plaintiff is suing to recover money damages for Falstaff's breach of contract in three separate instances: (1) Falstaff's "substantial discontinuance" of distribution of Ballantine products, or its failure to use best efforts to keep sales of them high; (2) Falstaff's underpayment of royalties prior to December 1975; and (3) Falstaff's discontinuance of royalty payments on Ballantine products sold after December 1975. We consider these claims separately.

[After trial, plaintiff abandoned its claims for substantial discontinuance and lack of best efforts for the period prior to May 1975, the date Mr. Kalmanovitz assumed operating control of Falstaff.]

I find that plaintiff has failed to prove "substantial discontinuance" under the contract. Falstaff now and at all times has distributed beer under the Ballantine name to all who would purchase it at a price above Falstaff's costs. Whether the totality of its merchandising efforts complies with the obligation to use "best efforts" presents a more difficult question.

Ballantine has, however, proved its claim that Falstaff failed to use its best efforts to promote sales of Ballantine products after May 1975.

The parties differ with respect to the meaning and effect of "best efforts". Defendant has urged on the Court the argument that the interpretation of such a clause requires the application of a subjective standard: Falstaff contracted to use "*its*" best efforts, and any determination of those efforts must include considerations of Falstaff's own allegedly precarious financial position. Plaintiff, on the contrary, cites substantial precedent holding that financial difficulty and economic hardship do not excuse performance of a contract, and argues for the application of an objective standard, that of the "average, prudent comparable" brewer. Arnold Productions, Inc. v. Favorite Films Corp., 176 F.Supp. 862, 866 (S.D.N.Y.1959), aff'd, 298 F.2d 540 (2d Cir. 1962).

The point of the argument appears to be defendant's contention that it promoted Ballantine to the full extent that its own straitened financial abilities permitted, and could do no more.

"Best efforts" is a term "which necessarily takes its meaning from the circumstances." Perma Research & Development v. Singer Co., 308 F.Supp. 743, 748 (S.D.N.Y.1970). In a patent assignment case, for example, in which the court found an implied obligation to use "best efforts," Judge Duffy examined the assignee's research capability and net earnings, and stated: "To properly evaluate Singer's performance under the patent assignment it is necessary to look first at Singer's capability." Id., 402 F.Supp. 881, 890 (S.D.N.Y.1975), aff'd, 542 F.2d 111 (2d Cir.), cert. denied, 429 U.S. 987, 97 S.Ct. 507, 50 L.Ed.2d 598 (1976). "Capability," however, is a far broader term than "financial ability." It includes the marketing expertise and experience attributable to the "average, prudent, comparable" brewer. It is obvious that any determination of the best efforts achievable by Falstaff must take into account Falstaff's abilities and the opportunities which it created or faced; Falstaff did not contract to promote Ballantine at the level or to the degree that Anheuser-Busch or Schlitz might have done. It did, however, contract to merchandise Ballantine products in good faith and to the extent of its own total capabilities, and this it failed to do.

The evidence in the case also shows that Falstaff's financial position during most of the period in litigation was far from that depicted by defendant, and that Falstaff failed to use even its own temporarily circumscribed abilities and resources to promote the sale of Ballantine products.

As a consequence of this precipitous departure from the New York City market area, Ballantine registered no sales there for the month of September 1975. In October and November 1975, Falstaff, on the initiative of several independent distributors, selected Thomas Fatato, Inc. to distribute them in New Jersey. The performance of these two has been less than impressive, and, indeed, at the time of their appointment, strong concern about their ability to cover the metropolitan area adequately was expressed by Mr. Griesedieck, President of Falstaff. Fatato, for example, services only about 1,500 to 2,000 of the approximately 15,000 to 17,000 retail accounts formerly serviced from North Bergen. In the first month of his operation (October 1975), sales dropped to 2,500 barrels from some 7,000 barrels sold in August. There was convincing testimony from defendant's own employees that Mr. Fatato's ownership of a competing brand, Milwaukee Beer, on which he earns both the distributor's and manufacturer's profit would naturally result in his giving preference to his own brand in the competition for shelf space, rather than aggressively marketing Ballantine. Since Fatato has been distributing Ballantine in the New York City area, sales of Ballantine draught beer have declined more than 90 percent. Despite all this, Mr. Kalmanovitz testified that Fatato's performance as a distributor was better than expected.

Under its union contract with its employees at the North Bergen depot, Falstaff considered itself legally bound not to appoint an official distributor for the tristate area to whom Falstaff would make shipments from its brewery in Cranston, Rhode Island. Both Fatato and Piccirrillo bought Ballantine Beer in Rhode Island and transported it themselves into the New York City area. This union contract would have expired in May 1976, but Falstaff's failure to terminate it with proper notice resulted in an arbitration award extending the contract until May 1977. Falstaff urges the existence of this contract as the excuse for its failure to take advantage of a very significant opportunity in the fall of 1975 which would have cost it nothing to exploit, but Ballantine may not be charged with Falstaff's negligence in failing to terminate its labor contracts properly.

In September or October 1975, Mr. John Molyneux, Vice President and General Manager of the Guinness-Harp Corporation, an importer of foreign beers, and distributor of various American brands including Schlitz, Schmidt's, Pabst and Piels, journeyed to San Francisco to discuss with Mr. Kalmanovitz the possibility of undertaking the distribution of Ballantine products. Mr. Molyneux testified that his company would be able to handle all of the Ballantine products (except Munich Beer) at the prices quoted by Mr. Kalmanovitz and would be able to distribute them profitably through the Metrobeer Division of Guinness-Harp, to about 13,000 of the 15,000 retail licensees in New York City. On October 20, 1975, however, Falstaff wrote to Mr. Molyneux that even that offer was withdrawn because Falstaff wanted to give Mr. Fatato a chance in New York and did not want to "invite competition" by other wholesale operations.

I find that Guinness-Harp presented Falstaff with an opportunity to promote Ballantine products that an "average, prudent, comparable brewer" situated as was Falstaff reasonably would and should have explored and sought to exploit. Existence of the union contract was not an obstacle to such an arrangement. There is no credible evidence that Mr. Molyneux demanded an exclusive "appointment" in the New York City area. In any event, after May 1976, any inability to appoint such an exclusive distributor in the New York area was caused by the fault or negligence of Falstaff. To the extent such fault or negligence prevented it from using effective marketing methods in the area which Molyneux proposed to serve, it is answerable in damages to Ballantine.

Defendant argues that it had the right, and even the duty to use in good faith its best business judgement in all matters arising under the contract, and also had the right to look to its own interest. This argument has some validity, but Falstaff has gone beyond that point. As the New York Court of Appeals said in a similar situation:

"Although a publisher has a general right to act on its own interests in a way that may incidentally lessen an author's royalties, there may be a point where that activity is so manifestly harmful to the author, and must have been seen by the publisher so to be harmful, as to justify the court in saying there was a breach of the covenant to promote the author's works." Van Valkenburgh v. Hayden Publishing Co., 30 N.Y.2d 34, 46, 330 N.Y.S. 329, 334, 281 N.E.2d 142, 145 (1972).

*   *   *

Some of this apparent callousness towards Ballantine sales is undoubtedly caused by the fact that even though the liquid in a can of Ballantine Beer and in a can of Falstaff Beer is identical, and accordingly costs exactly the same amount to produce, sale of Falstaff Beer produces a greater profit for Falstaff. In part this is the result of the fact that Falstaff is a "premium" beer and nets Falstaff about $4.20 more a barrel than does Ballantine, even before the $.50 Ballantine royalty is subtracted from the latter. Also, Mr. Kalmanovitz testified, the process of changing a production line over from Falstaff to Ballantine Beer "cost[s] a lot of money."

In addition to Falstaff's refusal to entertain Mr. Molyneux's proposals despite the apparent inadequacy of the Fatato-Piccirrillo distributorships, Falstaff has also failed in several other notable respects to promote Ballantine products with its best efforts. After

Mr. Kalmanovitz's assumption of control of Falstaff, the company severely cut back personnel in distribution, sales, marketing, administrative and warehousing areas. It virtually eliminated its promotion and advertising of Ballantine Beer and closed its advertising department, all this despite the repeated assertions by experts for both sides (for example, Mr. Weinstein for plaintiff and Mr. Dependahl, former Vice-President of Falstaff, for defendant) that personal contact, merchandising and advertising were essential to the marketing of any beer. While some cutbacks may have been temporarily justified in late 1975, the situation was quite different in 1976 and 1977 when Falstaff continued its stated policy of simply making the beer available, and when solicited by distributors, funding one-half of "co-op" promotional costs. After Mr. Kalmanovitz assumed control of Falstaff, the company even discontinued the establishing of goals for its remaining salesmen, an essential step in any marketing effort, and one which would have cost the company nothing to implement. This is not "best efforts."

Defendant has stressed the argument that Falstaff's policies after 1975 were evenhanded, that is, that Falstaff's cutbacks and marketing strategy affected Falstaff and Ballantine performance equally. Even if this were the case, which it is not, Falstaff's relationship to Ballantine is essentially different from its relationship to its own products. In the latter case, it may promote, continue or discontinue its products as it wills subject to its duty to shareholders; in the former case it is bound by a contractual duty to the promisee. As the court said in a case cited by the defendant here:

> " '[B]est energies' meant such effort as in the exercise of sound judgment would be likely to produce the most profitable results to the promisee in view of the nature of the business and the extent of the territory over which it was to be conducted." Randall v. Peerless Motor Car Co., 212 Mass. 352, 374, 99 N.E. 221, 226 (1912).

Additionally, Falstaff has not treated both products equally. Robert Thibaut, a Falstaff Vice-President, testified that Falstaff but no Ballantine had been advertised extensively in Texas and Missouri. In the same areas Falstaff, although a "premium" beer, was sold for extended periods below the price of Ballantine. These actions and failures to act were not consistent with those of the average, prudent, comparable brewer in the same circumstances seeking to promote a beer to the extent of his best efforts. The "business judgement" argument is of no help to Falstaff in this regard.

* * *

Accordingly, I find that from September 1975 until the present, Falstaff has breached the covenant in its agreement with plaintiff's predecessor, in that it failed without justification to use its best efforts to promote the sale of Ballantine products and has neglected to act in the manner required of the average, prudent, comparable brewer in marketing his product.

* * *

Damages

Falstaff has breached its contract with Ballantine to use its best efforts to promote sales of Ballantine products and thus assure fair royalty payments to Ballantine. The period of this breach extends from September 1975 when Mr. Kalmanovitz's policies began to take effect, through the date of trial, and anticipatorily, through March 31, 1978, the end of the royalty period. Since December 1975, moreover, Falstaff has, as a set-off against its claims against Ballantine, withheld royalty payments admittedly due on sales of Ballantine products. In the light of our discussion of defendant's counterclaims, these set-offs were not justified. Finally, it is undisputed that royalties to Ballantine for the period from April 1, 1972 through November 30, 1975 were underpaid in the amount of $41,399.50. During that period Falstaff sold 5,108,908 barrels of Ballantine brands, for which the royalty payments should have been $2,554,454.00, rather than the $2,513,054.50 actually paid.

Damages for Breach of Contract

"In simple terms, the measure of the damage [for failure to use best efforts] is the amount necessary to put the injured party in the exact position he would have been if the contract had not been breached." Perma Research & Development v. Singer Co., 542 F.2d 111, 116 (2d Cir.), cert. denied, 429 U.S. 987, 97 S.Ct. 507, 50 L.Ed.2d 598 (1976). In this case the position Ballantine would have enjoyed but for the breach is established by reference to the sales achieved by "comparable" brewers between mid-1975 and the present. This method of computing damages has often been employed by the courts. In Autowest, Inc. v. Peugeot, Inc., 434 F.2d 556 (2d Cir. 1970), which involved a claim of wrongful termination of a franchise to sell Peugeot automobiles, plaintiff proved his damages by, among other methods, comparison of the sales of Volvo automobiles, which had increased from 5,000 to 10,000 between 1965 and 1968, with sales of Peugeot automobiles which only rose from 700 to 900 during the same period. Contemporary Music, Inc. v. Famous Music Corp., 557 F.2d 918 (2d Cir. 1977), was an action to recover damages for defendant's failure to use reasonable efforts to promote Contemporary's records, specifically the song "Fear No Evil", which had reached No. 61 on the Hit Parade at the time it was wrongfully withdrawn by defendant. After stating the general rule that a plaintiff who has proved injury "need only show a 'stable foundation for a reasonable estimate of royalties he would have earned had defendant not breached,' " id. at 926, quoting Freund v. Washington Square Press, Inc., 34 N.Y.2d 379, 383, 357 N.Y.S.2d 857, 314 N.E.2d 419 (1974), the Court approved a statistical method of comparison which tended to show that 51% of songs reaching No. 61 on the Hit Parade went on to reach No. 20 and consequently to achieve greater sales. Finally, in Bigelow v. RKO Radio Pictures, Inc., 327 U.S. 251, 260, 66 S.Ct. 574, 90 L.Ed. 652 (1946), the Supreme Court approved a method of computing damages based on a comparison of the profits of plaintiff's theater, which had been deprived of first-run motion pictures by defendant, with the profits of a theater of comparable size which had access to such films.

[Here the court engaged in a lengthy discussion of the evidence presented by Messrs. Weinberg and Horowitz, expert witnesses for plaintiffs and defendants, respectively, as to the performance of "comparable" brands during the contract period. Both experts considered Schaefer and Rheingold to be products with market opportunities comparable to those of Ballantine. The court therefore found that the experiences of these two brands reveal what Ballantine's performance would have been had it not been for Falstaff's breach. Specifically, the court found that Ballantine's sales in each of the years 1975–1977 should have been the same percentage of base-year 1974 sales as experienced by the "comparable" brands. Actual Ballantine sales were then compared to this benchmark level for each year and the shortfall used to compute the lost royalties.]

Accordingly, the damages for Falstaff's breach amount to $628,528.10. These damages are reasonable under all the circumstances presented here. As our Court of Appeals stated in Contemporary Mission, Inc. v. Famous Music Corp., 557 F.2d 918, 926–27 (2d Cir. 1977):

"[T]he burden of uncertainty as to the amount of damages is upon the wrongdoer, Perma Research & Dev. v. Singer, supra, 542 F.2d at 116, and the test for admissibility of evidence concerning prospective damages is whether the evidence has any tendency to show their probable amount. Duane Jones Co. v. Burke, 306 N.Y. 172, 192, 117 N.E.2d 237, 247–48 (1954). The plaintiff need only show a 'stable foundation for a reasonable estimate of royalties he would have earned had defendant not breached.' Freund v. Washington Square Press, Inc., supra, 34 N.Y.2d at 383, 357 N.Y.S.2d at 861, 314 N.E.2d at 421. 'Such an estimate necessarily requires some improvisation, and the party who has caused the loss may not insist on theoretical perfection.' Entis v. Atlantic Wire & Cable Corp., 335 F.2d 759, 763 (2d Cir. 1964). '[T]he law will make the best appraisal that it can, summoning to its service whatever aids it can command.' Sinclair Rfng. Co. v. Jenkins Co., 289 U.S. 689, 697, 53 S.Ct. 736, 739, 77 L.Ed. 1449 (1933)."

Underpaid Royalties

It is undisputed that between April 1, 1972 and November 30, 1975 Falstaff sold 5,108,908 barrels of Ballantine products, on which a royalty of $2,554,454.00 was due. It has been stipulated that during that period Falstaff paid to Ballantine only $2,513,054.50. The underpaid royalties due for that period thus amount to $41,399.50.

Withheld Royalties

Plaintiff is also entitled to receive its $.50 per barrel royalty on all sales of Ballantine products after November 30, 1975. These were unjustifiably withheld by Falstaff in anticipation of its counterclaims against Ballantine, all of which have been found lacking in merit. In the period from December 1, 1975 to December 31, 1977, Falstaff sold 1,159,241 barrels of Ballantine products, and the royalty due is $579,620.50. Using the method described above, Falstaff would have sold 105,525 barrels of Ballantine products (30% of Ballantine's 1974 volume) during the first quarter of 1978. The royalties due for this period amount to $52,762.50.

The sum total due to Balco is thus $1,302,310.60. Pre-judgement interest at 6% *per annum* is awarded, with the computation to be made in accordance with New York CPLR Section 5001(b), with costs to be taxed.

QUESTIONS

1. Did Falstaff fail in what was described earlier in the chapter as its "diligence insurance" obligation? In what way? Would it surprise you to know that most of the litigated cases involve a diligence failure? Does that constitute strong evidence in favor of the "diligence" construction of "best efforts" as opposed to the "joint maximization" interpretation?

2. What is the meaning of the discussion of "evenhandedness" by the court? Why would Falstaff not have been evenhanded?

3. In a contract case, the method of computation of the damages usually permits one to infer the performance standard. Why? In the *Bloor* case, the method of damage computation is consistent with the joint maximization criterion. Why? Do you think that this consistency is deliberate, or could it have been inadvertent?

4. If Bloor had wanted to protect itself against this type of situation, how could the contract with Falstaff been rewritten?

RICHARDS v. ALLSTATE INSURANCE CO.

United States Court of Appeals, Fifth Circuit, 1982.
693 F.2d 502.

Before CLARK, Chief Judge, RUBIN and WILLIAMS, Circuit Judges.

Larry Richards filed this diversity suit against Allstate Insurance Company, seeking actual damages for injuries he sustained in a motorcycle accident and punitive damages for Allstate's bad-faith refusal to honor his claim for those injuries. The jury returned a verdict of $2,500 in compensatory damages and $750,000 in punitive damages. The district judge subsequently ordered a remittitur of $375,000, which Richards accepted, albeit reluctantly. Allstate contends here that the award of punitive damages was without basis in Mississippi law. Richards cross-appeals, challenging the propriety of the remittitur. We affirm.

Mississippi law requires all automobile insurance policies to provide at least $10,000 coverage for personal injuries sustained in accidents caused by motorists who have no insurance. See Miss. Code Ann. Sec. 83–11–101. The focal point of this litigation is Exclusion 2 of the policy issued by Allstate to Richards, which attempted to limit such coverage. This provision, which was for many years part of Allstate's standard Mississippi automobile policy, totally excluded from uninsured motorist coverage injuries suffered by an insured while occupying a vehicle owned by him but not specified as insured under his policy.

Allstate retained Exclusion 2 in its standard policy until 1981 despite the fact that in 1973 the Mississippi Supreme Court struck down a similar exclusion in another company's policy in Lowery v. State Farm Mutual Automobile Insurance Co., 285 So.2d 767 (Miss.1973). Allstate officials admittedly were aware of the *Lowery* decision and its fatal effect on Exclusion 2. They did not, however, delete the exclusion from their standard policy. Nor did they make any effort to inform their insureds or their sales agents of the effect of *Lowery*. Instead, mid-level claims personnel were instructed to honor claims that otherwise would have been denied in reliance on Exclusion 2. Unfortunately, as the result of a series of mistakes, this procedure failed in Mr. Richards' case and his claim was denied.

The incident that gave rise to Richards' claim occurred in August of 1977. Early in that month he was injured in a motorcycle accident caused by the negligence of an uninsured motorist. After Richards contacted an Allstate sales agent in an unsuccessful attempt to recover for the damages to his motorcycle, he brought his accident to the attention of Pete Quave, who worked for Richards' retained counsel. Quave was an ex-employee of Allstate and had handled a similar claim while working there. He contacted Allstate on Richards' behalf and spoke with Marinella Davis, one of Allstate's telephone claims handlers, describing the accident and the terms of Richards' policy, including the fact that the motorcycle was not an insured vehicle. After discussing the case with her supervisor, Margaret Kessler, Davis informed Quave that Allstate planned to deny coverage in reliance on Exclusion 2. At this point Quave brought the *Lowery* decision to Davis' attention and urged her to reconsider. He then talked to Kessler, again emphasizing the effect of *Lowery* on Richards' claim. Quave also asked to speak to Cecil Snodgrass, who he knew was aware of *Lowery*. Because Snodgrass was unavailable, Quave asked Kessler to discuss the case with him. The message somehow got garbled in transmission, and Snodgrass concurred in the denial. After receipt of Allstate's letter of denial, Richards filed suit.

Allstate contends first that this is not a proper case for an award of punitive damages. The leading Mississippi case on punitive damages in an insurance claim setting is Standard Life Ins. Co. of Indiana v. Veal, 354 So.2d 239 (Miss.1978). There the court recognized that punitive damages are not to be awarded unless the breach of the insurance contract is attended by an intentional wrong or such gross negligence as to amount to an independent tort. But the court allowed punitive damages, finding that the company had denied a legitimate claim for a reason clearly contrary to the express provisions of the policy. The court equated gross negligence with a refusal to pay not based on a legitimate or arguable reason.

This circuit has recognized *Veal's* two-part "legitimate or arguable reason" rule to mean that the absence of (1) a justifiable reason, or (2) an arguable basis under Mississippi law, for refusal to pay a valid claim creates a jury issue on punitive damages. Black v. Fidelity & Guaranty Insurance Underwriters, 582 F.2d 984, 990–91 (5th Cir. 1978). In this case we conclude that under *Veal* submission of the punitive damages issue to the jury was compelled by the proof.

At trial Richards alleged that three separate but related actions of Allstate justified a punitive award: (1) retention of the invalid Exclusion 2 in the standard Allstate policy; (2) failure to provide an adequate procedure to prevent erroneous denials; and (3) denial of Richards' claim itself. The jury was properly instructed on all three. We need go no further than the first allegation to uphold their verdict under the facts in this record.

As we have noted, the *Lowery* decision in 1973 invalidated Exclusion 2. Although aware of *Lowery*, Allstate decided not to delete the exclusion from its standard policy. Instead, a procedure was established within the claims department that Allstate thought would be adequate to prevent erroneous denial of claims that were valid but for Exclusion 2. The court instructed the jury that if they found an adequate procedure was established they could not assess punitive damages unless Richards proved that reliance on the procedure amounted to gross negligence.

Allstate urges that its procedure was successful in every case except Richards'. Even accepting this as true, this procedure provided no remedy for those policyholders who read Exclusion 2, assumed their injuries were not covered, and failed to file claims. Failure to delete Exclusion 2 in effect represented a corporate decision by Allstate not to inform its policyholders of undisclosed coverage required by Mississippi law. Whether this conduct was sufficiently culpable to justify an award of punitive damages was a question for the jury. The jury obviously believed that it was.

Allstate contends that retaining Exclusion 2 was justified in spite of *Lowery* and makes two arguments in support of this claim. Both are wholly without merit. First, Allstate asserts that Exclusion 2 was valid insofar as coverage in excess of that required by law was concerned. But this does not explain the fact that Exclusion 2 eliminated all coverage, not just that above the statutory minimum. In this case, for example, Richards' claim was within the statutory minimum, but it was denied based on the language of Exclusion 2. Second, Allstate contends that Exclusion 2 was in effect erased by provision 5 of the policy, which stated: "[S]uch terms of this policy as are in conflict with statutes of the state in which this policy is issued are hereby amended to conform." In Allstate's view, this provision corrected any deficiency in the policy. Therefore, it contends that deletion of Exclusion 2 was not required. This argument strains credibility. If it were accepted, Allstate could include in its policies any sort of invalid exclusion and then rely on change provision 5 when challenged. This would mean that policyholders, not insurance companies, would bear the burden of keeping abreast of changes in the law. Clearly this is not the intent of Mississippi's insurance code.

Exclusion 2 as written and as retained in Allstate's policies from 1973 until well after 1977 was invalid under *Lowery*. Under the court's instructions the jury necessarily found that Allstate's failure to remove Exclusion 2 from its standard automobile policy until after this suit was filed was grossly negligent. This finding is supported by the proof.

Allstate also claims that the punitive award is excessive in light of the actual injuries suffered by Richards. Although the punitive award here, even after remitted to $375,000, may be characterized as unusually large where actual damages are only $2,500, this disproportionality does not mandate reversal.

Punitive damages are awarded not as compensation to the plaintiff but as "punishment for the wrongdoing of the defendant and as an example so that others may be deterred from the commission of similar offenses * * *." Snowden v. Osborne, 269 So.2d 858, 860 (Miss.1972). Given the jury's determination that Allstate's actions were grossly negligent and that Allstate's financial statement disclosed its latest annual addition to surplus was $390,046,821 and its cumulated policyholders' surplus is $2,371,135,879, we cannot say that the award of sixteen ten-thousands of that surplus was greater than necessary to serve these twin rationales. See Standard Life Ins. Co. of Indiana v. Veal, 354 So.2d at 249. An additional consideration in determining whether a punitive damage is excessive is whether the plaintiff has performed a public service by bringing the wrongdoer to account. See Fowler Butane Gas Co. v. Varner, 244 Miss. 130, 151, 141 So.2d 226, 233 (1962). Here Richards' suit has benefitted all Allstate policyholders by directly causing deletion of Exclusion 2 from the standard Mississippi policy. These factors, together with the fact that Mississippi has never articulated any requirement that punitive damages be rationally related to actual damages, convince us that the award was proper.

Finally, Richards contends that the district judge erred in ordering a remittitur of half of the jury's punitive award. Because Richards accepted the remittitur, however, he is barred from challenging it on appeal. Donovan v. Penn Shipping Co., 429 U.S. 648, 97 S.Ct. 835, 51 L.Ed.2d 112 (1977). This is true whether the objection is voiced on appeal or cross-appeal. Keene v. International Union of Operating Engineers, 569 F.2d 1375, 1381 (5th Cir. 1978). Therefore, we do not reach the merits of Richards' claim.

For the foregoing reasons, the decision of the district court is Affirmed.

QUESTIONS

1. Did plaintiff Richards receive his bargained-for expectation interest in his insurance contract with Allstate? Is there any sense in which Allstate "broke its promise" to Richards? Is this a contract claim? If not, what?

2. Why did Allstate keep the unenforceable provision in the contract if its contention is true that Richards' case is a "slip-up" in a general policy of actually honoring claims that would have been barred by the term in question?

3. Suppose that *all* claims similar to that of Richards had been honored. Would anyone have a cause of action against Allstate? If so, for what damages?

4. The judge apparently thought that $750,000 in punitive damages was excessive on a claim of only $2,500 in compensatory damages. What factors should determine the amount of punitive damages, if any?

5. Most states now have landlord-tenant statutes that restrict the terms that may be written into residential leases. Would it surprise you to find that terms contrary to the statutes are fairly widely used? Why?

6. "Resolved: Anyone who shall induce another to transact on terms known to be contrary to law or public policy shall be liable for punitive damages." Comment.

Chapter VI

SUPPLY AND SYSTEMIC INTERACTIONS

COSTS AND MARKETS

This chapter deals in large part with "systemic" interactions among firms or other kinds of economic units. The traditional economic environment of "markets" is the principal system analyzed below, but reference is also made to non-market systems, such as inter-community migration (see the *Petaluma* case below). When individual units are linked in some form of interdependent system, it is necessary to trace the process whereby a large number of individualistic decisions become aggregated in a system result such as a market price, an industry-wide output, etc. Conversely, it may also be of interest to ferret out the impact on individual units arising as a consequence of some change in the structure of the system itself.

In order to understand the supply side of markets, one must first have some minimal familiarity with the standard "theory of the firm" and the way in which individual producers are understood to make their production decisions. Considerations of *cost* are, obviously, paramount in production planning. The first few sections of the chapter are therefore designed to raise some preliminary issues about the nature of cost and its relevance to several different kinds of legal problems. *Inter alia*, the sections on costs should demonstrate how important and illuminating it is to consistently adhere to an "opportunity cost" concept of cost.

The preliminary materials on cost are followed by some extremely simple models of market adjustment where individual decisions are aggregated into an industry-wide outcome. One should beware of taking these models too seriously as a description of the real world. They are offered here for the more limited purpose of supplying stripped-down constructs whose mechanics are hopefully simple enough to be intelligible while at the same time retaining some analogical relevance to the forces that operate in real situations.

375

Although there has been nothing really exotic about the economic concepts used in earlier chapters, they were imbedded in a legal context that is a bit removed from the traditional focus of economic literature. The underlying economics of this chapter is, by contrast, precisely the area in which standard economic texts have lavished a great deal of attention and sophistication. Be assured, therefore, that we are not about to undertake the task of re-inventing the wheel. The appropriately abbreviated and relatively non-technical view provided below will nonetheless permit access to a number of stimulating legal issues. The more interested reader may find it useful to follow up by consulting any of a number of excellent economic theory texts and applied works that deal more or less directly with the topics touched upon later in this chapter.

PRODUCTION COSTS AND CONTRACT BREACH

Firm S is a producer of standprods. It has contracted to deliver 6 lots of three units apiece to six different buyers, B1, B2, B3, B4, B5, and B6. All orders are to be delivered on June 1. Normally, production commences one working day before delivery is due. On April 29, before S has produced any of the standprods involved in these orders, market conditions undergo a dramatic change. Standprods become much less desirable to buyers and a series of breaches by S's buyers takes place. First B1 breaches his order of three units, followed by B2 on an order of three, etc. After the final breach by B6, all of S's orders have been lost.

We shall assume that S will file suit against each of the six breachers separately. Our problem will be to determine the "proper" recovery from each breacher. The costs that the firm would have had to incur in order to perform the contracts is an important determinant of that recovery. Exhibit 6.1 is a schedule of production costs for the firm in question. (We will also use this schedule for a subsequent problem.) One issue will be the appropriate treatment of what are sometimes called "overhead" costs.

Economists classify production costs in several ways that are relevant here. One important distinction is between "fixed" and "variable" costs. Fixed costs are whatever costs that remain even if output is shut down to zero. They are exemplified by items such as rental payments on a term lease of the plant, contractual obligation to pay the wages of the overseer, etc. In our Exhibit 6.1 example, such costs are $100. Variable costs are *avoidable* by adjusting output. Marginal costs are equivalent to the rate of change in these variable costs as output is varied. "Total" costs are, of course, the sum of both fixed and variable costs.

Variable costs are sometimes further subdivided to distinguish a category of "unallocable" costs. Such costs may be avoidable by shutting down completely, but for positive levels of production, it may be difficult to impute them to any particular item of production. In the example, it is assumed that a $15 license fee per period is necessary if any production takes place. Hence, the cost of the first unit of production is listed as $20: $15 for the license and $5 for variable inputs specifically attributable to the first unit of product.

EXHIBIT 6.1   Costs at Alternative Outputs

Output	Variable Cost	Total Cost	AVC	ATC	MC
0	NA	100	NA	NA	NA
1	20	_____	20.0	120	20.0
2	25	_____	12.5	_____	_____
3	30	_____	_____	_____	_____
4	35	_____	_____	_____	_____
5	40	_____	_____	_____	_____
6	45	_____	_____	_____	_____
7	50	_____	_____	_____	_____
8	56	_____	_____	_____	_____
9	63	_____	_____	_____	_____
10	71	_____	_____	_____	_____
11	80	_____	_____	_____	_____
12	90	_____	_____	_____	_____
13	101	_____	_____	_____	_____
14	113	_____	_____	_____	_____
15	126	_____	_____	_____	_____
16	140	_____	_____	_____	_____
17	155	_____	_____	_____	_____
18	171	_____	_____	_____	_____
19	188	_____	_____	_____	_____
20	206	_____	_____	_____	_____
21	225	_____	_____	_____	_____
22	245	_____	_____	_____	_____
23	266	_____	_____	_____	_____
24	288	_____	_____	_____	_____

QUESTIONS

1. Fill in the column of Exhibit 6.1 labelled "Total Cost." The column labelled "ATC" provides space for Average Total Cost, computed by dividing Total Cost by the relevant output quantity. "AVC" signifies Average Variable Cost, a concept analogous to ATC. Fill in however much of this "average" cost information as you deem useful or relevant.

2. Determine the incremental cost of each unit and place the resultant information in the column headed "MC".

3. Suppose that each of the contracts was for a price of $15.95 and the current market price has dropped to $6.95. How much does S need to collect in total in order to be as well off as if the contracts had been performed? Should each breacher pay the same amount? Why?

4. What do you understand to be meant by "efficient breach"? How is this concept relevant to the answer in the question immediately preceding?

5. Same facts as above, but the market price has fallen only to $7.95. What answer now?

6. If the fixed costs had been $150 rather than $100, how would the answers to the last two questions have changed? Of what relevance is the ATC column of Exhibit 6.1?

7. "Fixed costs are not really costs at all. They don't matter." Comment.

JERICHO SASH AND DOOR CO. v. BUILDING ERECTORS, INC.

Supreme Judicial Court of Massachusetts, Middlesex, 1972.
362 Mass. 871, 286 N.E.2d 343.

The defendant appeals from a final decree for the plaintiff on this bill in equity to reach and apply assets of the defendant to the plaintiff's claim of damages for breach of contract. The sole question presented is whether the trial judge erred in allowing damages for "profit (including reasonable overhead)" under G.L. c. 106, Section 2–708(2), in the absence of evidence showing separate figures for profit and for overhead. The plaintiff delivered 1,420 pairs of assorted sizes of window sash, for which the defendant admitted liability, and the defendant then repudiated the undelivered balance of 5,580. The plaintiff introduced evidence showing the "weighted average sales price per pair" and the "weighted average direct cost per pair" of the delivered sash. Subtraction of cost from price gave "lost profit and overhead per unit," and multiplication by the number of undelivered units gave "total lost profit and overhead," and the judge awarded more than $21,000 on that account. There was no error. The judge followed the statutory injunction that the remedy "be liberally administered to the end that the aggrieved party had fully performed." G.L. c. 106, Section 1–106(1), as appearing in St.1957, c. 765, Section 1. Damages need not "be calculable with mathematical accuracy. Compensatory damages are often at best approximate: they have to be proved with whatever definiteness and accuracy the facts permit, but no more." Comment 1 to Section 1–106(1) of the Uniform Commercial Code, 1 U.L.A. (Master Ed.). See Dyecraftsmen, Inc. v. Feinberg, Mass., 269 N.E.2d 693; Coyne Industrial Laundry of Schenectady, Inc. v. Gould, Mass., 268 N.E.2d 848. There is no requirement that "overhead" be separated from "net profit" in the computation. As the plaintiff's witness and the judge clearly understood, "profit (including reasonable overhead)" in the statute is the equivalent of "gross profit," including fixed costs but not costs saved as a result of the breach.

Decree affirmed with costs of appeal.

QUESTIONS

1. Even if you have never heard the accounting term "direct cost" before, what can you infer that it must mean?

2. What do you understand to be meant by the phrase in Sec. 2–708(2) of the Uniform Commercial Code allowing the seller to recover "profit (including reasonable overhead)" lost as a result of a buyer's breach? Is the discussion in the case unnecessarily muddy? How would you explain the point?

NOBS CHEMICAL, U.S.A., INC. v. KOPPERS CO., INC.

United States Court of Appeals, Fifth Circuit, 1980.
616 F.2d 212.

Before CHARLES CLARK, RONEY and HENDERSON, Circuit Judges.

HENDERSON, Circuit Judge:

[Koppers contracted with the plaintiffs, Nobs Chemical and Calmon-Hill Trading Corp., to purchase 1000 metric tons of cumene, an oily additive for high-octane motor fuel, at a contract price of $540,000. Plaintiffs had arranged to purchase the cumene in Brazil for $400 a ton and to expend $45 per ton for the cost of transporting the cumene to the defendant, for a total expense of $445,000. The district court applied Tex.Bus. & Com.Code Sec. 2.708(b) and determined that the plaintiffs were entitled to recover lost profits of $95,000 ($540,000 minus $445,000). The district court ruled that the plaintiffs could not recover the extra $25 per ton they allegedly were forced to pay their Brazilian supplier when the price per ton increased because their total order with the supplier was reduced from 4,000 metric tons to 3,000 metric tons because of Kopper's breach. The court decided this lost quantity discount amounted to consequential damages and was, therefore, not recoverable.]

* * *

We first turn to the issue of whether the district court was correct in applying the lost profits measure of damages to the plaintiff's loss. According to Tex.Bus. & Com.Code Ann. Sec. 2.708 (Vernon)

(a) * * * the measure of damages for non-acceptance or repudiation by the buyer is the difference between the market price at the time and place for tender and the unpaid contract price together with any incidental damages provided in this chapter (Section 2.710), but less expenses saved in consequence of the buyer's breach.

(b) if the measure of damages provided in Subsection (a) is inadequate to put the seller in as good a position as performance would have done then the measure of damages is the profit (including reasonable overhead) which the seller would have made from full performance by the buyer, together with any incidental damages provided in this chapter (Section 2.710), due allowance for costs reasonably incurred and due credit for payments or proceeds of resale.

The plaintiffs urge that subsection (a) should govern in this case. Because the market value of cumene dropped to between $220.40 and $264.48 a metric ton at the time of the breach, the plaintiffs contend that they should recover the difference between the contract price ($540,000) and the market price (between $220,400 and $264,480), substantially more than the $95,000 awarded them under subsection (b).

* * *

Because there does not appear to be any law directly on point, we take the liberty of looking to those more learned on the subject of the Uniform Commercial Code. Professors White and Summers, recognizing that Sec. 2.708(b) is not the most lucid or best-drafted of the sales article sections, decided that the drafters of the Uniform Commercial Code intended subsection (b) to apply to certain sellers whose losses would rarely be compensated by the subsection (a) market price-contract price measure of damages, and for these sellers the lost profit formula was added in subsection (b). One such type of seller is a "jobber," who, according to the treatise writers, must satisfy two conditions: "[f]irst, he is a seller who never acquires the contract goods. Second, his decision not to acquire those goods after learning of the breach was not commercially unreasonable. * * *"

J. White & R. Summers, Uniform Commercial Code Sec. 7–10, at 228 (1972). Nobs and Calmon-Hill clearly fit this description. The plaintiffs never acquired the goods from their Brazilian supplier, and, as White and Summers point out, an action for the purchase price or resale was therefore unavailable. See also, American Metal Climax, Inc. v. Essex International, Inc., 16 U.C.C.Rep. 101, 115 (S.D.N.Y. 1974) ("[C]ompensatory damages as provided in the contract-market formula of Sec. 2–708(1) [Sec. 2.708(a)] are realistic only where the seller continues to be in a position to sell the product to other customers in the market.").

The plaintiffs argue, however, that in this case the measure of damages under subsection (a) would adequately compensate them and therefore, according to the terms of subsection (a), subsection (b) does not control. This is an intriguing argument. It appears that the drafters of Sec. 2.708(a) did not consider the possibility that recovery under that section may be *more* than adequate. White & Summers, supra, Secs. 7–12, at 232–233.

It is possible that the code drafters intended subsection (a) as a liquidated damage clause available to a plaintiff-seller regardless of his actual damages. There have been some commentators who agree with this philosophy. [Citations omitted.] But, this construction is inconsistent with the code's basic philosophy, announced in Tex.Bus. & Com.Code Ann. Sec. 1.106(a) (Vernon), which provides "that the aggrieved party may be put in as good a position as if the other party had fully performed" but not in a better posture. * * * No one insists, and we do not think they could, that the difference between the fallen market price and the contract price is necessary to compensate the plaintiffs for the breach. Had the transaction been completed, their "benefit of the bargain" would not have been affected by the fall in market price, and they would not have experienced the windfall they otherwise would receive if the market price-contract price rule contained in Sec. 2.708(a) is followed. Thus the premise contained in Sec. 1.106 and Texas case law is a strong factor weighing against application of Sec. 2.708(a).

Our conclusion that the district court was correct in applying Sec. 2.708(b) brings us to the second issue—was it error for the district court to refuse to award the plaintiffs the additional $75,000, which they were required to pay when they lost their quantity discount?

We believe the trial court was correct in declining to award the plaintiffs the extra $75,000. Under Sec. 2.708(b), in addition to profit, the seller may recover "incidental damages" and "due allowance for costs reasonably incurred." The code does not provide for the recovery of consequential damages by a seller. Tex.Bus. & Com.Code Ann. Sec. 1.106(a) (Vernon); Petroleo Brasileiro, S.A. v. Ameropan Oil Corp., 372 F.Supp. 503, 508 (E.D.N.Y.1974); Cf. Tex.Bus. & Com.Code

Ann. Sec. 2.715 (Vernon) (buyer's remedies). "Incidental damages" are defined in Tex.Bus. & Com.Code Ann. Sec. 2.710 (Vernon) as "any commercially reasonable charges, expenses or commissions incurred in stopping delivery, in the transportation, care and custody of goods after the buyer's breach, in connection with return or resale of the goods or otherwise resulting from the breach." The draftsmen's comment to the section states that the purpose is to "authorize reimbursement of the seller for expenses reasonably incurred by him as a result of the buyer's breach." We think it is clear that Sec. 2.710 was intended to cover only those expenses contracted by the seller after the breach and occasioned by such things as the seller's need to care for, and, if necessary, dispose of the goods in a commercially reasonable manner. See, Guy H. James Construction Co. v. L.B. Foster Co., No. 17,473 (Tex.Civ.App.1979) (cost of replacing material in stock for resale recoverable as incidental damages).

* * *

QUESTIONS

1. Of what relevance is the sum that Nobs "expected" to make when it entered into the contract? Would giving it this sum be the same as expectation damages?

2. A careful reading of the case will suggest that Nobs was not contractually bound to purchase any fixed amount from the Brazilian supplier and had not yet acquired the cumene at the time of breach. If it had been able to perform on the contract, at what price do you think it would have been able to buy the necessary cumene?

3. Suppose that Nobs had already purchased the cumene for $400 per ton as originally contemplated and was holding it in inventory at the time of breach. What costs does it save if it does not have to deliver the cumene?

4. What is the "correct" recovery due to the plaintiff? Is it properly recoverable under subsection (a) of 2–708?

5. Could the plaintiff have plausibly argued that it had "purchased" the right to sell cumene at $540? What consideration did it give in exchange?

6. Does the court properly discuss the circumstances under which recourse to the second section of 2–708 is appropriate? See Goetz and Scott, "Measuring Sellers' Damages: The Lost Profits Puzzle," 31 Stanford L.Rev. 323 (1979).

CURT'S TRUCKING CO. v. CITY OF ANCHORAGE

Supreme Court of Alaska, 1978.
578 P.2d 975.

RABINOWITZ, Justice.

An overhead telephone cable belonging to the Anchorage Telephone Utility was severed when struck by the raised body of a dump truck operated by Gerald Curt on Minnesota Drive in Anchorage. The Anchorage Telephone Utility is a public utility owned by the City of Anchorage; and City employees repaired the damaged cable. The City then brought an action in superior court alleging that $45,349.23 in damages resulted from the negligence of Gerald R. Curt and Curt's Trucking Company.

The parties stipulated that Curt's Trucking was liable for the direct costs of repairing the damaged cable. The direct costs of material and labor amounted to $4,457.72. However, Curt's Trucking disputed the City's claim to an additional 20% for "overhead" and the trial in superior court was directed only to that issue.

The City introduced evidence indicating that its 20% overhead figure was derived from two separate sources: (1) general administrative overhead applicable to all reimbursable City services, comprising 13% of the 20% overhead figure, and (2) expenses incurred by the City's Risk Management Office in processing claims against third parties who damage City property. The superior court concluded that the entire 20% "overhead" charge should be allowed and awarded total damage in the amount of $5,349.23, i.e., $4,457.72 for direct costs of labor, materials and equipment plus $891.54 for indirect costs.

*   *   *

Curt's Trucking argues that the 13% charge for administrative expenses applicable to all reimbursable City services was not a proper element of damages because it is too remote or too speculative. Both parties have cited opinions of this court explaining that the general principle underlying the assessment of damages in tort cases is that an injured person is entitled to be placed as nearly as possible in the position he would have occupied had it not been for the defendant's tort. This principle also applies where the injured party performs the repairs itself. Many courts considering this problem have concluded that indirect expenses are proper items of damage and are not too remote or speculative when the evidence establishes a sufficient connection between the overhead expense and the necessary repairs.

In Baltimore and Ohio Railroad Co. v. Commercial Transport, Inc., 273 F.2d 447 (7th Cir. 1960), the court affirmed the inclusion of overhead in a damage award arising out of a collision between plaintiff's diesel locomotive and defendants' tractor-trailer. The railroad had applied various overhead percentages to its costs of materials and labor; the specific percentages had been taken from formulas established by 25 major railroads for use, in part, in billing each other for self-repair of their own track or equipment damaged by another railroad. The Seventh Circuit concluded that the reasonable cost of repairs made by the railroad's own employees should not be limited to the dollar amount actually paid workmen and suppliers because "[s]uch a limitation would ignore the facts of business life." The court also determined that the percentage formulas were properly submitted to the jury:

> On the basis of the facts adduced in the instant case as to the establishment of the percentage formulae contained in the Rules of the General Managers Association, and their long use and continued acceptance in the industry, we are of the opinion that the district court did not err in admitting the testimony and exhibit in question. This evidence was material and relevant in proof of plaintiff's damages. It is infrequent that damages are measurable with mathematical certainty or that a plaintiff can prove all elements from his own records or experience. The factors here employed and submitted for the jury's consideration were not designed to produce a profit. Methods accepted in everyday business affairs as fixing fair measures of value are not to be excluded from a jury's consideration in arriving at damages. [Idem.]

Other federal courts have also permitted recovery of properly calculated overhead expenses. In Bultema Dock & Dredge Co. v. Steamship David P. Thompson, 252 F.Supp. 881 (W.D.Mich.1966), plaintiff recovered overhead expenses in connection with repair of its underwater construction project, which had been struck by defendant's vessel. The district court explained, in part:

> Had it been necessary for an outside company to repair the damage, the cost of such repairs would include similar charges. There is no reason to free respondent of these costs simply because the injured party is in a position to make the repairs itself.

However, in Crain Brothers, Inc. v. Duquesne Slag Products Co., 273 F.2d 948, 952–53 (3d Cir. 1959), the Third Circuit explained that the reason a party which performs its own repairs may recover an amount including such overhead elements is that its actual loss would be the full amount charged by the independent contractor, as if it paid that amount out-of-pocket. Thus, where plaintiff has carried out the repairs itself, the losses and expenses actually incurred as a result of the accident should be included in a damage award. Costs which would have been recoverable had plaintiff hired someone else to do the work are a useful indicator of reasonable costs of repair only if plaintiff actually expends such an amount.

Although the state courts are not unanimous in awarding overhead expenses, many have concluded that such costs are properly included in damage awards. Courts permitting recovery generally have required plaintiffs to show that the claimed indirect costs were actually incurred and that the formula used to calculate overhead was accurate. Sufficient accuracy has been found where the overhead calculation was based on sound accounting principles; where the accounting methods used to allocate indirect expenses had been approved by government regulatory bodies; or where the formulas were widely accepted in plaintiff's trade or business as correct measures of overhead when self-repairs are performed.

We are persuaded that a party which repairs property tortiously damaged by another should be permitted to recover indirect expenses incurred in making such repairs if its calculation of overhead is shown to be a fair and reasonable measure of actual costs. A plaintiff need not identify the particular dollar amount of each overhead component which was expended in connection with specific direct costs; it is sufficient if reasonably accurate formula allocations or percentages are used to calculate the overhead. Whether such estimates are sufficiently accurate must be determined from all the facts and circumstances of the particular case.

In the case at bar, the City introduced the deposition of its internal auditor, Lawrence Campbell, a certified public accountant who explained how the 13% charge for administrative costs of reimbursable City services had been calculated. Campbell stated that the City performs a variety of services for which it recovers its costs. These services are known as "reimbursable City services," and they range from thawing water pipes for private citizens to maintaining streets for the state highway department. Included in "reimbursable City services" are repairs to property damaged by third parties. Campbell conducted a study and determined that the average overhead attributable to all City departments which perform reimbursable services was approximately 13%. * * *

Curt's Trucking called its own expert witness, Frederick M. Strand, a certified public acccountant who was present at the taking of Campbell's deposition. Strand observed that the 13% overhead figure had been computed in accordance with sound accounting principles. Curt's Trucking Company introduced no other evidence suggesting that the overhead figure was not an accurate measure of the indirect costs actually incurred in connection with repairing the damaged telephone cable.

As noted previously, we have determined that overhead expenses incurred by a party in repairing its damaged property are proper items of damages if such costs actually have been expended and have been allocated accurately to the repair work. In the case at bar, the superior court applied the correct principles of law in permitting recovery of these costs. In addition, the record contains nothing which indicates that the 13% overhead calculation was inaccurate. Thus, we conclude that the award of 13% of the direct costs was not clearly erroneous.

Curt's Trucking Company next asserts that the additional 7% charge representing expenses of the City's Risk Management Office are not proper items of damage because they are in the nature of costs incurred in preparing for litigation. The records shows that the 7% figure was derived in a different manner than the 13% charge associated with the cost of making repairs. The City's internal auditor, Lawrence Campbell, testified that his administrative cost study which established the 13% figure did not consider the Risk Management Department's expenses because the office had not yet been created. Both Campbell and Frederick Strand, the expert called by Curt's Trucking, stated that the functions presently performed by the Risk Management Office were formerly spread among the City's various departments. Thus, to the extent these activities were carried on by departments which performed reimbursable City services, the costs associated with claims preparation may have been reflected in the 13% overhead calculation. Edward Hite, head of the City's Risk Management Office, testified that to the extent claims processing occurred prior to creation of his position in 1973 it was conducted by personnel within the utility which had suffered damage. However, Hite stated that many of his office's functions had never been performed prior to 1973.

Hite also described the tasks of the Risk Management Office in some detail. According to Hite, his office collects information about the incident, takes statements of employees involved, coordinates with any police investigation, determines whether the other party was negligent, evaluates the validity of potential claims, consolidates possible claims of different departments arising out of the same incident, estimates damages or costs of repair, and sends the claim to an adjuster for collection or to the City's insurance company. Hite explained that the Risk Management Office does not send out investigators and rarely corresponds with the people who have damaged City property or with their insurors. On cross-examination, counsel for Curt's Trucking asked Hite what his office actually does with respect to a claim; Hite stated, in part:

> The same thing you as an individual would do if someone came along and smashed into your car. You're going to take that car down and get yourself an estimate on it. You may have to go to three different places. You're probably going to have to arrange for a rental car. You're going to sit down and try to figure out how much money you have been out and you're probably going to

end up arguing with an adjusting firm on how much money you have really got coming. And you're going to spend an hour or two and probably a lot of tears in trying to get your money. * * * Someone has come along and damaged our goodies and we're going to try to get our money back for the damage that is done. Someone from the municipal point of view has got to keep track of that money. Someone's got to keep track of who owes whom and what we're going to pay and why we're going to pay it. And if we don't, we're not handling your tax money right.

Even if the testimony could be understood as suggesting that some costs of preparing claims possibly were included in the 13% overhead figure as computed in 1971, we are not persuaded that the superior court's allowance of the full 13% was clearly erroneous. Both parties' accounting witnesses agreed that a 13% charge accurately reflected the indirect costs to the City of making repairs; no evidence was introduced to indicate the unrelated costs had been included. In addition, Campbell testified that his 1974 reevaluation of the 13% figure showed it was still accurate; in March, 1973 the City's risk manager had taken over claims processing functions which previously had been performed by the individual utilities.

* * *

QUESTIONS

1. Is all overhead fixed cost? What does it mean to require that "such costs actually have been expended and have been allocated accurately to the repair work"?

2. Should the treatment of "overhead" costs differ in any way because this is a tort and not a contractual relationship? Consider this issue also in regard to the *Lund* case immediately below which involves a criminal theft of services.

LUND v. COMMONWEALTH

Supreme Court of Virginia, 1977.
217 Va. 688, 232 S.E.2d 745.

Defendant, Charles Walter Lund, was charged in an indictment with the theft of keys, computer cards, computer print-outs and using "without authority computer operation time and services of Computer Center Personnel at Virginia Polytechnic and State University [V.P.I. or University] * * * with intent to defraud, such property and services having a value of one hundred dollars or more." Code Sec. 18.1–118 were referred to in the indictment as the applicable statutes.

* * *

The computer used by the defendant was leased on an annual basis by V.P.I. from the IBM Corporation. The rental was paid by V.P.I. which allocates the cost of the computer center to various departments within the University by charging it to the budget of that department. This is a bookkeeping entry, and no real money is involved. The departments are then issued "computer credits [in dollars] for their use [on] a proportional basis of their [budgetary] allotments." Each department manager receives a monthly statement showing the allotments used and the running balance in each account of his department.

An account is established when a duly authorized administrator or "department head" fills out a form allocating funds to a department of the University and an individual. When such form is received, the computer center assigns an account number to this allocation and provides a key to a locked post office box which is also numbered to the authorized individual and department. The account number and the post office box are the access code which must be provided with each request before the computer will process a "deck of cards" prepared by the user and delivered to computer center personnel. The computer print-outs are usually returned to the locked post office box.

Defendant came under surveillance on October 12, 1974, because of complaints from various departments that unauthorized charges were being made to one or more of their accounts. When confronted by the University's investigator, defendant initially denied that he had used the computer service, but later admitted that he had. He gave to the investigator seven keys for boxes assigned to other persons.

The director of the computer center testified that the unauthorized sum spent out of the accounts associated with the seven post office box keys, amounted to $5,065. He estimated that on the basis of the computer cards and print-outs obtained from the defendant, as much as $26,384.16 in unauthorized computer time had been used by the defendant. He said, however, that the value of the cards and print-outs obtained from the defendant was "whatever scrap paper is worth."

The defendant contends that his conviction of grand larceny of the keys, computer cards, and computer print-outs cannot be upheld under the provisions of Code Sec. 18.1–100 because (1) there was no evidence that the articles were stolen, or that they had a value of $100 or more, and (2) computer time and services are not the subject of larceny under the provisions of Code Secs. 18.1–100 or 18.1–118.

* * *

The Commonwealth concedes that the defendant could not be convicted of grand larceny of the keys and computer cards because there was no evidence that those articles were stolen and that they had a market value of $100 or more. The Commonwealth argues, however, that the evidence shows the defendant violated the provisions of Sec. 18.1–118 when he obtained by false pretense or token, with intent to defraud, the computer print-outs which had a value of over $5,000.

Under the provisions of Code Sec. 18.1–118, for one to be guilty of the crime of larceny by false pretense, he must make a false representation of an existing fact with knowledge of its falsity and, on that basis, obtain from another person money or other property which may be the subject of larceny, with the intent to defraud. See Hubbard v. Commonwealth, 201 Va. 61, 66, 109 S.E.2d 100, 104 (1959).

At common law, larceny is the taking and carrying away of the goods and chattels of another with intent to deprive the owner of the possession thereof permanently. Code Sec. 18.1–100 defines grand larceny as a taking from the person of another money or other thing of value of five dollars or more, or the taking not from the person of another goods and chattels of the value of $100 or more. The phrase "goods and chattels" cannot be interpreted to include computer time and services in light of the often repeated mandate that criminal statutes must be strictly construed. See Commonwealth v. McCray, 430 Pa. 130, 133, 242 A.2d 229, 230 (1968).

At common law, labor or services could not be the subject of the crime of false pretense because neither time nor services may be taken and carried away. It has been generally held that, in the absence of a clearly expressed legislative intent, labor or services could not be the subject of the statutory crime of false pretense. McCray, supra; 2 Wharton, Criminal Law and Procedure Sec. 604 at 369 (Anderson ed. 1957). Some jurisdictions have amended their criminal codes specifically to make it a crime to obtain labor or services by means of false pretense. We have no such provision in our statutes.

Furthermore, the unauthorized *use* of the computer is not the subject of larceny. Nowhere in Code Sec. 18.1–100 or Sec. 18.1–118 do we find the word "use." The language of the statutes connotes more than just the unauthorized use of the property of another. It refers to a taking and carrying away of a certain concrete article of personal property. See People v. Ashworth, 220 App.Div. 498, 222 N.Y.S. 24, 27 (1927). There it was held that the unauthorized *use* of machinery and spinning facilities of another to process wool did not constitute larceny under New York's false pretense statute.

We hold that labor and services and the unauthorized use of the University's computer cannot be construed to be subjects of larceny under the provisions of Code Secs. 18.1–100 and 18.1–118.

The Commonwealth argues that even though the computer print-outs had no market value, their value can be determined by the cost of the labor and services that produced them. We do not agree.

The cost of producing the print-outs is not the proper criterion of value for the purpose here. Where there is no market value of an article that has been stolen, the better rule is that its actual value should be proved. See 50 Am.Jur.2d, Larceny Sec. 45 at 211 and Sec. 148 at 329. Compare, Hancock v. State, 402 S.W.2d 906, 18 A.L.R.3d 1113 (Tex.Cr.App.1966), where the prosecution was based on a statute and there was evidence of the monetary value of the computer programs.

Here the evidence shows that the print-outs had no ascertainable monetary value to the University or the computer center. Indeed, the director of the computer center stated that the print-outs had no more value than scrap paper. Nor is there any evidence of their value to the defendant, and the value to him could only be based on pure speculation and surmise. Hence, the evidence was insufficient to convict the defendant of grand larceny under either Code Sec. 18.1–100 or Sec. 18.1–118.

For the reasons stated, the judgment of the trial court is reversed, and the indictment is quashed.

Note:

Following the decision in Lund supra, the Code of Virginia was amended as follows:

18.2–98.1. Computer time or services or data processing services or information or data stored in connection therewith is hereby defined to be property which may be the subject of larceny under Sec. 18.2–95 or 18.2–96 or embezzlement under Sec. 18.2–111, or false pretenses under Sec. 18.2–178.

QUESTIONS

1. Suppose that the defendant had stolen special purpose goods, such as an orthotic shoe device made by a podiatrist to a mold of defendant's foot and therefore of no use to anyone else. The materials of the device are about three dollars worth of plastic composition and an eighty-cent leather cover. Such devices are regularly sold by the podiatrist for $145. Defendant is charged with grand larceny under a state statute that requires a value of $100 or more for the goods illegally obtained. Would the fact that tangible goods are involved avoid the problem raised in Lund above? Does such an orthotic device involve both tangible goods and a service? If so, how are the values to be separated for purposes of the minimum valuation called for in the statute?

2. Is the Lund court correct in rejecting cost of production as an index of value? If cost of production were to be used, what elements (e.g., pro rata share of computer rental charges paid by university, labor of computer center personnel, etc.) should be included in the cost?

3. If "cost" to the University is construed as how much worse off it was made by not being able to exclude Lund from obtaining services illicitly, then what was the cost of the services taken?

4. At various times of the year, such as the ends of terms, most University computer facilities become overwhelmed with excess demand for the limited amount of processing time available on the system. This results in long waiting times, sometimes as long as several days, between the submission of a "job" and the reception of finished output. Assume that a significant portion of Lund's use occurred during such periods. What "costs" did he impose? Could they be quantified in any way? Do such costs have any legal relevance? If not, should they?

ADJUSTMENT OF A COMPETITIVE INDUSTRY

Up to this point, we have dealt exclusively in terms of the adjustments made by single decisionmakers or small groups; there has been no attempt to aggregate the behavior of individuals into "market" results. This section takes up the manner in which individual firms' decisions are translated into market prices and aggregate supply of a product. The treatment here is sketchy since the behavior of markets is the principal topic of traditional economics books, many of which deal with the subject very elegantly and in great detail. The material supplied below is, however, designed to provide the essential "flavor" of the process of market adjustment.

We present the traditional textbook case of a competitive market. The firms in this industry produce a homogeneous product and are "price-takers," i.e., *respond* to market prices but do not individually have the power to *set* prices. The indirect manner in which individual firms affect prices will be illustrated through a problem that has been used in economics classes for many years.

The problem is loosely based on a simple model of competitive market adjustment attributed to Professor Henry Simons. This model is explicitly a pedagogical one and, in order to maintain its simplicity, necessarily incorporates certain artificialities. Anyone who has reason to understand the process of market adjustments should nevertheless take the time to work through an exercise of this type at least once.

FACTS. At the beginning of the period under analysis, the industry which produces "standprods" (which are perfectly standarized goods) contains exactly 500 firms, each of which operates only a single plant. The per-period cost of producing standprods consists of "overhead" costs of $100 imputable to the plant itself, plus certain variable or "operating" costs imputable to different levels of output. The costs are identical for each firm and are the same as indicated above in Exhibit 6.1 used for the buyers' breach hypothetical problem.

The type of plant being used deteriorates completely in 500 weeks, regardless of how much it is used. At the beginning of the scenario, there is a uniform distribution of plant ages, i.e., one plant one week old, one plant two weeks old, etc. Plant construction takes ten weeks and, once initiated, is an irreversible process. Hence, there are initially 10 replacement plants "in process" which cannot be cancelled.

The demand curve faced by the industry can be represented by the equation price $= 65 - (Q/170)$ where Q is total industry output. This implies that price will fall a little more than half a cent for every unit produced. *But*, the number of competitors is sufficiently great that no single producer feels that his own output will affect price at all.

PART I. INITIAL EQUILIBRIUM STATE

a. Fill in any remaining blank columns of Exhibit 6.1. Using graph paper, plot the approximate shapes of the marginal cost, average variable cost, and average total cost curves as Exhibit 6.2.[1] (The abbreviations MC, AVC, and ATC are commonly used.)

b. Using a smaller scale than for Exhibit 6.2,[2] construct Exhibit 6.3 to show the supply curve of the present 500-firm industry. This will be the horizontal sum of each firm's marginal cost curve, *except* for the part of MC which lies below the AVC curve. [Why?] Superimpose the industry's demand curve onto Exhibit 6.3 and ascertain the equilibrium price where the supply and demand curves intersect. Why is this an "equilibrium" price? What will happen at a higher or lower price?

---

1. In order to facilitate the creation of a convenient format for the plot, do not plot the values less than 5. Also, you should assume that the maximum vertical ordinate necessary will be 32 and the maximum horizontal value will be 24. A correctly plotted Exhibit 6.2 is attached as Exhibit 6.2A in the Appendix to this chapter, but you are urged to attempt your own construction before looking at it.

2. A convenient format for Exhibit 6.3 will involve vertical (price) values in the range from 7 to 24 and horizontal (output supplied or quantity demanded) values between 4,000 and 13,000. An accurate version of Exhibit 6.3 is supplied as Exhibit 6.3A in the Appendix to this chapter.

EXHIBIT 6.2

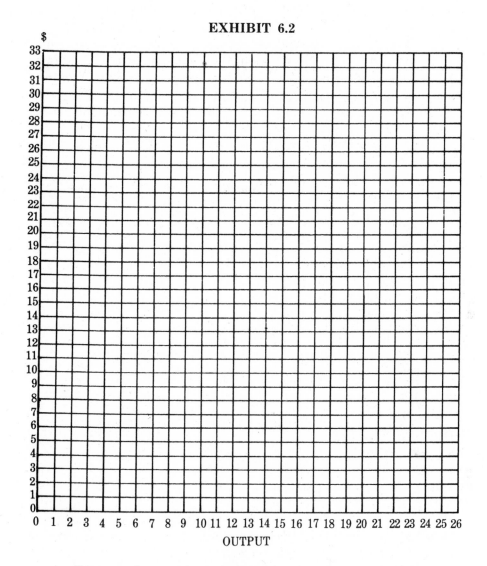

c. Suppose the world rolls on with the original situation basically unchanged. Will there be any tendency for changes to occur in price, the number of firms, etc.? Why?

PART II. DISPLACEMENT AND SHORT–RUN EQUILIBRIUM

Evidence is presented to Congress that the use of standprods causes significant environmental damage. A statute is subsequently passed requiring that standprods be rendered "environmentally harmless." Fortuitously, the AZD Corporation reveals that it has a patented process which will eliminate the environmental damages otherwise produced due to the use of standprods. The process in question is essentially a clever improvement in fabrication technique and does not in any way change the real resource costs of production. After estimating the market value of the technique, AZD Corporation fixes a $4 per standprod royalty for the use of its patented process.

    a.   Other than what is in effect a legal requirement to use the AZD process, no other changes in the conditions facing the industry

EXHIBIT 6.3

 = Demand Curve

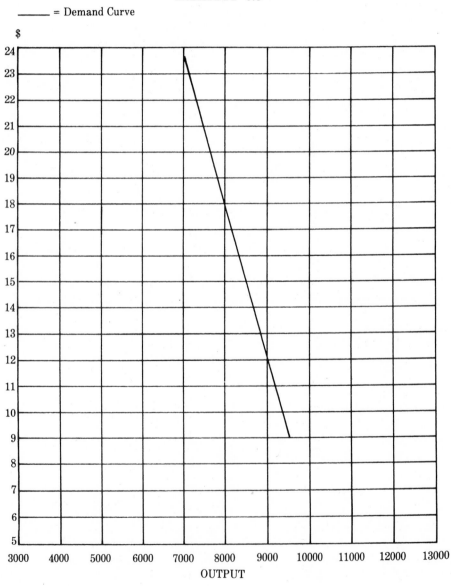

occur. Fill in Exhibit 6.4 as the revised version of Exhibit 6.1, reflecting the cost of the royalty for using the AZD process.

b. Add to Exhibit 6.2, in red or some distinctive manner, the new cost curves for a firm, based on Exhibit 6.4.

c. Add to Exhibit 6.3 the *new* industry supply curve and determine the new (short-run) equilibrium price immediately after imposition of the necessity to use the AZD process.

d. What is your answer now to the same question as asked in Part I-c above?

EXHIBIT 6.4 Cost to Firm Paying AZD Royalty

Output	Variable Cost	Total Cost	AVC	ATC	MC
0	NA	100	NA	NA	NA
1					
2					
3					
4					
5					
6					
7					
8					
9					
10					
11					
12					
13					
14					
15					
16					
17					
18					
19					
20					
21					
22					
23					
24					

PART III.   PROGRESS TOWARD NEW EQUILIBRIUM

a.   When (after how many weeks) will firms begin to leave the industry? Why? Draw the industry supply curve and determine the price when the time elapsed after enactment of the new law is 10 weeks, 30 weeks, 50 weeks. Why would these prices be regarded as only *short run* equilibrium prices"? Draw the short run supply curve that would exist if firms kept exiting for 70 weeks. How many firms would there be? *Would* firms keep leaving for 70 weeks? Why?

b.   What is happening to the output of a *single firm* as the short-run equilibrium price adjusts?

c   When do firms stop leaving and things "settle down" to a long run equilibrium? What makes this an "equilibrium"?

PART IV.   ADDITIONAL IMPLICATIONS

After the industry has reached a new long-run equilibrium it is revealed by a *Washington Pillar-and-Post* investigative reporter that AZD's patent was fraudulently obtained and is certainly invalid. Assuming this to be the case, AZD may be liable for treble damages under the antitrust statutes.

a.   Who should have the cause of action to sue? The standprods producers? The standprods consumers? Someone else? Explain the implications of the relevant alternatives. At this point, try not to be influenced in your response by what you know about the present stance of the courts in cases such as *Hanover Shoe, Inc. v. United Shoe Machinery Corp.*, 392 U.S. 481, 88 S.Ct. 2224, 20 L.Ed.2d 1231 (1968) and *Illinois Brick Co. v. Illinois*, 431 U.S. 720, 97 S.Ct. 2061, 52 L.Ed.2d 707 (1977). These cases are presented below. You may wish to reassess your answer after reading them.

b.   Suppose that ultimate consumers of standprods (the indirect users of AZD process) are to be plaintiffs. What is the measure of their damages? In what way, if at all, do such damages differ from those that a producer might ask if he were the antitrust plaintiff?

A SIMPLE MATHEMATICAL MODEL [OPTIONAL]

This is an optional section. Readers who are absolutely appalled by the slightest use of mathematics may wish to skip this section. Indeed, those who will be more confused than enlightened by the mathematical formulation can be assured that the results of this section are not crucial to what follows. On the other hand, the modest effort necessary to read this material will be well repaid in terms of increased understanding for many people, especially those who have never studied any type of mathematical economic model.

Even a vague recollection of 9th grade elementary algebra will suffice to follow the rudimentary methematical model of a competitive market about to be presented. Indeed, this model will be merely a translation into simple algebra of the graphical version of the Henry Simons model already discussed above.

Recall that the facts of the Simons model contained a stipulation of the market demand curve in the form of an equation:

[1] $P = 65 - (1/170)Q$

where P is the maximum market price that consumers will pay if Q units are to be sold. Since this relationship is really the equation of the *demand curve*, the Q should be identified as quantity *demanded* by appending an identifying subscript *d*. Then we can merely manipulate equation [1] in order to yield its more useful form:

[1a] $Q_d = 170 (65 - p)$

Equation [1a] says that quantity demanded, Q_d, is inversely related to price.

Now we need to model the supply side of the market. We know that each individual firm will produce out to the quantity where marginal cost equals the marginal revenue it receives. For competitive firms, price equals marginal revenue, so that the profit-maximizing output of a single firm will be where MC = P. In the relevant range of outputs (where price exceeds average variable cost), the behavior of marginal cost can be summarized by the following equation:

[2] $MC = k + q$

where the lowercase q is the single firm's output. The parameter k is equal to –2 in the situation before the AZD royalty fee was necessitated; i.e., MC = –2 + q. If the marginal costs are affected by the \$4 royalty fee, they become MC = –2 + 4 + q, so that k would then be (–2 + 4) or +2. If we wish to identify the profit-maximizing q, we must set MC = P by substituting the solution for MC from [2]

$$k + q = P$$

and then solving for q on the left:

[3] $q = P - k$

Since we are working with a simple "identical firms" model, the industry supply is the quantity supplied by any individual firm multiplied by the number of firms operating:

[4] $Q_s = nq$

where Q_s is the quantity supplied. We can also substitute equation [3] for the q term in equation [4], yielding

[4a] $Q_s = n (P-k)$

so that [4a] represents a short-run "supply curve" of the kind used in the graphical models.

Now the demand and supply relations can be put together to express the industry equilibrium condition that price must adjust until consumers desire to buy exactly the quantity supplied:

[5] $Q_d = Q_s$

Of course, it will be necessary to substitute the demand curve and supply curve equations derived in [1a] and [4a] for Q_d and Q_s, respectively, in order to solve for the equilibrium value of the price P. That substitution yields:

[5a] $n(P - k) = 170 (65 - P)$

as the equilibrium condition of the market. Finally, solving for P,[1] we have the "solution" of the model in terms of an equilibrium price:

[6] $P = (11050 + nk) / (n + 170)$.

By substituting $+2$ for K, as indicated for the with-fee situation, we can use equation [6] to follow the market adjustment process.

It would be desirable to express the number of firms, n, in terms of the time period involved. Thus, for the first week $t = 1$, for the second week, $t = 2$, etc. Because 10 new plants have irrevocably been ordered, $n = 500$ for the first ten weeks after the AZD fee is imposed. After that, n will decrease by one for each week as long as price remains lower than average total cost for the producers. Hence, from week eleven until a new equilibrium is established, n will be representable as $500 - (t - 10)$, or $n = 500 - t + 10$. What will be the situation in week 12, for instance? If we substitute the right values for k and n in equation [6] above, we will have:

$$P = [11050 + 499(2)] / (499 + 170)$$
$$P = 12040 / 669 = \$18.00.$$

At an $18 price, what will a single firm's output be? The answer can be gained from equation [3] above.

The model just created can be used to address the issue of when a new equilibrium will occur. In essence, this question really asks how many firms must enter or leave in order for price to become exactly equal to the *minimum* average total cost (ATC) of production for an individual firm. Do you understand why? Those interested in doing so may attempt to formulate this question as an algebraic equilibrium condition. [Hint: In the relevant range of outputs, Total Cost = Fixed Cost + 32.875 + $.5(q + 2.5)^2$.] Those less interested in such

1. Here, in some detail for those whose algebra is rusty, are the series of intermediate steps that might be followed in getting from [5a] to [6]:

$n(P - k) = 170(65) - 170P$
$nP - nk = 11050 - 170P$

$nP + 170P = 11050 + nk$
$P(n + 170) = 11050 + nk$
and thence to the result in the text.

an exercise should at least examine Exhibit 6.4b below and attempt to understand how it is possible to fill in the blanks. This exhibit uses the simple model just developed, together with the original facts of the Simons problem, to indicate the values of critical market parameters at various numbers of weeks after the AZD fee was imposed.

EXHIBIT 6.4b　Solutions of Market Model

Week	Firms	Firm Output	Firm Profit
11	499	16.0	_____
31	479	16.5	_____
50	460	_____	_____

Note that Exhibit 6.4b demonstrates the possibility that output solutions (for q in equation [3]) may take on non-integer values. Is there any interpretation of the original cost data that could make sense out of fractional outputs? Or must these models impose an additional mathematical condition that the solutions be integers?

BANKRUPTCY LAWS AND FIXED COSTS

There is a famous "quotation" that economists are fond of giving as a "comment" question on economic theory exams:

Economists are crazy. Obviously, recovering fixed costs is very important and necessary to businessmen. Economists, though, say that in the short run fixed costs don't matter and in the long run they don't exist.

The position attributed to economists is not so crazy at all, of course, as long as one understands costs in the opportunity cost sense. Past decisions to which one is irrevocably committed may require outlays, but they can never represent opportunity costs imputable to current activities.

There is, nevertheless, at least one important respect in which it would be incorrect to say that fixed costs do not matter at all. Fixed costs are often legal obligations to third parties. If the firm is unable to pay such obligations, judgments may be secured against it, attaching its working capital, physical assets, inventory, etc. Even though the firm would, through continued operation, be able to pay all *future* costs, it may be put out of business through its inability to satisfy creditors who have covered past costs. Bankruptcy laws play an important role in coping with this situation. Consider, for instance, the following scenario, one whose facts should have a familiar ring.

Universal Standprods, Inc., has just brought on line a new physical plant financed by a loan from Westhamden Guaranty & Trust and secured by a first mortgage on the building used for standprod production. Machinery in the plant was financed by various unsecured loans from five other financial institutions. A three month inventory of the raw materials and chemicals used in the production process is stored in Universal's factory warehouse. Most of this inventory was acquired from suppliers on 60 to 90-day open book credit. Standprods had been selling until last month at a price of $15, an amount exactly sufficient to provide Universal with the cashflow necessary to cover its costs and provide a normal return on equity capital. Unfortunately, a new EPA regulation has just increased unit costs by $4.00. Market price has risen in reaction, but is hovering around the $18 level. At any price below $19, Universal will have insufficient cash flow to cover production costs and the payments on its obligations to creditors. Universal has only a very small amount of liquid assets. It does possess wholly-owned standprod metering equipment purchased new for $500,000 shortly before the EPA regulation was announced. Creditors are beginning to become very nervous, since it appears that the present discounted value of Universal's liabilities exceeds that of its expected operating income.

QUESTIONS

1. Do you think the metering equipment could be sold for anything near its $500,000 cost? What factors determine its current value?

2. Under what circumstances could it be said that the creditors are in a difficult Prisoner's Dilemma? (Be as specific as possible in explaining the dilemma, using the concept of expected value where appropriate.) How do bankruptcy laws respond to this situation?

3. Who is made better or worse off by bankruptcy laws?

INCIDENCE ANALYSIS: SHIFTING AND PASSING ON

As presented above, the simple graphical and mathematical models of a competitive market demonstrate an interesting point: a cost initially levied on producers turns out, after the passage of some time for adjustment, to be "shifted" entirely to consumers. The tracing out of this process in an attempt to discover the ultimate consequences of a market change is called incidence analysis. Traditionally, incidence analysis has been used by economists primarily to investigate the burdens imposed by various forms of taxes. The same analytic principles are, however, applicable to other kinds of costs and benefits, notably including those created by the legal system.

If it were always the case that costs are ultimately shifted 100% to the consumer of the affected product, the world would be a simpler place. In that respect, however, the models used above are based upon an assumption that will not always be satisfied in the real world.

In order to understand what actuates—and limits—shifting, one needs to understand the fundamental equilibrium conditions of competitive markets. Two time periods are relevant. In what is called the "short run," the firm is "stuck" in the industry and outlays on so-called fixed costs are not economically relevant. Subject to the proviso that average variable costs are covered, the single firm's "supply curve" is its marginal cost curve and the market supply curve is the aggregation of the single-firm supply curves. When cost variations cause the firms' marginal cost curves to shift upward or downward, the effect is directly translated into a shift of the short run market supply curve, and therefore a change in price.

In what is called the "long run," firms are free to exit from or enter the industry. The actuating principle here is the relationship between price and average total cost. If price is greater than average total cost, a firm can do *better* in the industry than anywhere else, thus motivating new entrants whose increased supply will move price downward. If price is less than average cost, exit will take place, supply will fall, and price will start to rise. Equilibrium exists when price is exactly equal to average total cost. (Remember that cost is in terms of opportunity cost, so that when revenues and costs are equal the firm is doing just as well in the present industry as in the next best opportunity.) In sum, long-run equilibrium requires that price rise or fall, as may be required, to the level of average total cost.

In our earlier models, the average cost curves of the firms were assumed to be affected only by the change in the royalty fee. Obviously, then, price would in the long run have to track the fee variations exactly. The long run supply curve would be a horizontal line at the level of the low point on the ATC curve; at that price, firms will enter without limit to accommodate demand, while at any lower price nobody will continue to produce in the long run.

But what if the cost curves of the individual firms were also affected by the volume of output produced by the industry? For instance, as industry output expands, certain inputs may become scarce or have to be lured away from other uses. As the best inputs become fully employed, recourse to inferior inputs may be necessary. Such conditions would mean that costs to the individual firm will shift upward as industry output grows and, similarly, decline when it contracts. Graphically, this condition would be manifested by an upward sloping long-run supply curve. The degree of the slope depends on the strength of the scarcity factor as industry output fluctuates. A high slope of the supply curve is likely to be associated with the use of specialized inputs in an industry; when the industry output expands, these inputs can command a scarcity premium, but when output declines, their very specialization causes them to accept lower returns rather than shift to some other use or employment.

Of course, the degree to which industry output does expand or contract is in part determined by the *demand* conditions. If the slope of the demand curve is relatively flat, it means that consumers will adjust to any supply cutback principally by switching to some other form of consumption rather than raising their bids for the product and hence its price.

In sum, the incidence of a change in market conditions depends on the relative slopes of the demand and supply curves. In turn, the slopes of these curves depend upon the substitutability of other goods for consumers and the mobility of productive inputs, respectively. In general, we might expect that part of a cost increase will be passed on to consumers and some part may also be borne by the producing sector. Unfortunately, the relative degrees of incidence borne by particular parties is strictly an empirical question. For a more detailed discussion of the theory and practice of incidence analysis, see any standard public finance textbook.

The difficulty of doing accurate incidence analysis is an issue that troubles the Supreme Court in the following cases.

HANOVER SHOE, INC. v. UNITED SHOE MACHINERY CORP.

Supreme Court of the United States, 1968.
392 U.S. 481, 88 S.Ct. 2224, 20 L.Ed.2d 1231.

Mr. Justice WHITE delivered the opinion of the Court.

Hanover Shoe, Inc. (hereafter Hanover) is a manufacturer of shoes and a customer of United Shoe Machinery Corporation (hereafter United), a manufacturer and distributor of shoe machinery.

* * *

Hanover's action against United alleged that United had monopolized the shoe machinery industry in violation of Sec. 2 of the Sherman Act; that United's practice of leasing and refusing to sell its more complicated and important shoe machinery had been an instrument of the unlawful monopolization; and that therefore Hanover should recover from United the difference between what it paid United in shoe machine rentals and what it would have paid had United been willing during the relevant period to sell those machines.

* * *

The District Court found that Hanover would have bought rather than leased from United had it been given the opportunity to do so. The District Court determined that if United had sold its important machines, the cost to Hanover would have been less than the rental paid for leasing these same machines. This difference in cost, trebled, is the judgment awarded to Hanover in the District Court. United claims, however, that Hanover suffered no legally cognizable injury, contending that the illegal overcharge during the damage period was reflected in the price charged for shoes sold by Hanover to its customers and that Hanover, if it had bought machines at lower prices, would have charged less and made no more profit than it made by leasing. At the very least, United urges, the District Court, rejected this assertion of the so-called "passing-on" defense, and we affirm that judgment.

*   *   *

If in the face of the overcharge the buyer does nothing and absorbs the loss, he is entitled to treble damages. This much seems conceded. The reason is that he has paid more than he should and his property has been illegally diminished, for had the price paid been lower his profits would have been higher. It is also clear that if the buyer, responding to the illegal price, maintains his own price but takes steps to increase his volume or to decrease other costs, his right to damages is not destroyed. Though he may manage to maintain his profit level, he would have made more if his purchases from the defendant had cost him less. We hold that the buyer is equally entitled to damages if he raises the price for his own product. As long as the seller continues to charge the illegal price, he takes from the buyer more than the law allows. At whatever price the buyer sells, the price he pays the seller remains illegally high, and his profits would be greater were his costs lower.

*   *   *

*   *   * The rule, United argues, should be the subject to the defense that economic circumstances were such that the overcharged buyer could only charge his customers a higher price because the price to him was higher. It is argued that in such circumstances the buyer suffers no loss from the overcharge. This situation might be present, it is said, where the overcharge is imposed equally on all of a buyer's competitors and where the demand for the buyer's product is so inelastic that the buyer and his competitors could all increase their prices by the amount of the cost increase without suffering a consequent decline in sales.

We are not impressed with the argument that sound laws of economics require recognizing this defense. A wide range of factors influence a company's pricing policies. Normally the impact of a single change in the relevant conditions cannot be measured after the fact; indeed a businessman may be unable to state whether, had one fact been different (a single supply less expensive, general economic conditions more buoyant, or the labor market tighter, for example), he would have chosen a different price. Equally difficult to determine, in the real economic world rather than an economist's hypothetical model, is what effect a change in a company's price will have on its total sales. Finally, costs per unit for a different volume of total sales are hard to estimate. Even if it could be shown that the buyer raised his price in response to, and in the amount of, the overcharge and that his margin of profit and total sales had not thereafter declined, there would remain the nearly insuperable difficulty of demonstrating that the particular plaintiff could not or would not have raised his prices absent the overcharge or maintained the higher price had the overcharge been discontinued. Since establishing the applicability of the passing-on defense would require a convincing showing of each of these virtually unascertainable figures, the task would normally provide insurmountable. On the other hand, it is not unlikely that if the existence of the defense is generally confirmed, antitrust defendants will frequently seek to establish its applicability. Treble-damage actions would often require additional long and complicated proceedings involving massive evidence and complicated theories.

In addition, if buyers are subjected to the passing-on defense, those who buy from them would have to meet the challenge that they passed on the higher price to their customers. These ultimate consumers, in today's case the buyer of single pairs of shoes, would have only a tiny stake in a lawsuit and little interest in attempting a class action. In consequence, those who violate the antitrust laws by price fixing or monopolizing would retain the fruits of their illegality because no one was available who would bring suit against them.

*   *   *

  *   *   * We recognize that there might be situations—for instance, when an overcharged buyer has a pre-existing "cost-plus" contract, thus making it easy to prove that he has not been damaged—where the considerations requiring that the passing-on defense would not be permitted in this case would not be present. We also recognize that where no differential can be proved between the price unlawfully charged and some price that the seller was required by law to charge, establishing damages might require a showing of loss or profits to the buyer.

*   *   *

ILLINOIS BRICK CO. v. ILLINOIS

Supreme Court of the United States, 1977.
431 U.S. 720, 97 S.Ct. 2061, 52 L.Ed.2d 707.

[Suppliers of concrete block in Illinois pleaded *nolo contendere* to an indictment charging them with price-fixing. When a number of private suits were subsequently filed, the suppliers settled out of court with all of the contractors who had directly purchased the block. There were, however, also other suits by indirect purchasers, such as the purchasers of the buildings that the contractors had constructed.   The Court of Appeals held that these indirect purchasers could recover for any of their provable damages.]

Mr. Justice WHITE delivered the opinion of the Court.

* * *

The parties in this case agree that however Sec. 4 is construed with respect to the pass-on issue, the rule should apply equally to plaintiffs and defendants—that an indirect purchaser should not be allowed to use a pass-on theory to recover damages from a defendant unless the defendant would be allowed to use a pass-on defense in a suit by a direct purchaser.   Respondents, in arguing that they should be allowed to recover by showing pass-on in this case, have conceded that petitioners should be allowed to assert a pass-on defense against direct purchasers of concrete block; they ask this Court to limit *Hanover Shoe's* bar on pass-on defenses to its "particular factual context" of overcharges for capital goods used to manufacture new products.

Before turning to this request to limit *Hanover Shoe*, we consider the substantially contrary position, adopted by our dissenting Brethren, by the United States as *amicus curiae*, and by lower courts that have allowed offensive use of pass-on, that the unavailability of a pass-on theory to a defendant should not necessarily preclude its use by plaintiffs seeking treble damages against that defendant.   Under this view, *Hanover Shoe's* rejection of pass-on would continue to apply to defendants unless direct and indirect purchasers were both suing the defendant in the same action, but it would not bar indirect purchasers from attempting to show that the overcharge had been passed on to them.   We reject this position for two reasons.

First, allowing offensive but not defensive use of pass-on would create a serious risk of multiple liability for defendants.   Even though an indirect purchaser had already recovered for all or part of an overcharge passed on to it, the direct purchaser would still recover automatically the full amount of the overcharge that the indirect purchaser had shown to be passed-on; similarly, following an automatic recovery of the full overcharge by the direct purchaser, the indirect purchaser could sue to recover the same amount.   The risk of duplicative recoveries created by unequal application of the *Hanover Shoe* rule is much more substantial than in the more usual situation where the defendant is sued in two different lawsuits by plaintiffs asserting conflicting claims to the same fund.   A one-sided application of *Hanover Shoe* substantially increases the possibility of inconsistent adjudications—and therefore of unwarranted multiple liability for the defendant—by *presuming* that one plaintiff (the direct purchaser) is entitled to full recovery while preventing the defendant from using that presumption against the other plaintiff; overlapping recoveries are certain to result from the two lawsuits unless the indirect purchaser is unable to establish any pass-on whatsoever. As in Hawaii v. Standard Oil Co., we are unwilling to "open the door to duplicative recoveries" under Sec. 4.

Second, the reasoning of *Hanover Shoe* cannot justify unequal treatment of plaintiffs and defendants with respect to the permissibility of pass-on arguments. The principal basis for the decision in *Hanover Shoe* was the Court's perception of the uncertainties and difficulties in analyzing price and out-put decisions "in the real economic world rather than an economists' hypothetical model," and on the costs to the judicial system and the efficient enforcement of the antitrust laws of attempting to reconstruct those decisions in the courtroom. This perception that the attempt to trace the complex economic adjustments to a change in the cost of a particular factor of production would greatly complicate and reduce the effectiveness of already protracted treble-damage proceedings applies with no less force to the assertion of pass-on theories by plaintiffs than to the assertion by defendants. However, "long and complicated" the proceedings would be when defendants sought to prove pass-on, they would be equally so when the same evidence was introduced by plaintiffs. Indeed, the evidentiary complexities and uncertainties involved in the defensive use of pass-on against a direct purchaser are multiplied in the offensive use of pass-on by a plaintiff several steps removed from the defendant in the chain of distribution. The demonstration of how much of the overcharge was passed on by the first purchaser must be repeated at each point at which the price-fixed goods changed hands before they reached the plaintiff.

It is argued, however, that *Hanover Shoe* rests on a policy of ensuring that a treble-damage plaintiff is available to deprive antitrust violators of "the fruits of their illegality," a policy that would be furthered by allowing plaintiffs but not defendants to use pass-on theories. We do not read the Court's concern in *Hanover Shoe* for the effectiveness of the treble-damage remedy as countenancing unequal application of the Court's pass-on rule. Rather, we understand *Hanover Shoe* as resting on the judgement that the antitrust laws will be more effectively enforced by concentrating the full recovery for the overcharge in the direct purchasers than by allowing every plaintiff potentially affected by the overcharge to sue only for the amount it could show was absorbed by it.

* * *

Permitting the use of pass-on theories under Sec. 4 essentially would transform treble-damage actions into massive efforts to apportion the recovery among all potential plaintiffs that could have absorbed part of the overcharge—from direct purchasers to middlemen to ultimate consumers. However appealing this attempt to allocate the overcharge might seem in theory, it would add whole new dimensions of complexity to treble-damage suits and seriously undermine their effectiveness.

As we have indicated, potential plaintiffs at each level in the distribution chain are in a position to assert conflicting claims to a common fund—the amount of the alleged overcharge—by contending that the entire overcharge was absorbed at that particular level in the chain. A treble-damage action brought by one of these potential plaintiffs (or one class of potential plaintiffs) to recover the overcharge implicates all three of the interests that have traditionally been thought to support compulsory joinder of absent and potentially adverse claimants: the interest of the defendant in avoiding multiple liability for the fund; the interest of the absent potential plaintiffs in protecting their right to recover for the portion of the fund allocable to them; and the social interest in the efficient administration of justice and the avoidance of multiple litigation.

Opponents of the *Hanover Shoe* rule have recognized this need for compulsory joinder in suggesting that the defendant could interplead potential claimants under 28 U.S.C.A. Sec. 1335. But if the defendant, for any of a variety of reasons, does not choose to interplead the absent potential claimants, there would be a strong argument for joining them as "persons needed for just adjudication" under Fed. Rule Civ.Proc. 19(a).

*   *   *

It is unlikely, of course, that all potential plaintiffs could or would be joined. Some may not wish to assert claims to the overcharge; others may be unmanageable as a class; and still others may be beyond the personal jurisdiction of the court. We can assume that ordinarily the action would still proceed, the absent parties not being deemed "indispensable" under Fed. Rule Civ.Proc. 19(b). But allowing indirect purchasers to recover using pass-on theories, even under the optimistic assumption that joinder of potential plaintiffs will deal satisfactorily with problems of multiple litigation and liability, would transform treble-damage actions into massive multiparty litigations involving many levels of distribution and including large classes of ultimate consumers remote from the defendant. In treble-damage actions by ultimate consumers, the overcharge would have to be apportioned among the relevant wholesalers, retailers, and other middlemen, whose representatives presumably should be joined. And in suits by direct purchasers or middlemen, the interests of ultimate consumers are similarly implicated.

There is thus a strong possibility that indirect purchasers remote from the defendant would be parties to virtually every treble-damage action (apart from those brought against defendants at the retail level). The Court's concern in *Hanover Shoe* to avoid weighing down treble-damage actions with the "massive evidence and complicated theories," involved in attempting to establish a pass-on defense against a direct purchaser applies *a fortiori* to the attempt to trace the effect of the overcharge through each step in the distribution chain from the direct purchaser to the ultimate consumer. We are no more inclined than we were in *Hanover Shoe* to ignore the burdens that such an attempt would impose on the effective enforcement of the antitrust laws.

Under an array of simplifying assumptions, economic theory provides a precise formula for calculating how the overcharge is distributed between the overcharged party (passer) and its customers (passees). *If* the market for the passer's product is perfectly competitive; *if* the overcharge is imposed equally on all of the passer's competitors; and *if* the passer maximizes its profits, then the ratio of the shares of the overcharge borne by passee and passer will equal the ratio of the elasticities of supply and demand in the market for the passer's product. Even if these assumptions are accepted, there remains a serious problem of measuring the relevant elasticities—the percentage change in the quantities of the passer's product demanded and supplied in response to a one percent change in price. In view of the difficulties that have been encountered, even in informal adversary proceedings, with the statistical techniques used to estimate these concepts, it is unrealistic to think that elasticity studies introduced by expert witnesses will resolve the pass-on issue.

* * *

It is quite true that these difficulties and uncertainties will be less substantial in some contexts than in others. There have been many proposals to allow pass-on theories in some of these contexts while preserving the *Hanover Shoe* rule in others.

* * *

We reject these attempts to carve out exceptions to the *Hanover Shoe* rule for particular types of markets. An exception allowing evidence of pass-on by middlemen that resell the goods they purchase of course would be of no avail to respondents, because the contractors that allegedly passed on the overcharge on the block incorporated it into buildings. An exception for the contractors here on the ground that they purport to charge a fixed percentage above their costs would substantially erode the *Hanover Shoe* rule without justification. Firms in many sectors of the economy rely to an extent on cost-based rules of thumb in setting prices. These rules are not adhered to rigidly, however; the extent of the markup (or the allocation of costs) is varied to reflect demand conditions. The intricacies of tracing the effect of an overcharge on the purchaser's prices, costs, sales and profits thus are not spared the litigants.

More generally, the process of classifying various market situations according to the amount of pass-on likely to be involved and its susceptibility to proof in a judicial forum would entail the very problems that the *Hanover Shoe* rule was meant to avoid. The litigation over where the line should be drawn in a particular class of cases would inject the same "massive evidence and complicated theories" into treble-damage proceedings, albeit at a somewhat higher level of generality. *Hanover Shoe* itself implicitly discouraged the creation of exceptions to its rule barring pass-on defenses, and we adhere to the narrow scope of exemption indicated by our decision there.

*   *   *

QUESTIONS

1. For the simple case of the "standprod" industry given earlier in the chapter, review who are the injured parties and what is the quantum of their damages. In the real world, which of the facts would be difficult to know, and how would they affect the damage calculations?

2. Recall that the standprod hypothetical depicts a "constant cost" industry, the cost of whose product is not affected by the magnitude of industry output. How would the presence of scarce or specialized inputs complicate matters?

3. The *Illinois Brick* rule substantially undercuts the compensatory function of antitrust damages, does it not? What about the deterrent function? Does a party who has not really been injured have enough incentive to sue?

4. Are direct purchasers more likely to be able to detect and prove the violation? Does a fragmentation of the recoveries—as might occur when indirect purchasers must sue—affect the incentive to bring suit? See Landes and Posner, "Should Indirect Purchasers Have Standing to Sue Under the Antitrust Laws? An Economic Analysis of the Rule of Illinois Brick," 46 U.Chi.L.Rev. 602 (1979).

5. Might limitation of recovery to direct purchasers result in underdeterrence of antitrust violators?

ANTICOMPETITIVE SUPPLY RESTRICTION

The antitrust cases in the previous section provide the occasion to comment at least briefly on non-competitive markets, i.e., those in which producers' own decisions are capable of materially influencing the prices that they obtain. An assumption of our simple competitive model was, after all, that the producer acts as a "price taker" rather than as a "price maker." It is worth exploring why a producer who is one of many in a market is, in general, neither willing nor able to engage in output-restricting activities that will raise price. In sum, our message will be that a producer who is only one among many does not have the necessary incentives to try to influence price, nor would he be likely to have much impact if he did try to do so.

It is quite true that even a producer in a competitive market can put any price tag he wants on his products; the problem is that the price at which he can actually *sell* the product is set by the demand conditions of the market, not by any decision controlled by the producer himself. As the Henry Simons model earlier in this chapter illustrated, the market demand curve reflects the maximum price that consumers are willing to pay for different quantities placed on the market. For each possible quantity supplied, the corresponding price is really determined by the demand curve alone. The power to control price, therefore, can effectively be exercised only by controlling quantity supplied.

Still, it may seem that a competitive producer could control the price he gets, at least to some extent. As a competitive firm contracts or expands its own production, does not the aggregate quantity supplied on the market change, moving the price up or down the demand curve within the range of the producer's own quantity variations? Why does the competitive producer not take this price-changing effect into consideration? One facile answer is "Well, a competitive producer is too small to have much effect on price." Bright principles of economics students are sometimes troubled by this response, and rightly so.

"Wait a minute," they reason. "These economics books insist that the monopolist is sensitive to the effect that even a one-unit quantity variation has on his market price, that he regards the 'marginal revenue' of an extra unit sold as always less than the price he gets for that incremental unit. I can see how the impact of, say, a one-unit output variation on price would be small, but what I can't understand is why it would be any more perceptible when a monopolist varies quantity than when an output variation by one of many producers creates precisely the same small movement along the market demand curve."

It is, of course, quite true that equal quantity variations in aggregate quantity supplied would have the same effect on price no matter whether they were accomplished by small producers or large ones. Understanding why large and small producers act differently requires that one adopt a slightly different perspective on the problem, one that can be appreciated by using the simple market demand curve model embodied in Exhibit 6.5. Assume that the quantity supplied would be 10. At that quantity, the demand curve tells us that the market-clearing price would be $20. If one more unit were to be supplied, however, price would have to fall to $19 in order to induce consumers voluntarily to purchase the larger quantity. At the original quantity, the total revenues paid by consumers to producers will be $10 \times \$20 = \$200$ while at the larger output the payments from consumers are $11 \times \$19 = \$209$. For producers in the aggregate, therefore, the marginal revenue of the 11th unit is only $9 even though it sells at a price of $19.

It is instructive to observe the price and revenue change in terms of Exhibit 6.5 where the components of the change can be analyzed

EXHIBIT 6.5

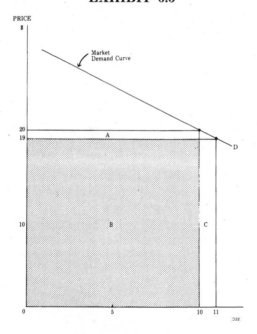

graphically. The total revenue corresponding to each situation is equivalent to the area of the rectangle formed by each price-and-quantity combination. These large rectangles have in common the large, shaded rectangle labelled B, so that the net change in revenues can be seen as the additional tall vertical segment C minus the loss of the horizontal segment A. Segment A represents what we can call a "market spoilage effect" whereby the sale of the 11th unit requires that the price on the other 10 units be cut by $1 apiece. The area of segment A is $(10 \times \$1) = \$10$. In turn, segment C is the revenue increase attributable to selling the incremental product at its market price and will be referred to as the "expansion effect." Since C's area is $(1 \times \$19) = \$19$, the net of these two areas, $\$19 - \$10$, is exactly the $9 change in producers' receipts derived in the previous paragraph.

But we have been analyzing the impact of the output variation in terms of producers in the aggregate rather than a single producer. The dawning of insight into the problem should come when one realizes that the seller of the additional unit gets the full benefit of the revenue increment that has just been called the expansion effect, but normally suffers only part of the loss flowing from the market spoilage effect. For instance, suppose that the original quantity supplied came from three suppliers, I, II, and III, who would have marketed 1, 3, and 6 units, respectively. If producer I markets an extra unit, his *individual* market spoilage effect only extends to the single unit he would have sold at original $20 price. Thus, his marginal revenue from the one-unit volume expansion is the $19 expansion effect minus only a $1 market spoilage effect, for a net of $18. Similar computations for II and III, yield figures of $16 and $13, respectively.

You should now recognize the rather direct application of the externality and Prisoner's Dilemma models of Chapter I to this context. "Market spoilage" due to supply expansion is an external cost borne by producers *in proportion to their market share*. "Expansion" is an internal benefit whose magnitude bears no relation to market share. A small producer bears so little of the market spoilage effect that his incentives are dominated by the expansion effect. As his market share increases, the market spoilage effect is less and less exported to others and becomes a significant internal cost of the producer's own output variations. The limiting case is, of course, the single seller (monopolist) for whom the market spoilage effect is felt undiluted.

A bit of a generalization in symbolic form will recap the argument thus far and also pave the way for the next step. Let Q represent the total quantity supplied before a one-unit variation, q the original quantity suplied by some particular producer, $\triangle P$ the price diminution required to accommodate the one-unit change, and P the market price after the change. Then the individual producer's own marginal revenue will be:

$$MR = P - (q/Q) [Q \triangle P]$$

where the term in parentheses is the producer's market share, the term in square brackets is the market spoilage effect, and P is of course the expansion effect. For the monopolist—or any producer with a large market share—the value of (q/Q) approaches one and the market spoilage effect becomes a significant output-restraining cost. For such producers, marginal revenue is always significantly less than market price P. By contrast, a small producer will find that $MR \approx P$ as market share (q/Q) approaches zero.

"But wait," our critical student objects. "The textbooks say that for the competitive firm $MR = P$ not that $MR \approx P$. Markets are represented as competitive when single firms have 5% or more of the market." Fair enough. All we have done thus far is to show why competitive firms would have little incentive to forego any profitable expansion effect (by failing to produce a unit when $MC < MR \approx P$). An additional step remains. Even if a single producer were *willing* to produce one unit less, our argument can be completed by showing that this restraint may have little or no effect on aggregate quantity supplied. Unless there is some effect on aggregate quantity supplied, the desired price maintenance impact will obviously not be achieved.

Rather than analyze the effect of a single-unit forebearance from producing, let us first over-dramatize by assuming a very large such forebearance. The principles derived from this more emphatic case can then easily be analogized to the single-unit situation. Specifically, suppose that, in the Henry Simons model, 10 firms unaccountably decide to do everyone else a favor by withholding their normal production, q, from the market and, instead, produce nothing. Will the reduction in actual quantity brought to market be equal to $10 \times q$? No. As soon as price begins to rise slightly in response to the initial supply constriction, other producers will be motivated to respond by expanding to fill the "hole" left by the forebearing producers.

In the short run, this "hole filling" effect will not completely counterbalance the reduction by the missing 10 producers. The other producers must, after all, expand out along their own short run supply curves, i.e., the upward-sloping marginal cost curves of the individual firms. You can, however, use the Exhibits earlier in the chapter to tell exactly what the impact will be. Recall that the situation is now, in effect, one wherein ten too many firms have left the industry. What is the relevant supply curve for that situation? What is its intersection with the demand curve? And, ultimately, how much difference did the complete forebearance of ten producers make?

The previous paragraph addresses only the short run hole-filling effect. If the ten firms were to persist in their behavior, how long would it take before the productive "hole" will be filled without a remaining trace? All that is necessary for this to happen is that somewhere out there are ten other investors who are willing to replace the ten who are attempting to create a reduction in the aggregate quantity supplied.

One of the opening questions in this section was: "As a competitive firm contracts or expands its own production, does not the aggregate quantity supplied on the market change, moving the price up or down the demand curve within the range of the producer's own quantity variations?" Despite its superficial plausibility, that question should be answered negatively.

In sum, a competitive firm tends to ignore the effects of its own output on price for two conceptually distinct reasons. One is that, even *if* such output variations affected industry output, what we have called the market spoilage effect is very dilute. The second is that a firm may have good reason to believe that aggregate output, and therefore price, will be about the same whatever its own output decisions. In combination, these factors justify the MR = P assumption of the competitive model.

Implicitly, our discussion above also suggests how anticompetitive supply restrictions may come about when the factual underpinnings of the competitive model are violated by factors such as small numbers of ("oligopolistic") producers, firms with large market shares, explicit collusive arrangements, and barriers to entry of new firms.

QUESTIONS

1. Review the Prisoner's Dilemma and externality concepts developed in Chapter I, especially the problem of the lawyers who wished to collude in the bidding for an assignable personal injury claim.

2. The standard price-and-output determination model for a monopolist is not provided in this text. (Many people are already familiar with it. If you are not, you may now know enough to guess at how it works. If not, look it up.) Draw that standard diagram and indicate the monopoly price and output. If the monopolist could be made to act like a competitive firm, i.e., ignore his own effect on price, what would price and output be? Who gains and loses as between the two outcomes? Show that consumers lose more by the monopolistic output reduction than the monopolist gains.

3. The text of this section deals with competitive *selling* markets. To what extent do the same considerations carry over to buying markets, i.e., competitive purchases rather than sales?

SEGREGATED MARKETS: PROVING "EXPLOITATION"

The opinions that follow are from a Chicago housing discrimination case that involves both a novel legal theory and interesting facts. On the one hand, you should reflect on what the future implications for the housing market would be if plaintiffs' liability theory were both accepted as a matter of law and were, as a practical matter, likely to be provable against developers in a substantial number of cases. On the other hand, it will be interesting to see what facts would have to be adduced in support of the discrimination allegation and how it is possible to support them with credible evidence.

Although the opinions do not of course provide a full picture of the evidence proffered by the parties, a careful reading indicates the substance of the arguments and the kinds of testimony elicited. Take the opportunity to "second guess" both the judges and the attorneys in the case.

CLARK v. UNIVERSAL BUILDERS, INC.

United States Court of Appeals, Seventh Circuit, 1974.
501 F.2d 324.

SWYGERT, Chief Judge.

This appeal is from a grant of a directed verdict for defendants at the close of the plaintiffs' case in chief. Plaintiffs are a class of black citizens who purchased newly constructed houses in Chicago from defendants under land installment contracts during the period from 1958 to 1968. Defendants include the building contractor of the houses and the various land companies through which the houses were sold to plaintiffs. In the district court plaintiffs claimed that as a result of intense racial discrimination in Chicago and its metropolitan area there existed at all pertinent times a housing market for whites and a separate housing market for blacks, the latter confined to a relatively small geographical area in the central city. Plaintiffs contended that the demand among blacks for housing greatly exceeded the supply of housing available in the black market and that the defendants exploited this situation by building houses in or adjacent to black areas and selling the houses to plaintiffs at prices far in excess of the amounts which white persons paid for comparable residences in neighboring urban areas, and on onerous terms far less favorable than those available to white buyers of similar properties, all in violation of plaintiffs' rights under the Thirteenth and Fourteenth Amendments and under the Civil Rights Act of 1866. Plaintiff's exploitation theory of liability was sustained by District Judge Hubert Will as stating a claim for relief under section 1982 of the Civil Rights Act of 1866. Accordingly, Judge Will denied defendants' motion to dismiss plaintiffs' complaint. The case then went to trial before District Judge Joseph Sam Perry, and plaintiffs, pursuant to Judge Will's approval of their exploitation theory of liability under section 1982, presented evidence before a jury of defendants' alleged exploitation of the discriminatory housing situation prevalent in Chicago during the period 1958 through 1968. Upon completion of plaintiffs' case in chief, Judge Perry granted defendants' motion for directed verdict, holding in opposition to Judge Will's theory of the case that:

> * * * [C]ounsel for the plaintiffs have not painted a pretty picture of the defendants, but that picture is a picture of exploitation for profit, and not racial discrimination.

*   *   *

> Nowhere in the six weeks trial is there one scintilla of evidence that the defendants or any of them or their agents ever refused to sell to a white person or a black person or a non-white person any house or refused to sell one or the other at a higher or lower price, absolutely no positive evidence of discrimination in this record

*   *   *

> Accordingly, for want of any evidence in support of the complaint, the motion for a directed verdict by all of the defendants now on trial is hereby granted, and the complaint of all of the plaintiffs is hereby dismissed as to all of the defendants.

Under Judge Perry's theory of the case, absent evidence of defendants' sales of the same or similar housing to whites on more favorable terms and prices, namely, the traditional theory of racial discrimination, plaintiffs failed to make out a case of liability under section 1982.

Plaintiffs raise numerous issues in this appeal the most important of which of course is the correctness of the grant of a directed verdict for the defendants. The other issues can broadly be categorized as challenges to the correctness of certain of the trial judge's evidentiary rulings and other procedural rulings.

In judging the propriety of the grant of the directed verdict, we are confronted with two issues. We must first resolve the conflict as to the scope of section 1982. That is, we must determine whether section 1982 covers only the so-called traditional type of discriminatory conduct, or whether a claim may be stated under section 1982 by proof of exploitation of a discriminatory situation already existing and created in the first instance by the action of persons other than defendants. If we determine that section 1982 is violated under the latter theory we then must determine whether the evidence, both the admitted evidence and erroneously excluded evidence, when viewed in the light most favorable to plaintiffs, together with all inferences that may be reasonably drawn therefrom, is such that it can be found that plaintiffs have made out a *prima facie* case.

I

Section 1982 of the Civil Rights Act of 1866 provides:

> All citizens of the United States shall have the same right, in every State and Territory, as is enjoyed by white citizens thereof to inherit, purchase, lease, sell, hold, and convey real and personal property.

Plaintiffs' "exploitation" theory of liability under this section can briefly be restated as follows: As a result of racial discrimination there existed two housing markets in Chicago, one for whites and another for blacks, with the supply of housing available in the black market far less than the demand. Defendants entered the black market selling homes for prices far in excess of their fair market value and far in excess of prices which whites pay for comparable homes in the white market and on more onerous terms than whites similarly situated would encounter. Plaintiffs contend that by so acting defendants seized upon and took advantage of the opportunity created by racial residential segregation to exploit blacks in violation of section 1982.

It is asserted that to countenance such actions by the defendant would be in direct contravention of the express language of section 1982 which provides by clear implication that black citizens "shall have the same right * * * as is enjoyed by white citizens * * * to * * * purchase * * * real * * * property." Moreover, plaintiffs claim that a ruling which would hold defendants' asserted acts of exploitation to be outside of the coverage of section 1982 would be contrary to the Supreme Court's declaration in Jones v. Mayer Co., 392 U.S. 409, 443, 88 S.Ct. 2186, 2205, 20 L.Ed.2d 1189 (1968), and that section 1982 was meant to be a vehicle through which "to assure that a dollar in the hands of a Negro will purchase the same thing as a dollar in the hands of a white man."

Defendants contend that absent a showing of the traditional form of discrimination, namely, that defendants refused to sell to blacks because of their race, or offered to sell the same houses to whites at lower prices or on more favorable terms than they offered to sell to blacks, plaintiffs have not made out a case under section 1982. Defendants assert that the houses they sold to plaintiffs in the black market were available to whites and would have been sold on the same terms and for the same prices as sales to the black plaintiffs. Therefore, defendants argue, plaintiffs enjoyed "the same right" as enjoyed by white citizens to purchase houses in the black market. Moreover, it is urged that other sellers and not defendants discriminated against plaintiffs in the first instance by refusing to sell to plaintiffs housing in other urban areas, thereby excluding them from the white market. The defendants claim that an extension of section 1982 so as to proscribe their alleged acts of exploitation would be tantamount to holding defendants liable for the discrimination of others without a showing of any discrimination by defendants. With respect to the Supreme Court's decision in Jones v. Mayer Co., the defendants suggest that it lends no support to the plaintiffs' desired interpretation of section 1982. Rather, defendants view Jones v. Mayer Co. as authority for their contention that section 1982 prohibits only the so-called traditional type of discrimination and does not encompass plaintiffs' theory of exploitation liability. Also, defendants urge that plaintiffs' interpretation of section 1982 would render that section unconstitutionally vague and would expose defendants to risk or detriment without fair warning of the nature of the proscribed conduct. It is on the basis of these arguments that defendants claim that no case can be made under section 1982 for exploitation absent a showing that defendants offered to sell the same or similar homes to whites at lower prices and on more favorable terms than they made available to blacks. We do not agree.

At the outset we note that section 1982 is framed in broad yet clear language. It provides that:

> All citizens of the United States shall have the same right * * * as is enjoyed by white citizens thereof to * * * purchase * * * real * * * property.

Facially, therefore, the scope of section 1982 would appear to be rather far reaching; indeed such a reading of the statute is supported by the Supreme Court's interpretation of section 1982 in Jones v. Mayer Co., 392 U.S. 409, 88 S.Ct. 2186, 20 L.Ed.2d 1189 (1968). In that case the Court was confronted with questions as to the scope and constitutionality of section 1982. The plaintiff in that case, a black person, brought an action pursuant to section 1982 claiming that the defendants refused to sell him a house on the basis of his race. The district court dismissed the plaintiff's complaint, and the court of appeals affirmed, concluding that section 1982 applied only to state action and not private action. The Supreme Court rejected the argument for a narrow construction of section 1982, holding in broad language:

> [T]hat section 1982 bars *all* racial discrimination, private as well as public, in the sale or rental of property, and that the statute, thus construed, is a valid exercise of the power of Congress to enforce the Thirteenth Amendment. 392 U.S. 413, 88 S.Ct. 2189 [Emphasis in original].

The Court went on to note that section 1982 was an attempt by Congress to provide "that the right to purchase and lease property was to be enjoyed equally throughout the United States by Negro and white citizens alike" and that Congress "plainly meant to secure that right against interference from any source whatever, whether governmental or private." 392 U.S. at 423–424, 88 S.Ct. at 2195. The Court concluded its analysis by stating that section 1982 must be accorded " 'a sweep as broad as its language.' " 392 U.S. at 437, 88 S.Ct. at 2202. Observing that "when racial discrimination herds men into ghettos and makes their ability to buy property turn on the color of their skin, then it too is a relic of slavery," the Court proceeded to uphold the constitutionality of section 1982 stating:

> Negro citizens, North and South, who saw in the Thirteenth Amendment a promise of freedom—freedom to "go and come at pleasure" and to "buy and sell when they please"—would be left with "a mere paper guarantee" if Congress were powerless to assure that a dollar in the hands of a Negro will purchase the same thing as a dollar in the hands of a white man. At the very least, the freedom that Congress is empowered to secure under the Thirteenth Amendment includes the freedom to buy whatever a white man can buy, the right to live wherever a white man can live. If Congress cannot say that being a free man means at least this much, then the Thirteenth Amendment made a promise the Nation cannot keep. 392 U.S. 443, 88 S.Ct. 2205.

Clearly the Court's decision in Jones v. Mayer Co. does not, contrary to defendants' assertions, detract from plaintiffs' contention as to the scope of section 1982. Rather, the decision is support for plaintiffs' theory for in *Jones* the Court viewed section 1982 as a broad based instrument to be utilized in eliminating all discrimination and the effects thereof in the ownership of property. Accordingly, Jones v. Mayer Co. does not stand as an obstacle to plaintiffs' case, but supports it.

Defendants insist that section 1982 cannot be construed to encompass other than the traditional type of discrimination, that is, that defendants offered to sell to whites on more favorable terms and prices than to plaintiffs. Keeping in mind the Supreme Court's admonition in Lane v. Wilson, 307 U.S. 268, 275, 59 S.Ct. 872, 876, 83 L.Ed. 1281 (1939), that the Constitution and statutes promulgated in its enforcement nullify "sophisticated as well as simple-minded modes of discrimination," we reject defendants' notion of adherence to a strict, rigid, and traditional type of discrimination. We need not resort to a labelling exercise in categorizing certain activity as discriminatory and others as not of such character for section 1982 is violated if the facts demonstrate that defendants exploited a situation created by socioeconomic forces tainted by racial discrimination. Indeed, there is no difference in results between the traditional type of discrimination and defendants' exploitation of a discriminatory situation. Under the former situation blacks either pay excessive prices or are refused altogether from purchasing housing, while under the latter situation they encounter oppressive terms and exorbitant prices relative to the terms and prices available to white citizens for comparable housing.

To avoid this conclusion, defendants contend that even though the results obtained under both the traditional and exploitation theories are similar, they come about through significantly different means. Under the traditional theory a black man is denied the "same right" as a white man in that the seller offers to sell the same house to each but at different prices and terms due to the differences in race of the prospective buyer. It is defendants' position that they offered the plaintiffs the same terms and prices they would offer whites. Therefore it is asserted that plaintiffs had the same right as white citizens. This argument ignores current realities of racial psychology and economic practicalities. Defendants can find no justification for their actions in a claim that they would have sold on the same terms to those whites who elected to enter the black market and to purchase housing in the ghetto and segregated inner-city neighborhoods at exorbitant prices, far in excess of prices for comparable homes in the white market. It is no answer that defendants would have exploited whites as well as blacks. To accept defendants' contention would be tantamount to perpetuating a subterfuge behind which every slumlord and exploiter of those banished to the ghetto could hide by a simple rubric: The same property would have been sold to whites on the same terms.

Defendants urge that other sellers and not they were the active agents of discrimination. That is, blacks were excluded from the white market by other sellers who refused to sell to plaintiffs and that accordingly plaintiffs' action lies solely against those other owners and real estate operators and not the defendants. But, we repeat, defendants cannot escape the reach of section 1982 by proclaiming that they merely took advantage of a discriminatory situation created by others. We find repugnant to the clear language and spirit of the Civil Rights Act the claim that he who exploits and preys on the discriminatory hardship of a black man occupies a more protected status than he who created the hardship in the first instance. Moreover, defendants' actions prolong and perpetuate a system of racial residential segregation, defeating the assimilation of black citizens into full and equal participation in a heretofore all white society. Through the medium of exorbitant prices and severe, long-term land contract terms blacks are tied to housing in the ghetto and segregated inner-city neighborhoods from which they can only hope to escape someday without severe financial loss. By demanding prices in excess of the fair market value of a house and in excess of what whites pay for comparable housing, defendants extract from blacks resources much needed for other necessities of life, thereby reducing their standard of living and lessening their chances of escaping the vestiges of a system of slavery and oppression. Indeed, defendants' activity encourages overt discrimination by offering the long oppressed black an unattractive yet alternative choice to that of a confrontation for equal buyers' rights in a white neighborhood.

Defendants in effect contend that this is solely a matter of economics and not of discrimination. We cannot accept this contention for although the laws of supply and demand may function so as to establish a market level for the buyer in the black housing areas, it is clear that these laws are affected by a contrived market condition which is grounded in and fed upon by racial discrimination—that is, the available supply of housing is determined by the buyer's race. In other contexts the law has prevented sellers from charging whatever the market will bear when special circumstances have occasioned market shortages or superior bargaining positions. In such instances sellers were denied the opportunity to exploit others merely because the opportunity existed.

Contrary to the trial court's stance, the shortage of housing here was triggered not by an economic phenomenon but by a pattern of discrimination that has no place in our society. Accordingly, neither prices nor profits—whether derived through well-intentioned, good-faith efforts or predatory and unethical practices—may reflect or perpetuate discrimination against black citizens. We agree with Judge Will's statement that "there cannot in this country be markets or profits based on the color of a man's skin." Contract Buyers League v. F & F Investment, 300 F.Supp. 210, 216 (N.D.Ill.1969). Price and profit differentials between individual buyers may be justified on a multitude of grounds; for example, the prospective purchaser's reputation or his financial position and potential earning power. But price or profit may not turn on whether the prospective buyer has dark or light pigmentation.

Defendants urge that acceptance of plaintiffs' asserted interpretation of section 1982 would render the statute unconstitutional and that the standards of liability utilized to deploy such an expanded interpretation would be unconstitutionally vague and indefinite. They argue that a narrow interpretation is compelled so as to sustain the constitutionality of the statute and to prevent the exposure of "a potential actor to some risk or detriment without giving him fair warning of the nature of the proscribed conduct." Rowan v. Post Office Dept., 397 U.S. 728, 740, 90 S.Ct. 1484, 1492, 25 L.Ed.2d 736 (1970). Defendants' argument misses the mark for we have not here a penal statute to be strictly construed. Rather, we have a civil statute which is remedial in nature and, as viewed by the Supreme Court, is to be accorded " '*   *   * a sweep as broad as its language.' "

Jones v. Mayer Co., 392 U.S. 409, 437, 88 S.Ct. 2186, 2202, 20 L.Ed.2d 1189 (1968) citing United States v. Price, 383 U.S. 787, 801, 86 S.Ct. 1152, 16 L.Ed.2d 267 (1966).

With respect to the standard of liability upon which a violation of the statute may be predicated within the factual context here depicted, we hold that the benchmark for guiding a seller's conduct in the black market is reasonableness. That this is a constitutionally sufficient standard by which to gauge one's conduct in the real estate market was long ago recognized by the Supreme Court in Levy Leasing Co. v. Siegel, 258 U.S. 242, 42 S.Ct. 289, 66 L.Ed. 595 (1922). In that case the Court held that the usage of a standard prohibiting "* * * reserving unjust, unreasonable and oppressive" rent and terms of renting was constitutionally definite so as to satisfy the demands of due process. Commenting on the *Levy Leasing Co.* decision, the Court in Small Co. v. American Sugar Refining Co., 267 U.S. 233, 241–242, 45 S.Ct. 295, 298, 69 L.Ed. 589 (1925), stated:

> Real property, particularly in a city, comes to have a recognized value, which is relatively stable and easily ascertained. It also comes to have a recognized rental value—the measure of compensation commonly asked and paid for its occupancy and use—the amount being fixed with due regard to what is just and reasonable between landlord and tenant in view of the value of the property and the outlay which the owner must make for taxes and other current charges. These are matters which in the course of business come to be fairly well settled and understood. A standard thus developed and accepted in actual practice, when made the test of compliance with legislative commands or prohibitions, usually meets the requirement of due process of law in point of being sufficiently definite and intelligible.

By demanding prices far in excess of a property's fair market value and far in excess of prices for comparable housing available to white citizens the seller ventures into the realm of unreasonableness. The statute does not mandate that blacks are to be sold houses at the exact same price and on the exact same terms as are available to white citizens. Reasonable differentials due to a myriad of permissible factors can be expected and are acceptable. But the statute does not countenance the efforts of those who would exploit a discriminatory situation under the guise of artificial differences.

* * *

When a seller in the black market demands exorbitant prices and onerous sales terms relative to the terms and prices available to white citizens for comparable housing, it cannot be stated that a dollar in the hands of a black man will purchase the same thing as a dollar in the hands of a white man. Such practices render plaintiffs' dollars less valuable than those of white citizens—a situation that was spawned by a discarded system of slavery and is nurtured by vestiges of that system. Courts in applying section 1982 must be vigilant in preventing toleration of this deplorable circumstance.

We hold accordingly that plaintiffs state a claim under section 1982 since they allege that (1) as a result of racial residential segregation dual housing markets exist and (2) defendant sellers took advantage of this situation by demanding prices and terms unreasonably in excess of prices and terms available to white citizens for comparable housing. If the plaintiffs sustain the burden of proof on these elements they make out a *prima facie* case, whereupon, as recently made clear by the Supreme Court, the burden of proof shifts to the defendants "to articulate some legitimate, nondiscriminatory reason" for the price and term differential. McDonnell Douglas Corp. v. Green, 411 U.S. 792, 802, 93 S.Ct. 1817, 1824, 36 L.Ed.2d 668 (1973).

II

Having determined the substantive framework upon which an action may be brought pursuant to section 1982 we address ourselves to the correctness of the directed verdict entered in favor of the defendants at the close of plaintiffs' case in chief. Keeping in mind that we must view all the evidence, plus the reasonable inferences to be drawn therefrom, in the light most favorable to the plaintiffs, Hannigan v. Sears, Roebuck & Co., 410 F.2d 285, 287 (7th Cir.), cert. denied, 396 U.S. 902, 90 S.Ct. 214, 24 L.Ed.2d 178 (1969), we hold that the admitted evidence was sufficient to establish a *prima facie* case under section 1982 pursuant to the exploitation theory of liability and, accordingly, warranted submission of the issues to the jury for resolution. Moreover, we rule that on the basis of the evidence erroneously excluded by the trial judge the plaintiffs have made out a case for section 1982 liability under the so-called traditional theory of discrimination and that, therefore, a directed verdict for defendants on this separate ground was likewise improperly granted. To demonstrate the error committed we proceed to review the evidence adduced at trial.

There was sufficient evidence to establish, *prima facie*, the existence of dual housing markets in the Chicago metropolitan area as a result of racial residential segregation. Dr. Karl E. Taeuber, a professor of sociology, testified as an expert witness about the results of his extensive research on the dispersion of population in the city of Chicago. His statistical analysis indicated that Chicago was a highly segregated city and that there was a very high degree of residential segregation between whites and blacks. Moreover, despite the decrease of white population in the city accompanied by a rapid increase of the black population, the supply of new housing available to whites was much greater than that available to blacks. Also, during the pertinent time period the expanding suburban housing market was limited almost completely to whites. Dr. Taeuber testified that the main obstacle to the movement of blacks into the white areas of Chicago and suburban residental areas was the high degree of discrimination against blacks in the white market. As a result the supply of housing available to whites was far greater in both absolute and relative terms to the supply of new housing available to blacks.

Plaintiffs produced additional proof concerning the existence of dual housing markets through the testimony of another expert witness, Scott Tyler, a real estate broker and appraiser with many years of experience in the real estate business in Chicago. Significantly, defendants seemingly concede the existence of a dual housing market in Chicago. Nor do we think it beyond the strictures of judicial notice to observe that there exists in Chicago and its environs a high degree of racial residential segregation.

We turn to the second element of the case, whether there was a sufficient *prima facie* showing of an unreasonable differential in price and sale terms between the housing sold or offered by defendants to plaintiffs and comparable housing available to whites. With respect to this phase plaintiffs offered the appraisal testimony of five expert witnesses; the testimony of two, however, was excluded from the jury by the trial judge. Concerning the testimony of Scott Tyler and John Hank which the judge did allow, both witnesses utilized the market data method of appraisal in arriving at a fair market value of a sampling of plaintiffs' homes. The fair market value appraisals were based on sales of comparable homes in all-white neighborhoods which were located in close geographical proximity to plaintiffs' homes and had similar communal amenities such as transportation, schools, churches, and quality of neighborhood. Both witnesses testified that the comparable white housing was sold at prices substantially below the prices commanded by defendants. Expert witness Tyler's appraisals demonstrated that on the average the contract prices charged by defendants exceeded the fair market value of the homes by $6,508, or 34.5 percent. Expert witness Hank was of the opinion that on the average defendants' prices exceeded fair market value by $4,209, or 20.6 percent. Plaintiffs adduced additional appraisal testimony from Paul Underwood who had been an appraiser for a savings and loan association which had loaned money to one of the defendant land companies for construction of houses sold to plaintiffs. Pursuant to this financing arrangement Underwood appraised thirty of defendants' houses for which he testified that the sales prices charged by defendants, on the average, exceeded fair market value by $4,296, or 20.9 percent.[11]   Based on the foregoing we think a jury could reasonably reach the conclusion that defendants' price differential was unreasonably in excess of fair market value and prices available to white citizens for comparable housing.   Accordingly, there was sufficient evidence on the price differential to send the case to the jury.

Turning to the issue of the reasonableness of the sale terms differential the evidence at trial indicated that defendants refused to sell other than on land contract to plaintiffs.   There was testimony to the effect that defendants refused to participate in any sales through a deed and mortgage arrangement despite the prospective buyer's ability to obtain mortgage financing.   The evidence indicates that plaintiffs were of the equivalent economic status as many whites who routinely obtained mortgages to finance the purchase of houses and that a competing construction company in the black market sold the vast majority of its homes on deed and mortgage to blacks similarly situated economically to plaintiffs.   Also, the evidence demonstrates that some plaintiffs made down payments of up to forty-five percent of the contract price—well above the amount needed to qualify for mortgages—and yet defendants refused to deal on terms other than contract.   On the basis of this evidence it could reasonably be inferred that defendants utilized the contract method of sales to facilitate their exorbitant pricing practices and not because of significant differences between plaintiffs' economic status and that of whites similarly situated who were able to utilize mortgage financing.   Hence, a jury could find that the different treatment accorded plaintiffs by defendants' sales terms was discriminatory.

Furthermore, plaintiffs offered evidence, which was erroneously excluded by the trial judge, sufficient to establish a *prima facie* case pursuant to the traditional theory of discrimination.   Under that theory there must be a showing of "treating, in similar circumstances, a member or members of one race different from the manner in which members of another race are treated."   Love v. DeCarlo Homes, Inc., 482 F.2d 613, 615 (5th Cir. 1973).   That is, a black prospective buyer of a dwelling demonstrates discriminatory conduct if he proves that an owner utilizes different pricing policies with respect to blacks and whites similarly situated.

---

11. The trial court improperly excluded appraisal evidence of Walter Tomlinson and Francis Parker. See, e.g., Illinois Power & Light Co. v. Talbott, 321 Ill. 538, 543, 152 N.E. 486 (1926). Tomlinson and Parker were employed by savings and loan institutions and as a consequence thereof they had appraised certain of defendants' constructions, for the purpose of extending construction mortgage funds. Tomlinson was of the opinion that defendants' sales prices were, on the average, $4,099 or 20.4 percent in excess of appraised value while Parker's appraisals reflected an average excess of $3,729 or 16.6 percent over the fair cash market value of the respective houses.

The proffered evidence which was rejected at trial involved the sales of new houses to white buyers in Deerfield, Illinois and Park Forest South, Illinois, both being suburban residential developments. The sellers of the houses in Deerfield were Universal Construction Company and a joint venture comprised of the Deerfield Home Development Company and Universal Builders, Inc., while the houses in Park Forest South were sold by the P.F.S. Development Company. The plaintiffs contended that these corporations were owned and managed by the same persons that owned and managed defendants and that these persons were engaged in discriminatory conduct through the use of different pricing practices in Deerfield and Park Forest South from those used in pricing defendants' houses. The trial judge excluded the evidence on two grounds: (1) the plaintiffs were not allowed to disregard the separate identities of the three corporations and (2) the lack of a basis of comparability for homes in Deerfield and Park Forest South with those of plaintiffs in Chicago. We rule that the trial court erred in excluding plaintiffs' evidence on the Deerfield and Park Forest South pricing policies.

Defendants' argument that the corporate formalities should not be disregarded in the context of the issues is without worth. As this court has stated, corporate formalities "may be disregarded in exceptional situations where it otherwise would present an obstacle to the due protection or enforcement of public or private rights." Ohio Tank Car Co. v. Keith Ry. Equip. Co., 148 F.2d 4, 6 (7th Cir. 1945), cert. denied, 326 U.S. 730, 66 S.Ct. 38, 90 L.Ed. 434 (1945). In situations such as here, where common ownership and management exists, corporate formalities must not be rigidly adhered to when inquiry is made of civil rights violations. Accordingly, the objection raised by defendants presents no obstacles to the comparison of defendants' pricing policies implemented in Deerfield and Park Forest South by the other selling organizations.

Turning to the second reason given for excluding the Deerfield and Park Forest South evidence we find that there was sufficient comparability between those operations and defendants' sales in the relevant black market so as to render the exclusion an abuse of discretion. Factors such as geographical proximity, the date of the sale, type of construction, and materials used are factors going only to the weight to be accorded the evidence by the jury and do not go to its admissibility. See, e.g., Winston v. United States, 342 F.2d 715, 721 (9th Cir. 1965); United States v. 124.84 Acres of Land, Warrick County, Ind., 387 F.2d 912 (7th Cir. 1968). Plaintiffs met the requirement of sufficient comparability through the use of a comparative statistical analysis of accounting data reflecting defendants' sales operations and pricing policies in Chicago with those of Deerfield and Chicago and with those of Deerfield and Park Forest South. We find plaintiffs' statistical evidence to have been sufficiently competent; see United States v. Certain Interests in Property, etc., 326 F.2d 109 (2d Cir. 1964), cert. denied, 377 U.S. 978, 84 S.Ct. 1884, 12 L.Ed.2d 747 (1964), and probative of plaintiffs' claim that defendants sold houses to blacks on price terms different from those they sold to white buyers similarly situated. Indeed, as the Eight Circuit has stated, "statistical evidence can make a prima facie case of discrimination." Carter v. Gallagher, 452 F.2d 315, 323 (8th Cir. 1972), cert. denied, 406 U.S. 950, 92 S.Ct. 2045, 32 L.Ed.2d 338 (1972).

Plaintiffs' expert witnesses testified that in the housing industry prices are established on the basis of direct costs, consisting generally of the investment in the land and the cost of construction, including materials. Once the direct costs are calculated, an allowance for overhead and profit is added to the direct costs to attain the sales price. The allowance for overhead and profit is added to the direct costs to attain the sales price. The allowance for overhead and profit is the gross profit on sales which plaintiffs' expert witness testimony indicated was generally found in the real estate industry to be from fifteen to nineteen percent of the sales price.[16] Defendants testified to the utilization of this method of pricing in their sales to plaintiffs; however, the statistical evidence presented by plaintiffs tends to refute that assertion.[17]

Viewing the evidence, first in absolute terms, it shows that defendants' pricing policy in Chicago produced an average gross profit substantially in excess of that produced by the Deerfield and Park Forest South operations.[18] In relative percentage terms defendants

16. To the extent that differences in land location and building materials affect sales price, those differences are reflected in the absolute amount of direct costs. The differences do not affect the pricing methods employed. That is, the expert testimony and defendants were agreed that the type of house or area in which it is built does not affect the method of setting prices. The selling price is arrived at by establishing direct costs and adding an amount for overhead and profit. The amount added for overhead and profit represents the gross profit and is an important comparative figure in analyzing the substance of the pricing methods employed by defendants.

17. Plaintiffs' statistical evidence was prepared by John Royer, an independent certified public accountant. To assure a substantial basis for statistical comparability between the Chicago and suburban operations, Royer made appropriate adjustments for differences in accounting methods and financial presentations between the various operations. Moreover, with respect to percentage comparisons of gross profit and mark-up, Royer testified that before calculating such percentages he determined that the components of direct costs were the same for the suburban companies as for the defendant companies.

18. In those instances where direct costs were comparable in absolute amounts, the gross profit garnered by defendants was substantially in excess of that obtained in the suburban operations. For example, the following chart compares the operations of Universal Con-

reaped a gross profit of 27.6 percent of sales, well above the industry figure of 14 to 19 percent and considerably in excess of the gross profit percentages of the Deerfield and Park Forest South operations.[19] Second, analyzing the same data in terms of the mark-up of the sales price over the direct costs, it is clear that the mark-up—as a percentage of direct costs—was much higher in the sales to plaintiffs than in the sales to white buyers in Deerfield and Park Forest South.[20]

The statistical evidence substantiates the claim that defendants priced plaintiffs' houses much higher relative to direct costs than the houses sold in Deerfield and Park Forest South and belies any defendants utilized comparable pricing policies in their sales to plaintiffs. Plaintiffs presented Dr. Richard Freeman, a Professor of Economics, who analyzed the statistical data pertaining to the difference in gross profits between defendants' sales to plaintiffs and suburban operations. His analysis demonstrated that the difference in pricing practices was due to the race of the buyer and not economic factors.

In summary, it is difficult as a *prima facie* matter to infer that the substantial disparity between the pricing practices of defendants in the black real estate market and the pricing practices in the white market was attributable to some factor other than the race of the buyers. Whether defendants afforded plaintiffs the "same right" to

struction Co. in Deerfield with defendants' efforts in Chicago:

	(1) Universal Construction Company	(2) Chicago Operation	(3) Difference (Column 2 Minus 1)
Average Sales Price	$22,644.60	$25,172.53	$2,527.93
Average Direct Costs (Land Plus Building)	$18,779.45	$18,246.14	$—553.31
Average Gross Profit	$ 3,865.15	$ 6,926.39	$3,061.24

Although the average direct costs were slightly lower in the Chicago operations, the average sales price and average gross profit were substantially higher in those operations than in the Deerfield operations.

19. In Deerfield, Universal Construction realized a gross profit of 17.1 percent while the gross profit of the Deerfield Home-Universal Builders joint venture was 17.6 percent. The operations in Park Forest South turned an average gross profit of 15.5 percent of sales price.

20. The average mark-up or ratio of gross profit to direct costs was 20.58 percent for Universal Construction while the Deerfield Home joint venture operations reflected a mark-up of 21.42 percent; the mark-up in Park Forest South was 18.35 percent. In contrast, defendants' mark-up on their sales to plaintiffs averaged 37.96 percent.

purchase housing as offered white buyers was, based on the foregoing evidence, an issue to be properly submitted to the jury.

* * *

QUESTIONS

1. Assume that all of the factual contentions made by plaintiffs are true. Looking to the future, would application of the legal theory advocated by plaintiffs be more likely to help or to hurt potential home purchasers who are blacks?

2. A "market-clearing" price is one which equates quantity demanded at that price with the quantity supplied. Does the court's holding require a builder such as Universal to charge less than a market-clearing price? If so, how does the quantity available get rationed out among the potential purchasers? Would resold houses presumably be subject to the same rule?

3. One reading of this case is that the seller must sell the houses at the price they would have sold for "but for" the segregated condition of the housing market? What difficulties would there be in knowing exactly what this price would be? Could the rule be attacked as unconstitutionally vague?

4. The assumption in this case is that racial bigotry and segregated housing markets will result in higher housing prices for blacks. In fact, the same premise is consistent with a result in which the price of housing to the discriminated-against group is *lower* rather than higher. What are the theoretical effects that work in opposite directions on the price of housing for blacks? How would one know what the true empirical result is? See Lapham, "Do Blacks Pay More for Housing," 79 J.Polit.Econ. 1244 (1971).

5. Is entry into the house building industry in downtown Chicago limited by any substantial obstacles? What implications can be drawn from your answer?

6. Did the defendant have a "monopoly" or substantial price-fixing market power over any product? If so, what? Of what relevance is cross elasticity of demand in answering this question?

7. Which of the factual assertions of plaintiffs' case seem most dubious? What kind of empirical evidence or theoretical arguments might be adduced to rebut them?

8. Pursuant to the remand ordered by the Seventh Circuit, the *Clark* case was subjected to a full trial on the merits several years later. The opinion in that case is excerpted below. Before reading the opinion, however, try to guess what evidence would have been presented by each party and how persuasive the evidence would have been.

CLARK v. UNIVERSAL BUILDERS, INC.

United States District Court, N.D.Illinois, 1983.
No. 69 C 115.

BUA, Judge.

* * *

III. The Traditional Theory of Discrimination

The traditional theory of discrimination requires proof that the defendants utilized different pricing policies in their sales of homes to the plaintiffs than they did in selling comparable homes in Deerfield to similarly situated white homebuyers.

  A. Plaintiffs failed to show either that the Deerfield and South side areas were comparable community environments or that the houses built in those communities were similar in terms of lot size, building materials, design and layout.

The plaintiffs attempted to prove that homes sold to whites by Universal Construction Company and Deerfield Home Development Company (DHDC) were comparable to those sold to the members of the plaintiff class by the South side land companies. This they failed to do.

The evidence shows that Universal Construction Company and DHDC sold approximately 50 homes in Deerfield between 1953 and 1958. During these years, Deerfield was a developing suburb that still retained a somewhat rural character. Ample evidence of this fact was presented at trial. For example, it was not until 1958 that the Tri-State connector was opened linking Deerfield to the Tri-State highway system, and the Kennedy-Evans expressway system was not opened to link Deerfield to downtown Chicago until late 1960. Additionally, Deerfield did not have a high school during this period, making it necessary for local high school students to attend school in Highland Park. Finally, Deerfield residents were dependent on local roads and a single railroad line for commuter service to Chicago.

In contrast, the South side neighborhood in which the defendants operated was a mature urban environment with extensive mass transit and railroad service available to its residents, and with shopping, schools, churches, parks and other facilities in the area.

In addition to the dissimilarity between Deerfield in the years 1953 to 1958 and Chicago in the years 1958 to 1969, the evidence indicates that the homes built in Deerfield were not comparable to the homes sold to plaintiffs. The plaintiffs offered the testimony of Edward Noonan, an architect and real estate developer, in their attempt to establish the comparability of the Deerfield and South side homes.

Mr. Noonan's testimony that the homes in Deerfield were comparable in size and superior in quality to the South side homes was based on his inspection of two homes in Deerfield constructed by DHDC and 12–20 homes on the South side. All of the inspected homes were selected by plaintiffs' counsel. Moreover, Mr. Noonan did not identify which models he inspected, and did not state whether he inspected one model or 20. It is to be noted that defendants constructed approximately 30 different home models on the South side. Mr. Noonan conceded that houses with the same direct costs of construction cannot be said to be comparable from the point of view of "living or location," or "value to the purchaser." Noonan, p. 678. In fact, he admitted that sales prices are not necessarily related to construction costs. Additionally, the ranch houses built in Deerfield in 1956 and 1957 were of frame construction. Many did not have basements. In contrast, the South side homes were brick and were typically built with basements. In addition, many of the South side homes were bilevel, split level, or two story homes.

In sum, this court concludes that Mr. Noonan's testimony is unpersuasive on the issue of comparability, and that the evidence as a whole shows a complete dissimilarity between the Deerfield and South side homes in terms of community environment, lot size, building materials, design, and layout.

> B. Evidence of the Appraised Value of the Deerfield and South side homes does not support the inference that defendants discriminated against plaintiffs in setting the sales price.

In order to sustain their burden under the so-called traditional theory of discrimination, the plaintiffs submitted in evidence appraisals of the value of homes built in Deerfield and on the South side. These appraisals were made by a number of savings and loan associations that provided construction and long term mortgage financing to the defendants. At the time these appraisals were made, Illinois and federal law required savings and loan associations to prepare written appraisals of the value of any real estate given as security for a mortgage loan. The appraisal reports were offered as evidence of the fair market value of the homes appraised in an effort to show that the average sales price approximated the appraised value for the Deerfield homes but greatly exceeded appraised value for the South side homes. Plaintiffs argue that this evidence demonstrates that the defendants' pricing policies on the South side were discriminatory. This court is not persuaded.

The testimony establishes that an appraisal is a subjective estimate of property value that may vary considerably with regard to a single parcel of real estate depending on the individual responsible for the appraisal. Plaintiffs presented no persuasive evidence that the appraisal reports offered in evidence are reliable indicators of the fair market value of the homes appraised. In fact, the testimony of defendants' expert Mr. Shlaes indicates that there is no necessary relationship between an appraised value and fair market value or actual sales price.

Additionally, plaintiffs' own witnesses in several instances refused to assert that the appraisal reports reflected fair market value. For example, Mr. Langworthy of Rogers Park Savings & Loan Association testified that appraisals made for that association were used for the purposes of determining the size of the loan that could be approved for a particular home. Likewise, Mr. Del Campo, a field appraiser for three years, testified that the appraisal reports to Fairfield Savings & Loan Association were made to enable Fairfield to render an opinion of the mortgage dollar amount it might grant to a borrower. Testimony also indicated that the appraisal values for homes financed by Chicago Federal Savings & Loan Association were based solely on an estimate of the reproduction cost of a home derived from cost manuals containing data six months to a year old. The Chicago Federal appraisals were not intended to reflect the fair market value of the property appraised.

The testimony of defendants' expert, Mr. Shlaes, casts a further shadow on the probative value of the appraisals. His testimony indicates that mortgage lenders "tend to use the appraisals they commission to support their own decisions which are based on underwriting concerns [i.e.] whether or not they want to make loans at the time or in the area to the borrower." (Shlaes 1498). If the savings and loan association is reluctant to make the mortgage loan, it may express or imply to the appraiser a desire for a low appraisal so that it can avoid making the loan in the amount requested. If the lender is eager to make the loan, it may encourage the appraiser to take a liberal approach in his or her estimate of value.

Shlaes' testimony also corroborates the testimony of Mr. Tomlinson that at the time the appraisals were made cost manuals relied on in estimating reproduction costs did not contain current data. Moreover, plaintiffs' comparison of the average appraisal and average sales price of homes sold by Universal Corporation Company and DHDC in Deerfield with 15 homes sold on the South side in the year ending January 31, 1958 fails to support an inference that the defendants were using different pricing policies on the South side than were used in Deerfield. Plaintiffs' argument predicated on averages is a distortion. It avoids individual comparisons of price to appraisal. Individual comparisons show that on the South side some of the ratios of average sales price to average appraisal were higher and some were lower. The range of such averages relating to both Deerfield and South side homes were similar.

  C. Comparisons of gross profits realized on homes sold on the
     South side with those sold in Deerfield do not justify a conclu-

sion that defendants utilized discriminatory pricing policies in their sales of homes to plaintiffs.

The plaintiffs also argue that evidence of the gross profits made by defendants on the South side homes when compared to the gross profits made on homes sold by Universal Construction Company and DHDC in Deerfield justifies the inference that defendants utilized different pricing policies on the South side than did Universal Construction and DHDC in Deerfield.

The Keystone of plaintiffs' argument is their assertion that the evidence demonstrates that in the homebuilding industry, builders and developers set their prices in relation to the direct costs of construction and seek to recover a certain gross profit. As used in this case, "gross profit" is the difference between sales price, on the one hand, and the direct costs of constructing the building and purchasing the lot on which the dwelling is built, on the other. Indirect costs generally include wages for clerical help, salary, and other expenses associated with a business but which cannot be directly allocated as part of the cost of a particular house.

The plaintiffs have presented voluminous evidence comparing the "gross profit ratios" of Deerfield and South side homes. A "gross profit ratio" is obtained by dividing gross profit by the total sales amount, and is expressed as a percentage.

The plaintiffs presented testimony in an attempt to demonstrate that during the period 1957 to 1969, there existed a standard gross profit ratio of between 15% and 20% which was generally sought by members of the homebuilding industry. This court finds that the preponderance of credible evidence does not support such a conclusion.

Plaintiffs' evidence consists, in the main, of the testimony of Mr. Edward Noonan and Mr. Herbert Rosenfeld. Mr. Noonan has been identified earlier in this opinion. See p. 18, supra. Mr. Rosenfeld is an accountant and real estate developer and was a one-third owner of Surf Builders from 1963 to 1969. Surf Builders was one of the defendants' competitors during this period, constructing and selling homes in the same area as the defendants on the South side of Chicago.

Mr. Noonan's testimony does not establish that home builders set prices based on an estimate of cost plus a standard gross profit. Rather, his testimony establishes at most that, in his opinion, builders during the period 1957 through 1969 enjoyed on the average a 15%–20% gross profit ratio.

Mr. Rosenfeld's testimony indicates that his company sold approximately 150 homes during this period to black purchasers. In choosing plans for homes to be constructed he first viewed Universal's models and noted defendants' prices. While his testimony at one point indicates that he hoped to make a gross profit equal to 15% to 20% of sales price, he admitted that the gross profit figure was determined by market conditions and the amount of earnings the company wished to achieve. Like Noonan's, Herbert Rosenfeld's testimony does not support plaintiffs' contention that a standard gross profit percentage existed or that such a desired percentage dictated pricing policies.

Therefore, it is difficult for this court to infer that a comparison of gross profit percentages of homes sold on the South side with homes sold in Deerfield evidences discriminatory pricing by the defendants. Moreover, the defendants presented credible evidence that there is no standard gross profit percentage in the housing industry and that no standard gross profit percentage is used as a price setting mechanism.

Defendants offered the testimony of Martin Bartling, Jr. on this issue. Mr. Bartling has been the executive vice president of the Home Builders Association of Greater Chicago since February 1, 1978 and in 1960 was the president of the National Home Builders Association. Prior to moving to the Chicago area, he had over 23 years experience as a builder of single family homes in Tennessee. Mr. Bartling credibly testified that he had never heard of a standard gross profit in all of his years in the industry or that builders set their sales prices with regard to a formula based on or related to a standard gross profit. This court finds it hard to believe that a standard gross profit or standard gross profit ratio could have existed or been recognized by real estate developers or home builders as an aid in setting sales prices in the face of this testimony. Mr. Schlaes' testimony corroborates this conclusion.

Mr. Turoff's testimony indicates that prices were set after taking into account estimated costs including indirect costs, competitive factors, and differences between models with an eye toward achieving a net profit of 10%–15%. No attempt was made to determine gross profit. In setting prices, a variable dollar figure was added to estimated direct costs. This figure varied depending on overhead, intention to advertise, the number of homes it was believed would be sold and competition. Price adjustments were then made to preserve marketing differences between different model homes.

IV. The Exploitation Theory of Discrimination

The Court of Appeals' opinion in this case, Clark v. Universal Builders, Inc., 501 F.2d 324 (7th Cir. 1974), held that "plaintiffs state a claim under section 1982 since they allege that (1) as a result of racial residential segregation dual housing markets exist, and (2) defendant sellers took advantage of this situation by demanding prices and terms unreasonably in excess of prices and terms available to white citizens for comparable housing." This court begins by noting that judicial notice has been taken of the fact that during all time periods relevant to this case Chicago residential patterns have been characterized by a high degree of racial segregation.

Dual Housing Markets

In order to sustain their burden of proof on the existence of "dual housing markets" plaintiffs relied primarily on the testimony of Karl E. Taeuber, Ph.D. Mr. Taeuber is a Professor of Sociology and the Assistant Director of the Institute for Research on Poverty at the University of Wisconsin. His area of specialization within sociology is demography. The McGraw Hill Dictionary of Scientific and Technical Terms, Second Edition, defines demography as, "The statistical study of populations with reference to nationality, mortality, migratory movements, age, and sex, among other social, ethnic, and economic factors."

Prof. Taeuber has studied and published on the demographics of the black population, residential and school segregation, and population redistribution trends in the United States. His educational and professional background do not, so far as the evidence shows, include training, experience, or expertise in the field of economics, more specifically in the area of price theory and the effects of racism or racial segregation on prices.

Prof. Taeuber testified that there was a "dual housing market" in the Chicago metropolitan area during the 1950's and 1960's. The segments of the dual housing market cannot be identified on a geographical basis. As used by Prof. Taeuber, the term "dual housing market" refers to the operation of two separate markets: in one market housing is made available almost exclusively to whites, and in the other market, housing is made available primarily to blacks. The so-called white market in housing presents a number of barriers to the entry of blacks as a result of several factors including race discrimination on the part of white sellers. The so-called black market presents few impediments to the entry of white buyers other than the lack of white demand for housing in areas that are commonly thought of as populated by black residents.

Prof. Taeuber testified that the ability to afford housing does not explain the pattern of residential segregation because both blacks and whites are represented at all income levels and that most members of both races are in middle income brackets. There was no testimony as to the distribution of income by race, however, and defendants' expert, Pierre De Vise, testified that there were both black and white residents in virtually every census tract in the metropolitan area. Thus, Taeuber's testimony does not exclude the ability to afford housing as a factor affecting racial residential patterns.

Taeuber also testified that most areas of Chicago contain a mix of high and low-priced housing and thus, even considering the ability to afford housing as a factor affecting residential patterns in the city, this factor would not serve to explain the exclusion of blacks from those areas of the city containing both high and low-priced housing. However, as pointed out above, exclusion of blacks from identifiable areas is a relative thing and the existence of racial discrimination cannot alone serve to explain racial residential patterns.

Taeuber concludes that blacks suffer from a form of discrimination different from that encountered by white ethnic minorities. However, such a conclusion is not relevant to the issue of how that discrimination affects the price that blacks must pay for housing. Taeuber's testimony indicates that when various immigrant groups came to Chicago from Europe, their initial areas of settlement were concentrated in core residential areas. As they gained experience in the city and secured a sound economic base, they quickly adopted the American preference for living in single family dwellings removed from poor areas and this resulted in their dispersal throughout the metropolitan area.

However, black "migration" to the city has not resembled this pattern. Although black "immigrants" from the South, after the first World War, had the advantages of speaking English, citizenship, and a preference to live in single family residences removed from poor areas, the same degree of dispersal did not take place. According to Taeuber, these observations support the conclusion that race discrimination caused residential segregation.

While race discrimination has clearly been a substantial contributing factor in creating patterns of past and present residential segregation, the evidence offered by plaintiffs through Taeuber is inadequate to persuade this court that these conditions presented the defendants with the ability to charge a price unreasonably in excess of that which white homebuyers would be charged for comparable housing, or a price in excess of what plaintiffs would have paid for their homes in a perfectly integrated market.

Thus, try as it might, this court is unable to find that plaintiffs have met their burden of showing that the patterns of residential segregation existing in Chicago and contributed to, in significant degree, by race discrimination, presented the defendants with the opportunity to charge exorbitant prices amounting to a tax on plaintiffs' race.

In attempting to show that market conditions tainted by race discrimination made it possible for defendants to charge excessive prices to black homebuyers, Taeuber testified that population trends are related to the need for additional housing. Taeuber stated that an increase in population, or an increase in the number of households in an area, causes a need for additional housing. However, such testimony bears little, if any, relation to the defendants' ability to extract exorbitant prices for their homes. A desire for single family homes cannot be translated into a statement of economic demand for housing that affects its price.

A simple and common example suffices to illustrate the leap of logic made by Taeuber in offering his opinion to the contrary. It is clear at the present time that there are many people who desire to purchase single family homes who do not constitute part of the demand for those homes available due to economic reasons. On the other hand, everyone needs housing but many prefer to rent, or are unable to afford the down payment or make the periodic payments necessary to purchase.

In short, this court has been presented with absolutely no persuasive evidence from which to infer that market conditions in the so-called black segment of the "dual housing market" presented the defendants with the opportunity to create a monopoly or oligopoly for single family homes in their market area. In other words, there is no persuasive evidence from which this court can conclude that the demand for new homes among blacks exceeded the supply to a proportionately greater extent than among whites, giving defendants the opportunity to exploit the "dual housing market" by charging plaintiffs unreasonably high prices. This court simply does not believe that Taeuber's testimony regarding the "demand" for new single family housing among blacks is credible, and the court is not persuaded that Taeuber has the expertise to draw such a conclusion. Furthermore, given the plaintiffs' failure to show by a preponderance of the evidence that a standard gross profit existed in the housing industry, this court is unwilling to draw the conclusion that the difference in gross profits earned on the South side homes and the Deerfield homes supports the inference that defendants were able to exploit plaintiffs by setting prices at an unreasonable level.

In addition, the testimony of defendants' experts, Brian Barry, Pierre De Vise and Yale Brozen, support the conclusion that the defendants did not, and were unable to, extract higher prices from plaintiffs because of the operation of a "dual housing market" and that the prices charged would not have been lower in the absence of the pattern of racial residential segregation existing in Chicago during the years defendants operated on the South side.

The fact that defendants sold homes to plaintiffs on installment contracts, rather than through a mortgage financing arrangement, does not support the inference that the homes were sold on terms more onerous than those available to white citizens. The record in the present case demonstrates that white citizens do purchase homes on installment contracts and that white citizens did purchase homes on contract from Universal Construction Company and DHDC. In addition, none of the witnesses stated that they actually applied for a mortgage in connection with the purchase of these homes, nor did the plaintiffs present any evidence from which this court could determine whether they would have qualified for a mortgage if in fact they had applied. Plaintiffs' evidence with respect to the size of the down payments made is inconclusive on this question. Also, many homes were sold with down payments substantially below the then current 10% standard down payment.

More significant, however, is the fact that the installment contracts contained a full prepayment privilege without penalty which allowed the buyer to obtain mortgage financing at any time. Additional evidence that the terms of the sale were not onerous is the fact that 275 of the purchasers were represented by attorneys and they advised their clients to proceed with the transaction. Furthermore, 18 of the homes were sold with mortgage financing. On the basis of the above factors, the court is unwilling to conclude that the terms of the sale were onerous or oppressive. In addition, the court is not persuaded that defendants engaged in deceptive practices related to the negotiation of the contracts of sales.

V.   Conclusion

The above findings of fact, analyzed in relation to the applicable legal standards, results in the following legal conclusions. In order to establish a traditional violation of 42 U.S.C. Sec. 1982, plaintiffs must prove by a preponderance of the evidence that a seller of realty has sold comparable homes in comparable areas to black persons at prices which were higher, or on terms which were more onerous than those sold to white persons. Jones v. Alfred J. Mayer Co., 392 U.S. 409, 88 S.Ct. 2186, 20 L.Ed.2d 1189 (1968). In addition, plaintiffs must demonstrate that the difference in prices or terms was due to the race of the purchaser, and that the seller's actions were motivated by a discriminatory purpose or intent. Mescall v. Burrus, 603 F.2d 1266 (7th Cir. 1979); Resident Advisory Board v. Rizzo, 564 F.2d 126, (3d Cir. 1977), cert. denied, 435 U.S. 908, 98 S.Ct. 1458, 55 L.Ed.2d 499 (1978); Chicano Police Officer's Association v. Stover, 552 F.2d 918 (10th Cir. 1977); Croker v. Boeing Co., 437 F.Supp. 1138 (E.D.Penn. 1977); Lewis v. Bethlehem Steel Corp., 440 F.Supp. 949 (D.Md.1977); cf. Washington v. Davis, 426 U.S. 229, 96 S.Ct. 2040, 48 L.Ed.2d (1976); Village of Arlington Heights v. Metropolitan Housing Development Corporation, 429 U.S. 252, 97 S.Ct. 555, 50 L.Ed.2d 450 (1977); Mt. Healthy City School District v. Doyle, 429 U.S. 274, 97 S.Ct. 568, 50 L.Ed.2d 471 (1977). The evidence in the present case failed to demonstrate by a preponderance of credible evidence that the Deerfield and South side community areas were comparable, or that the homes sold were similar in design, layout, lot size, or building material. In addition, the evidence presented by plaintiffs, specifically the evidence related to appraised values, comparison of gross profits, and the method of financing purchases, does not persuade this court that the seller's actions were motivated by a discriminatory purpose or intent. For these reasons, plaintiffs have failed to establish a violation of 42 U.S.C. Sec. 1982 under the traditional theory of discrimination.

Plaintiffs have also offered evidence to establish a violation of 42 U.S.C. Sec. 1982 under a theory of exploitation of a dual housing market. To establish a violation of 42 U.S.C. Sec. 1982 under the "exploitation" theory, plaintiffs must establish by a preponderance of credible evidence that as a result of racial residential segregation dual housing markets exist and that defendants took advantage of this situation by demanding prices and terms unreasonably in excess of those prices and terms available to white citizens for comparable property. Clark v. Universal Builders, Inc., 501 F.2d 324 (7th Cir. 1974); Mescall v. Burrus, 603 F.2d 1266 (7th Cir. 1979). Plaintiffs have demonstrated by a preponderance of credible evidence the existence of a dual housing market that exists by virtue of the historical patterns of residential segregation in the City of Chicago. Plaintiffs have failed to demonstrate, however, that defendants were presented with the opportunity to extract unreasonable prices or terms which amounted to a tax on plaintiffs' race, or that the prices and terms charged were motivated by a discriminatory purpose or intent.

* * *

Finally, plaintiffs have alleged that defendants' activities were conducted in a willful and wanton manner and that plaintiffs are therefore entitled to punitive damages. As previously stated, the court has concluded that plaintiffs have not established by a preponderance of the evidence the claimed statutory violations. Even assuming that these violations had been established, the court concludes that punitive damages could not be imposed as a matter of law. The alleged statutory violations occurred prior to Jones v. Mayer, 392 U.S. 409, 88 S.Ct. 2186, 20 L.Ed.2d 1189 (1968) which held for the first time that Sec. 1982 was applicable to private action until the decision in Griffin v. Breckenridge, 403 U.S. 88, 91 S.Ct. 1790, 29 L.Ed.2d 338 (1971). As a matter of law, one cannot be held to have wilfully violated a statute which one would have legitimate reason to conclude was inapplicable. See generally Jones v. Mayer, 392 U.S. 409, 88 S.Ct. 2186, 20 L.Ed.2d 1189 (1968); Lee v. Southern Home Sites Corporation, 429 F.2d 290 (5th Cir. 1970).

All findings of fact deemed to be conclusions of law, and all conclusions of law deemed to be findings of fact are incorporated herein by reference.

For the foregoing reasons, the court concludes that the plaintiffs did not meet their burden of proof and judgment is therefore entered in favor of defendants.

QUESTIONS

1. The opinion relates that "the testimony of defendants' expert Mr. Shlaes indicates that there is no necessary relationship between an appraised value and fair market value or actual sales price." Does this testimony surprise you? Is there a sense in which it could be true and not be damaging to the plaintiffs' evidence (consisting of a group of appraisals)?

2. What about the testimony that mortgage lenders "tend to use the appraisals they commission to support their own decisions which are based on underwriting concerns [i.e.] whether or not they want to make loans at the time or in the area to the borrower"? Is this plausible? Is it damaging?

3. The court regarded as the "Keystone" of plaintiffs' argument their assertion that builders and developers set prices in relation to the direct costs of construction and seek to recover a certain gross profit. Gross profit is the difference between sales price and the direct costs of constructing the building and purchasing the site. Other "indirect" costs were acknowledged as including items such as wages for clerical help, salary, and other expenses associated with a business but which cannot be directly allocated as part of the cost of any particular house. Can you think of any indirect costs which might systematically be greater (or smaller) in downtown Chicago than in the suburbs?

4. In comparing two somewhat different products, would you expect the profit margins (or "markups") over *all* costs to be very similar if computed over some reasonable length of time? Why? Would the same hold true for subcategories of costs such as variable costs, direct costs, etc.?

5. In deciding that Deerfield and downtown houses are not comparable, the trial court alludes to significant differences in local facilities and infrastructure: mass transit, parks, shopping, schools, etc. Is the trial court incorrect in thinking (fn. 16) that the values of such amenities would be reflected in the cost of land acquisition and, hence, in the direct cost comparisons?

6. Assume that the defendants in fact had no exploitative power. Why would they have been willing to sell on contract to some buyers who presumably could not qualify for a mortgage loan? (After all, doesn't the mortgagee bank in effect have title to the house much as the contract seller does?) Would it provide one hypothesis if you found out that there was a state usury law? If there were no usury

law, is there an alternative explanation: that the developer is a better risk-bearer than an ordinary lending institution? Why?

7. Plaintiffs offered evidence that at least one of Universal's competitors, Surf Builders, sold what were alleged to be comparable homes on substantially better terms (lower prices, mortgages instead of contracts, etc.). Are we to understand that Surf sold *below* market price or that Universal sold *above*? Surf sold homes in the same neighborhood, and therefore presumably the same market, as Universal. What could account for substantially the same product selling at two different prices in the same market?

8. If Universal were indeed attempting to be exploitative, why might it prefer the contract sale to sale via mortgages?

9. On what basis could defendants' experts have testified that "defendants did not, and were unable to, extract higher prices" due to what was admittedly a "dual housing market." Is that conclusion a logical proposition derived from economic theory or is it an empirical question?

10. If you could decide the issues of law and fact in *Clark*, what would your holdings be? If there are additional factual inquiries that would affect your opinion, indicate what they are, why they are relevant, and what sort of evidence might resolve them.

THE THEORY OF THE SECOND BEST

Many of us learned at our mother's knee the old adage that "Two wrongs don't make a right." Nonetheless, an economic axiom known as the "Second Best Theory" cautions us that the time-honored cliche may sometimes be incorrect, that two wrongs may indeed be better than only one.[a]

Reduced to simple terms, the Theory of the Second Best points out that what appears to be an improvement in one part of an interdependent process or system may have undesirable feedback effects in another. (In the field of systems analysis, a similar problem is captured in the warnings against "suboptimizing," i.e., optimizing the solution to one component part of a large problem while disregarding the effects on other aspects of the overall problem.) In the economic context, the Second Best Theory teaches that we can be sure that perfecting one market will also improve overall resource allocation only when all markets except the one being tinkered with are already working perfectly. In this case, the solution reached is a "First Best." If, however, some of the other markets are functioning incor-

a. Although the notion involved is a common-sense one, the theorem was first formalized and named by Lipsey and Lancaster, "The General Theory of the Second Best," 24 Rev.Econ.Stud. 11 (1956).

rectly, optimization of a related market may make things worse, rather than better, from an overall perspective.

Most of the applications of the Second Best theorem in the economic and legal literature have been drawn from antitrust and regulatory economics.[b] A typical contrived pedagogical example will illustrate. An earlier section in this chapter suggested why "too little" of a monopolized product is sold as judged by the product's production cost and its value in use: price is set higher than marginal cost. Suppose, then, that potatoes were monopolized and pasta (spaghetti, macaroni, noodles, etc.) were not. Too few potatoes would be consumed, but some of the demand for starchy food would be shifted to a substitute, pasta. Relative to the First Best quantities of potatoes and pasta that would be purchased if both markets were functioning ideally, we would now find too few potatoes and too much pasta being consumed. A Second Best theorist would then suggest that, rather than allow the competitive pasta market to produce out to where P = MC for pasta, pasta should be taxed with the purpose of artificially raising the pasta price above its (net of tax) marginal cost and causing consumers both to cut back on pasta and also shift some of their demand back to potatoes. This Second Best policy involves, in effect, the interposition of a second distortion in order partially to counterbalance a preexisting distortion. The First Best solution would, of course, be to get rid of the monopoly in the potato market in the first place.

Although the monopoly application is technically correct, students of the law frequently find the application an infelicitous one. One reason is of course, that the *distributive* consequences of the Second Best policy are in this case seen as improving the position of the monopolist, even though the *efficiency* of resource use is arguably improved. Once one understands the principle of offsetting distortions, however, more attractive applications of the Second Best principle can easily be supplied.

One rather persuasive example is supplied by the problem of pricing urban transportation. Ordinarily, economists would argue that the cost of a ride on an urban mass transportation system should be set equal to its marginal cost. Since consumers will buy rides up to the point where the marginal benefits of a ride equals its price, a price below marginal cost will result in inputs being used that produce less output value than their resource cost: MB = P and P < MC, and therefore MB < MC. In this case, however, little or no charge at all is made for the use of public highways, one of the substitutes for mass transit rides. By subsidizing transit rides, travelers

b. See, for instance, R. Bork, The Antitrust Paradox 113–14 (1978); R. Posner, Economic Analysis of Law 202–03 & n. 1 (2nd ed. 1977); W. Baumol, Welfare Economics and the Theory of the State 30 (2d ed. 1965).

may be pulled away from the highways, where their resource use is even more wasteful. First Best would be an appropriate user-charge for highways rides, but if this is impractical the Second Best may require "too low" prices for mass transit rides.

In the legal literature, a thought-provoking example of the application of Second Best theory is James Henderson's analysis of the extension of strict liability to segmented markets. See Henderson, "Extending the Boundaries of Strict Products Liability: Implications of the Theory of the Second Best," 128 U.Pa.L.Rev. 1036 (1980). Imposition of strict liability is often premised upon some defect in the affected product market. Even assuming *arguendo* that underlying premise, strict liability may make matters worse if the relevant market is divided into segments—such as commercial and non-commercial sellers—and one (or more) of these is not reachable by the strict liability. For instance, one of Henderson's discussions compares the sale or lease of used products through commercial and non-commercial channels. If political or other exigencies require that non-commercial channels will not be included within the strict liability rule, then imposition of the rule on commercial markets may motivate a shift into non-commercial outlets. Why might this "half a loaf" be worse than an environment in which a "needed" strict liability is imposed on *neither* sub-market?

The basic logic of the Second Best principle is easily extended to other interdependent systems or processes, including adjudication. If a bias in one direction can be identified and it is impractical to correct that bias directly (the First Best solution), then the toleration or even creation of an offsetting bias may be desirable.

Taken to its logical extreme, the Second Best theorem is a counsel of agnosticism. Since it is seldom the case that one can have confidence that the rest of the system is optimally fine-tuned, it is technically true that apparent improvements of subsectors of the system may make things worse.[c] Some might prefer, however, to couch the issue in terms of rebuttable presumption. An apparent improvement might then be regarded as a *prima facie* case in favor of a policy and the burden shifted to those who oppose it. That this burden can sometimes be met is demonstrated by some of the examples given above. Generally speaking, the Second Best principle will have a practical relevance in the economic environment when there is a defective but "uncorrectible" market that has a "closely related" market of either complements or substitutes. How does the policy reac-

---

c. See Markovits, "A Basic Structure for Microeconomic Policy in Our Worse-Than-Second-Best World: A Proposal and Critique of the Chicago Approach to the Study of Law and Economics," 1975 Wisc.L.Rev. 950; L. Sullivan, Handbook of the Law of Antitrust 4–5 (1977).

tion depend on whether the related market involves substitutes or complements?

QUESTIONS

1. Could a Second Best analysis be applied to the treatment of damages for future lost income? (Recall the knotty problems discussed in Chapter IV above.)

2. Are some kinds of punitive damages a reflection of the Second Best principle?

3. Outline in some detail how a parallel might be drawn between (a) Henderson's example of the commercial and non-commercial markets and (b) the urban transport pricing problem. What is the loss if the Second Best principal is not applied?

4. Following on the example in the text above, suppose that the pasta market were monopolized. What implications does this have for the market in spaghetti sauce?

5.   "In applying the Second Best theorem to economic systems, it is better to look at the way in which quantities are distorted than the way in which prices are distorted." What does this mean? Return to this question again after you have reflected on the application in the following section.

STATEMENT OF U.S. DEPT. OF TRANSPORTATION BEFORE THE INTERSTATE COMMERCE COMMISSION, WESTERN COAL INVESTIGATION—GUIDELINES FOR RAILROAD RATE STRUCTURE

Ex Parte No. 347, Aug. 4, 1978.

[The ICC was investigating appropriate rate guidelines for large-volume western coal movements originating in the Rocky Mountain-Upper Missouri River Region. These routes represent areas where the railroads occupy a strong competitive position with respect to alternative transport modes such as trucks or barges. Hence, the railroads would, with ICC approval, potentially be able to recover not only the variable costs of shipping on these routes but also to partially amortize fixed costs. DOT's statement is sympathetic to the railroads' desire to extract differentially higher prices on western coal shipments since the competitive situation makes it possible to do so and higher general rates on all shippers would otherwise be required to cover fully allocated costs.]

* * *

IV. Setting a Ceiling on Rates for Western Coal Rail Movements

A. *Considerations of National Energy Policy*

* * * DOT notes that this nation's energy policy is based in large part on conservation of energy resources as well as on a shift, wherever possible, to coal, a plentiful energy resource, and away from scarce petroleum products. Much of our dependence on petroleum fuels is due to an artificial reduction in the price of those fuels through a history of price controls. DOT is anxious to assure that in shifting to coal, market tests of resource allocation efficiency are retained in order to prevent this sort of misallocation in the future. As long as the delivered price of coal does not rise above the delivered price of alternative energy resources, our nation's fuel resources can be said to be efficiently and desirably allocated.

To assure that energy is appropriately priced and resources are properly allocated, DOT believes that the Commission should establish the principle that, in general, the maximum rate on coal is one that will equate the delivered price of coal per BTU to the delivered price per BTU of any other available fuel. Such a ceiling on transportation rates for coal would encourage a shift by utilities toward the use of coal and away from less desirable sources of energy.

Specifically, DOT believes that where a utility does have the opportunity to select from a number of fuels, including western coal, the Commission should not (except in a few circumstances described below) permit the imposition of a rate for large-volume coal movements which would result in the delivered price of coal being higher than the delivered price of other competing fuels. In a properly functioning market, this is the maximum a railroad could charge and still retain the traffic. However, where legal or institutional constraints require a utility to burn coal, DOT contends that the Commission should permit railroads to set rates up to a level that equates the delivered price of coal per unit of electricity with the delivered price of alternative fuels as though there were no price controls on those fuels. Such rate levels will contribute to the health of the railroads, allow allocational efficiency, and encourages conservation of energy.

B. *The Market Structure For Fuels*

In an efficiently functioning market, electric utilities would determine what fuel, as delivered to the plant, was least costly and would contract to purchase both the fuel and any transportation services needed to secure that fuel. Today's markets for energy and transportation do not match this ideal. The institutions and information necessary to simultaneously get price quotes on all alternatives, and to make long-term contracts for the lowest cost fuel and transportation combination, are simply not currently available. In the absence of contract rail rates, those utilities which choose (or are required) to employ coal for generation of electric power must enter into contracts to buy coal without knowing what their rail transportation costs will be over time.

Another evident market defect is created by the price controls on oil and natural gas which make those fuels artificially attractive relative to coal and incidentally work to frustrate national energy policy. Finally, a host of laws, directly or indirectly, work to influence the decision as to what fuel a particular utility will burn.

* * *

D. *Establishment of a Rate Ceiling Where the Utility is Required to Utilize Coal*

Where a particular utility is required to use coal to generate electricity, energy policy considerations are already achieved. Under those circumstances, economic efficiency and the policies of the 4R Act require only that the maximum rate for any new coal movements should leave the delivered price of coal per BTU no higher than the "economic cost" of using any other energy source.[26] Such an analysis permits the setting of railroad rates at levels no higher than they could be set were there economically efficient markets for both energy and transportation.

In light of the serious market imperfections described in Section IV B above, DOT contends that in order to ascertain the maximum rail rate for coal, it is necessary to calculate a "shadow price" associated with the delivery and purchase costs of other fuels.[27]

For a variety of historical reasons, price controls have been established on domestic oil and natural gas which encourage excessive use of those fuels relative to coal. This has artificially forced down coal prices and rail coal rates.[28] Limiting coal rates to a level that left the delivered price of coal no higher than the artificially depressed delivered prices of oil would unreasonably reduce railroad revenues without improving allocation of fuel or transportation resources in the economy. The major reason why there has been pressure to shift from other fuels to coal has been to conserve dwindling supplies of natural gas and to reduce dependence on oil. It would be inconsistent to require use of coal to conserve use of other fuels while at the

---

26. The economic cost of any resource is the price determined in the market in the absence of price controls or other constraints on the market.

27. A shadow price is the price which would exist had the market been operating properly and efficiently and had all

alternatives been available to the utility at the time the decision to utility coal was made.

28. The current government energy policy encouraging a shift from petroleum fuels to coal has, to some degree, corrected this artificial imbalance.

same time treating the price of those fuels as though they were lower than the free market level. Using the free market price of the alternative fuels, rather than the artificially low regulated price results in rate ceilings set on the basis of economic values of alternative resources. It also allows the railroads to obtain necessary revenues to maintain operations and to attract and retain capital.

QUESTIONS

1.   In the text at footnotes 27 and 28, the DOT staff uses "serious market imperfections" to advocate higher delivered prices for coal. In which markets are the imperfections? How does this affect the coal market? How is the concept of cross elasticity of demand (see Ch. V) relevant here?

2.   By the DOT argument, what would be the "First Best" solution to the alleged imperfections in energy markets? Why doesn't DOT argue for that solution?

3.   Is it fair to characterize DOT's position as based on Second Best considerations?

4.   Suppose that you represented western utilities who are obligated to burn coal. How could you argue that, on its own premises, the DOT recommendation is exactly 180 degrees around from the correct conclusion?

5.   If the best argument were made in the previous question, is there any way in which the DOT position might be reformulated so that it at least arguably follows from a line of Second Best logic?

GHEN v. RICH

United States District Court, D. Massachusetts, 1881.
8 F. 159.

NELSON, D.J.

This is a libel to recover the value of a fin-back whale. The libellant lives in Provincetown and the respondent in Wellfleet. The facts, as they appeared at the hearing, are as follows:

In the early spring months the easterly part of Massachusetts Bay is frequented by the species of whale known as the fin-back whale. Fishermen from Provincetown pursue them in open boats from the shore and shoot them with bomb-lances fired from guns made expressly for the purpose. When killed they sink at once to the bottom, but in the course of from one to three days they rise and float on the surface. Some of them are picked up by vessels and towed into Provincetown. Some float ashore at high water and are left stranded on the beach as the tide recedes. Others float out to sea and are never recovered. The person who happens to find them on the beach usually sends word to Provincetown, and the owner comes to the spot and removes the blubber. The finder usually receives a small salvage for his services. Tryworks are established in Provincetown for trying out the oil. The business is of considerable extent, but, since it requires skill and experience, as well as some outlay of capital, and is attended with great exposure and hardship, few persons engage in it. The average yield of oil is about twenty barrels to a whale. It swims with great swiftness, and for that reason cannot be taken by the harpoon and line. Each boat's crew engaged in the business has its peculiar mark or device on its lances, and in this way it is known by whom the whale is killed.

The usage on Cape Cod, for many years, has been that the person who kills a whale in the manner and under the circumstances described, owns it, and this right has never been disputed until this case. The libellant has been engaged in this business for ten years past. On the morning of April 9, 1880, in Massachusetts Bay, near the end of Cape Cod, he shot and instantly killed with a bomb-lance the whale in question. It sunk immediately, and on the morning of the 12th was found stranded on the beach in Brewster, within the ebb and flow of the tide, by one Ellis, seventeen miles from the spot where it was killed. Instead of sending word to Provincetown, as is customary, Ellis advertised the whale for sale at auction, and sold it to the respondent, who stripped off the blubber and tried out the oil. The libellant heard of the finding of the whale on the morning of the 15th, and immediately sent one of his boat's crew to the place and claimed it. Neither the respondent nor Ellis knew the whale had been killed by the libellant, but they knew or might have known, if they had wished, that it had been shot and killed with a bomb-lance, by some person engaged in this species of business.

The libellant claims title to the whale under this usage. The respondent insists that this usage is invalid. It was decided by Judge Sprague, in Taber v. Jenny, 1 Sprague, 315, that when a whale has been killed, and is anchored and left with marks of appropriation, it is the property of the captors; and if it is afterwards found, still anchored, by another ship, there is no usage or principle of law by which the property of the original captors is diverted, even though the whale may have dragged from its anchorage. The learned judge says:

"When the whale had been killed and taken possession of by the boat of Hillman (the first taker) it became the property of the owners of that ship, and all was done which was then practicable in order to secure it. They left it anchored, with unequivocal marks of appropriation *   *   *"

In Swift v. Gifford, 2 Low. 110, Judge Lowell decided that a custom among whalemen in the Arctic seas, that the iron holds the whale, was reasonable and valid. In that case a boat's crew from the respondent's ship pursued and struck a whale in the Arctic Ocean, and the harpoon and the line attached to it remained in the whale, but did not remain fast to the boat. A boat's crew from the libellant's ship continued pursuit and captured the whale, and the master of the respondent's ship claimed it on the spot. It was held by the learned judge that the whale belonged to the respondents. It was said by Judge Sprague, in Bourne v. Ashley, an unprinted case referred to by Judge Lowell in Swift v. Gifford, that the usage for the first iron, whether attached to the boat or not, to hold the whale was fully established; and he added that, although local usages of a particular port ought not to be allowed to set aside the general maritime law, this objection did not apply to a custom which embraced an entire business, and had been concurred in for a long time by every one engaged in the trade　*　*　*

I see no reason why the usage proved in this case is not as reasonable as that sustained in the case cited. Its application must necessarily be extremely limited, and can affect but a few persons. It has been recognized and acquiesced in for many years. It requires in the first take the only act of appropriation that is possible in the nature of the case. Unless it is sustained, this branch of industry must necessarily cease, for no person would engage in it if the fruits of his labor could be appropriated by any chance finder. It gives reasonable salvage for securing or reporting the property. That the rule works well in practice is shown by the extent of the industry which has grown up under it, and the general acquiescence of a whole community interested to dispute it. It is by no means clear that without regard to usage the common law would not reach the same result. That seems to be the effect of the decisions in Taber v. Jenny and Bartlett v. Budd. If the fisherman does all that it is possible to do to make the animal his own, that would seem to be sufficient. Such a rule might well be applied in the interest of trade, there being no usage or custom to the contrary. Holmes Com. Law, 217. But be that as it may, I hold the usage to be valid, and that the property in the whale was in the libellant.

The rule of damages is the market value of the oil obtained from the whale, less the cost of trying it out and preparing it for the market, with interest on the amount so ascertained from the date of conversion. As the question is new and important, and the suit is contested on both sides, more for the purpose of having it settled than for the amount involved, I shall give no costs.

Decree for the libellant for $71.05, without costs.

QUESTIONS

1. For expository simplicity, consider the whale industry to be composed of two stages of production, harpooning and finding. Harpooners actually produce two distinguishable "outputs"; (1) the harpooned whales that they are immediately able to retrieve; and (2) the "found" whales that initially got away. A case such as Ghen v. Rich determines the extent of the harpooners' property rights in the second type of output. Let β be the fraction of a found whale's value that a harpooner can appropriate (implicitly, the finder's share is $1 - \beta$) and V the market value of a whale. If the fraction of whales that get away initially is f and the fraction of those ultimately found is $\propto$, then the marginal revenue curve that a harpooner sees is $[(1 - f) V + (\propto f) \beta V]$ for each whale harpooned. Why? Would a harpooner want the magnitude of β to be as high as possible?

2. A finder produces only one kind of output: found whales. The marginal revenue curve that a finder sees is $(1 - \beta)V$, since his share of the whale's value is the remainder not kept by the harpooner. As the value of β moves toward zero, the finder's cost curves are likely to shift upward. Why? From the finder's perspective, what determines the optimal value of β?

3. Do you think that the finders may have wanted to lose this case? Is there anything in the opinion pertinent to this question?

4. What is the "best" value for β from the standpoint of society: the harpooners, the finders, and the users of whale products? Why might this value change over time? Should a court readjust it? How else might it be done?

5. Show that any value set for β falls short of a "First Best" result. [Hint: Do both the harpooners and the finders underproduce? What would be the joint maximization outcome and why do they not achieve it?]

6. What problems in earlier chapters are related to that of the harpooners and the finders? Does this current context present any difficulties that were not involved in the earlier problems?

NONMARKET SYSTEMS: INTERLOCAL MIGRATION

Although markets are perhaps the most important and well analyzed type of interactive economic system, other important systemic processes are amenable to economic analysis. For instance, attempts to regulate local development and, implicitly, interlocal migration patterns have raised some provocative legal issues. Although spatial location models can be among the most complex of all economic models, the flavor of the problem can be conveyed in the form of a very simplistic model.

Assume a very simple world with two possible living sites, City A and City B. City A is for various reasons—climate, topography, access to other resources, etc.—a more "favorable" site to develop. At each site, however, the net benefits of residence depend upon the number of other people sharing the location. Exhibit 6.6 has been drawn to reflect the net benefits per capita obtainable at each site as a function of the number of residents. Over an early range of population growth, there are "agglomeration economies" as the ability to share the cost of facilities and to interact beneficially increases. After the "optimal" population size is reached, the effects of congestion and other unfavorable interactions become dominant and increasing population causes benefits to decline.

EXHIBIT 6.6

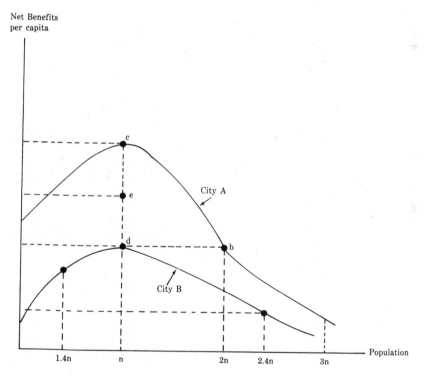

Be forewarned that Exhibit 6.6 has been drawn in a particular way in order to make a number of pedagogical points. The really important underlying assumption, however, is only that there are both economies and diseconomies of population size change over certain ranges. For simplicity, we shall also assume that the world is full of more or less homogeneous people who evaluate the two sites in similar ways.

If the world starts with one person, Exhibit 6.6 suggests that the person will choose to locate in City A. As population size increases up to the optimal size N, everyone is perfectly happy with the influx. Now let population increase to 2N. The "quality of life" in City A will deteriorate, but the B2 benefit level in A is still as good as the best one can do at the site of the potential City B. Is there any sense, then, in which a misallocation of population might be said to exist? At what point will people begin to leave A and move to B?

Although the Exhibit 6.6 model is a very crude one, it will suffice to pose some interesting questions. Relaxation of the model's simplifying assumptions raises even more fascinating issues, but those intricacies are beyond the scope of the present treatment.[d]

QUESTIONS

1. Assume the 2N level of total population. Show that *average* benefits of the population would be maximized if there were N people in each city. How could that population distribution be achieved, or maintained if it were achieved?

2. At 2.4N, all of the people would still be at site A. Why? Wouldn't the last 0.4N be better off if they moved to A? Who bears the "entrepreneurial" costs of developing B?

3. What "externalities" are involved in this interlocal migration process? When the second N people move into City A, do the external costs that they impose exceed the internal benefits they receive from being in A rather than B?

4. Does the law in any way seek to "internalize" this type of externality? Should it?

d. Exhibit 6.6 is taken from Goetz, "Fiscal Incentives for the Cities," Committee on Urban Public Economics Seminar series, Nov. 1969. The additional "intricacies" and their policy implications were in fact developed in that paper.

CONSTRUCTION INDUSTRY ASSOCIATION OF SONOMA COUNTY v. CITY OF PETALUMA

United States Court of Appeals, Ninth Circuit, 1975.
522 F.2d 897 (1975), certiorari denied 424 U.S. 934, 96 S.Ct. 1148,
47 L.Ed.2d 342 (1976).

CHOY, Circuit Judge:

The City of Petaluma (the City) appeal from a district court decision voiding as unconstitutional certain aspects of its five-year housing and zoning plan. We reverse.

Statement of Facts

The City is located in southern Sonoma County, about 40 miles north of San Francisco. In the 1950's and 1960's, Petaluma was a relatively self-sufficient town. It experienced a steady population growth from 10,315 in 1950 to 24,870 in 1970. Eventually, the City was drawn into the Bay Area metropolitan housing market as people working in San Francisco and San Rafael became willing to commute longer distances to secure relatively inexpensive housing available there. By November 1972, according to unofficial figures, Petaluma's population was at 30,500, a dramatic increase of almost 25 per cent in little over two years.

* * *

Alarmed by the accelerated rate of growth in 1970 and 1971, the demand for even more housing, and the sprawl of the City eastward, the City adopted a temporary freeze on development in early 1971. The construction and zoning change moratorium was intended to give the City Council and the City planners an opportunity to study the housing and zoning situation and to develop short and long range plans. The Council made specific findings with respect to housing patterns and availability in Petaluma, including the following: That from 1960–1970, 88 per cent of housing permits issued were for single-family detached homes; that in 1970, 83 per cent of Petaluma's housing was single-family dwellings; that the bulk of recent development (largely single-family homes) occurred in the eastern portion of the City, causing a large deficiency in moderately priced multi-family and apartment units on the east side.

To correct the imbalance between single-family and multi-family dwellings, curb the sprawl of the City on the east, and retard the accelerating growth of the City, the Council in 1972 adopted several resolutions, which collectively are called the "Petaluma Plan" (the Plan).

The Plan, on its face limited to a five-year period (1972–1977), fixes a housing development growth rate not to exceed 500 dwelling units per year.[1] Each dwelling unit represents approximately three people. The 500-unit figure is somewhat misleading, however, because it applies only to housing units (hereinafter referred to as "development-units") that are part of projects involving five units or more. Thus, the 500-unit figure does not reflect any housing and population growth due to construction of single-family homes or even four-unit apartment buildings not part of any larger project.

The Plan also positions a 200 foot wide "greenbelt" around the City, to serve as a boundary for urban expansion for at least five years, and with respect to the east and north sides of the City, for perhaps ten to fifteen years. One of the most innovative features of the Plan is the Residential Development Control System which provides procedures and criteria for the award of the annual 500 development-unit permits. At the heart of the allocation procedure is an intricate point system, whereby a builder accumulates points for conformity by his projects with the City's general plan and environmental design plans, for good architectural design, and for providing low and moderate income dwelling units and various recreational facilities. The Plan further directs that allocations of building permits are to be divided as evenly as feasible between the west and east sections of the City and between single-family dwellings and multiple residential units (including rental units), that the sections of the City closest to the center are to be developed first in order to cause "infilling" of vacant area, and that 8 to 12 per cent of the housing units approved be for low and moderate income persons.

In a provision of the Plan, intended to maintain the close-in rural space outside and surrounding Petaluma, the City solicited Sonoma County to establish stringent subdivision and appropriate acreage parcel controls for the areas outside the urban extension line of the City and to limit severely further residential infilling.

The purpose of the Plan is much disputed in this case. According to general statements in the Plan itself, the Plan was devised to ensure that "development in the next five years will take place in a reasonable, orderly, attractive manner, rather than in a completely haphazard and unattractive manner." The controversial 500-unit limitation on residential development-units was adopted by the City "[i]n order to protect its small town character and surrounding open

1. The district court found that although the Plan is ostensibly limited to a five-year period, official attempts have been made to perpetuate the Plan before 1977. Such attempts include the urban extension line (see text infra) and the agreement to purchase from the Sonoma County Water Agency only 9.8 million gallons of water per day through the year 1990. This flow is sufficient to support a population of 55,000. If the City were to grow at a rate of about 500 housing units per year (approximately three persons per unit), the City would reach a population of 55,000 about the year 1990. The 55,000 figure was mentioned by City officials as the projected optimal (and maximum) size of Petaluma. See, e.g., R.T. at 135–43, 145–46.

space." The other features of the Plan were designed to encourage an east-west balance in development, to provide for variety in densities and building types and wide ranges in prices and rents, to ensure infilling of close-in vacant areas, and to prevent the sprawl of the City to the east and north. The Construction Industry Association of Sonoma County (the Association) argues and the district court found, however, that the Plan was primarily enacted "to limit Petaluma's demographic and market growth rate in housing and in the immigration of new residents." Construction Industry Assn. v. City of Petaluma, 375 F.Supp. 574, 576 (N.D.Cal.1974).

*   *   *

Substantive Due Process

Appellees claim that the Plan is arbitrary and unreasonable and, thus, violative of the due process clause of the Fourteenth Amendment. According to appellees, the Plan is nothing more than an exclusionary zoning device,[10] designed solely to insulate Petaluma from the urban complex in which it finds itself. The Association and the Landowners reject, as falling outside the scope of any legitimate governmental interest, the City's avowed purposes in implementing the Plan—the preservation of Petaluma's small town character and the avoidance of the social and environmental problems caused by an uncontrolled growth rate.

In attacking the validity of the Plan, appellees rely heavily on the district court's finding that the express purpose and the actual effect of the Plan is to exclude substantial numbers of people who would otherwise elect to move to the City. 375 F.Supp. at 581. The existence of an exclusionary purpose and effect reflects, however, only *one* side of the zoning regulation. Practically all zoning restrictions have as a purpose and effect the *exclusion* of some activity or type of structure or a certain density of inhabitants. And in reviewing the

---

10. "Exclusionary zoning" is a phrase popularly used to describe suburban zoning regulations which have the effect, if not also the purpose, of preventing the migration of low and middle-income persons. Since a large percentage of racial minorities fall within the low and middle income brackets, exclusionary zoning regulations may also effectively wall out racial minorities. See generally Aloi, Goldberg & White, Racial and Economic Segregation by Zoning: Dean Knell for Home Rule?, 1969 U.Tol.L.Rev. 65 (1969); Bigham & Bostick, Exclusionary Zoning Practices: An Examination of the Current Controversy, 25 Vand.L.Rev. 111 (1972); Davidoff & Davidoff, Opening the Suburbs: Toward Inclusionary Land Use Controls, 22 Syracuse L.Rev. 509 (1971); Note, Exclusionary Zoning and Equal Protection, 84 Harv.L.Rev. 1645 (1971).

Most court challenges to and comment upon so-called exclusionary zoning focus on such traditional zoning devices as height limitations, minimum square footage and minimum lot size requirements, and the prohibition of multifamily dwellings or mobile homes. The Petaluma Plan is unique in that although it assertedly slows the growth rate it replaces the past pattern of single-family detached homes with an assortment of housing units, varying in price and design.

reasonableness of a zoning ordinance, our inquiry does not terminate with a finding that it is for an exclusionary purpose. We must determine further whether the *exclusion* bears any rational relationship to a *legitimate state interest*. If it does not, then the zoning regulation is invalid. If, on the other hand, a legitimate state interest is furthered by the zoning regulation, we must defer to the legislative act. Being neither a super legislature nor a zoning board of appeal, a federal court is without authority to weigh and reappraise the factors considered or ignored by the legislative body in passing the challenged zoning regulation. The reasonableness, not the wisdom, of the Petaluma Plan is at issue in this suit.

It is well settled that zoning regulations "must find their justification in some aspect of the police power, asserted for the public welfare." Village of Euclid v. Ambler Realty Co., 272 U.S. 365, 387, 47 S.Ct. 114, 118, 71 L.Ed. 303 (1926). The concept of the public welfare, however, is not limited to the regulation of noxious activities or dangerous structures. As the Court stated in Berman v. Parker, 348 U.S. 26, 33, 75 S.Ct. 98, 102, 99 L.Ed. 27 (1954): "The concept of the public welfare is broad and inclusive. The values it represents are spiritual as well as physical, aesthetic as well as monetary. It is within the power of the legislature to determine that the community should be beautiful as well as healthy, spacious as well as clean, well-balanced as well as carefully patrolled." (citations omitted). Accord, Village of Belle Terre v. Boraas, 416 U.S. 1, 6, 9, 94 S.Ct. 1536, 39 L.Ed.2d 797 (1974).

In determining whether the City's interest in preserving its small town character and in avoiding uncontrolled and rapid growth falls within the broad concept of "public welfare," we are considerably assisted by two recent cases. Belle Terre, supra, and Ybarra v. City of Town of Los Altos Hills, 503 F.2d 250 (9th Cir. 1974), each of which upheld as not unreasonable a zoning regulation much more restrictive than the Petaluma Plan, are dispositive of the due process issue in this case.

In Belle Terre the Supreme Court rejected numerous challenges [13] to a village's restricting land use to one-family dwellings excluding lodging houses, boarding houses, fraternity houses or multiple-dwell-

---

13. The plaintiffs in Belle Terre claimed inter alia that the ordinance interfered with a person's right to travel and right to migrate to and settle within a state.

The Supreme Court held that since the ordinance was not aimed at transients, there was no infringement of anyone's right to travel. 416 U.S. at 7, 94 S.Ct. 1536. Although due to appellees' lack of standing we do not reach today the right to travel issue, we note that the Petaluma plan is not aimed at transients, nor does it penalize those who have recently exercised their right to travel. See CEEED v. California Coastal Zone Conservation Comm'n, 43 Cal.App.3d 306, 118 Cal.Rptr. 315, 332–34 (1974); cf. Dunn v. Blumstein, 405 U.S. 330, 342, 92 S.Ct. 995, 31 L.Ed.2d 274 (1972).

ing houses. By absolutely prohibiting the construction of or conversion of a building to other than single-family dwelling, the village ensured that it would never grow, if at all, much larger than its population of 700 living in 220 residences. Nonetheless, the Court found that the prohibition of boarding houses and other multi-family dwellings present urban problems, such as the occupation of a given space by more people, the increase in traffic and parked cars and the noise that comes with increased crowds. According to the Court, "A quiet place where yards are wide, people few, and motor vehicles restricted are legitimate guidelines in a land-use project addressed to family needs. This goal is a permissible one within Berman v. Parker, supra. The police power is not confined to elimination of filth, stench, and unhealthy places. It is ample to lay out zones where family values, youth values, and the blessings of quiet seclusion, and clean air make the area a sanctuary for people" 416 U.S. at 9, 94 S.Ct. at 1541. While dissenting from the majority opinion in Belle Terre on the ground that the regulation unreasonably burdened the exercise of First Amendment associational rights, Mr. Justice Marshall concurred in the Court's express holding that a local entity's zoning power is extremely broad: "[L]ocal zoning authorities may properly act in furtherance of the objectives asserted to be served by the ordinance at issue here: *restricting uncontrolled growth*, solving traffic problems, keeping rental costs at a reasonable level, and making the community attractive to families. The police power which provides the justification for zoning is not narrowly confined. And, it is appropriate that we afford zoning authorities *considerable latitude in choosing the means by which to implement such purposes.*" 416 U.S. at 13–14, 94 S.Ct. at 1543 (Marshall, J., dissenting) (emphasis added) (citations omitted).

Following the Belle Terre decision, this court in Los Altos Hills had an opportunity to review a zoning ordinance providing that a housing lot shall contain not less than one acre and that no lot shall be occupied by more than one primary dwelling unit. The ordinance as a practical matter prevented poor people from living in Los Altos Hills and restricted the density, and thus the population, of the town. This court, nonetheless, found that the ordinance was rationally related to a legitimate governmental interest—the preservation of the town's rural environment—and, thus, did not violate the equal protection clause of the Fourteenth Amendment. 503 F.2d at 254.

Both the Belle Terre ordinance and the Los Altos Hills regulation had the purpose and effect of permanently restricting growth; nonetheless, the court in each case upheld the particular law before it on the ground that the regulation served a legitimate governmental interest falling within the concept of the public welfare: the preservation of quiet family neighborhoods (Belle Terre) and the preservation of a rural environment (Los Altos Hills). Even less restrictive or exclusionary than the above zoning ordinances is the Petaluma Plan which, unlike those ordinances, does not freeze the population at present or near-present levels. Further, unlike the Los Altos Hills ordinance and the various zoning regulations struck down by state courts in recent years, the Petaluma Plan does not have the undesirable effect of walling out any particular income class nor any racial minority group.[16]

Although we assume that some persons desirous of living in Petaluma will be excluded under the housing permit limitation and that, thus, the Plan may frustrate some legitimate regional housing needs, the Plan is not arbitrary or unreasonable. We agree with appellees that unlike the situation in the past most municipalities today are neither isolated nor wholly independent from neighboring municipalities and that, consequently, unilateral land use decisions by one local entity affect the needs and resources of an entire region. See, e.g., Golden v. Planning Board of Town of Ramapo, 30 N.Y.2d 359, 334 N.Y.S.2d 138, 285 N.E.2d 291, appeal dismissed, 409 U.S. 1003, 93 S.Ct. 436, 34 L.Ed.2d 294 (1972); National Land & Investment Co. v. Kohn, 419 Pa. 504, 215 A.2d 597 (1965); Note, Phased Zoning: Regulation of the Tempo and Sequence of Land Development, 26 Stan.L. Rev. 585, 605 (1974). It does not necessarily follow, however, that the *due process* rights of builders and landowners are violated mere-

---

16. Although appellees have attempted to align their business interest in attacking the Plan with legitimate housing needs of the urban poor and racial minorities, the Association has not alleged nor can it allege, based on the record in this case, that the Plan has the purpose and effect of excluding poor persons and racial minorities. Cf. Board of County Supervisors of Fairfax County v. Carper, 200 Va. 653, 107 S.E.2d 390 (1959). Contrary to the picture painted by appellees, the Petaluma Plan is "inclusionary" to the extent that it offers new opportunities, previously unavailable, to minorities and low and moderate-income persons. Under the pre-Plan system single family, middle-income housing dominated the Petaluma market, and as a result low and moderate income persons were unable to secure housing in the area. The Plan radically changes the previous building pattern and requires that housing permits be evenly divided between single-family and multi-family units and that approximately eight to twelve per cent of the units be constructed specifically for low and moderate income persons.

In stark contrast, each of the exclusionary zoning regulations invalidated by state courts in recent years impeded the ability of low and moderate income persons to purchase or rent housing in the locality. See, e.g., Southern Burlington County NAACP v. Township of Mount Laurel, 67 N.J. 151, 336 A.2d 713 (Mar. 24, 1975) (zoned exclusively for single-family, detached dwellings and multi-family dwellings designed for middle and upper income persons); Oakwood at Madison, Inc. v. Township of Madison, 117 N.J.Super 11, 283 A.2d 353 (1971) (minimum one or two acre requirement and severe limitation on multi-family units); Appeal of Kit-Mar Builders, Inc., 439 Pa. 466, 268 A.2d 765 (1970) (two to three acre minimum lot size); Appeal of Girsh, 437 Pa. 237, 263 A.2d 395 (1970) (prohibition of apartment buildings); National Land & Investment Co. v. Kohn, 419 Pa. 504, 215 A.2d 597 (1965) (four acre minimum lot); Board of County Supervisors of Fairfax County v. Carper, 200 Va. 653, 107 S.E.2d 390 (1959) (rezoning to minimum two acre lots with the effect of keeping poor in another section of municipality).

ly because a local entity exercises in its own self-interest the police power lawfully delegated to it by the state. See Belle Terre, supra; Los Altos Hills, supra. If the present system of delegated zoning power does not effectively serve the state interest in furthering the general welfare of the region or entire state, it is the state legislature's and not the federal courts' role to intervene and adjust the system. As stated supra, the federal court is not a super zoning board and should not be called on to mark the point at which legitimate local interests in promoting the welfare of the community are outweighed by legitimate regional interests. See Note, supra, at 608–11.

We conclude therefore that under Belle Terre and Los Altos Hills the concept of the public welfare is sufficiently broad to uphold Petaluma's desire to preserve its small town character, its open spaces and low density of population, and to grow at an orderly and deliberate pace.

Commerce Clause

The district court found that housing in Petaluma and the surrounding areas is produced substantially through goods and services in interstate commerce and that curtailment of residential growth in Petaluma will cause serious dislocation to commerce. 375 F.Supp. at 577, 579. Our ruling today, however, that the Petaluma Plan represents a reasonable and legitimate exercise of the police power obviates the necessity of remanding the case for consideration of appellees' claim that the Plan unreasonably burdens interstate commerce.

It is well settled that a state regulation validly based on the police power does not impermissibly burden interstate commerce where the regulation neither discriminates against interstate commerce nor operates to disrupt its required uniformity. Huron Cement Co. v. Detroit, 362 U.S. 440, 448, 80 S.Ct. 813, 4 L.Ed.2d 852 (1960). As stated by the Supreme Court almost 25 years ago: "When there is a reasonable basis for legislation to protect the social, as distinguished from the economic, welfare of a community, it is not for this Court because of the Commerce Clause to deny the exercise locally of the sovereign power of the [state]." Breard v. Alexandria, 341 U.S. 622, 640, 71 S.Ct. 920, 931, 95 L.Ed. 1233 (1951). It is wholly beyond a court's limited authority under the Commerce Clause to review state legislation by balancing reasonable social welfare legislation against its incidental burden on commerce. Brotherhood of Locomotive Firemen & Enginemen v. Chicago, Rock Island & Pacific Railroad Co., 393 U.S. 129, 136, 89 S.Ct. 323, 21 L.Ed.2d 289 (1968).

Consequently, since the local regulation here is rationally related to the social and environmental welfare of the community and does not discriminate against interstate commerce or operate to disrupt its required uniformity, appellees' claim that the Plan unreasonably burdens commerce must fail.[18]

Reversed.

QUESTIONS

1. Allegedly, the Petaluma Plan was not directed at size *per se* but, rather, "haphazard" development. Assuming that this is true, the model in Exhibit 6.6 does not directly apply. To what extent can an analogy with the model be drawn?

2. The development cases such as Petaluma may be viewed as a question of who "owns" development rights, earlycomers or latecomers. What is your sense of how the courts seem to be answering this question?

3. Suppose that the latecomers are held to own a certain type of development right, and that right is protected from uncompensated expropriation by the earlycomers. Is there any way in which the earlycomers can keep that right from being exercised?

---

18. Our decision today conforms with others which have upheld reasonable state environmental legislation despite some burden incidentally placed on interstate commerce. See, e.g., Huron Cement Co. v. Detroit, supra (air pollution statute); Proctor & Gamble Co. v. City of Chicago, 509 F.2d 69 (7th Cir.), cert. denied, 421 U.S. 978, 95 S.Ct. 1980, 44 L.Ed. 2d 470 (1975) (ban on phosphate detergents); American Can Co. v. Oregon Liquor Control Commission, 15 Or.App. 618, 517 P.2d 691 (1973) (ban on non-returnable beverage containers).

Appendix to Chapter VI

EXHIBIT 6.2A

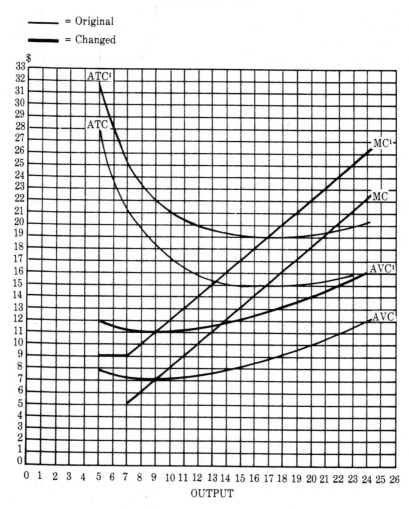

———— = Original

━━━━ = Changed

EXHIBIT 6.3A

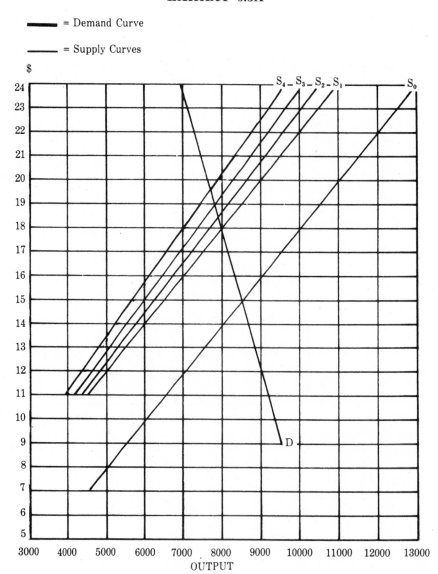

Chapter VII

ECONOMIC EXPERTISE IN LEGAL PROCEEDINGS

The previous chapters introduce important elements of economic-type reasoning and illustrate their relevance within a legal context. Many possible practical applications of the economic concepts have therefore been implicit in the preceding materials. Even so, the picture would not be complete without at least a brief attempt to survey in a somewhat more explicit fashion the use of economic expertise in legal proceedings and the institutional constraints on that use.

The treatment here is broadly divided along three lines. First is the use of economic insights by the lawyer himself in the hope of illuminating or clarifying the issues in controversy. Second is the traditional use of expert witnesses who provide testimonial evidence of a more or less orthodox type. Third is the possible use of economic expertise, whether through witnesses or other forms of submission, to inform a court on what has sometimes been termed "legislative" fact. Although the latter two themes fall within the traditional ambit of law school classes in evidence and civil procedure, it is worth illustrating some of the important issues in terms of explicitly economic materials. As a matter of practical necessity, the illustrative case materials in this chapter are heavily skewed toward the antitrust context. Although similar questions also arise in contracts, torts, and most other areas of the law, antitrust cases provide the most concise and explicit discussions of the use of economic expertise.

THE LAWYER–ECONOMIST

Relatively little perhaps needs to be said about the role of the lawyer-economist, since this role comes closest to being the implicit rationale for study of economics by modern students of the law. Indeed, this conception of the lawyer as a person with sensitivity to economic-type conceptions of legal doctrine is central to most of this book. One need not espouse one of the sweeping theories of economic efficiency as the fundament of the common law in order to find professional utility here. Surely the most hostile critic of economic analysis of law must concede a number of points on which the analysis is at least insightful, even when it is more or less seriously defective from certain points of view.

Whatever its ultimate merits, economic analysis of law frequently does give one a new perspective or understanding about legal issues. "Understanding the case" is, of course, always a notable asset in prosecuting it effectively. A potentially powerful benefit is the ability to convey a useful insight in a persuasive way to the judge, finder of fact, or even another party. Whenever an insight derives from concepts that have traditionally been alien and unfamiliar to the law, special practical precautions are in order. One is that pains need to be taken to translate the jargon of economics into suitable legal equivalents. Sometimes the translation is merely that of the terms themselves (i.e., risk aversion, discounting), but many terms involve a penumbra of conceptual ramifications (i.e., efficiency, opportunity cost) that are dismayingly difficult to convey in a succinct but clear fashion.

Lawyers who learn economic language should bear in mind the analogy between the translation of legal terms of art to laymen or clients and the presentation of economic concepts to judges, juries and other participants in the judicial process. Sometimes the terms of art are mere jargon in the sense that there is an equivalent vernacular word or phrase that is every bit as good: a "vendee" is a "purchaser" and "fixed costs" are "outlays that would have remained unchanged regardless of the level of output." On the other hand, sometimes a potentially significant element is lost in translation: "negligent" is not quite the same as "careless" nor is a "Prisoner's Dilemma" just a "situation with a tough set of behavioral incentives." Here, the terms of art summarize expansive concepts with great conciseness or involve shades of meaning that vary from the popular sense. Since truly valuable terms of art do have a role in sharpening one's analysis, a lawyer-economist may be well advised to adopt a somewhat schizophrenic approach. The precise technical language should be preserved in working out one's own thinking and communication with others who are conversant with the "language" but a facility for translation of any argument into a "common sense" version must also be developed.

With the exception of specialized areas—such as antitrust law and regulatory hearings—attempts to inject economic concepts and modes of reasoning into legal processes are of comparatively recent vintage. If and when key economic constructs prove their usefulness in legal argument, the translation problem will tend to be mitigated by the substantial incorporation of the most useful economic concepts into the vocabulary of the lawyer and jurist.

Perhaps fortunately, the understanding that derives from an analytic approach need not always be conveyed to other parties in any direct fashion. Frequently, early understanding of pivotal conceptual issues will be of enormous assistance in discovery and case preparation. For instance, in the initial stages of discovery, opposing parties may be caught substantially "off guard" when the importance of a factual issue has not yet been fully appreciated. If the proper questions are posed at this point, the responses may be more candid or helpful than would later be forthcoming. The converse, of course, applies to preparation of one's own early responses.

Even where early isolation of key issues does not yield tactical advantages, it represents an opportunity to use litigation resources more effectively. As a practical matter, the preparation of most cases is affected by time and cost considerations. Effort may be squandered on the preparation of issues that careful analysis would have identified as not having much promise of ultimate probative value. Conversely, key issues may be identified only at an advanced stage of the preparation process when it is either too late to repair the omission at all or when rectification requires costly re-working of previous preparation.

If a case goes to trial, economic insights may assist the lawyer's own presentation in the form of oral argument, briefs, and requests for jury instructions. For appellate cases, the lawyer has a particular opportunity to craft a brief that supplies the reviewing court with a thoughtful review and integration of the facts and theory of the case. The so-called "Brandeis Brief" technique is named for the effort of then-Assistant Attorney General Brandeis in defense of the constitutionality of an Oregon statute that was one of the first to set maximum work hours for women in certain industries. Of Brandeis' 113-page brief to the Supreme Court in Muller v. Oregon, 208 U.S. 412, 28 S.Ct. 324, 52 L.Ed. 551 (1908), barely two pages were devoted to legal arguments while the remainder reviewed economic and other data describing the arduous working conditions in the industries covered by the statute. A recent example of the use of this technique is the invocation, in the series of death penalty cases heard by the Supreme Court, of scholarly econometric research that tests the deterrent effect of capital punishment. See the excerpt from Gregg v. Georgia, 428 U.S. 153, 96 S.Ct. 2909, 49 L.Ed.2d 859 (1976), supplied later in this chapter.

The principal economic content of a case commonly involves expert witnesses. In addition to his own presentations, therefore, the lawyer's interaction with expert witnesses will frequently benefit from a sensitivity to economic analysis, its relevance and its limitations. With respect to his own expert witnesses, the lawyer must organize the preparation and presentation of the direct testimony in a fashion that is both coherent and persuasive. Many experts are not sensitive to the expository demands of a legal forum, and it is the lawyer's job to orchestrate the testimony so that it is as intelligible as possible to the trier of fact:

> The reports by the experts—one noted economist plus assistants for each side—are less helpful than they might have been for the simple reason that they do not begin from a common data base, they disagree over crucial statistical assumptions and they reach different conclusions. *Having hired their respective experts, the lawyers in this case have a basic responsibility, which they have not completely met, to put the hardcore statistical demonstrations into language which serious and concerned laymen could understand* * * * The court has been forced back to its own common sense approach to a problem which, though admittedly complex, has certainly been made more complex than was necessary.

Judge J. Skelly Wright, Hobson v. Hansen, 327 F.Supp. 844 (D.D.C. 1971) (emphasis supplied). With respect to the opposing testimony, it is of course possible to employ economic analysis in searching out substantive weaknesses that can be explored in cross-examination. Many practicing lawyers assert that they do not relish examining well prepared experts "because it's always a matter of playing in *their* home territory." A little knowledge of the basic topography of that territory can nevertheless often be surprisingly helpful.

In addition to the substantive aspects of expert testimony, there are a variety of possible pitfalls that arise out of the expert's possible unfamiliarity with legal procedural rules. This subject is explored more fully in the following section. Suffice it to say at this point, however, that the admissibility of expert testimony may hinge not only on a bare knowledge of the black letter rules of evidence, but also on a sense for the proper economic technical bounds of the "expertise" embodied in the proffered testimony. Such a sense demands some melding of the worlds of economic and legal knowledge. Here, the lawyer's job requires him to rescue his own expert either from errors of omission (with respect to foundation, etc.) or excess (testifying beyond proper scope). Conversely, alertness to the occurrence of those errors may provide an opportunity to exclude some or all of the expert testimony that the other side desires to use.

QUESTIONS

1. Identify two cases, each used in one of the preceding chapters, wherein the lawyer's briefs or oral argument would benefit significantly from an economic insight but where an expert witness is not necessary or feasible to make the point involved. One of these

should be a case that exemplifies an "easy translation," i.e., where the economic argument can be rendered quite straightforwardly in terms of more traditional legal language. The other case should be an exemplar of a more convoluted economic argument that poses formidable translation problems. Then select two other such exemplar cases drawn from cases not discussed earlier in this book.

2. Identify a case in which a Brandeis Brief of a substantially economic character would be particularly helpful. What would be the exact content of such a brief? What advantages and disadvantages does it have as compared to an oral presentation?

3. The text above quotes Judge Wright's complaint in Hobson v. Hansen. There are, arguably, several distinguishable aspects to that complaint. What are they? Are the lawyers involved potentially able to be more responsive on some of these grounds than others? Why?

4. Consider the issues in Clark v. Universal Builders, discussed at length above in Chapter VI. What guidance could economic knowledge have supplied to the process of discovery? Does your reading of the case suggest that there were wasted efforts or missed opportunities by either side?

5. Assume that depositions are being taken early in a case. Supply an illustration of a situation in which an unprepared deponent might make an ill-advised response because of failure to appreciate how an economic fact is important to the case.

6. Suppose that a properly qualified economic expert witness wished to testify that the prices charged to blacks by Universal were the result of discrimination. Would this be proper testimony? Would it make any difference if the expert based his opinion in part on a real estate transaction survey undertaken in the Real Estate Finance class at a local university? (You may wish to distinguish the questions carefully and also to reassess your answer after considering some of the materials in the next section.)

ECONOMIC TESTIMONY FROM EXPERTS

When the subject matter of a dispute is such that an untrained layman would be incapable of making an intelligent and understanding determination, recourse may be made to an "expert" who has specialized knowledge of the subject matter in dispute. The Federal Rules of Evidence expanded somewhat both the scope and form of expert testimony beyond that allowed under common law rules. Although state rules in some jurisdictions may be more conservative, the approach of the F.R.E. represents the dominant tendency. The case excerpts provided below illustrate some of the common pitfalls encountered in economic testimony.

Perhaps the best single judicial discussion of economic testimony is Judge Becker's evidentiary opinion in Zenith Radio Corp. v. Matsushita Electric Industrial Co., 505 F.Supp. 1313 (E.D.Pa.1981). Unfortunately, the length and complexity of the *Zenith* opinion make it impractical to edit into acceptable summary form. Instead, some of the same ground is covered below in the form of the *Litton* case, which draws heavily on the theoretical principles articulated in *Zenith*. Following that are a few short *Zenith* excerpts that illustrate specific problems with the testimony of economic experts. Obviously, the cases should be read with a view to understanding why much of the testimony involved was ruled inadmissible. Less obvious, however, may be a more constructive perspective. Could much of the impact of the excluded testimony have been preserved by offering it in a different—and therefore admissible—form? What guidance do nonlawyer professionals need in structuring their research and testimony for a legal forum?

AMERICAN BEARING CO., INC. V. LITTON INDUSTRIES

United States District Court for the Eastern District of Pennsylvania, 1982.
540 F.Supp. 1163.

RAYMOND J. BRODERICK, District Judge:

This case comes before the Court on the post-trial motion of defendant Litton Industrial Products, Inc. for judgment notwithstanding the verdict or, in the alternative, for a new trial. The jury returned a verdict finding Litton liable for both monopolization and attempted monopolization in violation of Sec. 2 of the Sherman Act and assessed damages in the amount of $958,691.00. For the reasons set forth below, the Court has determined to grant a new trial with respect to plaintiff's Sec. 2 Sherman Act claims.

* * *

Litton's arguments in support of its motions for judgment n.o.v. and a new trial are for the most part grounded upon the expert testimony of plaintiff's economist. At trial, Litton moved to strike his testimony in its entirety, asserting that it was speculative, misleading, based on unsupported assumptions and based on hearsay statements of a type not reasonably relied upon by experts in the field. Litton now asserts that the Court erred in denying its motion to strike and relying essentially on these same arguments, asserts that the testimony of the economist was not sufficient evidence upon which a jury could have determined the relevant market and market shares, the existence of proximate cause and the amount of damages. Since the Court has determined that certain critical portions of the economist's testimony should have been stricken for reasons hereinafter discussed and that there has been a miscarriage of justice, the only appropriate remedy is a new trial. Therefore, a lengthy review of the sufficiency of the evidence would be fruitless since, under these circumstances, even if the remaining evidence is insufficient to support the jury's verdict, the Court, in the interest of justice, will exercise its discretion under Fed.R.Civ.Pro. 50(b) and will order a new trial and will deny the motion for judgment n.o.v. in favor of Litton. Cone v. West Virginia Pulp & Paper, 330 U.S. 212, 67 S.Ct. 752, 91 L.Ed. 849 (1947); 5A Moore's Federal Practice para. 50.11.

The Applicable Legal Principles

Rule 703 of the Federal Rules of Evidence provides:

> The facts or data in the particular case upon which an expert bases an opinion or inference may be those perceived by or made known to him at or before the hearing. If of a type reasonably relied upon by experts in the particular field in forming opinions or inferences upon the subject, the facts or data need not be admissible in evidence.

Under Rule 703 an expert may testify to an opinion based on information which is not necessarily admissible into evidence provided the information is "of a type reasonably relied upon by experts in the particular field in forming opinions or inferences upon the subject." Zenith Radio Corporation v. Matsushita Electric Industrial Co., Ltd., 505 F.Supp. 1313, 1322 (E.D.Pa.1980) [hereinafter *Zenith Radio*].

When an expert bases a opinion upon facts or data which are not in evidence the question as to whether the facts or data are of the type reasonably relied upon by experts in the particular field in forming opinions or inferences upon the subject is a matter to be determined by the court. As stated by Judge Becker in *Zenith Radio*, supra at 1325, " * * * it is nonetheless plain that courts routinely make the decision whether a particular expert has reasonably based his opinions upon trustworthy underpinnings. * * * Moreover, any other result would open the door to wholesale admission of otherwise inadmissible evidence before the jury not, to be sure, as probative of the truth, but to explain the expert's opinion. Such a result could not have been contemplated by the rule."

In *Zenith Radio*, supra, a case in which the court determined, in advance of trial, the admissibility of opinions expressed in various expert reports, the court noted that Rule 703 had evolved from an exception to the hearsay rule which had been employed in a number of jurisdictions and which was originally limited to a "traditional mainstream" of cases which the court identified as: cases in which a physician was permitted to testify based upon information received from nurses, patients, radiologists, pathologists; etc.; cases involving expert testimony relating to land valuation based upon comparable sales, and cases in which courts permitted experts to testify as to the valuation of businesses based upon diverse background sources, including accounting data. See discussion of the history of Rule 703 in *Zenith Radio*, supra at pp. 1321–1324. Based upon a thorough review of the cases precursing Rule 703, the cases applying Rule 703, Rule 703 itself, the Advisory Notes, and the history of the Rule, Judge Becker set forth a list of factors to be used to guide a court in determining the reasonableness of reliance under Rule 703 in cases falling outside this traditional mainstream of cases. These factors are:

1. The extent to which the opinion is pervaded or dominated by reliance on materials judicially determined to be inadmissible, on grounds of either relevance or trustworthiness;

2. The extent to which the opinion is dominated or pervaded by reliance upon other untrustworthy materials;

3. The extent to which the expert's assumptions have been shown to be unsupported, speculative, or demonstrably incorrect;

4. The extent to which the materials on which the expert relied are within his immediate sphere of expertise, are of a kind customarily relied upon by experts in his field in forming opinions or inferences on that subject, and are not used only for litigation purposes;

5. The extent to which the expert acknowledges the questionable reliability of the underlying information, thus indicating that he has taken that factor into consideration in forming his opinion; [The court added in a footnote that it would limit the applicability of this criterion to close cases of admissibility because an expert who was a true "hired gun" could always surmount it.]

6. The extent to which reliance on certain materials, even if otherwise reasonable, may be unreasonable in the peculiar circumstances of the case.

Zenith Radio, supra at 1330. * * * [W]e believe the above factors are a relevant and useful guide for determining whether certain critical portions of the economist's testimony should have been stricken pursuant to rule 703.

Another rule relevant to this Court's determination as to the admissibility of certain portions of the economist's testimony is Rule 403 of the Federal Rules of Evidence which provides:

Although relevant, evidence may be excluded in its probative value is substantially outweighed by the danger of unfair prejudice, confusion of the issues, or misleading the jury, or by considerations of undue delay, waste of time, or needless presentation of cumulative evidence.

It is apparent that when considering the admissibility of expert testimony, Rules 703 and 403 somewhat overlap in that an opinion which is deemed inadmissible under one of the rules may also be deemed inadmissible on the basis of the other. As the court noted in *Zenith Radio*, supra at 1328, after reviewing a number of cases in which expert testimony was excluded by the court,

> Even when the issue is plainly admissibility, it is not always clear what rule is used as the basis for the court's decision. For example, as alternative theories, some courts deem an opinion based on unsupported assumptions to be unhelpful to the jury under F.R.E. 703. In any event, all of the above cited cases [see *Zenith Radio* at pp. 1327–28] refuse to countenance expert testimony based upon what the courts determine to be unreasonable assumptions. Despite the variety of procedural contexts and variety of F.R.E. pigeonholes, they indicate that the assumptions which form the basis for the expert's opinion, as well as the conclusions drawn therefrom, are subject to rigorous examination.

Therefore, in light of the above discussion, this Court will carefully examine the underlying assumptions, inferences drawn and conclusions reached by the plaintiff's economist. In so doing the Court will consider the various elements heretofore set forth with respect to reasonable reliance under Rule 703 and whether the probative value of the testimony is outweighed by the danger of unfair prejudice, confusion of issues, misleading the jury or by the other considerations set forth in Rule 403.

The Economist's Testimony on the Size of the Relevant Market and Market Shares

In his testimony relating to the size of the relevant market and Litton's and American Bearing's respective shares of the relevant market, the economist testified that for the years 1976, 1977, 1978, and 1979 American Bearing had, respectively, market shares of 5%, 5%, 5%, and 17%. Based upon the deposition and trial testimony of some of the buyers of thermal bearings (bearings which operate at 400 degrees F. 3000 pounds p.s.i. with a 3% coefficient of friction) he concluded that American Bearing and Litton were the only sellers of thermal bearings during 1976, 1977 and 1978 and, therefore, that during these years Litton maintained a 95% share of the thermal bearing market. Since a third company entered the market with a 20% share in 1979, Litton was attributed a 63% share for 1979.

To arrive at his calculation of the overall market, and the market shares of Litton and American Bearing, the enonomist relied on the testimony of Albert Judson, an expert witness testifying on behalf of American Bearing, that the ratio of the cost of bearings in electrostatic precipitators to the total flange to flange cost of the precipitators is .3% (.003) and that this same ratio exists between the cost of bearings used in baghouses and the total cost of baghouses. [Baghouses are huge structures used to control pollution by removing harmful elements from industrial discharges.] The economist used this .3% figure in conjunction with figures supplied by, and testified to at trial, by Robert McIlvaine, another expert witness who testified on behalf of American Bearing. The figures supplied by Mr. McIlvaine represented the total cost for each year beginning in 1976 of all sales of hot side precipitators and baghouses, that is, precipitators and baghouses operating at temperatures in excess of 250 degrees F. By multiplying Mr. McIlvaine's annual figures for baghouse and precipitator sales by Mr. Hudson's .3% figures, the economist arrived at what he considered to be the size of the relevant market in dollars for thermal bearing sales for each year, beginning in 1976. By comparing American Bearing's total sales of thermal bearings, determined from its invoices, for each year, with the figure purportedly representing total sales of thermal bearings for each year, the economist arrived at American Bearing's share of the relevant market and attributed the remaining share to Litton.

Litton asserts that the economist's method of calculating the overall market was far too speculative in that the testimony of Mr. McIlvaine showed that his figures included precipitators and baghouses which used bearings outside the market defined by the economist. The Court agrees.

The economist testified that in his opinion there existed a separate definable market for "thermal" bearings which he defined as bearings which operate at 400 degrees Fahrenheit, 300 pounds p.s.i. with a 3% coefficient of friction; while other types of bearings were occasionally used in baghouses and precipitators, and that other bearings were not relevant to the market because they did not have the performance characteristics of thermal bearings. However, in calculating the size of the relevant market, he employed figures which included bearings outside the market which he had defined. Specifically, he relied upon the figures supplied by Mr. McIlvaine showing the dollar value of precipitator and baghouse sales. Mr. McIlvaine had testified that his figures included *all* precipitators and baghouses operating at temperatures in excess of 250 degrees F. and thus included "hot side" precipitators operating at temperatures of about 700 degrees F. and some experimental precipitators which operate at about 1000 degrees F. Since the record in this case shows that the teflon slide bearings at issue in this litigation, and around which the economist based his relevant market, sublimate at approximately 620 degrees F., it is clear that these bearings could not have been used in all the precipitators included in Mr. McIlvaine's figures. In addition, the evidence showed that although thermal slide bearings were used in precipitators operating between 250 degrees to 350 degrees F., other types of bearings were also occasionally used. There is nothing, however, in the record to establish what percentage of the baghouses and precipitators included in Mr. McIlvaine's figures contained bearings other than "thermal" bearings.

Since Mr. McIlvaine's figures clearly were not tailored to fit the market which the economist was attempting to quantify, the use of Mr. McIlvaine's figures by the economist could only result in speculation as to the size of the market and the parties' shares of that relevant market. The economist made no effort to adjust his figures to account for the baghouses and precipitators outside the market he had defined, nor was there any reliable evidence in the record upon which he could rely to determine the actual extent of the relevant market. The economist did testify that *Mr. Hudson* had told him that hot-side precipitators would only account for 5% of Mr. McIlvaine's figures. Neither Mr. Hudson nor Mr. McIlvaine had so testified when they were on the stand. This statement was hearsay and is clearly not the type of statement upon which an expert economist should reasonably rely. Furthermore, when asked by the Court whether he had subtracted this 5% figure, he admitted that he performed no arithmetic in his calculations to reduce Mr. McIlvaine's figure or his own figure to reflect the 5% of "hot side" precipitators outside the market.

In conclusion, based on the fact that the economist, in quantifying the size of a narrow and carefully defined thermal bearing market, relied on figures which were shown to include baghouses and precipitators which used bearings outside his defined market and the fact that there was no reliable or admissible evidence upon which the jury or the economist could determine the extent to which bearings outside the market should have been deducted, the Court has determined that the economist's testimony in this respect was misleading and speculative and should have been excluded pursuant to F.R.E. 403. Furthermore, his testimony based upon the alleged out of court statement of Mr. Hudson that only 5% of Mr. McIlvaine's figure included "hot side" precipitators was clearly not admissible under Rule 703 in that it is not the type of evidence that expert economists reasonably rely upon. The 5% figure attributed to Mr. Hudson was objectionable hearsay. Mr. Hudson testified prior to the economist and made no mention of the 5% figure in his testimony and the defendant had no opportunity to cross-examine him concerning it. Rule 703 was never intended to permit an expert in any field to base an opinion upon such basic data which another expert had told him under such circumstances. As Judge Becker pointed out in *Zenith Radio,* supra, one of the factors to be considered by a court in determining the reasonableness of an expert's reliance under Rule 703 is "the extent to which the materials on which the expert relied are within his immediate sphere of expertise." Professor Bowman is well qualified as an economist, however he admitted that he had no expertise concerning the use of bearings in baghouses and precipitators.

The Testimony of the Economist Relating to Damages

The economist prepared and testified with respect to a chart, Exhibit P29, which purported to show in three columns: his calculations of the profits American Bearing would have earned from sales in the thermal bearing market from 1976 through 1983 absent Litton's alleged unlawful conduct; his estimate of American Bearing's actual profits through 1983 in the thermal bearing market, the latter figure assuming the absence of Litton's alleged unlawful conduct; and, the profits American Bearing lost from 1976 through 1983 as a result of Litton's allegedly unlawful activities.

To obtain the first set of figures showing the profits American Bearing would have earned from 1976 to 1983 in the absence of Litton's alleged unlawful conduct, the economist began by multiplying the total dollar amount of sales of thermal bearings for each year (the figure he had estimated by multiplying Mr. McIlvaine's figure for the sale of "hot" precipitators and baghouses by Mr. Hudson's .3% figure) by his estimate of the percentage of the market American Bearing would have controlled each year (12.5% in 1976; 37% in 1977; 50% for 1978) in the absence of the alleged unlawful conduct. The product of these two figures purported to be the revenues American Bearing would have achieved in the absence of Litton's alleged unlawful conduct.

The economist determined American Bearing's actual profits for the years 1976 through 1980 by adding up American Bearing's invoices for the sales of thermal bearings and deducting from that total his cost estimates for producing the bearings. To calculate American Bearing's lost profits he deducted American Bearing's actual profits from his estimate of the American Bearing's profits absent Litton's allegedly unlawful conduct.

The Court has determined that the economist's testimony with respect to the amount of lost profits should have been stricken for several reasons. First among these is the fact that the initial figure in his calculations (the estimated profits in the absence of Litton's alleged unlawful conduct) was based upon his opinion as to the total dollar amount of sales of thermal bearings for each year, an opinion which this Court has heretofore determined was too speculative and misleading to have been admitted at trial. The use of this figure by the economist as a basis upon which to determine American Bearing's lost profits rendered the result speculative and misleading.

In addition, the economist's testimony and the accompanying exhibits relating to the amount of lost profits are also inadmissible in that they were based on certain unsupported assumptions and, therefore, were unreliably based under F.R.E. 703, and were speculative and misleading in contravention of Rule F.R.E. 403. For example, his projection of American Bearing's fair competition profits for the years 1976–78 was based upon his estimate that American Bearing would have achieved market shares of $12^{1}/_{2}\%$ in 1976, 37% in 1977 and 50% in 1978. His estimated market shares were based on his oft repeated assumption that American Bearing was offering a better product, with better service, at a lower price. The only support in the record for any of these assumptions is the testimony of Mr. Roman, President of American Bearing, that American Bearing generally sold its bearing at a cost 40% lower than that charged by Litton and could deliver faster. There is no evidence in the record that any comparative tests were performed on the two bearings to determine relative superiority in terms of performance or durability. Furthermore, insofar as the economist assumed that these conditions, in particular that of lower price, would continue to exist as American Bearing's market share increased to 50% and Litton's share declined, his projections fail to account for any lawful competition and rational economic reactions on the part of Litton. As the United States District Court for the Middle District of Pennsylvania recently stated in addressing post-trial motions which attacked the sufficiency of proof of plaintiff's economic damage model,

> Perhaps the most blatant defect in plaintiff's damage model for lost profits is its failure to account for any lawful competition. Surely plaintiff cannot have expected the defendants to sit idly by while it proceeded to grasp 25% of the road construction market and maintain its roughly 12% of the blacktop production market, when each market began to dry up. As defendants point out, they were well integrated, established firms in the area. To postulate damages on the assumption that they would not individually react by reducing their prices and therefore require plaintiff to further reduce its price, thus reducing its net profit, is absurd. Nor did plaintiff present any evidence from which the jury could, without speculation, determine what the effect of lawful competition would have been and reduce the damages accordingly.

R.S.E., Inc. v. Pennsy Supply, Inc., 523 F.Supp. 954, 966 (W.D.Pa.1981).

Likewise, in Murphy Tugboat v. Crowley, 658 F.2d 1256 (9th Cir.1981), the Ninth Circuit, in commenting on the expert witness' testimony as to a plaintiff's projected share of the market absent the defendant's unlawful conduct, stated

> A reasonable jury could not, however, indulge in the assumption that a competitor would follow a course of behavior other than that which it believed would maximize its profits * * *. In a hypothetical economic construction such as the one underlying Murphy's theory on lost profits, economic rationality must be assumed for all competitors, absent the strongest evidence of chronic irrationality. Otherwise it will be impossible to keep speculation in check.

658 F.2d at 1262. Similarly, the Third Circuit, in Coleman Motor Co. v. Chrysler Corp., 525 F.2d 1338, 1353 (1975), granted a new trial in a Sherman Act antitrust case based in part on the ground that the expert, in calculating plaintiff's damages, failed to take into account the effect of sales which would be lost as a result of lawful competition.

In this case there was no reason for the economist to assume that if Litton had begun to lose a substantial portion of its market to American Bearing that it would not or could not have reduced its prices in order to remain competitive. The economist, in making his projection as to market shares and profits, did not take into consideration the effect a change in price by Litton would have had on market shares and American Bearing profits. His estimates, therefore, were speculative and misleading as to the damages attributable to Litton's unlawful activities. Thus, the economist's reliance on the unsupported assumptions discussed above rendered his opinion excludable under both Rule 703 and 403.

The economist also testified that in order to determine American Bearing's cost of manufacturing its bearings, he went to American Bearing's plant, reviewed the way the bearings were made, looked at the various materials required to manufacture the bearings, examined invoices to determine the costs of the various materials, looked at the accounts of the firm to determine the overhead percentage attributable to the manufacture of the thermal bearings and relied upon a time study prepared by Mr. Furchak, the secretary-treasurer and a stockholder and co-founder of American Bearing. Although Mr. Furchak testified at trial, he did not testify as to the preparation of the time study.

* * *

QUESTIONS

1. One reading of Rule 703 is that the expert, as a skilled professional, is the ultimate judge of what constitutes information of sufficient reliability to constitute a sound basis for his opinion on a matter. That view is, of course, rejected by the courts in the text above.

Common sense suggests that there may, at the very least, be some lack of objectivity in giving the witness free rein to decide the reasonableness of his own research methodology. In addition to that personal form of bias, however, there may also be problems with the admissibility of opinions based on procedures that are widely used by a class of professionals. Can you think of any illustrations of this (even if they are from non-economic areas)?

2. Can Rule 403 reasonably be interpreted as a kind of cost-benefit analysis of proffered testimony? Might this rule be applied to complex forms of testimony about the types of damage calculations discussed in Chapter III?

3. Could the objection to the economist's reliance on McIlvaine's information reasonably have been foreseen by the economist? By the American Bearing attorneys? If so, what should have been done? Would that have substantially "saved" the economist's calculations?

4. Your information about the facts of this case is, of course, sketchy. Nevertheless, is there anything in the facts that suggests the possibility of a strong attack on the economist's market definition from a perspective other than an evidentiary one?

5. The economist's testimony on market shares was excluded partially because it was admittedly based on "his oft-repeated assumption that American Bearing was offering a better product, with better service, at a lower price." What part, if any, of that assumption might have been capable of validation? How? Are all three parts of the assumption necessary? Experts are frequently told by counsel to assume certain facts in preparing their testimony. Is this a sound practice?

6. The damage estimates were also attacked on the grounds that they did not allow for the effects of lawful competition by Litton. Allowing for this would have required the economist to predict Litton's responses to forms of price and non-price competition by American Bearing within a free market. Are there any economic data that might permit predictions of this type? Would such conjectures be hopelessly "speculative" under Rule 403? In the event that no helpful conjectures about Litton's future behavior could be made, how could this testimony have been structured to meet the objection actually made?

7. American Bearing might well have been interested in making a showing that Litton's responsiveness to competition—in the form of price-cutting, for instance—would have been small in an unfettered market. What possibility would there be of eliciting helpful statements from Litton personnel during discovery?

ZENITH RADIO CORP. V. MATSUSHITA ELECTRIC INDUSTRIAL CO.

United States District Court for the Eastern District of Pennsylvania, 1981.
505 F.Supp. 1313.

EDWARD R. BECKER, District Judge:

Although the case law is limited, and adds little beyond examples to the Advisory Committee Note and F.R.E. 703 itself, it makes several things plain. First, expert opinion must be approached on an expert by expert—or even opinion-by-opinion—basis, and the court must * * * carefully examine each opinion offered by the expert to assess its helpfulness to the jury. Second, while it is not immediately obvious whether the inquiry should proceed under F.R.E. 702, 703, or 403, it is clear that the court may—indeed must—carefully scrutinize the underlying assumptions, inferences drawn, and conclusions reached by the experts before reaching a decision on admissibility of the expert's opinion. Opinions which contain inferences which cannot logically be drawn are no more helpful to the jury than are opinions based upon reliable information. Third, and of critical importance here, opinions do not assist the jury when they are cumulative of evidence already before the jury, or when the expert has sifted through that evidence reaching a conclusion which in essence attempts to tell the jury how it should decide the case. Rather, the expert must utilize specialized knowledge, not ordinarily possessed by the layman, to reach an opinion which truly aids the jury in understanding the evidence or in determining a fact in issue. We think one of the best expressions of this principle is contained in Stern, Toward a Rationale for the Use of Expert Testimony of Obscenity Litigation, 20 Case Western L.Rev. 527, 546 (1969): "The expert should strive to instruct the court *in the ways of his work*, whether it be psychology, literature or whatever, and to explain the nature of the judgments made in that work" (emphasis added). We shall refer to this formulation from time to time.

If, as defendants contend, the expert opinions in this litigation stem merely from a rehash of the evidence already before the trier of fact without adding a component of expertise, i.e., without instructing the trier of fact, "in the ways of his [the expert's] work," those portions will be found inadmissible because they are the unhelpful "oath-helping" of a "conspiracyologist." If, on the other hand, the experts' economic sophistication enables them to explain the evidence to the jury in a permissible manner otherwise beyond the jury's sphere of knowledge, the opinion would be admissible. We note that expert testimony may not be used merely to interpret a factually complex record. The test for admissibility of an expert's opinion turns not on complexity but on the subject matter of the opinion, i.e., on whether the expert's specialized knowledge enhances the jury's understanding.

The task of the court is to sift through the reports, parsing out those portions which will aid the jury. We reiterate that we are not considering the admissibility of these reports *qua* reports as documents to be admitted into or excluded from evidence. Rather, we are assessing the admissibility of the key opinions expressed in the reports, purged of their rhetoric and stylistic devices, as though they were being carefully framed at trial.

* * *

[Here the Court discussed the "DePodwin Report" by Dr. Horace J. DePodwin, an economic consultant and Dean of the Graduate School of Business Administration at Rutgers University. The initial part of the discussion was described as a line-drawing exercise to define what materials, although otherwise inadmissible in evidence, are encompassed within those permitted by F.R.E. 703 as being "of a type reasonably relied upon by experts in the particular field." This type of issue is dealt with in the *Litton* case above. The portions of *Zenith* excerpted here, however, deal primarily with the independent issue of the "helpfulness" and "special knowledge" requirements of F.R.E. 702 which provide that:

If scientific, technical, or other specialized knowledge will assist the trier of fact to understand the evidence or determine a fact in issue, a witness qualified as an expert by knowledge, skill, experience, training or education, may testify thereto in the form of an opinion or otherwise.

When an expert's testimony goes beyond an attempt to *assist* the trier of fact, the testimony may be attacked as improper.]

* * * As an alternative and co-equal basis for our holding of inadmissibility under [F.R.E. 703], we find [the] sections relating to conspiratorial meetings to be impermissible as expert testimony under F.R.E. 702.

What Dr. DePodwin has done is to step into the shoes of the factfinder and to set forth in narrative fashion what he believes the "evidence"—i.e., the materials he consulted—shows. He has described the Market Stabilization Council and the various industry groups as they appear from plaintiffs' documents, accepting the interpretation of those documents that plaintiffs have espoused throughout this litigation in their briefs and arguments, and concluding that certain activities of a conspiratorial nature—primarily exchange of information—occurred at industry group meetings. These activities are said to have constituted exercise of market control in the Japanese domestic television market. There is in this exposition no evident application of any economic expertise whatsoever. Dr.

DePodwin, in the process of reaching his conclusion, has not instructed us in any degree in "the ways of his work." Instead, he has done exactly what the jury is supposed to do—he has sifted through materials provided by plaintiffs, analyzed them factually, and reached certain conclusions regarding culpability of the defendants. This is precisely the oath-helping "conspiracyology" defendants object to so strenuously. It lends an unwarranted aura of scientific reliability to the arguments of plaintiffs' attorneys. We agree with defendants that such testimony neither utilizes special expertise nor assists the trier of fact, and that it is therefore inadmissible.

*   *   *

We wrap up our discussion of information exchange with a final illustration, one paragraph on page V–2, which reads:

> As pointed out in Part I, Outline of the Economic Analysis, a cartel's efficacy is enhanced if its members are provided with detailed information to reduce uncertainty, promote collusion, and police the observance of cartel agreements. The Japanese television cartel collected, organized, and distributed an extraordinary amount of information to its members.

The first sentence of this paragraph refers to Part I of the report, which outlined the economic methodology in reaching a conclusion, and as such we believe it to be permissible expert testimony under Article VII. The second sentence, however, is not permissible expert testimony for the reasons above discussed: it is a factual conclusion totally within the province of the factfinder. If there were at trial sufficient evidence in the record to support a finding in accordance with the second sentence of the quoted paragraph, the expert could assume the truth of the evidence presented and base a conclusion thereon. However, in this situation, the expert has not *assumed*, based on evidence in the record, that the Japanese defendants performed certain acts; he has simply categorically stated so. This he may not do.

*   *   *

The "Five-Company Rule" refers to a provision of the previously discussed JMEA rules, in effect from 1967 to 1973, which restricted each Japanese exporter to five U.S. customers. The rule was enforced by a registration and reporting requirement. Once again, DePodwin merely describes the rule and its use. The existence of and adherence to such a rule is not a matter which requires the application of specialized expertise, but is instead a matter uniquely within the competence of the fact-finder. Factual recitation such as that provided by Dr. DePodwin is not helpful to the trier of fact, hence excludable under F.R.E. 702.

We note that once independent evidence supports a finding that such a rule was adhered to, an expert could appropriately opine as to such a rule's potential effects on competition. This type of economic analysis is what DePodwin contemplated in his Outline of Economic Analysis in Chapter 1. It is not, however, what he has done.

Although we have dissected each discrete section of chapters IV and V of Dr. DePodwin's report, we still believe it would also be useful to examine the overall thrust of the opinions expressed in those chapters, as well as the manner in which they are expressed. What DePodwin has in essence done is to examine the myriad documents supplied to him by plaintiffs' counsel, to quote liberally from those documents, and to conclude, "Aha! Cartel! Conspiracy! Illegal concerted action!" Defendants maintain that a conclusion of conspiracy is never appropriate for an economist to draw, pointing out that they have, despite diligent effort, found no case which permitted an expert to testify in such manner. Drawing a distinction between conduct of defendants and industry structure, defendants offer the following quotation, which we find highly useful:

> The role of the economist as an expert depends upon the emphasis of the various antitrust statutes, with the scope of that role widening as the focus shifts away from conduct and towards structure or performance. An emphasis upon conduct will focus the attention of the trier of fact * * * upon whether particular acts were committed by the defendant. (*Collusion, for example, is not particularly the subject of economic expertise.*) In contrast, an emphasis upon the structure of an industry or firm or upon the performance of an industry—or of a firm within an industry—will focus the attention of the trier of fact upon economic issues that are the special subject of economic expertise.

O'Hara, "The Economic Expert in the Antitrust Arena," 12 Antitrust L. & Econ.Rev., 17, 19–20 (1980) (footnotes omitted) (emphasis added).

We need not decide whether an expert may ever testify that, in his opinion, based upon his economic analysis of certain behavior of defendants, a conspiracy exists, for, as we have discussed in some detail, Dr. DePodwin's analysis adds no increment of economic expertise which would aid the jury, and his analysis is further flawed by reliance upon a considerable body of untrustworthy materials. In short, there is no "economic value added."

* * *

[The following is part of the court's discussion of another expert's report written by Professor Kozo Yamamura, Professor of Economics and Asian Studies at The University of Washington. Yamamura's report was entitled "The Pervasive Use of Collusive and Company

Group (*Keiretsu*) Activities in Achieving the Rapid Increase in Japanese Exports of Television Receivers to the United States."]

We need not determine whether Professor Yamamura's use of the admissible protocols and testimony is so tainted by his equal reliance upon the unreliable diaries as to amount to a lack of reasonable reliance under F.R.E. 703, however, for Professor Yamamura has run afoul of F.R.E. 702 by engaging in the same oath-helping conspiracyologist exercise as did Dr. DePodwin. In fact, Yamamura's presentation is even less helpful than DePodwin's, for he has done nothing but quote the documents directly, after prefacing those quotations with a summary of their contents. But under our system of jurisprudence, we leave to lay jurors the task of sifting through the evidence presented, assessing its probative worth, and, aided by the arguments of counsel, the instructions provided by the court, and their own common sense, deciding for themselves the inferences and conclusions to be drawn. We do not delegate that task to expert witnesses. This is factfinding, not the application of expertise, and is totally inappropriate expert testimony.

Concluding his discussion of the Japanese domestic market, Professor Yamamura notes, as described in his summary:

> Of special importance in terms of the collusive activities of the defendant television producers in their domestic markets is the control they exercised over distribution, through employing collusive vertical restraints (Section A–3, pp. 118–125). Instrumental in this respect was the (1) "tight grip which each major Japanese manufacturer had on their respective distribution outlets" (the details of which are explained on pp. 118–124), which "constituted a very effective barrier to the entry of foreign sellers, Japanese discount stores, and Japanese as well as foreign producers into the Japanese market for television sets and other electric home entertainment products: (p. 124), (2) weak domestic antitrust enforcement (p. 125), and (3) cooperation between MITI and industry (pp. 125–126).

With regard to the first of these points, manufacturers' control over the distribution channels, Professor Yamamura rather astonishingly quotes verbatim for five and one-half single spaced pages from a publication which he neglects to identify, except by noting that it was written by "Komiya et al." We assume this is the same publication as that cited in subsequent section at p. 126 and listed in the bibliography for the report. If so, it is a Japanese language article in a Japanese journal, apparently about the electric home appliance industry, with an unknown translator. The quotation discusses the vertical, or distribution, *Keiretsu* in the home electric appliance industry, with specific factual reference to some of the defendants in this litigation.

This segment presents an admissibility problem different from the others we have addressed in this opinion. We can assume, although we may be incorrect, that the journal in question is an economics journal, and that Komiya et al. are economists. We can even assume that the article is of the highest scholarly caliber, and that it would be unquestionably reasonable for an expert witness to rely upon it in forming an opinion. But Professor Yamamura has not merely relied upon it in forming an opinion: he has imported it wholesale, incorporating it into his "dissertation" on the Japanese market structure. He has, in actuality, switched expert witnesses. Instead of Professor Yamamura expounding under the "or otherwise" clause of F.R.E. 702, we now have Komiya et al. providing their views. But those persons have not been qualified as expert witnesses in this proceeding. Nor has there been any attempt to qualify the Komiya publication under Rule 803(18), which permits materials "established as * * * reliable authority" and relied upon by an expert witness to be read into evidence as an exception to the hearsay rule. Indeed it would be extremely difficult to so qualify this article, for it presents such detail with respect to individual defendants as to demand a particularly firm foundation. Moreover, the publication is intrinsically tentative on factual matters and does not appear to espouse an opinion. It is replete with phrases such as "it is said that," "there are some manufacturers who," "it is estimated that," and "from a clue provided * * *." For these reasons, the quoted section is inadmissible.

* * *

"The Impact of Japanese Financial and Employment Practices on Japanese Production, Marketing and Price Behavior," by Gary R. Saxonhouse, is best summarized by Professor Saxonhouse himself:

> This paper shows that Japanese firms, in general, and Japanese electrical equipment manufacturing including radio and television manufacturers, in particular, had higher fixed costs than did their American counterparts. These exceptionally high fixed costs were the result of the special labor market and financing practices common to Japanese firms. These high Japanese fixed costs had three consequences which are pertinent to the present litigation.

> First, given their high fixed costs, Japanese radio and television manufacturers had a strong desire to avoid the risks of financially injurious, vigorous price competition. This, in turn created a very strong desire to collude among Japanese manufacturers.

> Second, the very high fixed costs meant, in a Japanese institutional context, that Japanese radio and television manufacturers would dump more output abroad with larger differences between

home market price and domestic price than would otherwise be the case.

Third, it is shown that collusive price increasing behavior by Japanese manufacturers in their home market enabled and sustained lower prices in Japan's export markets. There is an intimate connection between pricing behavior in Japan's home market and pricing behavior overseas. Higher prices at home subsidized lower prices overseas.

Saxonhouse Report at 1–2.

Defendants' primary objections to the Saxonhouse report are relevancy-based. They argue, first, that it is simply not a permissible inference to say that high fixed costs imply a wish to avoid risk, which in turn implies a motivation to collude. Second, they argue that, even if the assumptions about Japanese corporations in general were warranted, there is no basis for an inference that these particular defendants had any motivation to collude. And finally, they argue that propensity to collude is impermissible character evidence under F.R.E. 404(a). These are all potentially valid objections which we shall consider in conjunction with the conspiracy opinion. But the report is fundamentally flawed under Article VII as well.

The first portion of Professor Saxonhouse's report reviews statistics comparing (1) the debt-equity ratios of Japanese and American companies, as well as those of Zenith, NUE and various defendants; (2) the rates of corporate bankruptcy in Japan and the United States; (3) the rates of worker separation in the Japanese and American electrical equipment industries; and (4) expenditures for research and development by Japanese and American companies. Based upon these comparisons, he concludes that Japanese companies have higher fixed costs than American companies.

* * *

Having concluded that Japanese companies have higher fixed costs than do American companies, Saxonhouse states that "[t]his, in itself, makes predictable the necessity for collusive activity to minimize the risks entailed as a result of high fixed obligations." Saxonhouse Report at 5. This highly dubious inference is followed by the breathtaking statement that "[t]he following analysis will proceed on the *premise documented elsewhere that a calculated collusive decision had been made by Japanese radio and television manufacturers to take a continually increasing share of the American market*," citing the DePodwin and Yamamura reports. Saxonhouse Report at 5–6 (emphasis added). What Saxonhouse has done is to assume the very proposition which he then proceeds to "prove," and to base that assumption upon opinions which we have since found to be inadmissible, based in part upon their reliance upon untrustworthy information.

The ensuing pages of this brief report (14 pages of text, plus additional tables) are highly speculative, despite being adorned by impressive-appearing graphs charting the relationship between total costs and output and profit-loss curves. The following statement is illustrative:

> Studies of industries in the United States suggest that heavy fixed charges increase the desire and motivation of firms to collude. With fixed charges almost universally higher in Japan, the desire and motivation to collude in the home market and to carry that collusion to export markets must also have been stronger.

Saxonhouse report at 7–8 (footnote omitted).

Not only is the report speculative, but it repeatedly restates the fact that a collusive decision by the defendants has been explicitly assumed. Neither Rule 703, which excludes opinions based upon unreliable assumptions, nor Rule 702, which excludes opinion testimony not helpful to the trier of fact, condones the admission of such circular expert testimony. The opinions expressed in the Saxonhouse report are inadmissible.

*　　*　　*

QUESTIONS

1. Rule 704 of the F.R.E. states that "Testimony in the form of an opinion or inference otherwise admissible is not objectionable because it embraces an ultimate issue to be decided by the trier of fact." Why, then, would an economist be barred from rendering an opinion that a conspiracy existed?

2. At the first District Court trial of Clark v. Universal Builders discussed in Chapter VI above, testimony of plaintiffs' economic expert was excluded by Judge Perry on the grounds that "discrimination is not a technical matter." (Tr. 5294) The expert wished to testify that admitted evidence showed that (a) prices charged were above fair market value and (b) the large difference between the profits on the mainly-white and mainly-black developments were attributable to plaintiffs' race. How does this compare to DePodwin's conclusion about a "conspiracy" in Zenith?

3. Note the court's approving quotation of O'Hara's suggestion that the economic expert should focus upon structure rather than conduct. What do you understand to be meant by "structure"? Might the structure of an industry lead to strong inferences about likely conduct?

4. With respect to the Five Company Rule, do you think that De-Podwin might properly have been able to testify as to why the existence of such a rule was a *suspicious* phenomenon?

5. Note the paragraph quoted from Yamamura's report, in which he remarks upon the importance of controlling distribution. Why do you think this might be so important? If his testimony sought merely to embroider on that theme, should it have been admissible?

6. Suppose that the journal article used by Yamamura had cut in the opposite direction, i.e., contained facts and opinions contrary to those espoused by Yamamura. Could opposing counsel confront Yamamura with such an article on cross examination at trial?

7. Saxonhouse's report focussed on fixed costs. If the facts show that the Japanese firms had high fixed costs and very low marginal costs, what significance might this have in terms of (a) the incentive to form a cartel and (b) the likelihood of success of such a cartel. (You may wish to attempt to relate this to the cooperation and temptation differentials of the Prisoner's Dilemma as discussed in Chapter I above.) Does it seem likely that Judge Becker would have found an explanation of this to be admissible?

8. How might it be argued that each of the experts really did have something to say about "structure" in a way that would assist the trier in determining the motive for and likelihood of certain forms of anticompetitive conduct?

EXPERTISE ABOUT "LEGISLATIVE FACTS"

Economic expertise has traditionally been associated with the determination of what many legal commentators term "adjudicative" facts, i.e., those relating to the particular parties and actions at issue in the case at bar. Nonetheless, economic analyses—as well as other forms of technical expertise—have perhaps even greater potential importance in the area of "legislative" facts. The latter are theoretical or empirical *generalizations* about an aspect of "how the world works" that are relevant for the appropriate formulation of a legal principle or construction of a statute.

Loosely speaking, the distinction between adjudicative and legislative fact-finding corresponds to applying law and making law. Although courts most assuredly do make law, there remains a certain reluctance about confronting this rulemaking process overtly, especially at the trial court level. Trial courts are not, of course, in the business of overturning clear rules, but they not uncommonly find themselves in the position—at least implicitly—of engaging in gap-filling when a relevant rule either does not exist or is ambiguous as to its application in a new context. If expert testimony would assist a trial court in ascertaining legislative facts, what options are available? A court may be asked to take judicial notice of legislative facts that are undisputed. More elaborate procedures are, however, available if the facts are controversial or complex inquiry is required. As the cases below indicate, a court may take oral testimony and hold hearings with respect to legislative facts. The parties have little power, other than that of persuasion, to induce a reluctant court to take oral testimony. In such situations, written memoranda represent the principal means of introducing policy arguments based on technical analysis such as economics.

Appellate courts receive facts in documentary form, through submissions by the parties as a normal practice. Although brief oral arguments are conducted, these tend merely to embroider upon the written briefs. With increasing frequency, however, courts are found to reach out for sources of legislative fact that go beyond either the trial court record or party submissions. Judges have, of course, traditionally consulted authoritative legal treatises and the writings of commentators as a basis for opinions. The competence of the judiciary to apply sources of *legal* technical expertise is perhaps an assumption that must remain unquestioned. But if, for instance, appellate opinions come to turn upon interpretations from economic analysis, do the present procedures give one confidence that the inferences will always be correctly drawn?

O'HANLON v. HARTFORD ACCIDENT & INDEMNITY CO.

United States District Court for the District of Delaware, 1978.
457 F.Supp. 961.

STAPLETON, District Judge:

The sole question now before the Court is whether Section 3902 of Title 18 of the Delaware Code, pertaining to uninsured motorist insurance, applies to an excess liability insurance policy which, up to a limit of $1,000,000, insures the policy holder, *inter alia*, for bodily injury, death and property damage liability to a third party in excess of the $100,000/$300,000 retained limits of primary coverage. This issue was raised earlier on cross-motions for summary judgment. Although there was no dispute at that time regarding any relevant adjudicative facts, I nevertheless concluded that disposition of this action should await a fuller development of the record.[1] An evidentiary hearing was subsequently held at which the parties were afforded the opportunity to present any evidence which might shed

---

1. O'Hanlon v. Hartford Accident & Indemnity Co., 439 F.Supp. 377, 387 (D.Del.1977).

light on the "legislative facts" surrounding the enactment of Section 3902.

Legislative facts are "those which have relevance to legal reasoning and the lawmaking process, whether in the formulation of a legal principle or ruling by a judge *   *   * or in the enactment of a legislative body." [2] Advisory Committee Notes to Federal Rule of Evidence 201. The Federal Rules of Evidence prescribe no procedure by which courts are to go about receiving information regarding legislative facts, but the approach discussed there "leave[s] open the possibility of introducing evidence through regular channels in appropriate situations." Advisory Committee Notes to Federal Rules of Evidence 201.

Courts regularly and inevitably engage in findings of legislative facts. While these facts are not normally developed through the presentation of evidence,[3] there are instances when access to the pertinent data is most appropriately received through live testimony presented by the parties. This is one of those cases.

When a court is attempting to ascertain information relating to the marketing practices of an industry at a point in time, and to draw inferences from those practices regarding the intent of the legislature in fashioning legislation, the relevant data is most readily available through witnesses familiar with those practices.[4] Those witnesses not only can provide information through direct examination, but

---

2. See also, United States v. Gould, 536 F.2d 216, 220 (8th Cir.1976). Another definition of "legislative facts" is offered in Davis, 2 Administrative Law Treatise (1958 ed.), Sec. 15.03, p. 353.

Legislative facts are the facts which help the tribunal determine the content of law and of policy and help the tribunal to exercise its judgment or discretion in determining what course of action to take. Legislative facts are ordinarily general and do not concern the immediate parties.

See also, Davis, Judicial Notice, 55 Colum.L.R. 945, 952–9 (1955).

3. See Davis, An Approach to Problems of Evidence in the Administrative Process, 55 Harv.L.Rev. 364, 404–7 (1942); Davis, 2 Administrative Law Treatise (1958 ed.), Sec. 15.03, pp. 354–360. As Davis says in his Administrative Law Treatise (1970 Supp.), Sec. 15.03, p. 528.

A trial is normally required for finding facts about parties, but a tribunal may go anywhere to get facts used for molding law.

4. In Borden's Co. v. Baldwin, 293 U.S. 194, 210, 55 S.Ct. 187, 192, 79 L.Ed. 281 (1934), the Supreme Court said:

*   *   * where the legislative action is *   *   * challenged, and a rational basis for it is predicated upon the particular economic facts of a given trade or industry, which are outside the sphere of judicial notice, these facts are properly the subject of evidence and of findings. With the notable expansion of the scope of governmental regulation, and the consequent assertion of violation of constitutional rights, it is increasingly important that when it becomes necessary for the Court to deal with the facts relating to particular commercial or industrial conditions, they should be presented concretely with appropriate determinations upon evidence, so that conclusions shall not be reached without adequate factual support.

are also available for cross-examination [5] and to answer any inquiries which the Court might have. For these reasons, I agree that "[o]nce the court decides to advise itself in order to make new law, it ought not add to the risk of a poor decision by denying itself whatever help on the facts it can with propriety obtain." 1 Weinstein and Berger, Weinstein's Evidence (1977 ed.), para. 2000[03], pp. 200–16.

The hearing held in this case fulfilled its purpose. As the remainder of this Opinion will demonstrate, the evidence of legislative facts submitted at that time was of substantial assistance in understanding and resolving the issue before the Court.[6]

QUESTIONS

1. Assume a state court case similar to National Steel v. Gibbons, discussed above in Chapter II. National Steel wishes to present the testimony of an economist who will argue that the railroad is the least-cost bearer of the risk in question. On what grounds would opposing counsel be likely to object? And with what chance of success? Describe some other cases where expert testimony, although arguably useful in reaching a "good" decision, might be procedurally difficult to present.

2. Hearings of the type described in *O'Hanlon* are not very common. The text and footnotes to this case describe what Judge Stapleton viewed as ample authority for the hearing conducted. What authority would a state court trial judge have for a similar proceeding? Is the reluctance of judges to hold such hearings based on doubts about propriety? The non-traditional nature of the proceeding? Something else?

3. Rule 706 of the Federal Rules of Evidence specifically grants a federal court authority to appoint its own experts and grant them "reasonable compensation in whatever sum the court may allow." Although some jurisdictions do not allow the trial court judge this power, most jurisdictions grant judges the general authority to call witnesses. See Annot., 67 A.L.R.2d 538 (1959). What are the pros and cons of the court calling its own expert witnesses? Does the answer to the question depend in any way on whether the testimony is relative to adjudicative or legislative facts? (See Saltzburg, "The

5. It has been suggested that each party must have the opportunity to influence the Court's findings of legislative facts in order to comport with due process. Davis, Administrative Law of the Seventies (1976 ed.), pp. 364–5.

6. The evidence submitted included testimony from Professor Alan I. Widiss concerning the historical development of uninsured motorist insurance statutes, from Arnold Olsen of the Delaware Insurance Commissioner's Office regarding the 1971 amendment to Delaware's uninsured motorist insurance statute, and from David W. Detwiler, an insurance policy underwriter with the Insurance Company of North America concerning the marketing practices with regard to excess liability insurance policies.

Unnecessarily Expanding Role of the American Trial Court Judge,"
64 Va.L.Rev. 1, 75–81.)

GREGG v. GEORGIA

Supreme Court of the United States, 1976.
428 U.S. 153, 96 S.Ct. 2909, 49 L.Ed.2d 859.

[In Furman v. Georgia, 408 U.S. 238, 92 S.Ct. 2726, 33 L.Ed.2d 346
(1972), the Supreme Court had invalidated a Georgia death penalty
statute on the essentially procedural grounds that it accorded excessive discretion to jurors. Since *Gregg* addressed the justification of
the penalty itself, it was perhaps inevitable that the deterrence value
of the penalty be discussed by the Court. Justice Stewart's majority
opinion dismissed the statistical evidence on the deterrent effect of
capital punishment as inconclusive but "a complex factual issue the
resolution of which properly lies with the legislatures" which can
evaluate the evidence in light of their own conditions and goals. Justice Marshall's dissent considers the statistical evidence more explicitly.]

Justice MARSHALL, dissenting.

[I]n *Furman*, I canvassed the relevant data on the deterrent effect of capital punishment. 408 U.S., at 347–354, 92 S.Ct., at
2781–2785.[2] The state of knowledge at that point, after literally centuries of debate, was summarized as follows by a United Nations
Committee:

> "It is generally agreed between the retentionists and abolitionists,
> whatever their opinions about the validity of comparative studies
> of deterrence, that the data which now exist show no correlation
> between the existence of capital punishment and lower rates of
> capital crime." [3]

The available evidence, I concluded in *Furman*, was convincing that
"capital punishment is not necessary as a deterrent to crime in our
society." Id., at 353, 92 S.Ct., at 2784.

The Solicitor General in his *amicus* brief in these cases relies
heavily on a study by Isaac Ehrlich,[4] reported a year after *Furman*,
to support the contention that the death penalty does deter murder.
Since the Ehrlich study was not available at the time of *Furman* and

---

2. See e.g., T. Sellin, The Death Penalty, A Report for the Model Penal Code
Project of the American Law Institute
(1959).

3. United Nations Department of Economic and Social Affairs, Capital Punishment, pt. II, § 159, p. 123 (1968).

4. I. Ehrlich, The Deterrent Effect of
Capital Punishment: A Question of Life
and Death (Working Paper No. 18, National Bureau of Economic Research,
Nov. 1973); Ehrlich, The Deterrent Effect of Capital Punishment: A Question
of Life and Death, 65 Am.Econ.Rev. 397
(June 1975).

since it is the first scientific study to suggest that the death penalty may have a deterrent effect, I will briefly consider its import.

The Ehrlich study focused on the relationship in the Nation as a whole between the homicide rate and "execution risk"—the fraction of persons convicted of murder who were actually executed. Comparing the differences in homicide rate and execution risk for the years 1933 to 1969, Ehrlich found that increases in excecution risk were associated with increases in the homicide rate.[5] But when he employed the statistical technique of multiple regression analysis to control for the influence of other variables posited to have an impact on the homicide rate,[6] Ehrlich found a negative correlation between changes in the homicide rate and changes in execution risk. His tentative conclusion was that for the period from 1933 to 1967 each additional execution in the United States might have saved eight lives.[7]

The methods and conclusions of the Ehrlich study have been severely criticized on a number of grounds.[8] It has been suggested, for example, that the study is defective because it compares execution and homicide rates on a nationwide, rather than a state-by-state, basis. The aggregation of data from all States—including those that have abolished the death penalty—obscures the relationship between murder and execution rates. Under Ehrlich's methodology, a decrease in the execution risk in one State combined with an increase in the murder rate in another State would, all other things being equal, suggest a deterrent effect that quite obviously would not exist. Indeed, a deterrent effect would be suggested if, once again all other things being equal, one State abolished the death penalty and experienced no change in the murder rate, while another State experienced an increase in the murder rate.[9] The most compelling criticism of the

---

5. Id., at 409.

6. The variables other than execution risk included probability of arrest, probability of conviction given arrest, national aggregate measures of the percentage of the population between age 14 and 24, the unemployment rate, the labor force participation rate, and estimated per capita income.

7. Id., at 398, 414.

8. See Passell & Taylor, The Deterrent Effect of Capital Punishment: Another Year (unpublished Columbia University Discussion Paper 74–7509, Mar. 1975), reproduced in Brief for Petitioner App. E in Jurek v. Texas, O.T.1975, No. 75–5844; Passell, The Deterrent Effect of the Death Penalty: A Statistical Test, 28 Stan.L.Rev. 61 (1975); Baldus & Cole, A Comparison of the Work of Thorsten Sellin & Isaac Ehrlich on the Deterrent Effect of Capital Punishment, 85 Yale L.J. 170 (1975); Bowers & Pierce, The Illusion of Deterrence in Isaac Ehrlich's Research on Capital Punishment, 85 Yale L.J. 187 (1975); Peck, The Deterrent Effect of Capital Punishment: Ehrlich and His Critics, 85 Yale L.J. 359 (1976). See also Ehrlich, Deterrence: Evidence and Inference, 85 Yale L.J. 209 (1975); Ehrlich, Rejoinder, 85 Yale L.J. 368 (1976). In addition to the items discussed in text, criticism has been directed at the quality of Ehrlich's data, his choice of explanatory variables, his failure to account for the interdependence of those variables, and his assumptions as to the mathematical form of the relationship between the homicide rate and the explanatory variables.

9. See Baldus & Cole, supra pp. 173–177.

Ehrlich study is that its conclusions are extremely sensitive to the choice of the time period included in the regression analysis. Analysis of Ehrlich's data reveals that all empirical support for the deterrent effect of capital punishment disappears when the five most recent years are removed from his time series—that is to say, whether a decrease in the execution risk corresponds to an increase or a decrease in the murder rate depends on the ending point of the sample period.[10] This finding has cast severe doubts on the reliability of Ehrlich's tentative conclusions.[11] Indeed, a recent [s]tudy, based on Ehrlich's theoretical model but using cross-section state data for the years 1950 and 1960, found no support for the conclusion that executions act as a deterrent.[12]

The Ehrlich study, in short, is of little, if any, assistance in assessing the deterrent impact of the death penalty. Accord, Commonwealth v. O'Neal, 369 Mass. 242, 256, 339 N.E.2d 676, 684 (1975). The evidence I reviewed in *Furman*[13] remains convincing, in my view, that "capital punishment is not necessary as a deterrent to crime in our society." 408 U.S., at 353, 92 S.Ct., at 2784. The justification for the death penalty must be found elsewhere.

QUESTIONS

1. Ehrlich and other economists have suggested that punishment be viewed as a kind of "price" that affects the position of perpetrators along a negatively sloped demand curve to engage in criminal activity. Is this a useful conceptualization? Is it more useful for some crimes than others?

2. As a matter of *a priori* theory, is there any doubt that the threat of punishment would have *some* effect on the murder rate? To what extent are the studies a *quantification* of the effect rather than a proof of the existence of an effect? Ehrlich's 1975 study indicated a tentative conclusion that each execution might deter almost eight murders. Substitute the unknown value X for Ehrlich's estimate. How big does X have to be in order for the death penalty to be justified? Who bears the burden of proving what X is?

3. The Court cited a number of scholarly statistical studies bearing on this problem. How do you suppose it became aware of their existence and content? Are any problems raised if a court goes beyond the factual sources raised by the parties?

---

10. Bowers & Pierce, supra, n. 8, at 197–98. See also Passell & Taylor supra, n. 8, at 2–66–2–68.

11. See Bowers & Pierce, supra, n. 8, at 197–198; Baldus & Cole, supra, n. 8, at 181, 183–185; Peck, supra, n. 8, at 366–367.

12. Passell, supra, n. 8.

13. See also Bailey, Murder and Capital Punishment: Some Further Evidence, 45 Am.J. Orthopsychiatry 669 (1975); W. Bowers, Executions in America 121–163 (1974).

4. Ehrlich's study is a focal point of the scholarly controversy about the deterrence evidence. In addition to his conceptual model of deterrence, the empirical results are derived from an applied technical sub-specialty of economics called "econometrics." Do you know what "regression analysis" is all about? Does the Court? If a court is not in a position to evaluate the technical evidence proffered, what should it do?

5. Would it be appropriate for a judge to seek assistance by contacting an expert for interpretive advice on difficult technical points? To what extent do you think judges rely only on research or explanations provided by a law clerk who appears to possess familiarity with a technical subject matter?

6. Suppose that you were commissioned to write a set of guidelines for courts in dealing with legislative facts, including technical economic questions of either a theoretical or empirical nature. What are the problems, if any, with the present system? Would new procedures be desirable in order to improve things? Would the procedures have to be mandatory?

UNITED STATES v. AMERICAN TELEPHONE AND TELEGRAPH CO.

United States District Court for the District of Columbia, 1982.
552 F.Supp. 131.

GREENE, Judge:

These actions are before the Court for a determination whether a consent decree proposed by the parties is in the "public interest" and should therefore be entered as the Court's judgment. Over six hundred comments from interested persons, many of them objecting to various aspects of the proposal, have been received, and the Court has considered briefs submitted by the parties and others, and it has heard extensive oral argument. This opinion discusses the principal questions raised by these interested persons, and it embodies the Court's decision on the appropriateness of the proposed decree under the Tunney Act's public interest standard.

*   *   *

[The Court traces the history of the present proceeding back to another antitrust case, the "Western Electric" case, originally filed by the government against AT & T's manufacturing subsidiary in 1949.]

Periodic negotiations between AT & T and the government continued through 1954 and 1955, and by early December, 1955, the government and AT & T had reached an agreement.

The consent decree which was the product of this process included neither the divestiture of Western Electric nor any of the other structural relief originally requested by the government. Instead, an injunction was issued which precluded AT & T from engaging in any business other than the provision of common carrier communications services; precluded Western Electric from manufacturing equipment other than that used by the Bell System; and required the defendants to license their patents to all applicants upon the payment of appropriate royalties.

Despite the substantial differences between the structural relief requested in the government's 1949 complaint and the relief actually provided by the proposed decree, the District Court for the District of New Jersey accepted the proposal on January 24, 1956, after a brief hearing, stating:

> I feel that I can unhesitatingly accept the recommendations of the Attorney General, that this judgment is in the public interest, and that it is a satisfactory adjustment of this very, very vexatious problem; and I am therefore happy to go along with the recommendation made by the Attorney General and shall forthwith sign this judgment.

After the decree was approved, no major developments occurred in the case for the next several years. Until 1981, the entries in the court record concern primarily the patent licensing provisions.

This was the status of the *Western Electric* suit when the government filed a separate antitrust action on November 20, 1974, in this Court against AT & T, Western Electric, and Bell Telephone Laboratories, Inc. (Civil Action No. 74–1698). The complaint in the new action alleged monopolization by the defendants with respect to a broad variety of telecommunication services and equipment in violation of section 2 of the Sherman Act. In this lawsuit, the government initially sought the divestiture from AT & T of the Bell Operating Companies (hereinafter generally referred to as Operating Companies or BOCs) as well as the divestiture and dissolution of Western Electric. While the action was pending, the government changed its relief requests several times asking, at various times or in various alternatives, for the divestiture from AT & T of Western Electric and portions of the Bell Laboratories.

* * *

The trial itself began on January 15, 1981. At the request of the parties, the trial was recessed immediately after the opening statements for a period of six weeks in order to afford an opportunity for a negotiated settlement. When the settlement discussions proved fruitless, the trial resumed on March 4, 1981.

* * *

The Proposed Decree

On January 8, 1982, the parties to these two actions filed with the District Court for the District of New Jersey a stipulation consenting to the entry by the Court of the "Modification of Final Judgment" filed therewith. On the same day, they attempted to file in this Court a dismissal of the *AT & T* action pursuant to Rule 41(a)(1)(ii), Federal Rules of Civil Procedure. This Court ordered that the dismissal be lodged, not filed, and, in accordance with that order and the provisions of the Tunney Act, the dismissal has not yet been effected.

In their settlement proposal, the parties proposed that the Court enter the following judgment with respect to both lawsuits.

Section I of the proposed decree would provide for significant structural changes in AT & T. In essence, it would remove from the Bell System the function of supplying local telephone service by requiring AT & T to divest itself of the portions of its twenty-two Operating Companies which perform that function.

*   *   *

Section II of the proposed decree would complement these structural changes by various restrictions which are said to be designed (1) to prevent the divesting Operating Companies from discriminating against AT & T's competitors, and (2) to avoid a recurrence of the type of discrimination and cross-subsidization that were the basis of the *AT & T* lawsuit.

*   *   *

Procedures in Connection with the Settlement Proposal

The Tunney Act [15 U.S.C. Sec. 16(e)] provides that a proposal for a consent judgment submitted by the United States in an action brought under the antitrust laws may not be entered by the Court without prior compliance with certain procedures. These procedures include a sixty-day comment period, publication of a competitive impact statement by the Department of Justice, a sixty-day period for the receipt of public comments, and a determination by the Court that "the entry of such judgment is in the public interest." For the purpose of this public interest determination the Court may consider

(1) the competitive impact of such judgment, including termination of alleged violations, provisions for enforcement and modification, duration or relief sought, anticipated effects of alternative remedies actually considered, and any other considerations bearing upon the adequacy of such judgment;

(2) the impact of entry of such judgment upon the public generally and individuals alleging specific injury from the violations

set forth in the complaint including consideration of public benefit, if any, to be derived from a determination of the issues at trial.

Procedurally the Court may

(1) take testimony of Government officials or experts or such other expert witnesses, upon motion of any party or participant or upon its own motion, as the court may deem appropriate;

(2) appoint a special master and such outside consultants or expert witnesses as the court may deem appropriate; and request and obtain the views, evaluations, or advice of any individual, group or agency of government with respect to any aspects of the proposed judgment or the effect of such judgment, in such manner as the court deems appropriate; .

(3) authorize full or limited participation in proceedings before the court by interested persons or agencies, including appearance [as] amicus curiae, intervention as a party pursuant to the Federal Rules of Civil Procedure, examination of witnesses or documentary materials, or participation in any other manner and extent which serves the public interest as the court may deem appropriate;

(4) review any comments including any objections filed with the United States under subsection (d) of this section concerning the proposed judgment and the responses of the United States to such comments and objections; and

(5) take such other action in the public interest as the court may deem appropriate.

* . * *

* * * [T]he parties have now stated in various ways and before various forums (including before this Court) that, irrespective of their opinion of the technical applicability of the Tunney Act, they are willing to have the Tunney Act procedures applied by this Court.

* * *

Following the entry of [the Court's order applying the substantive Tunney Act procedures to the present settlement] and in compliance therewith, the parties filed the appropriate pleadings and reports.[58]

---

58. On January 28, 1982, the government published the proposed decree in the Federal Register (47 Fed.Reg. 4166 (1982)); on February 5, 1982, AT & T filed with the Court its description of the written and oral communications made on its behalf with any officers or employees of the United States regarding the proposed decree; on February 10, 1982, the government filed with the Court its Competitive Impact Statement, and on February 17, 1982 published it in the Federal Register (47 Fed.Reg. 7170 (1982)); beginning on February 19, 1982, the government made copies of the proposed decree available at the twenty-six district courts specified in the Court's order of January 21, 1982; over a period of two weeks in February, 1982, the government published in newspapers of general circulation in these twenty-six districts, a summary of the proposed decree and the

After the Court issued its January 21 order—and even prior to that time—a considerable number of individuals and entities sought to intervene in these proceedings for various purposes. On February 5, 1982, the Court issued an order denying all such requests. The Court also received a considerable number of comments from individual citizens. All such comments were filed in the Public Interest Docket, and duplicates were turned over to the Department of Justice for its response in accordance with paragraph 8 of the January 21, 1982 order.

During the months of April and May, 1982, the Department of Justice filed with the Court the comments it had received during the preceding sixty days, and on May 20, 1982, it filed its response to those comments.

On May 25, 1982, the Court issued a Memorandum governing further proceedings. The Memorandum identified a number of key issues that were raised by the comments and the responses, and it invited the parties and the various interested persons to brief these issues in a form more suitable to judicial adjudication than the necessarily somewhat diffuse comments. A hearing was held on June 29 and 30, 1982, at which time the issues were further elucidated and refined. The Court's substantive conclusions based upon the comments, responses, briefs, oral arguments, and the entire record herein, are discussed below.

Under the Tunney Act, the Court may approve the decree proposed by the parties only if it first determines that such approval is "in the public interest." Before discussing the substantive provisions of the proposed decree, it is appropriate to set out the standards which will guide the Court's public interest review.

* * *

Degree of Deference to the Proposal Submitted by the Parties

Where, as here, a court is evaluating a settlement, it is not as free to exercise its discretion in fashioning a remedy as it would be upon a

---

Competitive Impact Statement and directions for the submission of written public comments; from February 19 to April 20, 1982, there was a sixty-day public comment period; on April 21, April 23, April 27, and May 4, 1982, the government filed these written comments with the Court; as set forth in the Court's order of May 5, 1982 and in lieu of publishing all written comments, on May 10, 1982, the government issued a press release describing the procedures for obtaining copies of comments, and on May 17, 1982 published the press release in the Federal Register (47 Fed.Reg. 21214 (1982)); on May 17, 1982, the government published in the Federal Register the name and address of everyone who filed a written comment and the number of pages in each comment (47 Fed.Reg. 21214 (1982)); and on May 20, 1982, the government made available in each of the twenty-six districts referred to above a copy of every comment received.

finding of liability. For when parties enter into a consent decree, they

> waive their right to litigate the issues involved in the case and thus save themselves the time, expense, and inevitable risk of litigation. Naturally, the agreement reached normally embodies a compromise; in exchange for the saving of cost and the elimination of risk, the parties each give up something they might have won had they proceeded with the litigation.

United States v. Armour & Co., 402 U.S. 673, 681, 91 S.Ct. 1752, 1757, 29 L.Ed.2d 256 (1971). If courts acting under the Tunney Act disapproved proposed consent decrees merely because they did not contain the exact relief which the court would have imposed after a finding of liability, defendants would have no incentive to consent to judgment and this element of compromise would be destroyed. The consent decree would thus as a practical matter be eliminated as an antitrust enforcement tool, despite Congress' directive that it be preserved. See. S.Rep. No. 93–298, supra, at 6; H.R.Rep. No. 93–1463, supra, at 6.

It follows that a lower standard of review must be applied in assessing proposed consent decrees than would be appropriate in other circumstances. H.R.Rep. No. 93–1463, supra, at 12. For these reasons, it has been said by some courts that a proposed decree must be approved even if it falls short of the remedy the court would impose on its own, as long as it falls within the range of acceptability or is "within the reaches of public interest." United States v. Gillette Co., 406 F.Supp. 713, 716 (D.Mass.1975). See also United States v. Bechtel Corp., 648 F.2d 660, 666 (9th Cir.1981); United States v. Carrols Development Corp., 454 F.Supp. 1215, 1222 (N.D.N.Y.1978); United States v. National Broadcasting Co., 449 F.Supp. 1127, 1143 (C.D.Cal.1978). Although these decisions are not necessarily binding, this Court will follow a similar approach.

It does not follow from these principles, however, that courts must unquestionably accept a proferred decree as long as it somehow, and however inadequately, deals with the antitrust and other public policy problems implicated in the lawsuit. To do so would be to revert to the "rubber stamp" role which was at the crux of the congressional concerns when the Tunney Act became law. This consideration is especially potent in these cases, for several reasons.

First. This is not an ordinary antitrust case. The American Telephone and Telegraph Company, with its various components and affiliates, is the largest corporation in the world by any reckoning, and the proposed decree, if approved, would have significant consequences for an unusually large number of ratepayers, shareholders, bondholders, creditors, employees, and competitors. Beyond that, it is clear that the divestiture of the Operating Companies, combined with the entry of AT & T into new competitive markets, will be an enormous undertaking, fraught not only with many problems and difficulties, but also with a potential for substantial private advantage at the expense of the public interest. In view of these considerations, and of the potential impact of the proposed decree on a vast and crucial sector of the economy and on such general public interests as the cost and availability of local telephone service, the technological development of a vital part of the national economy, national defense, and foreign trade, the Court would be derelict in its duty if it adopted a narrow approach to its public interest review responsibilities.

Second. Some of those who during the legislative hearings took a narrow view of the judicial responsibilities under the Act suggested that the courts would generally not be able to render sound judgments on settlements because they would not be aware of all the relevant facts. But that factor is of relatively little relevance here, for this Court has already heard what probably amounts to well over ninety percent of the parties' evidence both quantitatively and qualitatively, as well as all of their legal arguments. It is thus in a far better position than are the courts in the usual consent decree cases [89] to evaluate the specific details of the settlement.[90]

Third. These actions, and this settlement, have an unfortunate history. The 1956 *Western Electric* consent decree was evidently the product of the very kind of influence and pressure that Congress subsequently sought to prevent through the Tunney Act procedures. That identical settlement, and the identical parties, are now before the Court. Nor can those events simply be dismissed as ancient history, irrelevant to the events of 1981–82. One needs only to recall the peculiar circumstances under which the instant settlement proposal was sought to be filed in the courts and the recurrence of an inappropriate collaboration in the course of the litigation between the Department of Defense and AT & T similar to that which occurred in 1952–54. See United States v. AT & T, 524 F.Supp. 1331 (D.D.C.1981). These circumstances do not foster a sense of confidence that the assessment of the settlement and its implications may be left entirely to AT & T and the Department of Justice.

None of this means, of course, that the Court would be justified in simply substituting its views for those of the parties. But it does

---

89. In United States v. Ling-Temco Vought, Inc., supra, 315 F.Supp. at 1309, the absence of a record forced the court to rely upon the parties' assurances that the proposed decree was in the public interest.

90. In fact, the parties sought review of the proposed decree in this Court precisely because of its "substantial expertise on the competitive situation in the telecommunications industry." Letter from Assistant Attorney General William F. Baxter, dated January 18, 1982.

mean that the decree will receive closer scrutiny than that which might be appropriate to a decree proposed in a more routine antitrust case.

The Court concludes that, taking into account the various legislative and decisional mandates discussed above, it will apply the following standard to its evaluation of the proposed decree. After giving due weight to the decisions of the parties as expressed in the proposed decree, the Court will attempt to harmonize competitive values with other legitimate public interest factors. If the decree meets the requirements for an antitrust remedy—that is, if it effectively opens the relevant markets to competition and prevents the recurrence of anticompetitive activity, all without imposing undue and unnecessary burdens upon other aspects of the public interest—it will be approved. If the proposed decree does not meet this standard, the Court will follow the practice applied in other Tunney Act cases and as a prerequisite to its approval, it will require modifications which would bring the decree within the public interest standard as herein defined.

* * *

CONCLUSION

The proposed reorganization of the Bell System raises issues of vast complexity. Because of their importance, not only to the parties but also to the telecommunications industry and to the public, the Court has discussed the various problems in substantial detail. It is appropriate to summarize briefly the major issues and the Court's decisions which are central to the proceeding.

A. The American telecommunications industry is presently dominated by one company—AT & T. It provides local and long-distance telephone service; it manufactures and markets the equipment used by telephone subscribers as well as that used in the telecommunications network; and it controls one of the leading communications research and development facilities in the world. According to credible evidence, this integrated structure has enabled AT & T for many years to undermine the efforts of competitors seeking to enter the telecommunications market.

The key to the Bell System's power to impede competition has been its control of local telephone service. The local telephone network functions as the gateway to individual telephone subscribers. It must be used by long-distance carriers seeking to connect one caller to another. Customers will only purchase equipment which can readily be connected to the local network through the telephone outlets in their homes and offices. The enormous cost of the wires, cables, switches, and other transmission facilities which comprise that network has completely insulated it from competition. Thus, access to AT & T's local network is critical if long distance carriers and equipment manufacturers are to be viable competitors.

AT & T has allegedly used its control of this local monopoly to disadvantage these competitors in two principal ways. First, it has attempted to prevent competing long distance carriers and competing equipment manufacturers from gaining access to the local network, or to delay that access, thus placing them in an inferior position vis-a-vis AT & T's own services. Second, it has supposedly used profits earned from the monopoly local telephone operations to subsidize its long distance and equipment businesses in which it was competing with others.

For a great many years, the Federal Communications Commission has struggled, largely without success, to stop practices of this type through the regulatory tools at its command. A lawsuit the Department of Justice brought in 1949 to curb similar practices ended in an ineffectual consent decree. Some other remedy is plainly required; hence the divestiture of the local Operating Companies from the Bell System. This divestiture will sever the relationship between this local monopoly and the other, competitive segments of AT & T, and it will thus ensure—certainly better than could any other type of relief—that the practices which allegedly have lain heavy on the telecommunications industry will not recur.

B. With the loss of control over the local network, AT & T will be unable to disadvantage its competitors, and the restrictions imposed on AT & T after the government's first antitrust suit—which limited AT & T to the provision of telecommunications services—will no longer be necessary. The proposed decree accordingly removes these restrictions.

The decree will thus allow AT & T to become a vigorous competitor in the growing computer, computer-related, and information markets. Other large and experienced firms are presently operating in these markets, and there is therefore no reason to believe that AT & T will be able to achieve monopoly dominance in these industries as it did in telecommunications. At the same time, by use of its formidable scientific, engineering, and management resources, including particularly the capabilities of Bell Laboratories, AT & T should be able to make significant contributions to these fields, which are at the forefront of innovation and technology, to the benefit of American consumers, national defense, and the position of American industry vis-a-vis foreign competition.

All of these developments are plainly in the public interest, and the Court will therefore approve this aspect of the proposed decree, with one exception. Electronic publishing, which is still in its infancy, holds promise to become an important provider of information—

such as news, entertainment, and advertising—in competition with the traditional print, television, and radio media; indeed, it has the potential, in time, for actually replacing some of these methods of disseminating information.

Traditionally, the Bell System has simply distributed information provided by others; it has not been involved in the business of generating its own information. The proposed decree would, for the first time, allow AT & T to do both, and it would do so at a time when the electronic publishing industry is still in a fragile state of experimentation and growth and when electronic information can still most efficiently and most economically be distributed over AT & T's long distance network. If, under these circumstances, AT & T were permitted to engage both in the transmission and the generation of information, there would be a substantial risk not only that it would stifle the efforts of other electronic publishers but that it would acquire a substantial monopoly over the generation of news in the more general sense. Such a development would strike at a principle which lies at the heart of the First Amendment: that the American people are entitled to a diversity of sources of information. In order to prevent this from occurring, the Court will require, as a condition of its approval of the proposed decree, that it be modified to preclude AT & T from entering the field of electronic publishing until the risk of its domination of that field has abated.

C. After the divestiture, the Operating Companies will possess a monopoly over local telephone service. According to the Department of Justice, the Operating Companies must be barred from entering all competitive markets to ensure that they will not misuse their monopoly power. The Court will not impose restrictions simply for the sake of theoretical consistency. Restrictions must be based on an assessment of the realistic circumstances of the relevant markets, including the Operating Companies' ability to engage in anticompetitive behavior, their potential contribution to the market as an added competitor for AT & T, as well as upon the effects of the restrictions on the rates for local telephone service.

This standard requires that the Operating Companies be prohibited from providing long distance services and information services, and from manufacturing equipment used in the telecommunications industry. Participation in these fields carries with it a substantial risk that the Operating Companies will use the same anticompetitive techniques used by AT & T in order to thwart the growth of their own competitors. Moreover, contrary to the assumptions made by some, Operating Company involvement in these areas could not legitimately generate subsidies for local rates. Such involvement could produce substantial profits only if the local companies used their monopoly position to dislodge competitors or to provide subsidy for their competitive services or products—the very behavior the decree seeks to prevent.

Different considerations apply, however, to the marketing of customer premises equipment—the telephone and other devices used in subscribers' homes and offices—and the production of the Yellow Pages advertising directories. For a variety of reasons, there is little likelihood that these companies will be able to use their monopoly position to disadvantage competitors in these areas. In addition, their marketing of equipment will provide needed competition for AT & T, and the elimination of the restriction on their production of the Yellow Pages will generate a substantial subsidy for local telephone rates. The Court will therefore require that the proposed decree be modified to remove the restrictions on these two types of activities.

D. With respect to a number of subjects, the proposed decree establishes merely general principles and objectives, leaving the specific implementing details for subsequent action, principally by the plan of reorganization which AT & T is required to file within six months after entry of the judgment. The parties have also made informal promises, either to each other or to the Court, as to how they intend to interpret or implement various provisions. The Court has decided that its public interest responsibilities require that it establish a process for determining whether the plan of reorganization and other, subsequent actions by AT & T actually implement these principles and promises in keeping with the objectives of the judgment. Absent such a process, AT & T would have the opportunity to interpret and implement the broad principles of the decree in such a manner as to disadvantage its competitors, the Operating Companies, or both, or otherwise to act in a manner contrary to the public interest as interpreted by the Court in this opinion.

For that reason, the Court is requiring that the judgment be modified (1) to vest authority in the Court to enforce the provisions and principles of that judgment on its own rather than only at the request of a party; and (2) to provide for a proceeding, accessible to third party intervenors and to the chief executives of the seven new regional Operating Companies, in which the Court will determine whether the plan of reorganization is consistent with the decree's general principles and promises.

* * *

QUESTIONS

1. Judicial review pursuant to the Tunney Act involves procedures that lift some of the cloak of secrecy that frequently is imposed upon settlement negotiations. What effect, if any, is the prospect of publicity likely to have on the negotiations?

2. Apart from the aspect of public scrutiny, the parties must reckon with the Court's power to reject or modify the terms of their proposed settlement. How much does it matter that the judge can modify terms rather than engage in a mere "take it or leave it" acceptance or rejection? What possible application does the Divide and Choose problem in Chapter II above have in this context?

3. In the AT & T case, Judge Greene had already heard a substantial portion of the evidence that was to be presented at trial. This arguably eliminated the need for any very substantial hearings to provide background necessary to evaluate the settlement terms. Suppose that the settlement had taken place before such factual input had been made available. What would be an appropriate format for the factual input to be provided?

4. Through his opinion excerpted above and his assertion of continuing jurisdiction over the administration of the settlement, Judge Greene has exercised an enormous regulatory power over a key industry. Arguably, this judicial authority conflicts at least to some extent with that of the Federal Communications Commission. Who should exercise such authority? Does the element of expertise significantly affect this question? How could the Tunney Act be redrafted to address this question?

5. What is the "worst case" scenario that one might use in arguing for reducing the scope of judicial review under the Tunney Act?

6. The judge in this case apparently exercises an enormous amount of discretionary control over the terms imposed on the parties. Is his discretion wider or narrower than if the case had gone to final judgment? In what types of *non*-antitrust cases does the judge have great discretion over remedies that have powerful economic implications?

7. Does this case fit the traditional dichotomy between legislative and adjudicative fact?

Appendix A

BIBLIOGRAPHY

The main text's chapters and other divisions are organized primarily in terms of underlying economic linkages. In order to assist readers who wish to identify literature in terms of more traditional legal categories, this appendix contains bibliographical references grouped to a greater extent by substantive areas of law.

I. Introduction to Economic Analysis of Law

II. Property Rights and the Coase Theorem

III. Torts: The Rule of Liability

IV. Torts: The Assessment of Damages

V. Contract Law

VI. Crime and Punishment

VII. Civil and Criminal Procedure

VIII. Family Law

IX. Corporation Law

X. Economic Perspectives on Collective Decisionmaking

XI. Federal Legal Systems

The groupings and their ordering follow the organization of a course in Economic Analysis of Law taught by Professors Michael J. Trebilcock and J. Robert S. Prichard of the University of Toronto Faculty of Law. Since the list had its genesis as supplementary readings for that course, the citations represent what has been found interesting or useful to law students; they do not purport to be an exhaustive catalogue of scholarship in the field. No attempt at all is made to supply listings for the "obvious" areas of economic analysis in law, such as antitrust and tax, on the grounds that standard texts in those fields already provide ample references to the economically oriented literature.

The bibliographical list is used with the permission of Trebilcock and Prichard, its original authors. The reading list has also been revised and updated successively by law students Paul Jones (University of Toronto) and Nancy H. Diamond (University of Virginia).

I. INTRODUCTION TO ECONOMIC ANALYSIS OF LAW

Ackerman, *Economic Foundations of Property Law*, (Boston: Little, Brown 1975), "Introduction," pp. vi–xvi.

Ackerman, "The Marketplace of Ideas: Comment on Posner," 90 *Yale L.J.* 1131 (1981).

Aivazian and Callen, "The Coase Theorem and the Empty Core," 24 *J.L. & Econ.* 175 (1981).

Baker, "Starting Points in Economic Analysis of Law," 8 *Hofstra L.Rev.* 939 (1981).

Baker, "The Ideology of the Economic Analysis of Law," 5 *Phil. & Pub.Aff.* 3 (1975).

Bator, "The Anatomy of Market Failure," 72 *Q.J.Econ.* 351 (1958).

Bebchuk, "The Pursuit of a Bigger Pie: Can Everyone Expect a Bigger Slice?", 8 *Hofstra L.Rev.* 671 (1980).

Becker, *The Economic Approach to Human Behaviour* (Chicago: Univ. Chicago Press, 1976).

Brenner, "Economics—An Imperialist Science?, 9 *J.Legal Stud.* 179 (1980).

Buchanan, "Good Economics—Bad Law," 60 *Va.L.Rev.* 483 (1974).

Buchanan, "The Institutional Structure of Externality," 14 *Pub.Choice* 69 (1959).

Buchanan and Tullock, *The Calculus of Consent* (Ann Arbor: Univ. Michigan Press, 1962).

Burrows and Veljanovski (eds.), *The Economic Approach to Law* (London: Butterworths, 1981).

Carroll, "Two Games that Illustrate Some Problems Concerning Economic Analysis of Legal Problems," 53 *S.Cal.L.Rev.* 1371 (1980).

Carroll, "Four Games and the Expectancy Theory," 54 *S.Cal.L.Rev.* 503 (1981).

Chapman, "Individual Rights and Collective Rationality: Some Implications for Economic Analysis of Law," 10 *Hofstra L.Rev.* 455 (1982).

Coase, "Economics and Contiguous Disciplines," 7 *J.Legal Stud.* 201 (1978).

Coleman, "Efficiency, Utility, and Wealth Maximization," 8 *Hofstra L.Rev.* 509 (1980).

Coleman, "Efficiency, Exchange, and Auction: Philosophic Aspects of the Economic Approach to Law," 68 *Calif.L.Rev.* 221 (1980).

Cooter, "Law and the Imperialism of Economics: an Introduction to the Economic Analysis of Law and a Review of the Major Books," 29 *UCLA L.Rev.* 1260 (1982).

DeAlessi, "On the Nature and Consequences of Private and Public Enterprises," 67 *Minn.L.Rev.* 191 (1982).

Diamond, "Posner's Economic Analysis of Law," 5 *Bell J. Econ.* 294 (1974).

Dworkin, "Is Wealth a Value?", 9 *J.Legal Stud.* 191 (1980).

Glasner, "On the Difference between Wealth and Liberty," 2 *Int'l L.Rev.* 227 (1982).

Goldberg, "Commons, Clark and the Emerging Post-Coasian Law and Economics," 10 *J.Econ.Issues* 877 (1976).

Gordley, "Equality in Exchange," 69 *Calif.L.Rev.* 1587 (1981).

Hansmann, "The Current State of Law and Economics Scholarship," 33 *J.Legal Ed.* 217 (1983).

Heilbroner, "On the Limited 'Relevance' of Economics," in *Capitalism Today* (eds. Bell and Kirstol, 1970).

Heller, "Is the Charitable Exemption from Property Taxation an Easy Case? General Concerns about Legal Economics and Jurisprudence" in Rubinfeld (ed.), *Essays on the Law and Economics of Local Governments* (Washington, D.C.: The Urban Institute 1979).

Hirsch, *Law and Economics: An Introductory Analysis*, (New York: Academic Press, 1979).

Hirshleifer, "Economics from a Biological Viewpoint," 20 *J.L. & Econ.* 1 (1977).

Horwitz, "Law and Economics: Science or Politics," 8 *Hofstra L.Rev.* 905 (1981).

Keating, "Standards: Implicit, Explicit, and Mandatory," 19 *Econ.Inquiry* 449 (1981).

Kelman, "Misunderstanding Social Life: A Critique of the Core Premises of Law and Economics," 33 *J.Legal Ed.* 274 (1983).

Kitch, "The Intellectual Foundations of Law and Economics," 33 *J.Legal Ed.* 1844 (1983).

Klevorick, "Law and Economic Theory: An Economist's View," 65 *Am.Econ.Rev., Papers & Proc.* 237 (1975).

Komesar, "In Search of a General Approach to Legal Analysis: A Comparative Institutional Alternative," 79 *Mich.L.Rev.* 1350 (1981).

Krier, "Book Review," 122 *U.Pa.L.Rev.* 1664 (1974).

Kronman, Wealth Maximization as a Normative Principle, 9 *J.Legal Stud.* 227 (1980).

Leff, "Economic Analysis of Law: Some Realism About Nominalism," 60 *Va.L.Rev.* 451 (1974).

Lekachman, "Law and Economics," 4 *J.Econ.Issues* 25 (1970).

Liebhafsky, "Price Theory as Jurisprudence: Law and Economics, Chicago Style," 10 *J.Econ.Issues* 23 (1976).

Lovett, "Economic Analysis and Its Role in Legal Education," 26 *J.Legal Educ.* 385 (1974).

MacCormick, "Adam Smith on Law" (Symposium International Perspectives of Jurisprudence), 15 *Val.U.L.Rev.* 243 (1981).

Macneil, "Economic Analysis of Contractual Relations: Its Shortfalls and the Need for a 'Rich' Classificatory Apparatus," 75 *Nw.U.L.Rev.* 1018 (1981).

Markovits, "Causes and Policy Significance of Pareto Resource Misallocation: A Checklist for Micro-economic Policy Analysis," 28 *Stan.L.Rev.* 1 (1975).

Markovits, "A Basic Structure for Microeconomic Policy Analysis in our Worse-Than-Second-Best World: A Proposal and Related Critique of the Chicago Approach to the Study of Law and Economics," 1975 *Wis.L.Rev.* 950 (1975).

McKenzie and Tullock, *The New World of Economics: Explorations into the Human Experience* (Homewood, Illinois: Erwin, 1975).

Michelman, "Politics as Medicine: On Misdiagnosing Legal Scholarship," 90 *Yale L.J.* 1224 (1981).

Michelman, "A Comment on 'Some Uses and Abuses of Economics in Law,' " 46 *U.Chi.L.Rev.* 307 (1978).

Michelman, "Norms and Normativity in the Economic Theory of Law," 62 *Minn.L.Rev.* 1015 (1978).

Mishan, "Pareto Optimality and the Law," 219 *Oxford Econ.Papers (N.S.)* 255 (1967).

Nutter, "On economism," 22 *J.L. & Econ.* 263 (1979).

Ogus, "Economics, liberty and the common law," 18 *J.Soc.Pub.Tchrs. L.* 42 (1980).

Okun, *Equality and Efficiency: The Big Tradeoff* (Boston: The Brookings Institute, 1975).

Oliver, *Law and Economics: an Introduction*, (London: Allen and Unwin, 1979).

Pejovich, "Law as a Capital Good" in Sirkin (ed.) *Lexeconics, the Interaction of Law and Economics* (Boston: M. Nijhoff, 1981).

Polinsky, "Economic Analysis as a Potentially Defective Product: A Buyer's Guide to Posner's Economic Analysis of Law," 87 *Harv.L.Rev.* 1655 (1974).

Polinsky, *An Introduction to Law and Economics* (Boston: Little, Brown, 1983).

Posner, *Economic Analysis of Law;* Ch. 1, "The Nature of Economic Reasoning," pp. 3–14; Ch. 2, "The Economic Approach to Law," pp. 15–23; Ch. 9, "The Theory of Monopoly," pp. 195–205.

Posner, *The Economics of Justice* (Cambridge, Mass: Harvard University Press, 1981).

Posner, "The Present Situation in Legal Scholarship," 90 *Yale L.J.* 1113 (1981).

Posner, "The Value of Wealth: A Comment on Dworkin and Kronman," 9 *J.Legal Stud.* 243 (1980).

Posner, "Some Uses and Abuses of Economics in Law," 46 *U.Chi.L.Rev.* 281 (1979).

Posner, "Utilitarianism, Economics, and Legal Theory," 8 *J.Legal Stud.* 103 (1979).

Posner, "The Economic Approach to Law," 53 *Tex.L.Rev.* 757 (1975).

Posner, "Economic Justice and the Economist," 33 *Pub.Interest* 109 (1973).

Prichard, Trebilcock and McDonald, "Selected Bibliography: Economic Analysis of Commercial Law" in Ziegel, (ed.), *Proceedings of the Seventh Annual Workshop on Commercial and Consumer Law,* pp. 153–164 (1979).

Renner, *Institutions of Private Law and Their Social Function* (London: Routledge & K. Paul, 1949).

Rizzo, "Uncertainty, Subjectivity and the Economic Analysis of Law" in Rizzo (ed.), *Time, Uncertainty and Disequilibrium,* (Lexington, Mass.: D.C.Heath, 1979).

Rubin, "Predictability and the Economic Approach to Law: A Comment on Rizzo," 9 *J.Legal Stud.* 319 (1980).

Samuels, "Introduction: Commons and Clark on Law and Economics," 10 *J.Econ.Issues.* 743 (1976).

Samuels, "Interrelations between Legal and Economic Processes," 14 *J.L. & Econ.* 435 (1971).

Samuels, "Law and Economics: Introduction," 7 *J.Econ.Issues.* 535 (1973).

Samuels, "Legal-Economic Policy: A Bibliographical Survey," 58 *Law Libr.J.* 230 (1965).

Samuels, "Law and Economics: A Bibliographical Survey, 1965–1972," 66 *Law Libr.J.* 96 (1973).

Samuels, "Maximization of Wealth as Justice: an Essay on Posnerian Law and Economics as Policy Analysis," 60 *Tex.L.Rev.* 147 (1981).

Samuels and Schmid (ed.), *Law and Economics: an Institutional Perspective*, (Boston: Martinus Nijhoff, 1981).

Schmid, *Property, Power and Public Choice: An Inquiry into Law and Economics*, (New York: Prager Special Studies, 1978).

Schnelling, "On the Ecology of Micromotives," 25 *Pub.Interest* 59 (1971).

Shipworth, "Economic Analysis for Attorneys," 71 *Ill.B.J.* 372 (1983).

Siegan (ed.), *The Interaction of Economics and the Law*, (Lexington, Mass.: Lexington Books, D.C. Heath & Co., 1977).

Sirkin (ed.), *Lexeconics, the Interaction of Law and Economics*, (Boston: Martinus Nijhoff, 1981).

Solow, "Science and Ideology in Economics," in *Capitalism Today* (eds. Bell and Kirstol, 1971).

Soper, "On the Relevance of Philosophy to Law: Reflection on Ackerman's 'Private Property and the Constitution,'" 79 *Colum.L.Rev.* 44 (1979).

Stigler, "Wealth, and Possibly Liberty," 7 *J. of Legal Stud.* 213 (1978).

Stigler, "The Law and Economics of Public Policy: A Plea to the Scholars," 1 *J.Legal Stud.* 1 (1972).

Strasser, Bard, and Arthur, "A Reader's Guide to the Uses and Limits of Economic Analysis with Emphasis on Corporation Law," 33 *Mercer L.Rev.* 571 (1982).

Trebilcock and Prichard, "Economic Analysis of Commercial Law" in Ziegel (ed.), *Proceedings of the Seventh Annual Workshop on Commercial and Consumer Law*, pp. 111–119 (1979).

Tribe, "Policy Science: Analysis or Ideology," 2 *Phil. & Pub.Aff.* 66 (1972).

Thurow, "Toward a Definition of Economic Justice," 31 *Pub.Interest* 56 (1973).

Tullock, *The Logic of the Law* (New York: Basic Books, 1971).

Turvey, "On Divergences Between Social Cost and Private Cost," 30 *Economica* 309 (1963).

Veljanovski, "Wealth Maximization, Law and Ethics—On the Limits of Economic Efficiency," 1 *Int'l Rev.L. & Econ.* 5 (1981).

Veljanovski, "The Economic Approach to Law: A Critical Introduction," 7 *Brit.J.L. & Soc'y* 158 (1980).

Weinrib, "Utilitarianism, Economics, and Legal Theory," 30 *U.Toronto L.J.* 307 (1980).

Williams, "The Static Conception of the Common Law: A Comment," 9 *J.Legal Stud.* 277 (1980).

Williams, "Collaboration Between Economists and Lawyers in Policy Research," 13 *J.Soc'y Pub.Teachers L.* 212 (1975).

II. PROPERTY RIGHTS AND THE COASE THEOREM

Ackerman, *Economic Foundations of Property Law* (Boston: Little, Brown, 1975). [Collection of readings.]

Ackerman, *Private Property and the Constitution* (New Haven: Yale Univ.Press, 1977).

Alexander, "The Concept of Property in Private and Constitutional Law: the Ideology of the Scientific Turn in Legal Analysis," 82 *Colum.L.Rev.* 1545 (1982).

Anderson and Hill, "The Evolution of Property Rights: A Study of the American West," 18 *J.L. & Econ.* 163 (1975).

Atiyah, "Liability for Railway Nuisance in the English and Common Law: A Historical Footnote," 23 *J.L. & Econ.* 191 (1980).

Ault and Rutman, "The Development of Individual Rights to Property in Tribal Africa," 22 *J.L. & Econ.* 163 (1979).

Beck, "Competition for Patent Monopolies," 3 *Research L. & Econ.* 91 (1981).

Berger, "A Policy Analysis of the Taking Problem," 49 *N.Y.U.L.Rev.* 165 (1974).

Brown and Holahan, "Taxes and Legal Rules for the Control of Externalities when there are Strategic Responses," 9 *J.Legal Stud.* 165 (1980).

Buchanan, "The Coase Theorem and the Theory of the State," 13 *Nat.Resources J.* 579 (1973).

Buchanan and Faith, "Entrepreneurship and the Internalization of Externalities," 24 *J.Legal Stud.* 95 (1981).

Burrows, "Nuisance, Legal Rules and Decentralized Decisions: A Different View of the Cathedral Crypt," in Burrows and Veljanovski, (eds.) *The Economic Approach to Law* (London: Butterworths, 1981).

Burrows, *The Economic Theory of Pollution Control*, (Oxford: Martin Robinson, 1979).

Burrows, "On External Costs and the Visible Arm of the Law," 22 *Oxford Econ.Papers* 39 (1970).

Calabresi, "Transaction Costs, Resource Allocation and Liability Rules—A Comment," 11 *J.L. & Econ.* 67 (1968).

Calabresi and Melamed, "Property Rules, Liability Rules and Inalienability: One View of the Cathedral," 85 *Harv.L.Rev.* 1089 (1972).

Chapman, "Coase, Cost and Causation," Law and Economics Workshop paper.

Cheung, "Private Property Rights and Sharecropping," 76 *J.Pol.Econ.* 1107 (1968).

Cheung, "The Fable of the Bees: An Economic Investigation," 16 *J.L. & Econ.* 11 (1973).

Coase, "The Coase Theorem and the Empty Core: A Comment," 24 *J.L. & Econ.* 183 (1981)

Coase, "The Lighthouse in Economics," 17 *J.L. & Econ.* 357 (1974).

Coase, "The Problem of Social Cost," 3 *J.L. & Econ.* 1, pp. 1–28.

Cooter, "The Cost of Coase," 11 *J.Legal Stud.* 1 (1982).

Crocker, "The Measurement of Economic Losses From Uncompensated Externalities," 14 *J.L. & Econ.* 451 (1971).

Crocker, "Contractual Choice," 13 *Nat.Resources J.* 561 (1973).

Dahlman, "The Problem of Externality," 22 *J.L. & Econ.* 141 (1979).

Dales, *Pollution, Property and Prices* (Toronto: Univ. Toronto Press, 1968).

Daly, "The Coase Theorem: Assumptions, Applications and Ambiguities," 12 *Econ.Inquiry* 203 (1974).

De Alessi, "The Economics of Property Rights: A Review of the Evidence," (Law and Economics Center, University of Miami School of Law, LEC Working Paper #78–2).

Demsetz, "The Exchange and Enforcement of Property Rights," 7 *J.L. & Econ.* 11 (1964).

Demsetz, "Some Aspects of Property Rights," 9 *J.L. & Econ.* 61 (1966).

Demsetz, "Toward a Theory of Property Rights," 57 *Am.Econ.Rev.Papers & Proc.* 347 (1967).

Demsetz, "Wealth Distribution and the Ownership of Rights," 1 *J.Legal Stud.* 223 (1972).

Demsetz, "When Does the Rule of Liability Matter?," 1 *J.Legal Stud.* 13 (1972).

Demsetz, "Ethics and Efficiency in Property Rights Systems" in Rizzo (ed.) *Time, Uncertainty and Disequilibrium,* at 97 (Lexington Mass.: D.C. Heath & Co., 1979).

Dewees, *Evaluation of Policies for Regulating Environmental Pollution*, (Ottawa: Economic Council of Canada, 1980).

Easterbrook, "Privacy and the Optimal Extent of Disclosure under the Freedom of Information Act," 9 *J.Legal Stud.* 775 (1980).

Ellickson, "Alternatives to Zoning: Covenants, Nuisance Rules, and Fines as Land Use Controls," 40 *U.Chi.L.Rev.* 681 (1973).

Ellickson, "Suburban Growth Controls: An Economic and Legal Analysis," 86 *Yale L.J.* 385 (1977).

Epstein, "Nuisance Law: Corrective Justice and Its Utilitarian Constraints," 8 *J.Legal Stud.* 49 (1979).

Feldman, "Liability Rules and The Transfer of Economic Rents," 3 *J.Legal Stud.* 499 (1974).

Frech, "The Extended Coase Theorem and Long-Run Equilibrium: the Non-equivalence of Liability Rules and Property Rights," 17 *Econ.Inquiry* 254 (1979).

Furubotn and Pejovich, (eds.), *The Economics of Property Rights* (Cambridge: Ballinger Pub., 1974).

Gifford, "Externalities and the Coase Theorem: A Graphical Analysis," 14 *Q.Rev.Econ. & Bus.* 7 (1974).

Ginsburg and Schechtman, "Blackmail: An Economic Analysis of Law," mimeograph.

Gjerdingen, "The Coase Theorem and the Psychology of Common-law Thought," 56 *S.Cal.L.Rev.* 711 (1983).

Gold, "The Welfare Economics of Historic Preservation," 8 *Conn.L.Rev.* 348 (1975–76).

Gordon, "The Economic Theory of a Common-Property Resource: the Fishery," 62 *J.Pol.Econ.* 124 (1954).

Gould, "Meade on External Economies: Should the Beneficiaries be Taxed?," 16 *J.L. & Econ.* 53 (1973).

Guttman, "The Economics of Tenant Rights in Nineteenth Century Irish Agriculture," 18 *Econ.Inquiry* 408 (1980).

Hirsch, "Landlord-Tenant Relations Law," in Burrows and Veljanovski (eds.) *The Economic Approach to Law* (London: Butterworths, 1981).

Hirshleifer, "Privacy: Its Origin, Function, and Future," 9 *J.Legal Stud.* 649 (1980).

Hsiao, "The Theory of Share Tenancy Revisited," 83 *J.Pol.Econ.* 1023 (1975).

Jaffe, "The 'Coase Theorem', A Re-examination—Comment," 89 *Q.J.Econ.* 660 (1975).

Janczyk, "Land Title Systems, Scale of Operations, and Operating and Conversion Costs," 8 *J.Legal Stud.* 569.

Johnson, "Meade, Bees, and Externalities," 16 *J.L. & Econ.* 35 (1973).

Johnson, Gisser, and Werner, "The Definition of a Surface Water Right and Transferability," 24 *J.L. & Econ.* 273 (1981).

Kelman, "Consumption Theory, Production Theory, and Ideology in The Coase Theorem," 52 *S.Cal.L.Rev.* 669 (1979).

Kennedy, "Cost-Benefit Analysis of Entitlement Problems: A Critique," 33 *Stan.L.Rev.* 387 (1981).

Kennedy and Michelman, "Are Property and Contract Efficient?" 8 *Hofstra L.Rev.* 711 (1980).

Kitch, "The Law and Economics of Rights in Valuable Information," 9 *J.Legal Stud.* 683 (1980).

Kneese and Maler, "Bribes and Charges in Pollution Control: An Aspect of the Coase Controversy," 13 *Nat.Resources J.* 705 (1973).

Knetsch and Borcherding, "Expropriation of Private Property and the Basis for Compensation," 29 *U.Toronto L.J.* 237.

Kronman, "The Privacy Exemption to the Freedom of Information Act." 9 *J.Legal Stud.* 727 (1980).

Liebhafsky, "The Problem of Social Cost—An Alternative Approach," 13 *Nat.Resources J.* 615 (1973).

Manne, *The Economics of Legal Relationships: Readings in The Theory of Property Rights* (St. Paul, Minn.: West, 1975).

Matthews, "Proprietary Claims at Common Law for Mixed and Improved Goods," 34 *Current Legal Probs.* 159 (1981).

Meade, "External Economies and Diseconomies in a Competitive Situation," 62 *Econ.J.* 54 (1952).

Michelman, "Property, Utility and Fairness: Comments on the Ethical Foundation of Just Compensation," 81 *Yale L.J.* 149 (1971).

Mishan, "The Postwar Literature on Externalities: An Interpretative Essay," 9 *J.Econ.Lit.* 1 (1971).

Mishan, "The Economics of Disamenity," 14 *Nat.Resources J.* 55 (1974).

Mishan, "The Effects of Externalities on Individual Choice," 1 *Int'l Rev.L. & Econ.* 97 (1981).

Monteverde and Teece, "Appropriable Rents and Quasi-Vertical Integration," 25 *J.L. & Econ.* 321 (1982).

Mumey, "The Coase Theorem: A Reexamination," 85 *Q.J. on Econ.* 718 (1971).

Munch, "An Economic Analysis of Eminent Domain," 84 *J. of Pol.Econ.* 473 (1976).

Note, "An Economic Analysis of Land Use Conflicts," 21 *Stan.L.Rev.* 293 (1969).

Note, "Eminent Domain: Private Corporations and the Public Use Limitation," 11 *U.Balt.L.Rev.* 310 (1982).

Note, "Efficient Land Use and the Internalization of Beneficial Spillover: An Economic and Legal Analysis," 31 *Stan.L.Rev.* 457 (1979).

Note, "Injunction Negotiations: An Economic, Moral and Legal Analysis," 27 *Stan.L.Rev.* 1563 (1975).

Nutter, "The Coase Theorem on Social Cost: A Footnote," 11 *J.L. & Econ.* 503 (1968).

Page, "Failure for Bribes and Standards of Pollution Abatement," 13 *Nat.Resources J.* 677 (1973).

Pejovich, "Toward an Economic Theory of the Creation and Specification of Property Rights," in Manne, *The Economics of Legal Relationships* (St. Paul: West Pub. Co., 1975).

Pigou, *The Economics of Welfare* (London: MacMillan & Co., 1960).

Polinsky, "Controlling Externalities and Protecting Entitlements: Property Right, Liability Rule, and Tax Subsidy Approaches," 8 *J.Legal Stud.* 1 (1979).

Polinsky, "Resolving Nuisance Disputes: The Simple Economics of Injunctive and Damage Remedies," 32 *Stan.L.Rev.* 1075 (1980).

Polinsky, "On the Choice Between Property Rules and Liability Rules," 18 *Econ.Inquiry* 233 (1980).

Posner, *Economic Analysis of Law*, Ch. 3, "Property," pp. 27–64.

Posner, "The Economics of Privacy," 2 *Regulation* 19 (1978).

Posner, "The Right of Privacy," 12 *Ga.L.Rev.* 393 (1983) and comments by Fried, Bloustein, Epstein, Baker, D'Amato, Rubin, Karafiol and Birmingham.

Posner, "Privacy, Secrecy, and Reputation," 28 *Buffalo L.Rev.* 1 (1979).

Regan, "The Problem of Social Cost Revisited," 15 *J.L. & Econ.* 427 (1972).

Roberts, "An Appropriate Economic Model of Judicial Review of Suburban Growth Control," 55 *Ind.L.J.* 441 (1980).

Sagoff, "Economic Theory and Environmental Law," 79 *Mich.L.Rev.* 1393 (1981).

Samuels, "The Coase Theorem and the Study of Law and Economics," 14 *Nat.Resources J.* 595 (1973).

Sax, "Takings, Private Property and Public Rights," 81 *Yale L.J.* 149 (1971).

Schwartz, "The Case for Specific Performance," 89 *Yale L.J.* 271 (1979).

Spitzer and Hoffman, "Reply to Consumption Theory, Production Theory, and Ideology in the Coase Theorem," 53 *S.Cal.L.Rev.* 1187 (1980).

Stigler, "An Introduction to Privacy in Economics and Politics," 9 *J.Legal Stud.* 623 (1980).

Weld, "Coase, Social Cost and Stability: An Integrative Essay," 13 *Nat.Resources J.* 595 (1973).

Wellisz, "On External Diseconomies and the Government-Assisted Invisible Hand," 31 *Economica* 345 (1964).

White and Wittman, "Optimal Spatial Location under Pollution: Liability Rules and Zoning," 10 *J.Legal Stud.* 249 (1981).

White and Wittman, "Long-Run versus Short-Run Remedies for Spatial Externalities: Liability Rules, Pollution Taxes and Zoning," in Rubinfeld (ed.) *Essays on the Law and Economics of Local Governments* (Washington, D.C.: The Urban Institute, 1979).

Williams, "Liberty and Property: the Problem of Government Benefits," 12 *J.Legal Stud.* 3 (1983).

Zerbe, "The Problem of Social Cost in Retrospect," 2 *Research L. & Econ.* 83 (1980).

III. TORTS: THE RULE OF LIABILITY

Akerlof, "The Market for 'Lemons': Quality Uncertainty and the Market Mechanism," 84 *Q.J.Econ.* 488 (1970).

Benham and Benham, "Regulating Through the Professions: A Perspective on Information Control," 18 *J.L. & Econ.* 421 (1975).

Bishop, "Negligent Misrepresentation: an Economic Reformulation," in Burrows and Veljanovski (eds.) *The Economic Approach to Law* (London: Butterworths, 1981).

Bishop, "Negligent Misrepresentation Through Economists' Eyes," 96 *L.Q.Rev.* 360 (1980).

Borgo, "Causal Paradigms in Tort Law," 8 *J.Legal Stud.* 419 (1979).

Browder, "The Taming of a Duty—The Tort Liability of Landlords," 81 *Mich.L.Rev.* 99 (1982).

Brown, "Toward an Economic Theory of Liability," 2 *J.Legal Stud.* 323 (1973).

Buchanan, "In Defense of Caveat Emptor," 38 *U.Chi.L.Rev.* 64 (1970).

Burrows, "Idealized Negligence, Strict Liability, and Deterrence," 2 *Int'l Rev.L. & Econ.* 165 (1982).

Calabresi, "Some Thoughts on Risk Distribution and the Law of Torts," 70 *Yale L.J.* 499 (1961).

Calabresi, "The Decision for Accidents: An Approach to Non-fault Allocation of Costs," 78 *Harv.L.Rev.* 713 (1965).

Calabresi, "Optimal Deterrence and Accidents," 84 *Yale L.J.* 656 (1975).

Calabresi, *The Costs of Accidents* (New Haven: Yale Univ.Press, 1970).

Calabresi, "Product Liability: Curse or Bulwark of Free Enterprise?" mimeograph.

Calabresi and Bass, "Right Approach, Wrong Implications: A Critique of McKean on Products Liability," 38 *U.Chi.L.Rev.* 74 (1970).

Calabresi and Hirschoff, "Toward a Test for Strict Liability in Torts," 81 *Yale L.J.* 1055 (1972).

Cayne and Trebilcock, "Market Considerations in the Formulation of Consumer Protection Policy," 23 *U.Toronto L.J.* 396 (1973).

Chelius, "Liability for Industrial Accidents: A Comparison of Negligence and Strict Liability Systems," 5 *J.Legal Stud.* 293 (1976).

Cooter, "Contract, Tort, and Contributory Negligence," 1982 *N.Z.L.J* 294 (1982).

Cooter, Kornhauser and Lane, "Liability Rules, Limited Information and the Role of Precedent," 10 *Bell J.Econ.* 366 (1979).

Darby and Karni, "Free Competition and the Optimal Amount of Fraud," 16 *J.L. & Econ.* 67 (1973).

Diamond, "Single Activity Accidents," 3 *J.Legal Stud.* 107 (1974).

Diamond and Mirrlees, "On the Assignment of Liability: The Uniform Case," 6 *Bell J.Econ. & Mgmt.Sci.* 487 (1975).

Englard, "The System Builders: A Critical Appraisal of Modern American Tort Theory," 9 *J.Legal Stud.* 27 (1980).

Epstein, *A Theory of Strict Liability—Toward a Reformulation of Tort Law*, (San Francisco: CATO Institute, 1980).

Epstein, "Nuisance Law: Corrective Justice and its Utilitarian Constraints," 8 *J.Legal Stud.* 49 (1979).

Epstein, "A Theory of Strict Liability," 2 *J.Legal Stud.* 151 (1973).

Epstein, "Causation and Corrective Justice: A Reply to Two Critics," 8(3) *J.Legal Stud.* 477 (1979).

Feiner, "Preferential Admissions from the Economic Perspective of Information Costs," 26 *UCLA L.Rev.* 162 (1978).

Fletcher, "Fairness and Utility in Tort Theory," 85 *Harv.L.Rev.* 537 (1972).

Gellhorn, "The Abuse of Occupational Licensing," 44 *U.Chi.L.Rev.* 6 (1976).

Goldberg, "The Economics of Product Safety and Imperfect Information," 5 *Bell J.Econ.* 683 (1974).

Green, "On the Optimal Structure of Liability Laws," 7 *Bell J.Econ.* 553 (1976).

Hamada, "Liability Rules and Income Distribution in Product Liability," 66 *Am.Econ.Rev.* 228 (1976).

Helms, *The Economics of Medical Malpractice* (1978).

Henderson, "The Boundary Problems of Enterprise Liability," 41 *Md.L.Rev.* 563 (1982).

Henderson, "Extending the Boundaries of Strict Products Liability: Implications of the Theory of the Second Best," 128 *U.Pa.L.Rev.* 1036 (1980).

Higgins, "Producers' Liability and Product-Related Accidents," 7 *J.Legal Stud.* 299 (1978).

Hodgson, "Restrictions on Unorthodox Health Treatment in California: A Legal and Economic Analysis," 24 *UCLA L.Rev.* 647 (1977).

Hubbard, "Efficiency, Expectation, and Justice: A Jurisprudential Analysis of the Concept of Unreasonably Dangerous Product Defect," 28 *S.C.L.Rev.* 587 (1977).

Knoeber, "Penalties and Compensation for Auto Accidents," 7 *J.Legal Stud.* 263 (1978).

Landes and Posner, "The Positive Economic Theory of Tort Law," 15 *Ga.L.Rev.* 851 (1981).

Landes and Posner, "An Economic Theory of International Torts," 1 *Int'l Rev.L. & Econ.* 127 (1981).

Landes and Posner, "Joint and Multiple Tortfeasors: An Economic Analysis," 9 *J.Legal Stud.* 517 (1980).

Landes and Posner, "Causation in Tort Law: an Economic Approach," 12 *J.Legal Stud.* 109 (1983).

Landes and Posner, "Salvors, Finders, Good Samaritans and Other Rescuers: An Economic Study of Law and Altruism," 7 *J.Legal Stud.* 83 (1978).

Leibman and Sandy, "Can the Open and Obvious Danger Rule Coexist with Strict Tort Product Liability?: A Legal and Economic Analysis," 20 *Am.Bus.L.J.* 299 (1982).

McKean, "Products Liability: Trends and Implications," 38 *U.Chi.L.Rev.* 3 (1970).

Mackenzie, "Some Reflections on Negligence, Damages and No-Fault Compensation," 10 *U.B.C.L.Rev.* 27 (1975).

Michelman, "Pollution as a Tort: A Non-Accidental Perspective on Calabresi's *Costs*," 80 *Yale L.J.* 647 (1971).

Murray, "Sindell v. Abbott Laboratories: A Market Share Approach to DES Causation," 69 *Calif.L.Rev.* 1179 (1981).

Note: "An Efficiency Analysis of Vicarious Liability Under the Law of Agency," 91 *Yale L.J.* 168 (1981).

Note, "Allocating the Costs of Hazardous Waste Disposal," 94 *Harv.L.Rev.* 584 (1981).

Note, "Assumption of Risk and Strict Products Liability," 95 *Harv.L.Rev.* 872 (1982).

O'Connell, "Elective No-Fault Insurance For Many Kinds of Accidents: A Proposal and an 'Economic' Analysis," 42 *Tenn.L.R.* 145 (1974).

Ogus and Richardson, "Economics and the Environment, A Study of Private Nuisance", 36 *Cambridge L.J.* 284 (1977).

Ordover, "On the Consequences of Costly Litigation in the Model of Single Activity Accidents: Some New Results," 10 *J. Legal Stud.* 269 (1981).

Ordover, "Costly Litigation in the Model of Single Activity Accidents," 7 *J. Legal Stud.* 505 (1973).

Peltzman, "An Evaluation of Consumer Protection Legislation: The 1962 Drug Amendments: A Reply," 83 *J.Pol.Econ.* 663 (1975).

Polinsky, "Strict Liability vs. Negligence in a Market Setting," 70 *Am.Econ.Rev.Papers and Proc.* 363 (1980).

Posner, *Economic Analysis of Law*, Ch. 6, "Tort Rights and Remedies," pp. 119–161.

Posner, "A Theory of Negligence", 1 *J. Legal Stud.* 29 (1972).

Posner, "Killing or Wounding to Protect a Property Interest", 14 *J.L. & Econ.* 201 (1971).

Posner, "Epsteins Tort Theory: A Critique," 8(3) *J. Legal Stud.* 457 (1979).

Posner, "Strict Liability: A Comment," 2 *J. Legal Stud.* 205 (1973).

Posner, "The Concept of Corrective Justice in Recent Theories of Tort Law," 10 *J. Legal Stud.* 187 (1981).

Posner, *Tort Law: Cases and Economic Analysis*, (Boston: Little, Brown and Co., 1982).

Prichard, "Professional Liability and Continuing Competence," in Klar, *Studies in Canadian Tort Law* (1977).

Priest, "A Theory of the Consumer Product Warranty," 90 *Yale L.J.* 1297 (1981).

Rabin, "Nuisance Law: Rethinking Fundamental Assumptions," 63 *Va.L.Rev.* 1299 (1977).

Rabin, "The Historical Development of the Fault Principle: A Reinterpretation," 15 *Ga.L.Rev.* 925 (1981).

Reder, "An Economic Analysis of Medical Malpractice," 5 *J.Leg.Studies* 267 (1976).

Rizzo, "Law Amid Flux, The Economics of Negligence and Strict Liability in Tort," 9 *J. Legal Stud.* 291 (1980). Cf. Rubin, "Predictability and the Economic Approach to Law: A Comment on Rizzo," 9 *J. Legal Stud.* 319 (1980).

Rizzo, "The Imputation Theory of Proximate Cause: An Economic Framework," 15 *Ga.L.Rev.* 1007 (1981).

Rizzo and Arnold, "Causal Apportionment in the Law of Torts: An Economic Theory," 80 *Colum.L.Rev.* 1399 (1980).

Rottenberg (ed.), *The Economics of Medical Malpractice*, (Washington, D.C.: American Enterprise Institute for Public Policy Research, 1978).

Sands, "How Effective is Safety Legislation?," 11 *J.L. & Econ.* 165 (1968).

Schwartz, "Contributory and Comparative Negligence: A Reappraisal," 87 *Yale L.J.* 697 (1978).

Schwartz, "Products Liability and Judicial Wealth Redistribution," 51 *Ind.L.J.* 558 (1976).

Schwartz, "Foreword: Understanding Products Liability" 67 *Calif.L.Rev.* 435 (1979).

Schwartz, "Tort Law and the Economy in Nineteenth-Century America: A Reinterpretation," 90 *Yale L.J.* 1717 (1981).

Schwartz, "The Vitality of Negligence and the Ethics of Strict Liability," 15 *Ga.L.Rev.* 963 (1981).

Schwartz and Komesar, "Doctors, Damages and Deterrence: An Economic View of Medical Malpractice," 298 *New England J.Med.* 1282 (1978).

Schwartz and Mitchell, "An Economic Analysis of the Contingent Fee In Personal-Injury Litigation," 22 *Stan.L.Rev.* 1125 (1970).

Schwartz and Wilde, "Intervening in Markets on the Basis of Imperfect Information: A Legal and Economic Analysis," 127 *U.Pa.L.Rev.* 630 (1979).

Shavell, "Accidents, Liability and Insurance" (discussion paper, 1979).

Shavell, "Strict Liability versus Negligence," 9 *J. Legal Stud.* 1 (1980).

Shavell, "An Analysis of Causation and the Scope of Liability in the Law of Torts" 9 *J. Legal Stud.* 463 (1980).

Simon, "Imperfect Information, Costly Litigation, and Product Quality," 12 *Bell J.Econ.* 171 (1981).

Skogh, "Public Insurance and Accident Prevention," 2 *Int'l Rev.L. & Econ.* 67 (1982).

Spence, "Consumer Misperceptions, Product Failure, and Product Liability," 44 *Rev.Econ. & Stat.* 561 (1977).

Spitzer, "Economic Analysis of Sovereign Immunity in Tort," 50 *S.Cal.L.Rev.* 515 (1977).

Steiner, "Economics, Morality, and the Law of Torts," 26 *U. Toronto L.J.* 227 (1976).

Stone, "The Place of Enterprise Liability in the Control of Corporate Conduct," 90 *Yale L.J.* 1 (1980).

Symposium, "Products Liability: Economic Analysis and the Law," 38 *U.Chi.L.Rev.* 1 (1970).

Veljanovski, *Economic Myths about Common Law Realities—Economic Efficiency and the Law of Torts,* (Oxford: Centre for Socio-Legal Studies, 1979).

Veljanovski, *Bibliography in Law and Economics—Legal Liability and Negligence,* (Oxford: Centre for Socio-Legal Studies 1979).

Veljanovski, "The economic theory of tort liability—toward a corrective justice approach," in Burrows and Veljanovski (eds.) *The Economic Approach to Law* (London: Butterworths, 1981).

Viscusi, "A Note on 'Lemons' Markets with Quality Certification," 9 *Bell J.Econ.* 277 (1978).

Whitford, "A Comment on a Theory of the Consumer Product Warranty," and Priest, "The Best Evidence of the Effect of Products Liability Law on the Accident Rate: a Reply," 91 *Yale L.J.* 1371 (1982).

Wittman, "Optimal Pricing of Sequential Inputs: Last Clear Chance Mitigation of Damages, and Related Doctrines in the Law," 10 *J. Legal Stud.* 65 (1981).

Wittman, "First Served: An Economic Analysis of 'Coming to the Nuisance'," 9 *J. Legal Stud.* 557 (1980).

Zeckhauser, "Coverage for Catastrophic Illness," 23 *Pub.Pol'y* 419 (1973).

IV. TORTS: THE ASSESSMENT OF DAMAGES

Bell, Bodenhorn, and Taub, "Taxes and Compensation for Lost Earnings," and Burke and Rosen, "A Comment," 12 *J. Legal Stud.* 181 (1983).

Blomquist, "The Value of Life Saving: Implications of Consumption Activity," 87 *J.Pol.Econ.* 540 (1979).

Blomquist, "The Value of Human Life: an Empirical Perspective," 19 *Econ. Inquiry* 157 (1981).

Brady, Brookshire, and Cobb, "Calculating the Effects of Income Taxes on Lost Earnings," 18 *Trial* 65 (1982).

Broome, "Trying to Value a Life," 9 *J.Pol.Econ.* 91 (1978).

Calabresi, "The Decision for Accidents: An Approach to Non-Fault Allocation of Costs," 78 *Harv.L.Rev.* 713 (1965).

Calabresi, "Reflections on Medical Experimentation in Humans," 98 *Daedalus* 387 (1969).

Conley, "The Value of Human Life in the Demand for Safety," 66 *Am.Econ.Rev.* 45 (1976).

Cooter, "Economic Analysis of Punitive Damages," 56 *S.Cal.L.Rev.* 79 (1982).

Curran, "Inflation and the Discount Rate in Estimating Damages in Tort," 56 *Conn.B.J.* 420 (1982).

Davis, "Damages for Personal Injury and the Effect of Future Inflation," 56 *Australian L.J.* 168 (1982).

De Alessi, "The Rule of Liability for Loss of Use When Property is Totally Destroyed: Some Economic Considerations," 32 *U. Miami L.Rev.* 255 (1978).

Ellis, "Fairness and Efficiency in the Law of Punitive Damages," 56 *S.Cal.L.Rev.* 1 (1982).

Fried, "The Value of Life," 82 *Harv.L.Rev.* 1415 (1969).

Jones-Lee, "The Value of Changes in the Probability of Death or Injury," 82 *J.Pol.Econ.* 835 (1974).

Linnerooth, "The Value of Human Life: A Review of the Models," 17 *Econ. Inquiry* (Jan. 1979).

Mishan, "Evaluation of Life and Limb: A Theoretical Approach," 79 *J.Pol.Econ.* 687 (1971).

Mishan, *Cost-Benefits Analysis* (New York: Praeger, 1971).

Note, "Adjusting Damage Awards for Future Inflation," 1982 *Wis.L.Rev.* 397 (1982).

Note, "Inflation, Productivity, and the Total Offset Method of Calculating Damages for Lost Future Earnings," 49 *U.Chi.L.Rev.* 1003 (1982).

Note, "Prejudgement Interest: Survey and Suggestion," 77 *Nw.U.L.Rev.* 192 (1982).

Owen, "Problems in Assessing Punitive Damages Against Manufacturers of Defective Products," 49 *U.Chi.L.Rev.* 1 (1982).

Owen, "Civil Punishment and the Public Good," 56 *S.Cal.L.Rev.* 1 (1982).

Priest, "Punitive Damages and Enterprise Liability," 56 *S.Cal.L.Rev.* 1 (1982).

Rhoads, "How Much Should We Spend to Save a Life?," 51 *Pub. Interest* 74 (1978).

Schelling, "The Life You Save May Be Your Own?", in Chase, *Pub. Expenditure Analysis* (1968).

Schwartz, "Deterrence and Punishment in the Common Law of Punitive Damages: A Comment," 56 *S.Cal.L.Rev.* 1 (1982).

Singer, "How to Reduce Risks Rationally," 51 *Pub. Interest* 93 (1978).

Thaler and Rosen, "The Value of Saving a Life; Evidence from the Labour Market" in *Household Production and Consumption* (Nester E. Terlecky, ed. 1975).

Votliek, "Tort Damages for the Injured Homemaker: Opportunity Cost or Replacement Cost?" 50 *U.Colo.L.Rev.* 59 (1978).

Zeckhauser, "Procedures for Valuing Lives," 23 *Pub.Pol.* 419 (1975).

V. CONTRACTS

Akerlof, "The Market for Lemons: Qualitative Uncertainty and the Market Mechanism," 84 *Q.J.Econ.* 488 (1970).

Ashley, "The Economic Implications of the Doctrine of Impossibility," 26 *Hastings L.J.* 1251 (1975).

Atiyah, *The Rise and Fall of Freedom of Contract,* (Oxford: Clarendon Press, 1979).

Barton, "The Economic Basis of Damages for Breach of Contract," 1 *J. Legal Stud.* 277 (1972).

Beatty, "Labour is not a Commodity" in Reiter and Swan (eds.) *Studies in Contract Law,* (Toronto: Butterworths, 1980) at 313.

Biger and Rosen, "A Framework for the Assessment of Business Damages for Breach of Contract," 5 *Can.Bus.L.J.* 302 (1981).

Birmingham, "Breach of Contract, Damages, Measures, and Economic Efficiency," 24 *Rutgers L.Rev.* 273 (1970).

Bowles and Whelan, "Judicial Responses to Exchange Rate Instability" in Burrows and Veljanovski (eds.) *The Economic Approach to Law* (London: Butterworths, 1981).

Bridge, "The Overlap of Tort and Contract," 27 *McGill L.J.* 872 (1982).

Carroll, "Four Games and the Expectancy Theory," 54 *S.Cal.L.Rev.* 503 (1981).

Cayne and Trebilcock, "Market Considerations in the Formulation of Consumer Protection Policy," 23 *U. Toronto L.J.* 396 (1973).

Cheung, "Transaction Costs, Risk Aversion, and the Choice of Contractual Arrangements," 12 *J.L. & Econ.* 23 (1969).

Clarkson, Miller, and Muris, "Liquidated Damages v. Penalties: Sense or Nonsense?," 101 *Wis.L.Rev.* 351 (1978).

Coase, "The Choice of Institutional Framework: A Comment," 17 *J.L. & Econ.* 493 (1974).

Cummins, "Incentive Contracting for National Defense: A Problem of Optimal Risk Sharing," 8 *Bell J.Econ.* 168 (1977).

Dalzell, "Duress by Economic Pressure," 20 *N.C.L.Rev.* 237 (1942).

Darby and Karni, "Free Competition and the Optimal Amount of Fraud," 16 *J.L. & Econ.* 67 (1973).

Diamond and Maskin, "An Equilibrium and Analysis of Search and Breach of Contract, I: Steady States," 10 *Bell J.Econ.* 282 (1979).

Dowie, "The Risks of Contract Law," 2 *Int'l Rev.L. & Econ.* 193 (1982).

Epstein, "Unconscionability: A Critical Reappraisal," 18 *J.L. & Econ.* 293 (1975).

Farber, "Reassessing the Economic Efficiency of Compensatory Damages for Breach of Contract," 66 *Va.L.Rev.* 1443 (1980).

Fleming, "The Collateral Source Rule and Contract Damages," 71 *Calif.L.Rev.* 56 (1983).

Fried, *Contract as Promise: A Theory of Contractual Obligation,* (Cambridge, Mass.: Harvard University Press, 1981).

Goetz and Scott, "Liquidated Damages, Penalties and the Just Compensation Principle: Some Notes on an Enforcement Model and a Theory of Efficient Breach," 77 *Colum.L.Rev.* 544 (1977).

Goetz and Scott, "Measuring Sellers' Damages: The Lost-Profits Puzzle," 31 *Stan.L.Rev.* 323 (1979).

Goetz and Scott, "Enforcing Promises: An Examination of the Basis of Contract," 89 *Yale L.J.* 1261 (1980).

Goetz and Scott, "Principles of Relational Contracts," 67 *Va.L.Rev.* 1089 (1981).

Goetz and Scott, "The Mitigation Principle: Toward A General Theory of Contractual Obligation,"—69 *Va.L.Rev.* 967—(1983).

Goldberg, "Institutional Change and the Quasi-Invisible Hand," 17 *J.L. & Econ.* 461 (1974).

Goldberg, "Competitive Bidding and the Production of Precontract Information," 8 *Bell J.Econ.* 250 (1977).

Goldberg, "Toward an Expanded Economic Theory of Contract," 10 *J.Econ.Inquiry* 45 (1981).

Goldberg, "The Law and Economics of Vertical Restrictions: A Relational Perspective," 58 *Tex.L.Rev.* 91 (1981).

Goldberg, "Relational Exchange: Economics and Complex Contracts," 23 *Am. Behavioral Scientist* 337 (1980).

Goldberg, "Pigou on Complex Contracts and Welfare Economics," 3 *Research L. & Econ.* 39 (1981).

Grossfeld, "Money Sanctions for Breach of Contract in a Communist Economy," 72 *Yale L.J.* 1326 (1963).

Grossman, "The Informational Role of Warranties and Private Disclosure about Product Quality," 24 *J.L. & Econ.* 461 (1981).

Hallagan, "Self-selection by Contractual Choice and the Theory of Sharecropping," 9 *Bell J.Econ.* 344 (1978).

Harris, Ogus and Phillips, "Contract remedies and the consumer surplus," 95 *Law.Q.Rev.* 581 (1979).

Hirsch, "Habitability Laws and the Welfare of Indigent Tenants," 63 *Rev.Econ. & Stats.* 263 (1981).

Jackson, "Anticipatory Repudiation and the Temporal Element of Contract Law: An Economic Inquiry into Contract Damages in Cases of Prospective Non-performance," 31 *Stan.L.Rev.* 69 (1978).

Joskow, "Commercial Impossibility, The Uranium Market and the Westinghouse Case," 6 *J. Legal Stud.* 119 (1977).

Kennedy, "Form and Substance in Private Law Adjudication," 89 *Harv.L.Rev.* 1685 (1976).

Klein, "Transaction Cost Determinants of 'Unfair' Contractual Arrangements," 70 *Am.Econ.Rev.* 356 (1980).

Kornhauser, "Unconscionability in Standard Forms," 64 *Calif.L.Rev.* 1151 (1976).

Kronman, "Specific Performance," 45 *U.Chi.L.Rev.* 351 (1978).

Kronman, "Mistake, Disclosure, Information and the Law of Contracts," 7 *J. Legal Stud.* 1 (1978).

Kronman, "Contract Law and Distributive Justice," 89 *Yale L.J.* 472 (1980).

Kronman and Posner, *The Economics of Contract Law* (Boston: Little, Brown, 1979).

Landa, "An Exchange Economy with Legally Binding Contract: A Public Choice Approach," 10 *J.Econ.Issues* 905 (1976).

Landa and Grofman, "Games of Breach and the Role of Contract Law in Protecting The Expectation Interest," 3 *Research L. & Econ.* 67 (1981).

Leff, "Injury, Ignorance and Spite—The Dynamics of Coercive Collection," 80 *Yale L.J.* 1 (1970).

Linzer, "On the Amorality of Contract Remedies—Efficiency, Equity, and the Second Restatement," 81 *Colum.L.Rev.* 111 (1981).

Lowry, "Bargain and Contract Theory in Law and Economics," 10 *J.Econ.Issues* 1 (1976).

Macaulay, "Non-Contractual Relations in Business: A Preliminary Study," 28 *Am.Soc.Rev.* 55 (1963).

Macaulay, "Elegant Models, Empirical Pictures and the Complexities of Contract," 11 *Law and Soc.Rev.* 507 (1977).

Macneil, "Efficient Beach of Contract: Circles in the Sky," 68 *Va.L.Rev.* 947 (1982).

Macneil, *The New Social Contract: An Inquiry into Modern Contractual Relations,* (New Haven, Conn.: Yale University Press, 1980).

Macneil, "Economic Analysis of Contractual Relations," in Burrows and Veljanovski (eds.), *The Economic Approach to Law* (London: Butterworths, 1981).

Markusen, "Personal and Job Characteristics as Determinants of Employee-Firm Contract Structure," 93 *Q.J.Econ.* 255 (1979).

Martin, "The Economics of Employment Termination Rights," 20 *J.L. & Econ.* 187 (1977).

Martin, "Job Property Rights and Job Defections," 15 *J.L. & Econ.* 385 (1972).

Milner, "Liquidated Damages: An Empirical Study in the Travel Industry," 42 *Mod.L.Rev.* 508 (1979).

Nelson, "Information and Consumer Behaviour," 78 *J.Pol.Econ.* 311 (1970).

Note, "The Economic Implications of the Doctrine of Impossibility," 26 *Hastings L.J.* 1251 (1975).

Ordover and Weiss, "Information and the Law: Evaluating Legal Restrictions on Competitive Contracts," 71 *Am.Econ.Rev.Papers & Proc.* 399 (1981).

Perlman, "Interference with Contract and Other Economic Expectance—A Clash of Tort and Contract Doctrine," 49 *U.Chi.L.Rev.* 61 (1982).

Perloff, "The Effects of Breaches of Forward Contracts Due to Unanticipated Price Changes," 10 *J. Legal Stud.* 221 (1981).

Perloff, "Breach of Contract and the Foreseeability Doctrine of Hadley v. Baxendale," 10 *J. Legal Stud.* 39 (1981).

Polinsky, "Risk Sharing Through Breach of Contract Remedies," 12 *J. Legal Stud.* 427 (1983).

Posner, *Economic Analysis of Law*, Ch. 4, "Contract Rights and Remedies," pp. 65–100.

Posner and Rosenfield, "Impossibility and Related Doctrines in Contract Law: An Economic Analysis," 6 *J. Legal Stud.* 83 (1977).

Posner, "Gratuitous Promises in Economics and Law," 6 *J. Legal Stud.* 411 (1977).

Priest, "A Theory of the Consumer Product Warranty," 90 *Yale L.J.* 1297 (1981).

Priest, "Breach and Remedy for the Tender of Nonconforming Goods under the Uniform Commercial Code: An Economic Approach," 91 *Harv.L.Rev.* 960 (1978).

Rafferty, "Concurrent Liability in Contract and Tort: Recovery of Pure Economic Loss and the Effect of Contributory Negligence," 20 *Alta L.Rev.* 357 (1982).

Rea, "Nonpecuniary Loss and Breach of Contract," 11 *J. Legal Stud.* 35 (1982).

Reiter, "The Control of Contract Power," 1 *Oxford J. Legal Stud.* 347 (1981).

Rubin and Shedd, "Human Capital and Covenants not to Compete," 10 *J. Legal Stud.* 93 (1981).

Sandor, "Innovation by an Exchange: A Case Study of the Development of the Plywood Futures Contract," 16 *J.L. & Econ.* 119 (1973).

Schwartz, "Seller, Unequal Bargaining Power and the Judical Process," 49 *Ind.L.J.* 367 (1974).

Schwartz, "Sales Law and Inflations," 50 *S.Cal.L.Rev.* 1 (1976).

Schwartz, "The Case for Specific Performance," 89 *Yale L.J.* 271 (1979).

Schwartz and Wilde, "Intervening in Markets on the Basis of Imperfect Information: A Legal and Economic Analysis," 127 *U.Pa.L.Rev.* 630 (1979).

Shanker, "The Case for a Literal Reading of U.C.C. Section 2–708(2) (One Profit for the Reseller)," 24 *Case W.Res.L.Rev.* 697 (1973).

Sharpe, "Specific Relief for Contract Breach," in Reiter and Swan (eds.) *Studies in Contract Law* (Toronto: Butterworths, 1980).

Shavell, "Risk Sharing and Incentives in the Principal and Agent Relationship," 10 *Bell J.Econ.* 55 (1979).

Shavell, "Damage Measures for Breach of Contract," 11 *Bell J.Econ.* 466 (1980).

Speidel and Clay, "Seller's Recovery of Overhead Under UCC Section 2–708(2): Economic Cost Theory and Contract Remedial Policy," 57 *Cornell L.Rev.* 681 (1972).

Trebilcock, "An Economic Approach to the Doctrine of Unconscionability," in B.J. Reiter and J. Swan (eds.) *Studies in Contract Law* (Toronto: Butterworths, 1980) at pp. 379–421.

Trebilcock and Dewees, "Judicial Control of Standard Form Contracts," in Burrows and Veljanovski (eds.), *The Economic Approach to Law* (London: Butterworths, 1981).

Trebilcock and Prichard, "Economic Analysis of Commercial Law," in Ziegel (ed.), *Proceedings of the Seventh Annual Workshop on Commercial and Consumer Law*, pp. 111–119 (1979).

Umbeck, "A Theory of Contract Choice and the California Gold Rush," 20 *J.L. & Econ.* 421 (1977).

Veljanovski, *Bibliography in Law and Economics: Contract Analysis*, (Oxford: Centre for Socio-Legal Studies, 1979).

Weicher, "Product Quality and Value in the New Home Market: Implications for Consumer Protection Regulation," 24 *J.L. & Econ.* 365 (1981).

Weinberg, "Sales Law, Economics, and the Negotiability of Goods," 9 *J. Legal Stud.* 569 (1980).

Williamson, "Contract Analysis: the Transaction Cost Approach" in Burrows and Veljanovski (eds.) *The Economic Approach to Law* at 39 (London: Butterworths, 1981).

Williamson, "Transaction-Cost Economics: the Governance of Contractual Relations," 22 *J.L. & Econ.* 233 (1979).

Yorio, "In Defense of Money Damages for Breach of Contract," 82 *Colum.L.Rev.* 1365 (1982).

VI. CRIME AND PUNISHMENT

Adelstein, "The Moral Costs of Crime: Prices, Information, and Organization", Sage in Gray (ed.) *The Cost of Crime* (London: Sage, 1979).

Adelstein, "Institutional Function and Evolution in the Criminal Process," *Research Study No. 2* (Oxford: Centre for Socio-Legal Studies, 1980) also 76 *Nw.U.L.Rev.* 101.

Adelstein, "Informational Paradox and the Price of Crime: Capital Sentencing Standards in Economic Perspective," 70 *J.Crim.L. & Criminology* 281 (1979).

Avio, "Recidivism in the Economic Model of Crime," 8 *Econ.Inquiry* 450 (1975).

Avio, "Capital Punishment in Canada: A Time Series Analysis of the Deterrent Hypothesis" 12 *Canadian J.Econ.* 647–676 (1979).

Avio, "An Economic Analysis of Canadian Corrections: The Canadian Case" 6 *Canadian J.Econ.* 164 (1973).

Backhaus, "Defending Organized Crime? A Note" 8 *J. Legal Stud.* 623 (1979).

Baldwin and McConville, "Plea Bargaining and the Court of Appeal" 6 *Brit.J.L. & Soc'y* 200 (1979).

Becker, "Crime and Punishment: An Economic Approach," 76 *J.Pol.Econ.* 169 (1968).

Becker, "Irrational Behavior and Economic Theory", in Becker, *The Economic Approach to Human Behavior,* (1976).

Becker and Landes, *Essays in the Economics of Crime and Punishment,* (Cambridge, Mass.: National Bureau of Economic Research, 1974).

Block and Lind, "Crime and Punishment Reconsidered," 4 *J. Legal Stud.* 241 (1975).

Block and Lind, "An Economic Analysis of Crimes Punishable by Imprisonment," 4 *J. Legal Stud.* 479 (1975).

Brier and Fienberg, "Recent Econometric Modeling of Crime and Punishment: Support for the Deterrence Hypothesis?" 4 *Evaluation Rev.* 147 (1980).

Danzinger and Wheeler, "The Economics of Crime: Punishment or Income Distribution," 33 *Rev.Soc.Econ.* 113 (1975).

Deininger, "The Economics of Heroin: Key to Optimizing the Legal Response," 10 *Ga.L.Rev.* 565 (1976).

Elzinga and Breit, *The Antitrust Penalties: A Study in Law and Economics* (New Haven, Conn.: Yale Univ. Press, 1976).

Erickson, "The Social Costs of the Discovery and Suppression of the Clandestine Distribution of Heroin," 77 *J.Pol.Econ.* 484 (1969).

Ehrlich, "The Deterrent Effect of Criminal Law Enforcement," 1 *J. Legal Stud.* 259 (1972).

Ehrlich, "Participation in Illegitimate Activities: An Economic Analysis," *Essays in the Economics of Crime and Punishment* (Becker and Landes eds., 1974) reprinted from 81 *J.Pol.Econ.* 521 (1973).

Ehrlich, "The Optimum Enforcement of Laws and the Concept of Justice: A Positive Analysis," 2 *Int'l Rev.L. & Econ.* 3 (1982).

Ehrlich and Gibbons, "On the Measurement of the Deterrent Effect of Capital Punishment and the Theory of Deterrence," 6 *J. Legal Stud.* 35 (1977).

Fernandez, "The Clandestine Distribution of Heroin, Its Discovery and Suppression: A Comment," 77 *J.Pol.Econ.* 487 (1969).

Friedman, *The Economics of Crime and Justice*, 1976.

Friedman, "Reflections on Optimal Punishment, Or: Should the Rich Pay Higher Fines?" 3 *Research L. & Econ.* 185 (1981).

Gibbons, "The Utility of Economic Analysis of Crime," 2 *Int'l Rev.L. & Econ.* 173 (1982).

Goff and Reasons, "Corporations in Canada: A Study of Crime and Punishment," 18 *Crim.L.Q.* 468 (1976).

Hannan, "Bank Robberies and Bank Security Precautions," 11 *J. Legal Stud.* 83 (1982).

Harris, "On the Economics of Law and Order," 78 *J.Pol.Econ.* 165 (1970).

Hellman, *The Economics of Crime* (St. Martin, 1980).

Komesar, "A Theoretical and Empirical Study of Victims of Crime," 2 *J. Legal Stud.* 301 (1973).

Mathieson and Passell, "Homicide and Robbery in New York City: An Economic Model," 5 *J. Legal Stud.* 83 (1976).

McKenzie and Tullock, The New World of Economics (1975), Chaps. 11 & 12.

Myers, "The Economics of Bail Jumping," 10 *J. Legal Stud.* 381 (1981).

Noam, "The Optimal Size of the Criminal Court System," in Sirkin (ed.) *Lexeconics, the Interaction of Law and Economics* (Boston: Martinus Nijhoff, 1981).

Noam, "Blindfolded Justice Led by an Invisible Hand: Criminal Justice as a Variable of Exchange Transactions," 3 *Law & Pol'y Q.* 490 (1981).

Note, "Daring the Courts: Trial and Bargaining Consequences of Minimum Penalties," 90 *Yale L.J.* 597 (1981).

Ozenne, "The Economics of Bank Robbery," 3 *J. Legal Stud.* 19 (1974).

Phillips, "The Criminal Justice System: Its Technology and Inefficiencies," 10 *J. Legal Stud.* 363 (1981).

Phillips and Votey, "Crime Control in California," 4 *J. Legal Stud.* 327 (1975).

Polinsky and Shavell, "The Optimal Tradeoff Between the Probability and Magnitude of Fines," 69 *Am.Econ.Rev.* 880 (1979).

Posner, *Economic Analysis of Law*, Chapter 7, "The Criminal Sanction and Criminal Law," 163–177.

Posner, "Excessive Sanctions for Governmental Misconduct in Criminal Cases," 57 *Wash.L.Rev.* 635 (1982).

Posner, "Retribution and Related Concepts of Punishment," 9(1) *J. Legal Stud.* 71 (1980).

Reder, "Citizen Rights and the Cost of Law Enforcement," 3 *J. Legal Stud.* 435 (1974).

Rhodes, "The Economics of Criminal Courts: A Theoretical and Empirical Investigation," 5 *J. Legal Stud.* 311 (1976).

Rizzo, "The Cost of Crime to Victims: An Empirical Analysis," 8 *J. Legal Stud.* 177 (1979).

Ross, *Deterrence of the Drinking Driver: An International Survey*, Report No. DOT–HS–805–820. (Washington, D.C.: U.S. Dept. of Transportation, National Highway Safety Administration, 1981).

Rottenberg, "Clandestine Distribution of Heroin, Its Discovery and Suppression," 76 *J.Pol.Econ.* 78 (1968).

Trumbull and Witte, "Determinants of the Costs of Operating Large-Scale Prisons with Implications for the Cost of Correctional Standards," 16 *L. & Soc.Rev.* 115 (1981–82).

Tullock, "Does Punishment Deter Crime?," 36 *The Pub. Interest* 103 (1984).

Tullock, "An Economic Approach to Crime," 50 *Soc.Sci.Q.* 59 (1969).

Votey, "Detention of Heroin Addicts, Job Opportunities, and Deterrence," 8(3) *J. Legal Stud.* 585 (1979).

Votey, Scandinavian Drinking-Driving Control: Myth or Intuition?", 11 *J. Legal Stud.* 93 (1982).

Witte, "Estimating the Economic Model of Crime with Individual Data," 94 *Q.J.Econ.* 57 (1980).

VII. CIVIL AND CRIMINAL PROCEDURE

Adelstein, "The plea bargain in England and America: a comparative institutional view," in Burrows and Veljanovski (eds.) *The Economic Approach to Law*, (London: Butterworths, 1981).

Becker and Stigler, "Law Enforcement, Malfeasance, and Compensation of Enforcers," 3 *J. Legal Stud.* 1 (1974).

Bernstein, "Judicial Economy and Class Actions," 7 *J. Legal Stud.* 349 (1978).

Blair, "Antitrust Penalties: Deterrence and Compensation," 1980 *Utah L.Rev.* 57 (1980).

Bowles, "Economic Aspects of Legal Procedure," in Burrows and Veljanovski (eds.) *The Economic Approach to Law* (London: Butterworths, 1981).

Brady, "Fee Shifting: An Institutional Change to Decrease the Benefits from Free Riding" in Sirkin (ed.) *Lexeconics, the interaction of law and economics* (Boston: M. Nijhoff, 1981).

Carroll and Gasten, "A Note on the Quality of Legal Services: Peer Review and Disciplinary Service," 3 *Research L. & Econ.* 251 (1981).

Chester, "Class Actions to Protect the Environment: A Real Weapon or Another Lawyers Word Game?" in Swaigen (ed.) *Environmental Rights in Canada* (Toronto: Butterworths, 1981).

Clermont and Currivan, "Improving on the Contingent Fee," 63 *Cornell L.Rev.* 529 (1978).

Cooter and Kornhauser, "Can Litigation Improve the Law Without the Help of Judges?," 9 *J. Legal Stud.* 139 (1980).

Cooter, Kornhauser and Lane, "Liability Rules, Limited Information, and the Role of Precedent," 10 *Bell J.Econ.* 366 (1979).

Dam, "Class Actions: Efficiency, Compensation, Deterrence, and Conflict of Interest," 4 *J. Legal Stud.* 47 (1975).

Dewees, Prichard and Trebilcock," An Economic Analysis of Cost and Free Rules in Class Actions," 10 *J. Legal Stud.* 155 (1981).

Domberger and Sherr, "Economic Efficiency in the Provision of Legal Services: The Private Practitioner and the Law Centre," 1 *Int'l Rev.L. & Econ.* 29 (1981).

Durand, "Note: An Economic Analysis of Fluid Class Recovery Mechanisms," 34 *Stan.L.Rev.* 173 (1981).

Easterbrook, "Ways of Criticizing the Court," 95 *Harv.L.Rev.* 802 (1982).

Easterbrook, Landes, and Posner, "Contribution Among Antitrust Defendants: A Legal and Economic Analysis," 23 *J.L. & Econ.* 331 (1980).

Eatherly, "Drug Law Enforcement: Should We Arrest Pushers or Users?," 82 *J.Pol.Econ.* 210 (1974).

Ehrlich and Posner, "An Economic Analysis of Legal Rulemaking," 3 *J. Legal Stud.* 257 (1974).

Ehrlich, "The Optimum Enforcement of Laws and the Concept of Justice: A Positive Analysis," 2 *Int'l Rev.L. & Econ.* 3 (1982).

Epstein, "The Static Conception of the Common Law," 9 *J. Legal Stud.* 253 (1980).

Goodman, "An Economic Theory of the Evolution of Common Law," 7 *J. Legal Stud.* 393 (1978).

Goldman and Marks, "Diversity Jurisdiction and Local Bias: A Preliminary Empirical Inquiry," 9 *J. Legal Stud.* 93 (1980).

Higgins and Rubin, "Judicial Discretion," 9 *J. Legal Stud.* 129 (1980).

Kaye, "The Laws of Probability and the Law of the Land," 47 *U.Chi.L.Rev.* 34 (1979).

Klevorick, "Jury Size and Composition: An Economic Approach," in *The Economics of Public Services* (eds. Feldstein and Inman, 1977), p. 75.

Komesar, "Legal Change, Judicial Behaviour, and the Diversity Jurisdiction: A Comment," 9 *J. Legal Stud.* 387 (1980).

Kornhauser, "A Guide to the Perplexed Claims of Efficiency in the Law," 8 *Hofstra L.Rev.* 591 (1980).

Krier and Montgomery, "Resource Allocation, Information Cost and the Form of Government Intervention," 13 *Nat. Resources J.* 89 (1971).

Landes, "An Economic Analysis of the Courts," 14 *J.L. & Econ.* 61 (1971).

Landes, "The Bail System: an Economic Approach," 2 *J. Legal Stud.* 79 (1973).

Landes and Posner, "Should Indirect Purchasers Have Standing to Sue under the Antitrust Laws? An Economic Analysis of the Rule of Illinois Brick," 46 *U.Chi.L.Rev.* 602 (1979).

Landes and Posner, "The Private Enforcement of Law," 4 *J. Legal Stud.* 1 (1975).

Landes and Posner, "The Independent Judiciary in an Interest-Group Perspective," 18 *J.L. & Econ.* 875 (1975).

Landes and Posner, "Legal Precedent: A Theoretical and Empirical Analysis," 19 *J.L. & Econ.* 249 (1976).

Landes and Posner, "Adjudication as a Private Good," 8 *J. Legal Stud.* 235 (1979).

Landes and Posner, "Legal Change, Judicial Behaviour, and the Diversity Jurisdiction," 9 *J. Legal Stud.* 367 (1980).

Leubsdorf, "The Contingency Factor in Attorney Fee Awards," 90 *Yale L.J.* 473 (1981).

Martin, "Justice and Efficiency Under a Model of Estate Settlement," 66 *Va.L.Rev.* 727 (1980).

Martin, "The Economics of Jury Conscription," 80 *J.Pol.Econ.* 680 (1972).

Mashaw, "Private Enforcement of Public Regulatory Provisions: The Citizen Suit," 4 *C.A.R.* 29 (1975).

Morris, "The Exclusionary Rule, Deterrence, and Posner's Economic Analysis of Law," 57 *Wash.L.Rev.* 647 (1982).

Noam, "A Cost-Benefit Model of Criminal Courts," 3 *Research L. & Econ.* 173 (1981).

Note, "The Allocation of Prosecution: An Economic Analysis," 74 *Mich.L.Rev.* 586 (1976).

Note, "A Framework for the Allocation of Prevention Resources with a Specific Application to Insider Trading," 74 *Mich.L.Rev.* 975 (1976).

Ogus, "Quantitative Rules and Judicial Decision Making" in Burrows and Veljanovski (eds.) *The Economic Approach to Law* (London: Butterworths, 1981).

Phillips and Hawkins, "Some Economic Aspects of the Settlement Process: A Study of Personal Injury Claims," 39 *Mod.L.Rev.* 497 (1976).

Polinsky, "Private Versus Public Enforcement of Fines," 9 *J. Legal Stud.* 105 (1979).

Polinsky and Shavell, "Contribution and Claim Reduction Among Antitrust Defendants: An Economic Analysis," 33 *Stan.L.Rev.* 447 (1981).

Posner, *Economic Analysis of Law*, Ch. 21, "Civil and Criminal Procedure," pp. 429–460; Posner, Ch. 22, "Law Enforcement," pp. 461–478.

Posner, "A Reply to Some Recent Criticisms of the Efficiency Theory of the Common Law," 9 *Hofstra L.Rev.* 775 (1981).

Posner, "The Ethical and Political Basis of the Efficiency Norm in Common Law Adjudication," 8 *Hofstra L.Rev.* 487 (1980).

Posner, "An Economic Approach to Legal Procedure and Judicial Administration," 2 *J. Legal Stud.* 399 (1973).

Prichard, "Private Enforcement and Class Actions," in Prichard, Stanbury and Wilson, *Canadian Competition Policy: Essays in Law and Economics* (1979).

Prichard and Trebilcock, "Class Actions and Private Law Enforcement," 27 *U. New Brunswick L.J.* 5 (1978).

Priest, "The Common Law Process and the Selection of Efficient Rules," 6 *J. Legal Stud.* 113 (1976).

Priest, "Selective Characteristics of Litigation," 9 *J. Legal Stud.* 399 (1980).

Rizzo, "Can There be a Principle of Explanation in Common Law Decisions? A Comment on Priest," 9 *J. Legal Stud.* (1980).

Rizzo, The Mirage of Efficiency," 8 *Hofstra L.Rev.* 641 (1980).

Roberts, "Beaches: The Efficiency of the Common Law and Other Fairy Tales," 28 *U.C.L.A.L.Rev.* 166 (1981).

Schwartz and Mitchell, "An Economic Analysis of the Contingent Fee in Personal Injury Litigation," 22 *Stan.L.Rev.* 1125 (1970).

Scott, "Two Models of the Civil Process," 27 *Stan.L.Rev.* 937 (1975).

Rubin, "Why is the Common Law Efficient?," 6 *J. Legal Stud.* 51 (1977).

Shavell, "Suit, Settlement and Trial: A Theoretical Analysis Under Alternative Methods for the Allocation of Legal Costs," 11 *J. Legal Stud.* 55 (1982).

Stigler, "The Optimum Enforcement of Laws," 78 *J.Polit.Econ.* 526 (1970).

Votey and Phillips, "Police Effectiveness and the Production Function for Law Enforcement," 1 *J. Legal Stud.* 423 (1972).

Wittman, "Prior Regulation Versus Post Liability: The Choice Between Input and Output Monitoring," 6 *J. Legal Stud.* 193 (1977).

Wright, "The Cost-Internalization Case for Class Actions," 21 *Stan.L.Rev.* 383 (1969).

VIII. FAMILY LAW

Becker, "An Economic Analysis of Fertility," in *The Economic Approach to Human Behaviour* (ed. Becker) (Chicago: Univ. Chicago Press, 1978).

Becker, "Privacy and Malfeasance: A Comment," 9 *J. Legal Stud.* 823 (1980).

Becker and Posner, "Sex Ratios, the Value of Men and Women, and the Incidence of Polygamy in Primitive Societies," Unpublished memorandum, University of Chicago.

Becker, Landes and Michael, "An Economic Analysis of Marital Instability," 85 *J.Pol.Econ.* 1141 (edited) (1977).

Becker & Lewis, "On the Interaction Between the Quantity and Quality of Children," in *The Economic Approach to Human Behaviour* (ed. Becker, 1978).

Becker, "A Theory of Marriage: The Economics of the Family," in *The Economic Approach to Human Behaviour* (ed. Becker, 1976) or *Economics of the Family* (ed. Schultz, 1974).

Becker, *The Economic Approach to Human Behaviour* (Chicago: Univ. Chicago Press, 1978).

Becker and Tomes, "Child Endowments and the Quantity and Quality of Children," 84 *J.Pol.Econ.* 143 (1976).

Benporath, "The Economics of the Family—Match or Mismatch? A Review of Becker's *A Treatise on the Family*," 20 *J.Econ. Literature* 52 (1982).

Butz and Ward, "Will U.S. Fertility Remain Low? A New Economic Interpretation," 5 *Population & Development Rev.* 663 (1979).

Carr and Landa, "The Economics of Symbols, Clan Names, and Religion," 12 *J. Legal Stud.* 135 (1983).

Cheung, "The Enforcement of Property Rights in Children and the Marriage Contract," 82 *Econ.J.* 641 (1972).

Chiswick, "Minimum Schooling Legislation, Externalities and a 'Child Tax,'" 15 *J.L. & Econ.* 353 (1972).

DeTray, "Child Quality and the Demand for Children," 81 *J.Pol.Econ.* 70 (1973) or *Economics of the Family* (ed. Schultz 1974).

DeTray, "Child Schooling and Family Size: An Economic Analysis, R–2301–NICHD (Santa Monica, Calif.: RAND, 1978).

Dixon and Weitzman, "Evaluating the Impact of No-Fault Divorce in California," 29 *Family Relations* 297 (1980).

Espenshade, "The Value and Cost of Children," 32 *Population Bulletin* (Washington, D.C., Population Reference Bureau).

Frieden, "The United States Marriage Market," 82 *J.Pol.Econ.* 34 (1974) or *Economics of the Family* (Schultz ed. 1974) p. 352.

Gardner, "Economic of the Size of North Carolina Rural Families," 81 *J.Pol.Econ.* 99 (1973).

Gollop and Marquardt, "A Micro-economic Model of Household Choice: the Household as a Disputant," 15 *L. & Soc'y Rev.* 4 (1981).

Goode, "Comment: The Economics of Nonmonetary Values," 82 *J.Pol.Econ.* 27 (1974).

Gronau, "The Effect of Children on the Housewife's Value of Time," 81 *J.Pol.Econ.* 168 (1973) or *Economics of the Family* (Schultz ed. 1974).

Hannan, "Families, Markets, and Social Structures: an Essay on Becker's *A Treatise on the Family*," 20 *J.Econ. Literature* 65 (1982).

Hermann, "An Economic Analysis of Incest: Prohibition, Behavior, and Punishment," 25 *St. Louis U.L.J.* 735 (1982).

Landes, "Economics of Alimony," 7 *J. Legal Stud.* 35 (1978).

Landes and Posner, "The Economics of the Baby Shortage," 7 *J. Legal Stud.* 323 (1978).

Leibowitz, "Home Investments in Children," *Economics of the Family* (Schultz ed. 1974), p. 432.

McKenzie and Tullock, *The New World of Economics*, (Irwin 3rd ed., 1981) chaps. 8, 9 and 10.

Michael, "Education and the Derived Demand for Children," 81 *J.Pol.Econ.* 128 (1973) or *Economics of the Family* (Schultz ed. 1974).

Note, "The Economics of Divorce in Georgia: Toward a Partnership Model of Marriage," 12 *Ga.L.Rev.* 640 (1978).

Rosenzweig, "The Demand for Children in Farm Households," 85 *J. of Pol.Econ.* 123 (1977).

Rosenzweig, "Educational Subsidy, Agricultural Development, and Fertility Change," 97 *Q.J.Econ.* 67 (1982).

Schoen, Greenblatt and Mielke, "California's Experience with Non-Adversary Divorce," 12 *Demography* 223 (1975).

Schultz, "The Value of Children: An Economic Perspective," 81 *J.Pol.Econ.* 2 (1973).

Schultz, "Fertility and Economics Values," *Economics of the Family* (Schultz ed. 1974), 3.

Schultz, *Economics of the Family: Marriage, Children, and Human Capital* (Chicago: Univ. Chicago Press, 1975).

Staffard, "Student Family Size in Relation to Current and Expected Income," 77 *J.Pol.Econ.* 471 (1969).

Tullock, "Welfare and the Law," 2 *Int'l Rev.L. & Econ.* 151 (1982).

Weitzman, "Legal Regulation of Marriage: Tradition and Change," 62 *Calif.L.Rev.* 1169 (1974).

Weitzman and Dixon, "Child Custody Awards: Legal Standards and Empirical Patterns for Child Custody, Support and Visitation after Divorce," 12 *U.C.D.L.Rev.* 473 (1979).

Willis, "A New Approach to the Economic Theory of Fertility Behaviour," 81 *J.Pol.Econ.* 14 (1973).

IX.   CORPORATION LAW

Alchian, "The Basis of Some Recent Advances in the Theory of Management of the Firm," 14 *J.Ind.Econ.* 30 (1965).

Alchian and Demsetz, "Production, Information Costs, and Economic Organization," 62 *Am.Econ.Rev.* 777 (1972).

Anderson, "Conflicts of Interest: Efficiency, Fairness and Corporate Structure," 25 *UCLA L.Rev.* 738 (1978).

Baker, "Interconnected Problems of Doctrine and Economics in the Section One Labyrinth: Is 'Sylvania' A Way Out?," 67 *Va.L.Rev.* 1457 (1981).

Barber, "The Customs Union Issue," in *OPTIONS*, Toronto: University of Toronto Press, pp. 213–32 (1977).

Barrett, "Restrictive Distribution and the Assault of the 'Free Riders,' " 7 *J.Corp.L.* 467 (1982).

Barry, "The Economics of Outside Information and Rule 10b–5," 129 *U.Pa.L.Rev.* 1307 (1981).

Bebchuk, "The Case for Facilitating Competing Tender Offers," 95 *Harv.L.Rev.* 1028 (1982).

Braithwaite, "The Limits of Economism in Controlling Harmful Corporate Conduct," 16 *Law & Soc'y Rev.* 481 (1981–1982).

Brudney, "Dividends, Discretion, and Disclosure," 66 *Va.L.Rev.* 85 (1980).

Calvani and Siegfried, *Economic Analysis of Antitrust Law*, (Boston: Little, Brown and Co., 1979).

Coase, "The Nature of the Firm," 4 *Economica* 386 (1937).

Davies, "Property Rights and Economic Behaviour in Private and Government Enterprises: The Case of Australia's Banking System," 3 *Research L. & Econ.* 111 (1981).

Easterbrook, "Insider Trading, Secret Agents, Evidentiary Privileges, and the Production of Information," 11 *Sup.Ct.Rev.* 309 (1981).

Easterbrook and Fischel, "Antitrust Suits by Targets of Tender Offers," 80 *Mich.L.Rev.* 1155 (1982).

Easterbrook and Fischel, "Corporate Control Transactions," 91 *Yale L.J.* 698 (1982).

Easterbrook and Fischel, "The Proper Role of a Target's Management in Responding to a Tender Offer," 94 *Harv.L.Rev.* 1161 (1981).

Easterbrook and Fischel, "Takeover Bids, Defensive Tactics, and Shareholder's Welfare," 36 *Bus.Law.* 1733 (1981).

Economic Policy and the Regulation of Corporate Securities (Manne ed.) (Amer. Enterprise, 1969).

Engel, "An Approach to Corporate Social Responsibility," 32 *Stan.L.Rev.* 1 (1979).

Fama, "Agency Problems and the Theory of the Firm," 88 *J.Pol.Econ.* 288 (1980).

Fischel, "Efficient Capital Market Theory, the Market for Corporate Control and the Regulation of Cash Tender Offers," 57 *Tex.L.Rev.* 1 (1978).

Fischel, "The Law and Economics of Dividend Policy," 67 *Va.L.Rev.* 699 (1981).

Gilson, "A Structural Approach to Corporations: The Case Against Defensive Tactics in Tender Offers," 33 *Stan.L.Rev.* 819 (1981).

Gordon, "Fair Use as Market Failure: a Structural and Economic Analysis of the Betamax Case and its Predecessors," 82 *Colum.L.Rev.* 1600 (1982).

Grenier, "Recent Development: Damages for Insider Trading in the Open Market: A New Limitation on Recovery Under Rule 10b–5," 34 *Vand.L.Rev.* 797 (1981).

Grossman and Hart, "Take-over Bids, the Free Rider Problem and the Theory of the Corporation," 11 *Bell J.Econ.* 42 (1980).

Grossman and Hart, "The Allocational Role of Takeover Bids in Situations of Asymmetric Information," 36 *J.Fin.* 253 (1981).

Halpern, Trebilcock and Turnbull, "An Economic Analysis of Limited Liability in Corporation Law," 30 *U. Toronto L.J.* 117 (1980).

Jackson and Kronman, "Secured Financing and Priorities Among Creditors," 88 *Yale L.J.* 1143 (1979).

Jarrel, "The Economic Effects of Federal Regulation of the Market for New Security Issues," 24 *J.L. & Econ.* 613 (1981).

Jarrell and Bradley, "The Economic Effects of Federal and State Regulations of Cash Tender Offers," 23 *J.L. & Econ.* 371 (1980).

Jensen and Meckling, "Theory of the Firm: Managerial Behavior, Agency Costs and Ownership Structure," 3 *J.Fin.Econ.* 305 (1976).

Langbein and Posner, "Market Funds and Trust Investment Law," 1976 *Am. Bar Foundation Research J.* 1976, "Market Funds and Trust Investment Law," II, 1977 id. at 1.

Langbein and Posner, "Social Investing and the Law of Trusts," 79 *Mich.L.Rev.* 72 (1980).

Levmore, "Monitors and Freeriders in Commercial and Corporate Settings," 92 *Yale L.J.* 49 (1982).

Lorie and Halpern, "Conglomerates: The Rhetoric and the Evidence," 13 *J.L. & Econ.* 149 (1970).

Lorie and Hamilton, *The Stock Market: Theories and Evidence* (Irwin, 1973).

Manne, "Mergers and the Market for Corporate Control," 73 *J.Pol.Econ.* 110 (1965).

Manne, "Our Two Corporate Systems: Law and Economics," 53 *Va.L.Rev.* 259 (1967).

Manne, "The Limits and Rationale of Corporate Altruism," 59 *Va.L.Rev.* 708 (1973).

Marris and Mueller, "The Corporation, Competition and The Invisible Hand," 18 *J.Econ. Literature* 32 (1980).

Marx, "Political Consequences of Conglomerate Mergers," 27 *Antitrust Bull.* 107 (1982).

McManus, "The Costs of Alternative Economic Organizations," 8 *Can.J.Econ.* 334 (1975).

Modigliani and Miller, "The Cost of Capital, Corporate Finance, and the Theory of Investment," 48 *Am.Econ.Rev.* 261 (1958).

Note: "The Economic Inefficiency of Corporate Criminal Liability," 73 *J.Crim.L. & Criminology* 582 (1982).

Note: "The Fraud-on-the-Market Theory," 95 *Harv.L.Rev.* 1143 (1982).

O'Hara, "Property Rights and the Financial Firm," 24 *J.L. & Econ.* 317 (1981).

Posner and Scott, *Economics of Corporation Law and Securities Regulation*, (Toronto: Little, Brown and Co. 1980).

Prichard, Stanbury, and Wilson, *Canadian Competition Policy: Essays in Law and Economics*, (Toronto: Butterworths, 1979).

Rosenfeld, "Between rights and consequences: A Philosophical inquiry into the foundations of legal ethics in the changing world of securities regulation," 49 *Geo.Wash.L.Rev.* 462 (1981).

Salmanowitz, "Note: Broken Investment Recommendations and the Efficient Capital Market Hypothesis: A Proposed Cautionary Legend," 29 *Stan.L.Rev.* 1077 (1977).

Scott, "Insider Trading: Rule 10b–5, Disclosure, and Corporate Privacy," 9 *J. Legal Stud.* 801 (1980).

Sidak, "Antitrust Preliminary Injunctions in Hostile Tender Offers," 30 *Kan.L.Rev.* 491 (1982).

Stone, "The Place of Enterprise Liability in the Control of Corporate Conduct," 90 *Yale L.J.* 1 (1980).

Strasser, Bard and Arthur, "A reader's guide to the uses and limits of economic analysis with emphasis on corporation law," 33 *Mercer L.Rev.* 581 (1982).

Vagts, "Challenges to Executive Compensation: for the Markets or the Courts?," 8 *Corp.L.* 231 (1983).

Winter, *Government and the Corporation* (1978).

X. ECONOMIC PERSPECTIVES ON COLLECTIVE DECISION–MAKING

Beales, Craswell and Salop, "The Efficient Regulation of Consumer Information," 24 *J.L. & Econ.* 491 (1981).

Berk, Poolman and Oppenheim, "Price and Prejudice: A Variance Components Analysis of Some Causes and Consequences of Regulating Chicago Storefront Banks," 14 *Law & Soc.Rev.* 7 (1979).

Clarkson and Martin (eds), "The Economics of Nonproprietary Organizations," 1 *Research L. & Econ. Supplement* 1 (1980).

Eckert, "The Life Cycle of Regulatory Commissioners," 24 *J.L. & Econ.* 113 (1981).

Economic Council of Canada, Responsible Regulation: An Interim Report by the Economic Council of Canada (Ottawa: Supply and Services, 1979).

Feis, "The Political Economy of Regulation," 5 *U. New South Wales L.J.* 80 (1982).

Hartle, *Public Policy Decision Making and Regulation* (Montreal: Institute for Research on Public Policy, 1979).

Jordon, "Airline Performance Under Regulation: Canada vs. The United States," 1 *Research L. & Econ.* 35 (1979).

Kormendi, "A New Remedy for the Free Rider Problem?—Flies in the Ointment," 1 *Research L. & Econ.* 115 (1979).

Latin, "Environmental Deregulation and Consumer Decisionmaking under Uncertainty," 6 *Harv.Envtl.L.Rev.* 187 (1982).

Mueller, *Public Choice*, (Cambridge: Cambridge University Press, 1979).

Peltzman, "The Growth of Government," 23 *J. Law & Econ.* 209 (1980).

Posner, "Theories of Economic Regulation," 5 *Bell J.Econ.* 335 (1974).

Quinn and Trebilcock, *Compensation, Transition Costs and Regulatory Change* (Ottawa: Economic Council of Canada Working Paper No. 18, 1981).

Trebilcock, Hartle, Dewees and Prichard, *The Choice of Governing Instrument: A Study Prepared for the Economic Council of Canada*, Chapters 1, 2, 3, 8 (Ottawa: Ministry of Supply and Services, 1982).

Trebilcock, Waverman, & Prichard, "Markets for Regulation: Implications for Performance Standards and Institutional Design" in *Government Regulation: Issues and Alternatives* (Toronto: Ontario Economic Council, 1978).

Yorio, "Federal Income Tax Rulemaking: An Economic Approach," 51 *Fordham L.Rev.* 1 (1982).

XI.   FEDERAL LEGAL SYSTEMS

Breton and Scott, *The Economic Constitution of Federal States* (U. Toronto Press, 1978).

Buchanan, "Beyond Pragmatism: Prospects for Constitutional Revolution" in *The Limits of Liberty: Between Anarchy and Leviathen*, (Chicago: Univ. Chicago Press, 1977).

Buchanan and Goetz, "Efficiency Limits of Fiscal Mobility: An Assessment of the Tiebout Model," 1 *J. Public Econ.* 25 (1972).

Ellickson, Public Property Rights, Vicarious Intergovernmental Rights and Liabilities as a Technique for Correction Intergovernmental Spillovers," in Rubinfeld (ed.), *Essays on the Law and Economics of Local Governments* (Washington, D.C.: The Urban Institute, 1979).

Flatters, Henderson, and Mieszkowski, "Public Goods, Efficiency, and Regional Fiscal Equalization," 3 *J.Pub.Econ.* 99 (1974).

Fischel, "The 'Race to the Bottom' Revisited: Reflections on Recent Developments in Delaware Corporation Law," 76 *Nw.U.L.Rev.* (1982).

Green and Parliament, "Political externalities, efficiency, and the welfare losses from consolidation," 33 *Nat'l Tax J.* 209 (1980).

Hartle and Bird, "The Demand for Local Political Autonomy: An Individualistic Approach," *J. Conflict Resolution* 443 (1971).

Hirscham, *Exit, Voice and Loyalty: Responses to Declines in Firms, Organizations, and States* (Cambridge, Mass.: Harvard University Press, 1970).

Michelman, "Microeconomic Appraisal of Constitutional Law: A Methodological Practice," in Rubinfeld (ed.), *Essays on the Law and Economics of Local Governments* (Washington, D.C.: The Urban Institute, 1979).

Michelman, "Constitutions, Statutes, and Theory of Efficient Adjudication," 9 *J. Legal Stud.* 431 (1980).

Ostrom, "Can Federalism Make a Difference?," 4 *Publius: J. Federalism* 3 (1974).

Riker, "Is the Federal Bargain Worth Keeping?," *Federalism: Origin, Operation, Significance* (1964).

Rose-Ackerman, "Risk Taking and Reelection: Does Federalism Promote Innovation?," 9 *J. Legal Stud.* 593 (1980).

Rubinfeld ed., *Essays on the Law and Economics of Local Governments* (Washington, D.C.: The Urban Institute Committee on Urban Public Economics [COUPE] Papers on Public Economics, No. 3, 1979).

Safarian, *Canadian Federalism and Economic Integration* (1974).

Shoup, "Interregional Economic Barriers: The Canadian Provinces," in Ontario Economic Council *Issues and Alternatives 1977: Intergovermental Relations*, 81 (Toronto: 1977).

Sproule-Jones, *Public Choice in Federalism in Australia and Canada* (1975).

Stigler, "The Tenable Range of Functions of Local Governments," in Joint Economic Committee, *Federal Expenditure Policy for Economic Growth and Stability*, pp. 213–19 (Washington: U.S.G.P.O., 1957).

Stigler, "Economic Competition and Political Competition," 13 *Public Choice* 91 (1972).

Stigler, "The Division of Labour is Limited by the Extent of the Market" in *Organization of Industry* 129 (1968).

Tiebout, "A Pure Theory of Local Expenditures," 64 *J.Pol.Econ.* 416 (1956).

Trebilcock, Kaiser and Prichard, "Restrictions on the Interprovincial Mobility of Resources: Goods, Capital and Labour," in *Intergovernmental Relations* (1977).

Usher, "How Should the Redistributive Power of the State be Divided between Federal and Provincial Governments?," 6 *Canadian Pub. Pol'y* 16 (1980).

West and Winer, "The Individual, Political Tension, and Canada's Quest for a New Constitution," 6 *Canadian Pub. Pol'y* 3 (1980).

West and Winer, "Optimal Fiscal Illusion and the Size of Government," 35 *Pub. Choice* 607 (1980).

INDEX

References are to Pages

†